D1196586

Prayers & Sermons from the City Pulpit

Prayers & Sermons from the City Pulpit

Joseph Parker

AMG
PUBLISHERS
Chattanooga, TN 37422

PRAYERS & SERMONS
FROM THE CITY PULPIT

Originally published in London
by Hodder & Stoughton, 1900.

ISBN 0-89957-208-1

Library of Congress Card Catalog Number: 96-84207

Printed in the United States of America.

Contents

Part II

Foreword

It is a privilege to present this collection of classic sermons from Dr. Joseph Parker. These sixty sermons, delivered at his famous London church, have been carefully selected from a three-volume work titled *The City Temple Pulpit,* first published in 1900 by Hodder and Stoughton. Each sermon is a powerful exposition in Parker's convincing style on topics that are as pertinent to the late-twentieth-century reader as they were to his congregation nearly a century ago.

Preceding each sermon are a prayer, the date the sermon was preached, and the passage of Scripture to which the sermon relates. Interspersed throughout the book are special sections of *Words for Preachers,* which contain excerpts related to the duties and characteristics of ministers written primarily by renowned men of God from the seventeenth century. Readers should note that the points of current history mentioned by Parker are from turn-of-the-century England.

In creating this volume, we at AMG Publishers have made a few minor changes to the original work to help make its content more clear for modern readers: We have updated spelling in accordance with how our language has changed over the years, and in some cases, unusual forms of punctuation have been simplified. However, Parker's original words have not been changed in any way, and his compelling messages have been preserved for generations to come.

Part I

Prayer

Thou doest as Thou wilt in the armies of heaven and amongst the children of men, and none may say unto Thee, What doest Thou? Thy will be done on earth as it is in heaven; not our will but Thine be done. Pardon our mistakes and our refusals, our impious rejections and non-compliances with the march of Thine own movement and with the purposes of Thine own will. We have sinned in ignorance, and we have sinned in intention, and Thou hast brought us to sore humiliation and uttermost self-contempt. We have done the things we ought not to have done, we have left undone the things we ought to have done. We have refused the Stone elect and precious, we have built upon sand of our own gathering; behold, our houses have fallen down from the roof to the basement, and they lie in ruins about our feet, for we have played the fool before God, and have not consulted the spirit of wisdom. We have trusted to ourselves, we have perished in self-confidence; we have not diligently and penitently inquired the way of the Lord that we might walk therein with steadfastness and ever-brightening hope: but Thou hast dashed us to pieces like a potter's vessel; Thou hast torn our nest to pieces, and scattered it upon the stormy wind; Thou hast barked our figtree, and taken away our one ewe lamb, and turned our vineyard into a wilderness. And herein is that saying true, God is a jealous God, full of burning zeal; He will have no rival, He will reign alone; for He is complete and sovereign, infinite in resource and in graciousness, and He will share His throne with none. Enable us to accept the throne of God, and to bow under His gracious scepter, and to say in our bitterest desolation that the Lord doeth what seemeth good in His sight, and, behold, He will bring it all out in the light and glory of love. Come to the weary ones, and give them rest; come to broken hearts, and bring them the balm that is in Gilead; come to those who are ill at ease, and whisper the seasonable word in the ear of their distress.

We pray at the Cross, we look upon the red blood; it is the redeeming stream; we look upon the five wounds, the five entrances into Thy love and Thy kingdom—make them five seals of our adoption and sonship and infinite security. Amen.

1

The Refused Stone

Preached on Thursday Morning, June 8th, 1899.

The stone which the builders refused is become the head stone
of the corner—Psalm 118:22.

How is this to be accounted for? You did all you could to hinder Him, and there He is at the head—the Savior of the world, the throned Son of God. You spat upon Him, and scourged Him, and crucified Him; and yet there He stands, fairest among ten thousand, and altogether lovely. You hated Him, but God loved Him; that is the reason of the exaltation and the immutable sovereignty. The Lord reigneth. The wrath of man He restrains; He keeps back the remainder of it that He may dash it in the face of His foes. Why will we not be wise? Why will we not kiss the Son whilst we are in the way with Him? Why do we set up our little impertinence and self-will, and say that we know what is right, and we will have this man and not that man?—whereas we have nothing to do with it. God reigns, God elects; whom He foreknows He predestinates to be conformed to the image of His Son. We can do nothing against the truth but for the truth; we can swing with gravitation, or try to swing against it and have our brains dashed out.

"The stone which the builders refused." But surely the builders could not be wrong? They were experts. We pay for an expert in our age; for we have high prices to pay for the most elaborate ignorance. They knew exactly what stone to choose and what stone not to choose, and they reported upon the case, and upon their report the

3

stone was cast away with a spitting of contempt upon it. Does God delight to baffle the malevolent ingenuity of man? Has He some special pride in taking the experts by the feet and dipping them into the river as if He would drown them in the waters of contempt? It is an awful thing to be an expert when you do not know anything about the business in which you profess to be a proficient; your aggravation is sevenfold. The common man would not feel it one tenth part so much as you do, because he is not an expert; he gives opinions as it were offhandly and superficially, but you are scribes and Pharisees and experts, and you only go into court for a fee of not less than fifty guineas, and would not shake your silk again over any brief under that sum which you call an honorarium. Surely the builders cannot be wrong, because they are experts. The stone which the builders refused has become the head of the corner. I am sorry for the builders, because they will every day have to pass by that stone and see their own condemnation written upon its election and coronation, and they will hasten past that stone whispering to one another, and trying that old familiar trick of changing the subject. Every day to have to face your folly; every day to read the black story of your wickedness! The builders cannot get to their city offices without passing the head stone of the corner, and remembering that they refused the Lord's election, and tried to cancel the predestination of the Eternal. You may wriggle as you please, and quibble with infinite subtlety of verbal dialectic, but when you have wasted all your breath in untoward polysyllables there remains the sullen, stubborn, unchangeable fact, that there is a sovereignty in the universe, a law that proceedeth and cannot be hindered; a decree that is being worked out little by little, hour by hour, from the dawn to the zenith, from the zenith to the occidental line; still the great march of the Divine purpose proceeds; and none can hinder.

But the builder has a redress; the builder has an uncomfortable and uncomforting consolation; he says he always knew that this stone had a meaning in it, and that even in his most wrathful moments he never denied that the stone was a good one, and might some day come to some kind of selection and win for itself some place in the total edifice of the Divine purpose. Away! Too many words! Yet who would dash the cup from his lips? Poor disappointed one—it is all he has to drink, and who would see even his enemy die of thirst? It is a sad thing when man takes upon himself the attributes of omniscience; it is a distressing and most agonizing thing for any man to undertake to say what is going to be done tomorrow. One has pity even upon the poor ill-paid weather prophet whose vaticinations are printed on the front page of the daily journal: which vaticinations never come to pass; but if they come to pass within a week he finds a kind of warmth and comfort about the soul, because he wishes to persuade himself, though he knows what a liar he is, that that was the week he really meant when he said the other week! Do not be prophets, that is to say, predictionists, fortune-tellers, people who know what stones are going to be first, midst, last. The Lord reigneth; He will put the stones in their right places; He knows where the rough blocks should be, and where the diamond should be set, and what stone is fittest to meet the morning kiss of the sun. Thy will be done on earth as it is in heaven.

Yet we cannot, I repeat, but be sorry for the builders, because having once been convicted of this most tragical and ludicrous mistake, they can never open their mouths upon any subject any more. Men would not allow them to be heard in the assembly; they would say, Ha, ha! These men refused the stone—down! They would never be heard again in any assembly of honest men or of honest hearts; such men and such hearts would cry out upon them, and say, You have no claim to be heard, you refused the stone that was meant to be the head stone of the corner: how dare you speak to the intelligence or to the moral agony of the age? It is thus that God closes the mouth of the enemy without saying one word to the impostor. He simply keeps on rearing His building, carrying up His temple to the dome, and when it is done He leaves the men to their own reflections, and those reflections darken into the unutterable darkness and the worm that cannot die.

Many persons have undertaken to refuse the Bible stone. God has made it the head stone of the corner. Every day brings a new witness to the truth of the Bible, and even to the science of the Bible, and one day even Moses will have what is due to him in the way of tribute and gratitude and coronation. Moses has stood many a test; our hearts have ached for the grand old man as he had to die without treading the land that was fruitful with the harvest of a promise. Our grief was premature. Do not interfere with God's way. He knows it is better to die here than to die there; let Him fix the place, and dig the grave, and write the epitaph; and as for us, let us stand back; we are of yesterday and know nothing. Moses was refused and cast out and utterly condemned, but today the hosts of the choir invisible lift up their voice in thunder-anthems; the song they sing is the song of Moses and the Lamb. God will work, must work; He began with a purpose, and to the last throb and pulse of its meaning He will work it out into music and beauty and completeness.

We read of men being self-made fools in this matter of refusals. It is always the builders who refuse; that is to say, the leading men, the architects, the upbuilders, the trained minds, the experts, the scribes and the Pharisees—men so learned in the law that it would be impossible for them to have the slightest conception of the spirit. "This Moses whom they refused, the same did God send." So we read in Acts 7:35. They refused the elect stone, they would not have Moses teach them beyond the terms of their own blind self-confidence. They wanted Moses to become a popular preacher —and popular preacher means the man who says with emphasis what other people try to say—a mere echo, an empty echo, a shadow-voice, without individuality, without the majesty and the tragedy of the Cross in his soul. These men are popular because they reject the stone which God has elected. God nominates our leaders; God appoints every man to his own place; God inverts sequences and prophecies. We should have said Aaron and Moses, but God says Moses and Aaron. God did not care for the three years' seniority over the younger man; He said, Stand back–Moses and Aaron. And old Jacob knew that there was a movement going on in his hands, magnetic, occult, incalculable, which made him crown and bless according to a law other than the law of primogeniture; and if some said, Nay, my father, this one first, and that one second, Jacob said, Let be, and groped his way in growing blindness to the working out of the Divine election. We are great at primogeniture. I wonder what we think it means. We are quite sure it ought to mean something, because it is so long; you can wind it almost around the body of a serpent, it lengthens itself out so wondrously. God has come down again and again in history, and said, No, not this, but that; not Esau, but Jacob; not Aaron, but Moses. The great voice has sounded through all the aisles and corridors of ever-rising history; the first shall be last and the last shall be first; and God thus shakes the nations and the buildings together and works out of the intermingling the final and perfect Man. Let alone! Thy will be done.

Ah, we have been wonderful in our arbitrary selections and elections. But God says, Accept the will, obey the discipline. And the apostle has said so in every grade of eloquence. "See that ye refuse not Him that speaketh. For if they escaped not who refused Him that spoke on earth, much more shall not we escape if we turn away from Him that speaketh from heaven." This business of refusal is a business connected with austere and inevitable responsibility. You cannot both reject the stone and have it; you cannot build upon the stone whose virtue you deny. Do not imagine that the stone and the sand are the same thing; what is built upon the rock is a house; what is built upon the sand is also a house; the difference is in the foundation, and you cannot decorate a sand house into a rock foundation; it cannot be done. And do you suppose that God allows all our refusals to end in nothingness and makes no account of them, saying, Well, so let it be; these people have refused Him, but I will think nothing further about it? That is not the case as it is stated in Holy Scripture: "Because I have called, and ye refused; I have stretched out My hand, and no man regarded, but ye have set at naught all My counsel and would have none of My reproof"— what then? Is He but a good-natured Deity that will smile at the infirmities and account our refusals as accidental mischances? This is the answer: "I also will laugh at your calamity, I will mock when your fear cometh as desolation and your destruction cometh as a whirlwind, and distress and anguish cometh upon you. Then shall they call upon Me, but I will not answer; they shall seek Me early, but they shall not find Me; for that they hated knowledge, and did not choose the fear of the Lord; they would none of My counsel; they despised all My reproof. Therefore shall they eat of the fruit of their own way, and be filled with their own devices." Life creates its own judgment-day; we need no pedagogue to deck a throne in white and set it in the air that we may gaze at it; that judgment-throne is in the conscience, in every man's own heart. Every man knows whether he is true to the inward voice or false; let every man decide.

Refusals do not end in themselves. Do not suppose that the matter is of no consequence; that we can refuse, and nothing more will be heard of it. It is not so written in the Book. They refused to obey, and the consequence is that the Lord mocked them and shamed them. We have to face our refusals. We cannot throw our lives behind our backs, and say, Nothing more will be heard of this. Everything more will be heard of it; we shall give an account to God for every idle word we have spoken; we shall have to account for our decisions and elections and preferences. It is so sad to think that the greatest blunders in all human history have been committed by the leaders, the preachers, the clergy, the statesmen, the scribes, the Pharisees. It is heart-breaking to think that they will one day have to face their own stupidity and their own crimes. We say, Surely the scribe and the Pharisee cannot be wrong. If the light that is in thee be darkness, how great is that darkness! No man can be so foolish as the wise man when his wisdom is not wisdom, when his light is not light; for there is an obstinacy of intelligence when it is only partial, and that obstinacy leads to the most disastrous results.

A writer has undertaken on his own suggestion, and happily at his own expense, to shatter the whole fabric of Christendom. What a man he must be! He has undertaken to show that the Bible and all the fathers, pagan and classical, all the antiquarian lore on which we build so much, is all the work of the monks of the twelfth century! The monks of that fruitful century wrote Moses and the prophets and the evangelists and the apostles, and wrote all the great learned works in the Greek and Latin language, and therefore Christendom is built upon a species of smoke. Let him be heard! He sent his book to me, saying, Why do you public teachers of Christianity not answer this book? I answered it in a sentence; I am afraid that sentence, though but one, was too long; said I, Many thanks for your book; I am not an antiquarian scholar, and I have next to no acquaintance with the monks of any century, I am specially unfamiliar with the monks of the twelfth century; I cannot follow all your learned argument, but I can follow you in one sentence in your own preface; that sentence is as follows: "The Americans are just about, in 1896, let us say, to celebrate the fourth anniversary of the discovery of America." Said I, If this is a specimen of your accuracy and archeology, I need not read any more of your book. He came to see me and said, This is perfectly true what I have said, that the Americans are in the year 1895 or 1896 about to celebrate the fourth anniversary of the discovery of America. I said, What! You surely mean fourth centenary, the four hundredth year. Well, said he, with uplifted hands, I never saw it until this moment! A man who can give himself to a blunder of that sort of his own manufacture, I am not going to trust too far in matters which I cannot bring to an equally severe and definite test. I always find that if a man cannot speak his own language correctly, there is some just suspicion to be attached to his speaking all other languages or speaking any of them. If a man does not know his own country, I do not think he can know very much about the mountains and valleys of the moon. And so the Book still stands, and the assailant books are never asked for. The stone which the builders rejected is become the head of the corner. Let us be just to fact.

There is a refusal which is right. That refusal is associated with the illustrious name just quoted. Moses when he was come of age refused to be called the son of Pharaoh's daughter. The offer was made to him, he might have had the honor, he might have occupied an exalted position; he was learned in all the lore of the Egyptians, he had been proved to be a man of capacity, of great physical beauty and majesty, of great moral force and dignity; and when the offer was made to him that he might be the son of the king's daughter, he said, No. Then what will you choose? I choose rather to suffer affliction with the people of God. These are the refusals that mark critical points in human history. These, too, are the refusals which bring character to completeness and to crowning majesty. Resist, refuse the devil, and he will flee from you. When he says, All these things will I give thee if thou wilt fall down and worship me, order him behind you as you would order a hound that had incurred your displeasure. Refuse the wrong king; send for the Jesus you have rejected, saying, We will have this Man to reign over us; and say to Him, God forgive us! Come and reign over us, Son of Mary, Son of God.

Understand, therefore, finally, that we cannot depose those whom God has called in His electing love to this position or to that. We can say to Him, Lord, make me much, little, nothing, but let me know that it is Thy doing, and I shall be calm with Thine own peace; I shall not know the burning of jealousy and of envy; I will know that He who set the stars in their places has appointed my habitation. That is the spirit in which to accept the providence of life, and work out the destiny fixed by the love of God. Understand that we cannot all be at the head of the corner. Honor enough for us if we be in the God-built edifice, whether in the base, in the midst, or at the top. God must be allowed to build His own temples in His own way. "He that buildeth all things is God." Let us further remember that every man is a living temple of the Holy Ghost, and that of the temple of his heart Christ must be the chief corner stone. We must not build even our own heart-temple from specifications and plans of our own invention. God plans the insect, and God plans the seraph. The marvel of God's wisdom is shown in the specialty of individual life. Man is many, yet man is one. No two men are identical. No two responsibilities can be so blended as to relieve any man of the entire burden of his own life. What is the head stone of our heart? Have we any idols to cast out? Jesus can have only one place; whatever we build, be it gold, silver, or precious stones, if it be not built on the one foundation it will be overwhelmed and broken down forever.

Prayer

Almighty God, how wondrous are Thy ways in manifoldness and beauty and suggestion! how great is the altar at which we kneel! All things praise the Lord. In this great utterance of psalm and reading and thanksgiving may no human heart be dumb; show us that silence is blasphemy, teach us that to be dumb is to be hostile; may we know Thy wonderful mercy which accepts the music of the heart as if it were also the music of the voice. Thou hast given us all things richly to enjoy; may we testify our enjoyment by our psalm; may we not be degraded by our own ingratitude. Teach us that thankfulness multiplies the gifts which it acknowledges; in all things may we be thankful, and in all things may we rejoice. Can we rejoice in Thy chastening? Thou dost lacerate us, and, behold, our weakness gives way; Thou dost desolate us, and we cannot sing in the wilderness. Is the stroke of Thine hand a stroke of love? Enable us to receive it as such, lest our hearts wax rebellious and kick against the four corners of Thy throne. Show us that Thou dost test our strength as well as our weakness by Thy chastening; show us that when Thou dost chasten us Thou art as a seedsman coming to receive the harvest—a harvest of obedience and acquiescence and of resignation. But to these things we must grow in the centuries to come; we cannot do these things here and now under skies so gray and on a sand which can hold no foundation for our life-house; mayhap in the centuries to come even our poor voices may join the acclaim, and we, even we, may be in haste to kiss the hand that held the rod. But we cannot kiss it now; in a thousand years maybe we shall see it all. Thou dost hide a great doctrine and a comforting hope in our desolated hearts; Thou hast only asked of us faith, and Thou dost first give that which Thou dost require. Wondrous has been Thy way towards us; Thou hast made us exultant with joy and all but mad with despair; Thou hast sent adversity to tear down our house, and grief to spoil the feast of our heart. Yet Thou art watching it all and directing it all, and Thou wilt bring it all to sanctification and completeness. We thank Thee for all Thy love; we see it in the darkness; it is a star before the morning, it is a star that is not afraid of the night. Thou dost send to us voices and visions and comfortings and evangels manifold, and adapted to our weakness and our forlorn misery. We bless Thee that Thou hast undertaken the great question of sin; the blood of Jesus Christ Thy Son cleanseth from all sin; behold the Lamb of God that taketh away the sin of the world. May we follow Thee and cling to Thee, and accept the offers of Thy love and fall in with all the overtures of Thine unspeakable mercy. Regard the stranger within our gates with favor; take away from his heart all sense of lonesomeness; may he feel that in Christ there is no more sea that all whom He loves are within the reach of His heart, and all of them can receive the breathing of His love, and he in return be enriched by all their honor and confidence and affection. Look upon all who have come from the marketplace; purge their ears of the noise of the world, give them the joy of silence—that quick, eager, sensitive silence that hears the going of God in the clouds. If any man has brought special sin here, having stained the week with deepest iniquity, and has come from the house of evil, from the pit of degradation, and from the solitude of shame, we leave him with Thee, we have no prayer great enough to include such noisomeness; but we have heard from a thousand voices of history that Thy mercy endureth forever. If any soul would be better, struggling out of beasthood into manhood, trying to recover lost ground, trying to escape the tempter, the Lord help such with a very tender mercy. Gather up all these little children as Thou wouldst gather flowers in Thine own garden, and kiss them and bless them and give them to feel that all the days will bring some joy of their own. Our old folks and sick ones, our friends who know the bitterness of grief, we lay them down at Thy feet; Thy look will be their heaven.

We pray all this at the Cross, already blossoming out of the winter of its desolation into the summer of its universal acceptance. Amen.

2
Manifold Grace

Preached On Sunday Morning, June 11th, 1899.

The manifold grace of God–1 Peter 4:10.

The whole verse reads thus, "Let every man that has received the gift even so minister the same one to another as good stewards of the manifold grace of God." What is "manifold"? Many? No. The word "many" would be misleading, though it does enter into the larger and truer interpretation of the term. Manifold in this case means variegated, many in color and light and bloom and beauty. Manifold is not in this relation a question of quantity or quality, but of variety; every color a poem, all the colors belonging to one another and totaling up into one ineffable whiteness. Every man hath received the gift, therefore let him minister the same, and let one give to another, and let every man bring his color to every other man's color, and let all the world see how variegated in charm and hue is the total grace or gift of God. Every man holds his own color of grace as a steward. Your color is not mine, mine is not the color held by some other man, but every man hath received his gift of God, his shade of color. The shades of color do not look well when they are taken away from one another; therefore they should be arranged into poems of brightness and bloom and fragrance; for God is the giver of them all. The holders of the variegated grace of God are only stewards.

Has there been any chaffering of contention in the green woods all these summer days? Not one word of such rivalry or foolish ambition or vanity has been heard. How many greens are there? Let those who have leisure count the number. And may one green live with another? One green may be essential to the interpretation of another, to its full showing-off. But shall the blue green fight with the gray green? They know better; nature more loyally serves her Lord. All the green forests sway in the music of unity: it is only man who makes a fool of himself. His color he is always magnifying above every other color; he says his is the right green, and other people's green is the wrong green. So we have botanized ourselves into little woods and special corners of plantations, and we publish annual reports to show that our green is the right green. Oh! that men were wise, that they understood these things, that they would consider the manifold grace of God, the many-sidedness of His gifts, the many colors in His gardens and in His forests, and that they would not compare one to the disadvantage of the other. But man must to the last be a fool. We cannot get people to praise one blue without pouring contempt upon another. You never heard any preacher praised except when you have been told that he is nothing like so beautiful a green as you may find in some other preacher. They will not take a man or a color or a plant or flower or tree for what it is. Who will pluck the apples of the apple-tree when he knows perfectly well that it is not a pear-tree? He lives for pear-trees only, to the exclusion of apples and plums and other fruits. This is what man is always doing, and he is always doing so to his own vexation and impoverishment. He says, Whilst acknowledging the merit—bless his dear little soul, if it is not too small to be blessed; he acknowledges the merit!—then let the universe take holiday and do what it pleases for one round of the clock. One man is not every man; one variety of grace is not the total grace of God; one minister is not the ministry; one book is not literature. A book on geography of Asia Minor is not to be contrasted with Milton's *Paradise Lost*. Why will not people distinguish, and allocate, and recognize the distribution of the Divine gifts by Divine hands, and let the Lord alone? Who refuses bread because it is not water? Who refuses wheat because it was not grown in a vineyard? Recognize the manifold grace of God, the many colored flowers, the variegated foliage. The variety is an illustration as well as a proof of the deity.

This word "manifold" occurs in many places, and it applies to good things and to bad things alike. There is nothing in the descriptive word itself, it is only when it is related to some substantive that it acquires a character or indicates a special utility of its own. Who expected to find this expression in Nehemiah, the busiest of the books, the wall-building book, the Balbus before the time. "In Thy manifold mercies thou forsookedst them not" (Neh. 9:19). The mercy is one, the mercies are ten thousand. Always distinguish between the substantial central quality and its raditations or offshoots or incidental distributions of forces. Mercy comes in many forms. They say—oh that we had ears to hear!—that chastening may be mercy. In the manifoldness of Thy mercies Thou didst not forsake Thy people. One had a small mercy; one had a glint of light; another had a little flower from Thy garden; another had a great vision of light, a kind of morning at midnight; one had a dream, another a psalm, another a deep consciousness that things were going right when they seemed to be going wrong; and they bore their testimony and contributed their various experience until the whole totaled up into mercy. It required all the mercies to represent the mercy. That is how God uses the singular in all the grammar of His providence, and that is the purpose He has in view in gathering up all the plurals. He has from the beginning been aiming at a great unity; He has had to break Himself up into many visions and many diverse indications, and He has had to proceed by a ministry of variegation, but all the time His object has been to build up a great unity. It is so in that grand final anthem that has to be sung the universe through; there shall one day go up a grand thunder hallelujah, sung as hallelujah has never been sung by lips on earth —"Hallelujah! the Lord God Omnipotent reigneth; the kingdoms (the plural) of the world have become the kingdom (the singular) of our God." Think of the mighty force that is handling kingdoms, uniting and relating empires! These are nothing to Him, for He unites and relates the constellations, and gathers the heavens into heaven. In the meantime we are in the land of plurals and in the land of manifoldness of representation and service, and what we have to recognize is that all these plurals are making their way as fast as time will open its gates into the grand singular, the infinite solidarity.

In that most wondrous of the psalms in many respects, the 104th, we read in the twenty-fourth verse, "O Lord, how manifold are Thy mercies!" Why not say, How great is Thy mercy! That should be said, that has been said, but most of us are still in the lower school, and we have not quite got into the way of amalgamating and unifying the diverse plurals and bringing them into one sublime and glowing unity. The apostle Paul, most wondrous of writers and speakers, in one unconscious effort united the plurals and the singular in one grand expression, Ephesians 3:10–that album of wisdom, that temple of the uppermost and innermost piety. Paul there speaks of "the manifold wisdom of God." It is another variety of the text, "the manifold grace of God"–the grace split up into attributes, into lines, separate individuality accentuated, and yet all gathering themselves up into grace, wisdom, love. Men will not learn this lesson; they expect to find all the colors in one flower, they cannot really believe that God made two flowers; they can appreciate one flower only, and although before their very eyes there are spread out many flowers, yet they have their pet flowers as they have their pet graces, their pet texts, their miserable and bewildering and misleading partialities. But how many minds can take in two ideas? how many minds are open to the reception of new ideas, thoughts, dreams, and visions? Not many. What a group of tender and ennobling thoughts!–manifold mercy, manifold wisdom, manifold grace. Recognize the manifoldness. Could you imagine any man saying that a piano is not a musical instrument because it is not a flute? There may be some such peculiarly wise man, but we have not met him, and therefore we shall dismiss the notion almost with contempt. Do you discard your little child because she has not the features which Phidias would have loved to sculpture? or the little boy because he is not the kind of creature that Raphael would have stolen from the streets in order to reincarnate him in paint? You recognize the excellence of the child, and that is right; and you should recognize the degree of grace which you can receive, and not dispute that another man has not the right grace because he has seen a different view of God from that which your own eyes have seen. Every man, every soul must get its own view of God. This is the rule through all life. Get out of the landscape what you can. We are all, if wise and reverent, artists and poets according to our own gift. Hear what you can in the air; see what you can see in all the outspreading wonders of God, and be thankful if you get any glance or peep of light and beauty; call that beauty your own, be faithful to it, and you will get more.

I must recall an idea just referred to, namely, that the word manifold is applied not only to things good, divine, beautiful, but to other things. "I know your manifold transgressions and sins" (Amos 4:12). Every man sins in his own way, and every man condemns the sins of every other man. That is how we come to have the little clay idol called Personal Respectability—that miserable imp, that worst species of infidelity, if exaggerated and unduly applied and construed. Every man tries to make himself respectable by remarking upon the want of respectability in the man who is sitting next him: as who should say, You observe how critical I am, and how different I am from this person, although we are seated near to one another and are actually in the closest bodily proximity; yet how different I am from him! But the other man is saying exactly the same thing! That is the awkward part of the criticism. Mind yourself, take heed unto thyself. Pulling down another man's house does not make your own any the more secure. Sin is manifold; some men sin in gray hues, others in ardent red and glaring greens; and others sin with a peculiar intermingling of all the hues, so that it is difficult to fix a name and fasten it on the particular quality and range of sin. O man, pierce thine own heart! Judge not that ye be not judged; for with what judgment ye judge ye shall be judged, and with what measure ye mete it shall be measured to you again. Consider not the mote that is in thy brother's eye; get the beam out of thine own. But that would put an end to conversation, and turn the school of human training into a school of the deaf and dumb.

The same word is applied by the very apostle of the text. In the same epistle (1:6): "Ye are in heaviness through manifold temptations." What is a temptation to one man is not a temptation to another. You rise in perfect decorum from the table; another man at the same table lost his manhood and went body and soul to the devil. Temptations come in various forms and in various forces. It is no temptation to you to do a certain thing, but it is an overpowering temptation to another person to do it. Consider thyself lest thou also be tempted. If thy brother has gone astray, say nothing about it, but as soon as possible go out into the darkness and find him, even if you have to grope for him and sit down beside him and kiss him back into manhood and hope and sonship.

So then the word "manifold" may be applied not only to the grace of God, the wisdom of God, and the mercy of God, but to the transgressions and the sins of men and to the temptations through which all souls that are being educated for heaven must needs pass. Be ye stewards of the grace which God has committed to you. It is a grace of wealth, a grace of leisure or of patience or of tenderness; you are gifted with the love of mankind, you have yearning hearts after the Lord; you have a great skill in seeing the best side of every man's character, and working upon the lost from the point of hope and the center of possible restoration. Oh, do not look at the weed, look at the flower; do not look at the hardships, but look at the enjoyments. Wondrous is the mercy, the grace of God. I see it in every beast and bird, in every dewdrop and in every flower; I see nothing but God in all the beauties of nature and in all the education and higher harmonies of life. I would never speak of theology and science; to me there is nothing but theology, that is to say, God. Science is religious, science has a pew in every church, science belongs to the altar. God has not amputated His own universe, and scattered it in little offcuttings and branches and schisms of spiritual and secular, theology and science, and sacred and something else contrastive. No, all things belong to the manifold grace of God. Do not permit a man to be a thief in the house of the Lord; everything that is precious belongs to the house. Arithmetic is part of the hymn-book, and science in its abstrusest inquires must needs return to the altar to recruit its strength or to relight the lamp of its hope. This is my belief. I see the grace of God in every season of the year, in spring and summer, in autumn and winter alike, and I see the mercy of God in all the moan and sorrow and in all the hope and joy of providential life. I see the throne of God in the midst of things; I feel the breath of God in the wilderness and in the tropical paradises of flowers and things blooming and fragrant.

But if I would see the grace of God in its broadest manifestation, in its morning and noontide glory, I would look at the Cross. That is the grace of God which bringeth salvation; that is the grace that sought us while we were wandering and brought us home in faith and penitence, in tears and love. The Cross of Christ should be interpreted from this point of view, namely, as the great appeal of the heart of God, the outgoing of the infinite pity of heaven to seek men, to save them, to bring them to God. Never be ashamed of the word grace. It is a charming sound, it has in it a deep philosophy; it means the heart of God, so to say, supreme above the hand of God, mercy greater than omnipotence. By grace are ye saved, and when the apostle would gather us all together in his great arms and make us most conscious of the Divine blessing, he says, "The grace of our Lord Jesus Christ be with you all." When he would stir us to the noblest endeavor, he says, "Ye know the grace of our Lord Jesus Christ." Let that be your inspiration, your sustenance.

The word "grace" is not popular today. It is by no means a modern word, for it goes back to the very heart of God. This is the day of materialism; of pomp and show and glittering spectacle; this is an age of mechanics, engineering, and what is called practical work. I claim for "grace" that it is the most practical work of all. It renews the heart, it purifies the motive, it gives life a new purpose, it makes conduct beautiful, and any ministry that can accomplish all these marvels is never to be described or despised as sentimental or theoretical. Brethren, until the grace of God has had free course in our lives and hearts we know not the highest meaning of our own manhood, nor can we get any clear view of our own eternal destiny. The grace of God is what we need—the purifying spirit, the clear vision, the high aim. God waits to be gracious.

Prayer

Almighty God, teach us by Thy Spirit that we know not what we do either in good or evil; teach us that we cannot calculate the value of our own actions or the range of our own influence. Teach the wicked man his folly when he says that he injures no one but himself; comfort the good man when he thinks that he is not doing anything to help forward the progress of Thy kingdom. Show us that influence attaches to all thought and all action; that we influence ourselves, that we sculpture our own faces and mold our own figures, and introduce music or discord into our own voices, and that we may make the air a living way up to heaven by constant, loving, trustful prayer. Show us that all things are in motion if we could but understand Thy method in things, and teach us that we see best with our eyes shut, with our bodies sent away from us, that the spirit may have larger franchise, ampler liberty, fuller delight. We thank Thee for religious aspiration, for the hungering and thirsting after better things, and we bless Thee that there is no aspiration of the soul after light and truth and beauty and music that does not rest upon the promise of the Infinite Righteousness and the unspeakable mercy. Teach us how solemn a thing it is to live; bring to bear upon us all considerations that can lift us out of the lower depths and from the lower levels, and carry us away into the great mountains, whence we may see the larger sanctuaries and the opening gates in the great light. The Lord pity us when we are low-minded and mean of soul, and when we make small calculations and arrangements; say unto us from Thine own heights, Arise, shine, for thy light has come, and the glory of the Lord is risen upon thee. Thus may we awaken to behold the morning, and to improve every shining moment of the dawn. We have brought our sin to Thee that we may leave it at the Cross, that we may heartily repent of the same and abandon it forever, saying, each for himself, God be merciful unto me a sinner! Turn all our thoughts, we humbly pray thee, Christward and towards the Cross, that we may know somewhat of Thy deeper meanings and come into closer audience with the King, so that the whispers of our heart may reach Him and the unspoken desires of our souls may affect Him like living prayers. Amen.

3

One of the Least

Preached on Thursday Morning, June 15th, 1899.

One of the least of these—Matthew 25:40.

Christ never despised little folks, little things, little occasions, little duties; Jesus never turned away from the small and the lame, the halt and the blind. Why was this? It was because He was Jesus. No man a mere man could have afforded to attend to us little creatures, persons of no consequence; it required God to stoop low enough to come down to us. The Deity is in the stoop, not in the grammar. He who holds a grammatical God has no God to hold. The Deity of the Lord Jesus Christ is in His pity, care, tears, mercy, His coming out after us in the dark times, in the stormy nights, sure that if we are to be found at all we must be found in the wilderness. That is His Deity; not some variable preposition or difficult word to construe with some other verbal difficulty.

"One of the least of these." This was His doctrine about the Church. If I might tell you why I chose a particular section or aspect of the Church I should have no hesitation in approaching your confidence, though I might instigate your criticism. Jesus Christ said, "Where two or three are gathered together in My name, there am I." I consider that where these circumstances concur I find the Church, the Christian Church, the redeemed and sanctified Church. I may be wrong; older and better men infinitely than I am may form some other opinion about the Church, and they are as much entitled to their construction of the terms as I am; let there

be no angry difference between us or amongst us. This is my definition of the Church: "Where two or three are gathered together in
My name, there am I in the midst of them." He did not choose a
great thousand or fix His unit at ten thousand; as usual, He stoops,
He condescends, and accepts the very lowest plural. "Where two
or three"—just the very smallest number of persons—"are gathered
together"—because they love Me, because they trust to Me, and depend upon My Cross for their salvation—wheresoever I find even
that little number I find My own Church, and the gates of hell shall
not prevail against it. Thus I am saved from many intricate questions which can do me no real good of heart or soul, but which
might very greatly perplex and distress me. I retire into the sanctuary built by the hands of Christ Himself, and that little sanctuary is
only as big as two or three, in the right name and with the living
Christ amongst them—that is the Church. But man will not have
it; man hath found out many inventions; he is in danger of cutting
himself to pieces with the sharpness of his own misled genius. If
this definition of the Church is right, and it seems to me to be absolutely and unquestionably right, then I get rid of a great number
of words which men are very fond of using. I hear of "weak"
churches. Where did Christ speak of them? He never alluded to
them. I hear of "poor" churches. Where are they? Christ never mentioned one of them. Poor churches are a simple impossibility; the
one word contradicts the other. I hear of "isolated" churches. Man
is so fond of adjectives—"poor" and "weak" and "isolated." Does
that word "isolated" ever occur in my Lord's speech? I have read
Him now for a lifetime; I hardly read any other teacher; I do not remember a single case in which my Lord used the word "isolated" in
reference to two or three broken hearts gathered together in His
name and healed by His grace. But man could not live without epithets; it would be poor living if we could not coin as many adjectives as we want, and therefore we have now called into existence
poor churches, weak churches, isolated churches, struggling
churches; and my Lord never heard of one of them. Be very careful

how you apply epithets to anything Christ ever did; it is impossible to fit an adjective to His substantive. So I am willing to be number two or number three in the little society which Jesus Christ condescends to recognize. Money is not essential to the constitution of a church; numbers have nothing to do with Christ's conception of His redeemed Church; isolated is simply an impossible word as applied to the two or three who can only meet behind a spring hedge or gather together by some well-side and drink His blood in water. It is not essential to the Church that there should be a minister. There we come upon a whole black seam of sophisms. People no sooner get together than they want a harmonium. I do not remember that my Lord ever spoke about a harmonium as essential to the constitution of His Church. It is no more necessary to the Church to have a minister than it is to a home to have a piano. But the people will have it so; they beg for harmoniums. When will we get back to the dear Lord's conception of the Church—a witnessing body, a body dependent upon Himself and the Holy Ghost for the doctrine and the inspiration and the beneficence and the whole outset and outline of Christian life? Yet if I were to talk so even my own brethren would cast me out. But sometimes I prefer to be cast out; I love the open air, I love the sky; in its bright dumbness it often makes me religious.

And Jesus Christ, looking upon lives and services, said, "One of the least of these." Supposing them to be all little, there are some that are less and some that are least; and some man expressed some other man's feeling in the hymn which has in it this line, "Oh to be nothing, nothing!" The least is essential to the whole; every stone in the building is essential to the entire masonry; not a brick in the minster can be dispensed with. But do not let the least think that he is the biggest; do not let the least show his piety in his touchiness. There are some persons less than the least in their own speech, but they do not recognize this when they are spoken of as such in the speech of others. This is a subtle distinction; the sword of the Lord is sharp, piercing, to the dividing asunder of the joints and the marrow, and it makes havoc in all our flimsy distinctions and in all our pious hypocrisies. When the Lord looks upon the services which people render, He often stops beside a cup of cold water, lifts it up, and smiles it into wine that makes glad the heart of God and man. That was all that the giver could give; being all that the giver could give, it became valuable, precious, priceless. "One of the least of these gifts." This woman hath cast in more than they all. Lord, how much has this woman given? ten thousand talents of silver or gold? we would see the glittery heap. Nay, said Jesus, more than that. This poor woman has cast in more than that, dost Thou say, sweet Lord? Ay. How much? All. The millionaire cannot give; no man gives except under the knife. Jesus Christ will not have it that any man can give Him anything except from the Cross, His own Cross, and the man's cross cut out of it; that is giving; the last bronze from the till—that is giving.

This alters our whole conception of Jesus Christ's thought, as we have misunderstood it. We thought He would be very careful about legions of stars, and He seems to be more careful of the poor man's one tallow candle that is set in the window on wintry nights to show the prodigal the way home. He will not allow that candle to sway in the storm; He guards it and keeps it steadily towards the window if mayhap the strayed girl or the prodigal boy may want to come home some night cold, and that candle is there, an evangel, a gospel, a luminous welcome. We have wholly misconstrued the idea of power. If we were required to describe power we should think of great magnitudes, immense distances; and God does not think of these things. He is great in pity, great in love, great in tears; never so much God to a fallen world as when saturated, drenched, drowned in the tears of pity. Poor man! Looking at a gigantic mass of mud called a mountain, he says, How noble, how vast, how grand! Why was this waste of epithets? They might have been sold for a bronze or two and given to the poor. Say my Lord is great when He cries over Jerusalem, saying unto the queen city of the world, Thine house is left unto these desolate. Great pity is much more than great strength. God does nothing by mere energy, He makes no display of mere power; He never worked a miracle for the sake of the miracle, He always worked it for the sake of the blind man or the lame creature or the suffering woman or the hungry ones that were feeling the pinch of starvation in the inhospitable wilderness. I will think of my Lord's greatness in this way; it brings Him nearer to me; perhaps He may weep over me some day and take me back into the heart which by my many sins I have forsaken or even distrusted. My hope is in the tears of God.

All through the Bible there is a wonderful care of little things; God noticing them, God caring for them, and God bringing them to perfectness of meaning. Said Jesus Christ on one occasion the most remarkable thing out of the beatitudes, and it is the beatitude that crowns the rest, "The very hairs of your head are all numbered." That is greatness. "He putteth my tears in His bottle"; that is condescension. "None of his steps shall slide," as if he numbered step by step all the going of His people. One of those people said, "Thou knowest my downsitting and mine uprising, my going out and my coming in." And another said, "Thou hast beset me behind and before, and laid Thine hand upon me, as if I were an only child." These are God's condescensions: sweeping the house diligently until He find the piece that was lost; leaving the ninety-nine in the wilderness, and going out after that which had strayed, and not returning until He had found it. This Shepherd undertakes no vain errands; He brings back the wanderer and completes the flock.

One of His disciples—he is quite a study in psychology, because he seems to be able to plunge into fire and to go through seas of darkness; and yet though he wrote very little he wrote some of the sweetest words that ever were written by mortal pen, and one of these words runs like this: "Now unto Him that is able to keep you from failing." In the Authorized Version it is "able to keep you from falling," but the finer distinction of the term is, Able to keep you from reeling, staggering, falling; able to save you before you fall into the ground, able to seize you in the very act of falling, and set

you up again, men. Once Jesus Christ said these words, showing
how great He is in tenderness and in human mercy, Give these people something to eat "lest they faint by the way." This is the Divine
economist; He does not wait until people are half-dead of starvation, and then give them something; He anticipates hunger, so that
when hunger comes it finds the table ready; not "because they are
hungry," but lest they become hungry, lest they faint by the way.
Oh the care! Mother never spoke a gentler word; fondest sister
never took such pains to prevent or anticipate recurring hunger.
There you have the deity of Christ; there you have the humanity of
the Savior. No man can define deity. If he could define deity he
could define God, for Deity is but another name for God. But who
can define that word which has become so large and glorious that it
fills the imagination, exhausting all speech, and beginning the creation of a language of its own? So we say "God" without being able
to define it. We must not think that we can take every mystery to
pieces and put it together again as a puzzle. We cannot touch the
sun, but we can receive its morning light and its midday crown. So
it is with language; no man can define God, and yet it is so wrought
into our Western thought and the very tissue, so to say, of our souls
that no other word can take its place, it stands alone; as well attempt to displace the firmament by some canvas canopy as to displace this word God by any number of man-invented polysyllables.
We misconceive greatness.

It is curious to know how the Church talks. Sometime if you
have half an hour to spare, which you ought never to have, it
would interest you to hear how the poor old Christian Church all
over the world talks. I could give you a short extract from the
speech of this withered beauty, the speech of her who ought to
have eclipsed the stars by her glowing splendor. She is talked about
now in this way: It is a very, very poor affair; I was there some little
time ago, and I think I am not exaggerating when I say that there
really could not have been more than about five-and-twenty of a
congregation. Ah, how they cut the Lord's heart to pieces with

sharp knives! They say, It was a very insignificant affair; there were
no people of any importance there. Ah, thou slighted Calvary, thou
often crucified Christ! Here is a definition of importance for thee!
The Church is in the little village, and there are no persons of importance in it. What is importance? For all these people Christ died.
But there are people of no importance! Sometimes the Church, as
discredited and discrowned, is made to talk a language bordering
on blasphemy, for she says, The resolution was carried by a very
great majority; in fact, the minority was so small as to be of no account. My Lord said, Where two or three are gathered together in
My name, there am I in the midst. Let us get back to the New Testament, back to Christ; let us redefine our position. I will have
nothing to do with your millionaire demonstrations; I would go
out after that which was lost, and by my Lord's strength I would
continue out until I have found it. I would recognize the smallest
worker, the Sunday-school teacher, the ragged-school teacher, the
city missionary. What have I heard the Church, as dismantled and
discrowned, say? She said that there was only a missionary preaching last Sunday. Only a missionary!—a man who has hazarded his
life for the Lord Jesus; a man who has left his children on this shore
that he may go to yonder land and tell the story of the Cross, its
shame and glory. But when he comes to our pulpit we go to hear
some popular preacher who never lost a night's sleep for the salvation of the world; and when asked why we have gone to hear him
we say, Because there was only a missionary in our own church.
Shame! That church can never win the world. It is a clumsily orga-
nized hypocrisy.

Then we must not make any mistake about this littleness. If we
do little when we could do much, then the little goes for nothing.
That is where your sixpence went! It was absolutely lost in ungrateful oblivion. Perhaps it was not wholly your blame, because you
had the two coins in the same pocket, the half-sovereign and the
half-shilling, and it was just by an accident that you took out the
white one. It may be so—may it, may it be so? If the little is all I

can do, my Lord takes a few grassblades as if I had brought Him a whole paradise. But if I could have brought Him rich flowers, and only plucked a weed out of the hedgerow, He will not take my gift. He who can stoop low will not stoop to be insulted when I offer Him a hedgerow weed when I might have given Him a garden of orchids.

I have said that it is not essential to the constitution of the Church that there should be a minister. This goes to the root of a very important matter. It is no more essential to the constitution of a Church that it should have a minister than that it should have a steeple. It is because Christians so largely differ, I may say so vitally differ, about the constitution of the Church that they spend so much of their time in bitter and futile controversy. What is the Church of Christ, as Christ Himself understood it? is the all-comprehensive and all-determining inquiry. Not what fathers and founders, prelates and popes, have thought the Church of Christ to be, but what Christ Himself intended the Church to be is the question which should never be shirked. According to one definition, the Church is merely an expression of national life, and is just what the national life is. The national sentiment determines the constitution of the Church. If the nation were atheistic, there would be no Church; if the nation were evangelically disposed, there would be an evangelical Church; when the nation is worldly or religiously indifferent, the Church follows the mood of the world and sleeps in irresponsible languor. There is another conception of the Church which diametrically differs from this. According to the second definition, the Church of Christ is the body of Christ—a body composed of regenerated or converted souls which by solemn oath and covenant have united themselves as living members of a living Church. The characteristic note of this Church is sympathy with Christ, love of Christ, work for Christ, brotherhood in Christ. It will be seen that these two conceptions cannot coexist. For my own part, as your voluntarily elected pastor and teacher, I frankly say that I have adopted the second definition. Repentance, confession, forgiveness, regeneration, are essential to membership in the true Church of the Savior. Distinctions and grades there will always be; some will be "of note among the apostles," some will "seem to be pillars," others will be nameless and socially of no consequence whatever, yet out of all these varying materials there will be built up a holy house unto the Lord; a sacred, tender, beneficent fellowship. To be one of the least in that fellowship is the greatest honor which any man can attain; it never means rivalry, jealousy, or unholy emulation; it means that the soul is content to be in Christ, whether as a little twig or a great branch; its joy is in being attached to the root which is itself attached to the very heart of the universe.

Prayer

God in the person of His Son has all His mightiest works outdone. We see not God, but we see Jesus. His name is Immanuel; He took on our flesh, He spoke to our hearts, His words are with us today. We live upon those words as upon bread and water from heaven's fountains; we want no other food, we would live upon the Son of God. As the branch abideth in the vine, so would we abide in Christ; without Him we can do nothing; we can do all things through Christ enabling us. We have come to the house of prayer that we might for a moment turn it into a house of praise; for the Lord hath done great things for us, and we will not be silent concerning them. Thou hast taken us by difficult roads, up high mountains, and down deep valleys which never caught the sunlight; Thou hast been with us in the burning wilderness, and for us Thou didst find honey in the bare rocks. How then shall we be silent in Thine house, and take no part in the song which is sung by the rest of Thy creation? Thou hast beset us behind and before, and laid Thine hand upon us; Thou hast gone before us and prepared the way; Thou hast said unto crooked paths, Be straight, and Thou hast commanded rough places to be plain, and the valleys Thou hast exalted, so that the morning light might shine upon them. We remember that we have done the things we ought not to have done, but wilt Thou permit us to lay our hand upon Thine and to lead Thee to Calvary and to ask Thee whether Thy grace has not infinitely abounded above our sin. O Christ of God! Behold Thine own Cross; recount Thine own wounds; feel again the deep spear-thrust, and tell us whether all this atoning, redeeming work is not infinitely greater than the sin of our short day. God be merciful unto me a sinner!—is the cry of every broken heart. Thou hast ordained that prayer; Thou wilt never refuse the answer of love to so sharp a cry; Thou wilt say to each of us, Thy sins, which are many, are all forgiven thee; and thus we will see in the Cross of Christ the way to pardon, thence to purity, thence to heaven. We pray for one another; it is well for the life that is bathed in prayer; no evil shall come nigh it, the pestilent night shall leave it untouched, and the darkening day shall leave it without a bruise. Happy are they who live in the sanctuary of Thine heart, Thou God of Abraham and Isaac and Jacob, Thou God of the redeeming Cross. Break up all our own little notions and poor devices for reforming and redeeming the world: show us that from eternity Thou hast planned to do this, and that nothing can hinder the final consummation of the purposes of Thy grace; we can do nothing against the truth but for the truth. Teach us how foolish we are if we depend upon ourselves to make God's world greener or give a deeper blue to God's own summer sky. Yet Thou hast been pleased to call us to cooperation, Thou hast made us part of Thine own husbandry, we are called fellow-workers with God; herein we find our inspiration and our courage and our pledge of final success; the mouth of the Lord hath spoken it. So everything opposing Thy word must disappear, must be dashed to pieces like a potter's vessel, and as a stone shall all hindering furrows be dropped into the midst of the sea. Give courage, we humbly pray Thee, to all evangelists, missionaries, preachers of the everlasting gospel and teachers of the holy doctrine, and may we, at home, abroad, in the school, in the wilderness, never change the subject. The enemy tempts us, he shows us how much fruit we might pluck off this tree and that tree and some other poor shrub; may we keep to the tree which Thou hast set for our eating; may we never change the theme! Blessed shall be that servant who at the last shall be preaching none other than the infinite Christ, the all-kindling light of all the firmament, the peace and the glory of God. Wilt Thou be pleased to bless us all. Leave none unblest. Remember the old man whose prayers are nearly ended; he is already beginning to put on his singing robes. And wilt Thou lovingly smile like a broad June morning upon all the little ones, and give them to feel that this life has no end, that it is already heaven, and that heaven has nothing more to do than to continue and to crown the present; then when the trial comes and the cloud and the stress, the broken vow and the shattered staff, and the old, old misery that sweeps down upon us all, it will be time enough to speak a language they can understand, of consolation and sympathy and hope beyond the death line. Wilt Thou look graciously upon the strangers that are within our gates, friendly folks that have come to mingle their hymns and prayers with ours; grant unto them a home blessing, destroy the nausea of home-sickness, give them to feel that in God's house there is a sense of home and fellowship and rest. God save the Queen, the Queen Victoria, whose coronation day we have been thinking of, whose accession we have been celebrating! Her eighty years are too few—make them eight hundred, and more. God save the Queen! Let the Queen live forever, and she will do us good and not evil, though she tarry with us through many centuries. And if others are praying for their kings, rulers, presidents, and magistrates, the Lord hear the prayer of patriotism, and answer it with a great answer.

We speak all this at the Cross, in the name of the red blood, in the power of the atoning sacrifice. Already we feel the balmy answer bringing its blessing. We wait a moment that we may catch it all. Amen.

4

Holden Eyes

Preached on Sunday Morning, June 25th, 1899.

Their eyes were holden—Luke 24:16.

Jesus Christ was walking with the two men. They knew Him perfectly well under ordinary conditions; it suited His purpose that they should not know Him for a little while, and therefore He held their eyes, so that they could not know Him. He did the same afterwards with Mary; He so held her eyes or transfigured Himself that Mary did not know the Lord she loved above all other lives. We are accustomed in the Bible to come upon such expression as "their eyes were opened"; now and again we come upon the corresponding remark, "their eyes were holden." The things were all there, the environment had not been changed one shade or whit; the change had taken place in the power of vision. Their eyes were not permitted to see, though they were wide open and though no oculist could see the slightest change in their formation. The same thing is happening today in both senses. Sometimes we say in our poor, mean language —for we drop into ineloquence when we are left alone very much— sometimes we say, That opened my eyes! I never saw it before; I cannot tell you exactly how it was, but from that moment my eyes were opened, and I saw it all. Poor man! He has now and then what he vulgarly calls an eye-opener. Yet a wonderful creature is this little man. He invents great machines which sometimes blow him up into the air fifty feet high, and he does many curious things for which he gets large pay; he makes a livelihood by his ingenuity. Yet every

35

now and then he confesses that he must have been undergoing a
process of partial or total blindness; for he says quite suddenly,
That opened my eyes! What opened your eyes?—an attitude, a sentence, a change of policy, a mere turning-round of the human figure that it might signal to some other figure? Yes, that is about what
it was. And you tell me that so simple a thing opened your eyes?
where were your eyes all the ten or twenty or fifty years before? The
eyes were there, but they did not see. Perhaps they were holden;
for the air is full of life, and that life takes our life into its keeping,
and does just what it pleases with our ears and eyes and general
sense of things, while all the time we are undergoing an expensive
process of what is termed education.

We may profitably consider what it is to have our eyes holden,
what a blessing it is, what a source of strength it is not to see things,
not to know things, not to hear things, not to have any senses at all.
There is a blessing on the negative side of the hedge; there is much
profitableness in the impenetrable gloom. Not to see may be a privilege; not to know may be a science.

How true it is that our eyes are holden so that we may not see
the perils of life by which we are constantly surrounded! We walk in
danger; the air is full of arrows and sharp darts and poisoned elements. Some things we could not enjoy if there were not an element of poison in them. The honey would soon be no honey, the
man of science tells us, if there was not inserted by the sting of the
bee just one little drop of poison. There is honey that has no keeping in it because it has no poison in it; so the man of science tells
us. On the whole, it is better for us not to be analytical chemists; it
ministers much to the comfort of the house not to know the chemical constituents of what we are eating and drinking. There are few
things more troublesome than to be on intimate terms with an analytical chemist who lives next door to you. The air is full of danger; every step you take is a step along the edge of your grave. All
the darkness has uncounted imps in it; the east wind brings them
from no man knows where in countless millions. The awful micro-

scope tells us that there may be more bacilli or some other hideous and distressing creature in one little point of butter than there are inhabitants in the total area of Europe. That had better not be widely known; there are nervous temperaments. Most Christians are timid people, or invalids, or incapable of hearing a preacher who says the word condemn in one syllable. My own twelve peers called the jury will not compensate me for my accident according to the value which I place upon my own life, because the learned judge has just told them (it was a work of supererogation certainly) that to go out of the house at all is to go into possible accident; he has told them in some learned apothegm that to breathe is to incur peril, and that therefore a man's accident is not to be estimated by itself as if it stood alone, as if that accident had not happened no other accident could have happened. What has happened is only one of a thousand possible accidents; and all that has to be taken into account when they assess the damages. It is well that we do not see these things. We do not know how near our death we were this morning; by a hair's-breadth we escaped a so-called accident that would have dashed us into eternity. Our eyes were holden. It is well we did not know.

Our eyes are holden that we may not see our own spiritual surroundings. It is a mercy that we cannot see God. Yet we rave about it as if He had inflicted an injury upon us because He will not show His face. We thus reject our greatest blessing. It is a mercy for us also that we cannot see our spiritual enemy the devil. If we could see him who could live? He is hidden from our eyes, or our eyes are holden that we should not see him; enough to feel the fiery breath of his temptation; enough to know that someone touched us as with a finger of flame and scorched our very blood! What are these tormenting passions, these hellish desires, these sudden temptations to do evil? What is it that brings the curse to our lips or the deeper curse unspoken to our hearts? There is a ministry of evil in the universe. The Bible does not conceal that fact; the Bible reveals it and magnifies it and puts us on our guard against it; but mercifully our eyes are holden that we should not see the evil power that would devour our very soul.

A great mercy it is also that we cannot see death—grim, gruesome, horrible death. Yet he is always looking at us; he seems to be saying in that interrogatory look, Whom shall I strike next? There is a fair bud growing on the tree of the mother's heart, I have a mind to snatch it; there is a fair lily that gives value to all the rest of the garden, without that lily the other flowers would droop and wither, I have a mind to break the owner's heart; why not strike at the root of that lily or put a worm there that shall little by little gnaw the root or suck the blood-juice? That image is in your garden, in your house, in mine, on the thoroughfares, everywhere. And yet we go laughing on, joke on joke, and the merriment heightens like foaming wine. Verily it is a mercy that our eyes are holden that we should not see these things!

And a great blessing it is that we do not see the future. We cannot see tomorrow. Whether you mean the future by day or month or year, we cannot see it; it is veiled from us, or our eyes are holden that they may not see it; and herein is a gracious, tender mercy. If you knew for a certainty that you would die this day ten years, you would feel that you were holding a wasting lease, and that it was not really worth your while to do this or that, for ten years are but a handful. Yet we may die tomorrow. It is better we should not know the time of death; better that some things should be known only to God. Jesus Christ plainly told us that there was one thing of which even He was ignorant, that none knew it but the Father, because He was the Father He kept it back—do not tell them when, or you will disorganize the universe. Infinitely better that some things should be kept in the iron safe, so to say, or the strong room, of eternity; better that the Father alone should know certain days and certain hours. There is an appointed time to man upon the earth, and God will not tell us when that time occurs. Otherwise we could not live; the joy would go out of the wedding day and the birthday, and the belfry accustomed to ring out in jubilance and clangor great anniversaries and splendid occasions would itself be turned, as it were, into frost and ice, and it would speak no more its metallic music. Under some circumstances therefore it is better not to know; infinitely better not to see. The life of which you are in quest is just within reach, but you do not know it; the life that would redeem your life from despair is only a day's march off, but no man can tell when the incoming train will give its last throb into the station. It is better so. Lord, Thy will, not mine, be done.

The occasion of opening our eyes shows us in what a big universe we live. Our tendency is to belittle everything. Some persons would be quite contented to regard their own particular parish, district, province, or congregation as the utmost limit of the universe; that is to say, there may be great territory beyond their privileges, but it is only unmapped territory, a chaotic geography, infinite masses of nothingness; the true universe is within the four walls of the house we live in, or certainly within the four walls of the church we worship in. Yet every now and then our eyes are opened; there is another man we never saw before; and yonder is a country of which we never dreamed; and I hear there are human voices. What is this universe? *What?* The question stands like a mark of interrogation in the very center of the sun. Only God knows how big His own universe is.

Poor Hagar was dying of thirst, and the great boy was tugging at her for help, and she had none; and the Lord opened Hagar's eyes, and she saw that she was within hand-reach of a well, and never knew it. The wells are all there if we did but know it. "There standeth One among you whom ye know not; He it is." The well was there all the time; God created no well for Hagar, He only opened Hagar's eyes that she might see the well that was there. In many ways God shows us how near His love is and how delicately His beneficent providence is addressed to our pressing necessities. We have all read of that shell that was shot by the Russians at Sevastopol into the British camp; we almost saw it, so graphic was the description, fall into the earth, and the great masses of earth leaping up, and presently, the British camp greatly needing water, there was a great gush of living water from a rock that had been shattered by the shell, and the stream was relieved, leaped up, and fell in blessings at the very feet of the men who needed the water. So it often is. The enemy shoots great shells into our lives, we ourselves are none the worse for this great rush of intended destruction, but the shell breaks some lid of a rock, and that lid being shattered the water leaps out, and comes to us as an unexpected blessing. Let God have His way; stand back, thou little meddler, and let thy Father rule!

Our eyes are holden that we should not see all the processes and opportunities of civilization. Man does not like the word revelation; he thinks it has a church odor. But the little creature has taken up with another word; he must have a word, poor two-legged insect! He will not have the word revelation, but he will have the word invention; it fits him better, it hits the measure of his little size. But, religiously interpreted, what is invention but revelation? The telephone was in Eden; not as a telephone, but in all that the telephone means. In Eden? Why, in Eden it is quite an old commonplace; it was in eternity; eternity is but a day old; go further, it was in God. Man liked it, however, better when he called it an invention and patented it and made a livelihood out of it, and said to his soul (excuse the poetry!), Soul, thou hast much goods laid up for many years, live on this telephone, eat, drink, and be merry, for I have patented it. I speak now under circumstances that to our forefathers would have been deemed laughable and incredible; in addressing you I am addressing the hospitals of London. I have been entreated to have microphones placed in this pulpit so that people at the hospitals, the hospital for Incurables and many other asylums of disease and distress, sufferers are gathered around their tables at this moment, and I am glad that they have heard the thrilling music which has resounded under this roof, and perhaps some word of prayer or meditation, uttered under the inspiration of God by my own lips, may find a lodgment in the memory of their hearts. I send my sympathetic love to all these listening invalids;

they hear every tone I am uttering, and I say to them in their solitude and in their pain, God help you, God be gracious unto you! "Invention" is an atheistic word; it shuts out God. Revelation is a religious term, and brings in God, and sets Him at the head of things. Man likes to play the atheist—for a little time. It may seem remarkably clever, cleverer than anybody that ever lived before in the whole universe, because the atheist knows that there is no God; and to know that there is no God must be to have been everywhere, as John Foster says, because if we have not been everywhere God may be in the very place where we have not been. But man loves the word "invention," there is something mechanical about it and a sniff of commercial air in it; it is something that one day may become the subject of a patent and a lawsuit, and man likes this kind of activity. He prefers speculation to religion: and verily I say unto you he has his reward.

Oh, if we could have foreseen some days we could not have lived! If you could have foreseen the ruin of your child, boy or girl! When the boy went away, when the girl was drawn aside, when your life was utterly changed; if you could have foreseen that day suicide might have been preferable to its realization. You died seven deaths when the child died; when the child died morally, spiritually; when that young tender life took itself out of the branch and out of the root; well that you did not see it! What a glorious privilege that our eyes were holden so that the tearing and the rending of our life came upon us quite suddenly, when the lifetime was crushed into three months; when all the nightmares and awful apprehensions of life were crowded into one day's pulsation. What a mercy that we did not see all this ten years ago! We should have been disabled for that period of time; we should have lost nerve and courage and hope and joy; it would have been a period of ten years' living dying; but our eyes were holden that we should not see it. If you could have foreseen the loss of all your money—it went, as it were, in a moment. But you got a good deal of enjoyment out of the wealth while you had it. Your eyes were holden that you should not see the thief that was coming to steal your treasure. So it is a privilege that we know not the day of our death. I know I may die tonight, I feel I may live a year or years. God says to me, Poor child of mortality, it is infinitely better that thou shouldst not know anything about it; go on steadily, loyally, hopefully, with thy work, and when it is time for thee to leave the plow, though it be left in mid-furrow, and another man shall complete that furrow, I will come for thee. Till I come, occupy!

Prayer

Almighty God, we have taken all Thy deliverances, and have not believed Thee. We have made use of God, we have found in Him an occasional theology; but we are bruised all over our heart by wounds inflicted by the enemy, wounds of unbelief and obstinacy and self-regard. We are poor creatures at the best; we have a long creed, but no faith; now and again we almost believe Thee, but not wholly; we do not take the decisive leap into the arms and bosom of God; we hold on to things seen and finite and vanishing by one hand, and dimly and uncertainly clutch at some superstition with the other. So the devil beats us in the war, the night vanquishes the most glittering stars, and the wind blows down our altars, which are built partly in belief and mainly in superstition. How broken is our life, how uncertain; how it trembles under the daily burden! We do not feed upon the grace of our Lord Jesus Christ, we do not live on the Cross, and for the Cross, and by the power of the Cross; our feet are still on the earth, and now and then we look down to the dust if haply we might find all the God we want lying at our feet. The Lord pity us; the Lord send showers of tears upon our broken lives! Amen.

5
Partial Truth

Preached on Thursday Morning, June 29th, 1899.

In this thing ye did not believe the Lord your God
—Deuteronomy 1:32.

These are the great battles of the world. Not the clang of swords
and the roar of kingdoms, but the conflict of man with God—man
calling God a liar; these are the disastrous and fatal wars. You shud-
der at the idea of military war; you cannot bear the noise of the guns,
the clash of the contending men; you are nervous and timid and
shrinking; you pride yourselves on sensitiveness and very tender-
hearted refinement. It may all be a lie! This very morning you may
have doubted the Word of God, and set up your little will in combat
against God's will, you may have lifted a fist against the heavens,
and then gone to church to sing psalms without souls. Why do we
not look at the reality and inwardness of things? Why are we so very
sensitive about war and bloodshed? and why do we get up memorials to governments about war and against war and for peace, all being
so very tender and so very sensitive? And this morning you may
have affronted the Most High and set up your will against the decree infinite. That was the point at which you should have been nervous and sensitive and refined. Pity us, angels! We think ourselves
refined because we shrink from the taste of hot blood, and then go
and secretly disobey the God that made us.

We are often called upon to contemplate what may be called partial faith. We have faith in spots; we are mainly bruises of unbelief,

wounds of unconfessed but deadly atheism; yet here and there, leopard-like or zebra-like, we are spotted and studded with pieces of detached piety. How true this is let every man bear witness on his own account. We do believe some things, but generally they are things of no importance. We believe things that cost us nothing. Who believes the thing that has a Cross, wet with red blood, in the middle of it? We are all partially religious, whimsically religious, religious after a very arbitrary and mechanical fashion. A discourse might be preached on whimsical religiousness. It is marvelous how the conscience is trained in little dots and short lines, and how the total manhood is left in a practically atheistic condition. Man is most whimsical when he is religious. He cultivates special points, and if you do not cultivate precisely the same points he is not sure that you can be going to heaven. How whimsical is semi-converted man! What poet can satirize him? What Juvenile can mock him with satire sufficiently biting? He will sell you at church a hymn-book on the Lord's Day, but if you asked to buy the sermon as well as the hymn-book he would call it Sabbath-breaking! He always dusts the soles of his boots, but if he were to clean the upper leather on Sunday morning, he would not for the world be seen in the act; for he observes the Lord's Day! Out upon this partial, whimsical, mechanical, hypocritical piety! Let us have health, reality, soundness of faith, and completeness according to our measure.

We see what is meant by partial faith when we contemplate a vision which comes before us every day of our life, and that is the vision of partial character. Where is there a man that is all reprobate? The son of perdition occurs but now and then in the rolling transient centuries. Who is there who has not some good points about him? How we magnify those points into character; how the man himself takes refuge in these scattered or detached virtues, and builds himself a reputation upon these incoherent fragments! Always the great challenge falls upon us from the angry clouds, In this thing, in that thing, ye did not believe; at this point you suspended your faith, at that point you were a practical atheist; and know ye, say the angry clouds, the chain is no stronger than its weakest link. Would you trust a chain thirty links long if you were sure that one of the links was very weak? What would you think of the reasoning which said, Certainly one of the links is not to be depended upon for a moment, but it is only one in thirty, there are nine-and-twenty links perfectly strong, thoroughly serviceable, you may trust your whole weight to them; and what is one in thirty? Which one? Why ask which one? why not go by the majority of the links—nine-and-twenty links—hands up for strength; one link in a base minority. Ay, but which link? You are quite right. Why not be logical, why not be consistent, and apply the same thing and the same doctrine to the integrity and the completeness of your own character? You are no stronger than your weakest point; study that weak point; repair, amend, or remove it, or replace it by some point worthy of the rest of the character. That would be commonsense, that would be downright logic worthy of the marketplace. Why not accept it and realize it?

We all believe in Providence. Which providence? How much providence? In what seasons do we believe in providence? We are great believers in blossoming-time, but what faith have we when the snow upon our path is six feet deep and the wind a hail and frost? The Lord has many fine-day followers. There is not a man in all the populations of the globe that would not believe in any God after receiving a fortune of fifty thousand pounds, no matter where it came from. That kind of hypocritical evaporation or sentiment is often mistaken for a belief in providence. When a man has had ten thousand pounds unexpectedly left to him, he is prone to sing, "God moves in a mysterious way." Hypocrite! He is mayhap, notwithstanding his psalm-singing, a hypocrite; he has no faith, he does not understand the meaning of faith, which is self-transformation into the very bosom of God. Faith is not to be measured by your assent to a few little critical, catechetical dogmas. A man is not saved as to his soul by simply assenting to so many points, items, or articles in an ecclesiastical creed. A man is what he is in his heart, no matter what he may profess. All things must be determined by the heart, for with the heart alone man believeth unto righteousness.

We often hear of some persons who are remarkably sound on certain doctrines. I dread to hear of any man who is particularly sound on any one doctrine, because I have the suspicion that he is magnifying his soundness upon that doctrine that he may ingratiate himself into my confidence so far as to inoculate me with some peculiar heresy of his own. Let us beware how we fix upon certain articles or upon certain dogmas, and judge all men by their acceptance or rejection of them. As we have said before, what would be thought of any man who was partial to certain letters of the alphabet, and remarkably sound upon the consonants, or who held two of the vowels with most pious and clinging faith, who would lay down his intellectual life for the vowel *a* and for the vowel *o*, but who would take leave to cherish his own suspicions with regard to the soundness of the other vowels? What of the man who is strong upon the letter *b*, but a little heretical upon the letter *z?* You would instantly, if silently, think whether the man was quite sane. Yet this is precisely what is done among the doctrines of the great Biblical theology. We are strong at points, we are furious about certain lines, we go into a passion in maintaining such and such dogmas; as for the others, they may take care of themselves. This is God's charge against us by the mouth of His prophets and apostles—"Yet in this thing ye did not believe." We must not only be careful about what we do believe, but about what we do not believe; we must see where our strength lies and where our weakness lurks. We must remember the doctrine we have just laid down, and which is the common property of the intellectual world, that a chain is no stronger than its weakest link.

Do we really believe in Providence?—in the shepherdly God, in the fatherly God, in the motherly God, in the God of the silent step, who comes with the noiselessness of a sunbeam into the chamber of our solitude and desolation? Do we really believe in the

God who fills all space, yet takes up no poor man's room, and who
is constantly applying to broken or wounded hearts the balm that
grows only in old sweet Gilead? Do we believe that the very hairs of
our head are all numbered? Are we perfectly sure that if God
should take away this one little child of ours, the only child, that all
would be well? How deep is our faith in Providence? I want Habakkuk's great sounding faith; he said about fig-trees and herbs and
flocks and olive-yards that if they were all swept away yet he would
trust in God and strike his harp to the praise of the Almighty Father. I am not so old in faith as mighty Habakkuk, I could see many
trees blighted without losing my faith, but there is one tree, if anything should happen to any single branch or twig of that tree, my
soul's faith would wither as a blossom would wither under the
breath of nightly frost; in that thing I should fail. What, then, can
be my faith, if it is true, and it is true, that a chain is no stronger
than its weakest link? Lord, save me, or I perish!

We believe in prayer. How much? At what time do we believe in
prayer? Do we believe in a particular providence, and do we so
deeply believe in that providence that we would ask God to inter-
vene and save us from the final disaster? Is there not a time when
prayer itself becomes dumb? Are there not periods of agony in life
in which we dismiss all around, and look with dumb sorrow upon
the unheeding heavens? It is in vain that we say we believe in prayer,
and that we lament for those who do not pray, if our prayer does
not stand us in good stead in the hour and article of life's extremest
agony. In that hour we may not be able to use the words of prayer,
but there is a wordless liturgy, there is a look that prays, there is a
sighing laden with supplications and petitions for which there are
no fit and adequate words. Will our faith in prayer go with us into
the deepest part of the valley, or is it a mocking faith that can exert
its influence only when the sun shines and the broad-fronted morning blesses the hills with a common kiss? Remember the possibility
of our having a partial faith, a partial faith in Providence, a partial
faith in prayer, and remember that the chain is no stronger than its

weakest point, and if in this thing or that we do not believe the Lord our God we may strike the rest of our faith dead as with a sword-stroke. Lord, save me, or I perish!

What we want, then, is an all-round faith; in other words, what we want is an all-the-year-round faith. But our faith comes in fits and starts. Perhaps this may be accounted for by the fact that we have confounded the word creed with the word faith. Creed is weather, faith is climate; creed is a variable alphabet, faith is an eternal poetry. We live on faith, we walk by faith; without faith we have no life. As to our creed, take it, leave it, read it, despise it, adopt it, do what you like with it, but faith abides forever, sometimes requiring new words and new modes, but never changing its inward and divine substance and meaning. Hast thou faith? I do not ask thee to fret me with thy poor money-bought creed. The year is three hundred and sixty odd days long, and I want a faith that will go with me to the last tick of the last hour of the whole year. I do not want my faith to glance at me or touch me occasionally or send balmy messages to me now and again; I say to my faith, Come not to sojourn, but abide with me; remain always in my heart! Never leave me, never forsake me; I leave the creed to the changing language, but my faith I never put into any custody but Thine own heart, Thou Father-Mother God, Thou King of the stars!

Let every man apply this text to himself. Let no man charge another about this merely occasional or spasmodic faith. Now and again we hear men say, My faith could not rise to that height. The words should never be lightly spoken; they are an impeachment against the soul, they throw a doubt upon the soul's name being written in the book of life. I can do all things through Christ enabling me. Sometimes I may ask for a little patience, now and again I may say, Give me time; once more I may assure you that I am faint yet pursuing; my face is in the right direction; do not judge me by sudden expressions or extemporaneous confessions of weakness, but judge me by the substance and essence of my character; for I am able to say through all the cloud of sin and all the misery

of self-impeachment, Lord, Thou knowest all things, Thou knowest
that I love Thee. That is the true faith. So long as that love lingers
in the heart hell shall not have thee, nor the gates of hell prevail
against the rock on which you build.

This is very serious. This reflection makes life very solemn.
Some of us have thought too much that we could take up our faith
and set it down, that we may believe a little of this and a little of
that; some of us have not thought much of the roundness of the
orb of faith. Let us not give way to censoriousness upon others.
You do not know how hard it is for some men to believe. It may be
comparatively easy for you and me to believe, but there is a natural
obstinacy for which we cannot account, a hardness and rebelliousness of heart which sets itself against God, against the supernatural,
and against what is termed the unthinkable. Others of us find a
tabernacle in ideality, a castle in the sunshine, a grand opening for
the exercise of the finest imagination in all the unmeasured space of
an incalculable firmament. But other men are born otherwise; they
are born with a rock in their hearts, they have no faculty of faith, as
we should say; they cannot imagine, they cannot dream, they cannot idealize; they never see a parable in the opening blade, in the
growing ear, and in the outfilling of the harvest purpose which
makes the landscape purple and fills the earth with a psalm of
thankfulness; to such men, all this is poetry, they do not follow it.
We must be gentle with them; they are not necessarily dishonest
men, nor are they necessarily bad men, but they are incomplete
men, and at one point of their character, and that the principle
point, they are weak men; we must regard them as warnings and
not as examples. But we who are strong should bear the infirmities
of the weak; we should be patient with the slow, we should desire
that other men may know the joy and the blessedness and the triumph and the glory of the full life. Blessed are the merciful; for
they shall obtain mercy. Blessed are the patient; for they shall be
patient with infirmity. Let us pray God that He will forgive our periods of not-believing. Though we saw His victories, and ate His

bread, and drank His water flowing out of the rock, yet we had our doubts about Him; we speculated where we should have adored, and we raised up questions where we should have preached with a deeper earnestness and served with a deeper obedience. Lord, save me, or I perish!

Prayer

Almighty God, Thou art the Redeemer of Israel, and Thou wilt perfect Thy purpose of love, and the whole earth shall be filled with the knowledge of Thy name and the splendor of Thy kingdom. We bless Thee that we live upon the oath of God, we stand back in the tabernacle of Thy covenant, we know that Thy purposes shall be redeemed and fulfilled, and that all Israel shall rejoice to sing the song of triumphant, divinest love. Thou didst thunder with a great thunder upon the Philistines and blind the warriors when they came up to assail praying Israel; Thou didst give godless Israel into their hands, and they trod them underfoot and held them in extreme contempt; when the prophet slew the sacrifice and the people cried unto him to pray for them continually, then Thou didst hurl Thy thunder upon the Philistines and utterly bewilder and dismay the foe. It is to this God we trust; Thou wilt bring in the fullness of the Gentiles, Thou wilt drive away by the power of the Cross, the atoning, redeeming Cross, all evil, all darkness, and Thy Church shall be beautiful as a jewel made for Thine own wearing. Amen.

6

Re-Conquests

Preached on Thursday Morning, July 6th, 1899.

The cities which the Philistines had taken from Israel were re-stored to Israel—1 Samuel 7:14.

The whole verse reads: "And the cities which the Philistines had taken from Israel were restored to Israel, from Ekron even unto Gath; and the coasts thereof did Israel deliver out of the hands of the Philistines. And there was peace between Israel and the Amorites." The Amorites liked neither the Philistines nor Israel, but they all thought it preferable to fall into the hands of the latter. We are driven to the adoption of alternatives. On one great occasion a sufferer said, Let me fall into the hands of God; for it is better to fall into the hands of God than to fall into the hands of men.

The cities were "restored"; that is to say, they did once belong to Israel, but Israel had a period of unbelief, even of practical atheism. Unbelief is weakness, in the marketplace as certainly as in the Church. Do not suppose that unbelief is a theological term; it is a term that runs right through the whole web and woof of human language and intercourse. Israel has sinned grievously. Technically Israel would not abandon the true Jehovah, but practically Israel said, Can there be any harm in the multiplication of gods? We have no wish to depose Jehovah, we desire above all things to honor Jehovah, but we want some gods of our own that we can more immediately bring into action, and gods will take the word from our lips instead of our taking the word from their lips; can we not have some strange gods—

Ashtaroth and Baalim and others? The Lord will not have a divided
heart, He will not occupy the house with Ashtaroth; either the Ark
must give way or Dagon must fall; they cannot both abide on equal
terms under the same roof: choose ye this day whom ye will serve.
You can have all the gods you want, but you cannot have Jehovah
along with them; you can have Jehovah, but all the other gods must
go. Israel had a period of vacillation, not knowing for one whole
day together whether to have one God or many gods; Israel went a-
lusting and a-whoring after other idols, and the Lord forsook Israel.
Then Israel became as dry paper before a scorching fire; the
Philistines came down upon them, and utterly overwhelmed them,
and trampled them underfoot. This was the Lord's doing. Now and
again He lets us see what we are when we are not His, when we do
not keep the oath, when we trifle with the holy covenant; then all
the winds are against us and all the stars, and the four seasons are
four enemies. Who can stand before the anger of the Lord? Israel
came to see this, and Israel cried to Samuel, saying, We have done
wrong; sacrifice for us; cry continually unto the Lord on our behalf. Cowardly Israel was afraid because the Philistines were too
many when the Lord was not on the side of His own army. And
Samuel slew the sacrifice, and offered it, and Israel repented, and
the Lord turned; and one day when the Philistines came up against
Israel the Lord shouted at them with thunder, and they knew not
whence that terrible voice came, their knees knocked together, and
their hands lost their expertness, and their eyes mistook friends for
enemies and enemies for friends; and the Lord turned the battle
against the Philistines, and all the cities which they had taken from
Israel were restored to Israel when Israel got back her faith. Faith is
power; unbelief is weakness.

How poetical and suggestive is the word "restored"! They were
brought back again. The cities that had been taken by the Philistines
were recovered by Israel; that is to say, by believing and penitent
and broken-hearted Israel; all the cities were taken back, from Ekron
even unto Gath, and in the hand of the Philistine there was no relic

of triumph; the Lord stripped the enemy, and drove him out naked and trembling and ashamed. "Restored"–the word comes into use in many departments and phases of life. We speak of a man being restored to confidence. For a time confidence had been forfeited by some real or imaginary demerit; then came the period when the public mind was enlightened, when fuller evidence was produced, when a calmer judgment prevailed; little by little suspicion was dispelled, and finally the suspected and injured man was restored to confidence, and to more than confidence, to honor, was welcomed with enthusiasm, and was set among the uncrowned kings of men. What the word restoration must mean to a man like Dreyfus! Who can explain his conception of that term? He stands today the most ill-used man these nineteen centuries. But it is not Dreyfus that will need to be restored, it is France that needs restoration. How France is to be restored to the confidence of civilization I know not. Shame upon shame be to those who, even if the verdict had been just, have heaped torture upon torture, indignity upon indignity, upon the unfortunate and miserable victim of the wrath of an army on whose behalf I cannot conceive any honest man speaking one word of favor. Does not a case like the case of Dreyfus belong to a nation? It does not, it belongs to humanity, it belongs to civilization, and civilization ought to speak out fearlessly and unmistakably. I would not give three months' purchase for the tranquility of a nation that has acted as France has acted in this case of Dreyfus. Thanks be to every duke, earl, king, prince, author, journalist, who has sent some message of sympathy to the man who is loaded with such ineffable sorrow. How I should welcome him to this place today if such an honor were permitted to me! Whatever he has done, he has suffered too much. That Isle of the Devil should be bought by civilization, and either burned out of existence or planted as a garden in which there should be memorials of repentance and sorrow over the most wicked of all outrages. If I could send a message to Dreyfus in my own name and yours, it would be to keep up his heart and trust in God and have faith in the people.

Coming to the historical lines of the narrative, we have to dwell upon reconquests, upon the taking back of cities which we ought never to have lost. I do not speak of cities in the ordinary sense of the term, but I speak of the great losses which the Church—meaning by the term Church all its sections and communions—has forfeited or lost or unworthily abandoned. There will be a great day of restoration; the Church of Christ has much property to reclaim. The Philistines must be stopped; they have run away with much, and we have not been robust enough and fearless enough to cry, Stop, thief! We have let the enemy take nearly everything, and we have recushioned our pews, and sat more softly that we might the more easily drop into slumber. The watcher of the Church is dead; the great spirit that should have arrested this pilfering, thieving, and depletion, is soaking itself in the literature of the day, and modernizing eternity into an anecdote or a sentence of the most trivial gossip. The thief likes it; the thief says, The Church is going to permit us to take more; let us take all we can, let us sack the Church, and let her wake up some day to find that she has nothing, and that the so-called cities which she holds are not worth the paper on which their names are written. But there shall come another day, a great day of restoration and reclamation; "kings shall minister unto thee; in my wrath I smote thee, but in my favor have I had mercy upon thee. . . . The nation and kingdom that will not serve thee shall perish; yea, those nations shall be utterly wasted." The Lord is on the warpath, and He will redeem His people, and the enemy shall disgorge the stolen plunder. The Church is very guilty in all this matter; the Church has let one thing slip after another. (Always understand that by the word Church in such discourses is meant the whole redeemed Church throughout the world, apart from denominationalism or sectarianism or limitation of any kind whatsoever.) The consequence is that the Church is surrounded by a number of little military houses from the windows of which popguns are being continually fired, largely in mockery, and mainly because nearly all the Church property has been stolen.

We shall reclaim all that has been pilfered. Agnosticism will have to give up its purse and its passbook and its checkbook and its balance. Agnosticism is the meanest of the thieves. Its name was invented only yesterday; it was baptized in a ditch, it has done no good for the world, but it has troubled a good many people in the Church on the subject of the unknowableness or unthinkableness of God. The Church ought never to have been troubled or disturbed for one moment. Agnosticism is one of its own Bible doctrines; we as Christian believers are all agnostics, in the true Biblical sense of the term: "No man hath seen God at any time; no man can see God and live; God is great, and we know Him not; who can find out the Almighty unto perfection?" That is the true agnosticism. There is a line where knowledge ceases or vanishes away, and where the great spiritual kingdom becomes a kingdom without words, without definitions of a final kind, a kingdom of light and song and joy unspeakable. Why do we not realize this? Why do we, poor invalids—for the most of believers, I am afraid, are not well—allow persons to steal one of our principal doctrines, the doctrine of the unknowableness of God? To know God is to be God; only God can know God; time cannot grasp eternity. But we believe in revelation, having the revelation of God in the person of Jesus Christ His Son, and we hail the Son of God under the great name Immanuel, God with us—looking at us, stooping to us, teaching us, dying for us and rising again that we may share the triumph and the peace of His immortality. It was thought at one time that the Philistines, having taken to themselves a great city called Agnosticism, would overthrow the Church. The Church of Christ in the degree of her penitence and faith is firmer today than she ever was. No man can take her crown if she keeps up her praying; everything depends upon that arrangement. The poorest, meanest thief can steal your diadem if you cease your intercession. So long as we live in God, so long as we live and move and have our being in God, the Lord will not suffer the depletion to continue; He will thunder upon the Philistines, and drive them away before the uproar of His

thunder into any wilderness that will bid them welcome to its in-
hospitableness.

And then the Philistines have built another hut which is called
Secularism. Man likes a word which he thinks is practical and in-
telligible. Man loves to keep up a shop with a counter in it; man
would not be happy if he had not a till, that is a box or drawer, unseen by the public, admission into which, so far as the public are
concerned, is by a very small slit in the counter. Man calls that
business. He does not care for religion, he cares for the secular aspects of life; he can understand these, but he cannot understand
metaphysics, philosophies, theologies; so he puts another penny in
the slot and sees that nobody else takes it out. This he thinks is
commerce. He does not pray, he does not sing, he attends no place
of worship. The poor foolish man forgets that this world is God's as
well as any other world that may be gleaming in the nearer universe
or shining in a universe beyond the ken of our telescope. He forgets
that godliness has the promise of the life that now is and of that
which is to come. Christianity is the religion of industry, honesty,
thrift, neighborliness, cleanliness, and all the social virtues and ex-
cellencies. One would think, from certain observations made by
people who have no imaginable right ever to open their mouths,
that religion was nothing but an attitude of clasped hands and up-
turned eyes, a religion that leaves the whole earth to cultivate itself
or to go to ruin. That is not so; God is the creator of the plowman;
God teaches the husbandman how to go about his work; the har-
row belongs to God, and all the harvesting is part of the Divine
Providence. He who does not work should not eat: we only say,
Seek first the kingdom of God and His righteousness, and then all
these things shall be added unto this great wealth. So when your
young disciples—I speak now to ministers and teachers—run away
with the idea that they are secularists, you should call after them,
So am I, but we must come to definition and to the right application of terms. No Christian treats wealth without regard, no truly
pious man despises business; the man who prays best will work best

in the city or in the field or on the sea. Prayer is genius in all directions. He who prays best conquers most. We ought never, therefore, to have allowed the secularist to take anything from the Church. Anything that the secularist holds which is really precious and good belongs to the Church, and we should have it back, and take all the cities again in honest restoration which for the moment have been wrenched from the grasp of our unbelief.

There is now a wonderful partition, mainly of lath and plaster, put up between religion and what is called science. There ought to be no such partition. Science is theological; there is nothing excluded from the grasp and the dominion of a true theological genius and conception of things. The laboratory is a chamber in the Church; every retort ought to be claimed by the Church as a special instrument or resource or piece of furniture; the Lord has made the inventory, and that retort belongs to God. Stop, thief, back! The Church has itself to blame. There is nothing in all the empire of true knowledge that is not ruled over by the spirit of a true theology. We cannot be equally strong at all points, so far as our individual gift or faculty is concerned; one man may be stronger in philosophy than in science, another may be stronger in science than in philosophy, but they may both belong to one another. The theologian and the man of science ought not to live on hostile terms; it does not become either of them to abuse the other. Let us welcome all discoveries; and if the man of science calls them discoveries, and the man of piety calls them revelations, well, they may really both be meaning the same thing; they speak different languages. Let us understand, therefore, that whatever is true in arithmetic, geology, astronomy, chemistry, or any other science is part of the sacramental plate of the Church, and no man must run away with it without being proclaimed a sacrilegious thief. We must enlarge the definition of the Church. It has largely been reduced to a very small account of hymn-books, and chant-books, and to ministers more or less underpaid. We have famished the word Church, we have reduced that great word to an almost skeleton; whereas the

Church, redeemed by the blood of Christ, regenerated and sanctified by the Holy Ghost, is the Bride of the Lamb, and on her head
she wears a diadem in which there are jewels of every color, of science and art and learning and civilization. We must therefore re-
take from Philistinian hands terms and properties and provinces
which have been stolen from us, either while we were faithlessly
slumbering, or in some hour in which our belief gave way and let
the devil come in like a flood. I call upon young preachers of every
name and class to reclaim stolen cities for God. All the cities belong to God, and He must have them every one. But there may be
a city of darkness. Bring it! God in His power has stars enough to
light the gloomiest city that darkens any corner of His universe.

When rights are restored there will be a new distribution of
cities and of all manner of wealth. Then the missionary will stand
very near the head of the conquering host. The man who has created civilization, meaning by that term the civilizing and refining
influences of Christianity, is the great man. The poor missionary
will one day be recognized, hailed. At present he has a hard time of
it; he is seldom on the sunny side of the wall. If you mention some
great missionary to some frivolous-minded drinker of the cup of
blood, the cup of sacrament, he or she may ask, Who is he? The
missionary, that ought to be better known than tsar or kaiser or
king, is inquired about as if he were an anonymous character. If I
could send word to the mission field today in India and New
Guinea, in Africa and in Polynesia, it would be, Let not your hearts
be troubled; go on with your work; many that are first shall be last,
and many that are last shall be first; and when the cities are re-
claimed and redistributed the men who created civilization or up-
rooted barbarism will be reckoned among the princes of God. They
are seldom welcomed now. The teacher will one day be better
known than the warrior. We write poems to warriors, we hail them
at civic feasts. I have never known a teacher, a great teacher, toasted
and saluted at a civic revel. What matter? Hearts up! Peace hath her
conquests no less renowned than war; your day is coming, and the

man who has taught another mind shall be hailed when the warrior is forgotten. But we are all more or less tainted with the disease of littleness. Somebody is now making, according to a journal whose name at this moment escapes me, and I do not regret that fact, a sword with a gold handle and a blade set in precious stones. Who is the man for whom the sword is made? A city missionary? A teacher, a preacher, a philosopher, a leader of the gentler ministries of life? No! The sword shall perish, and moral enthusiasm, spiritual purity, true holiness of heart, shall live when swords are turned into agricultural instruments, and the wearers and bearers of them are forgotten. There will be a great reclaiming of cities, cities of property, cities of fame, cities of gold, cities that have been taken from us in a moment of unbelief; all coming back if we be faithful, and we shall only be rewarded in the degree of our faithfulness, not in the degree of our intellectual brilliance, not in the degree of our power of unbelief, not in the degree in which we have been doing mischief, not in the degree in which we have been shouting hallelujah to some unworthy hero; but all will come back to Christ's Church in the degree in which Christ's Church is pure, simple, true, wise, vigilant. Then kings shall minister unto her, and it will be the highest renown to have one's name written on her imperishable records.

Prayer

Lord, teach us how to pray! If we pray well we shall live well. Lord, teach us how to pray! Show us that prayer must come from the heart, and must pass by way of the Cross to the footstool of the throne. There is none other way; it is broad, brighter than the day, and written with the words of welcome expressive of Thy love. Let no man despair; may the dumb pray, may the lifelong silent break out into praise; let this be creation day and resurrection morning in one glad revelation of Thy mercy and Thy grace. We would praise Thee; we are fearfully and wonderfully made, and fearful and wonderful have been Thy ways towards us and concerning us; our life is bathed in mystery, we cannot tell the springs thereof, and the outgoings thereof no man may calculate. We accept our life as a divine trust, we bow before its awful mysteries, we are thankful for the revelations which gladden it, and we would pray for the obedient spirit to follow Thee in all Thy leadership, thou God and Father of our Lord Jesus Christ. Wherein we have taken our lives into our own hands, we bow down before Thee in burning shame; we thought to displace God! Our ambition and our selfishness conspired against the Most High; behold, we were taken in our own net, we fell into the pit which our own hands had dug, and we are here to say, God pity us—for we have done wrong, and let us cling to the Cross, wherein is all our hope! We were led away by our own vanity, and ensnared by our own ambition, and we thought we might boast of tomorrow; when lo! Thou didst suddenly send upon us sevenfold darkness, and we stumbled and fell, and lay down in utterest helplessness, not knowing one way from the other. But Thou hast broken down our spirit, Thou hast by sore chastening of our life brought us to humbleness of mind, and filial dependence of will; Thou hast rebuked our imagination, and led us into the temple of faith. We review our life, and are lost in wonder, love, and praise; we see now how near the edge of the precipice we were now and again and yet again; we now understand Thy rebukes, and how suddenly Thou didst bring us back from the way our hearts longed to walk in. We praise Thee because Thou didst not answer some of our prayers; for they were conceived in vanity and spoken in foolishness, and we knew not what we said when we took our life into our own hands. Jesus, still lead on! May we have grace enough to live one day at once; may we depend upon the Arm that cannot weaken; may we look to the light which no storm can blow out; may our eyes be unto the hills where stands God's own eternal temple. May we no longer live in the external and circumstantial and transient, but in the internal, the spiritual and the everlasting; may we know that we are ordained to the altar, consecrated to the sanctuary, that upon us is the mark of the blood of Calvary, and we are no longer of the mob wandering in the ways of darkness. May we know our calling and our election of God, and answer the same with pureness and patience and thanksgiving, thus making our life a lifepsalm, a daily holy sacrifice. We live among broken hearts, we build our houses by the brink of the grave; the living and the dead are housed under one roof: teach us to number our days that we may apply our hearts unto wisdom; give us that sense of dominion over things outward and calculable that shall also give us the higher sense of things divine, eternal, things in which we may rest, finding there eternal Sabbath. Some are weary, disappointed, sorely vexed, deeply afflicted, not knowing which way to turn; the house is dark even on this sunny summer morning, the shades of death have put out the lights of summer: the Lord look upon such, and see them through the tears of His pity. Some are full of life and plan and high ambition and song, as if they would never grow old or never know the bowing-down of weakness: the Lord teach them gently, softly, that there is an appointed time to men upon the earth, and show them the outline of the near-lying grave; and yet do not take from them their youth and red blood and hopefulness, but may they live well, for life's noon, and life's afternoon, and life's quiet evening. God be with the sons and daughters of affliction, with the children of pain, with those whose lifework is now concluded, and who are waiting in the shadows till the invisible chariot draws near. Heaven's broad blessing be upon us, and may we feel, through the power of the Cross, the atoning, redeeming blood of Christ, that we are now called to festival and joy and holy song. Amen.

7
Looking for the Wrong Thing

Preached on Sunday Morning, July 9th, 1899.

He hoped to have seen some miracle done by Him
—Luke 23:8–11.

Man is always fond of conjuring and frivolity and entertainment.
He divides the word into many different meanings, parts of meanings and applications, but it all comes to the same thing, that man
likes to see something, or kill something, or be amused by something, or be entertained in any way, the less costly the better.

The case before us is that of Herod. When Pilate knew that Jesus
Christ belonged to Herod's jurisdiction he was right glad of it, an
immense burden of responsibility was taken off his shoulders. Pilate sent Jesus to Herod, who happened to be at Jerusalem at that
time. Never was weary man more glad of unexpected rest than Pilate
was when he heard that this illustrious but mysterious Prisoner belonged to some other man's jurisdiction. When Herod saw Jesus he
was exceeding glad; it was in very deed the thing he had been waiting for day after day. Kings and rulers cannot rush into the streets to
see all the irregular and eccentric characters which perplex the mind
of the general populace; so they must have shows by command,
and opportunities created by sovereign fiat or by personal charge.
When Herod heard that Jesus Christ was actually in the house, he
was not only glad, he was exceeding glad; for he was desirous to see
Him of a long time, because he had heard many things of Him; he
hoped to have seen some miracle done by Him. A miracle all to

oneself, a miracle at home, a domestic festival, an opportunity of seeing the Conjurer close at hand, and watching the cunning manipulation, tracing the action of every finger, and marking well the expression of the eyes. This was Herod's opportunity. We all have that opportunity according to our varying conception of the term. When Herod saw Jesus he was exceeding glad. Then enroll him, if you please, as a disciple! No, he is not a disciple. But is not every man who attends a place of worship with a laugh upon his face a disciple of the living God? Not necessarily; a man may bow his head in prayer, and look down all the time into the face of the devil. The time comes, therefore, for analysis, discrimination, careful apportionment of claim and standing; the day of judgment comes wherein every Christian must judge himself. When a man is seen hastening to church with a broad smile upon a benignant face, hastening that he may take part in the first hymn or psalm, may he not be enrolled as a disciple? Perhaps not; the evidence you have supplied is not sufficient; more must be known about the case. We approach Christ through the heart; in relation to Christ and all Christly matters a man is what he is in his heart. There may be sadness on his face, great deep furrows torn up by the plow of grief, and the man may seem to be going rather to the house of sorrow than to the house of song. Judge nothing before the time; he may be happiest who looks least happy. There is a joy in melancholy. Where in joy there is not a touch of melancholy about the joy, dash the wine-cup to the dust, for there is no festival in such fire. The question therefore becomes very critical and very serious. It is awful to think that a man may be interested in religion, and yet may be irreligious. There is an irreligious religion; there is an interest in piety which is impious.

Let us look at this almost domestic idyll. "When Herod saw Jesus, he was exceeding glad." No Christian was he, but he had heard the popular rumor and the common gossip about a young man, fair, solemn, of gentle face, who had spoken words that seemed to have no relation to the voice in which they were pronounced; a young man that could say, Woe unto you—through a sob that was choking his throat; a new rhetoric, a new music, a new way of delivering judgment and forecasting doom. Herod did not trouble himself with the ethics of Christ, with the evangelical conception which He gave of the kingdom of God; Herod knew nothing about these things, but he had heard of tricks, conjurings, miracles, things quite marvelous; and where there is a will there is a way; and busy Herod, who could have turned off a thousand applicants on the ground that he was engaged, created a space for Christ, and was prepared to give Him the whole day for the study of those marvelous signs and tokens which were said to accompany His ministry.

Do we really understand the occasion? What was the effect on Christ of Herod's peculiar gladness? Shall we imagine Jesus Christ speaking this monologue: My time has now come; I knew it would come and probably come unexpectedly; I have had to encounter public hostility, social animosity, the contempt of the proud, but now a great man, having heard of me, welcomes me to his house, and makes me almost a guest instead of a prisoner; the occasion comes at last to men, we have only to wait and we shall get our deserts in the long run; I feel gratified and honored by the attention of Herod, and I will now work any number of miracles for his entertainment, I will indeed show him miracles I have not shown to the public; he has asked for a whole day of my time, he is willing to suspend his judicial or official or regal functions in order to give me an opportunity of showing what I can do; I feel already free with a large liberty than I have yet enjoyed. In such a speech the gospel would have died. Jesus cannot be patronized; the Creator cannot be flattered; He returns all their lies to all the hypocrites. Jesus does not accept the glittering opportunity, He declines it; He walks on higher levels, He breathes a purer air. But surely Herod was a man worth placating? No. A man?—an insect, a worm. In relation to the eternal God there is no man worth placating in the common vulgar sense of that term. The only man with whom Jesus

Christ will speak is the man of a broken heart; a broken and a contrite spirit He will not despise. If an old broken-down woman, carrying seven sorrows like seven wounds, had tugged His robe, and asked Him to read the twenty-third psalm to her, He would have read it all, and waited until the holy balm had got well into the festering sores. Do you know that this Man is King of kings, Lord of lords? He who thinks he can do Christ a favor, in the sense of conferring a patronage, has not begun to understand even the outline of the infinite character of the Son of God.

The same thing is going on today, going on in this house, going on in nearly every heart. So the text is modern; it comes up with the hoar of nineteen centuries upon it, and with the hoar of all the centuries and all the ages, and yet it expresses the experience of the men of today. What do the men of today do? They go in search of the wrong thing; they miss the point. We are going to church, can that be wrong? Possibly; it may be an acted blasphemy. We have seats in the church, can that be wrong? It may be; it might be truer to my character to have seats in the synagogue of Satan. All depends upon spiritual realities, the inmost inwardness of things, the metaphysic of the metaphysic; God is a Spirit, and He must be worshiped in spirit and in truth; the Father seeketh such to worship Him. I am glad to go to church. Why? I like to hear good congregational singing. That is no reason. I like to hear a good sermon. What do you mean by a good sermon? Foam, froth, nothingness, entertainment, intellectual titillation? What do you mean—to have conscience roused, memory of guilt refreshed, pardon offered through the blood of the Cross? That is a good sermon, and there is no other sermon worth listening to. To hear the public estimate of preachers and their preaching! Let a man be doctrinal, Biblical, practical, and he will be voted heavy, dry, old. Yet he is on the only line that is worth traversing; he goes at the right pace, he goes along the right lines, he is destined to the right goal. Hear him, pray for him, account him prophet of the Lord, clothed with a mantle of sunshine, ordained by hands invisible. "I like to read the Bible."

Why? What parts do you like? The historical parts, the short stories, the graphic narratives, the household idylls. Very good; what more? If nothing more, you have hardly begun to read the Bible at all; the Bible is a revelation of God to man and a revelation of man to himself, and a revelation of sin to itself; and until we get into these deeper and more inward mysteries, we know nothing about the Bible. What is your standard? Into what haunts do you flee when the soul is ill at ease? Your daily Bible is your autobiography; he who has eyes to read character and conduct aright could discover from my daily Bible what I am, what I have suffered, enjoyed, what I long for, hope for, live for. There is nothing in the Bible that is unimportant, but there is a central Bible, a Bible within the Bible, full of the spirit of revelation and worship, prophecy and evangelical exposition, and into that innermost circle of all the concentric circles we must find our way before we can form any estimate of the real compass and the real spirit of the Bible. Few men have read thee, O Book of God, for thou art a letter to the heart, to be read in the dusk of life, or in the morning twilight, when no one is present, when the air is listening as if nervously to take back to the Author of the letter some answer given in sigh or sob.

Jesus Christ answered Herod nothing. It is one of two things. When accused you must either answer nothing, or if you begin a defense you must complete it. This was the policy of Christ; He answered him never a word. He looked at Pilate as if Pilate were not in existence, through him, beyond him; and to Herod the face of Christ was the face of a stone. Jesus Christ would never talk about His miracles. The only man that was ever likely to elicit anything from Him about His miracles was Nicodemus. That ruler of the Jews came to Jesus at night with this great compliment, and this most veracious compliment: Rabbi, we know that Thou art a teacher come from God, for no man can do these miracles that Thou doest except God be with him; they are not only miracles, they are miracles of a certain range and quality, they have an accent and a note of their own; they are not to be ranked with the conjurings and the necromancies of the ages; they are singular, peculiar, distinctive; no man can do these miracles, the miracles that Thou doest, except God. And Jesus answered, Except a man be born again he cannot enter the kingdom of heaven—the supreme miracle, the culminating miracle, the miracles towards which all other miracles were moving; the new man, the living miracle. We are not called upon to study the miracles, but to be the miracles. We are to be the deaf, the dumb, the blind, the lame, the dead, on whom the great revivals of Christ's energy shall operate, calling us up into speech and hearing and song and agility and manhood: that is the miracle towards which all other miracles of mine were lamely moving. I am not called upon to entertain some advanced thinker and to discuss with him the miracles of Christ; I am called upon to say, I was blind, and now I see. The Christian is to be the miracle, and not to write commentaries upon the miracles. No man can understand the manner of the miracles or has any right to speak about them until he has undergone the major or final miracle, testified in his own new life, expressed in his own consciousness, and verified by his own conduct.

And Herod and his men-of-war set Him at naught, and mocked Him, and arrayed Him in a gorgeous robe—the purple of Rome, or the cambric of the rabbinic priesthood; anything gorgeous enough will do to express contempt of this man who in the presence of Herod is dumb, and accounted demented or infamously discourteous. We may not literally put on a purple robe, in fact we should never dream of doing such a thing, but in an ideal way we may send Christ back into the shadows of history clothed with the purple of admiration, or of some sort of literary appreciation; we may even go so far as to praise His moral system and then hand it over to oblivion because its very ideality makes it impracticable in an age of growing civilization. Evolution has its perversion as well as its proper application. We may, if the word may be allowed, "evolute" Christ backward, or we may evolute Him into a shadow, a whisper, an echo, anything that removes Him from a dominating and disciplinary position in human life. We go to Christ with a standard which He never approved, or apply to Him a test which He has never regarded other than as with contempt, and because He does not satisfy our prejudices, and our aspirations, we send Him back into shadows where He is forever lost. The worst kind of homage that can be rendered to Christ is that of mere intellectual or even moral admiration. Christ does not reveal Himself to our wit, our imagination, or our aesthetic taste; He reveals Himself to broken and contrite hearts, and to them only will He show the infinite loveliness and charm of His personality. Christ came not to excite admiration, but to preach the kingdom of God, and to offer the love of God to all men conscious of sin, its burden, and its cruel torment. We cannot break up Christ into a miracle worker, a moralist, a speculator, the Socrates or the Solon of His own day or of any succeeding day. Christ must be received by the penitent heart as a whole, for if He is not received in the totality of His claim and offer He will consider Himself rejected and despised. We know the value of Herod's appreciation when we come to consider how Herod eventually treated the Lord. Herod the man was not filled with interest in the Christ; but Herod the speculator, the lover of mere excitement and wonder, was no doubt sincerely interested in the small matter of miracle working. This will never do. With my whole heart I beseech you to consider that Jesus Christ is not to be treated as a conjurer, or to be applauded as an idealist; He is to be received as the only and the infinite Savior of the world.

We repeat all this, let me say again, in our own experience. We get from Christ just what we bring to Him. If we bring a humble heart to Christ we receive a blessing; if we come behind Him and touch Him with the fingers of faith, then the wound is stanched and our youth is renewed. If we come, saying, Lord, I am blind and poor and ignorant, what wouldst Thou have me do? Teach me Thy will, O God, and give me grace and strength to obey it all; then Jesus Christ will hold the sun standing still and the moon shall not depart from Ajalon till the great largess of His heart be poured out upon such suppliant penitence and sincerity. The proud He sendeth empty away. He has no message to pride. The Son of Man is come to seek and to save that which was lost; this Man receiveth sinners and eateth with them. He that is whole needeth not a physician, but he that is sick. Jesus Christ cured the sick, but He never cured a painted wound. Paint your flesh in all the colors of simulated agony, and Jesus will pass you with contempt: show Him one deep heart-gash—loss of husband, wife, child, friend—deep, holy, tender sorrow; conviction of sin, bitter self-accusation, and say, Jesus of Nazareth, look at me and help me—and you will be restored to youth and hope and highest consecration. After that your burden will still be there, but without weight; the tears will still be there, but without the salt and bitterness of sorrow. The Son of Man came to the sick, the afflicted, the sore of heart, but the proud, the respectable, the self-sufficing He sendeth empty away, and after them a wind of contempt.

Prayer

Let it please Thee, our Father in heaven, to receive our humble song and answer our contrite petition. We will sing of mercy and judgment, we will praise the Lord, yea, we will sing a new song unto our God, for He hath done marvelously, and His right hand is outstretched in wonder and power. We will not be dumb in the courts of our God, nor sullen, nor self-involved; we will go out of ourselves, and pour out our life in song—a sacrifice of the heart, a sweet-smelling savor unto the Lord. We cannot take all these things and not be thankful for them, for then would we divide their number and kill their quality; by thankfulness we multiply Thy mercies, and by a love-offering of the soul we see new things and revelations and lights in all the way of Thy providence. We will remember Thee for good; Thou dost make the light of the morning, and set the evening star in its place; Thou dost water every herb of the field, every grassblade, and Thine is the wondrousness of color with which Thou dost clothe the shoulders of the summer. Thou dost grow wheat for us; the vineyard and the oliveyard are of Thy planting, and Thine angels watch them and bring them to the harvest fullness. As for our life, Thou dost beset us behind and before, and lay Thine hand upon us, and count the hairs of our head. How can we then be dumb in Thy courts? Our hearts would praise Thee, our souls would go out in ardent love, because the hand of the Lord hath touched us and we have dwelt in the tabernacle of His power. If we have done the things we ought not to have done—and these we humbly and penitently confess—it is because we are still on the earth, and in the flesh, and hunted by the enemy, and limited by time and space; but there is a better law in our members, there is a holier tone in our voices, and all the miserable sordidness of the week is run through and through as with the chords of a sacred song. Let the Lord hear us when we confess our sins and abase ourselves before the Cross and call upon the atoning blood to cleanse us from all our sins. Thou hast set us in wondrous difficulties, Thou hast smitten our tower and thrown it down, and only the foundation thereof remains; Thou hast smitten the choicest apple-tree in the garden; Thou hast taken away the one ewe lamb that was bleating for Thee on the hills, not knowing what it was bleating for. But if Thou hast shown us great and sore trouble Thou wilt surely revive us again; for the third day is Thine, and the seventh, and the day of sudden coming, and the morning of startling vision. So we lay ourselves down on Thy bosom, Thou Son of God, and rest there until we hear Thy voice, Thy next command, Thy completing benediction. We give one another into the keeping of the hand of God; except the Lord keep the city the watchman watcheth it but in vain; the Lord keep us, keep our mouth, our lips, the outgoing of our mind and our heart, and the secret doors of the temple of our manhood, lest the enemy cunningly and silently approach, and overthrow the lifehouse while we are slumbering. Some are sad of heart; Thou dost meet them in Thine house with great delight, and Thou bringest with Thee balm from the unseen and far-off Gilead. Some are tired of life; it is a dream that has darkened into nightmare, it is an expectation that falls short of a hope; it is a blighted ambition, and a dead trust. Is there no reviving with the Lord? Is He, who made the heavens and the earth, tired, and has He gone back from us in exhaustion and fatigue? Blessed be God, Thou art still near us, Jesus still lives and prays for us; we will bring our little crosses and lean them against the infinite Cross of His unspeakable grief. Amen.

8
Unreported Interviews

Preached on Sunday Morning, July 16th, 1899.

When they were alone, He expounded all things
to His disciples—Mark 4:34.

These were unreported interviews; these were secret conferences.
We do not speak our best things in the public air; our whispers are
costlier than our thunder; they may have more life in them, more
tenderness, more poetry. We cannot report what we have heard, except in some poor dull way of words. That is hardly a report at all.
To hear any man tell over what he has heard you say, that is punishment! He may speak your very words, and leave out your soul;
with the best intention, he may report the interview upside down.
Communications are not in words, except in some rough, commercial, and debtor-and-creditor way. Communications are in the
breathing, in the looking, in the touching, in the invisible and the
inaudible. You say you have it in black and white. That is impossible; that is the fundamental error of some minds—to imagine that
they can have anything worth keeping in black and white, in a cast-
iron form, in a mechanical environment. It was not a word, it was a
tone that smote you; not a photograph, but a look that held you
entranced in a most willing, consenting captivity.

Jesus Christ had two speeches. The one to the great multitude.
For them He had toys and stories and miracles and parables; He
knew them well, He knew precisely what was adapted to their re-
ceptive power and their then state of intellectual culture. He always

took out with Him toys enough to amuse and interest and haply instruct the gaping mob. To hear Jesus you must wait until He comes into the house; let Him read the Scriptures to you when your number is but small. His greatest tones are in the minor key; the way in which He finds the heart is a way of His own; never man spoke like this Man. We are thankful for His great public utterances; without them we could not live; they constitute what is at least the framework and apparatus of His redeeming Gospel and His eternal kingdom; but His whisper was His eloquence. When we were most hushed we were most applauding. There is an applause of tears, there is a cheering of the radiant face, the radiant dumbness. Have we ever been closeted with Christ? Have we taken our four gospels and apostolic epistles, and asked Jesus Christ to read them to us just as He always meant them to be read? Have we taken to Him civilization, history, providence, the daily story of grief or joy, of loss or gain, and asked Him to read them to us in the right tone? Have we had secret interviews with Christ? Do we live in solitude, or in the thronged park, amid the rattle of wheels and the high-stepping horses? The only man who can interpret Christ is Christ Himself. Surely a man can interpret his own letter better than any other man can interpret it for him; for he has expressed the sincere desire of his heart. Jesus Christ is still accessible; Jesus Christ is still a house-to-house minister; He ought to be a member of every household, He ought to have a chair at every table, He ought to be welcomed on every occasion. Think of Jesus in the house, close at hand, a friend, a brother, a guest, who speaks the blessing and thus multiplies the feast.

I live with Christ, and He has taught me that there are two ways of reading everything. Sometimes I have thought my Lord partly amused at the greatness of us when we were really least. I am not quite literally sure, but I think I have sometimes seen the outline of a smile upon His face as He has watched the development of what we call our civilization. He has spoken very frankly to me upon this matter, He has told me that civilization must be very carefully watched, or it will become our ruin; He says that civilization unsanctified is a breach of the very first commandment of the decalogue.

My Lord, said I, we are proud of our civilization, we thought it Thine. It was then I thought I saw the ghost of a smile flit over the fairest of faces, when He said, It may be mine, or it may not; I have forbidden you in the decalogue to make to yourselves any graven image, and, behold, you have taken my gold and stamped it with the faces of your kings; I have looked into your houses, and found that they were no better in some instances than graven and molten images before which you bowed down and said, as you bowed before the idols' feet, Behold great Babylon which I have built! We may have made civilization atheistic. Civilization in the higher sense is in the purpose of God, and He is leading all things towards the accomplishment of that purpose; God is the God of order and civilization and the highest intellectual life and energy; God is the Father of all beauty and loveliness and music, and He wishes us to have all these things, and more and more if we hold them as His gifts and use them as His trustees. Never let your civilization be bigger than your humanity; always let the worker be greater than his work; let the cabinet-maker be more in quality than any chair he ever put together and sold for mean silver. We are proud of our civilization, and Jesus Christ says, Do not be proud of it in any sense that excludes its higher symbolism; the tree is nothing, and the fruit is nothing, and the summer that warms them into fullness of expression is nothing, when stripped of symbolism, typology, the indication of the higher meaning, the right tree, the right fruit, the eternal summer.

I have said to Jesus Christ, speaking as a minister to my instructing and inspiring Lord, This is my great difficulty, Thou sweet Jesus, that I have to preach faith, and, taking the people in their multitudinousness, they do not know what faith is; they think it is something metaphysical or theological, or something that has to do some way or other with churches, and they reject my poor message. And He said to me, It is indeed unspeakably curious and psychologically most interesting, if it were not morally painful and disastrous, to watch the ways of people about faith; for people who will not be saved by faith are willing to be lost by fear; it is most paradoxical, said He; now fear is just as psychological and spiritual and metaphysical and inwardly inward as faith; yet they take so kindly to fear, and look upon faith as some ghost of the Church. I thank Thee, Lord, for that illuminating word. It is even so. Fear destroys strength, fear ruins men, fear clouds the imagination, fear enfeebles the will, fear eats out the soul; and men are willing that it should be so, and they make a kind of boast of their fear; but when I speak to them of their faith, they think it is Sunday and that I am preaching. My Lord, help me, for this ministry is an ineffable burden and sadness!

Then said I to Jesus, The people believe in what they can see. Nay, said my Lord, that they do not, poor minister of mine. But, said I, they say that seeing is believing. Then quoth my Lord, It is quite right, but no man sees; the eyes were not given that men might see, but that they might look; body cannot see soul, therefore how can eyes, which are body, see thoughts, which are spirit? They have a theory of adaptation amongst themselves, these poor half-civilized creatures who boast of their civilization, that one instrument is adapted to one thing, and another instrument is adapted to another thing, and yet they think that the eyes of the body can see the things which belong to the soul. *That* is their fatal fallacy; over that stumbling-block they will drop into hell. Oh! said He, after a moment's interval, that I had made men without eyes—for then their souls might have had fair play, and their thoughts might have been optical instruments by the use of which they could have penetrated into the inwardness and the metaphysic of the kingdom of God. Lord, said I, canst Thou—now that we are in the house together and the door is shut—canst Thou speak to me about all these fluttering things, stars and comets and worlds, and forests and seas; these things look as if they were realities. No, no, said He, poor child of mine and preacher, thou art looking at things from the wrong end and in the wrong light—thou, a pulpit man! Lord, teach me! And He taught me, saying, The things that are seen are not the real things; what thou canst see is all outside, symbolic, intermediate, perishable; the real things never can be seen; they can be prayed for, aspired after, and deeply thought about, until the soul becomes transfigured into the image of the invisible: what thou seest is the unreal; thy palace is a decorated grave; thy grave, if rightly read, may be a postern-gate opening into the King's gardens. Then all things became new to me, and I longed to tell the people what I had heard, because if they could have heard Jesus as I heard Him, and if they could see things as I now see them, all the world would be Christian—the earth an altar, the air a living and acceptable incense. Jesus Christ, however, pities us because we are still in the body, surrounded, limited, bewildered, blinded; our eyes are holden that we should not see; we are to be trained by the Holy Ghost into a deep and right and final interpretation of the mystery of God. There are people who believe in the body because they can see it; Jesus almost smiles when He hears such men talk such infantile talk. The men to whom reference is made say there can be no doubt about the body, and Jesus answers, That is the only thing that may be doubted; the body is ever changing, always casting off its yesterdays, continually struggling into a new carcass, always urging it towards a nobler manhood, when it is under right control. The only real thing, the Lord continuing said, is the soul; that never dies; you will never see each other in the body again, but you will not want to see each other in the body when you step over the last black river and see the meaning of things; you will no more want to recover the old body than to recover the clothes you wore in infancy; you have shed them off, forgotten them; now you enter into a higher fellowship, a broader, deeper, more lasting life. We believe in the resurrection of the dead; the resurrection of the body is another thing altogether: but even that may rise again in your tenderest imaginings, in your deepest love. The only thing that

God has promised to me just now is revision, reunion, larger fellowship, wedding in a new sense—wedding as the angels understand it. Enough!

These expositions of mystery and sorrow the Lord gave to us when we were alone, walking up the hills, sauntering in the valley, hesitating by the riverside, or when sleep draws its curtains around the tired head, and the ministering Lord can speak more closely to the soul because the body is otherwise and meanly engaged.

Then said I to my Lord when we were alone, There are so many churches. No, said He, no, there is only one Church. That one word was a deliverance, a revelation, a new beginning in the higher thought. They say, Lord, that this system is right and that system is wrong. No; they are both right. The Congregationalist tells me that his idea of the Church is right because it is self-governed. So, said my Lord, are all my other churches. The Congregationalist amuses himself with that annual mistake. It is only the unit that is changed. Congregationalism has its little unit, the individual church; Presbyterianism has its larger unit, all the churches of its order; Episcopalianism is as truly self-governed as is Congregationalism: it will not allow some other church to interfere in its affairs, as it calls its particular business. It is only the unit that is different. The Congregationalist is in danger of becoming rather narrow-minded, it may be, and self-idolatrous; he thinks that when he has got his little crowd of men of a certain quality in a little corner that that is the Church of Christ. So it is, if the spirit is right, and if I myself, the Redeemer of the Church, be present in the midst of that company. But there is a larger unit of all the churches that think the same, and they are as self-governed as any little individual church may be that lives by begging and thinks it respectable to avoid starvation. My son, said my Lord to me, keep thine heart up; the bigger centuries are coming, the larger definitions are at hand; I will sweep all these little dust-heaps out of the way. The Lord will suddenly come to His temple! Faith, hope, charity, these three, but the greatest of these is charity. Knowledge vanished away, ashamed of its own ignorance; prophecy, thrown down its horoscope, for it says, The Lord is at hand, and in His eyes all things shine as visions that men can read; but charity abides, eternal love, great, sympathizing, brotherly, redeeming love. Sectarianism, where is it? Dead! Who wrote its epitaph? It has none.

So Jesus takes us one by one, according to our gift and function, and talks to us alone. What lovely, tender, inspiring talks we may have with our Lord! We come out of them filled with His own inspiration, and enriched with His own patience and forbearance. We, being young, inexperienced, and foolish, want to have everything settled tomorrow. Jesus says, It takes a long time to make a rock; I have been a million ages in making this little pebble at the bottom of the stream, and thinkest thou that a man can be made in no time? If it required a million ages to make half-a-dozen smooth pebbles, how long will it take to make a redeemed and sanctified Church? Be patient, take larger views of things; the whole process is going on; there are firstborn sons in knowledge, as well as in nature; firstborn sons in prophecy and revelation and song, as well as in estates and titles and inheritances; the whole mystery was settled from the beginning of the creation, and long before the creation was in existence. All things are primordially in God; out of God they come, and God's will must be done on earth as in heaven, but day by day, five thousand more years, fifty thousand more risings of the sun, a million more revolutions of this planet or of that. But all the revolutions, all the silent dancing of the planets mean final music, beauty, rest.

Prayer

Almighty God, wilt Thou send a plentiful rain upon Thine inheritance, and make souls that are athirst rejoice because of great gladness. Thou hast the key of the rain; the river is Thine, and it is full of water; every drop Thou dost count, every shower Thou alone dost give. Thou dost look upon the earth, and satisfy its thirst abundantly; Thou baptizest the meads and the flowers and the great acres of corn, that there may be food for man and beast, and that Thy providence may be vindicated in annual season. Blessed are they that hunger and thirst after righteousness! For this thirst we pray, the keener thirst, the inner thirst: the Lord hear us when we ask that we may be satisfied out of the river that flows by His own throne. None can quench the thirst of man but Thyself; Thou hast made man in Thine image and likeness, and none may trifle with him and mock him. Thou art the God and Father of us all; Thou knowest our whole nature, our pain, our need, our sin, our helplessness, and Thou hast made ample provision to meet us at every point of our life. We will not go after other gods, no idol shall dwell in our house; our whole life shall be the temple of the living God, and He shall dwell with us. We thank Thee for these gracious decisions and for these lofty aspirations; for they also come forth from the Lord of Hosts, excellent in counsel and wondrous in working. We bless Thee for the queenliest of the days, the day that makes all other days quiet, calm, and gives unto every other day a golden value. May we be in the spirit on the Lord's day, may our hearts burn with a great glow, and shout because they must praise the Lord. Thou hast done great things for us, whereof we are glad; and our gladness cannot be dumb, it must utter itself loudly and sweetly, and keep in accord with all the other voices that bless Thy goodness and Thy love. It is at once our joy and our terror to know that Thine eye sees everything in our life; there is nothing hidden from the fire of Thine eye; Thou dost pierce us through and through. While we tremble before this vision we also rejoice in it, because if there is anything in us on which Thy smile can alight Thy smile will be withheld, and because everything that is good in us is as a flower from Thine own garden and planted in our hearts by

Thine own hand. Some are in great joy because Thou hast caused a light to shine into their house, and they are full of gladness because they have seen Thy presence with the vision of their love; Thou hast redeemed them in distress, their extremity has been to Thee an opportunity, Thou hast made Thy servants and handmaidens glad with surprises of grace; they bring today their thankoffering of love and praise; Thou wilt deign to accept it, for the Lord's name is love and His attitude is one of condescension. Others are in great trouble; all Thy waves and Thy billows have gone over them; they do not know why they should be thrown down into the trough of the sea and that the waves should threaten to swallow them up. Some are concealing disease; others are carrying sin unconfessed, though not unrepented. Others have a wound in their heart which they will not and dare not show to other eyes; from day to day they say, A wounded spirit who can bear? Others are all in youth and light and energy and hope and active dream; behold, they see Thee in every color, hear Thee in every breeze, and they are not afraid of the thunder, because it is the tabernacle of God. Seeing that we represent so much experience and so much variety and diversity, to whom can we come but to the God who made us all; and by whom can we come but by the Son who died for us all? He gave us our hope; He is our peace; He hath made atonement, He is the daysman who can lay His hand upon God and upon the sinner and can make reconciliation with His own blood. Through His Cross we come; at His Cross we lie in hopeful prostration. No man ever died whose arms were thrown around the Cross. Amen.

9

Dwell Among Your Own

Preached on Sunday Morning, July 23rd, 1899.

And she answered, I dwell among mine own people
—2 Kings 4:13.

The whole incident is full of idyllic beauty, and is also vital with modern suggestion and application. "And it fell on a day, that Elisha passed to Shunem, where was a great woman; and she constrained him to eat bread. And so it was, that as oft as he passed by, he turned in thither to eat bread. And she said unto her husband, Behold now, I perceive that this is a holy man of God, which passeth by us continually. Let us make a little chamber, I pray thee, on the wall; and let us set for him there a bed, and a table, and a stool, and a candlestick; and it shall be, when he cometh to us, that he shall turn in thither. And it fell on a day, that he came thither, and he turned into the chamber, and lay there. And he said to Gehazi his servant, Call this Shunammite. And when he had called her, she stood before him. And he said unto him, Say now unto her, Behold, thou hast been careful for us with all this care; what is to be done for thee?"—I do not like to take such hospitality for nothing, I must make some recognition, what is the most acceptable form in which this recognition can express itself? "Wouldest thou be spoken for to the king?" how would that do? "Or to the captain of the host?"—one of the most distinguished men; he has gifts to give and promotions to confer. What about the king or the captain? "And she answered, I dwell among mine own people"—let me alone, I want to speak my mother tongue; I know my customary environment, and I do not want to break through it or reconstruct it in any way; I am quite contented and happy. A woman beyond patronage; a soul not to be bribed, even if bribery were intended, which it was not in this case. Said the woman in effect: I am quite content, I do not want the king's notice, the captain of the host can do nothing for me; I have my husband, my house, my daily task, I am well content; if I were otherwhere I should feel as if I were a stranger: I would rather be just where I am. If this woman's spirit should take hold of us the most precious blessings would immediately and permanently be realized by every soul. It is vanity that disturbs the world; it is illegitimate, unnatural ambition that troubles and divides and torments lives that might otherwise be placid and content. A man is not always able to pass from one environment to another, and to retain the full use of his faculties. He who is really of consequence in one place would be of no consequence in another: the same man, but not the same environment.

It is so socially. If you allow the man to remain upon his native heath; if you allow him to pursue his honest, quiet, healthful occupation of plowing the land which he owns or rents; the man is quite content, he feels that he is in his right place. If you took that same man and planted him down in Park Lane, in Broadway, in the chief streets of the capitals of Europe and other countries, he would want to be back to the old plow, the old field, the old stacks of corn. He was then equal to the occasion, but he is not equal to the other occasion that has been forced upon him; in the depths of his heart he cries, Let me dwell among mine own people: oh for a day at home—in the old pastures, stroking the old cattle! The man is quite right. Disturbance of environment is loss of power and loss of peace and loss of self-respect.

It is so educationally. A man may be well informed and what is popularly called well read, and yet not be an educated man, and not be qualified to take any part in educated society. The very first time he opens his mouth the people know that he may be a well-filled sack, but not a man of education. He has information, facts in piles; he is like a well-filled grate, full of coal and paper and wood, but lacking the spark that makes the poetry and that fills the house with pictures. He will be the first to cry out when he is forced into new conditions, Oh that I could dwell among mine own people! I am but a well-informed artisan, my soul has not been bathed in rivers of knowledge and wisdom; I only know things from the outside, I have not that peculiar insight or prevision which sees the whole figure immediately in front of me, the background behind, the sky above, the darting, flashing lights that create all the mystery and poetry of color: let me alone; I can then talk with my own comrades; they think I am quite a well-read man; in my soul I am not; I have read the opinions of other men, but I have not entered into the mystery of the higher communion with the spirits of light and blessedness. Much better that a man should know exactly what he is, what he can do, and what place he can adequately occupy.

Do not read the text in any spirit of narrow-mindedness or sectarianism, saying, I never go beyond my own house, I never inquire into the opinions or the sentiments of other people. That is not the spirit of the text when it is properly interpreted. You have a home, but you also have a neighbor; you have a house, but that does not prevent you accepting the hospitality of those of your own class. Do not therefore read sectarianism or bigotry into the text, but take it in its broad, deep, common-sense applications, and you will have rest, content, strength, and live the life of gracious and cooperative independency. How restless is the man who thinks he could be better and do better if he were only some ten stories higher in the great house! How divided is the strength of the man who always wants to add another story to his dwelling-place, another field to his estate; how mischievous is the influence which tells a man that if he could only be in some other place he would be the man of the day, the foremost man, the coming man—nay, the man come and crowned.

It is so in commerce. You think that if you had only another kind of stool to sit on it would be equal to a throne; but, you say, who can sit on this tripod, this three-legged stool? If I had an easy chair covered with morocco my customers would see at once that I am a prince in the camp, or a king, and they would respect me as such; after all, it is morocco that creates the occasion! Foolish man, and self-disappointing man! If he could say, I am now in a position which by the providence of God I can fill; if enlargement comes to me I shall be glad to welcome it, but it must come in a legitimate way; he that is industrious or diligent in his own business shall stand before kings; I will not trouble my mind about standing before kings, but I will be down to my business early in the morning and stay at it late at night, and I will always be on the spot, and no chance shall pass by me; I shall not be talking about other things, and neglecting the importunity of the commercial age; if the kings come along and ask me to come out and be saluted by them, well, I shall be on the ground, but what I have to do is to dwell in my own position, to do my immediate duty, to occupy well the talents I have; and as for the kings, I shall have as much of them as is good for me. It is an infinite mischief for a man to get it into his head that he ought to be somebody else; he loses his own power; he is not really what he might be and what God intended him to be; he is a wavering and double-minded man, and he can receive nothing of the Lord and he can receive nothing of men; for he is here and he is there, and he is nowhere. When shall we cultivate calmly, educationally, domestically, religiously, a steady, deep, quiet, urgent, loving life? Shall we in the broadest and most generous sense dwell among our own and be their ornament as they are our complement?

We are all tempted to think that if we were somewhere else we would be somebody. What we are does not satisfy us; it is well enough to be going on with, but we want another kind of thing, and to be somewhere else; and the devil tells us that a man of our attainments and faculties ought to be somewhere else. The old liar! he was a liar and a murderer from the beginning, and he has never been able to change his certificate. There are some persons who think that they could be very great people if they were only some-where else. That is what they want. If it was only around the corner, or in the next street; if they could only come out more publicly and definitely! It is so life-wasting. It is one of my very brief and occasional amusements to see the bird take up the snail in its shell and drop it on a hard brick, and then take the snail out of the shell. So many people want to come out of their shell! The devil wants them to do so; and he takes them up, and dashes them against hard stones, and drinks up their poor little soul, and leaves the empty shell in a thousand pieces little. Why not be happy at home? Why not make the best of the situation? Why not say, The environment is very small and very poor, but it is the very best thing that I can do at present, and I will make the best of my opportunities and be cheerful, and I shall wait and watch and pray, and when God wants me elsewhere He will send for me; meanwhile, I dwell among mine own people.

Some persons think that they confer a great honor, for exam-ple, upon Dissenters by remaining with them. No! No man can confer an honor upon Dissent; it is the life of the world, it is the guarantee of progress. Some persons posture as if they were mar-tyrs: if they were not surrounded as they are they might sometimes be invited to a garden party at the vicarage. Oh what I lose, one of such people may say, by being a Dissenter! They do not ask me to a tennis party or to a bowling party or to a cycling club just because I belong to that little conventicle. No, there are no "little conventi-cles"; they are testimonies, witnesses, revelations of the higher truth; and if you want to go to a garden party elsewhere, go; I dwell among mine own people. Anybody that would not admit me be-cause I have convictions I am quite willing to dispense with; I could do better without such patronage than with it. Where I go my con-victions must go; I have not a movable conscience that I can leave behind me, and laugh the fool's laugh on some other ground.

What a temptation to any man it is to be told that a man of his talents and powers might be the manager of the business! The moment that idea gets into a man's mind he is ruined. When a man says, Of course I know well what my capacity is; I know that if I had gone aside from the pulpit and gone to the bar, I might now have been receiving my thousands a year. If you were really called to the pulpit you make no sacrifice for Christ's sake by abiding in it. I owe all I am and have to Christ's grace and Christ's ministry. I have lost nothing by it; I have gained everything. I thank God I have never received the temptation that if I would only turn talents of such and such a kind in other directions I might be a figure in the capital and have a very large fruit garden. Get thee behind me! Avaunt! Out, foul fiend! It is a lie, and I know it. Resist the devil, and he will flee from thee. There is the temptation, and we had better recognize it, and expect the tempter to come along that line. He says to you, You living in a little place like this—a man of your powers! If you came to London, why I can almost promise you, and do it in writing, that in less than twelve months you will have London at your feet; yet here you are wasting your power preaching to three or four dozen poor yokels who never read anything beyond the serial literature of the day; why, yours is a metropolitan style; if you were to come to London, London only could hold the people that would wait upon your ministry. A man likes to be told that; he knows it is exaggeration, and he says so, "but at the same time—" now the mischief has begun! The moment the man said, "But at the same time," he began the reasoning that ends in perdition. He should have said, I am Christ's servant; I put myself wholly into the hands of Christ; if I have to labor in this little village I dwell among mine own people; they are kind-hearted people, simple-minded, sincere, generous to a fault; they make everything of me that mortal man can make of a minister; when Jesus Christ wants me to go and overwhelm London by the splendor of my genius and the energy of my passion, He will drop me an indication to that effect: meanwhile, I dwell among mine own people; I stand here, and I am happy in their friendship and rich in their love. Young minister, take that lesson; remember it when I am not here to give it. He who is faithful over a few things shall be made ruler over many things, and it is neither in your power nor in mine to confer distinction or luster on the Christian pulpit; by its message, its redeeming gospel, its grand, revealing, eternal kingdom, it looks down upon us, and accepts us only as we are willing to accept its spirit.

You would like to get back to the old village after being lost in London for some two years and a half. But the old village has forgotten you, because you forgot the old village. You did not leave in the right spirit; you labored under the influence of a contemptuous feeling; you thought you were so much superior to your poor few people. Sir, you were not! I care not how few or how poor the people, if the Spirit of Christ is in them they are worthy of any genius that you and I may have been mistakenly entrusted with.

Now there is nothing narrow or little in Christ's conception of life. He does not want to make us hermits or dissatisfied hearts, known by what name soever. Christians must remain among Christians. You do not know how good the very meanest Christian is until you get into the society of men who have no God, no reverence, no religious aspiration. There is blasphemy in their wink, there is hell in their hot breath; they are incarnate lust, embodied selfishness or sordidness that can never do you good. Do not venture beyond the Christian circle; understanding by the Christian circle all that is holy, beautiful, benevolent, philanthropic, and redeeming. You need not leave Christ if you want great subjects of contemplation and study. Christianity holds in its keeping the greatest themes on which the greatest intellects can dwell. Nor need you leave Christian society if you want to be wealthy with the true riches. The true riches consist of thought, ideas, broad conceptions, brilliant outlooks, consciousness of the nearness and helpfulness of the spiritual world. He who has these things has the true wealth, and moth and rust are shut out from the house in which such treasures are preserved. You need not leave Christ if you want to enjoy the most exalted and the most exalting communion. We are come to the spirits of just men made perfect. All history in its saintliest moods and influences is at our service. God is not the God of the dead, but of the living. Abraham is ours, and Samuel, and David, and the man of visions, and the man whose soul's ear can catch the music of the spheres. There is nothing little, tawdry, deteriorating, and demeaning and belittling in the Christian life. If some men have made it so, blame the men, not the idea. Jesus Christ intends us to have lofty conceptions, brilliant outlooks, magnificent spheres of service, and to enjoy opportunities for doing good on the largest possible scale. When the dear Lord says to one and to another, Will ye also go away? Our answer is, Go away? To whom shall we go? Ay, verily, to whom shall we go? To cisterns, broken cisterns, that can hold no water; to conjurers and necromancers and theorists; to the fool who laughs with me today, and will laugh at me tomorrow? To whom shall we go, sweet Lord, to whom? What other man is there? Thou hast the words of eternal life.

I accept the teaching of the text; my vanity, my self-importance is quenched; I am set back in my own environment, great or small; I am told to make the best of my surroundings, and I accept the will of God. This should be the outcome of all such meditations as ours today. One of the most capable pastors I have ever known was a man who never had a hundred people in his congregation; but he thought there was no such congregation in the world. That was his power. He did not take me aside and say, You see how I am surrounded by these poor creatures; you can see for yourself that they are persons of a very inferior quality, and I necessarily, as a man of some reading and culture, feel a little dissatisfied with this surrounding; if there is anything in London that you can introduce me to I feel that I should now like a little change. Never! They were "my people," true people, godly, excellent people; everyone of them doing the best he could for Christ's cause. And he never wanted to be introduced to a pastorate in the London that in two days would have forgotten him.

Prayer

O Lord, Thou art not far from any one of us. We can whisper to Thee in the depths of our hearts; Thou dost incline Thine ear and hear us; Thou dost stoop to gather us to Thy breast. We have heard of Thee as the great Shepherd, having sheep in this fold and in that fold, and Thou knowest where all Thy flock is, whether among the rocks or in the green pastures, whether in the daylight or whether in the darkness sevenfold. Thou dost cause every one of Thy flock to pass under the rod that Thou mayest know whether all Thy followers are at home; Thou dost count them one by one, not laying the rod upon them in chastisement, but in indication that Thou dost notice everyone that comes home. May we thus pass under Thy rod, not to be smitten, but to be counted and to be enrolled as members of the great flock under the great Shepherd. We have always been under the eyes of Thy love, we have like sheep gone astray and turned every one to his own way, but Thou hast come after us all. Thou hast died for us all, and now we have returned to the Shepherd and Bishop of our souls, and we have forgotten our wandering and all its sore distress. Deliver us from the gloom of the past, from the great weight of guilty memory; enable us to look upward to the Cross and forward to the glory, and to think less of our sins than of Thy redemption. It is in the name of Jesus we now come before Thee; He taught us how to pray, He built the altar, He inclined His ear, He offered the great answer to our heart's supplications; we therefore pray in the name of Jesus, and ask Thee to answer us in the power of His grace. We would bring Thee our little song, some flower from the summer garden of our gratitude; for Thou hast done great things for us, and art doing them day by day, so that our whole life is a miracle of surprise and deliverance. We will not be dumb in the courts of the Lord; each man has his own story of deliverance and release to tell; the heart knoweth its own bitterness, and under the sunniest face there lies a bruised heart. Thou knowest our distress, our loneliness; Thou knowest how long the time is, and how heavy are the slow-passing hours. Some of us are watching by the sick bed in hope, in fear; in fear, in hope; now this, now that; now a great light, and now a great gloom; and we hasten away into privacy lest we hurt the sufferer by our tears. And some are in great joy, for all the heaven is blue; when the nighttime comes the stars overspread it with light; they are full of joy and gladness, so full of gladness that is holy that they would give a portion to him that has none, and seek out the case that is far off, and help to include some other life in their great festival of love. And some are weary of the world, and dare not leave it; longing for suicide, but may not commit it; praying for death, but death fleeth from them: for life is a weariness, everyday a bitter disappointment, every summer a mockery of hope. And others are simple-minded, sincerely waiting for the Lord, saying, Not my will, but Thine, be done; quite sure that the Lord is at hand, and sure that the Lord is at hand as the great apostles were; for the Lord was just there, a figure in the light, an outline in the noonday, an attitude in the sun; always coming, always nearly come, always sending a promise, and always assuring a fulfillment. And some are wondering about the other hearts that are not in this assembly, the far-away hearts, those who could not afford to come because the distance was long, the voyage tedious, and some who dare not leave lest the little one should die or the oldest friend should pass away. Some are wondering about the boy that has not written so long, they wonder if anything has happened, and their hearts are more there than here, and would not be here at all were it other than the house of God. Now that Thou knowest our condition, and that our hearts and hands are spread out unto Thee in posture of expectation, now that we are gathered at the Cross, what wait we for but some answer that will lighten the burden, cheer the sadness, and give hope to desolation that dare hardly open its eyes?

The Lord hear us and comfort us and be with us on our way from Bethel to Jericho, and to the further city, and to the place where the chariot will come down, and the angels will bid us take our seats, and rise. Amen.

10
Victories, Not Victors

Preached on Sunday Morning, July 30th, 1899.

Now thanks be unto God, which always causeth us to triumph in Christ, and maketh manifest the savor of His knowledge by us in every place—2 Corinthians 2:14.

This is a difficult text to remember; let us beat it out into more words, if haply in the multiplication of words we may here and there catch something of the idea. "Now thanks be unto God, which always causeth us to triumph in Christ." We never go to any city but the magistrates and the leaders of that city fall down before us in a kind of social homage; they are delighted to see us; they say, These are men of fame, this is a special event, a historical opportunity, and all the people turn out of all the houses to shout Huzza! It is a wonderful ministry to which we are called; every rival is put down, no competition can live when we present ourselves; we have only to speak, and the waters fall to obedience and silence, and all the social atmosphere is a blessing. You now begin to see something of the meaning of the apostle's exclamation. I hope you do not, for the apostle said nothing of the kind; he hardly spoke of himself or of his brother apostles at all. The text would read just the contrary way. "Now thanks be unto God, which always causeth us to triumph"—nothing of the kind; that would be a poor speech, altogether unworthy of apostolic dignity and sanctification. This is not egotism, this is worship; this is not self-exaltation, this is falling down before Christ and hailing Him Lord of all. The apostle never

93

said, See how great a victor I am; if I go out to hunt I bring back with me prey of all sorts; never, not even Nimrod, stood mightier hunter than I am. That is not the apostolic tone; it is the tone of folly, of self-ignorance, and of guilty ambition. The text has been read thus: "But thanks be unto God, which always leadeth us in triumph in Christ, and maketh manifest through us the savor of His knowledge in every place." What was the first picture like? It was like a number of boasting men all gathered together and praising one another as persons who drew upon themselves the recognition and the applause of every society into which they entered. What is the second and true picture? That all these men have been arrested, converted, blessed by Jesus Christ, and He as conqueror points to them and says, Behold the men I have taken at the spearpoint. So we are not victors, but victories; not little greatnesses that have strutted our hour of vanity upon the stage, but we are the prey of Christ, the consenting and happy victims of His spear; He wounded us that He might make us immortal in His own blessedness.

This, then, is a beautiful picture. The subject ought to be treated pictorially. We should see a great king with a great procession of chariots behind him, and those chariots full of saved men, and the Captain of their salvation at the head pointing to these men as proofs of the reality and energy and beneficence of His redeeming and saving grace. Let the heart keep the picture vividly before its eyes: Christ at the head, miles of chariots, all golden, all filled with living hymns, all wounded men, but wounded to their own salvation; and as they come along they say, We have been taken by Christ at the spearpoint; if you want to know what Christ can do, read the record of our experience. Christ says in effect, If you would know what my Gospel can do with men, look at all these consenting and grateful arrests of mine, and you will understand the purpose of the redeeming grace of heaven. So egotism is dead; it is the Lord that is magnified, and not the apostle or preacher or flaming evangelist. Stand back! it is the Lord's trophy; it is the Lord's day; we will rejoice and be glad.

This reading of the text does two things: first, it puts Christ in His right position, and, secondly, it puts Christians in their right position, and not Christians only, but Christian apostles and martyrs, the leaders and heads of the visible Church upon earth, appointed by Christ, clothed by Him with some mantle which is the truest honor of the soul. Christ is put in His right position by being put at the head of the great procession. Who is this that cometh up from Edom with dyed garments from Bozrah, this that is red in his apparel, traveling in the greatness of his strength? And who are these that follow Him, and sing as they follow? It is the army of the saved, it is the caravan of the blessed, it is the host on every member of which is sprinkled the saving blood, and by these grand trophies of His grace Christ spreads the news of His kingdom over all the waiting earth.

It would be interesting to look at one or two of these men and to ask one or two questions about them. They all seem to be distinguished men; the Lord has conquered in high places. May we interrupt the caravan for a moment and ask who are these marked with red blood, sealed with a seal, and claimed by a mighty King? Yes, we may interrogate the whole of them. Take two or three typical instances, and they will do for the rest, as explaining the idea and putting it in pictorial form and color.

Who is this first man following immediately after Christ? His name is Paul. Was that always his name? No; at first he was called Saul. A man of any family or standing, any pedigree—can he produce any documents to establish his identity as belonging to the house of history and antiquity? He can; he was a Pharisee of the Pharisees, a Hebrew of the Hebrews; as regarding the law, a man blameless; a person of great intellectual capacity, keen-sighted; and as for will, no fortress of rock could keep him back. He hated the Christian religion, he hated Christ; he thought he was doing God service by opposing the name and claim of Christ; and he went out to seek those who prayed in the name of Christ, that he might exterminate them. A blameless man, as regards the law. How comes he in this chariot, and so near the Captain of the whole host? He is the joyful, grateful prisoner of Christ. Does he want to be in that chariot? He does, or nothing could keep him there. He calls himself the slave of the Lord Jesus—slave in its poetic sense, slave as involving ownership and consent and obedience and invincible attachment to the house of the King. What has Christ to say about this man? He has this to say, namely: Self-righteousness is conquerable by grace. There is the proof. Do not go into any argument of words; one word fights another; let the wordy contest go on: there is the man. Paul has taken up all his pedigrees, genealogies, hereditary rights and claims, and, gathering them up into one little bundle, he has deliberately thrust the whole into the very hottest center of the fire, and says, Things that I counted gain to me I count but loss; yea, I count all things but loss, refuse, σκυβαλα, nothing worth. It would take some great argument to convince this man, it took Christ Himself, the embodied grace of God; it was that great force that came into conflict with him at the gate of Damascus, and there with a white flame as a sword the Lord Jesus smote this man, and points to him today and forever as an illustration of what the grace of God can do, when man does not obstinately and to his own ruin resist the pleading and sweet entreaty of the Spirit. The most self-righteous man among us may be conquered by the grace of Christ. Surely the conquest of self-righteousness is the supreme miracle of the Cross. Man loves his own miserable piety; man loves to have a righteousness that he can measure and lay his hand upon and estimate and appreciate in plain figures; a morality that can be plainly seen by plainest folks. To cast away that righteousness and take upon the soul and into the soul a spiritual righteousness, with new motives, new purposes, new aspirations, and new realizations of destiny—never! Yes, now! There's the conflict, and Christ will win. We must get rid of our self-righteousness, we must cast ourselves upon the grace of God, we must fall down dead as it were at the foot of the Cross, and cry for the pity and for the healing grace of the Lord Jesus.

Who is that not far behind Paul? That is a very remarkable man; if you knew his history you would at once acknowledge that he is a remarkable man. That man is the dying thief. Jesus spoke to him, got an entrance into his heart, told him that he need not be a thief any longer. Only tell a man that he need not be a drunkard anymore, nor a thief, nor a bad creature, and you instantly bring the morning of hope to shine upon the night of his despair. That is the dying thief; he said, "Lord, remember me!" He called Jesus "Lord"—more than Sir, more than a mere title of courtesy; this was not the time for playing off the tricks of gentlemanliness, this was an hour of agony, when the real man expressed himself in adequate terms. He called Jesus Lord, and recognized Jesus as the King of a kingdom, and recognized that Jesus Christ had power in more worlds than one. If the grace of God could get at that man's heart, why should it not get at mine, at yours? The man was half in hell; the man was swiftly sinking down the line that ends in the pit. We can be saved from going into it: Now is the accepted time, now is the day of salvation. Do not go into some little miserable verbal argument, here is the man; he was taken at the spearpoint, and that spear has lost nothing of its strength or keenness; yield to that gracious thrust, and die that you may forever live.

And there sits a man not far from him who uttered a prayer the world will need until its latest day. It was a short prayer, it was great in its brevity; it was a Bashan in an acorn, it was a great forest in a little seed. This man is known throughout all history as the publican who prayed side by side with the Pharisee. He said, "God be merciful unto me a sinner!" God was merciful to him; the man went down to his house justified. It is evident, therefore, that even self-contempt is conquerable. The man repudiates himself, dare not look heaven in the face, is afraid of the white stars by night, and he will hardly look at the earth, for it is rich with blooming and pure flowers; he knows not where to look: where can shame look and self-conviction? He looks within and sees the putridity of the sin of which he is guilty, and his lips move, saying, "God be merciful to me!" The prayer that always brings the key from the throne; the prayer which God never answered but in the affirmative and immediately in the affirmative; no time was lost, the prayer was hardly uttered until heaven's grand amen came down and filled the air as with the presence of angels. Are we really filled with the spirit of self-contempt? I do not inquire whether we do in some moments cantingly describe ourselves under very contemptuous names; that may all be hypocrisy of the very meanest and cheapest sort; but do we in our soul's soul hold ourselves as before God in contempt? If so, here is the answer; not an answer in words, for words can be answered by words; here is the answer in life, in a living personality, in a definite and ascertainable character. It is by such miracles that Christ makes His way, the Conqueror, the King.

All these, some hearer may say, do not represent my case; I left my father and my mother, I am a mean wretch; I have not written to them except to beg for many a day; I dare not think about myself, I have murdered my father and mother; they used to sit up for me, thinking I would come home, and I never went; they used to trust messages to people in the hope that they would someday and somehow meet me and deliver the message of perpetual love; there is no man in that procession that represents me; I am not the publican, I am not the dying thief, I am not Saul of Tarsus; I am the prodigal son. Here he is, in the very next chariot, the prodigal son returned, and the Lord Jesus would not permit him to tell out the last tone of his prayer; the Lord Jesus saw what his heart was going to say, and stopped him, and said, Bring forth the best robe and put it on him. Was that not so, returned prodigal? And the answer comes ringingly forth, Yea, that was my case; I came home, and my father received me, and my mother became young again, and the house was a castle of sunshine, and the whole atmosphere became a very near and appreciable heaven. The argument to the living prodigal is this: If the grace of God could triumph over the prodigal son's obstinacy and selfishness, why may it not triumph over yours? Go home today, take the prayer of a guilty, self-condemning heart with you, tell your father and mother and other friends exactly how it was, keep nothing back, pour out the wretched tale, and get rid of it, or it will injure you like a hidden scorpion: out with it! When you have made up your mind to this, the grace of God will come into your heart and fill it with gladness and with hope, and though you may never be able to forgive yourself, and have no business to think about yourself after the great transaction has been completed. When Christ's grace has spoken the word to you, you may say, Christ Jesus came into the world to save sinners, of which saved sinners I am chief. You do not go back to your villainy, you go forward to your adoption and your sonship. Many men find it to be almost impossible to get rid of their old selves. What sanction is there in Scripture for keeping up the penance of self-reproach? Surely there comes a time when grace is utterly to destroy the memory of sin. If there is a struggle between sin and grace in the human heart, there must necessarily be a vivid memory of the unholy things which degraded and disgraced our past lives. But when the Gospel has been received in all its redeeming energy and uplifting music, all its holy grace and its tender sympathy, the memory of sin should be blotted out and the spirit of grace should fill the whole horizon of life and hope. Penitence is an act which in a sense may be completed and glorified; but grace continually comes into the heart day by day, and will come in until the whole soul is saturated with the love of God and with the spirit of holiness. In the degree in which that process is completed we may come to forget the very name of sin as one day we shall forget the name of sorrow and the name of sighing, for both sorrow and sighing shall flee away. I will not look continually and depressingly at my sins, I will look at the Cross where they were forgiven, and I will listen to the Savior, who says, Go in peace—a command He never could have given if He had intended me to lacerate my heart with self-reproach to the very end of my days.

We are, then, to be specimens of Christ's victorious grace. What an honor, what a responsibility, yet what a danger—lest we should be self-deceived and be but half-subdued. The argument of Christ is, Believe me for the work's sake; here is the man, the man is the best argument; personal character is the best defense; remember what the man was, what the man is, to what energy he ascribes the change. He tells you it was the miracle of the grace of God; believe the man. Why should you be keeping outside God's gracious kingdom, chaffering with some fellow-disputant, neither of you being able to discuss the mysteries of the kingdom of heaven with any adequacy of intellectual force or spirit fitness? Why should you be asking hard questions in words? There is the man, the soul, the publican, the thief, the prodigal—there! You have not to answer an argument in words, you have to destroy a logic in life, a grand syllogism in fact, in experience, in ascertainable consequence. Do not, I pray you, especially the young, be going and buying books that will puzzle you with long words and difficult arguments. Look at the instances you yourselves have known of the energy of the grace of Christ; know that Jesus Christ calls you to consider what victories He has already won. Whatever your case or mine may be, there is an analogy, a parallel, an almost identical instance in the record of Christ's victories. Read it, and say, If Christ could conquer that man, He can conquer me. Jesus of Nazareth, take me at the point of Thy victorious spear!

Prayer

Thou dost confound us with questions. We are utterly bewildered and stupefied by the inquiries which Thou dost put in thunder, we are afraid and scared and driven off. We cling to our own little tether, we can go but so short a way. We have lifted up our eyes and beheld, and, lo, we cannot count the stars; we have no names for them; we name a few, but our names exhaust themselves: what are these further ones, these brighter ones, the star-faces that look upon us from the infinitely glorious line? We are of yesterday, and know nothing. If Thou wouldst by Thy grace teach us that we know nothing, we shall begin to be wise. If any man think that he knoweth anything, he knoweth nothing as it is. We sit down self-rebuked, utterly humiliated; our breath is in our nostrils, and the grave opens its mouth and laughs at us from under our feet. The Lord keep us within our own lines; Thou hast fixed the bounds of our habitation: oh that Thou wouldst fix the bounds of our fancy, ambition, and speculation! Then we should have time to work, and in service we should find all the revelation we need. Thou hast been very good to us; Thou hast given to us with both hands, and the left hand has been as the right, and Thy generosity sevenfold and beyond all our imagining. If any man has seen the white face of death, show him the radiant countenance of immortality; if any man thinks he has sounded all the depths of sorrow, teach him he has not yet begun to know it as compared with the infinite grief of the Son of God. We take our little crosses and set them up beside His great Cross, and we are ashamed of their meanness.

The Lord be with us, a beauteous morning, a spring day, a summer dawn, an autumnal benediction. Let the Lord hear us, and His attention will be an answer. We speak it at the Cross. The Lord will hear us when we kneel before that altar of blood and love. Amen.

11
Limits

Preached on Thursday Morning, September 21st, 1899.

What canst thou do? . . . what canst thou know?—Job 11:8.

These questions were put by an extraordinary contradiction of human manner. They were put by Zophar, a citizen of the fair Naamath—a lovely place, full of flowers: a place that the summer might have haunted, and have lingered until the last beam of light faded behind the hills. Yet this was one of the most rough-spoken men of his day; in this respect the environment and the man were mismatched. Zophar was an accuser, a man of rough tongue; he could not be civil until after he had been rude. He told Job that he, the wasted one, was "a man of lips," in the Hebrew tongue—a word-chopper, a gabbler in the face of the heaven's patience, and that Job knew nothing about his own case. The ideal and poetic Eliphaz had spoken, and Bildad—the sort of middleman that interprets poetry to prose, and makes the dull dog try to understand a word here and there—and Zophar comes up with the climax of brutality. There is a candor that is not lovely, there is an outspokenness that had better have choked itself before it began to speak. Yet every now and then—for we have called the man a self-contradiction—Zophar comes squarely down on the bedrock of fact and experience, and treats the whole deitic question with wonderful pith, setting it out in glittering generalizations and stunning Job as if by new proverbs.

This is illustrated by the text: It is high as heaven; what canst thou do? It is deeper than hell—man, hear me! Why bruise thy knuckles on that door? This whole question is deeper than Hades, deeper than the grave, deeper than the burning pits below the ocean; what canst thou know? It was a rough way of preaching, and yet not without its own grim grandeur. Zophar called Job back to beginnings, to realities, to limitations. Said he in effect, See thee, this is the length of thy tether; thou hast seen a dog straining his neck as if he would get beyond the length of his iron chain, and he could not do it, but he nearly choked himself in the process; be wise; this thing deitic, is higher than heaven; what canst thou do? deeper than hell what canst thou know? "Do," "know"—nearly all the verbs in one couplet.

Everywhere man, proud man, is set back, is stung with rebukes, is driven off from the front line as if it were already pre-engaged. Great man, so great that he speaks about—hear it!—the inferior animals! He has even taken some of the inferior animals under his protection; he has made refuges for them, and collected subscriptions for them, and called them dumb creatures. I have never met any dumb dogs or dumb lions or dumb fowls of the air; each had its crow, or its little utterance of smallest music. When men talk about the dumb animals, I wonder what they mean; when man, full six feet high, and knowing it, speaks about the inferior animals, he is at his worst. In one sense they are inferior, but in many other senses they are superior. Can you fly as high as the eagle? If the standard of comparison is flying, I think that man will have to occupy a very humble seat somewhere where it is impossible to see him. What can you do with the lion or the tiger? Can you stand foul weather as he can? Can you sleep in the jungle? And yet my lord talks about the inferior animals, and sometimes addresses Sunday-schools on that grim subject. The dog rebukes his master; the bloodhound says, Stop at home, proud man, and I will find the hidden, the self-concealed murderer; let me but catch one sniff of anything he ever wore, and I will hunt him to the death. And proud man buys him a kennel and a collar. Stop at home, and for the nonce be the inferior animal.

Explain it how you may, man is being continually rebuked, reduced in magnitude, put in a very sober place. In some other respects we know how godlike he can be, how sweet in prayer, how
tender in sympathy, how noble in charity; but always distinguish
between the inferior and the superior, and understand, O man, that
thou art tethered, and beyond thy chain thou canst not go. If you
will know so much, you will begin to be wise. Why, we say this in
poetry and literature, and science and preaching, and in everything
else indeed; we speak of a man who knows exactly what he can do.
Professor Huxley said that to keep within the range of your own
ability is power; to try to get beyond it is weakness. If man could
know but once now and then that he is not God, he might sometimes stumble on the eternal throne and begin to pray. It would
seem as if God had placed man in an environment of rebuke. Man
is snubbed on every hand. The hills rebuke his strength; futurity
rebukes his insight; the sky mocks his stature; nature never visits
his academy except to laugh at him. When man charges you to go
into his academy, the great nature-academy—the rocks and trees and
forests and rivers and seas—says, Come, behold the works of the
Lord and the wonders of His hand. Man publishes a catalogue,
God publishes the universe. Nature is very severe sometimes; when
she is in a satiric mood there is no satire so acid and so biting as
hers. Sometimes she looks upon a landscape which some man has
painted; then her countenance is a sight; she looks upon the trees,
and wonders where the poor creature got the idea from; she rejects
his portraits, and will not buy his photographs. She stands alone—
an original. So man is continually rebuked; he is continually hearing thundered into his ear, It is as high as heaven; what canst thou
do? Deeper than hell; what canst thou know? Thou poor dog, sleep
in thy kennel, and dream thyself into more bigness and wisdom.

I could show you some little pictures that would preach better
on the text than I can ever hope to do or any other man. Let me
show you one or two. I say to this man, On what business art thou
bent today? He says, I am going to measure the sun. With what

instruments? With this yard wand; I shall be back when I have finished. I say, I am sure you will, but not until then, I hope. It is higher than heaven, man; what canst thou do with thy yard wand? Go home, stand behind thy village counter, and earn an honest loaf, but never attempt to measure the sun with a yard wand. Let us walk by the seaside; here is a man who seems to be very busy. May we ask you what you are doing? Certainly. Then tell us how you are occupying your time. The answer is, I am occupying my time by counting one by one all the sands upon the seashore. What would you think of that man? Would you require to retire from the jury box in order to consider the case? Would you not stop the argument before it went one sentence further? Well, that is precisely what you—I speak to the unbelieving or doubting man—are doing when you are trying to measure the infinite with a finite instrument, measure, or standard. Man, it cannot be done; why not know it, and take to honest breadwinning and healthy praying and rational watching? And here is a third man who is going to do something that will paralyze the world. I pray thee tell me what thou art after this sunny September morning. I am after a new idea. Relate it; we have not heard any new ideas for many a century, what is thine? To devise a method by which I can put the whole Atlantic Ocean into a thimble. Need we remain long with this man? Have we not had enough of him in this one little sentence? Shall we not go forward and look at the blue sea, and wonder concerning that underheaven that holds by reflection all the suns and stars of the sky? Much better, I trow. Why laugh at these men when we ourselves may in some degree be doing the very self-same thing—trying to sound the infinite with a cord made heavy with lead at one end? Why try to know God when He is not to be known? Why endeavor to find Him out to perfection, when His perfection no mind can conceive and no tongue express?

But are we to leave the sun unmeasured? Certainly not, but take with you adequate instruments. But may we not try to count the sands upon the seashore? No; I will tell you why: if you could count them you could not state the result of your inquiry; arithmetic would abandon you, figures would say, We cannot now pronounce our own name; we are good from millions to nonillions; there we can speak with a wide mouth, though we do not understand what we are saying, but when you get to cubed nonillions we have no name for that mighty sum. Thus you come, even along the line of arithmetic, upon the unknowable and the inconceivable and the unthinkable; but when you come upon God along that line you become a new species of insect—an agnostic! Why, you are as much an agnostic along the arithmetical line as along the theological line. Space is as mysterious as God; duration is as inconceivable as the deity; all things go into the unknown and the unknowable. Space says, I have no more words with which to explain myself, I melt into the infinite. Time says, My little chronometer has ticked off all its moments, and now I am absorbed in eternity. And speech—proud, eloquent—having finished its last perspiring climax, says, I can add nothing, now I will take to music.

So with this greatest of all subjects, the Godhead. We cannot know it, for it is higher than heaven, deeper than Hades; it belongs to all the unmeasured space, all the infinite intellectual territory, which has not yet been crushed into maps and made part of some elementary geography. But though I cannot measure the sun, I can enjoy the sunlight. That is my province, then; I cannot measure his diameter, but I can hail his summer and welcome his morning and bathe my cold life in his warm radiance. That is what we can do, and that we are called upon to do. We cannot count the sands upon the seashore, but we can walk over the golden path, and let the blue waves break in white laughter on our feet as we traverse that highway of beauty and vision. We cannot put the Atlantic into a thimble, but we can traverse it, sail upon it, turn it into a highway, utilize it, and make it not the separator, but the uniter of the nations.

So our not knowing and our not being able to do, need not prevent our enjoyment and our service and our discipline. Do not imagine that you can get rid of religion by any intellectual act: there still remain the moral duties, the ten commandments, the eternal Sinai. Fool is he who thinks that there is no field beyond his own hedge, and that he has really nothing to do with religion because he cannot find out unto perfection the Almighty Father and Creator of all. To know that we do not know, that is wisdom; to know just where we ought to end, that is understanding. It is something to know that we are not artists; it is the next best thing to being artists. What trouble a man saves himself who never buys any paints or any brushes, and never spends a shilling upon palette or easel; what vexation and rubbing-out, what erasure and disappointment, the man saves himself when he knows that he is not a painter, and never will be one. He sees what time is left to him for what he can do by so clearly knowing what he cannot do. It is very sad—I could almost weep over it if I had not something better to weep over—to see a man doing water-colors that his own family will laugh at; but he thinks it is "in" him, and he is developing himself, and he persuades himself that he has the artistic temperament, and therefore must have his own way in the house. It is a sad thing when a man thinks he has got the artistic temperament when he has not got it. Blessed is he who knows that he does not know. Why, it is something for a man to know that he is not a giant; then he would save himself all the trouble that he takes in secret to measure himself against every bedroom door in the whole house to see if he cannot by stretching make himself at least one inch higher. But the man is a simple, an honest-hearted, a right trustable soul, that says, I know exactly what I am, I am five feet eight inches, and I am not going to stretch myself to try to make myself six feet six inches. If men would be just what they really are, if they would not seek to be what they cannot be, what time would be saved, what useful energy would be satisfactorily applied. If a man knew really that he could not preach—on that I need not say anything, for the public are as candid as Zophar the Naamathite, and will soon let him know the truth.

"What canst thou do? What canst thou know?" We can know Jesus; He speaks the language of little children; we have heard Him say, "Come unto Me, all ye that labor and are heavy laden, and I will give you rest," and it was just like our mother talking. Sometimes I have heard the greatest preacher spoken of in this way, "It was not like preaching, it was more like as if he were talking to you." I said, That is the preaching I want; for a man to face me and say, Hear the word of the Lord; thou art in the wrong way; this is the way that is right; here is the profitable doctrine; I have come to thee to speak definitely and directly and responsibly to thee; arise—the Master calls for thee!

"What canst thou do?" We can do the commandments; at least, we can begin to do them; it will take us a long time to penetrate into their metaphysic, but we can begin to do their practical commands at once; we can make an effort in that direction. You would like to do something very great and sublime? Do not attempt it; it is as high as heaven; what canst thou do? You would like to have five thousand orphans? Have one to begin with; I know it would not suit the grandeur of so high and mighty a man as you are, but it would please Jesus; if you wait until you get the five thousand you will never get them, but if you take the first little child that is fatherless and motherless, and say, I will be feet to thee and eyes to thee and wisdom to thee, and I place myself in Christ's name and for the sake of Christ's Cross at thy service, dear little one, then you are already in the kingdom of God. "What canst thou do?" I will tell you; it shall be no message of my own conception, hardly a message of my own delivery: "What doth the Lord require of thee, but to do justly." It is such disciplinary commands that makes Christianity unpopular. If Christianity had scented pillows to offer on which the head of weariness could rest, and if it could have some comfortable provision made on its return from slumber, Christianity would become quite a popular religion, but it is known by the badge called the Cross; its home is in Gethsemane and on

Golgotha; its command is, Do justly, love mercy, walk humbly with God.

Instead, therefore, of drowning yourselves in some sea of metaphysics, why not take up with these grand ethical commandments, these great moral attempts and endeavors, and work your way? And by-and-by the darkness will depart, and the white light of the morning shall kiss the hills of the east, and thou shalt know that the day of the Lord has come. This would be severe teaching; it would be impossible doctrine but for the grace of God that lies behind it: "My grace is sufficient for thee." I can do all things through the Christ that enables me; our sufficiency is of God. We will not be called great scholars, perhaps, but God will call us good scholars. I do not know that God cares much for the word "great"; I have heard Him again and again in His book say "good," "faithful"— terms of universal application because of universal utility. Do not wait until we can be great; let us try in the grace of God to be good. Do not wait until we can give a million pounds; throw in the two mites: and who knows to what harvests of gold they may one day come? What we do know let us put into practice; what we can do let us do with both hands earnestly; and if we do the will we shall know the doctrine, and if we obey the law we shall come into a great inheritance of reward. One day the Master will say, Well done, good and faithful servant; thou couldst not find Me out unto perfection, but thou didst touch the hem of My garment, and thou didst go upon My errands in the night-time, and do good by stealth, and help men without ever giving in thy name to swell thy reputation.

Let us not, therefore, think that we are called upon to give great intellectual answers to unfathomable questions, but we are called upon to do good according to our opportunities, and to redeem the time, and to wait patiently for the Lord, who will give us wider horizons and more enduring suns.

Words for Preachers

I am more and more convinced that as preachers we must go back to the great Masters of the Evangelical pulpit if the Christian ministry is to flourish in its ancient power. Puritan preaching had no small share in the making of heroic and spiritual England. It had a specific and definite Message which it thundered with vehement energy, and which the country was compelled to hear. We must recall the days of consecration—the Altar, the Cross, the Holy Ghost! The political essay, the literary pedantry, the polish that never grapples with the most strenuous conditions and the most eager aspirations of the human heart, must be driven out forever, and replaced by the true culture, the deeper piety, and the more ardent zeal of the invincible Puritanism. The Twentieth Century is upon us, how is the Christian Pulpit going to meet it? It will be an exacting century. The hope of the pulpit is in distinctiveness, not in colorless neutrality. The pulpit is not to be an adaptation of the printing press; it must realize its own peculiar function and pursue a course which admits of no rivalry and no blending either with passionless commonplace or frenzied sectarianism. With my whole heart I pray God to raise up in England an army of Puritan preachers, men who know the Cross, and are not ashamed of its stigma—men who know the Throne and have power with the King.—*Dr. Joseph Parker*

Like as a woman who taketh a child to nurse and feed for hire, although she should pray for it one part of the day, and sing to it another part of the day, and should wash and keep it as clean as possible the third part of the day, and yet should give it no milk, nor feed it, but suffer it to die from hunger, nevertheless, for all her singing and saying, washing and praying, she were a murderess; or, as if a watchman were hired of the citizens to watch the city, and should leave his place and go into the city and help the masons to build the walls, or be occupied about some other affairs which he had no charge of, and in the meantime the enemy should come and kill some within the city, in thus doing he should be guilty of their death; even so the minister who taketh a congregation to feed, although he be diligent in reading the service, singing of psalms, ministering the sacraments, or occupied about some affairs of the commonwealth, if he should leave undone the most principal part of his calling, which is preaching and catechizing, and so the people perish for want thereof, in thus doing he is a soul-murderer, and guilty of all those that thus perish.—*Cawdray, 1609*

Prayer

Almighty God, our Father, Thou dost come to us. We cannot find Thee out, but Thou canst find Thy child, and speak to him in little words which he can understand. We cannot find out the Almighty, but the Almighty can find us out, and speak to our hearts, to our sin and sorrow and whole necessity. It is from this point that we now humbly and in the name and at the Cross of Jesus Christ approach Thee with some boldness of love, that we may obtain mercy and Thy grace to help in every time of need. Every time is a time of need; every moment is a cry unto God, everyday brings its own hunger and thirst and conscious necessity. Come to us and reveal Thyself to us while we tarry at Thy bleeding feet. The Cross never disappoints us; the Cross fills the whole firmament; it, too, is longer than the earth and deeper than the sea. It comes to us as Thine own heart, an expression of Thine own infinite pity; we throw the arms of our love around it, knowing that there, on Golgotha, no man who believes can die.

12
Man's Freedom

Preached on Thursday Morning, September 28th, 1899.

It is as high as heaven; what canst thou do? deeper than hell;
what canst thou know?–Job 11:8.

Let us continue the interesting and profitable mediation which we commenced last Thursday upon this inquiry, "What canst thou do?" Sometimes man is so conscious of strength that he feels he can practically do anything and almost everything, and yet I expect it will turn out before we conclude the meditation of this hour that we can do next to nothing. It pleases man to think that he is a free agent. So he may be, but we must first hear and consider his definition of the principal word in the terms of the assertion–the word "free." Always be clear about your definitions, and it is quite wonderful how you will curtail controversy. Nearly all discussion ranges round the qualifying terms, the adjectives or epithets; very little discussion ranges around the substantive term. So here we are confronted with the large word "free." Almost every man who knows anything about himself declares himself to be a free agent and a free man; and I think the Englishman's voice is loudest in the unmusical chorus. He likes to think himself free, and he is not free for one single moment in all the four-and-twenty hours of the day. "What canst thou do?" Let us take the self-boasting free man at any point, and ask him some simple but searching questions.

Had you any choice about coming into this world? Was it ever proposed to you in some anterior state whether you would come into this world or come into some other world? You are a free agent—tell me, when did your freedom begin in this particular matter? Have you any freedom in the matter of going out of this world? Can you go any day? Do you prefer the summer to the winter for going out of this world? You are a free man, and you have invented certain little vulgar songs upon your freedom; tell me now, can you select the day of your death, the day of your exit, the season of your departure, the environment of your recession into the shadows? You do not seem to have much to say upon this question. Had you any freedom, choice, or election in the matter of your nationality? Did anybody or any soul ever ask you before you became clothed with this mortal body whether you would like to be born in sunny Italy, in classic Greece, in imperial Rome, in western seas, with their shivering and often sterile islands? You are a free agent; why did you select England, Ireland, or Scotland as your birthplace? Why did you not enter this European continent by the sunny door of sunny Italy?

Had you any choice about your name; even your surname? Your so-called Christian name, which is no name at all, was discussed by father and mother at a council table, and several letters were written to absent friends for suggestions as to the name you should bear. Your freedom is dwindling quickly; when shall we see this free man and free agent and free Briton? Had you any freedom of action in the matter of your stature? Why did you elect to be five feet seven inches instead of six feet two inches—were you not consulted on the matter? But you are a free man and a free agent, and you revel in a great liberty; and you were never consulted as to your own height! It seems as if things had gone heavily against you; it appears to me that your cage is fast shrinking, and we shall hardly be able to see you within its iron bars presently. But let us wait. Had you any freedom of action in the matter of your complexion? You are a free agent; when did you take up your freedom? Why were you not born black instead of white, or yellow instead of cream and pink? Have you absolutely no choice about your own complexion? It is your own, it is not the complexion of the man who sits next to you, it is your own; how did it become your own? You believe in free will; where does it begin, end?

Ay, it is when we get into citizenship, when we get into the larger life of the commonwealth, the larger space of the State, that we gain our freedom, and take up the franchise and sign our names as belonging to the liberty of great cities and great provinces. Believe me, it is not; I must ask you even here some penetrating and humbling questions. Why did you not bring out your house six inches further or set it six inches back? Because there is a Metropolitan Building Act, and by that Act we are bound to follow a certain line. But I thought you were a free man, and had on the livery and dined with the liverymen; do you tell me that you had to set back your house six inches from the line you would like to have chosen? Yes. Then where does your liberty begin? And as to that matter of taxation; of course there you have the liberty of a philanthropist and the freedom of a poet; there should be no doubt about that; you are so anxious to give to the State that you always take care to be out of the way when the tax-collector calls. I thought you were a free man and had a great liberty, and that you had made certain little vulgar, silly tavern songs about your freedom as Englishmen. Where is your freedom in the State? You cannot make your own dictionary, or if you can make it you dare not use it. You may have a hundred dictionaries in that secret drawer of yours for anything I know to the contrary, and you will be obliged to keep them there; the State will not allow you to publish them, or will not allow you at least to act upon them. You must not change the language in which you were born; there is no private interpretation of the English tongue, or of any other national language; it is a common right, and must be interpreted by a common grammar. Already I think your freedom is shrinking a good deal in magnitude.

You will not be allowed to alter even the pence table. That is a most extraordinary thing for a man who boasts of being so very free and so very independent and so highly individualistic. For a man who lives in a villa and in a mansion and in a castle and in a palace, or even in a flat—no such man can alter the pence table that as little children we all chattered—"four farthings one penny, twelve pennies one shilling, twenty shillings one pound." Can I not alter all that? There are certain ways of altering it which would lead you into the undesirable companionship of a constable. But I thought you were free, a great free agent! You may be free at some points, but we have not found them yet. You cannot alter the multiplication table, and you say, "Britons never, never, never will be slaves!" They are slaves all the time—to the multiplication table, to a common idea, to a national testimony and standard. Am I not at liberty—a man fourteen stone avoirdupois and living in a large house and paying taxes—am I not at liberty to say there are nineteen shillings in a pound? You are at perfect liberty to say it, but you are not at all at liberty to pay it; you can have what idiotic ideas you like as to how many shillings there ought to be in a pound, but if you go on reasoning as you have already suggested, you will land first in the bankruptcy court, and then be sent to penal servitude. Freedom is dwindling; we shall have presently to say that we are in a cage, that we are bound, and that we belong to one another, and therefore that the State could not continue for a single day if we allowed individual opinions to control the points which have been thus incidentally raised. But can we not say that twelve times twelve are a hundred and forty-two? Certainly; you are at perfect liberty to say that if it will give you the slightest possible enjoyment, and you may say that twelve times thirteen are a hundred and four if it will relieve your feelings or in any way contribute to your realization of a high ideal of manhood. But you must not go further; you must take care how you trifle with common property.

There is a language the grammar of which you cannot change; there is a pence table which will be turned one day it may be into a standard of your honesty; there is a multiplication table with which you must not trifle, or you may throw the whole State into confusion by giving new reckonings, new additions, and subtractions, and divisions. We must act in a common sense, under a common standard, at a common bidding; we must allow the commonwealth to absorb mere individualism. So the State is very severe; the State takes into its care our very grammar. There are certain men within almost two throws of a stone in wigs and gowns sitting for the purpose of interpreting grammar. What business have they to interpret grammar—have we not all been to school? Are we not in some sense grammarians? Do we not all speak our mother tongue? Yet there are bewigged and begowned men within some three or four hundred paces of this church who undertake to tell you what your own writing means and what your father's writing means, and you are not at liberty under certain circumstances to interpret your father's own will. I thought you were free! Free in what sense? You are not at liberty to kill your own child. The child, you say, is your own. I deny it; that is your fundamental sophism and utter mistake; the child is not yours, it is ours, it is God's; it is life, and every red blood drop is God's. He will call us to account for our cruelty even to the animals that we often denominate inferior. The State will not permit you unduly to beat your horse, and the State will interpret the meaning of the word unduly, and you will not be permitted to interpret it for your own uses. The child is not yours, it is God's: then momentarily yours; and all the time, since it came into being, it has belonged to civilized, law-abiding society. The great mistake which people make is that anything is theirs individually, independently, and to be used according to individual will. All society gathers around the little cradle with the little stranger, and all society will hang you if you kill that child; every mother will lead you to the gallows, every father will give you short shrift, if you take away the life of your so-called own child. Where is your freedom? Where is your boasted independence, and where your foolish cry a man may do what he likes with his own? Possibly he may, but he must first prove that it is his own. Your money is not your own, because the hand that holds it is not your own. All things are under a beneficent, unchangeable sovereignty.

But may I not kill myself? No, society will not allow you, and if you do it, society will bury you under quicklime, and no epitaph shall mark the place of your unholy rest. Even the national Prayer Book, often so great in charity, will not pronounce its benediction over your grave if you put an end to your own life, but vagabonds of the baser type will dig a hole for you in the earth and fling you into it, and cover you up with quicklime, and you will be forgotten as a murderer of yourself. Take care, O thou boasted free man! Where is thy freedom, thy great liberty, thy Magna Charta of self-independence?

But is not a nation sovereign? Is not convocation or conference or union sovereign? May not any one of these do what it pleases? No; the first thing a nation has to do is to give away its own sovereignty, or it cannot be a nation. The first thing convocation or conference or general assembly has to do is to limit itself. Civilized institutions are only sovereign within the four corners of their own constitution. You must give notice of change; you can hardly alter a bye-law without giving three months or six month's notice of your intention to suggest such a change. Suppose convocation or conference could all be there at a given moment, has it not the power to proceed in a sovereign capacity? It has not; it has given away its independence and handed it to the custody of a certain constitution or law, and any deed done without consulting that constitution would be challenged in chancery and invalidated, and the boasted freedom trampled in the dust.

"What canst thou do?" Where is thy liberty? Art thou not hidebound? Is not a watcher set over the sea? Is not leviathan under supervision? "I would be free as the ocean waves." Exactly; that you are at perfect liberty to be; but the ocean waves are all in prison. "I would be free as the wind." Be so; the wind is in jail. All things are under law, control, definition, and so to say in a very serious measure responsibility. The stars must keep up their pace; if a star were to stagger for one moment it could never recover itself. One chance, one lapse, and–hell! It is an awful universe, a solemn place to live in, but a glorious sanctuary if accepted at the Lord's bidding, wrought out under the Lord's inspiration and direction; then every dewdrop is a jewel, every star the beginning of a sun.

May not a man hold what opinions he pleases? I think so, but he is not at liberty always and under all circumstances to express them or to carry them out. I could myself, if I were so disposed, give you permission today to go to your house and build the largest cupboard that carpenters ever made, and shelve that cupboard from the top right away down to the floor, and fill all the shelves with divisions, and call all the divisions pigeon-holes, and put a label over every pigeon-hole, and I could give you permission to save up so as to have twelve opinions in every pigeon-hole. If that would at all relieve your feelings, I think that is about the most innocent idiocy I know of; there is really nothing violent about it; it does not put the life of the State in jeopardy. So if you please to have a cupboard fifty feet long by proportionate breadth and depth, by all means have it, and stuff it full, as if it were a feather-bed, with opinions—*your* opinions, not your wife's opinions, or my opinions, or the opinions of Parliament, but your own opinions; you, six feet high and a taxpayer, go and do that, and enjoy your liberty! But take care how you permit those opinions to find expression and application. You may have it as your solemn conviction that there ought to be no kings or queens; you may say that it is wrong for England to have a queen or a monarch of any kind; you may so say that as to be comparatively innocent as against the law, but just along that line there is a certain pale ghost called Sedition, and beyond that pale ghost is a blood-red figure called Treason, and if you promote sedition or perpetrate high treason, though you may do so conscientiously, and you may hold it strictly as a personal opinion, I do not guarantee your life, though you are a very free man, and sometimes you deliver lectures on free thinking and free speech, the like of which is not to be found in any history.

There is but one will, there is but one freedom. God's will settles everything. You can oppose it, you can, as we have just said, kill yourself, you can kill your own child, you can use your so-called freedom in that base manner, but that is not the right use or the right interpretation of freedom. You are free to obey gravitation, not to oppose it; if you oppose it, which you may do, you will be crushed, you will be ground to powder. I am free to walk with the stars, to keep pace with the constellations, but I am not free to go the other way, and to back the stars out of their places. Gravitation is in this sense a poor symbol, but it will do for the immediate purposes, of the greater gravitation which we may describe reverently as the will of God—"Thy will be done on earth, as it is in heaven." Now you are in freedom; if the Son shall make you free, then you are free indeed, because He leads you to the movement of the eternal throne and the eternal decrees. The very hairs of your head are all numbered. To realize this conception of things, to accept it in the name of Jesus, and to keep it by the grace of Jesus, is the true freedom, the glorious liberty of the sons of God. If the stone fall upon you, you will be ground to powder, but if you fall upon the stone your obstinacy shall be broken, and your false, idolatrous conception of free will will be taken out of you, and soon after you will begin to pray.

I offer you a large universe, I offer you an immediate heaven of liberty, the liberty of faith, the heaven of grace, the security of obedience, and protection by the Omnipotent Arms. I do not want any liberty but the love of God; there is room enough there for all I need, for all I should desire. "Thy will be done on earth, as it is in heaven." A right sense of law is a true conception of liberty. God Himself has environed us by law. You have allowed the little bird to escape out of the cage. You have not; you have allowed it to escape out of *a* cage, but not out of *the* cage. No pebble on all the shore of the blue sea can get out of its cage; it may move from one shore to another, but it is still in the cage. And we may go out of the cage of the present and the cage of the visible, but we are only in the larger cage of a higher school and a nobler occupation. The finite can never be more than finite. There is of necessity but one Infinite. "Thy will be done." I ask no wider liberty.

Words for Preachers

The law of truth was in his mouth, and there was no iniquity
found in his lips: he walked with me in peace and equity, and
did turn many away from their iniquities—Malachi 2:6.

This may teach us why the ministry of the Word, and the ministers of
it, are so harsh and so unacceptable unto most men, if they be faithful
and will seek by all means to convert men to God because they must turn
them from their sin, separate them and their iniquities which they love so
dearly (as Micah 6:7). Sin is either natural or by custom, or both; natural
diseases are almost incurable, and no less diseases that grow into a custom, which is another nature. And the physician that should go about to
cure these against a man's will, should have little thanks for his pains,
and not be greatly welcome, when such things cannot be removed without some sharp and bitter medicines, great pain and grief. So in this. And
here is the cause why a man's ministry, at the first coming to a place, is
very acceptable for a while, because he speaks things good and wholesome, but somewhat generally, because he knows not the state of his flock
and people; but after he has lived some years, and sees their sins, and begins to speak home unto them, then he is unacceptable, because he
would part them and their sins; as the minister that should persuade a di-
vorce betwixt a man and his wife whom he loves most dearly, should
never be welcome to his house or company, so in this. It may be it is but
the same he has often spoken of before, but then it was borne because
they probably conjectured he meant not them; but when he has been a
while with them, and may know them to be guilty of the sin, though
haply, and ten to one he did not, then it is intolerable, because they think
he would separate them and their beloved sin, their profitable and delightful sin. All the while he will preach peace and comfortable things to
them and bring the word of reconciliation, and tell them of God's love
and God's mercy, and that he is sent to woo them to be married to God;
all the while he shall be kindly welcome. As he that should sue for a

prince, to win the love of a woman to him, all the while he tells her of his honor and riches, and beauty, and such things, he shall be kindly welcome; but if he come to tell her that she must separate herself from some place and company she loves well, and change her manners, and forsake her friends and father's house, he shall find his entertainment both for usage and countenance changed; so in this. This makes oftentimes ministers, if they be not the more faithful, grow cold and careless, and so fall into many grievous sins.—*Stock, 1568–1626*

Prayer

Almighty God, we thank Thee that we have come to the general assembly and Church of the firstborn, whose names are written in heaven; to a great invisible assembly, yet making the air balmy around us by breathing upon it. This is none other than the house of God, and this is the gate of heaven; where Thou art heaven is: may we enter into the spirit of this assurance, and comfort ourselves as those to whom a great inheritance has been given. We thank Thee for the things we have overcome and laughed at in holy banter and mockery, even death itself, saying, Death is abolished, and asking where is its sting, and the grave, where its victory—poor overthrown opponents of life! We rejoice in heart coming to heart, in reunited lives, in old hopes and loves remingling, and knowing that they mean more than can be expressed in words—a higher companionship, a diviner association, an eternal masonry. Enable us to lift up our thoughts, we humbly pray Thee, to these great conceptions and radiant ideas, lest we be slaves of the dust and victims of the devil. Thou hast given us a great portion, and we have not seized it all; it is so great that we are almost ashamed to claim it every whit. Who can set forth the goodness of the Lord or count His mercies or set a limit to His love? Behold, we cannot follow Thee in all Thy tenderness; Thou carest for us, and Thou dost consider us in Thine heart. We thank Thee for every human touch, for every gentle word of kindness and comradeship; we would cheer one another in the valley of the shadow of death, we would speak comfortably in the name of Jesus to those who are appointed to walk in lonely places and sometimes to linger in the isle of the devil. Thou knowest the way of this life, its trouble, its storm, its dark skies, its glorious summers, its gracious autumns; Thou knowest it, and it is all within the plan of Thy love; oh that we could live it and rest our souls on the breast of Jesus Christ! We say to one another, All hail! We are glad to have come back from the sea and the mountain and the desert place and the garden of beauty, back to old haunts, old services, and old associations; and if we have left old age behind us and have taken on the beauty of youth, and if our flesh has come again as the flesh of a little child, it is because the river of God runs through the deserts of earth. We thank Thee, we praise Thee, we would worthily magnify Thy name, for Thy daily mercy, for the constant bread given to us by Thine own hand. We have done the things we ought not to have done, and we have left undone the things that we ought to have done, and we have hardly voice enough to confess our sin, for our throat is choked with self-accusation. God be merciful unto us sinners! Remember the Cross; we would venture to take Thee Thyself to the Cross, and to say, If Thou didst this for us Thou canst also forgive our added sin; where sin abounds grace doth much more abound. O Lord God, remember the Cross of Thine own Son, and pity us, and take us again into Thy family and Thine heart. Some are overborne; the load is too heavy, the road is too long, and there is a keenness in the wind that means coming winter, sealed fountains, killed flowers. Wilt Thou come to them, with the Sun of Righteousness with healing in His beams, and give Thy fainting ones heart again, and renew their youth. When Thou dost come Thou dost not bring old age with Thee, but childhood and youth and morning, and Thou art the God of the blossoming spring. And some are full of joy and laughter and holy merriment, for things have gone well with them; may they not wax fat and kick, may they interpret Providence largely and not narrowly, and may they know that they have the sunshine that they may the better endure the darkness. And if any are disposed to leave Thee because they think they can do all they want to have done in their own strength, cut them not down in their folly, but spare them that they may learn to pray. Bless the strangers within our gates, the good kind hearts that have come together to help to sing our common hymn and to say amen to the common prayer. Tarry by the seaside or on the mountains, with those who have not yet returned to us, and may they think kindly of this day and send a smile of their heart to the house which they love. The Lord be kind to us as He has ever been, the Lord hear us at the Cross, and bring all old people and young people, and little children, and may we all constitute one redeemed and grateful family. And let the Lord's blessing be upon the whole world; it is in Thine hand and in Thine heart, and Thou wilt conduct its affairs, let men do or not do as they please.

To Father, Son, and Holy Ghost, the eternal mystery, the eternal blessing, be the hallelujahs of all the ages! Amen.

13
The Morning Star

Preached on Sunday Morning, September 24th, 1899.

And I will give him the morning star—Revelation 2:28.

The Lord has brought us back again in the sunshine; let us accept the sunshine as a happy omen. The Lord has not done with us yet. As I came along through your city I perceived that in all things you were too fearful and panic-struck and atheistic. For I saw upon the city walls this very beautiful September morning such words as "Threatening attitude," "Grave situation in the Transvaal," "Great disturbance" here and there. Him therefore whom ye ignorantly fear reveal I unto you by the grace of God; I will tell you his name, it is the devil. It is the devil who is at the root and base of all this Dreyfus business and Transvaal agitation; it is only the devil, and you are afraid of him! Do not turn your religion into cant; if you have a religion assert it, live it, do not take out of it all its morning hope and cheer. "Grave situation" indeed! "Menacing attitudes"! Ah me! The atheists say these things, not the believers. My only fear is that the believer may be entrapped and betrayed, and that he may sing his morning psalm, and repeat his standard creed, and then hasten with his poor penny to buy the devil's Bible about a threatening attitude somewhere and a grave situation. I am ashamed of such socalled Christian faith. The Lord reigneth. There will be no war; reason is against it, and civilization, and the righteousness of God, and all things beauteous and true and kind. There will one day be a great war; America will be on the one side and not England on the other, but Europe; and that war will not be without educational effect and without Christian hopefulness, for the Lord will direct it, and the issue will be a benediction. Why do we forget that it is the business of some men to get up wars? It is worth the while of a thousand men in the City of London to foment a war between England and the Transvaal; it would be like a lucky turn of the wheel to them; they are gamblers, speculators; they belong to the baser sort of the Stock Exchange community; it is worth their while to get up a war that they may refill their purses. Do not heed them; He that sitteth in the heavens shall laugh at them, the Lord will have them in derision. It is pitiable, it is most ghastly, to see how Christian people run hither and thither to know what the latest telegram was from the Transvaal. The Lord reigneth; I want a lightning message from the eternal throne.

Jesus comes to us this morning in a tone of benediction. I love the stillness of the text; receive that text as an assurance that the Lord is the distributor of the prizes and the rewards, and He has promised in these wondrous letters to the Seven Churches of Asia that one day He will have a grand prize distribution: I will give, I will give, I will give—as if He would distribute His universe among those who have turned it into an altar. It is wondrous music. "To him that overcometh I will give to eat of the tree of life." Observe, it is to him that overcometh. Expect war, expect strenuous contest; the Lord is watching the contestants, and He is breathing down the hot thunderous air this Gospel message: To him that overcometh. . . . Cheer thee, strike again, contest once more, now again, hearts up! To him that overcometh will I give a great festival; I will pluck the fruit from the tree of life, and he shall have abundance. Nothing for the coward, nothing for the runaway, nothing for him who would magnify his weakness into a kind of piety; but everything to him that overcometh; he that endureth unto the end shall be saved. Salvation is at the end; to him that overcometh will I give the hidden manna, I will give him a white stone, and in the stone a new name written. Who writes it? Who writes all the names on all the rocks?

Read me the moss; stand before some hoar rock, and read me the moss. Why be blind, why insensate, why make a little universe when we might have heaven upon heaven? He that overcometh will I clothe with white raiment, and no soot shall blacken it, no foulness pollute it; whiter than the snow, more enduring than the ages; I will give, I will give, I will give; it is prize day, and God is the creator and the distributor of the prizes. Shall there be one of us to whom no prize is given? Shall we turn away unprofitable servants, men who knew the Lord's will and did it not, men who turned the beggar from the door, men who said to the poor, Be ye warmed and be ye filled, but gave not the wherewithal to make them as they ought to be? Is there to be a thousandfold crowd not receiving a prize? Him that overcometh will I make a pillar in the temple of My God, and I will write upon him My new name. Are not all these minor prizes? Is there not some larger reward? Yes. What is it? "To him that overcometh will I grant to sit with Me in My throne, even as I also overcame, and am set down with My Father in His throne"; and the Father shall have countless millions of sons, mighty giants, sons of the winning war, yet by the grace of God become entitled to sit with Christ on the sapphire throne.

In the meantime what I like best, because my heart needs it most, is the promise made unto the faithful in Thyatira: "I will give him the morning star." The Lord would seem not to keep any of the universe to Himself; He divides His creation with His children. What have you done? By Thy grace I have fought strong temptations, and I have won. Come thou, sit down under the shadow of the tree of life, and I will pluck fruit for thee. What hast thou done? I have had a strenuous time, every nerve has been strained, temptations were poured upon me like fiery darts. Sit down; thou shalt be recruited with the manna of God. And what hast thou done? I have endeavored to keep Thy Word in difficult positions and situations; I have been sore pressed to disobey Thee, but by Thy grace, and by Thy grace alone, I have overcome. Stand! I will give thee the morning star—sign of royalty, signet of the King, pledge of more. Morning is the poetry of the day. Who can count its jewels of dew? Morning means more than it seems to mean, for it means vanished night. Where is the night? Gone! Where that darksome, fearsome midnight? Fled away! Where is it? None can tell. The morning star has nothing to do with nightly gloom. The nightmare is past, the sorrowful traveling alone is ended, solitude is a conquered enemy, and the man who has overcome by the grace of Jesus Christ shall have the morning star. Is it a living star? Yes. Have I not heard of it in another relation? Is the morning star but some flash of perishing radiance? Oh no! It is clothed with personality. Tell me how. "I am the bright and the morning star." It is a star within the star, a Redeemer, a personality. The stars are embodiments of God. I will pluck for the faithful and true, the valiant and the conquering, heaven's chief jewel, and he shall wear it on his glowing heart. I will give him the morning star.

"Morning." Jesus Christ never associates Himself with night. We have a few peculiar, anonymous, unmanageable people who club themselves together and conduct their affairs at small expense, and try to warm one another into a kind of ghastly enjoyment, but the effort always fails; the people to whom I refer are the pessimist, and they live at an unknown address. Do not let the pessimists overcome you; have in you a light that will burn out their darkness. Jesus Christ is the light of life, the light of the world; you are so constituted it may be—I speak to the few, not to the many—as to be soon nervously depressed, and those grim pessimists would soon persuade you to give up your faith in God. Pessimists never did anything for the world. We cannot judge them by their fruits, for fruits they have none; they are men who darken the soul, their very shadow is descending night; in their voices there is no music, on their face there is no illuminating smile. Jesus Christ always associates Himself with morning: "When the morning was come." And God has always associated Himself with the morning: "Come up early in the morning," said He to Moses; and He has always been talking about the morning. Christianity is associated with morning fullness, morning impulses, morning ideas and conceptions and brightness; and not with night-reflections and pessimistic meditations and the killing of the heart by self-impeachment. Always Jesus Christ is associated with the morning light, the white gleam on the eastern hills, the opening portal, the rising of the sun. They misunderstand the Christian faith utterly who associate it with decayed empires and decayed ideals and wasted ambitions and sickening fear. There are some people whose names I have forgotten, because I never took any pains to learn them, who always say that Christianity is an effete faith, it is outworn, it is obsolete, it has had its day. It is our joy as Christian believers to feel that the morning of Christ is always coming, the light is always rising, the fighting line is thrown out a thousand miles ahead, and the light cannot be blown out by storm or by wrath of man.

The time will come when these ideas will be seized, will be believed, and will be applied. Christianity is always new. A sermon is never old if it is true; a discourse upon Christ is never old if it touches the immediate sore of the heart and the overpowering darkness of the soul. The beatitudes are as new today as when they were breathed across the dew of the morning. What we want is not a new book, but a new reader of the old Book, the man who can put the music of his experience into the eloquence of the Divine testimony. Christianity has always a new program, a new opportunity, a new inspiration, a new possibility. But our young men seem to be dying; they are so taken up with frivolities as really to have no kingdom of God and no orient conception of the radiance of the Divine kingdom. We are dying for want of young men. When the prophet was asked how this thing was to be done, he said, By the young men, the young princes; agricultural laborers they may have been in actual position, but princes of God in the royalty and dignity of their spiritual convictions. Let that be the motto of all coming centuries, By the young men, by the young princes, by the morning, by the early light. Oh, pray your first prayers before the first dewdrop has been exhaled by the sun.

He who has the morning star has the noon. I wish that idea could penetrate our minds, and hold them; then should we be strong men, and no longer panic-driven and dumb because of fear. He who has the morning star has in that star the pledge that he shall have the noon, the midday, the zenith gleam. He who has Christ has heaven. If we really believed the promises of the Cross, we should now be in the upper sanctuary, there should be no separation, no distance, no sensible disseverance of soul from soul. He who has the acorn has the oak. Why do we not realize the promises, and carry them out in all the fullness and poetry and idealism of their suggestiveness? Instead of that how prone we are to droop our heads and to be alarmed by placards that announce threatening situation and serious menaces, and a very unexpected telegram from any quarter of the world. And these poor sickly creatures seem to like it. If ever they are cheerful for one moment in the day in the house, it is when they announce that there is a grave situation. I suppose that such people must be provided for, the Lord in His providence must not leave them in utter neglect, and so they become funereally and most ghastly cheerful, and speak to people they have never spoken to before, to announce that there is a grave situation. Where? I do not know exactly where, but I saw it on the walls as I came along. You will see a delightful situation on the same walls tomorrow morning. Better wait a while! Now he who has the Christian faith has the Christian realization; it is a completed fact in his experience; he must live a few days or years longer in order to see the detail of it carried out, but he who has the witness of the Holy Spirit in his own heart has heaven, and is already throned on the sapphire hills, and is already permitted within the golden and jasper walls of heaven.

"I will give him the morning star." Everything else goes out but the Christian faith—which, in other words, is, everyone goes down but Jesus Christ, and the man to whom Jesus Christ has given Himself—Himself who is the bright and morning star. Shall I startle any fearful friend if I say that nothing really endures but the Gospel? If you watch the processes of literature and statesmanship and general civilization, you will find that each one of them lives only to rub out what it did yesterday. But the Gospel of Christ has a message for every morning, a star for every opening day, a hymn, a psalm, a resilient anthem for every valley. I hear the soldiers tramping down that deep valley, and methinks I hear them sing as they go, and they sing, It shall not be always thus; tomorrow shall bring us deliverance; already the ground is ascending, the grade is heightening, and in a few more days we shall see the high trees on the high hills, and the wide sky—that great blue revelation of God whose reading is difficult to acquire, but which being acquired is an eternal joy and an enduring satisfaction. "Whom the gods love die young." I believe it because the god-loved soul is never old. They go the right idea of things in the olden times when they reckoned six and seven hundred years of age as nothing, simply putting it down in the record as a mere family fact. It is we poor atheists with our small books in our hands that talk about a man being eighty-four, eighty-five, and then the open mouths of ignorant wonder and the exclamations about eighty-seven. Why, in the old, old time—call it poetry or idealism; call it what you like—in the old register, the true idea is given, that hundreds of years mean mere breathings, mere accents in the psalm of duration. When the old man dies at eighty, ninety, he dies young; the proverb is quite right. Or if you substitute the word "early" for the word "young" you do not take away the meaning which I wish to indicate. "Whom the gods love die early"; whenever they die they die into the morning, and the morning is round about them while they are yet dying. There is no old age in love. O soul of man, put away from thee the idea of old age! It does not belong to the new temple, the new sanctuary, the final revelation in Christ Jesus. Bid it begone; old age is not among the jewels of God. But the morning star is chief of those jewels. If thou wouldst always be young, be good; if thou wouldst not know when old age cometh, be stooping to serve some little child, and thou wilt not know that old age has come, and gone, and left thee—a child!

Prayer

Lord of our life and God of our salvation, we have come up to Thine house with a purpose. We are here at the bidding of our own hearts, and here by the constraint of Thy Holy Spirit, and here because Thy bounty to us has been so great that we must unite in common prayer and common psalm and shout together the praises of the Lord. We thank Thee that we are here under no other constraint, no penalty hangs over us; we are here because of the inspiration of love and gratitude and hope. We must praise Thee, we cannot be dumb, our love is not a silent love, it comes with its exclamation and hallelujah and shout of joy. The Lord has done great things for us, why should we not be glad? For us Thou hast built the mountains and lighted the stars and made the earth to grow its fruits; for us Thou hast shed the blood of Thy Son. We know not the fullness of the mystery, we cannot penetrate into the secret of such love, but it is round about us, high beyond us, a perpetual blessing, a perpetual challenge to our devotion and our thankfulness. We bless Thee for the spaces we cannot measure, for the things we cannot understand, for the things which are far away from these fleshly eyes; we would not be without these true riches. Once we thought to understand God and to find out the Almighty unto perfection, and, lo, we found it was higher than heaven, what could we do, deeper than Hades, what could we know? So now we rejoice to be within our cage, and to see through all the split bars the far-away horizons and the coming days and the advancing kingdoms. We come to praise Thee for Thy gifts to us personally, socially, nationally; Thou hast given every man something, every little child has had some little flower from the garden of Thy love; and the lame and the blind, yea, the deaf and the dumb, has his token of love. We will not look at the darkness and the infirmity and the fear and the great darkness of night that broods upon many a life, we will look out towards the morning, and the stars rising before the dawn, and we will think of the times of gladness we have already enjoyed, the old psalms and the sacred songs and the minstrelsy that is love without words. We praise Thee for all these. Oh the childhood sunshine, the girl-and-boy delight of the old, old time, and the finding of new paths, and the hearing of new voices in the air, and the watching of the pure blossoms of the spring, and all the dreams and delights and forecasts and anticipations, and words of written love, and love unutterable. May we not brood over these as if they were all gone, may we think of them as the husbandman thinks of the seed he has sown, and may we wait patiently and hopefully for the harvest coming and the time of the sickle and the gathering-in of ripe fruits and golden corn. Look upon us in all our distresses and tribulations; rebuke us if we fear too much and allow fear to triumph over faith. Lord, increase our faith; teach us that all things are under Thy government; Thou slumberest not, neither dost Thou sleep; when Thou dost see the nations surging upon one another in unaccountable wrath, dost Thou not say, Why do the heathen rage and the people imagine a vain thing? We have forgotten God, we have trusted to our own sagacity and statesmanship and far sighted wisdom—that greatest of all blindness. Oh that we had never spoken; that we had simply, silently put our trust in the living God. The Lord stay the sword, and turn back the cannon, and speak peace into the hearts of the nations, that they may no longer delight in war. The Lord have us all in His holy keeping. Give wisdom to our guides, rulers, and directors, and to the heads of all nations and kingdoms, and may we see the Son of man triumphing over the lust of the unsubdued heart. If any soul has come into Thine house sad, depressed, wholly overcast, the Lord meet such in the darkness and whisper to such words which their hearts alone can understand. And if any are here with new joys and great delights and cloudless hope, the Lord bless them, comfort them, and put the spirit of wisdom in their hearts, lest in their joy they should forget to pray. Be with all our dear ones everywhere, by the seaside, and on the mountain and on the sea and in far-away lands: the Lord be with them all as we think of them in the dream of our love. If any man would do evil, the Lord break both his arms; if any mouth would be opened in slander and lying and blasphemy, the Lord put gravelstones between the teeth. If any man would do good and show light and sweetness and charity, the Lord's angels be round about such a thousandfold, that their holy purpose may be completed. The Lord be with the stranger within our gates, the kindly heart that wishes us well, and that says, Peace be within thy walls, O Zion, and, Jerusalem, the Lord fill thee with His light. And then some other day we shall remember that we met this morning amid cloud and rain and fear, and yet had a secret light and a true inward joy that we could hardly tell.

We always gather at the Cross; we always pray at the Cross; we always bring our distresses to the Cross; and we would never take them back again to ourselves, for in the Cross are our sins forgiven, and our burdens are dissolved and dispersed like morning clouds. Amen.

14

Seen . . . Not Seen

Preached on Sunday Morning, October 1st, 1899.

While we look not at the things which are seen, but at the
things which are not seen; for the things which are seen are
temporal, but the things which are not seen are eternal
—2 Corinthians 4:18.

I have been thinking much about words you will find in the
Second Epistle of Paul to the Corinthians in chapter 4, verse 18.
"Seen . . . not seen; temporal . . . eternal"—the two languages each
with a grammar of its own; two styles of music, two gamuts, two
different ranges altogether of utterance. We shall get into the profitableness of the theme if we read the whole verse and the verse before as well: "For our light affliction, which is but for a moment,
worketh for us a far more exceeding and eternal weight of glory;
While we look not at the things which are seen, but at the things
which are not seen; for the things which are seen are temporal, but
the things which are not seen are eternal." Here is a new standard of
proportion and a new light of color and a new expression of life;
here, indeed, is a new language bigger and better than our mother
tongue. "Our light affliction"—of which we made so much and
groaned so deeply; we turned the summer into winter and the day
into night: and, lo, a voice came to us suddenly, and found our
hearts in a thrilling whisper, saying, "light affliction," hardly anything worth mentioning, quite a matter of the surface; there is no
duration in it. You should look in the right direction if you would
see your own self, O soul; what is now accounted by you as a severe

affliction is working out something beyond itself; it is working out for you a far more exceeding and eternal weight of glory. What does "eternal weight" mean? I never heard these two words put together before; what is the relation of "eternal" to "weight" or of "weight" to "eternal"? It should be thus expressed: Weight upon weight of glory, dawn upon dawn of light, morning upon morning of blaze and radiance. And how does this wondrous vision come about? It comes about while we look not at the things which are seen, but at the things which are not seen. But how can we look at things that are not seen? That you must find out. We misconceive this passage frequently; we set earth and heaven in antithesis. But that is not the proper apposition of the words. It is not earth and heaven, the things which are seen are of the earth earthy, and the things that are not seen are of the heavens heavenly; that is not the right reading of the text at all. The very things that are round about you, yea, the very things on which you can lay your hands, are both seen and not seen. You need not go to heaven for your completion of the analogy; it is in your own breath, it is in your own words; it is within thee, without thee, round about thee; written on the whole belt of things; on the great broad band of gold that keeps all things together are the words, The things which are seen, and the things which are not seen. This is not a theological term at all, we need not go to church to find it out; we have only to look into our own consciousness and our own habit of mind, and we shall find that we carry both man and God, a moment and an eternity.

This may all be simplified, so that the slowest and youngest mind can comprehend and appreciate it. Here are Acts of Parliament; they are things that are seen; they are sold, they might be sold by weight. Are there any things within the Acts? There is one thing within them—Law. The Acts are seen and temporal; Law is unseen and eternal. In having the Acts of Parliament we have Law? No; you have a law, or for the time being the law, but Law stands alone without adjective or epithet or qualifying article. You can change the Acts of Parliament, they are seen and temporal, and they were made to be broken; otherwise the country would have little or nothing to do at headquarters, there would be a great dearth of employment; but you cannot change Law. *That* is the force that keeps things together, subtle, impalpable, imponderable, the gravitation that has no shape, and that must condescend almost infinitely to put itself even partly into words. So we need not go into the Bible and into theological books and ecclesiastical places in order to find the very secret of this great passage written by the immortal apostle. We have the whole of it in this one simple illustration: Acts of Parliament seen, Law unseen; Acts of Parliament temporal, Law eternal. And we are only wise in the degree in which we catch the spirit of Law and put it into formal words and give it civic and imperial applications. It is not for us to make Law, but it is for us to make little saleable toys called the laws. Unless we penetrate into the very marrow of that distinction we shall lose the text.

The creed is seen; Faith is unseen; that is the distinction. You can alter a creed, you cannot alter Faith. I do not say a faith, or the faith, or some faith, but Faith; a word so grand as to need no adjective, a solitude so sublime as to be a trinity. The creed comes and goes. If churches had only understood the difference between creed and Faith, we should have had very little controversy. We may all be believers in the deepest and best sense, but we may not all be creedists. As if Faith could be written upon the back of an envelope; as if Faith could be issued in an octavo volume; as if Faith gave the printer anything to do! Creeds keep men busy. Their opinions, their views, their theories, their orthodoxies of the moment: Faith, sublime, solemn, still, eternal, may keep the whole world together, without the world being able to analyze the fires that consolidate it into holy unity. Sometimes men talk about their creeds as if their creeds were revelations; they are only guesses, clever conjectures, something resolved upon by one generation to be amended or forgotten by another; but Faith abides, Faith rules. By making creeds we make infidels; where we make laws we make offenders; let the laws alone, the offenders would never be created, and therefore would not need to be dealt with. But we make creeds, and therefore separate men; if we preached Faith, we should unite them. But what would the world be without controversy?

Denominationalism is a thing seen; Worship is a thing not seen. Sectarianism is temporal, the Church is eternal. There are many persons who give themselves much needless trouble by not distinguishing between Church and churches, between denominations and the Church. And many persons are running up and down the earth endeavoring to create what they call unity. They can neither create it nor destroy it. It would be like a man running up and down the earth offering to brighten the stars; it would be exactly the same. The Church and the unity of the Church are beyond the touch of Pope or Archbishop or minister or layman. The Church never wants uniting; it was always united; it is best represented by the seamless chrysolite without flaw or break. But it is not seen; it is the inner force that keeps the peace, secures and consolidates and perpetuates the true holiness. But we have our consultations and conferences, and we offer to meet one another. Good God—that one of the smallest of the intellectual insects should offer to meet another! It is too solemn, it is too farcical. The Church is in her Lord, in her Savior, in His blood crimson with the redness of it, and is one all the world over; not in form, not in creedal subscription and attitude, but in that unseen gravitation-like force that binds hearts to a common center. Oh, waste of energy that we have seen about the denominations, and what we call in the language of a very tumid charity various Christian communions. Why not think of the Church, the Bride, the Lamb's Wife, the great heart union between the Lord and those who have yielded to the persuasions and redemptions of His grace? Why not say, We are all one in heart and soul and purpose, though we may have our cutaneous and superficial distinctions, differences, and even hostilities?

The day is a great controversy. We call it Sunday, Sabbath day, the Lord's day, the first day, the seventh day; we wonder if it began on Friday and went over Sunday, or if it began late on Saturday night, or if it began on what we should call Monday morning; and we have written pamphlets upon this, wonderful pamphlets, hardly ever read, but still there to be read if anybody has time to read them. What is the eternal thing, the grand Platonic conception of the universe? Not Wednesday, Thursday, Saturday, Sunday, but Rest. And that you cannot change; man claims it, God accords it, heaven blesses it. Men will wrangle at the wrong point; they are stormy in their wrath about things that are really of hardly any consequence whatever; now what I want to be at in all my searching is this, not the Act of Parliament, but Law; not the formal creed, but Faith; not the local hospital, but the universal Philanthropy; not the particular day as a mere term in the calendar, but a day set apart for Rest, joy, high festivity, realization of the family masonry and love—a grand religious conception of time, and a connecting of little perishing day with the eternal rest.

We might apply the same thought in even the highest direction of all. The Bible in a certain sense is but a book; it was written by men, copied by men, printed by men. We do not look at the merely mechanical book; when we speak of the Bible in our highest moods we speak of the revelation. We do not ask the printer's permission to read it, we know it; we do not ask the priest, the robed fraud, to read it for us, we claim to read it for ourselves, for it is the Father's speech to the son's heart, and between the Father and the son, meaning by son the whole human race, there is a confidence, subtle, impenetrable, all but omnipotent. All the controversy rages about the mechanical book: Who wrote it? Was this written in the Maccabean period? Can we trace this psalm to post-exilian sources or pre-exilic dates? Hence the controversy and the expensive communication between man and man. The critic says that David could not have written the twenty-third psalm because he says he will dwell in the house of the Lord forever, and David did not build the temple. Oh, the folly, the madness! Jacob, long before David was ever thought of, said in the rocky place where he slept, This is none other than the house of God—the unbuilt house, not built by hands; not seen, but eternal; the house in the clouds, in shadow, in outline; the precursor of all the temples and altars yet to be reared by human hands. Why no look into the poetry, spirituality, and the true idealism of things, and catch the morning ere it dawns?

We have now great discussion about adult baptism and infant baptism, paedo-baptism and anti-paedo-baptism. Have I not often told you that these controversialists are lost amid the adjectives of their own creation? If you were to take away their adjectives you would destroy their comfort in controversy. I believe, not in adult baptism or infant baptism or water baptism, or sprinkling or plunging; I believe in Baptism. He that believeth and is baptized with the Holy Ghost, with the water of fire, shall be saved. By all means let every man be fully persuaded in his own mind if it is worth while being persuaded upon any such subject. For my part, I baptize little children—wee, wee mites of things; I do not think I dare have done it with so much joy if my Lord had not whispered to me, as the mothers were bringing the little ones to my arms, "Of such is the kingdom of heaven." He told me, and I will not refuse anything which He denominates the kingdom of heaven.

As for the public profession of this great faith, never profess any creed. I have said again and again that I would not subscribe any creed that my own hand had written; I have told you the reason, namely, that language changes, words have not the same weight or color in one century that they have in another; I will sign it for the day, but not for the morrow. We do not want an ism, we want a Person. Who is that Person? The Son of God, the Son of man, the atoning Savior of the world. I would not go to the last great assembly having on a coat with ism written on the back of it; I would rather go naked, crawl round to my Father's back door, and ask Him to take me into His arms. Jesus Christ is the Church, the Savior of the Church, and the Creator of the Church, and I do not want anything to do with any ism under heaven; I want to love my Lord, Son of man, Son of God.

Remember that the great things in life are all not seen. You cannot see Love, you can only see its incarnations. You cannot see Faith, you can only see its conduct, for it becomes a motive and turns the soul into action and into deeds of purity and charity. Thus would I rest. The little child can see the rosy-cheeked apple that its mother brought away from the orchard; the child can see the apple, but not the love that plucked it. As a little child it must begin where it can; the apple is an apple to the child, the metaphysical or penetrating force of the soul has not yet begun to assert itself, and therefore the little fingers and knuckles clutch the apple, and the little mouth shapes itself into an unspeakable, doxology, and the whole earth is a beautiful place so long as that apple continues to exist. But the little child did not see the love that thought of it, the love that asked for it, the love that put it in a safe place, the love that dreamed for the child a sweet surprise; the child does not see the love that folded the apple in the tissue paper, and the fingers that moved so deftly and opened the cotton wool in which the little prize lay snugly. All the little child could see was the rosy-cheeked apple; all the ministry of preparation and love and forecast the little child knows nothing about. One day it will be explained in heaven!

Prayer

Almighty God, we thank Thee for Thy Son Jesus Christ, the only Savior of the world, in whose great name we now approach Thy throne. Great is the Savior and greatly to be praised, and His name is to be had in everlasting remembrance by those who have felt the comfort of His grace and the cleansing of His blood. We thank Thee that Thou wast manifest in the flesh, we bless Thee for One whose name was Immanuel, God with us. For all His wondrous sayings we thank Thee. He was the express image of Thy person, Thy very glory incarnate. When we see Jesus we see God. Enable us to look with reverent eyes and to direct a reverent expectation towards the Lord; then shall we be abundantly satisfied with the provisions of Thine house, and our hearts shall be lifted up with new and imperishable joy. Bring us more closely to Christ that we may be brought more closely to Thyself. May we look back to the eternities which Thou hast partially revealed, and see Thee from before the foundation of the world planning our salvation, purposing the redemption of the entire race of man, and may we stand as in a temple of vision and be grateful that we are connected with all the ages past and coming. Thus by the enlargement of the vision may we lose our littleness and all its woe. Amen.

15
God Made Visible

God was made manifest in the flesh—1 Timothy 3:16.

This does not come upon the reverent reader as a surprise; it comes upon him as the culminating point in a most wonderful plan. If you open the Bible at 1 Timothy 3:16, and know nothing about what has gone before, you will be stunned as if you had suddenly come upon a blasphemy. That is not the way to read any text in Holy Writ. You must first read the context; indeed, as an expositor of the Scriptures and an occasional teacher of young men who are preparing to preach, I have ventured to say that in order to give out a text so as to secure the confidence and the gratitude of the hearer, you must read the Bible from the very beginning up to the text of the day. If the people were really in earnest about preaching, and all its redeeming and ennobling purpose, they would revel in this method of preaching; it would be new, it would be like being present at the creation of the universe; people would then see behind things, and be able to trace how things came to be. In order to understand fully 1 Timothy 3:16, we should begin at Genesis, chapter 1, verse 1, and steadily and musically read through the whole revelation, and then 1 Timothy 3:16 would be the very thing we had been waiting for all the time. Selecting the local text, which some foolish people are so fond of doing, we miss all the light, all the music, and come upon the face of a stranger when we ought to warm ourselves in the countenance of a friend.

"God was made manifest in the flesh." Impossible! That is what you would naturally exclaim if you had read nothing before

1 Timothy 3:16. You would feel that it was irreverent; you would say, No, this surely could never be—God in flesh, God in shape and form and figure, God visible; it is a profanity, it is a lie. I am not surprised that you should pronounce that verdict, because it is the verdict of absolute ignorance. If you had steadily read through from "In the beginning God created the heavens and the earth," you would have said, This 1 Timothy 3:16 is a natural and adequate climax; it accounts for everything, it is a sun within the sun and above it; the light of the universe. But people do not care for wise preaching; they are impatient with sound, thoroughgoing Biblical exposition; and this accounts for so-called unbelief or misbelief or worldliness or indifferentism. If they would always begin the Gospel of John by reading all the books prior to it, there would be no infidels, there would be no unbelief, and the world would fall away into its right perspective, and the eternal would be seen to be the great. That age will come—long after you and I have crossed the river.

I cannot read the Bible from the very beginning (I live it, I have no other companion, I love it, I do not preach it, I rebreathe it out) without feeling that Someone is coming. You speak of this and that being in the air; you speak of omens and signs and premonitions; perhaps we hardly know what we mean when use these pregnant and significant words. We do not feel that the right man has yet come, though we read in Genesis and to the end of the Pentateuch; the leaves are stirring with an air blown from another book; and when we read all the history volumes we still feel that Someone, be His name what it may, is on the road—I saw a flash of light, I heard a voice, I felt as it were the darkness of a transparent shadow—a most curious and self-contradictory thing, now an angel, now a dream, now a prophet, now a great thunder voice, now a still small whisper comforting the heart. He has not yet come, but He is coming, He is on the way: did I not catch the blast of a trumpet millions of miles away, a rising, falling cadence? Is it a signal that the King approaches? I know not, but I read away through my prophets and my psalms sure that perhaps tomorrow, today, there may be another Personality among us. Thus coming upon 1 Timothy 3:16, the text of the morning, I am not surprised; I have received an explanation, I know now what it all meant: God was made manifest in the flesh; I expected nothing else.

Now if I had no other corroborative and illustrative Scriptures available, I might have the fear of the Revised Version before mine eyes; I rejoice, however, to find that this is not a text only, but is part of a revelation, that it is sustained, supported, and illuminated by other passages as distinct, as graphic, and as comforting as itself. "I and my Father are one. . . . My Father worketh hitherto, and I work. . . . He that hath seen me hath seen the Father." That is enough; we now come to the doctrine of Paul fortified by the doctrine of Christ Himself; they preach the same doctrine of the Sonship and the Godhead, and I feel that my heart is, so to say, face to face with a God not invisible, but seen, palpable, at hand. The comforting idea, therefore, is that if we study Jesus Christ rightly, we are keeping company with the Eternal God Himself. When we say, What would God do? we have only to inquire what Jesus did; when we wonder about the transcendental metaphysics of the Godhead, a voice says to us, You cannot go far along that line, but you can see God in Jesus Christ. Never ask any questions beyond the visual line; put your feet in Christ's footprints, stop where He stops, move as He moves; for he that hath seen Christ hath seen the Father. It is, therefore, not our business to trouble ourselves with some philosophy of the Deity, it is our glorious and ever-comforting privilege to keep company with the Son of God, and to study all His ways, and receive all His teaching in the simplicity of tenderest love. See, then, what an opportunity is before us! We can see God! "He that hath seen me hath seen the Father. . . . God was made manifest in the flesh. . . . The Word was made flesh and dwelt among us, and we beheld His image." We shall not, therefore, longer talk about the invisible God, the unseen God, the mysterious God; we shall also speak about the visible God, the God nigh at hand, the God who has come to us through the medium of our mother tongue; we have seen Him who molded the stars and set the constellations in their places.

This makes the New Testament a new book to me. Am I told that God is as approachable, as simple, as beautiful in brotherliness or fatherliness as Jesus Christ was? Yes. You cannot see the glory of the Godhead, but you can see the incarnate Deity. But Jesus Christ was so simple and so peasant-like sometimes; Jesus Christ accepted food at our hands; Jesus Christ talked to us now and again as if He were simply our equal: we cannot imagine that God is to be so imaged to the mind. Yes, I think God is as simple and peasant-like and brotherly and motherly, and all that. Who made you speak of the peasant with a lingering sneer in your voice? The peasant was the first man, the so-called king came down by a wrong way a long time after the peasant began; it is the peasant who is ancient, it is the peasant who makes the Plantagenet modern. Yet you must not think of Jesus Christ only as simple and childlike and unostentatious, houseless and almost friendless and breadless. That is one aspect of the Christ, but I tell you that now and again there came a look into the Man's face that frightened us; now and again a tone lighted up the gamut of His voice, and made it like no other voice that was ever heard. You must bring in these elements and qualities if you would represent the Godhead of Jesus Christ in sufficiency of expression and sentiment. Sometimes we could go quite closely to Him and speak to Him as if we were exchanging the salutations of the hour, and in a moment, without notice, He blinded us with lightning, and we stood back and said, What manner of man is this? You must put the two aspects together, if you would acquire and appreciate the totality of the person and priesthood of Jesus Christ.

We are taught that there is a great scheme of providence at work round about us. It is a very mysterious providence; if you look at it in the wrong light, it is so mysterious as to be painful and destructive in its expression and energy. If I would study the providence of

God, I would read all that Jesus Christ did. What shall I get from such a perusal of His record? A clear vision of what at present is regarded as the invisible providence. We talk about a providence within a providence; we speak thus almost atheistically. The providence of God is as plain as the sunlight, as beautiful as the summer landscape. How can we approach it? By studying Jesus Christ; the daily life of Christ was the daily life of God. Then why tear the clouds asunder to see some at present invisible providence? It is needless, it may soon become impious. We need not batter the cloud-door, and say, Admit us to see the machinery of the universe. No need of that; read the life of Jesus Christ, and you will see what God is doing, what God can do, and what God has been doing all the undated and uncalendared ages.

This brings the matter very closely to us. The kingdom of God is among us, the kingdom of God is within you. Why stretch your necks to see something beyond the horizon when God Himself is standing in your midst and manifesting Himself in your own flesh? Then we will study Jesus, and see what He thought about the people and about life, and how He sought comfort for all the persons that trusted to Him, how He made the orchards grow and the wheatfields and the vineyards and the yards of olives. That is right; now you are becoming religious.

How does God deal with the poor? Ask Jesus. What does Jesus say? He says to His disciples when they mention the necessities of the people to Him, Give ye them to eat. Yet we are the men who want to know what God does for the poor in His providence! He gives to me that I may give to the man sitting next me. He has made the man sitting next me rich in gold that he may hand some of it over to me. He sets up the great doctrine of mutual interdependence; not the bastard socialism of a card-up-the-sleeve with which some swindler may seek to win the game, but the true socialism and masonry of brotherhood. That is too simple a plan for many persons; they like something more intricate, something that needs to be explained in long and resounding words; whereas God in Christ says to every man who has a loaf, Give some of it to the man who has no bread; I gave you the loaf, not that you might keep it, but that you might distribute it, and I have so arranged the economy of life that distribution is multiplication, and that whoso gives the bread most freely will be surprised at the last to find that he had more to end with than he had to begin with. Man does not like that kind of providence; he prefers a program, a demonstration in some London park, howling and shouting and waving red banners—where dyed I know not, but I suspect—to the simplicity of handing over to the man who is needy part of the loaf which God has entrusted to him. I wonder that men, seeing these things, do not stand up and say, Hail Him! Crown Him Jesus Lord of all! His plan was so fundamental, vital, impartial, Divine, my wonder is that any man is ashamed of Jesus or turns his back on the sanctuary where His name is worshiped.

What does the invisible and unthinkable God do in the matter of the prodigality and sinfulness of the world? Read Jesus Christ's life and you will get the answer at once. What is God's plan about a lapsed and ruined world? "The Son of man is come to seek and to save that which is lost." That is what God is doing all the time; He is seeking and saving the lost; He is keeping the door of His own heart open that the very least and worst of His children may enter in and be saved. But we have theological lectures upon this point. Better not have any such lectures! We have a great scheme of explaining all these mysteries. There is no need for such a scheme. Read the life of Christ; He was God manifest in the flesh; He said, He that hath seen me hath seen the Father. Read His word. What is God doing today? Seeking men; saying, Behold I stand at the door and knock; if any hear my voice and open the door I will come in." We have a pleading God, a self-humbling God, a God we keep standing out in the dews of the midnight and amid all its boisterous winds; and we are asking profound or foolish questions about God's method of dealing with the world He made and loved and redeemed.

What is God's relation to so-called sinners, sinners of the baser type also; not respectable and well-dressed sinners who have a dress for the summer day and another kind of dress for the day of snow, and who have so many meals per day drenched in wine. But what does God do when He meets a sinner of the baser sort? He goes home with him, and if the poorest of the city's women-sinners should ask Him to share her crust He would go and do it, and leave a thousand wheatfields behind Him. We dare not do that because we are, possibly, the worst of sinners. There are most damnable sinners with fine cloaks on and feathers and jewelry, and studs of horses, and betting books and books of prayer and praise all huddled in one wild wardrobe and library. They murmured that He was gone to be guest with a man that is a sinner. You dare not have gone, because you have a visiting card, and a list of calls, and a very intricate system of hypocrisy and falsehood—call, and do not want to call; hoping that when you leave the grand door some person will observe that you have been inside it, and will respect you for your greatness. Away! That is my Lord who comes out of the sinner's house, rich or poor, who talks to the poor woman and smiles her back into girlhood, and lifts her up into her proper divinity. That is what God does; and we sit smoking and wondering in a cloud about the mysteries of Providence, when there are no such mysteries when properly apprehended, and when we approach them along the line so clearly indicated by the doctrine and by the example of our Lord Jesus Christ. God pities the world; God dies for the world; God dies everyday; God sheds His blood from the foundation of the world that He may thus wash out forever the stain of sin and the taint of crime.

If, therefore, we would see God we must see Jesus. This is the Gospel simplified, and the Gospel definitely applied. I have been adopting now what I believe to be a very proper and wise scheme of philosophy in the interpretation of things. There are two ways along which we may proceed: we may begin with the greater and come down to the less, or we may begin with the less and gradually ascend to the higher. We may begin with eternity and find our way down by broken pieces of duration into so-called time; or we may begin with time and proceed from days to months, from months to years, from years to centuries, from centuries to millenniums, and pile the millenniums one upon the other, until our arithmetic is dazed and lost; and describe that as the highway to the palace of eternity. We may begin with the invisible, metaphysical, unthinkable Deity, and leave Him in His unspeakable solitude, because we cannot bring Him within the four points of our own intellectual limitation; or we may take the other and better plan, to begin with man, prophet, poet, dreamer, Immanuel, the living Jesus, the great word, the great deed, the marvelous revelation, and so work our way upward to the Ineffable and the Everlasting. That is what I daily try to do. Begin where you can, and proceed with diligent obedience into the further and larger spaces.

What is God's method of judgment? We read of a great white throne, we read of a day of final audit and trial. We need not wonder about that; Jesus Christ has gone through the whole process; if we study Him we know all about it; and the day of judgment may be no longer than one flash of light, than the twinkling of an eye. What is God's plan of judgment as shown by Jesus Christ? He said, Where much is given much will be required; where little is given little will be expected. Where there is poverty and difficulty about doing certain things, yet there sounds this sweet music, She hath done what she could. That is the judgment; that is the day of judgment. Why not judge ourselves now? We need not wait until the after-death judgment: set up the day of judgment now. I have much, do I give much? I have little, do I give out of the little? Do I do what I can? Oh, so small, yet given with a kiss of the heart. Let this Divine revelation come nearer and nearer to us. Let us go to Jesus when we would know about God. Let us study His example when we would apprehend somewhat of Divine metaphysics. With Christ at hand no man need be at a loss for God.

Prayer

Thou openest Thine hand and satisfiest the desire of every living creature. We are all guests at the table of the Lord, the first archangel and the meanest insect; we gather around the Lord, for He made us, and by His power only are we sustained. We are one universe, one life; we would be the glory of the Lord. Enable us, by the ministration of Thy Spirit and the wondrous miracle of Thy grace, to show that we were made in the image and likeness of God. Take away from us all that is merely earthly, purge the gold of all its dross; relieve us of all that is ungainly and unlovely and undivine; may the Spirit itself, yea God's own Spirit, witness with our spirit that we are the children of God, and may we know this by our pureness and unselfishness, by our modesty and love and service of others; thus may we reincarnate the Son of God, and show the meaning of the Divine, eternal love. We bless Thee that we have heard the Gospel; Thou hast proved it in our own experience to be true; we want no man's argument, we only want the history of our own heart, our joy and sorrow, our sin and trouble, and then we would see the glorious light shed upon the whole mystery of life by the incoming of Him whose name is Immanuel. Deliver us from the narrowness and the bondage of the letter; save us from the temptation to know everything; and the Lord deliver us from explanations which men would tender of the infinite counsel and the eternal purpose. We bless Thee for the spiritual forces that are operating upon our souls; we thank Thee that the old horizon no longer binds us; by the power of Thy Spirit we see beyond it—new mornings, new kingdoms, new summers. We have been fettered and belittled by the men who would bring everything down to explanation and definition and cold letters cast in iron. Now we have the Spirit we see now what the blood means, we see now that doctrine is bread and that true bread is doctrine, and that Christ being a door is no figure but a great emancipation, a new and glorious liberty, and by the opening of that door we are welcomed into paradises undreamed in fancy or in love. We do the things we ought not to do, we leave undone the things that we ought to accomplish; we know it, but we are struggling towards a higher life; by Thy grace we will be better tomorrow, and tomorrow, and in that ever-coming time which brings with it the descending kingdom of God. Pity us, we humbly pray Thee, in our littleness and blindness and narrowness; we misjudge one another; we misjudge our Father; we are led away by our own fancies and prejudices and foolish conceits. Let the Lord pity us, for it is the Lord who built the Cross! Amen.

16
Reality in Religious Inquiry

Preached on Sunday Morning, October 8th, 1899.

Jesus answered him, Sayest thou this thing of thyself, or did others tell it thee of me?—John 18:34.

That makes all the difference in the world. How do we come to ask questions? What is the occasion or the motive of our inquiry? Are we mere gabblers and gossipers, or are we thinkers and students? Do we ask questions which other people have prompted, or do we ask only the questions of our own heart? Here, as ever, Jesus Christ is the teacher and the example. Pilate entered into the judgment hall again, and called Jesus and said unto Him, Art Thou the king of the Jews? Jesus answered him, How did you come to ask this question? Have you any real deep interest in the inquiry, or have you only picked up the rumor of the day? Does the question come from your tongue or from your heart? Tell me that, and I will answer. Thus He sits in His heavens, and everyday talks in the same grand frank manner. Jesus does not answer the gossip of the ages, the new attacks that are made upon His name and upon His kingdom, the clever sallies and the bitter sneers He heeds not; but if any soul will come to Him sunk right down in penitence and brokenheartedness, and say, Lord, I want to know what this means; wilt Thou tell me? Oh let me lay my weary head for one moment on Thy lap and sob out all that is in my troubled heart—then Jesus will stay the sun, and the moon shall hang over Ajalon till the great colloquy is complete in the man's redemption. Sayest thou this thing of thyself, Pilate? I shall be so glad if so; then I shall feel the Gentiles are coming to the brightness of my rising, then I shall feel and know that Ethiopia is stretching forth her hands unto God: if this is only an intellectual puzzle, a little trick in curiosity, I will answer in stony silence; if the inquiry comes from a heart that wants something better than it is, then I arrest all processes, and I will talk to thee light!

It is just the same today. We could apply the text to all manner of spiritual and religious inquiries and difficulties. I have no interest in the doubter, as he calls himself. A curious word altogether that and made up of a special kind of India-rubber that may be twisted into any shape. If the man is giving expression to his own doubts— I mean his own, own doubts—I will stop with him till overborne by sleep, and will then ask God to deliver me from slumber that I may continue still to talk to the burningly earnest inquirer. There is the difficulty that men come to you with other men's doubts. Away with them! You have read in a halfpenny pamphlet that some man doubted something somewhere, and you want to know what we have to say to it. Nothing! We cannot be refuting the infidelities of the fourth century and the indigestions of yesterday. But if you, dear heart, have a question that really pains your own soul, tell it, let us hear what it is, and on the understanding that it is your own, your very own, we will talk it out. All depends upon that. Only retail your own infidelity, and you will find in the course of conversation how very little of an infidel you are; when you are really thrown down into your own soul to find out what infidelity you hold there you will find an empty cupboard. But if you bring to me all the works of all the heretics that ever lived, and pile these books round about me, and say, Now I give you five minutes to give me an answer to all these things, I will not answer them, and I will not detain you; I am a busy man, and I have not time to entertain hawkers who cart about in a traveling basket some other people's unbelief. But if you are the very poorest man that ever lived, I will welcome you to the softest chair in my study if you really are going to talk to me out of your own heart, and tell me about your own sin and doubt and fear and perplexity; I will stop the clocks, I would stay the sun, that we might have time to sound the depths of the troublous problems and find some balmy answer to your wounded faith. Have you ever sat down, so to say, with pen in hand just to write out a full account of your own infidelity? It is an interesting exercise, and a very brief one. There is not a man probably in this audience who can infidel over half a page, and even there his writing is full of quotation marks; it is what somebody else believed or disbelieved or troubled about the day before yesterday.

When coming to church only bring your own questions with you; do not trouble with other people's business until your own is settled, and when you have found an answer to your own doubt and fear, then go out and find some other man, and tell him that if he wants the same balm he must go to the same Gilead. This would abbreviate conversation, this would stop many theological reviews; this would do a world of good by first doing a world of mischief among the poor petty things that are set up against the incoming of the kingdom of God. Beware of those people who have reduced life to an illegitimate science of explanations. It will be a poor religion that can be explained, a poor little withered, shriveled sky that you can get under your plaster ceiling. Never imagine that even your house, though so lofty and so richly gilded, can entertain with any adequacy the firmament, the spaces of the stars. Blessed is he who has got beyond the region of explanations in the quiet sunlight and uplands of truest rest and peace—peace in the faith that we are undergoing part of a great process inscrutable and ineffable, and that all we have to do in relation to many of the mysterious outposts of the universe is to let God alone. You cannot put God into a catalogue. No man can exhaust God by explanations. He explain! Poor creature, starved hound, born yesterday, seeking for lodgings tonight, and carried out into the grave the day following. And he is going to explain the universe, and have a rational religion, a measurable piety, an arithmetical dream! Ah me! To know that we cannot know is the beginning of knowledge.

The same inquiry which Christ put to Pilate may be put to our various religious exercises; as, for example, it may be put to the great exercise of what is called preaching. Now what is this preaching? Preacher, you are talking to me—is it out of a book you have borrowed, or out of a soul that has sinned to damnation and been redeemed with the redness of God's heart-blood? Is your preaching a recitation or a revelation, is it the latest trick in German text? Or is it a sacrifice, great drops of blood-sweat issuing from its mad agony? Preaching will in very deed lose its place and go down, and I will hasten it down, if it be not the supreme effort of the soul. When it is an unburdening of the memory I would call upon the preacher to sit down; when it is an unloading of the heart, the story and the song, the agony and the joy of a deep abysmal experience, I say, God save the preacher and make him strong as a host of men! It is not preaching that is going down in some quarters, it is the want of preaching, it is a mistake as to the true nature of preaching. To hear a human soul tell what it knows of light and darkness, sin and sorrow, penitence and forgiveness, and to hear a great, warm human soul pouring out its experience upon other hearts, *that* can never go down. The essay will be burned, but the Gospel no fire can touch. Sayest thou, then, this thing of thyself, O preaching man, or did some other man tell thee what to say? Do not deliver other men's messages; deliver your own; though it be short, it may be pregnant; though it be poor and stumbling in words, the wise hearer will hear the music inside the stumbling, and will answer it with a great, glowing, loving gratitude.

So, then, we want personal experience, personal testimony, personal affirmation. That was the great power of apostolic preaching. When the Apostle Paul stood up anywhere he always said, Men, brethren, and fathers, I—It was a right royal egotism, a magnificent audacity in personality; the man told what he was, what he is, how he came from the was to the is, and it was a great turnpike of facts, personal and well-attested incidents; and so clear, ample, definite was the testimony that before you could disbelieve the argument you must destroy the character of the man. That was preaching, and under it men used to rise from their seats, which they never do now; under such apostolic preaching men were pricked to the heart, and they cried out—that would be indecorous now. We have run theology into a science, and piety into a decorum. When men want to know the truth because there is a pain in their hearts they will surely get that truth, God will not deny such dumb prayers. He looks down upon all who come to His house, and He says in effect, Here is a man whose very muteness is eloquence; here is a soul whose look is consecration; here is a broken-hearted inquiry, the tears shall be turned into waters of baptism and shall fall again in great blessing on the troubled and bleeding heart.

Suppose we could personify some of the Christian doctrines and verities, they would be able to ask of us the very question which Christ asked of Pilate, Sayest thou this thing of thyself, or did others tell it thee of me? I hear sweet Prayer, describable by my own imagination as the most beauteous of the beauties, an angel of angels, and when she hears someone speaking about prayer, either answered or unanswered, she says—oh, with what sweetness and subtlety!—Sayest thou this thing of thyself? Tell me, hast thou been answered? Open the portals of thine heart to me and let me see God's autograph on the tablets of thy soul: or did someone tell it thee of me, saying that I was never answered, that I was only another exercise in breathing, a peculiar effort in vocalization? Did somebody try to trouble thee about me, saying I was never answered and never heeded in heaven? Put away all that evil report, and if thou dost come with doubt and difficulty and objection and challenge, come in thine own name and for the sake of thine own soul, and I will talk it out with thee, I will explain what prayer is, how prayer is prayed, upon what range it operates, what singular answers it secures, how it plucks the lightning from the eternal throne and uses it in the ministries of daily life: but be honest, talk out your own heart to me, and not somebody else's heart: oh, tell me, and I will tell thee, and we shall have a sweet interview. If we could get to such sharp points and issues as these we should soon have a revival of religion, and we should not be long in knowing the mystery of what is meant by growth in grace; all other subjects would sink into insignificance or would fade away to a vanishing point by a rearrangement of spiritual perspective, and when it came to be known that a man without the intervention of a priest could go to God and tell Him even his infidelity and his blasphemy and his impiety, and could tell God the tale of shame, and ask Him at the right place and in the right name to be forgiven, all other subjects would vanish out of sight. There *are* no other subjects; there are diverse points of gossip, but subjects, themes that get down to foundations and rise up into the heavens, there are none but this— the relation of the soul to God, and the relation of God to the soul; and all other subjects, if they so miscall themselves, stand back and let spirit talk to spirit. That is the true spiritualism; all other spiritualism is but groping in a decreasing twilight.

If we personify the Bible we shall find the Bible putting the same question to us that Christ put to Pilate. When we praise it, the Bible says, Doest thou this of thyself, or because it is an old custom in the house? Thy grandfather and grandmother dusted me and set me upon uppermost shelves and took me down reverently, and put me back again, and nothing came of it. You say that the Bible is a good book and full of wisdom and glorious with guiding light; now, sir, wait: sayest thou this thing of thyself? Have you read me? Have you read the Bible through and through, every word of it, and before giving out any verse in the New Testament have you qualified yourself by graduating in the Old Testament, and do you take the last text you have read as part of an infinite background of history, and do you relate the immediate text to all the revelation that has gone before and to all the opening possibilities that fill the great sky with doors of entrance? Is your Bible a fetish, or a living power—is your notion of the Bible something traditional and superstitious, and a mere repetition of what somebody else has told you to think and believe about it? Then you have no Bible, and the very smallest infidel insect can steal from you what you have: there would not be much burdened if he had to carry away all the Bible that you have left in your house; though you dust it and put it under a dome, and are very careful how you refer to it, it is no Bible to you. But if you can say to your soul's soul, I have read it, tasted it, we have been companions night and day these fifty years; it has the answer to every riddle, a balm for every wound, a reply to every wise and profitable inquiry, a song that fits the night and an anthem that fills the summer, I know it—that testimony I love to hear; we want to hear more about such experience. Alas—the world for the time being has no immediate care for Bible reading; almost anything will do to substitute for the Bible; and men that used to read the Bible so lovingly and so long are now so affected by the spirit of the age that they have barely time to read just one little verse before catching the train or the omnibus to the City to make more money. I do not despair; old fashions come around; evangelical interpretations of the Bible will have their turn next, and it shall come to pass in this City of London that he shall be the most original and powerful preacher who gets back to old Puritan evangelical doctrines of salvation by the blood of Christ. In the meantime the Bible is undergoing diverse processes and examinations. I do not know at this moment that I would stop any one of them; I have faith in the Bible, in the revelation of God, in the testimony written and unwritten, harmonious and cooperative, and I believe that all bubbles—blue, beautiful, iris-like bubbles—will round themselves and split themselves and be forgotten; but the Word of the Lord abideth forever. Young preachers, do not strain to preach to the times, to be abreast with the age, and to borrow expensive magazines that you may quote from more or less benighted and impecunious writers; you stand fast to the revelation known to us as the Bible, and you will never be wanting in subjects, you will never be less than original, and you cannot be less than poetic, ideal, in the truer sense of these terms that indicate the whole range of intellectual possibility.

Now when men went to Jesus He always put to them this question, or He always operated as if He presupposed the individuality and consequent reality of the appeal. Once a man crept into his house by night, and he was detained there until the morning. You may depend upon it Jesus saw in him something worthy of attention. The man was deferential, more than deferential, he was truly reverent, and he said, Master, we know that Thou art a teacher sent from God, for no man can do these miracles—miracles with this peculiar quality and accent, *these* miracles—that Thou doest except God be with him. Miracles that require testimonials are poor miracles, but when men recognize in the miracles their own testimonials, the quality being so rich, and the purpose of their being wrought so beneficent, then there will be a great incoming to see and to testify the wonders and the realities of the kingdom of God. Nicodemus was kept all night; he heard such a sermon as no other man ever heard; the sermon has, blessed be God, been published for the instruction and edification of the world. I wonder how many of us could repeat that sermon by heart? There is no way over that sermon into the blank desert land of infidelity; it is so rich, so utterly comely, so spiritual, so comforting and sustaining; it brings with it such a great light and such a glorious redemption that when it has ceased we wonder that such music should ever come to an end. He who has read the interview of Christ with Nicodemus cannot be an infidel, does not want to be one; he finds in it enough for intellect, heart, imagination, and the immediate claim and responsibility of life.

And once Jesus Christ recognized that a certain person represented to Him individuality, reality of soul and of outlook, and He made His first grand revelation to her by the well's mouth. It was a wondrous time; the disciples had gone away, a woman whose life was written in her face, written in wrinkles, ciphers that only experts can translate, looked at Christ with a woebegone face; there was a great tragedy in her heart; she mentioned the name Messias, she said that she knew and all knew that when Messias came He would teach them all things. And Jesus looked at her as He never looked at any other person, and He said, I am He. And she knew it, and fled away, and preached it, could not help preaching it; left her waterpot and her Jacob's well to tell some great story of pity and love and thankfulness. Do not imagine that you will get anything from Christ if you come to Him in a mood of curiosity. If you ask Him to sit down and hear you read Hume's argument on the miracles—poor Hume!—as if he could argue about anything under heaven! and if you imagine that you can entertain Christ when you read to Him some of the latest difficulties, and set up before Him the alabaster no-God of rationalism and measurableness of piety, He hath no time, the King's business requireth haste. But say, Lord, hear me, for my heart moans with sorrow and wants to ask Thee a question, and He will sit down, and the King's business will be to liberate you. But do be real, do be personal. Do not carry about with you from door to door some other man's lame, empty, miserable atheism.

Prayer

If I may but touch the hem of His garment I shall be made whole. Lord, increase our faith; give us the holy touching power; may we come into daily, loving, healing contact with the All-Living: then shall we have life in ourselves, and Thy word shall be in us like a well of water springing up to everlasting life: we shall know the beauty and the music and the gladness of eternal spring. We have come to touch the hem of the Savior's robe; we put out our groping fingers towards the Cross; if our heart's love may but touch it, death will flee away. But we are in great fear and trembling when we remember the penetration of Thy Spirit, Thy Holy Spirit. Thy word itself is sharper than any two edged sword, piercing to the dividing asunder of the joints and marrow; Thine eyes search our hearts; we cannot hide ourselves from God. If Thou wouldst slumber for one moment we should have another kind of gladness, the gladness which comes of deceiving God and His righteousness; but Thou dost search Jerusalem as with a candle; all things are naked and open to the eyes of Him with Whom we have to do. Thou knowest our thought afar off; before we have time to be ashamed of it, lo, Thou dost blush over us in the heavens: our thought is so mean, so poor, so deficient, oftentimes so hideous and so cruel. We keep a silent chamber in the heart into which no one is admitted, and out of which we would gladly exclude Thyself if we could. We are bad souls, we are conscious of guilt, we defy the law, but we fear the righteousness, the holiness of God. Pardon our expertness in comparative morals; comparing ourselves with ourselves, into what foolish delusions we fall—but setting ourselves against Thine own holiness, behold, who dare open his own eyes on his own deeds? Grant unto us spiritual criticism, the penetration of holiness, and may we measure ourselves by the standard of God's character, and not by the fickle wand of our own treacherous inconsistency. In Thine house we invoke Thy Spirit; we would trifle not in the presence of God, we would rebuke ourselves lest we vaunt before God; ours shall be a penitent spirit and a prostrate attitude, for we are sinners before God, if not before one another. We talk one another into a belief of our mutual respectability, but when we speak to God we cannot see Him for His radiance, and we dare not ask Him to look upon our holiest attempts. But the blood of Jesus Christ Thy Son cleanseth from all sin. To that blood we come; to the redemption wrought for us by Christ Jesus we trust; we venture again and again, in morning light and evening shadows, to look up to God, and say, For Christ's sake, pity us, pardon us, make us good! Amen.

17

Motive Detected

Preached on Sunday Morning, October 22nd, 1899.

For he knew that for envy they had delivered Him
—Matthew 27:18.

He was a Roman, and they were Jews; but he saw through them. Men are seen through much more than they imagine. Pilate had heard all their hypocritical protestations about Caesar and loyalty and the high treason of this young Culprit; Pilate never knew before that the Jews were so fond of Rome; this was a kind of revelation to Pilate. On this occasion, however, the Jews were the most loyal of Caesar's subjects; they hugged their chains, they paid all their taxes and tributes with both hands and with unutterable generosity, and were thankful to have an opportunity of paying homage to the throne of Caesar. But Pilate saw through them. We are more seen through than we think. Pilate was a discerner of the thoughts and intents of the heart. If we could have heard Pilate speaking his own language, he would have spoken after some such manner as this: Ye hypocrites, ye detestable people! You envy this young Man, you are jealous of Him, in some way or other He hurts your pride, and if you could only have Him legally murdered that would satisfy your hellish desire: ye hypocrites! You talking about Caesar, and my not being Caesar's friend—you beasts of hell! Pilate knew that for envy they had delivered Him. Only get rid of this Jesus, the pretended King of the Jews, and all would be well, and it would be worth while to believe any number of lies in order to get rid of

Him. We will kiss Caesar's foot, we will ask Caesar to redouble his chains, and we will sing Caesar's praises morning, noon, and night, if we can only get rid of this critical, awful Judge of our lives. Away with Him—anywhere! Oh, how pious they were, and how exceedingly patriotic, and how delightfully subservient! But Pilate saw through them, mocked them in his heart, despised them in his bedchamber, hated the very fall of their feet as they approached him; he saw through the hypocrisy and the bloodthirstiness.

The awful reflection is that men may deceive themselves and put one motive at the front and keep the real motive at the rear; and the self-deception may go to such an extent that if you charged the men with the baser motive they would feel annoyed—they are so sensitive, so honorable. May the Lord deliver us from self-blindness! We make a great pother about color-blindness; we will not admit a man into army or navy unless he be very quick-sighted as to the distinctions between colors. If we would apply the same criticism to our own motives and our own hearts, we would have revelation enough, and we might even yet be saved. I do not know whether it lies within the compass of the Divine mercy to save envy, jealousy, hatred, that springs out of the heart and that pretends to be justice; I do not deny that God may save the jealous, but I doubt it. Jealousy is never so hideous and never so dangerous as when it denies its own existence. If I could personify envy, which is another name for jealousy, or jealousy, which is another name for envy, I think I could put words into its mouth: Jealous, indeed! What an insinuation! What is there to be jealous of? I have no need to be jealous of him; what need have I to be jealous of her? What an extraordinary suggestion to make, that *I* am jealous! Then was the devil born in the evil Bethlehem of that heart! Envy says, What is there to envy? You talk about his powers, what are they? You talk about her beauty, what is it? There is nothing to be envious about; if there were anything to be envious about, well, of course, I might be envious, but until there is something to be envious about I must defend myself against the infamous impeachment. Her singing—

what is it? His literature; why, the man can hardly write at all; he has written a book, but there is no literature in it, it is mere gabble. His painting; why, I would not have such a daub in my house; I do not call it painting. Show me something to be envious about, and then I may perhaps be envious, but until them hold me guiltless. *Then* envy, jealousy, is at its worst. And such miserable disposition is clearly seen through by Pilate and by alien and by stranger and by everybody.

We can easily tell when it is envy or jealousy that is running down a public man or a private character. The people have a spirit of judgment; trust the people when they have had time to become sober; they will protect you, and your book, and your singing in the concert hall, and your merchandise, and your family life; they see through all the attacks that are made upon you; leave it all to them and to God. Know this—a statement absolutely incredible, if we did not know it to be absolutely factual—that the Son of God was delivered for envy; jealousy hunted Him to His death. If they did these things to the Lord, will they spare His people? Will the Master be persecuted and the disciple be allowed to go without criticism or hostility? The point of comfort in this case is that Pilate saw through the Jew, the Roman governor saw through the Jewish tributary. It is a sad thing to know that great searching, clear, righteous eyes are reading us all through and through. Even in the act of listening to us persons may be criticizing our statement regarding others. Have you suffered from jealousy? You are a rising young man, and it is the business of those who are just a little older than you are to put you down. Are you suffering in your little trade and commercial life? It is the one business of the man who has a shop twelve inches wider than yours to buy you up, to sneer at you, and to wonder what you have come there for—not that he is envious or jealous! He is a most magnanimous man, if lies are true. Are you a young artist in painting, in music, in literature? it is the business of those people on the other side of the curtain to depreciate you. Some of the more skillful of them are very excellent; they depreciate you by praising you; they know the stopping-places, they know the gradations of verbal color, they know the mystery of moral emphasis. The wrestler lifts his opponent a few inches in the air that he may the more surely dash him to the ground. The mischief is that you never in your life met a man who confessed to jealousy. That is the woe of it; that is where the murder blushes into its guilty redness: because the man or woman charged with jealousy says, What is there to be jealous about—that is what I want to know. Thus the devil comes of age and claims his right over the human heart. Beware! Resist beginnings. I have never known a jealous person saved; I do not deny the salvation of persons who are jealous, but I have never known it: that I give as a personal testimony.

Now see what envy or jealousy or hatred of the heart will do by studying the case of Jesus Christ. What did these people seek to get rid of? They sought to repulse the gentle advances of mercy. Mercy is the name of the Son of God, mercy was the purpose of His heart. He came to seek and to save that which was lost; He came to bind up the broken-hearted, to give joy to the joyless, and to set the captive free. But He did not come in the conventional way; He did not come from the expected place; He did not bring with Him what were deemed orthodox credentials; so He and His Gospel, His mercy, His love, His pity were cast away; herein is that saying true, He was despised and rejected of men. See what envy will do; see what doors it will close, see what light it will quench, see what opportunities it will abuse. And, rejecting Christ, the people rejected His discipline. Jesus was a disciplinarian.

Want of discipline is killing England today; it is altering commerce, trade of all kinds, occupations of all sorts; it is eating out all family veneration, all social reverence, and is asserting self above law and right, above decency and social beauty. The great disease that is eating up England, and will finally destroy it, is want of discipline, order, obedience, punctuality, decorum, self-restraint. Want of discipline now discloses itself on the public streets; every thoroughfare may be said to be placarded with lack of discipline—every man doing just what he likes in his own eyes, coming at his own time, going at his own time, doing what pleases himself, and mixing up engagements and enjoyments that ought to be inconsistent with the daily observance of decent life. The Gospel cannot be popular; it will take a millennium multiplied by itself to give the Gospel any substantial foothold in what are called the economic and the practical departments of life because men do not like discipline: whereas the Gospel has but one time, *Now;* one duty, *Go;* one reward, enduring to the end means the final crown. But we have lost our pith, our sinews; we are athletics in the joints and paralytics in the nerves of the soul; great jumpers, poor soldiers; great at running when nobody wants you to run, poor at standing still and keeping the fort. Until the spirit of discipline gets back I have no hope of family unity, of business integrity, of national prosperity, of world-wide evangelization. The children on the streets have now taken to tricks and practices that would not have been allowed for a moment a century ago when England was younger, not older, than she is today. When people rejected Christ they rejected the sense of responsibility; they did not like to be called to account: and Christianity is the religion of responsibility; that is, of accounting for itself, accounting for the expenditure of its time and the expenditure of its money, and the outgoing of its energy and its influence. Christianity and responsibility are to a large degree interchangeable terms. Where is thy brother? What have I to do with my brother? Everything. Where art thou? To whom have I to give an account of my retreat, of my privacy and solitude? To God.

This is not likely to be a popular Gospel. There will be more people at the country fair where the clown thrusts his head through a hoop than there will be at the church festival of sacrifice and responsibility and oath-taking as to better life and better deed. It is apparently pleasanter to be at the fair—there, that is the drum, that the band—away! Ah me, these people will never do any good for their country; they may be conscripts someday, but willing patriotic soldiers, never! It is not their nature, it is not in their blood.

Of course responsibility means that Christians are to reincarnate Christ. He is to be incarnated in every man who believes in Him and gives his heart to Him. Thus we are to be in the world in our poor degree just as Christ was. When we read our marching orders and our orders of discipline it is very hard reading: When He was reviled, He reviled not again; when He suffered, He threatened not; He gave His back to the smiters, and His cheeks to them that pluck off the hair. And what have we to do? Read your orders: Love your enemies, pray for them that despitefully use you and persecute you: if thine enemy smite thee on the one cheek, turn to him the other also. Pilate, crucify Him! His blood be on us and on our children; we cannot have this; life would not be worth living under such law: crucify Him! crucify Him! He hurts our pride, He disestablishes our pomp and our houses and our great ancestral delights and honors; He plucks all our decorations from us, and sets us out stark naked under the burning midday sun: Pilate, crucify Him! Prove thyself Caesar's friend! We cannot alter the law, we cannot alter the morality of the Gospel, we cannot accommodate Christian requirements to human prejudices. When the great Christian criticism plows its way through our life, we hate it, it tells us we are all descendants of one father, a sinful man; and we want to fix our genealogy where we like, going seven centuries before the first century if possible, and to say we were born then, and we were the only inhabitants of the universe for two million ages; that would suit us. But Jesus traces us all to one root, to one parentage, and He includes us all in one condemnation; and His great universal, unqualified cry is, Repent! If He had gone down to the slums and out-of-the-way quarters of the city we would gladly have subscribed a trifle to any little home mission in which He was foolish enough to engage Himself. When He stands at the center of things and directs His inclusive glance upon all the generations, all the evolutions of human life, and cries with thunderous voice, Repent! –Pilate, crucify Him!

Men do not always disclose the real motives under which they operate. I return to that point to make it more emphatic. We may give one motive to the public and keep the real motive in our heart. In every heart there is a chamber of imagery, a hidden place where we keep the idols, the unclean pictures, and in which we enjoy without suspicion on the part of the public the unholy revel. While we are in the church we may be in some house of ill-fame; while we are singing out of the hymn-book or joining the public anthem we may be reveling in the bed of lust. We want a searching light, a penetrating criticism; we want, indeed, to be revealed to ourselves. Self-deception, I repeat, is the worst of all deceptions. And as for our glibness and expertness in substituting one motive for another to suit the public exigency or the private contingency, then, alas—is salvation possible? I have known a man leave the church because he could no longer profit by the preaching of the pastor—poor wounded soul, sensitive creature, he could no longer be edified by the preaching which once built him up; and the poor weak-kneed creatures that are in every church got around him and sympathized with him, and petted him and treated him to diverse sorts of impious confectionery, and hoped that by patience and forbearance he might one day be restored and take up his old delights. All the time the villain was making a subterranean passage through which he could escape from a charge of falsification of accounts, malfeasance in commerce, and he was lacerating his poor pastor, and bringing him into sore mental straits under the pretense that he no longer profited, when—blessed be God!—he was weaving a rope for his own neck, and he was hanged as one who had wounded society. In the meantime, what some men may have to suffer on account of others, and these poor weak-kneed creatures that somehow get into every Christian community—I would that all the windows were barred that they could not get in!—all get around this poor creature, whose soul is drooping down for want of the food which he once enjoyed and for which he was once thankful. Pilate would have seen through him; Pilate had the critic's eye; he saw the hypocrite in the pretended patriots that were around him.

Then let us go to the other side for one bright moment. Jesus Christ knows when we are doing our best to quench the evil; He listens nightly to our prayers which we dare not pray at the family altar, saying, Lord Jesus, I did it for envy, I did it for jealousy, and this cruel devil in my heart is eating my very life out and telling me that I have nothing to be envious about or jealous about; but I know better, I know that I am doing this for envy, and I am self-tormented by my jealousy, for jealousy torments all its victims; I dare not tell my father, my mother, my dearest one about it, but in reality this devil jealousy is drinking my blood and killing my human nature, and is poisoning me against Thyself, and is telling me to give up praying and take to reveling: let me put my arms round Thy feet, Thou Son of Mary, Son of God, and help me: Thou knowest what envy did in Thine own case; Thou knowest what it is doing in my heart, in relation to other men better infinitely than I have ever been: come to me this night in this darkness and cast out the devil! On such a scene the morning shall arise and the spring shall break, and transgression shall be rolled as a thick cloud and cast forever behind the Lord! Behind the Lord, behind the Infinite, where is that? It is there our transgressions are cast by our loving Lord, in the degree in which we kiss His five wounds with the lips of our heart, and in the degree in which we make those five wounds five starting-places under the providence of the Holy Spirit towards a new life and a final heaven.

Prayer

Almighty God, we thank Thee with all our love for the gift of Thy dear Son our Savior Jesus Christ. To us He is Emmanuel, He is God manifest in the flesh, He is Thyself made visible. We heard Him say, and our souls delighted in the saying, He that hath seen Me hath seen the Father. Yet men saw Him with the bodily eyes and crucified Him; may we have the heart-vision, eyes of the soul; blessed are the pure in heart, for they shall see God. Enable us to look, therefore, with the attention of our souls, that nothing may escape us of the Lord's condescending revelation and perpetual beauty. Open our eyes that we may behold wondrous things out of Thy law; open our understanding that we may understand the Scriptures; bring us away from the market place where we have been idling too long, and give us work to do in Thy vineyard or in Thine house. We would have God for Master, we would obey the Lord, we would be fellow-workers with God, we would be of His husbandry and of His household. Enable us to work while it is called day; may we waste no daylight, may we work even into the night-time; so urgent and so desirous should we be to do something for Him who gave His life for us. The Lord be with all godly workers, with all missionaries, teachers, evangelists, with all who work in the field of home missions, on their own hearthstone, under their own roof-tree; and thus the Lord send upon us the spirit of consecration, that we may be strong souls, given in the power of the Cross and by the oath of love to the service of the Son of God. Amen.

18
Daily Service

Preached on Thursday Morning, October 26th, 1899.

As every day's work required–1 Chronicles 16:37.

That was the law. "So he left there before the ark of the covenant of the Lord Asaph and his brethren, to minister before the ark continually, as every day's work required." Not as yesterday's work required, not as tomorrow's work might require, but as every day's work required within its own twelve hours or twenty-four. That was order. The men had been singing. A musical man cannot be disorderly; he would refute his own song, he would annihilate his own music. "As ever day's work required"–morning by morning; now much, now more; now not quite so much; now a little variety; but every day had its duty; every morning had its opportunity. That is the secret of success. For want of knowing such a secret and applying it many men are without bread today; honest men, well-meaning men, but without faculty, without conscience that is well disciplined; the intention is perfectly good, the conscience is not faulty, except in the particular that the conscience is not ruled by the conscience. Here is a great subject for a great City lecture; here might be compiled a manual for young men, for merchants, for ministers, for housekeepers. There is infinitely more in the text than there seems to be. So there was in every saying of Jesus Christ; you could not fathom the wisdom of the Speaker. If we could obey any one thing that Jesus Christ ever gave us to do, we should be saved, and the world would be arrested, contented, and happy. He said,

Let your Yea be yea. The world will not, and therefore the world is torn by a restless demon. The Lord Christ said, Let your Nay be nay. But the world will not. If the world would let Nay be nay, or Yea be yea, the world would be saved; but it will have rearrangements, modifications, covenants that are reserved; it will have a speech that is qualified by mental reservation; it will have ornaments and sacraments that are modified by unspoken and to us unintelligible intention. We have often said that he who really and truly values a blade of grass must pray; and so we say, he that obeys anyone of the ethical laws of Jesus Christ must be plunged in the fountain filled with blood drawn from Emmanuel's veins. The whole creation is a unity; life is a sublime integrity; herein is that saying true, He that breaks one breaks all; he that is obedient in one is obedient in all. You cannot split up the commandments and the ethics of the Lord and his Christ into little detached isolations and make pets and toys of the Lord's great inclusive and eternal word.

"As every day's work required." There is only one time—Now "Now is the accepted time, now is the day of salvation." Now is God's great opportunity given to us all. Yesterday is gone, tomorrow is unborn, today is now, and the golden portal rolls back to let us into the larger liberty. Things are not to be done at any time. That is where so many people go into confusion and into final bankruptcy, and spend their days at the public expense, and complain that it is very hard to go to the workhouse at the last. There is no need for any man to go to the workhouse; if every man will do as every day's work requires, he need never bend his head under the doorway of a workhouse. To so many people there is no regular time; that is the reason of failure, that is the leak. They were going to do this, but they forgot. What! A man forgetting? He was going to do this at ten o'clock, but he was busy at that moment, and now he will do it in the afternoon. I do not read of any provision made for such people; and when they go to the workhouse with a heavy heart and a long-drawn sigh the last thing they would ever think of doing is to blame themselves; they would blame their relations, and they would blame the Government of the day, and they would blame people not yet born, so absurd and ridiculous and unjust is the spirit of those people who break the law of time and violate the discipline of responsibility. Never ask if you can do this tomorrow; no man has a right to promise you that liberty. Will it do if I attend to it after supper? Where is that man going? To the workhouse. The great secret of successful life is discipline, promptitude, military obedience—now, altogether, the best I can; as every day requires.

That was the way that Jesus Christ lived. In that apparently coldly ethical doctrine there is a great evangelical gospel; the Son of God is hidden in that disciplinary prose: I must work the works of Him that sent Me: are there not twelve hours in the day? I must work while the light lasts; the night cometh wherein no man can work: I must not postpone Monday's duties to be done in Tuesday's light. That is success, mastery; he who obeys that rule is king, no man can take his crown. It is the little man fussily doing nothing that comes to disappointment, confusion, and pennilessness. There is a daily sacrament of work. I must do my allotted work in this allotted time. "How is it possible for you to do so much?" we say to this great king of labor, and that great leader of civilization; and he makes answer, Only by doing the day's work within the day. I must have my chapter a day, and there is no bed for me until the last verse of that chapter is read and understood. There are a great many persons who have out-of-the-way places in which they store things to be attended to sometime; the fact being that there is no peace in that household, no music, no deep content; there is always something tugging at the conscience and reminding the memory of the arrears. Never have any arrears; keep abreast with your duties, and let who likes keep abreast with the times—those great, gigantic, immeasurable ciphers who always keep abreast with the times in things that do not concern them and let their own homes and their own business go to waste. Is that the Gospel? Yes! That was Christ's rule, and he that obeys in one obeys in all—must do it, or his soul would be ill at ease till he had struck the last blow due on the day's responsibility.

What does a well-spent day mean? It means Sabbath every night, satisfaction; it is finished, it is enough; I have told my tale, I have woven my thread, there is nothing more to be done today; then comes the sleep of the laboring man, and that is sweet. The lazy man cannot sleep, he can only snore. Only he who works, works for God, with God, in the spirit of Christ, can sleep, and God will make up all that is due to him whilst he is sleeping. The Authorized Version reads, "He giveth His beloved sleep": better read, "He giveth His beloved sleeping": while the hard worker is sleeping the angels are doing things for him, and he will find the morning beautiful with a large door of opportunity set before him and a day's store of grace prepared for his nourishment and comfort. God giveth to His beloved when they are sleeping; He says, in effect, "Now what are the little knots that puzzle My beloved?"; and He sends the angels to disentangle them; and the sleeper on waking says, I see it now! The Lord says, "Now what is the burden that is crushing his dear, loving, loyal heart?"; and He sends the angels to take the load away, so that on recovering consciousness after dreamless sleep he, the Christian believer, says, I feel that I am able to go forth as a giant whom God has refreshed. So many things are done for us in sleep. If even the burden remains the strength has been increased, so that the burden ceases to be a weight. It is God's way. There is morality in sleep. Some men have no right to sleep. And they who have worked well shall sleep on the Father's bosom, they shall not know when fear cometh. I must work the works of Him that sent me, I must work while it is called day; the night cometh wherein no man can work. But even God has a church of darkness, a church of sleep, a temple of restfulness, of vision, of slumber, and the stars can talk as well as the burning midday sun.

Secondly. Let us enlarge the meaning of the word "day." The term day is one of the most flexible terms in the Holy Scripture, in poetry, and in general experience. "In six days the Lord made heaven and earth." I have no doubt of it; but I do not know what "day" means. We speak of "our day": does it mean from eight o'clock in the morning until eight o'clock in the evening? Is the word "day" there a term of clock-time, or does it relate to centuries, eras, epochs? We say, "Our little systems have their day": does that mean a chronometer day, or a larger and variable period? Evidently it means the latter. So the text may be expanded without a change of word. "As every day's work required,"—as the time needed, as the exigency demanded, as the epoch called for, as the century required. You are fully aware that every day, in the larger sense of age, epoch, or era, has its own peculiar revelation and its own peculiar truth and special and even unique duty and obligation. We cannot go back upon the centuries and fit the expired eons into the framework of the immediate day in which we are breathing. So with Truth in its forms—creedal, ecclesiastical; we cannot be taking yesterday and fitting it into this day—meaning by yesterday not twenty-four hours ago, but a thousand years since. Every age-day has its own work which must be done within its own limits. The apostle did not hesitate to speak of "the present truth," the truth of this particular day, with all its thrill and pulse and feverishness; the present truth, precisely adapted and suited to the immediate intellectual and spiritual condition of the times. We often say that our fathers would preach differently if they could be replaced in the pulpit today. Differently they might preach, but in the degree in which they were prophets of God, rich with insight into spiritual mystery and verity, they would make their sermon for the age, and not for an age that expired long ago. Speak to those who are present; do not address the antiquities, and only use antiquity in the degree in which it can be spiritually and profitably modernized. Thus the eternal is brought into the present moment, and we know that we are not cut off from the provinces and continents and globes of eternity because we have an immediate truth with a special, unique, and it may be temporary application.

We read of men who fell asleep after serving their generation—
"and having served his generation, he fell on sleep." And he serves
the next generation best who serves the present generation well.
Your influence will not be cut off, it will run on when you are no
longer visible; it will be a memory, and inspiration, an enthusiasm,
an ever-recurring poem, lifting life's prose into nobler music. We
must catch the very spirit and genius of the time; our question
should be, What will the people hear; not in any groveling or degrading sense, but, What is the supreme necessity of the human
heart just at this hot moment? Shall we preach to the English people in Latin? No. Shall we deliver to them terms which are so ar-
chaic as to be utterly without immediate meaning to their panting
and needy souls? No. We must show them that the old Gospel, old
as the love of God, is adapted to this very moment and can take
upon itself the hue and complexion of the transient time. There is
no need to fear the resources of eternity. We may have to remold
testimonies in a new form. We have translation after translation of
the written word. No translator can do final justice to the Scriptures. The Scriptures are more than grammar. Grammar is often a
very inadequate and disappointing tool to work with; we must get
within the grammar; that is, at the very soul of things, and the most
modern application of that soul to this day's necessity and obligation. So we do not want verbal translations, but spiritual transub-
stantiation; as we have said in another discourse, a carrying on of
all the meaning as to its substance and purpose from age to age and
from land to land, so long as man lives and the Cross stands the
hope of the world.

What is it, then, that covers and sanctifies all days?—the little
day of twenty-four hours or twelve, and the great day of long centuries and piled millenniums? That permanent and all-sovereign
quantity of or force is Jesus Christ. It is said of Him, He is the same
yesterday, today, and forever; He describes Himself as He that is
and was and is to come—Alpha, new as the dawn; Omega, venerable as the sunset of millenniums. He abides in the Church, He is

ever on the throne, He gives the order of the day, He has a message for every morning. If we could lay hold of that great truth we should have a united Church at once. In fact, the Church is united in its soul, in its innermost, in its deepest purpose. It is when the Church begins to arrange things and to dress itself and to publish small editions full of various readings—for all of which I could find an ample space in the waste-paper basket—it is then that the Church is apparently divided. What is it that endures? It is Christ; it is not ecclesiasticism, it is not forms, it is not a series of scaffoldings and frameworks. What we, therefore, should be anxious to get at is the internal and unchangeable quantity, the warm heart, the radiant face of the Son of God. Of course we shall always have little creatures, if I may personify them by taking wide grammatical license, called Opinions and Views. One of Dr. Vaughan's sweetest sermons—I mean the great Dean, the illustrious Master of the Temple, who has been with us in our Thursday morning service—is upon Views; as who should say, My view, His view, Her view, Their view. And the whole of them may be dead tomorrow morning! We do not want your view, and you do not want my view; I was born yesterday, and I almost hope to die tonight, and therefore to trouble you with my view would be impertinence. We want the Christ, the Cross, the blood, the atoning priesthood; these abide forever, and views and hypotheses—I was most thankful for the idea of cremation when I heard of somebody's views—the little creature that was measured for a suit yesterday and will be measured for a shroud tomorrow. Some persons apparently imagine that they are only singing right when they are singing out of a particular hymn-book. If Christians would only believe that it is not the hymn-book we want, but the praise, the song, the eternal music, we should get liberated from a thousand bigotries, and should be the richer for our deprivation of a thousand superstitions. Now it is not by theology, but by religion, spiritual religion, that we truly live. It is not by the letter, for even the letter of the Bible, if separated from the spirit, may be grievously misunderstood and most mischievously applied.

When I read the Bible I must say to the Writer of it, Open Thou mine eyes that I may behold wondrous things out of Thy law! I do not want the iron-bound letter, I want the ever-living, all-sanctifying Spirit; not the alphabet, but the power is what I am in quest of when I shut myself up with my God and His Book.

So much for working on the broader scale; so much for working within day, meaning century, age, epoch. We are not all working in the same way or all doing precisely the same kind of work. If the Church would but believe this she might have summer all the year round. We will compare one man with another; it would seem as if there were no escape from this lunacy. We think that unless a man shall begin where we expect him to begin, and continue as we expect him to continue, and conclude as we expect he will conclude, that such man is wrong. Never forget that that man could criticize you if he thought it worth while to stoop so low. It would seem to be supposed that only one party can criticize; it is a miserable, profitless little game that all parties can be experts in if they please. Every man in his own order. The greatest sermon I ever heard in my life was preached by a Roman Catholic priest in the city of Montreal. When I go away from home it is to hear other people and visit other churches, and to know somewhat of the extent and variety of the kingdom of heaven. I would God we could hear all preachers and read all manner of books! The wider, the brighter the mind, the deeper, the sweeter the charity.

Day–day–day–in its usual sense it means so short a space of time. Take short views of life. Mayhap I am speaking to someone who is worrying himself about the day after tomorrow. Where is that day? Who has seen it? What will it be like? Who told you about it? What rights have you in it? Today is thy limitation. He who works well today shall have holiday tomorrow—holiday in the sense of renewed strength, increased vigor, and power to deal with the problems and handle the difficulties of life. You are wondering who will live in your house two years after you are dead. Why should you trouble yourself about two years after? You will not be there to see, why trouble about it now? Use your house well while you are in it, make every corner of it holy with prayer, make every part of it sweet with the breath of charity; so that when the people come to your house after you have gone they will say, I know there is a blessing in these walls, I feel it; it may be superstition, but it is a good sort of superstition; I know good, sweet, honest, high-minded people have lived under this roof, and I am getting the advantage of their having been here. So live, and thou shalt be blessed. Do not turn tomorrow into an enemy; you have enemies enough, without turning tomorrow into another hostile force. Tomorrow is with God; tomorrow is lingering by the lakes of heaven; tomorrow has not yet left the eternal throne. Why fret and worry and tear thyself about tomorrow? It may be the brightest day that ever shone upon thee; and if thou wouldst make it so, today be up and doing, and tomorrow thou shalt have joy in thy Lord.

It is not forbidden to us to dwell for a moment on the past. I often live in the past. My Gospel is in the past, the Cross is in the past, all sweet providences are in the past. I will think of Him who took me up and led me by a way that I knew not; I will recall all the friends that have brought me roses and gifts of fruit from God's own vineyard; I will think of all the songs, the true music, the sweet hymns that helped to make me what I am when I am my best; I will bind the psalms around me as men wear chains of gold, and I will think of the Lord's doing; and thus I shall not be too lonely, thus I shall be saved from uttermost despair. And when I go to the sanctuary of darkness night by night I will hear a sweet voice teaching me this little song:

> His love in time past
> Forbids me to think
> He'll leave me at last
> In trouble to sink.

Yesterday is my Sanctuary—tomorrow my Hope.

Words for Preachers

Ministers must often enter into this meditation with themselves, that they are as actors upon a stage, or as beacons set upon a hill to give light to others. They are seen afar off, and a little blemish is soon espied in their coats. Everything that they speak or do is observed and marked.
—Attersol 1618

Take heed to yourselves also, because there are many eyes upon you, and therefore there will be many observers of your falls. You cannot miscarry but the world will ring of it. The eclipses of the sun by day-time are seldom without witnesses. If you take yourselves for the lights of the churches, you may well expect that men's eyes should be upon you. If other men may sin without observation, so cannot you. And you should thankfully consider how great a mercy is this, that you have so many eyes to watch over you and so many ready to tell you of your faults, and so have greater helps than others, at least for the restraining of your sin.
—Baxter, 1615–1691

Knowledge is so fundamental to the work and calling of a minister, that he cannot be without it: *"Because thou hast rejected knowledge, I will also reject thee, that thou shalt be no Priest to me"* (Hos. 4:6). The want of knowledge in a minister is such a defect as cannot be supplied by anything else; be he never so meek, patient, bountiful, unblameable, if he hath not skill to divide the word aright, he is not cut out for a minister. Everything is good, as it is good for the end it is appointed to; a knife, though it hath a haft of diamonds, yet if it will not cut 'tis no knife. A bell, if not sound, is no bell. The great work of a minister is to teach others, his lips are to preserve knowledge, he should be as conversant in the things of God, as others in their particular trades. Ministers are called lights; if the light then be darkness, how great is the darkness of that people like to be! I know these stars in Christ's hands are not all of the same magnitude; there is a greater glory of gift and graces shines in some than others; yet so much light is necessary to every minister as was in the star the wise men saw at Christ's birth; to be able out of the word to direct sinners the safe and true way to Christ and Salvation. O, sirs, it is a sad way of getting a living by killing of men, as some unskillful physicians do; but much more to get a temporal livelihood by ruining souls through our ignorance. He is a cruel man to the poor passengers, who will undertake to be pilot, when he never so much as learned his compass.—*Gurnall, 1617–1679*

Prayer

If we may but speak unto the Lord for one moment our souls shall be lightened of many a burden and our life will lie before us as a plain path. We have come into Thine house in the name of Jesus Christ our Blessed One, our infinite and only Savior, in the hope that our hearts may catch some glimpse of God. All things weary us, they exhaust themselves; the time-vessel is emptied, and behold, there is nothing remaining to refresh and encourage the soul. The things that are eternal can alone comfort us, because of our own quality; they bring with them messages from the hills of heaven and from the chambers of eternity. We want to hear the ineffable music, we lay open our souls that they may receive the morning gospel from the morning heaven. We thank Thee for Thy great goodness, continual, increasing, multitudinous; we cannot number Thy mercies, they are more in number than the sands upon the seashore; we cannot count up all Thy goodnesses towards us, for they are greater in multitude than are the stars. So we will sing of Thy mercies, our song shall be of mercy and judgment; unto Thee, O Lord, will we sing, and we will say of Thy mercy that it endureth forever. We thank Thee for the use of great words, such as forever, eternal, everlasting; these words belong to our souls; if we have lost them it is by self-impoverishment, our sins have kept good things from us, and have stood between our souls and our inheritance in God. Oh that we had hearkened unto Thy commandments! Oh that we had been obedient children; then had we reaped the harvest of obedience, and our barns would have been too poor and small to hold all the largess of Thine answering love! We have done things we ought not to have done, but we would remember this no more, because in Christ Jesus Thou hast Thyself ceased to remember it. Where sin abounds grace doth much more abound; we will think of the grace rather than of the sin, we will see the Cross of Christ triumphing over all the destruction of the enemy. May our souls never lose sight of the Cross, may that great radiant image raise itself through all the sevenfold night of darkness and misery and shine upon us an infinite hope. We have but a few days to live, our breath is in our nostrils; while we do live in sight of one another may we be kind, gracious, charitable, all-hoping, all-forgiving; may no root of bitterness spring up to trouble us, may we spend our little time together in increasing joy, in deepening confidence, and in brightening hope. This day we would in Thy name, O Christ, renounce all evil, we would recall every bitter word, we would withdraw every hotly spoken accusation against good men, and we would humble ourselves before the Cross that through its blood we may be forgiven.

Let the Lord hear us in these things, and remember that our breath is in our nostrils, and that we fly with sinking sins to our little grave, and may His love abound over our sins, and give us light at eventide. Amen.

19
To the Ephesians

Preached on Sunday Morning, October 29th, 1899.

I would like to read to you in the second chapter of Paul's Epistle to the Ephesians. Would you like to hear the reading? We must stop now and then to modernize and apply the deep sweet meaning.

The Apostle Paul is not always just the same. He is consistent, but never monotonous. He is a sevenfold man; his epistles are his truest photograph. Have you ever read the epistles in the light of that suggestion?—not only to find out what the epistles are, but what their author was. He never wearies us, because he has a great gift of escaping monotony. He is rugged, incoherent, sometimes almost verbally self-contradictory; he is full of parentheses, he makes great use of bracketings and asides and literary diversions, yet all the while there is a wholeness which eyes that love him can perfectly discern. In some epistles he is argumentative, almost contentious; he is pushing a point upon the attention of his correspondents, and he wants to establish a plea. He is not so enjoyable in such epistles. He sometimes elicits pity for the other man. He is heroic in his logic and destructive in his conclusions; then I sometimes prefer to turn over a page. To the Colossians, the Ephesians, he is as it were in another sense more vividly and tenderly and approachably the Apostle of the grace of God. In the Galatians he talks to the Galatians; in the Corinthians he talks to the Corinthians; they have their local disputes and matters to adjust and to determine. But to the Ephesians and the Colossians he speaks universals, he reveals solar systems;

his strides are constellations; they are infinitely wondrous in intellectual conception, in imaginative and ideal color and emphasis—catholic epistles in very deed; addressed to one church, but meant for all men and all ages.

We need such epistles many a time in traversing the hills and the dales of life. There are times when we are impatient with special messages to special people, with letters of explanation and contention; we want something more, we feel as if we could receive all the sunshine and breathe all the air and accommodate all the sparkling, flashing fountains of living water. When we are in such spiritual mood we find all we want in the great father-mother-brother-sister letters to the Ephesians and to the Colossians. It would be the soul's fortune in the sterling gold of heaven if our memories could charge themselves with all the philosophy, theology, and poetry of the two epistles to the Colossians and to the Ephesians. They are great banqueting-tables; if we change the figure, they are great highland scenes with wondrous panoramas of light and color and mystery and consolation. There are, I repeat, times when we need every word of them, times when we need the whole Godhead, for we are poor, alone, and sad, and lost, and God Himself is hardly enough to satisfy the creature He has created. Who knows the epistles to the Ephesians and the Colossians? He who knows them has bread to eat that the world knows not of. Yet these very epistles, so deep in their theology, so wide in their outlook, so piercing in their appeals, are full of ethical teaching and moral reminiscence and penetrating rebuke. Paul preached a full-orbed Gospel; he went around the entire circle of Divine thought insofar as it is revealed to human imagination.

Take the first verse as an example: "And you hath He quickened, who were dead in trespasses and sins."

That verse is theology in one sentence; you need no more. As we found in Genesis 1:1 all the Bible, so we find in Ephesians 2:1, the whole scheme of God and the whole revelation of human history. You—dead, quickened; you alive, brought from the dead.

There are moral resurrections as well as physical. How we boggle over some poor little miracle in bodily resurrection, and forget the infinitely grander and greater miracle of spiritual resurrection—the awakening of the soul, the calling-back of strange thoughts, whispering into the ear of moral death, blowing some silver trumpet over the grave of conscience, and awakening conscience to newness of life. But it is the trick of man to worry himself over the lowest points of things, to make a great stir about minor quantities and subsidiary agencies and applications; it is the nature of the creature when he is left to himself. He is greatly excited about the coming-again of a poor body that is not worth while bringing back from the dust, but he passes over in silence the bringing-back of a dead soul, the quickening of an inspired conscience, the reconstruction of a moral temple: that he cares not for. He says, "With what body will the dead come?" Poor worrying creature; always wasting himself at the wrong points and waiting midnight after midnight at the wrong door! If God has quickened man He will see to all the rest. Recall our lessons upon words that teach by implication. We have seen that created means provided; that provided means redeemed; that redeemed means ultimate sanctification and perfectness of manhood. So with the word "quickened"; it carries all the other evolution along with it; the oak is in the acorn.

> Wherein in time past ye walked according to the course of this world, according to the prince of the power of the air, the spirit that now worketh in the children of disobedience (Verse 2).

There is the world for you in one gloomy sentence. This is Paul's reading of moral history. Paul was no fancy lecturer; Paul did not write out a course of dreams and call them a course of lectures: Paul recognized that the air is full of the devil. The devil has hardly left room for the summer in all that air which he breathes and poisons. He would edge out the summer if he could; he tempts the spring; he says to that sweet young thing, the vernal spirit, Blight,

O blossoms! Arise, O East Wind, and kill the buds! Choke those little birds in their homely nests! It is the devil. Do not attempt to argue him out of existence. Some people try to argue him into existence; they have a devil on paper and in the middle of a sealed creed which they feel themselves to be at liberty to take into the Court of Chancery to have the deed grammatically interpreted by a man who is learned in the analysis of letters. But the Apostle Paul assumed the devil, revealed him, declared him, took him into account, lectured upon him, defied him, sometimes was rebuffed by him—"Satan hath hindered us." There is probably no way of getting the idea so thoroughly into our dense minds as by representing the air, the whole atmosphere, as in some mysterious and inexplicable sense the sphere of the devil's ministry. You can for yourselves see what difficulty the sun has with the atmosphere, the fog, the rain, the east wind, the sea tormented, the crops blighted, the fields naked when they should be clothed with verdure. All this is but for a time. Never undervalue the enemy; never underestimate his resources; take it for granted that, whether you are fighting spiritually or physically, you have a great enemy to meet, and prepare yourselves accordingly, or you will lose the battle, and you will deserve to lose it.

> Among whom also we all had our conversation in times past in the lusts of our flesh, fulfilling the desires of the flesh and of the mind; and were by nature the children of wrath, even as others (Verse 3).

That is not modern talk. We have schooled ourselves by false schooling out of these great solemn, bedrock verities. The apostle never would have suffered for our poor superficial theories; the apostle would not have endured suffering and gloried in tribulation because he had received into his fancy some cobweb theory of creation, its evolution and its destiny. Not for such things did men preach in sorrow and seal in blood. If we have little conceptions about man and God, we shall have a little crumbling church, always at war with itself, and always losing the sham fights which it challenges and invites. Marvelous master was Paul! What deftness, what magnanimity, what wondrous subtlety of persuasiveness! "We all had our conversation." This is no pedantic priest coming with ferrule or rod to scourge some minor generation of men; this is a brother soul, this is a kindred experience: I know it, I have suffered it, I recall the darkness, I remember the mercy. It is preaching of Paul's kind that will reconstruct the Church. The Church of Christ does not need reform. We have chosen that little milk-and-water word, and we carry it about with us as a kind of evening-party trick or toy. We say, This or That must be reformed. Jesus Christ never said so; He did not like diluted terms; He never spoke a pale hesitant language into which you could thrust a thousand qualifying parentheses. He said, Repent! Ye must be born again: make the tree good; do not paint the branches, hew down to the root and get the poison out. We do not want a reformed Church, we want a regenerated Church, a reconstructed Church, a Church of the Holy Ghost; not a framework, scaffolding, or apparatus of our own hired ecclesiastical imagination; we want a regenerated Church, every fiber, every filament made pure, made chaste with the sanctity of God. Beware of these little church-jobbers who are going about reforming any institution. When an institution needs reforming it needs destroying, that destruction may precede reconstruction, and that sense of inadequacy or unfaithfulness may lead to a cry for the baptism of regeneration.

> But God, who is rich in mercy, for His great love wherewith He loved us,
> Even when we were dead in sins, hath quickened us together with Christ, (by grace ye are saved;)
> And hath raised us up together, and made us sit together in heavenly places in Christ Jesus (Verses 4–6).

"Us," "us," always "us"—a priest who invokes a benediction upon himself as well as his people. That is brotherhood, that is holy masonry. "God, who is rich in mercy"—not rich in thunderbolts only, not rich in lightnings and tempest and great whirlwinds. Mercy is the greater part of Him; if we could but see it, His wrath is sometimes an aspect of His mercy; He slays the sinner that He may save him; He strips me naked that He may clothe me with a finer linen; He tears my nest to pieces that He may show me how to find a larger and warmer in some tree I had never thought of. "Rich in mercy," so that we may go to Him at all times, and we see Him most when we cannot see Him at all because of the burning tears of our unquenchable grief. Put God's mercy to the test; He can bear a greater pressure still; lean hard, harder, hardest, again; you cannot fatigue Omnipotence. It was "when we were dead in sins" that God showed the richness of His mercy. It was not when we were partly recovering ourselves, it was actually when we were dead in sins, and, being dead, helpless, lost; it was then that the Sun of Righteousness arose with healing in His wings. God makes us now sit in heavenly places; that is, in the unseen kingdom. We trust the naked eye, and therefore miss the grand astronomy. We call our eyes of the body instruments of vision: whereas they are only instruments of deception or misinterpretation. True seeing is of the soul. Every son of man is in heaven while he is on the earth. This is a great mystery, but I speak concerning Christ and His Church. They who go about with a made candle lighted by a made match will sometimes come into passages where the swirling wind will blow the lighted tallow out. What then? Live in the eternal, live in the heavenlies, have a throne spiritual, a crown imperishable, beauteously called a crown of life. O man, why be put a little higher than the brutes when thou mightest be but a little lower than the angels?

> That in the ages to come He might show the exceeding riches of His grace in His kindness toward us through Christ Jesus.
> For by grace are ye saved through faith; and that not of yourselves: it is the gift of God (Verses 7, 8).

Salvation is not by intellect, knowledge; because then heaven would be full, if full at all, of grammarians. I question whether any grammarian can enter the kingdom of heaven. I am now speaking of him in his purely pedantic relationship. He must be more than a grammarian; a grammarian he may be, and a great grammarian, and a grammarian of whom his fellows are justly proud, but in relation to the kingdom of heaven he must be something other, greater, wiser; he must have a faculty within a faculty that can see Jesus Christ as a little child might see Him. If salvation were not as the apostle has placed it here, it would be an intellectual feat, perhaps sometimes degrading itself into an intellectual trick. But it is of grace—"by grace are ye saved through faith." The world never invented these two great words; the world does not understand either of them. "Grace," "faith," that is a foreign tongue. It is! It is heaven's tongue; it is the tongue of the Infinite Love. Grace means favor, pleasure, kindness, pure simple love, appreciation; it is a gift, not a bargain; it has no equivalent; the number stands alone, and the sign of equal-to never follows it. It is above algebra, above grammar.

Not of works, lest any man should boast (Verse 9).

That is the very point. There must be no boasting; we must simply stand out, and say, It is the Lord's doing, and marvelous in our eyes. "Not by works of righteousness which we have done, but according to His mercy hath He saved us, by the washing of regeneration, and the renewing of the Holy Ghost." We have nothing to do with our own making. We had nothing to do with our physical birth, we have nothing to do with our superior or spiritual birth. For the next verse says:

> For we are His workmanship, created in Christ Jesus
> unto good works, which God hath before ordained
> that we should walk in them (Verse 10).

Into what beautiful English might this be rendered! Instead of saying "workmanship" speak the word that is almost Greek in its very form—"we are God's poems." God is the Poet, we are the poems; He makes us now in this measure, now in that measure; now sublime, now more friendly and approachable, but always pregnant with thought and love and music and mercy. Our souls, like our bodies, are all dissimilar, yet each soul is the poem of God. How so, Master, how so? Through Christ Jesus, in Christ Jesus, by the power of Jesus: the mystery of the Cross. Man, if thou knowest not these things in thy soul, and only through some worm-eaten book of man's writing, thou canst not discuss this high theme, thou art not in this great encounter with evil. Thou art an outsider ill-fed, ill-nourished, self-exiled. Come in, and learn the language of the house, the home!

Prayer

Almighty God, we are killed by the letter of Thy law. We cannot accept it; our souls loathe this strange meat. Thou knowest our frame, Thou rememberest that we are dust; we are self-regarding children. The words of Thy law are hard for us to listen to: the law came by Moses, but grace and truth came by Jesus Christ. What the law could not do, in that it was weak, Christ did by grace accomplish. We are saved by grace, by faith; not of works, lest any man should boast. Yet we bless Thee for Thy law, for all its terribleness and severity and impossibility; it is Thy law, it is the law of righteousness and integrity, and behold we stand before it amazed, and say, Lord, help us: who can reach this great height? Who can do these wondrous things? Who can keep back his hand or his heart from evil? We have done the things we ought not to have done, we have left undone Thy law; we have heard Thee say, Thou shalt not, and we have gone and done it with both hands greedily and earnestly and wantonly. Hear our poor soul as it cries to Thee from a depth of self-accusation, saying, God be merciful unto me a sinner! Open Thou our eyes, that we may behold wondrous things out of Thy law; open Thou our understanding, that we may understand the Scripture; may these words of Thy law be no longer to us as pieces of rock, hard stones which we cannot break, but stones covered with fruit, of which if a man eat plentifully he shall hunger no more. We will bring Thy law to Thy Cross, we will ask Thee to help us by Thy love to do Thy law; then we shall know the meaning of the wondrous words, My yoke is easy, my burden is light. Amen.

20
Spirit and Letter

Preached on Thursday Morning, November 9th, 1899.

The letter killeth, but the spirit giveth life—2 Corinthians 3:6.

This is always so, in all life, in all business, and the whole evolution of the human story. It is important to notice this, because we think that so many things are in the Bible and in the Bible only. We are apt to imagine that many things would have no effect if they were not named in the Bible, whereas you will find that the Bible gathers up and vividly expresses all that is most common and all that is most profound in human life. Just as many people think that the Revelation of John the Divine or the Apocalypse is a most wonderful book, that never was heard of until John wrote it; that is how many people blunder over the interpretation of the Apocalypse. Why, the Revelation of John the Divine is just all the former part of the Bible over again; there is not a word in the Revelation of John the Divine that has perplexed all the commentators through all the ages that they ought not to have known before they came to the Revelation at all. But we *will* begin at the wrong point. Some people read Revelation first, it has a fatal fascination for them: hence all these nonsensical calculations and forecasts which help to while the time away. If they would only begin at the Book of Genesis—but you cannot get them to do that, they do not like such commonplace and routine reading—and steadily plow their way through, they would find that the Revelation of John the Divine was the only way of ending the great record. But if the world were not unutterably and all but incurably stupid, where would the preachers be?

"The letter killeth"—in all things. In merchandise, in the statute book, in the family, in reading, in literature, the letter killeth; no man can live on cast iron: but the spirit giveth life—the poetry, the meaning, the purpose, the inmost intent and content; there you have immortality. Let us see how far this can be simplified, and especially how far it can be applied; because if we could get into the music of this text we should all be living Christians, ecstatic saints, glorious forerunners of the coming Lord.

We may have the right letters, but the wrong word. There is absolutely nothing in the letters except under certain conditions, and these conditions we are prone to overlook or to undervalue. Everything depends upon the letters being brought into the right relation. Every letter must not only be in the right place, but it must be uttered singly and collectively in the right tone. If people understood this the whole world, in the event of its being practically applied to conduct, would be full of light, full of music; we should realize a new brotherhood, we should be almost in heaven. We may deliver the right words in a wrong tone. The soul gives the tone. The printer's press gives you the letters at so much a box or a case; it is the tone that vivifies, it is the tone that has in it welcome and summer and resurrection, the *Come forth!* that startles the grave into surrender and bows it down in conscious and pitiable humiliation. We all know how almost impossible it is to deliver a message. Yet the messenger can prove that he said the very words he was told to say. We must allow that the messenger delivered the very words, the *ipsissima verba,* not one word missed; and yet the message was not delivered. "The letter killeth." The letter mispronounced, misconceived, the letter with a false emphasis, the letter with a false color, kills the original meaning of the speaker who sent the message. Hence you cannot report a speech, you cannot report a sermon; that is to say, you may give all the words and miss the emphasis. But where would Christian controversy be if we had not a very marked genius for putting the emphasis on the wrong word? That is how we live. The speaker who assails you quotes it may be in some rare cases your very words, but imports his own tone into them, and tells a lie without meaning it—in some cases. It is not enough to know the letter, we must know the spirit; it is not enough to deliver the message, we must deliver it in the spirit of the man who gave it. We could so pronounce some sentences in the Bible as to blaspheme God. I have heard a man so deliver this word that I have screamed as it were with laughter and sense of comedy, and that word was none other than this, "Come unto Me, all ye that labor and are heavy laden, and I will give you rest." But the sweet message was torn to pieces, delivered without any sympathy, shouted, screamed, and the whole tone was such an anti-climax to the spirit of the words that they could excite no other sense than that of piteous comedy. Yet the words were the very words of the Bible, but torn, shattered, without soul, without tenderness, without hospitality; and no man should crack a horsewhip over such music as that most beautiful of the welcomes of Christ. We may therefore, I repeat, deliver the right words, in the right order, but in the wrong tone; and may preach the Evangelical Gospel without the Evangelical spirit: and a morning without dew is like a morning without a blessing.

Secondly. We may be correct in our letters and utterly wrong in our words. Can a man be both right and wrong at the same time? Certainly; that is what we are doing all the day. We must psychologically understand this if we would recover ourselves from the disease of heart-folly. Observe what the proposition is: We may have the right letters, and yet have the wrong word. The letter is nothing, the letter is confusing; the letter needs companionship, atmosphere, historical relationship, and, above all, a penetrating and uplifting, a redeeming and sanctifying spirit. Let us grope our way into the meaning of this strange paradox, that we may have the right letters and yet the wrong word; the right letters, and yet the wrong sermon; the right letters, and a doctrine degraded from a revelation to a profanity. Here are six letters; R, H, E, T, M, O. What does that mean? "You must have given us the wrong letters," you say, in reply, and I answer, No, I have given you the right letters, and just the right number of letters; I could swear it. There is no mistake at all about this; these are the letters, and I leave them with you. Now you put on your consideration cap, and tell me what you can do with R, H, E, T, M, O. "Are you sure that you have got the right letters?" Certainly! Ask another man, Are these the right letters which this first man has given to me? "Yes; I did not hear them exactly as you heard them, but I know these are the exact letters; I thought they ran like this—H, E, R, M, O, T." Are you sure these are the right letters? "Perfectly sure." "I can make nothing of them, but you may depend upon it," is the response, "they are the right letters." Will some third man help me? Two persons have been to my house today, and they have delivered these letters; the one said R, H, E, T, M, O; the other said, H, E, R, M, O, T. Can you read me this riddle? The third man looks at the letters; in a moment his face is alight with an expository smile. He answers, "The letters are perfectly right, but they are in the wrong order; what both the men wanted to convey to you was this word M O T H E R." "What! 'Mother'?" "Yes!" I never imagined that Mother, even as a word, could be so basely treated. They gave me the exact letters, and the exact number of the letters, but they were as men who babbled nonsense to me; but now you have come with some insight into the meaning, and you tell me that the order should have been MOTHER. I welcome the word; "the letter killeth," there is nothing in it; but the spirit, the right order, the music is Mother. That is just how the Bible is often read. The people reading it may have the right letters and the wrong meaning. They can only see that the letters are right; beyond that they can see nothing, and they stupidly and stubbornly insist that they have given the right letters, and they have founded denominations upon them. They cannot run the letters into music, they cannot set the letters in their intended consecutiveness, and therefore though they may have the Bible words they have no Biblical doctrine, they have little detached letters broken up into all sorts of relationships, but spelling nothing. Open Thou our eyes that we may behold wondrous things out of Thy law; open Thou our understanding that we may understand the Scriptures; send some Philip to us who will leap upon our chariot and read the words to us as they ought to be read; then shall we find a summer in the wilderness and great fatness in the desert of rocks. The prosaic shepherd, a man who had so much a day for doing it, could drive the flocks around the foot of Horeb and see nothing: Moses saw the tabernacle of God, the burning bush was to him more than fire; within that unexpected place there must be something—what is it? The other man saw the flame, but heard no voice, saw an instance of spontaneous combustion as he imagined it to be, but saw no shekinah, no temple-flame, no robe of deity. These two men shall read the Bible, each of them shall give the exact words of Scripture; to the one man the revelation shall be a series of inconsistencies and contradictions; to the other man it shall be as it were the very living, warm, balmy breath of God.

There is a very singular word, which requires to be approached with some cautious introduction, but which very strikingly exhibits what is intended to be conveyed by these references. Printers have a word called *pye*. The case of letters has been set up, all is in readiness to be transferred to its proper place, but in transferring the case to the press an accident occurs, and all the letters become confused, so that the first letter is the last of the paragraph, and the middle line is the first, and three or four lines displace one another, and then you have some very, very perplexing reading. But you have all the letters, the same as you have in your little denominational box that you would die for, if you could not help it; and the letters are the right letters, and just the number of letters, and yet no man in the civilized world can read the result. That is what is meant by not having the meaning in the letter. The letter is nothing. You must have the letter, the right letter, the right letter in the right place and in the right relation before you can get at the right meaning: and it is the meaning we live in, not the confusion of the letters. We may obey and disobey at the same time. That is very remarkable; it would be more remarkable still if it were not absolutely true. "The letter killeth." We do the letter, but we do not obey the spirit. You can shut a door, and offend everybody in the house by doing it. A child may be requested by the father to shut a door, and he can so shut the door as to carry his father away into contempt and oblivion. He obeyed? He did, he did not: "The letter killeth, the spirit giveth life." The child could have shut the door so benignly and heartily as to give his father pleasure; he did carry out the letter of the father's request, but in doing so, in his spirit and meaning, he disobeyed his father. We know what this means in relation to work, to the common work of the common day. A workman may not do the work in the spirit, and therefore it is poorly or badly done. If a man shall take no pleasure in his work he cannot do it, except in a perfunctory and utterly unsatisfactory manner. It is this dislike of work that is killing England and losing England all her battles. Men who do the work only in the letter are liars and thieves and anything but patriots. When the right estimate of labor goes down, the country goes down. When men go to their work at the rate of three miles an hour and leave it at the rate of seven, they are not patriots, and they ought not to win any battles; the God of order is against them, the spirit of the spring condemns their action and dismisses them from all holy and responsible relations. And this holds good in the pulpit and out of it. Unless a man really love his work and long for it, he cannot do it. We cannot live on painted fire. No man can continue the holy ministry of the Cross for a lifetime and have as much joy in it at the end as at the beginning, except in the spirit of the Cross that he preaches; then he will be eternally young—an amaranth that no snow can chill into death. This holds good, therefore, in all sections, departments, and relations of life. The young man in the Gospel had kept all the commandments from his youth up; having heard the decalogue from a lower slope than Sinai, and yet from an infinitely higher height, namely, from the lips of Jesus Christ Himself, the young man said, All these have I kept from my youth up, I have been doing nothing else in life. Jesus said unto him, One thing thou lackest. What is that one thing? The spirit. It is the spirit that giveth life. In a certain technical and mechanical sense you may have been keeping all the ten commandments from your youth up, but one thing is lacking--the all-transfusing and uniting spirit, that turns a burden into a delight, a duty into a song.

If we could receive these instructions we should have fewer Bible-readers, but better; we should know that the letter killeth, but that grace and truth give life and hope and music to the soul. Blessed be God, there are some people who get at the spirit of the commandments before they get at the letter. There are some poor stumbling readers that could not read the grammar, the literal code, Mosaic or other, but yet who by the power of the mighty Spirit see the meaning, and are away doing the commandments without hardly knowing the critical meaning of the code. There is hope for us all; salvation is not of grammar, salvation comes of the spirit: "Marvel not that I say unto you, Ye must be born again." We must have a spiritual perception of the letter; then it will become spiritual and beautiful and the delight of our lives. Oh, how the Spirit enables me by such words to cut down the pride of men, how it is teaching me on this memorable morning to lay the ax at the root of the tree! We must get rid of the literalists, the men who only read the iron letter, and do not read the Bible in the Bible's own atmosphere. What do we want? I will tell you: the Holy Ghost; he only can read the book which he only wrote; we must become acquainted with the Author before we can read his writings with deep spiritual, lasting advantage. If any man lack wisdom, let him ask of God. If ye then being evil know how to give good gifts unto your children, how much more shall your heavenly Father give the Holy Spirit to them that ask Him? It is expedient for you that I go away; when I go away I will send unto you another Paraclete, the abiding Comforter; he shall not speak of himself, he shall take of the things that are mine, and show them unto you. We must get our dear mothers, the daughters of trouble, who have been bathed in rivers of misery, to read us the Bible. The Bible is not an academical book. The academician has his place, and the wisest academician will be the first to define his place as very narrow, very limited. We must bring in the sons and daughters of a deep, genuine, long experience, and they will bid us sit down beside them while they take the holy book and read it to us; there will be tears in their tones, there will be music in their cadence, there will be meaning in every vocal punctuation; every pause will have its high significance; and we shall say when these readers whose faces are marred with sorrow have finished their reading, It was never so heard in Israel! Never man spoke like this man. Our iron taskmasters pointed to the letters, showed us nothing beyond the cold iron type; we were obliged to say, Yes, that is the letter; but in our souls there was a great hunger, and when the experienced motherly, fatherly, brotherly reader came along, we said, Read this to us; we can read the letter, but it is like knocking at a door and nobody opens from within. Then the Philips, the prophets, the apostles, the great readers of the great word, who have been schooled in sorrow and refined in heaven, shall give us the self-same words, but with such a wondrously different meaning. Jesus, come to me, and read me all Thine own sayings; let me hear them in the drip and the plash of Thine own vocal music; and I will know that Thou art the Savior of the world!

Prayer

Almighty God, Thou hast cared for us with all the care of love. Thou hast saved us by the shedding of blood. We have peace with Thee only through our Lord Jesus Christ, by Whom we have received the Atonement. We do not know the meaning of the words we use in all their depth, and tenderness, and mystery; yet we must use these very words, for they fit our heart's necessity. We need them all; they are music without which we could not live. While we were yet sinners Christ died for us; all we like sheep have gone astray, we have turned every one to his own way; but Jesus Christ Thy Son has carried the iniquities of us all. He brings with Him the eternal glory and the eternal love; where sin abounds grace doth much more abound. Who can measure the Christ? Each cries after another, oh the depth, the height, the breadth! Who can measure the infinity of God's loving heart? We stand in Thy love, and there we have security, and song, and light, and hope. May we not hew unto ourselves cisterns, broken cisterns, that can hold no water; may we ever come to Thee, the fountain and living stream, and there be refreshed and purified. Surely we are not worthy of all this condescension and all this love, expressing itself through sacrificial blood; we are filled with self-contempt, yet we remember that we are made in the image and likeness of God, that though fallen, we belong to the family redeemed. Enable us, we humbly pray Thee, to remember these things, lest we accuse ourselves beyond all hope, and fret ourselves by our self-helplessness. Our help is not in ourselves, it is in the living God. We have told lies unto ourselves, and we have reaped the black harvest of the sowing; but now we know that there is no help in man, that the true help is in the eternal, in the infinite, in God. These mysteries are beyond us, but so are the blue heavens, yet out of those heavens we receive morning, and summer, and golden harvest. The Lord deliver us from our own little reason and reasoning, for we were not born to live our days in such iron cage. Enable us to stretch out the wings of faith and hope and a holy and imperishable confidence, and dare the spaces of the firmament.

The Lord hear us evermore, hear us while we tremble and pray and wait at the Cross. Amen.

21

A Watered Garden

Preached on Sunday Morning, October 15th, 1899.

A watered garden–Isaiah 58:11.

In another discourse we have spoken about a garden that had no water. We see the other side of the picture in this most musical text, "watered garden." "The Lord shall guide thee continually, and satisfy they soul in drought, and make fat thy bones; and thou shalt be like a watered garden, and like a spring of water, whose waters fail not." Only God could have spoken such a promise; there is in it spring and summer and autumn; it is like the voice of many waters; it is in infinite and ineffable comfort. How wonderfully cared for are some people, and have always been from their very first breath in this cold earth climate! They have been reared amidst a multitude of attention; they have been considered, watched, fed, nourished, cultivated, enriched. How different have some lives been! Yet perhaps there is not a life which has not its own little song or its own glint of sunshine. We have all seen little children in out-of-the-way places singing, dancing, playing at their mirthful games, and we have wondered that they could so express themselves considering their surroundings. But life is greater than environment, and no slum or alley is big enough for an immortal soul. What comforts some lives have had!–too many sometimes. They would have been stronger lives if they had had fewer luxuries; but every want has been anticipated, every outlook has been answered, as if it were an expectation directed towards heaven itself. Such people have had beautiful nurseries, silver cradles, toys, pictures, festivals, entertainments, companionships. It is sometimes very hard to begin at that end of life. Other men have been like watered gardens; not gardens only, but gardens that had within them their own fountains; hence they have had flowers all the year round, they have traveled with the strawberries, they have gone step for step with violets; or in this form, or in that form, or in some other form, there has always been near them the plash of fountains, the fragrance of flowers, the ripple of music. They do not know what life is; they have had no brown bread yet, they have never walked on the shady side of the wall; they are poor companions in many instances, for they cannot speak the mother tongue of misery, and loss, and unutterable sadness; they have been themselves so much like a watered garden, that they begin to doubt whether there is any trouble in the world, or whether, if there be trouble, it be not self-made and easily accounted for, and to be treated punitively rather than sympathetically. Blessed is the man who has walked on both sides of the road, without being overborne with despair on the one side or unduly elated by the sunshine of the other.

"A watered garden." There is too much music in these two words; we could have done with one of them. "A garden"–beautiful; "Watered"–music in itself, but "a watered garden," both things together and both things in our possession, and we ourselves representing that dual wealth. Who can handle a psalm so magnificent, so majestic?

Yet even this text may give us pause, may lead us to the asking of some piercing questions. The further such questions penetrate the soul the better for the soul's health. "A watered garden": cannot a garden water itself? No. That is the answer, definite, cold–discouraging, encouraging, as we may take the term. Is it not enough to be a garden? What matter about the sunshine? Who cares about the rain or the dew? Is it not enough to be a garden, a geometric form, pearled and diamonded with many a flower? The king's gardens cannot do without rain; Solomon's parterres wither away but for the morning dew and the summer shower. We need something from without. We are always reminded that there is no one world; you may write it up and sneer at the other worlds, and enclose yourselves in little square cages in which there is no room for an altar; you can do this; but again and again the Lord of the vineyard cometh to seek fruit, and if we have not supplicated His sunshine and His rain, His morning dew, we shall have no fruit for Him when He comes to visit His own land. Is it not enough to be a garden? Not without water, not without culture; the Lord Himself made a garden and also made a man to take care of it. Never rest satisfied with your garden; be thankful you have one, and enjoy it, but remember that it belongs to the acreage of the universe; it is not self-enclosed in any sense that shuts off the rest of God's creation, it is part of a greater garden, and there is a common baptism, a universal rain, a gracious benediction of dew and storm. Does a bust need feeding? No: but your child does. It is greater to be the least child than to be the greatest bust or statue set on marble or pedestalled on bronze. You do not invite the bust to come and partake of your morning feast or your evening meal; you smile at the idea of asking that marble face to sit down at your table; but, looking round the table you say, Are we all here? There is one little creature absent. No matter, the little creature is standing beside the bust, and they are talking together, and they have no need of food. That will not satisfy you. But it satisfies you in religion! What you contemn at the trough, condemn as an impossibility, you applaud at the altar, and you cast contempt upon the sanctuary. O fools, fools, sad, unpardonable, hopeless; men who are wise in a pantheon of marble are fools when they deny their need of the rain of heaven and the dew that drops from the eyelids of the morn.

Cannot a man sustain himself by his own resources? He cannot. If any man has tried to do so he will be the loudest in his confirmation of my reply. We soon exhaust ourselves, we want the other man, the other hand to touch, the other eyes to look into, the other voice to fill the dull vacancy of our solitude. Is it not enough to be a man? What do you mean by being a man? A figure is not a man, a corpse is not a man; a mere personality, if it could be detached from all other personalities, would not be a man. We cannot live upon stature or figure or anything that our hand can hold. Life is deeper; there is a sanctuary of life, a well far away, where spring water bubbles and gurgles and flashes out in the sunlight like a great gospel preached to the thirst of man. You think you can do with your own resources; let us test your foolish argument for one moment, if we may dignify it by the name of argument.

Self-sustenance is not the law of the body; why should it be the law of the mind? Let us reason from the lower to the higher. Every day every man has to go out of himself to keep himself going. If he would study that simple philosophy, he would soon begin to pray. But he will not: he is led captive by Satan at his will. Who can believe that the body not living upon its own resources proves to the soul that it has resources enough within itself? What a haze of words, what a palpable irony, what an evident lie! If men were as wise about their souls as they are about their bodies, the throne of religion would be established amid the nations of the earth, and the whole life of men would be an expectation, which is the next best word to a prayer. My expectation is from the heavens, my help from the hills; not the little hills, but the great hills unseen which we can sometimes almost see through the webwork of the clouds. But the mind is not sustained by itself. You have books; lay them down, be your own book. You cannot. You need some other man to write you a book, and sometimes to explain it to you. You have libraries. What are libraries but wheatfields for the mind? If I ask you in the autumn, "What do you want with all these golden growths, all these purple riches and vegetable and fruit?" you say, "We require all these things for the sustenance of the body." And what do you want with all these libraries, and museums, and academies, and colleges, and schools of every name and degree? These are the wheatfields which the soul reaps, and it needs them every one, for the soul is bigger than literature. That is all I want you to admit; that admission carries with it everything that is relevant to the spiritual argument. You want something outside yourself–a book you have not written, a study you have not explored. And the soul lives by friction with some other soul. God is fire. To come into happy attrition with Him, or contact, or friction, who can tell what may come out of that soul touching soul, man praying to God? Prayer is a kind of friction if truly wise and honest, and out of that friction come sparks to lighten the night and put out the common sun.

We are continually undergoing a process of education. There is an unshaped and unpaid education going on constantly in the world. We are gathering from one another; by one another we are helped, assisted, stimulated, and inspired. There is a common life as well as an individual life. The brick that is in the wall is more than a brick; it is part of the wall. It is not a brick, it is a brick in relation; it helps to complete the massiveness, or to illustrate the beauty of the architectural idea. So a little human soul is not detached, and orphaned, and isolated; it is part of a greater soul, a grander socialism, a diviner commonwealth. If you had to live upon your own bodily resources, I question whether after six months you would be visible to the naked eye; if you have been living upon your spiritual and intellectual resources, you will be invisible to the highest telescopes known in all the universe. A man's soul needs refreshment as well as his body. There are men who starve their souls, feed their bodies, and rot into oblivion.

What hast thou that thou hast not received? The reception is itself a kind of religion. To receive gratefully and appreciatively is almost to pray, or sing a holy psalm, or offer a sacred, sacrifice. What hast thou that thou hast not received?–thou who didst ask but a moment ago whether it were not enough to be a garden without being dependent on morning dew, or dew of the twilight, or rain of the black cloud. What hast thou that thou hast not received? We take every man from every other man something for the common sustenance and for the common completeness. The book you read gave you an idea; the song you heard lifted your soul to another level, if but for a moment, just long enough to show you that there are higher levels than you have yet attained. Who can tell what ministries are playing upon him? You say, Pay for an idea? Certainly; in fact, there is nothing else to pay for, and the only man you do not sufficiently pay is the man of ideas. An idea is light, liberty, inspiration, encouragement. You have shaped the iron, and have labeled it in plain figures; but the shaping of it was the carrying out of an idea. That poor piece of iron or large piece, as we call large—though there is really nothing large—that piece of iron has been melted, hammered, shaped at some other man's bidding. Behind the blacksmith is a mental goldsmith, who says, Not so, but thus; and the distinction between the so and the thus is an idea. We only pay for merchandise because we are hardly yet out of the brute stage. By-and-by it will be realized that the only man worth giving to is the man who says, Blessed are the pure in heart, for they shall see God; blessed are the merciful, for they shall obtain mercy. Let not your heart be troubled, ye believe in God, believe also in me. The feeder of the soul will be welcomed one day as the only true philanthropist.

What care God has taken of every one of us; what rains He has poured on the earth; what sunshines has He poured upon the whole globe! The lines have fallen unto us in pleasant places, we have a goodly heritage. We did not make the libraries, and if we sowed the seed it was seed we caught from some other harvest. The whole evolution of life is a continuity—vital, sensitive, marvelous in its power of self-enlargement, which is but another form of enlargement in God.

As we do not leave a garden to take care of itself, neither should we leave ourselves to ourselves. How foolish is the man who says, I leave my children to bring themselves up, to do very much in life as they please; I let them have their own undisciplined way; no superintendence over them is exercised or thought of. If you will do the same with your garden you will be a consistent man, you bestow less attention on a child than you bestow upon a dog; for I have heard you order him to his kennel and bid him be silent. If you will leave your garden to itself as you say you leave your little child, then I shall see what will become of the child, after I have studied the issue of your policy in the garden. Have you ever seen a garden that has been left to itself? What do you think of it? It has never been pierced by the spade, it has never had any growth pruned, its hedge has never felt the cut of a knife, there has been no renewal from season to season of the roots and bulbs and seed: shall I go with you and look at that garden? I would, but I should be compelled to take it as a text and to preach to you and ask if that is the kind of way which you have treated your own soul, without discipline, without study, without literature, without intellectual sustenance, without that kind of intercourse which means friction, and which means after friction and with friction light.

God waits to give us everyone more water, more sustenance, more sunshine. What we might be if we would enjoy our privileges! Into what great distance we might have entered the sanctuary if we had really cared to be at the upper and inner altar that we might be blessed by its sacrifices! Oh that thou hadst hearkened unto me! then had thy peace flowed as a river and thy righteousness had been as the waves of the sea. A branch cannot bear fruit except it abide in the vine, and the Vine is Christ, and except we be in Christ our souls cannot receive the true culture or the true nourishment. We draw our heart's blood from Him, we live in Christ; and he lives nearest the heavenlies and nearest the conscious immortality who lives most and most deeply in the Lord. Blessed are they who have Jesus Christ as their bread and their water, and they will have bread to eat that the world knows not of; they will be mysteries to men; people will be unable to understand them in common ways or to express them in common symbols and quantities. The Christian ought to be as Christ in his own little degree—a mystery to the world. How he lives who can tell? None.

Prayer

Almighty God, grant us the seeing eye and the understanding heart and the obedient will. To this end do Thou grant us a plenteous pouring out of the Holy Spirit into the soul of man. God is a Spirit; the spiritual alone can discern spiritual things. Grant unto us, we humbly pray Thee, the spiritual faculty; teach us that morality is the guarantee of vision; teach us by Thy Spirit that it is character that sees not genius. Blessed are the pure in heart: for they shall see God. Would that all the Lord's people were seers! We should have less unrest and godless disquiet and tribulations and mutual distrust. May we see beyond the wall, may we see beyond the cloud, may we see the meaning of things; teach us that all this embroidery and robing and garniture of stars and constellations and blue heavens and the great earth and the throbbing sea, that all this is but part of an infinite parable. Help us to read the symbolism, to be true idealists, to enter by the spirit into the temple of the spiritual. We are now in the earth sphere, in the time space—a poor sphere, a poor space! We are surrounded by dilapidations, we are convulsed by needless terrors: oh that by Christ, who gave sight to the blind, we might see the permanent within the transient, the real beyond the parabolical! The Lord help us herein by the power of the Cross of Christ, else we shall assuredly be the victims of ignorance and superstition. Amen.

22
Seer and Prophet

Preached on Thursday Morning, October 19th, 1899.

He that is now called a Prophet was beforetime called a Seer
—1 Samuel 9:9.

So long as they both meant the same thing, what does it matter what they were called? If they did not always mean the same thing, then it signifies a great deal. We must not have old names with new meanings, nor must we invent new ideas to suit old terms. The parable of the old wine and the new bottles, the old bottles and the new wine, old ideas and new conceptions, affords a very tempting ground for fancy and invention and diverse knavery. When we have a word, let us know exactly what its meaning is. When we change the word, publish the fact; do not let us have any vocal or verbal legerdemain; let us beware of trifling with terms, let us beware of meddling with the currency of the King's language.

"He that is now called a Prophet was beforetime called a Seer." Probably there was really no change of a vital kind, and therefore the change of terms resolved itself into the popular question, What's in a name? But there is a principle here; there is a great moral possibility just at this very point; let us have no verbal ambiguity or ambiguity in deed, and then tell others that we really meant in substance the same thing, when we did not. There is a morality of language, there is a currency of words; and we must not keep some little private mint in which we counterfeit the inscribed and superscribed glory of the heavenly realm. Let us apply this change of names to the circumstances in which we find ourselves in our own day.

First, that which is now called a Discovery was beforetime called a Revelation. I prefer the beforetime word; it is deeper, it holds more, it is intellectually and spiritually more capacious; it is ideally and imaginatively more poetical and ideal. We speak now of discoveries; the old, old people that read human history spoke of revelations, visions: "The word of the Lord came unto me." I like the older language; it is more religious, more spiritual, more morally sensitive and tender. When a man says, "I have discovered," he may possibly put himself in a false position. When he says, "It has been revealed to me," he at once takes his right place in creation, and what is more, he gives God His right place in His own universe. We speak of So-and-so as a great discoverer. He who is called a discoverer was beforetime called a receiver; and it is better: what hast thou that thou hast not received? And does science lose anything by coming to us with her austere face in which some tenderness is hidden, notwithstanding the severity of the facial line, when she says, I have been communing with the Lord, and He has turned over a page for me, and I will tell you what I have read on the new page? Science would lose nothing by such modesty; she would gain much; she would challenge a larger area of human confidence; she would kneel with Ignorance, and taking the hard horny hand of Ignorance in her white soft palm, they would both say together, Our Father which art in heaven. It would be better.

He that is now called an Agnostic was beforetime called a Blind Man. I prefer the beforetime description; it seems to get nearer the truth. It would be impossible, I think, to find a proud blind man. Did you ever in all your companionship and confidences find a proud blind fellow creature? It would be difficult for a blind man to be proud, but it is the natural air of my lord the agnostic. You never found a humble agnostic; he could not be humble; he has eloquence enough to pretend to be humble, but in the soul of him, if he has a soul, he is as proud as Lucifer. He wants to get rid of sundry moral obligations. Besides, I think it is a fine thing to have a Greek name as well as an English one; there is a classical flavor about it to those who do not know better. A dear, sweet friend wrote to me three or four names beside the name given to her by her father and mother. I said, I do not know you. She said, These are my Roman Catholic names. It seemed to be quite a little fortune to be able to sign so much and almost to cover the breadth of a sheet of notepaper; it seemed to be a long way on towards making and signing a five-pound note. So I replied to her and signed myself Joseph Matthew Mark Luke and John Parker. She took it in good nature and said the hammer had struck the head of the nail.

"He that is now called a Prophet was beforetime called a Seer." So that which is now called an Accident was beforetime called Providence. I like the old term best; it covers more ground, it is nobler, it stands in a more royal majesty. I will not have any accidents in my little world; I have no room for accidents—little broken pieces of china that nobody can patch together again. I have in my little world of imagining and experience a ruling, loving, watchful Providence. We have high talks together; I have learned the language of Providence: Fear not; lo, I am with you alway; not a sparrow falleth to the ground without your Father; the very hairs of your head are all numbered; if God so clothe the grass which today is and tomorrow is cast into the oven, is He going to let you fall to the ground, man—the wreck of his own image, a reminiscence of Eden? And my soul says, No; and we have high revels of joy together on the green hillside when Providence in many a long soft sunny summer afternoon goes over the whole plan with me and says, See those beautiful little graves; they are graves of little ones that have been taken to heaven; and those larger graves, everyone of them is noted in the heavenly books, and every soul that has escaped the time sphere is enrolled in a loftier registry and secured by an inviolable protection. Then Providence teaches me a little hymn that the soul can understand, the music of which is very weird, and can only be safely entrusted to the summer wind, but the singing of it does the soul good like a summer rest. Which will you have—Accident, or Providence; a thing that happened without anyone knowing that it was going to be or for what purpose it came; or will you see in all life God's handiwork, the shaping of the great Creator, Redeemer, Father—this large, that small; the colors intermingled, rainbows in stones, in ideal marbles—which will you have? Man, say, and say distinctly, which, and play the fool no more!

Now, never suppose that a thing is changed simply because the name is changed; it may not be the same, but it may be. Many persons do not understand their own religion, unless they hear it from their own preacher, in their own place of worship—the only place that is sure of the benediction of God; the sun never shines upon nettles; the sun shines only upon broad, fragrant roses. There are people who do not think the Gospel is preached unless it is given out in numbers and in the same order. There are persons who can sing out of only one hymn-book; I do not know them by name, and I have no wish to ascertain what book it is they sing out of. I should like to sing out of all hymn-books. I go to all churches—to Roman Catholic and Protestant, and High Church and Low Church and Broad Church, and I can learn something from everyone of them. Every man sees his own angel of the kingdom of God, and I say to him, Dear sir, would you allow me just to put my feet in your footprints that I may, if possible, catch your view of the kingdom of heaven? The Lord deliver us from narrow-mindedness, from sectarianism, from living in one little cobwebbed corner and looking at God's blue universe through one cobwebbed chapel window.

That which is now called A better state of things was beforetime called Regeneration. And I like it better. Oh for the old, old Regeneration!—the metaphysical, penetrating, all-including new birth. There are many dusters and sweepers in the world, persons who go about with little dusters, and rubbing things and saying, Now they are all right. It is one thing to have a Hyde-Park-Sunday-afternoon-demonstration duster and another thing to have a Holy

Ghost. Between these two things lies an infinite distance; they are separated by the diameter of the universe. If I could speak to all young men in one thunder-breath it would be to the effect, Beware of dusters, sweepers, scavengers; all of which are very useful in their own sphere; some of them are indispensable within their own limitation, but only God, whom we adore and worship as the Holy Ghost, can get at the root and core of things, and create, not new works, but a new worker, and therefore new works. You are giving up all the grand old words; you have now discoveries, instead of Revelation; accidents, instead of Providence; a new state of things, instead of Regeneration. If a minister, however distinguished, were to announce a course of lectures on Justification by Faith, men would be too busy to hear him; they would call it theological, they would regard it as not being up to the times: whereas that doctrine is always up to date, and until you pass through that gate of justification by faith you cannot see the kingdom of God. That kingdom of God is not an intellectual conundrum, it is an internal experience, a communion of the soul with the soul's Creator. Until you become thus vitally theological you will make no progress in your studies of the upper and eternal kingdom.

That which is now called the Continuity of Law was beforetime called the Sovereignty of God. I prefer the latter designation. Man likes new words; man is still infantile, and still fond of amusingly clever mechanical toys. I have not known the human mouth so expressive of sensuous delight and complete torpor-like satisfaction as when it shaped itself into the phrase, the continuity of law. No one knew what it meant, but that was the beauty of it: to have ghosts whose names you know and whose addresses you have marked in your note-books are ghosts not worth knowing. To have a series of words that sound as if they meant something and that yet lay no moral responsibility upon you, that is a Bank Holiday of the soul. Beforetime called the sovereignty of God: The Lord reigneth; clouds and darkness are round about Him, righteousness and judgment are the habitation of His throne; He doeth all things well; He measureth out the heavens with a span, He spreadeth them out like a curtain to dwell in; and as for the stars, a million million host of stars, He calleth them all by name, and that He is great in power not one faileth, Arcturus and Pleiades and the whole mystery of the Milky Way, and the paths of the fire-flash, and the channels of the thunder, and the foundations of the unseen; all these are under His governance and continual and beneficient supervision. I therefore found the continuity of law very poor picking when my soul was in unutterable distress. I never invited the continuity of law to come and spend an evening with me when all the stars shrank from the vision of my sorrow; but I did invite the living Lord, the sovereign Father, the Father-Mother-Sister of all the worlds, to come and stanch the wound and dry the flood of tears. And He came. Never did morning break so brightly over the hills as morning broke after our night's conference in black Gethsemane. Do not expect me, therefore, to give up the old words. I cannot now undertake to invent a new gospel. These fifty years and more I have been preaching, by the grace of God and the comfort of His Spirit, the Gospel of our Lord Jesus Christ, the only Savior of the world, and that which beforetime was called the Gospel I cannot now have called a new idea, a novel theory, an invention which the inventor wishes everybody to try at their own expense. There are many inventors sitting round, seeing how you like the new invention; they would not drink the poison themselves, they wanted to practice upon some vile corpus, some poor body that was in search of a new poison. So I, standing here, after these thirty years of City life, standing in the very midst of London, in the midst of the week, and in the middle of the day, I am still enabled by the grace of Christ to preach the old, old Gospel, and to say with my heart what I love to hear children sing, "The old-time Gospel is good enough for me."

Do not, therefore, let us be victimized by phrases; do let us allow some scope for individuality of experience. The Lord hath been pleased to set diverse officers in His Church; He has made some prophets, and some pastors, some evangelists and teachers, and He has made some men mighty in prayer, and to me He has given the keys of invisible kingdoms and empires yet unmeasured. Let us recognize all the grades of the hierarchy, and let every man understand that whatever he holds he holds as Christ's trustee.

That which is now called the Survival of the Fittest was before-time called Predestination, election, foreordination: and these are the grand terms when properly defined and understood. I believe in destiny, I believe that every man comes into the world with a distinct gift, with an individuality all his own, and that it is his business so to work his individuality as to increase the common stock of intelligence and goodness and usefulness. I cannot understand how it is that things are now going, apart from the doctrine of pre-destination, foreordination, special election to office and special endowment of faculty. Here is a man sent into the world with a harp; I, listening to his harp, think I could do as well. The only revenge the harper wants is to let me try. He is a quiet man the harper, his soul is too large to be easily fretted; so he allows me to sit on his stool and to finger his harp, and leaves me to pronounce the verdict; and I never mention the fact to a single human creature when I have got out of his presence. But I have a harp of my own. What is that harp, O thou poor man? It is a harp whose name you know, and it is God's harp, God's invention, and a most useful, beautiful harp it is. What do you think the name of my harp is? It is a word of one syllable, only a word or two more than the name of the instrument which emits such thrilling music. He has a harp, I have a plow, and we are both singing the same tune, worshiping the same Creator, accepting a common stewardship. The plow when profitably and properly applied is an instrument of music. Do not take a low view of it. So is your task, whatever it be; so your ministry, your lowly occupation. Accept what is given as given by the loving hand of God, and under His grace and Spirit. Man, do the best with it, stand up and renew the fight! He that endureth to the end shall be saved.

Prayer

Almighty God, we bless Thee that we see through the letter into the spirit and meaning of Thy kingdom, and that we understand those who struggle to express that which is inexpressible. We thank Thee that things are unspeakable, we bless Thee for Thine unspeakable Gift; we bless Thee for those things that are immeasurable, so that we cannot ascertain their length and breadth and depth and height; we thank Thee for those things that pass knowledge; herein we become truly spiritual, intensely religious, transferring our life into the very spirit and love of God. These are the mysteries of the faith, these are the joys that shine upon us while we tarry in the temple of God. Lift us out of our narrow surroundings, and show us, we humbly pray Thee, the true and foreordained environment of the soul. May we remember that we are but dust as to the body, but of the nature of God as to the spirit; if we sow to the flesh we shall reap of the flesh corruption; if we sow to the spirit we shall reap life everlasting. To be carnally minded is death, to be spiritually minded is life and peace. May our life be hidden with Christ in God, may we have an inner life, a city of the mind, a sanctuary of the soul; may we have bread to eat that the world knoweth not of, and that no harvest-field of time ever grew amid all its golden grain. Feed us with Thyself, nourish us with Thine own grace, and bring us to the measure of the stature of perfect men in Christ Jesus. In His mighty name we pray, in His great grace we travel through the wilderness and make it blossom as the rose, and in His faith, the faith in God which is by Christ, we look into the grave until it smiles in flowers. Amen.

23
Ephesians 4:14–23

Preached on Thursday Morning, November 16th, 1899.

We are reading in Paul's Epistle to the Ephesians. It is more like walking through a forest than dallying in a garden. We must in many a case give up his grammar and acquaint ourselves with the music of his soul. Paul did not write much; when he did write he wrote as a blind man might be supposed to write, in large capital letters, saying, "Ye see how large a letter I have written unto you with mine own hand." Poor weak-eyed man, he could hardly see the boldest capitals which he inscribed upon his paper; and as a tired man he thought he had done more than he really had done; he thought it was a large letter because it took so much out of him. There are many standards of measurement.

This Epistle to the Ephesians must be true in its divinity because it is so palpably (and shall I say glaringly?) true in its humanity. Where the one thing which we can test is so true, the probability is that that which is beyond the present metaphysic, that which is spiritual and transcendental, is also true. What a grasp of human nature the Apostle always had! He seemed to lay a great grip upon us and explain us to ourselves. We are not dealing with a posture-master, nor are we in commerce with a man who gives small rules in etiquette and superficial interpretations in religious ceremony; we feel a great grip on the soul, and a man telling us through the ear of the body into the ear of the spirit what we are by nature, by conduct, under whose dominion we live; and we confirm his testimony, saying, with great tearful, terrible amen. It is as thou hast spoken. What a delight it is to have confidence in the teacher! How exceedingly disquieting it is to walk through perilous places with a man who is himself afraid! His fear doubles the peril. If we were within the shadow of a great strong man, within hearing of a man who could speak great sure words to us, we should feel that "well-begun is half-done," we should make a temple of his confidence and rest in it, yea, and sometimes fall to singing as if we were the happier for the danger. It is so we feel when we are in the companionship of the Apostle Paul. His benedictions are inspirations; his instructions are battles; his battles are victories.

We have come to the fourteenth verse of the fourth chapter.

> That we henceforth be no more children, tossed
> to and fro, and carried about with every wind of
> doctrine, by the sleight of men, and cunning crafti-
> ness, whereby they lie in wait to deceive.

Yet we must always be children. Children are so good that we baptize them; we receive them into our arms with this certificate, written in light and perfumed in the incense of the morning, "Of such is the kingdom of God," and we baptize them with the dew of the morning. Yet we must in another sense no longer be children, we must not tarry in the cradle; he would be a monster, not a man, who at thirty years of age still needed to be rocked to sleep in his cradle. It is in these things that we are not to be children; not in the child-sense, the childlike sense, the little clinging, trustful child-sense; always that; in that sense the heavens are full of cradles. To God we must always be beginning; to the Infinite we must always be little sparklets, mere specks and blossoms of things, holding within us great and solemn possibilities. In another sense we are not to be childish, foolish, receiving instruction and letting it fall out of the mind as soon as it gets into it; in that sense let us be no more children, tossed to and fro, carried about by every wind; that is the children's little game, and for children it is natural and it is pleasant. What is the child going to be? Ask the little creature to tell you on Monday what it is going to be, and the child has a Monday answer; on Tuesday, What are you going to be? Something other than was said on Monday. It is the privilege of little boys to be one thing one day and another another, and seven different things every year: that is natural and beautiful; but there comes a time when all this uncertainty and movableness of mind must end, a decision must be come to, we must make an election or a choice; henceforth we must be men with a definite program, an assured purpose, a worthy scheme of life. The mischief is that some people have no plan of existence; they live from hand to mouth, and generally at other people's expense; most of them have an idea that they could be something very great, which is a certain sign that they will never mount the ladder. The Apostle would have us fix upon a scheme, plan, or thought of life, and keep at it. Persistence is success. If you are seven different things on the seven different days of the week, what can you possibly come to? If a man shall be a lecturer, a politician, an adventurer, a painter, and a preacher, he will be a poor preacher. You cannot be all that and a preacher. A preacher is never thrown in; he is never mixed up under the indefinite designation of an et cetera. That is the reason why I have seen some men fail in the pulpit. They were so much more eager to get up on Monday morning to go to the picture gallery than they were to get up on Sunday morning to go to the pulpit; they deserved to fail. That is why I have seen other men succeed with but moderate talents; they have been faithful to their call, definite and certain in their convictions; patiently and lovingly they have continued at their work; and patient continuance in well-doing means a diadem at the last, a Well-done that is more golden than a golden crown. The Apostle Paul, therefore, insists that there must be a period put to childishness, and he further insists that we must begin with a meaning and work with a purpose and light our way through the wilderness with the lamp of hope.

Look what an image of human nature is given in these words— "alienated from the life of God." The whole of the 18th verse is a great nocturne, it is a picture struck out of a cloud, it is a statue hewn out of sevenfold midnight. "Having the understanding darkened, being alienated from the life of God through the ignorance that is in them." "Alienated from the life of God"–O how shall we represent that isolation, that desolated orphanage? Shall we imagine a tree taking its roots out of the earth and placing itself upon the face of a rock that it may have no more connection with the soil?–for the soil is full of light, the soil is full of dew; though there be no rain on the surface, there is dew at the core. We dig down to dew, and in all the strata through which we dig we are cutting sunshine to pieces; the earth is a store of morning, a gallery piled with sunshine. Shall we imagine the poor tree saying, I will have none of it, I will tear myself out of this place, and instead of seeking to plant myself in another part of the soil I will lay myself down on the rock and turn my roots to the morning sun? It cannot be; for a day or two it may seem as though it were a possibility and even a fact, but only for a day or two; the tree must be rooted in the earth as the earth is rooted in God, where all things grow harmonically, proportionately, sympathetically, and tree waves to tree as hymn might sing to hymn. There is a dread possibility of a man taking himself out of the current of things. The soul that takes itself out of the appointed currents shall die. No institution has a right to set itself outside the law of evolution. Evolution means purpose, scheme, predestination, sovereignty of God, the outworking of a grand beneficent plan; and no man has a right to set himself outside the law, and to let the law roll past him; if so, he does but make himself a nameless, hapless grave. Hence the folly of those persons who are always wanting to build themselves on a narrow interpretation of antiquity. We are thankful that antiquity is a word in the English language, because it has sometimes a kind of soothing and quieting effect upon a given species of mental adolescence and incompleteness. But the true antiquity is today; time has never been so old as it is at this moment; the hoar of the ages rested upon today as it was born into history. Let us, therefore, believe in spiritual evolution; let us get away from the nakedness of sin into the white linen of the saints, the purple and the true luxury of the Divine sonship. Many persons are trying to live without God; they are alienated from the life of God through the ignorance that is in them. They do not know that other people are praying for them, they do not understand the philosophy of intercession. We know not who may be praying for us in the general assembly and Church of the firstborn; but we know that Jesus Christ Himself ever liveth to make intercession for us. It would be like human nature to take favors from God, and to smite the hand that gives them. There may be atheists; I never met one; I have met not a few who have professed atheism; the word was greater than their understanding of it; the little boy who carries his yard of string in his pocket really cannot, however ambitious his intention, fathom the Atlantic.

There is another expression in the 18th verse that is so true—"the blindness of their heart." Do not pity the blind man on the streets with his little dog and his mendicant's little tin; that is not the man to pity; the man to pity may be the man who is pitying him: for the one man has lost only the eyes of the body, the other may be blind in his heart; he does not see moral distinctions, he does not recognize spiritual differences; he takes the right for the wrong, and the right for the left, and he goes up under the impression that he is going down, and he goes down under the impression that he is going up, and he lives in mental and moral confusion. There are moral lunatics; do not go to the lunatic asylum and say concerning the inmates, Poor creatures—how sad to have lost reason and understanding! It is a poor speech; the real lunatic may be outside the asylum. He is a lunatic who does not understand anything of God, truth, light, beauty, goodness. The first shall be last, and the last shall be first. What if we who pity the blind and the unseen should ourselves be blind in heart and darkened in understanding. Fool! I would say to my poor soul sometimes; thou art the blind, thou art the insane, for the King passed and thou didst not see Him; the whole universe is an argument in parable, and thou didst not understand the sun.

In the 19th verse there is an expression more terrible, if possible, than we have yet come upon. "Past feeling." Read the whole verse:

> Who being past feeling have given themselves over unto lasciviousness, to work all uncleanness with greediness.

"Past feeling." Is not he past feeling who for thirty years has heard the Gospel preached with simplicity and pathos and power, and is today a worm of the earth, a groveler in the mud? "Past feeling": the spring comes without being hailed and saluted, and the summer is allowed to pass by without a smile of recognition, and the golden autumn is only regarded as a contribution to the marketplace, and all the jewelry of frost and all the spotless linen of the mountain snow go for nothing, because he who was made in the image and likeness of God has lost sensibility and power of response to all poetic and ideal and spiritual appeals. On some people everything is lost; on some hearts we waste our kindness; on some lives fathers and mothers have thrown themselves away, their generous love being regarded as a commonplace that comes without appreciation or response. It is possible to be overfed religiously; it is possible to hear too much good preaching; it is possible to hear it under the impression that it comes as a mere matter of course; not knowing that every sentence is a blood-drop, every cry of the appealing heart a loss of nervous energy. To preach to people who are "past feeling," that must be solitude and desolation and unutterable misery. Given over, given themselves over to work with greediness all manner of badness—to work with the right hand, with the left hand, and work with both the hands, and love it, and kiss it, and work it over and over again, and roll it under the tongue as a sweet morsel; and then say they have been to church. To hell!

In all this magnificent portrayal of human nature there are top-lights, half-lights, bright lights, gleamings above the brightness of the sun. For example, Paul talks about coming "unto a perfect man." He will not despair at all the rubbish which he has been portraying and pathetically describing; he sees the possibility of growth. A perfect man means a mature man, a full-grown man who has reached the highest inch of his possible stature not a perfect man in any merely sentimental and pietistic sense, but full grown. The orchard is perfect when the apples are ready for plucking; the acres are perfect when the golden grain swings in the gentle breeze, and says without words, I am ready to be cut down and to be turned into bread.

And what a beautiful expression we find in the 15th verse— "speaking the truth in love": truthing it in love, doing everything in love; growing up into Him in all things in love; finding our duty in love. If we lose this power of love we cannot do any duty, we cannot be our best selves. It is motive that gives a man the true self-possession. His mere taste or his mere sense of duty might shrink from certain tasks and efforts. To mere duty the day is so long; to love, the longest day that June can show us is but a flash of light. If we go to church because it is our duty we shall never get there; we may get there in the body, a ton weight of stupidity; but if we go because we have been hungering and thirsting after the holy exercise, we heed nor rain nor snow nor burning sun nor long distance over the city streets; we fly in great expectation and with great warmth and glow of love. It is the same with everything else; with painting, with music, with writing books, with daily drudgery, with household tasks; if we do these things when we do not want to do them we will be burdened and utterly distressed, but if we work in the spirit of love, then let work come, and more and more of it, it does but multiply the acreage of a sunny and gladsome field. And then, in another sense, we are to be filled with a spirit of love that makes increase, love that edifies itself in love, love that doubles itself, love that says to the laborer, I will love you still more; if you will work another hour I will bring to your hands all you want, and we will both do it together. Love building itself up in love—tautology to the grammarian, poetry to the poet.

And how is all this to be done? By being renewed in the spirit of our mind, according to verse 23. "Renewed," that is great; "in the spirit," that is great; "in the spirit of your mind"—O that is getting to a very inward part of the soul, piercing through fold after fold, until the light, the grace of God, gets into the very beginning of manhood and renews it. That is regeneration; not a new notion, a new opinion, a new theory in morals, in theology, in politics, in patriotism; no, but a new man. Many persons are renewed in their opinions who are not renewed in the spirit of their mind. The Word of God is sharper than a two-edged sword, it pierces to the dividing asunder of the joints and marrow, and is a discerner of the thoughts and intents of the heart; and until we are cleansed in there, in that central center, we do not know the meaning of the kingdom of God; and nothing can get in there with cleansing power but one thing—the blood of Jesus Christ. Precious Savior, mighty Savior, send Thy cleansing blood through the innermost currents of my heart, that I may be without spot or wrinkle or taint or stain, holy after the quality of the Divine purity!

Words for Preachers

Common auditors receive not a doctrine in the abstract, only minding what is taught; but in the concrete, with reference to the person that teacheth it. Therefore, if your credit be cracked, it is as bad as if your brains were crazed: you may preach of heaven and hell until doomsday; and the truth will be truth in your mouths, not in their hearts.—*Adams, 1654*

If any people be wiser than to follow the examples of such men; yet the loathsomeness of their lives will make their doctrine the less effectual. Though you know the meat to be good and wholesome, yet it may make a weak stomach rise against it, if the cook or the servant that carrieth it have leprous or dingy hands. Take heed, therefore, to yourselves, if ever you mean to do good to others.—*Baxter, 1615–1691*

A cracked bell is a very harsh sound in every ear; the metal is good enough, and maybe was once well tuned; it is the rift that makes it so unpleasant by jarring. Just thus is a scandalous, ill-lived preacher; his calling is honorable, his noise is heard far enough; but (O, sad but!) the flaw which is noted in his life mars his doctrine, and offends those ears that would take pleasure in his teaching. It is possible that such a one, even by that discordous noise, may ring in others into the triumphant church of heaven, while there is no remedy for himself but fire, either for his reforming of judgment.—*Bishop Hall, 1574–1656*

Where do vices show so foul as in a minister, when he shall be heavenly in his pulpit alone? Certainly, they wound the gospel that preach it to the world, and live as if they thought to go to heaven some other way than that they teach the people. How unseemly is it, when a grave cassock shall be lived with a wanton reveler, and with crimes that make a loose one odious! Surely, God will be severest against those who will wear His badge, and seem His servants, yet inwardly side with the devil and lusts. They spot His honor, and cause profane ones to jest at His holiness. We see, the prince suffers in the fails of his ambassador; and a servant's ill action is some touch to his master's reputation: nor can he free himself, but by delivering him up to justice, or discarding him: otherwise he would be judged to patronize it. Other offenses God may punish, this He must, lest the enemies of His truth triumph against Him.—*Felltham, 1668*

Prayer

Thou hast given us cause to praise Thee; therefore will we not be silent in Thy courts, we will open our mouth and sing loudly unto the Lord; and our song shall be of mercy and judgment. Thy mercy endureth forever. May our whole life be a song of love and consecration and thankfulness. Thou dost come to us every morning with a psalm; the light is music, the growing day is a growing anthem. Thou openest Thine hand, and satisfiest the desire of every living thing. We live in Thy love; without Thy love there is no life: God is love. God is a Spirit; God is in us, and about us, and in Him we live and move and have our being. May we realize this glorious fact, that it may kill the spirit of fear and the spirit of self-reproach; for we have cut our heart to pieces when we have remembered our sin against God. But the blood of Jesus Christ Thy Son cleanseth from all sin: where sin abounds grace doth much more abound. We will look to the grace, and not to the sin; to the Savior, and not to ourselves. We humbly pray Thee come to us, and be our morning psalm, and in the twilight of declining day be the star of the evening, and between these star-songs set Thy great chorus of the sun; then shall our life be full of sacred music, and be a sacrifice of praise, and the house of the Lord shall be great as the universe which He has created. Amen.

24
Ephesians 5:8–18

Preached on Thursday Morning, November 30th, 1899.

For ye were sometimes darkness, but now are ye light in the Lord: walk as children of light: (For the fruit of the Spirit is in all goodness and righteousness and truth;) Proving what is acceptable unto the Lord. And have no fellowship with the unfruitful works of darkness, but rather reprove them. For it is a shame even to speak of those things which are done of them in secret. But all things that are reproved are made manifest by the light: for whatsoever doth make manifest is light. Wherefore he saith, Awake thou that sleepest, and arise from the dead, and Christ shall give thee light.

See then that ye walk circumspectly, not as fools, but as wise, Redeeming the time, because the days are evil. Wherefore be ye not unwise, but understanding what the will of the Lord is. And be not drunk with wine, wherein is excess; but be filled with the Spirit —Ephesians 5:8–18.

Observe the striking series of contrasts in this marvelous passage. Let us trace the series, and learn what we can from these contrastive pictures. The first is in the eighth verse. This word "darkness" is not indicative of mere dim or transient fog or inconvenient grading of light; it is a deeper, severer, ghastlier word. "Ye were sometimes darkness," not dark, but darkness itself, sevenfold night, yea, more than night ever was; for surely every night must have somewhere and somehow its relieving star. It was not so with you in your former state; you were living darkness, without ray or glint or beam of light, as far away from light as it is possible to be. That is a wonderful conception of human nature and of human condition before the

Father of lights. You were not merely broken lights, scattered beams, that it was impossible to put together; there was no beam in you, you had never been illumined, you had never been warmed, you had never even heard of the summer of holiness; ye were simply incarnate, embodied darkness. Who could call us out of that state? What matchmaker could strike a little flash that would drive away such gloom? Where the darkness is so dense God Himself must handle the occasion, or there is nothing for it but fatal night. Sometimes we have said of a great singer, He is not musical, he is music; that is to say, he is not a merely mechanical player, a man who has got into his memory what is written in a book, but the music is in him, a well of water springing up into everlasting melody. So, reversing the picture, the Gentiles were not dark, they were darkness; unpenetrated, and but for the divine mercy, impenetrable clouds. Occasionally we say of a man, He is not eloquent, he is eloquence, embodied, incarnate, breathing, walking, living eloquence; he has not learned something by rote, he has not recited something of which his memory is in charge, but the holy gift is moving in him like a spirit, a genius, a heavenly choir. Reverse the picture, and you have the Apostle's idea: Ye were not dark, you were darkness, the thing itself, sevenfold night; no imagination could conceive the intensity of the darkness of your condition.

Then the contrastive "but"–"but now . . . light"; not partial light, not a gray light, not a mere hint of light, but as truly as you were once darkness, so truly are you now light. "Walk as children of light." The miracle is as great on the one side as on the other. Chaos was not partial chaos; chaos was not a mere mood or transient phase of disorder; it was utter confusion, without date, without measure, without figure, a tumultuousness and disorderliness not to be spoken of in words in any adequate sense or with any adequate fitness. Chaos is not partly order and partly confusion; the old chaos on which the Holy Spirit brooded was utter chaos, shapelessness, amorphousness, that which could not be ruled into order by any skill created; but now, since the beginning, chaos has given place to order, proportion, music, perspective, and all the apocalypse and summer of color. That is the difference. Chaos has no history. People want to know when the creation began. They can never know it. All depends upon what you mean by creation. The thing upon which creation operated may be calculable, but the thing out of which creation took its materials may lie back, so to say, in the memory of God alone. Transfer the figure to the Christian life, and you have first the darkness, utter dense darkness, on which moon and star never shone, not to speak of dawning light and wakening morning. Then you have light, glory, midday, points of extreme. Unless we recognize the extremity of the points we shall lose the whole movement of the miracle. Let us keep our memories well refreshed with the fact that once we were darkness; let us pity those who are in darkness still. Do not imagine for a moment that the man on the street can come into the sanctuary of God and partake of it and be as one of the called saints of heaven all in a moment. He cannot; nor can he hear the Gospel, much less understand it. He is darkness. A great mystery of movement must take place in his soul by the power of the Holy Ghost. We want again Genesis first chapter and first few verses; we want especially the Spirit brooding over the infinite night, the infinite disorder, with a vew to having brought out of it proportion and harmony and rest.

As to these workers of darkness, verse 2 lays down the instruction succinctly and unmistakably: "Have no fellowship." Do we rest there? No; we come upon this remarkable "but" which recurs in the passage quite startlingly: "but rather reprove them." Do you mean rebuke them? No. Do you mean disallow them, or look unfavorably upon them, or look askance at them? No; all that, all that and something more: Convict them. The Holy Ghost shall reprove the world of sin, convict the world of sin. Do not hold any conversation with the unfruitful works of darkness; have nothing to do with them; repel them when they come near you, shrink away from them as if some horrible plague were in the air and you were afraid of being blighted by the fatal pestilence. Now we have escaped all that, and we have come to the age of toleration, and we call toleration charity, and thus we unwed that holy bride, and tear her away from righteousness and justice, and drive her out into the wilderness to talk an alien tongue. We have now great toleration for people who are of a contrary persuasion to our own; we compromise with the works of darkness; the day says to the night, Let us say no more about our differences, but let us compromise in a neutral tint or tone of color, and let us lay down the noble democratic doctrine that one thing is as good as another in its own sphere, and if taken in its own atmosphere and in its proper relationships to the universe at large. So we are feeble, we are a school of cripples, we are a home of incurables; we have lost the nerve, the muscle, the tremendous energy that moved the world some centuries ago. We now live comfortably with all our opponents and with regard to diverse social practices we have compromised upon them; we come to church in the morning, and receive our friends in the afternoon, and slander the absentees over the cup, which cheers but not inebriates. We used to go to church twice a day; now it is enough to get it over in the morning as early as possible, and then have the whole-day—mayhap for "the unfruitful works of darkness." Have we lost the sharpness of division? I am not now speaking about differences of opinion; opinion goes a short way in this great difference. This is not a matter of intellectual pedantry or ecclesiastical persuasion as to this form or that form: questions upon which men may honestly or even profitably differ. I am speaking about moral antagonisms, about God and the devil; and they cannot compromise; we belong to one or the other, we cannot serve God and Mammon: not the "cannot" of inconvenience, but the "cannot" of a transcendental necessity; the thing cannot be done. The Apostle Paul operated upon this grand doctrine of separation: Come out from among them, said he, and be ye separate; and he said he was speaking the word of the Lord; for what fellowship hath light with darkness? So he is consistent with himself in writing to the Ephesians and the Corinthians. Division, separation of a moral and spiritual kind, leaving all our necessary and not wholly unhappy differences of mere opinion to settle themselves; but the moral and immoral cannot sign the same document; they do not serve the same king; their souls are different, they are irreconcilable.

Then in verse 15 he says, "not as fools," then the inevitable "but." What a series of "not" and "but"! "Not as fools, but as wise." Fools is a word of many meanings in the Scripture: senseless, nouseless, having no shrewdness of mind, having no moral sensitiveness, confusing things that differ, making mistakes and thinking nothing of them, as to their moral value and their relationship to the remaining links and duties of life. Sometimes the "fool" means the withered heart; the intellect is there, sharp enough, shrewd enough, trying to live upon its own problems and its own rude guesses at life's conundrums; but the heart is gone. It has faded like a leaf, it has withered like a leaf that falls from a branch that seems to shake it down with contempt. "The fool hath said in his heart, There is no God": not the intellectual fool, but the withered heart, the heart that is desiccated, juiceless, pithless, that which is leather which was once flesh, the heart in its withered late autumnal days says, There is no God. And to the withered heart what God can there be? Is not the heart the man at his best? Does it not mean not only sensibility and tenderness and sympathy and all the words that belong to the line of high sentiment? Is not the heart the home of the man, the innermost sanctuary and altar of the soul? The heart sees, the heart becomes the noblest intellect; the heart under the right conditions will see more of God than the mere brain can ever see. Hear this word that comes through all the winds that blow through the ages, "Blessed are the pure in heart: for they shall see God." And sometimes the heart is the whole man; it is so in the first and great commandment of the law: "Thou shalt love the Lord thy God with all thy heart, with all thy soul, with all thy mind, and with all thy spirit"—with all thy mind: the heart will recover the brain; the heart will go out after the prodigal intellect and bring it back. Some may only be doubters intellectually; they are not doubters, but believers in the great necessities and sorest agonies of life; then they suddenly change their creed, and remember that away down in the heart's deepest places there lives not a creed, but a faith, a creating, redeeming, God-appropriating faith, which is itself the very creation of divine grace.

Yet again in verse 17, "not unwise"; then the inevitable "but"— "but understanding what the will of the Lord is." Getting at the very center of things; not living the little superficial life, but connecting the mind and the heart with the upper fountains and the ever-springing wells of the divine conception and the divine purpose. "Not unwise"; living from day to day; not seeing the connection of things, and not noticing that an increasing purpose runs through all the process of suns and stars, of all bodies solar, geologic, and other; not knowing that the whole conception is in the grip of God, that the Lord reigneth, that the fog is but for a moment, that the blue light and the everlasting morning will come, and in its glory we shall forget the night and cease to remember that we were once troubled by a cloud.

To what a great character does the Apostle call us in setting before us this series of *not* and *but!* He is talking as only a great spiritual statesman can talk. A passage like this is a great educational lesson to the soul. Everything is balanced, mutually related, and impregnated by the very spirit of humanity and of divinest love. To have read such a passage is to have incurred a great responsibility; how much greater does that responsibility become when we read the concluding or climacteric "not" and "but" in the eighteenth verse, "not drunk with wine . . . but"—the same style of argument—"filled with the Spirit," drunk with the Spirit, intoxicated and made enthusiastic by divine possession and inspiration. What insight into human nature! "Be not filled with wine, drunk with wine, wherein is excess." Upon that excess we soon come; first there is exhilaration, and then there is a higher degree of buoyancy, and then there is a taste of bitterness, and then there is a sense of surfeit, and then a sense of revulsion, and an act of revulsion; you have reached the limit of the wine; wine can go so far and no farther. But as to the Holy Spirit, be drunk with that Spirit, that holy wine; be intoxicated and transported by that high revelry and that noblest ecstasy, in which there is no satiety, no excess, no surfeit; for the mind grows by what it feeds on, and our capacity to receive the Spirit enlarges as we bid Him welcome to the hospitality of our love. There is a whole volume of philosophy in that eighteenth verse. All limited things will surfeit you, only the infinite will never cloy you. Why? Because you yourselves are meant to be immortal, you are intended to live with God, and in that life there is no monotony, no sense of weariness, but as we company with Christ we increase in desire to have further association still. I speak concerning Christ and His Church; no man can enter into this mystery but the man who lives and moves and has his being in God; he is never alone, he is never satiated; why, the water of Jacob's well would not be enough for him, he would drink of it and thirst again; but he who drinks of the water that Jesus Christ gives, he who drinks of the Holy Spirit, shall never thirst, and never know the meaning of satiety, but will evermore call upon the Lord to increase his faith that he may at once increase his service and his joy.

These are wonderful contrasts. Now we must go back a little upon our track here and there to pick out some peculiar words that seem to fit this mechanism of expression with exquisite adaptation. Quote a few of these remarkable words. Verse 9, "The fruit of the Spirit." Better translated as it is in the Revised Version, "the fruit of light." "Walk as children of light," we read in verse 8; in verse 9 the Apostle adopts a connective or logical word, and says, "For (because) the fruit of light is in all goodness and righteousness and truth; showing us what is acceptable unto the Lord." There is no more any darkness. The apple trees will not respond to great masses of gloom and cloud; there is no heroic little bird blithe enough to face the overpowering fog with even one little cheery note; no daisy or violet will come out to see the fog. But light makes all things come out; you cannot stop at home when it is light; light scatters them and yet unites them; light creates a common joy and a common sympathy, and people who never saw one another before are almost inclined to speak when the sun is doing its very best to make the earth merry and glad as with a new song. So long as we remain in darkness we shall bear no fruit; when we come out by the power of the Spirit into light there will be bud and blossom and shaking fruit. May no blight or cruel wind from the east discourage such buddings and outbursts of the vernal juice!

And then we read in the eleventh verse of "the unfruitful works of darkness." What did they all come to? When we were really bad men what did it come to when it was all totaled up in results? What did it come to? To loss of virility, to loss of reason, to paralysis of will, to the divestment of our best nature; it came to fear and trembling and self-accusation and beasthood; that is what it came to. What fruit had ye than in those things whereof ye are now ashamed? The bad man gets nothing; he thinks he makes a good bargain; he utters the fool's laugh at the devil's counter; and says what a wonderful arrangement he has made. And then come disappointment, social distrust, newspaper reports, halings before the courts; and then there may come more wine, a deeper draught of the devil's fluid to drown the devil's accusations; and then when it is all added up what does it come to? What the bill? Hell!

The Apostle urges us to walk as children of light, making his argument, in verse 13, run according to this line, "whatsoever doth make manifest is light," and light in three points, light almost in three qualities: light at the center, which illumines the whole man; light that discovers, throws itself upon objects and discovers them. The sun discovers, not creates the dust. You think the room has been well cared for; so it may have been: will you draw up the blind and let the sun be critic? And when he comes in with those eyes of light you are ashamed of the very room you were proud of an hour ago. And then there is a light that reflects, the mirror light, that throws back, so that you can see yourself in the light and abhor yourself, never before having seen your disfigurement and your un-worthiness and your utter decrepitude and miserable infirmity.

The Apostle gives the Ephesians a new word in verse 15: "See that ye walk circumspectly." It is a hard world to walk in at all; we need to have eyes in front and eyes behind and eyes on either side of us; because the enemy is watching us, and we are walking along a very narrow wall; on the top of that wall are sharp points of glass made as if in the cement, and we must walk very carefully, or we shall be undone. We walk along a very narrow precipice, we cannot turn around to speak to a companion or fellow-traveler; we say we must be perfectly silent till we get across this difficult place. Before you start on the journey look well around, be circumspect—round-about-lookers—exactly to see where you are and to what point you are moving. Do not live the careless life or the rootless life or the planless life, taking things just as they come and being unwise, and foolish with exceeding folly; but enter into calculation, relate one thing to another, and be wise in the Spirit of God, and let the word of Christ dwell in you richly that you may know how to answer the enemy, how to light a glory in the darkness, how to sing a song in the wilderness.

"Redeeming the time." The day of the Lord was always coming to Paul; the day of the Lord is always coming to us. We are to walk and work, to serve, to suffer, as if the day of the Lord would be to-morrow. He indicated a grand policy, he did not execute an arith-metical exercise; he did not sit beside the ticking pendulum, and say, Tell me when the Lord will come. To that have we brought our studies of the Scripture, whereas the Apostle indicates a grand pol-icy. This was a favorite philosophy of his, to get hold of the policy, and let the details relate themselves to it; and part of the Pauline policy was this, that the Lord may be expected at any moment. And there is no other wise way of living. Ye know not the hour that ye may know it; not to know it is to expect it, not to know it is to be solemnized by it. "The kingdom of heaven is at hand," said He who began to preach, and then finished by dying that He might afterwards rise from the dead and show how near His kingdom is. But so slow of heart are we that we want to know days and hours; we have our slate and our pencil, and if a prophet but drop a word that is arithmetical, we take him down in a moment, and if an apostle should indicate anything like a day, we begin to calculate and put another figure to it. By figures you can prove everything; by figures you can prove nothing. It is very sad indeed that men who have slates and pencils gave many of us a sleepless week this month by looking for meteors that never came, so far as I am aware. Personally, I did not care whether they came or not, but there was a great inroad made upon my sleep: they might be there, and I ought to rise and see if they have come after all. Better redeem the time, better turn the sunshine into labor, better serve the Lord with simplicity and honesty and godly fear, and then we shall be ready for Him when He does come. Convinced am I that this is a policy of the Apostle, and not the indication of an arithmetical expectation. "Ye know not what hour your Lord cometh." Christ Himself said so. What I say unto one, I say unto all, Watch. The kingdom of heaven comes every moment to the man who wants it, and asks to see in the coming of his Lord the way to a new opportunity, to suffer bravely, to work wisely, and to serve with the gratitude and the grace of a spiritual obedience.

Words for Preachers

Blots appear fouler in a strict life than a loose one: no man wonders at the swine's wallowing; but to see an ermine mired is prodigy.
—*Felltham, 1668*

Take heed to yourselves, lest your example contradict your doctrine, and lest you lay such stumbling blocks before the blind as may be the occasion of their ruin; lest you may unsay that with your lives, which you say with your tongues; and be the greatest hinderers of the success of your own labors. It much hindereth our work, when other men are all the week long contradicting to poor people in private, that which we have been speaking to them from the word of God in public; because we cannot be at hand to manifest their folly: but it will much more hinder if we contradict ourselves, and if your actions give your tongue the lie, and if you build up an hour or two with your mouths, and all the week after pull down with your hands! This is the way to make men think that the word of God is but an idle tale, and to make preaching seem no better than prating.—*Baxter, 1615–1691*

It is not a very likely thing that the people will regard much the doctrine of such men, when they see that they do not live as they preach. They will think that he doth not mean as he speaks, if he do not as he speaks. They will hardly believe a man that seemeth not to believe himself. If a man bid you run for your lives because a bear or an enemy is at your backs, and yet do not mend his pace himself in the same way, you will be tempted to think that he is but in jest, and there is really no such danger as he pretends. When preachers tell people of a necessity of holiness, and that without it no man shall see the Lord, and yet remain unholy themselves, the people will think they do but talk to pass away the hour, and because they must say somewhat for their money, and that all these are but words of course. Long enough may you lift up your voices against sin before men will believe that there is any such harm or danger in it as you talk of, as long as they see the same man that reproacheth it, to put it in his bosom and make it his delight. You rather tempt them to think that there is some special good in it, and that you dispraise it as gluttons do a dish which they love, that they may have it all to themselves. As long as men have eyes as well as ears, they will think that they see your meaning as well as hear it; and they are more apt to believe their sight than their hearing, as being the more perfect sense.—*Baxter, 1615 –1691*

Prayer

God is our refuge and strength, a very present help in trouble; therefore will not we fear, though the earth be removed and the mountains be carried into the midst of the sea. We will say, Why art thou disquieted within me? O my soul, why art thou troubled with unrest? There is a river the streams whereof make glad the city of God, the holy place of the tabernacles of the Most High. There is a still small voice after all the tribulation and thunder and destroying tempest; that whisper of love shall find our hearts; Thou wilt not break the bruised reed, Thou wilt not quench the smoking flax. Thou hast given unto Thy Son the tongue of the learned, that He may speak a word in season unto him that is weary. If Thou dost overthrow us by Thy thunder, Thou dost gather us again with Thy speaking tender love. God is love; before the wrath and after the wrath shall we see the love of God. We bless Thee for Thy Sabbath day, the day of days, the morning of rest and hope and song and joy; Thou hast been careful of the days, Thou hast made one of them Thine own jewel. This is the day the Lord hath made; we will rejoice and be glad in it. We come into Thy courts with praise and with loud sweet songs, and we approach Thee in the name of Jesus Christ, the Son of God, the Savior of the world, the promised Messiah that should redeem humanity. We pray in no other name; it is enough; He ever liveth to make intercession for us, and to multiply our prayers by His own solicitude and by His own love. Grant unto us a day of rest, a high festival day; may we order off all lower things, all mean enjoyments, all cups which exhilarate and then destroy; for one sweet short day may we live the upper life, may we be fed with corn from heaven and eat angels' food. Thou knowest how easily tempted we are to the lower levels of life, how any fool can stop our prayer and substitute his song for Thine. Oh! that men were wise, that they understood these things, that they would consider their latter end, that they would make diligent search into Thy will and Thy purpose, and serve Thee with deepening reverence and holy, filial, tender fear: then would all the week be a minor festival, all work would be sanctified by the Sabbatic song. Oh! that men were wise, that they understood these things, that they would not waste their time, that they would not degrade their vocation and election in God, but for one day might stand on the mountain top and feed at the table where there is no satiety. We have come to thank Thee for all Thy love during the week; if we have played the fool, it is because we are still in the body; if we have turned away to other altars, it is because we are utterly foolish in our heart, so small, so vain, so weak. But in this moment of consideration and deepest sobriety of spirit we remember our evil natures, our wasted days, our ignorant wisdom and our foolish talk. Oh! that men were wise, that they understood these things, that they would be men indeed, made in the image and likeness of God and redeemed with the blood of Christ, the precious blood, the blood infinitely precious. We have come to the tower from whose windows we can see afar; we have come to the temple of God, and out of its windows we can behold the landscapes afar off; and while we tarry under the sacred roof we hear voices of welcome and gladness and inspiration. Seeing these things, and obeying these voices, behold, the whole week shall lie under our feet like a conquered thing, and we shall be no longer slaves of time and space and limitation. Thou hast not neglected one day, Thy love has kissed us every morning, every night Thy fingers have drawn down our eyelids that we might enjoy refreshing slumber; behold, the angels have spread our table and replenished our cup of water, and Thou hast given us corn from heaven and angels' food; therefore are we strong, exuberant, full of passionate yet sober joy. Thou hast rocked the cradle, Thou hast blessed us in basket and in store; Thou hast comforted the sad, Thou hast given the ill and the dying a new lease of life; and we have come in memory of these things to praise Thee in a common psalm, and to seek Thy blessing in the name of Christ in a common supplication. We pray for one another: for the old man, for the little child, for the weary pilgrim, for those to whom life is a daily fight, and for those who are in danger of losing God by reason of the abundance of His blessings. May Thy harvests never quench Thine existence, may we never be blinded by Thy goodness to forget Thyself; the Lord help us to remember that He reigns over all things, and guides our lives, and will be with us in the eleventh hour, and when the twelfth hour doth strike we shall see the Lord's face in the Lord's heaven. Look upon the earth, we humbly pray Thee, upon our kings and queens our mighty men and councilors, our wise leaders and thoughtful writers, and upon all persons who would lead us in the upper and better way. The Lord burn the chariot in the fire, the Lord put an end to war; the Lord work out His own purposes in His own way; and may we have confidence in God and stand in that confidence as men might stand in an impregnable fortress. Pity the bereaved and the sorrowing; touch the broken heart with Thine own healing balm; plant some flowers around the grave; and may all life be offered to Thee in the name of Jesus at the foot of the Cross as a living sacrifice. Amen.

25
Soul Food

Preached on Sunday Morning, December 3rd, 1899.

Corn of heaven. . . . angels' food–Psalm 78:24, 25.

What do you live upon? How many lives have you? Who is the sustainer of your life? In what direction do you look for daily sustenance? Surely here in these two texts, which are in reality one text, we find exactly what man needs at his best estate–"corn of heaven, angels' food." Is such sustenance available? Yes. Are there any invitations to partake of this food? Certainly; invitations given as with the blast of trumpets to come and eat, to come buy wine and milk without money and without price. The Lord reasons with people who are sitting at the wrong tables and partaking of the wrong food, and points out to them that their souls can never flourish on such mean viands. But who thinks of eating anything for his soul's health? Man thinks of his body, he must have his meals regularly, he would complain were there any breach of regularity; but what of his soul? Who seriously, not occasionally, but seriously and continuously, thinks of feeding his best life? Who is there that does not in some way suppose that his best life must take care of itself? Feed the body, and let the soul do what it can in its own interests, is the mean creed of many a man who would be shocked if he were charged with being an atheist.

What do we live upon? Here is corn from heaven, here is angels' food, and we may perhaps never touch it. Let it not be supposed that God is responsible for our self-impoverishment; He never meant us to impoverish ourselves, He never meant us to attempt to satisfy our hunger with the husks that the swine do eat; He never meant us to be swine; if we are swine we are self-made, self-degraded, we have dishonored the image and likeness of God. And what you eat comes out in your face, in your skin, in your eyes; your food expresses itself in daily incarnations. It is possible to eat nothing but flesh, and to make flesh of it; it is possible to eat nothing but what the beasts may eat, and to make it no better than they make it. On the other hand, it is possible to eat viands meant for the body, and to turn those viands into poetry, inspiration, benevolence, charity, grace. How much good food is wasted on some people! The food was sufficient in quantity and it was excellent in quality, but it was unblessed food, therefore it came to nothing, fatness of flesh and leanness of soul; petted bullocks are some men.

It was God who gave Israel in the wilderness corn of heaven and angels' food; it was so to say doubly of heaven and doubly angels' food, because it was given in the wilderness; it was such a contrast, it was evidently a thing that could not be grown by the wilderness; it was something that had come into the wilderness and come into the wilderness from above. Yet it is possible for the devil so to deprave and thwart the imagination and the conscience of men as to make them believe that it was the wilderness that grew the corn and the very rocks that provided the angels' food. Man can be stupid; man is brilliantly clever in degrading and depraving things. I would not trust him with the stars; he would break them up, scatter them, take out their light and sell it. Lord, keep him on the ground out of which his body came, lest he spoil Thy universe! Whatever man touches he degrades. When he builds, nature begins to take off the roof before the man has wholly put it on. When man plucks a flower, the flower is dead at once; you cannot pluck and keep the flower. Let the Lord shut down this little all-spoiling sprite and keep him within his cage until he is fit for larger liberty. You can tell what a man has been feeding upon by looking at his face, by listening to his voice, by watching the light of his eyes, by hearing his proposals,

by consulting him in perplexity, by asking him to step into the silence of the shadow of the chamber of affliction; then his meat will
come out of him, a vulgarity or a poem, a degradation or an instruction; he will show at whose table he has been eating when he
tries to comfort over the dead body of husband, wife, child; such
food as he has been eating, and such food eaten in such a spirit as
his, can never be turned into a benediction, it goes into corruption.
That is the apostolic word; it sinks into rottenness and putridity.
Ay, the wheat, so golden, which was grown on the fields under
God's sunshine, may become nothing but despair and cursing ingratitude and red shame. Do not eat unblessed bread. You can ask a
blessing upon it in silence; you need not subject yourself to the
sneer of the enemy by asking the blessing aloud, but you can make
every mouthful of bread sacramental, and every drop out of the
cup you may drink as if it were red blood; then we shall see the
food in your shining face, and hear it in your tender voice, and feel
it in your masonic grip, and know it by your willingness to impart
its strength to others.

What a wonderful psalm this is! God had done all sorts of
beautiful and lovely things for this people Israel, and here He
brings an indictment against the children of the wilderness. When
God had piled gift upon gift, they sinned yet more against Him by
provoking the Most High, and they tempted God in their heart,
and they asked meat for their lust. They wanted bread to turn it
into passion, they wanted flesh to turn it into devil. Beware of these
subtle and almost unconfessed degradations of daily blessings; beware of tempting God to work miracles to gratify human passion.
That passion may be intellectual, imaginative, artistic, or it may be
sensual, and the lowest of the low desires. This wonderful psalm
shows the absolute futility of mere miracles. God seems to have
worked all His miracles in this seventy-eighth psalm; it is as full of
miracles as the Lord's sermons were full of parables. Yet all ended in
a deeper atheism; not an atheism as we understand the word, a
term emptied of God, but a term so filled with gods as to dethrone

God. The Israelites were not nominal atheists. Would God there were more nominal infidels today–more nominal pledged and badged atheists, that we might know them in the streets and feel their hot breath the moment the door of hospitality opened; then we would know into what hell we were going. But it is possible to have eaten bread of sacrament, and to leave God in the church where we paid no heed to Him. We are fast coming to this. Then we wonder that we do not win our wars. We ought not to win them –impious hounds, churchgoing hounds, creed-loving hounds, and yet devil-worshiping devotees! Yes, the casualties will be more and more, for the nation has cast off its Redeemer, and gone to selfishness and folly and madness, and it deserves to be crushed.

These people in the wilderness tempted God to do another miracle, and then another, and at last miracles became commonplaces to them, ceasing to be miracles and sinking below mere anecdotes or transient circumstances. Let us get back to the idea that God is the sustainer of man, God is the bread-giver; let us go back to our little child-prayer, Give us this day our daily bread. That prayer will do more for the world than atheism has ever done; that prayer will keep the world sweet when many a vain intellect theory will pervert its imagination and destroy its conscience.

"Corn of heaven, angels' food." Let the imagery stand for all that it really means. We cannot take out of it the idea that bread and water and honey and locusts and all the old wilderness fare may be so accepted and utilized as to become as if it were corn of heaven and angels' food. Surely it was angels' food in the most literal sense that Adam ate when he was in the Garden of Eden.

> Now morn, her rosy steps in th' eastern clime
> Advancing, sow'd the earth with orient pearl,
> When Adam waked, so custom'd for his sleep
> Was aery light, from pure digestion bred,
> And temperate vapors bland.

So sang Milton of the first Adam. A wondrous life that–first and second–when Adam bathed into pearl, and sat on the river banks, watching the sunset shine upon Pison, as it shone on the land of gold. Then came the forbidden tree, the interdicted fruit, and the apples sour, and the grapes that held in them the good wine took into themselves the devil's spirit and tore the drinker as if possessed by demons. We have got away from that long-ago simplicity; we shall be wise in the degree in which we endeavor to get back to it. Eat no unblessed bread; it will come out on you in blotches, in leprous spots, in drunken pimples, in all manner of physical degradation and shame; have nothing to do with such bread; a blessed crust means a feast; a blessed water-bottle, the bottle just filled from the running rill, means the true wine. Then there will be no poverty. The mental mood lifts up the whole life above the physical circumstances. Poverty is unknown to the good; poverty is not in the vocabulary of the man who truly prays. We have made a kind of clay poverty, a poor cold chill and chilling idol, that we gather around with our ignorant nostrums. The life that is hid with God in Christ knows nothing about poverty, and could receive no explanation of it; it is a language not unknown only, but unknowable.

Are we sustained by the living God? Do we live upon God? Do we understand how many kinds of food or elements of sustenance God can give to us? Jesus Christ revealed the great philosophy of living; He said, "Man shall not live by bread alone." The meaning is so often mistaken or perverted, as if the passage read, Man must have something more than bread, he must have something to his bread, it will not do to give him mere bread, bare bread. The passage has no such poor driveling meaning. Here is a great philosophy of sustenance; man shall not live only by bread, as if there were only one way of living, as if there were only one method of keeping man together in his personal identity. God can feed a man on the rocks or in the air or on the sea, away from civilization wholly. God can so sustain His own dear child that the child shall have no physical want, he shall be for forty days and forty nights away in the wilderness or on the mountain top, and hunger shall return to him as a forgotten consciousness. When men rightly live in God the world will be at rest, and not until then. There is no way of rightly living in God but through Jesus Christ His Son. That is the Gospel message; that is the evangelical doctrine; and, sirs, clever men, dreamers, conjurers, program-makers, that is true when all your frivolity is blown away.

Jesus Christ explained all this so beautifully when He spoke in John 6:32. He speaks of being the true vine. "Then Jesus said unto them, Verily, verily, I say unto you, Moses gave you not that bread from heaven, but My Father giveth you the true bread from heaven. For the bread of God is He which cometh down from heaven, and giveth life unto the world." And that so touched the imagination, the pathos, the conscious necessity of man, that those who heard the words cried out, "Lord, evermore give us this bread." That should be the exclamation of every audience at the close of every evangelical exposition and appeal. But audiences make no response now; they die of decorum, they rot in indifference; there are no echoes now, or few. Jesus said, I am the bread which came down from heaven, and they say, How can this man be the bread which came down from heaven? we know His father and His mother, and we know all about Him, and He saith He is the bread that cometh down from heaven. "Then Jesus said unto them, Verily, verily, I say unto you, Except ye eat the flesh of the Son of man, and drink His blood, ye have no life in you. Whoso eateth My flesh, and drinketh My blood, hath eternal life; and I will raise him up at the last day. For My flesh is meat indeed, and My blood is drink indeed. He that eateth My flesh, and drinketh My blood, dwelleth in Me, and I in him. As the living Father hath sent Me, and I live by the Father: so he that eateth Me, even he shall live by Me. This is that bread which came down from heaven: not as your fathers did eat manna, and are dead: he that eateth of this bread shall live forever." And the poor literalists, as all literalists will down to the end of the age, said, How can this man give us His flesh to eat? They were what we call rationalists; they said in effect, You see, it stands to reason; there is a limited body, here is an unlimited population, and the population of the world will go on from age to age, and this man says that only by eating His flesh can we enter into the kingdom of heaven; why, it stands to reason—O that shamed reason, that ill-judged and ill-treated reason! There is a reason that grows into faith and faith belongs to infinity. We are saved by faith. The literalist says, You have the bread laid on your sacramental plates, and you call this the flesh of Christ; some call it God, some say it is transubstantiated from the material into the spiritual and into the divine; why, it stands to reason—It does not; your reason is not reason; you are a literalist, you are a little slave of the little alphabet; you know nothing yet about the kingdom of heaven. In a crumb of bread there may be the Father and the Son and the Holy Ghost symbolically represented, and it may be accepted by faith as a great sacrament. Do not live, if you please, by your so-called reason. That is a poor light; I would not trust it. Faith is the Christian word; if you want a literary word, I will give you the word imagination, fancy, great power of transmutation and symbolization. When we eat the sacramental bread we do not eat the literal flesh, but we eat by faith, we partake of a grand symbolical element, and we partake of it symbolically, and it is to us as the flesh of Christ, and the wine is as the blood of His heart.

Have we eaten of the living bread? Have we partaken of the Son of God? Do we accept the Lord Christ as our Savior, our only Savior, our only because our sufficient and eternal Savior? Then our daily bread is blessed by that acceptance; the poor flesh bread that we eat at home by which we seek to stave off the gnawing of bodily hunger, even that bread becomes sacramental, symbolic, indicative. All other eating is waste; a waste that may end in momentary cleverness, and in a sufficiency of income, but when added up and appreciated at the last, the word waste will be the right word. Hence said the dear Christ, Father, I have kept all but one, and that one is the son of waste—not the word perdition, as we understand that word; I have lost none but the son of waste; I would have saved him if I could, but he is the child of waste, he has withered away, there was nothing in him that could grow up into life; Father, I have lost him.

Words for Preachers

The snuffers of the tabernacle were of pure gold: they who reprove and snuff the vices of others had need themselves to be free from those sins. The snuffers must be of gold.—*Watson, 1696*

The minister's miscarriage is dangerous to the people; therefore pray for them, lest you be led into temptation by their falls. The sins of teachers, are the teachers of sin. If the nurse be sick, the child is in danger to suck the disease from her that lies at her breast; if the minister be tainted with an error, it is strange if many of his people should not catch the infection; when, if he be loose and scandalous in his life, he is like a common well or fountain, corrupted and muddied, at which all the town draw their water. The devil aimed at more than Peter when he desired leave to try a fall with him: "Simon, Simon, Satan hath desired to winnow thee." He knew his fall was like to strike up the heels of many others. The minister's practice makes a greater sound than his doctrine; they who forget his sermon, will remember his example to quote it for their apology and defense when time serves. Peter withdraws, and other Jews dissembled with him (Gal. 2:12, 13).—*Gurnall, 1617–1679*

In your study acquaint yourself with the Word of God. That which may pass for diligence in a private Christian's reading and search into the Scripture, may be charged as negligence upon the minister. The study of the Scriptures is not only a part of our general calling (in common with him) but of our particular also; in which we are to be exercised from one end of the week to the other. The husbandman doth not more constantly go forth with his spade and mattock to perform his day labor in the field, than the minister is to go and dig in this mine of the Scripture. He is not to read a chapter now and then, as his worldly occasions will permit, or steal a little time from his other scholarly studies to look into the Bible in transitu, and bid it farewell: but it must be his standing exercise, his plodding work; all other must stoop to this. Suppose thou shouldst know what Plato, Aristotle (with the rest of the Princes of worldly learning) have writ, and hadst encircled all the arts within thy circumference, but art un-skillful in the Word of righteousness, thou wouldst be Paul's unlearned person; as unfit to be a minister as he that hath read all the body of the law is to be a physician, if ignorant of this art.—*Gurnall, 1617–1699*

Prayer

Almighty God, we bless Thee for the great Exemplar; we thank Thee for the Lord Christ, God manifest in the flesh, Emmanuel, God with us. May we make Him our example, may we copy none other; as He loved, so may we love; as He suffered, so may we suffer; may we make no reference to ourselves, but always refer to the great Savior, the Christ of God. Then will everything be unto us as it was unto Him; enduring the Cross, we shall despise the shame; accepting the discipline, we shall look beyond and see the crown, and hear the final hymn. May Christ dwell in our hearts by faith; may He rule our whole life; then shall our temper be sweet, our considerateness for others shall be full of tenderness; we shall bend over the sick with sympathy, and help the helpless with an open and generous hand. It is the Christ we want, the indwelling Savior, the all-ruling and all-subduing Cross; then everything will come easy to us, and we shall know what it is to carry a burden that is light and a yoke that is easy. We thank Thee for making all things so plain to us in Christ Jesus the Lord; we bless Thee that Thou dost not call us to any ventures on our own behalf or to any inventions of new and untried moralities; we thank Thee for the eternal temple in which we may hear the heavenly song and for the balances by which we may test all our doings and thoughts, our motives and purposes. We thank Thee for the fine gold; may we examine all pretended gold by its light and according to its quality; then shall we be men and women of solid character, high uprightness, noble magnanimity, and men shall take knowledge of us that we have been with Jesus. Amen.

26
Ephesians 5:19–22

Preached on Thursday Morning, December 7th, 1899.

Speaking to yourselves in psalms and hymns and spiritual
songs, singing and making melody in your heart to the Lord;
Giving thanks always for all things unto God and the Father
in the name of our Lord Jesus Christ—Ephesians 5:19–22.

Live the thankful life. Let us have no more groaning and com-
plaining, but let us have music and psalm and hymn and spiritual
song, an inward and outward melody. The Church has forgotten all
its exhortations to thankfulness and to music; it has made for itself a
series of threnodies very depressing and soul-enslaving, services and
tests of discipline and standards of heartless and often hypocritical
solemnity. The Apostle says, Let us have no more of this; there is a
sunny side even to Christian faith; there are whole days, long bright
summer days, in which it becomes us to sing one to another in
psalm and hymn and spiritual song and to match the summer with
a human melody. We are not the more pious because we are so depressed; melancholy is not one of the evidences of the Christian
faith; as well refer to death in proof that we are members of the kingdom of heaven. We have nothing to do with death; it is abolished,
sponged out; our subject is the resurrection. When the Church is
more cheerful it will depose the world from many a position of social charm and fascination to which it has no right whatsoever. Do
we contribute towards a cheerful Church? Did you ever know any
church that was really rationally and consistently vivacious and triumphant because of the nearness of the Savior and because the air

was made balmy by His presence and blessing? Let a cheerful life be added to the evidences of the truth of the Christian religion. Paul was never ashamed of his overflowings of joy; he mingled the cup of life so dexterously and with so sweet and sacred a cunning that no man ever drank such a cup as Paul drank; he said, Yea, we glory in tribulations also. Nothing could repress him or depress him; his religion forced its way through fog and smoke and storm and pain and loss; he took tribulation with a strong man's hand, and added it to his wealth. This is the victory that overcometh the world, even our faith. Always hear the music that is in everything. There is fire in ice; there is music in silence, there is music in the radiance of the face. Music is not a noise; music is an expression, a spiritual emphasis, a force within which makes all outward things palpitate as if in obedience to some fascinating charm. It would be better for us to have psalm and hymn and spiritual song than to have groaning and unbelief and fear and timidity. The heart should be so full of music as to leave no room for the devil. What the Apostle cautioned the Romans against was a void mind; a mind empty, idle, and either having nothing to do or being unwilling to do anything; that is the devil's chance! We hear a good deal about our temptations and difficulties and struggles. Silence! We want to hear something now about the psalm and hymn and spiritual song, and the triumph and domination in the infinite strength of the infinite grace. We are cautioned not to give way to depressing influences. Our singing spiritually with the right fervor and emphasis will keep the devil at bay. He hates all singing hearts; music tortures the damned spirit. If you had more music you would have less fear. Not mechanical music, not something that can be taught at a certain number of pence per half-hour; that is not the music meant by the Apostle Paul; it is melody in the heart, it is the whole life itself turned to music. The devil does not get very near to the heart that lives in real thankfulness and in spiritual melody. When we live in argument, he asks us questions; when we try to sustain the soul on controversy, he puts before us in a most skillful, almost professional manner the heresies of old centuries, and asks us what we make of them; as if long ago we had not buried them, and lost them and cursed them! You never should attempt to make an ancient heresy a modern difficulty. There are many temptations to depression. Some of those temptations arise from physical constitution. Some persons never can be otherwise than depressed; other persons would really be unhappy if they had no depression; they would wonder what had taken place because they feel a little better this morning. These are not our living epistles and letters of commendation. At the same time we are called upon to be patient with people who are constitutionally melancholy. We should never marry them; we should live as little as possible with them; but with these two reservations, we should be as kind as we can be to them.

If we have had our psalm and hymn and spiritual song, what then, thou great disciplinarian of the Church? I will tell you, says Paul; after the song must come the discipline. You will find all along the Christian line that song and discipline alternate; they seem to balance one another; in that, as in the record of Genesis, the evening balances the morning, and the evening and the morning are the whole day. Discipline succeeds melody:

> Submitting yourselves one to another in the fear of God. Wives, submit yourselves unto your own husbands, as unto the Lord.

We shall miss the whole point of this if we take it out of its connection and make a jest of it. There are no jests in the Bible. The buffoon can find them on the altar, almost on the Cross, but the wise man finds no such thing. Observe the atmosphere in which the apostle is now writing; take note of the atmosphere which he has created around these Gentile converts. Do not place the Ephesian converts on a level with Christian and experienced nations. When the temperature is at the highest, when joy is at the zenith, when all the summer fruits are growing and all the summer birds are singing, he says, Submit yourselves one to another in the fear of

God. And in that atmosphere it is impossible. That is the exposition. Where the atmosphere is right there will be no difficulty. What a cunning master of fence was this great brother of ours, the leader of the Christian host! Said he, "Submitting yourselves one to another." That is the key of all that follows. The submission is never to be on one side only; and where there is submission on both sides there is no humiliation, there is sympathy, there is union. Everything depends upon the point at which we approach difficult subjects or severe trials. The difficulty is not so much in the thing itself as in the point from which we proceed towards it and the atmosphere with which we invest it. All things are affected by atmosphere. It is the atmosphere that makes the beauty of the summer day. The sun would be but a clumsy artist painting in white too dazzling if he had not the help of atmosphere; that is where he gets his pictures; and yet we call him the great artist; in a sense he is the great artist, but he has wonderful appliances, God has given to him very great assistances and auxiliaries; he would be but a poor glaring white-faced thing, a merely frightsome thing, in yonder courts of his, if he were not attempered and colored and toned by that which no man ever saw, the air, the atmosphere, the mysterious something that clothes the earth like a garment, a garment invisible and yet full of a strange mystic color.

For example, many persons are broken down in mid-life and made cripples of for the rest of their days because of the great difficulty about the miracles. There is no difficulty about the miracles. Yet you were broken down at thirty-five, and have never been yourself since, because some fool of a man suggested to you the difficulty of Jesus Christ walking on the sea, and raising the dead, and giving sight to the blind. That man made you a sort of initial, elementary, and most infantile infidel some thirty years ago. Would God some nobler spirit had been within your calling! The miracles, what are they? Everything depends upon the point of view from which they are surveyed, or the point in their own circumference at which they are broken in upon. Here and elsewhere the question is

largely one of spiritual atmosphere. A poor little urchin brought up
in a very depressing village, reared in a room seven feet by six, with
a window in it so high that he was never able to look out of it, is
brought up to see some great city, and how affrighted he is, how
terrorstruck, how amazed! How will he ever get back again? Here is
a youth brought up in a large city, educated upon a liberal scale,
companying with persons of culture and travel and large information; how does he regard the city, even the city of London? Without fear, with appreciation; he has come down upon it from a high
point; the other visitor struggled up to it from the lowest possible
point: do these people view the city in the same light and estimate
it at the same value? Certainly not; they are two different people,
they approach it from two totally different points of view. So if I
come down from long companying with the Savior in heaven; if I
have spent with Him forty days and forty nights; if we have held
long, sweet, deep, vital intercourse, I come down upon its wonders,
and do not consider them worth looking at; I have been with the
Lord and everything else must be mean, small, contemptible; if I
have made myself by grace and the holy action of the blessed Spirit
familiar with the purposes of Christ, I shall approach the miracles
of Christ as very little things, as He Himself approached them; they
were never great efforts to Jesus Christ; He came from eternity, and
time can never be great to Immortality. Jesus Christ said concerning
His miracles in addressing His disciples, Greater works than these
shall ye do, because I go unto the Father: the further I am from
you, the nearer I am to you; the leverage will be greater, all the apparatus and appliances, spiritual and metaphysical, will be more
immediately under my command; I go that I may come; I vanish
that I may be seen by the heart.

So with this matter of submission. "Submitting yourselves one
to another." A man takes refuge in his vanity, in self-exaggeration,
in overweening and overwhelming self-importance: how do you account for that? Because he has come from a low communion, he
has struggled up to this position; he has not come down upon it, as

an eagle might alight upon a rock; so he asks why he should sub-mit—*he!* Was ever a little pronoun so loaded with false emphasis, so crushed by misinterpretation? He—a candle that a wind can blow out; he—a leaf that will fall with the winter wind blowing upon it; he—whose breath is in his nostrils; he—upon whose brain a cloud may descend at any moment, and he will grope at midday as if it were sevenfold night. He must approach himself from the right standpoint, he must come to himself from communion with God, and then he will understand what Jesus, the ever-blessed One, meant when He said, He that is greatest among you, let him be the servant of all. That is submission. Service is submission; help given to others out of a generous because regenerated heart is the sign and is the seal of a genuine submission. What is this wonderful sub-mission? It is two persons doing the same thing at the same time to one another. Where is the submission? These acts are not conse-quent one upon another; they are concurrent; you bowed just as I was bowing, I submitted just as you submitted, and the finest me-chanical or mathematical instrument ever discovered could not mark the point of coincidence. That is submission. There is nothing here of some high and mighty one waiting until some lowly and inferior one kisses his boots; there is no act of condescension on the part of some foolish person who does not understand himself or understand the discipline of life; there is no knavish trick in this. Observe the atmosphere in which we have been trained; we have been brought up to being filled with the Spirit, to singing with one another in hymn, psalm, spiritual song as unto the Lord; we have been taught to give thanks always for all things, unto God and the Father, in the name of our Lord Jesus Christ: then "submitting"—part of the psalm! I may be the closing note of the rolling, the sonorous anthem. But we delight to tear these little sentences out of their place and to found theories upon them, so that some poor miserable preacher, of whom his mother might be ashamed, claims to be the head of the wife; a man who can hardly get out of bed in the morning; a man who has great difficulty in making bread enough to sustain his wife and family; a little, miserable, poorly-made toy of a man who is the head of the wife because he could not make himself the head of anything else! That is not Christian teaching. The two are one; they submit themselves one to the other; how to be first in the act of submission is the great problem, the happy delightful enigma, which both the parties, if filled with the Spirit of Christ, can instantly and sufficiently answer and resolve.

You cannot lay down little rules upon any such matters of personal or household discipline. What then can we do? The Apostle has already told us—"Be filled with the Spirit." To rule without ruling, to lead without leading, to drive without cracking the whip, to be a man without being a fool; that is only possible when we are filled with the Spirit, when we are breathing the vital atmosphere, when we are one with Christ. There is a sovereign principle which simplifies and sanctifies the whole action, redeeming it from servility and lifting it up into a sacrament. What is that sovereign principle? Again and again it asserts itself in all these exhortations—"as unto the Lord," "as Christ," "even as the Lord of the Church." Christians, whether men or women, are never asked to do more than Christ did. That will solve everything. "Even as the Lord." Then again, "as Christ," and again, "as unto the Lord." It is not some little domestic claim; it is a living Christian principle. Does the wife do nothing, even for the most successful of men? She makes the income quite as much as he does; she sustains him, inspires him, lifts the burden from his shoulder, takes him to see some new vision, drops into his life some new note of music. I would not have a penny that my wife did not share and could not spend. She made it; I, a poor creature easily depressed and turned out of the way, whose only delight is that he can resign his position; and she, cheering, gladdening, inspiring, uplifting: to whom does the property belong? To her. When I told a certain half-grown old gentleman that my wife drew all the checks without consulting me or troubling me about such documents, he said, "You must have great confidence in your wife." The wretch! Confidence in your wife—what a life without her! A nightmare, an awful intolerable misery. But these things cannot be regulated by little laws and maxims. How then can they be regulated? I quote again the wholly sufficient answer, "Be filled with the Spirit, the Spirit of love." Love never thinks that anything has been given while anything has been withheld. Until, therefore, we are great in the Christian life, great in the conception of spiritual blessings in Christ Jesus, fore-ordained by the discriminating and loving wisdom of God, settled, rooted, grounded in Christ, we are not fit to have a house, we are not fit to handle the delicate and difficult problem of life. But if the word of Christ be in us and dwell richly in us there will be no difficulty; there will be music, there will be rest; and we shall say, poor man or great man, "Be it ever so humble, there is no place like home."

Words for Preachers

Keep a clear conscience; he cannot be a bold reprover that is not a conscientious liver: such a one must speak softly, for fear of awaking his own guilty conscience. He is like one that shoots with a foul piece; he reproofs recoil upon himself. Unholiness in the preacher's life will either stop his mouth from reproving, or the people's ears from receiving. Oh, how harsh a sound does such a cracked bell make in the ears of his congregation! "Let the righteous smite me," if any, is the language of all hearts.—*Gurnall, 1617–1679*

A wicked minister, or parent, may be earnest with his people or family to mend, because they lose not their own sinful profits or pleasures by another's reformation, nor doth it call them to that self-denial as their own doth. But yet for all this, there is none of that zeal, resolution and diligence, as is in all that are true to Christ. They set not against sin as the enemy of Christ, and as that which endangereth their people's souls. A traitorous commander, that shooteth nothing against the enemy but powder, may cause his guns to make as great a sound or report as some that are laden with bullets; but he doth no hurt to the enemy by it. So one of these men may speak loud, and mouth it with an affected fervency; but he seldom doth any great execution against sin and Satan. No man can fight well, but where he hateth, or is very angry; much less against them whom he loveth, and loveth above all.—*Baxter, 1615–1691*

It is fabled of a madman, that, talking with a lean, meager cook, he understood from him what dainty dishes he dressed for his guests; and hearing that they were all fat and fair liking, and thrived with it, he asked him why he did not feed on those meats himself, that he might be fat too. The cook answered, that, for his part, he had no stomach; but the madman replies, "Take heed how thou come near Bedlam; if the corrector find you, your punishment will be very sharp, for certainly, you are madder than ever I was." Thus, it is no better than madness for ministers, magistrates, and others in place of eminency to give light to others, and walk themselves in darkness, to distribute portions of meat to the family and starve their own souls, to rescue others from the enemy and suffer themselves to be taken, to forewarn others of the pit whereinto themselves run headlong, to give good counsel to others and not to be guided by the counsel themselves.—*Otho Melander*

Prayer

Almighty God, show us Thy purpose, we humbly pray Thee, in our creation, preservation, and redemption. By Thy Holy Spirit, teach us that we are being taught and educated, day by day, till we come to be perfect men in Christ Jesus. Now we are imperfect, sometimes utterly infirm, unequal to the task of the day, and sometimes we feel that we are not utterly forsaken, that God is still with us, and that His purpose will be completed in the perfectness of our manhood. For every beam of light we thank Thee, for every voice of encouragement which penetrates our dejection and dispels it we bless the name of the Lord. Help us to believe that our education in Christ Jesus is Thy sovereign will, and that, being Thy sovereign will, Thou wilt surely bring it to its fullest accomplishment. There is much to deter us, there is much that is hostile and fierce and cruel; enable us to believe that He who is with us is more than all that can be against us, and that through the power and the love and the grace of Christ we shall ultimately be more than conquerors. We bless Thee for all stimulus, for all spiritual encouragement, for daily sustenance; Thou dost feed us with corn of heaven and with angels' food, and thus our souls are preserved though the enemy be strong. Look upon us in our low estate; the clouds are thick, but Thy sunlight can penetrate them all; desolation and sorrow are on every hand, but the comforts of God are not exhausted. We commend one another to Thy tender care. Oh send us some rose from Sharon, some lilies from the sheltered valley! Amen.

27
Till and Until (I)

Preached on Thursday Morning, December 21st, 1899.

Till we all come–Ephesians 4:13.

The immediate point is not what we are coming to, but the fact that we are coming, and that something is coming to us, and that this double action is the secret of the inspiration, the culture, the strengthening of our innermost life. The text therefore is "till . . . until,"–the something that says, You have not finished yet; there is another hill to climb, and then you will see it; there is another stream to ford, and on the other bank of that stream you will see what flowers can grow, and how mean are all the plants on this side the river. Till the sunshine comes, till the heavenly band appears and sends its thundering anthem through the quivering sky; till then, hope on! You have not yet arrived, but you are proceeding, you are on the right road, and you have this little singing word to cheer you in all your climbing and in all your descending and in all your fighting and in all your sorrow, "until–!" It would be a most profitable study to collate all the main passages in which we have the music of this till and until, and we should rise from the perusal of the oracles satisfied that though we have yet much to do there is a climacteric point, there is a just-now-rising dawn, the many tints of which can just be seen over the highest hill. Blessed are the prophets, forerunners who catch the first gleam of that morning light! They cannot keep the intelligence to themselves; there are some gospels that must be preached. When a man who is out far beyond us sees the first rising of the light which the ages have been waiting for, he will cry, Come, the day has risen! Even selfishness could not stifle that gospel, mayhap because selfishness could never receive it. The reason that people do not receive the Gospel is because they do not know it, nor do they feel it; it is at present but an intellectual conception or a moral conjecture; it is a mere study in ethics. When the Gospel itself with all the heat of its own red blood gets into any of us we must preach the Gospel to every creature. Let us be thankful for the men who have gone ahead, the men who first see the morning. How long we have been waiting for it! It seems century after century as if the slumberer would never awake, yet now and again, from Genesis to Revelation, there comes a voice which says, Until! It may be tomorrow, it may be a century hence, but it will come, and what we have to do is to hold on until the dayspring break in all its soft radiance and its implied eternities of summer on the earth that has been so long moaning, waiting, and mingling its prayers with a large share of dejection and despondency.

The keyword, therefore, is till or until; the same word, the same idea, and that idea an idea of encouragement and assurance, a word to hide in the heart and to listen to in the darkness when there seems to be no "until," when there seems to be but one settled frown on the brow of time. Yet the custodians of God's decrees, the divinely appointed priests of the eternal ark, are enabled to hear the sweet word "until," and such men, unknown, mayhap despised, have kept the world alive.

Where does this word "till" or "until" occur? Where all the great words occur, as I have told you a thousand times. Where do all the great words occur? In the Book of Genesis; and you have never read it! I speak not to the few who are familiar with the Divine Word, but to the many who never read it. You do not read the Divine Word when you only read it in the letter. The Divine Word is not a letter, but a spirit; it is not written music, but music sung and music brayed out from brass and throbbed as it were on living drums. We must go to Genesis for our first grand "until" (49:10). Jacob is dying, he knows that his life is slowly but certainly trickling away; he calls all his sons around him, and made such speeches as mortal man never made either before or since; and most of you have never read them! Never was such eloquence heard before; there are no forged climaxes, no mechanically built periods, no half-forgotten and hesitant recitations; but great, grand, flowing eloquence. When the patriarch came to his son Judah he waxed almost as eloquent as when he came to his son Joseph, but not altogether as eloquent. The old man was at his best when his hands as it were groped for the head of Joseph, but he was beautiful when he spoke to Judah—Judah who bore an awful scar of unfaithfulness and badness, but which was much covered up, if not wholly healed, by processes of grace which only experienced souls understand. Said Jacob, "The scepter shall not depart from Judah, nor a lawgiver from between his feet, until Shiloh come." There is the "till" or the "until," the word of promise, the gleam of hope, the pledged morning. No man can tell us what "Shiloh" means; we have had the word in Hebrew and in Greek, and we have called around it a whole marketplace of expositors, a whole gallery and sanhedrim of learned men, but they can make nothing really final out concerning all the wells and fountains and springs that are hidden in this word Shiloh. But there is a Christian acceptation of the term, which is sufficient for us. The ancient Jews, indeed, associated the name Messiah with the word Shiloh, and regarded them as practically interchangeable terms; but the ancient Jews did not know Messiah as we know Him; therefore we must attach a Christian interpretation to Shiloh, and find him in Bethlehem, and on Calvary, and on Olivet, and away yonder in the city of the temple of intercession. Enough for the present exposition that there was a promised Man, soul, light, song, something away in the ages beckoning on the human race and feeding it with corn of heaven. You cannot empty the ages, you cannot deplete the future. The future itself seems to be a term of welcome and hospitality and most generous promise. We can look at it from any point of view we choose, and yet the human heart says, Your hope is in the future; tomorrow there may be One blessed among women who will give the world a Savior, and you cannot shut out that "until"; you can modify it, mutilate it, pervert it, but there is the "until." There shall be an evil reign until he come whose right it is to sit upon the uppermost throne. This song of faith also sings in each individual heart. It is tomorrow that Shiloh will be here, it is in a week or two that we shall hear from the far-away places that will make us glad. Why, in one little month we shall hear tidings that will more than compensate us for all our sorrow and dismay and self-accusation. In a century the world will grow greener grass and the heaven will be clothed with a diviner blue. In five centuries who knows what the old earth will be? In a thousand years there may not be a grave in all the mold of the globe. It is because we have these great shining, singing promises that we are able to suffer the present; if this were all, we could not live another day. There are points of agony and of misery which would end our poor feeble existence if there were nothing beyond, if no Shiloh were preparing to come, if no sweet spring with vernal flowers were lingering by the blue Tyrrhean sea. It is because we know that the Shiloh spring is coming that we can bear the darkness of these December days, which are hardly worthy to be called days at all. June and December could never talk about days, they would not understand one another; June has one lexicon and December another, which his dim eyes can hardly read. It is the Shiloh that is coming that keeps the world alive, and all the atheists and agnostics and scorners and mockers cannot keep out of view or out of the sphere of holy, happy influence this grand Shiloh idea. The child will be born, the man will grow, the king will ascend the throne, and then we shall know why the universe was created, and the explanation will be grand, solemn, sufficient.

Another "until" we find in Psalm 73:17, "Until I went into the sanctuary." Then I saw all about it. The sanctuary is the only place where you can see everything, Church or State, just as it is. You see nothing really until you see it from the point of the altar. The religious soul, the soul that bathes itself in the stream of the divine wisdom and the divine light, is the greatest soul under heaven. All other souls are little pedlars compared with the religious soul that has the key of heaven, the entree of the hospitable skies. A poor man was sadly troubled because wicked people were prospering exceedingly: their gardens were full of flowers, and they had roses with next to no thorns on them, and they had herbs and oliveyards and vineyards and all manner of increase, yet they never sang a psalm, they never laid a tribute on God's altar. Their eyes were standing out with fatness, they had more than heart could wish; God was excluded from their whole imagination; and yet as to banking, as we should modernly call it, and commerce and prosperity, they had it all; and poor Asaph was hardly strong enough to carry his own harp. When he saw these almost beasts, certainly these minus men, his feet well nigh slipped, he was as nearly down flat on his back as ever a man was on treacherous ice. And then, having just strength enough to crawl into the sanctuary, he said in effect, What are all these lights? What is this I hear? What are these explanations that are rising in my mind? Who speaks? Who makes the night dead? If there was any audible voice able to make him hear this music beyond the merest outline and beginning. But thought came on thought, reflection followed upon reflection; Asaph put this together with that, and finally he said, I see it! Behold, it was they who were set in slippery places, it was they who were as bullocks fattening in a succulent pasture: ay, thou didst train them and fat them for the knife: I see it now! We should see all things if we went into the sanctuary in their right proportion, because in their right perspective and their right light. We are so meddlesome, and we will discuss daily details, and we are first troubled by one man and then we are troubled by another, and then in the middle of the day there is a sure and certain lie that comes and perplexes us more than ever as to what we heard yesterday and heard this morning. Why can we not leave the detail alone, and why does every washerwoman suppose that she could settle better than any statesman what ought to have been done in certain great national crises? Only in the sanctuary can we get the solution of all things. Sometimes that solution comes in the form of increased patience, a deepening sense of our dependence upon the living God. We do not always get an explanation in words and in grammatical phrases skillfully and mechanically piled into paragraphs which we can measure and understand. It is not always so that God works. Somehow in the sanctuary there is an atmosphere, as there is in the chamber of death. Tell me what is that weird, wondrous atmosphere that gets around the soul in the sight of the dead body. You are then really in the sanctuary, though not nominally so. The chamber of sickness may be a sanctuary; the chamber of your own closet where you offer secret prayer to God and commune silently with the Spirit may be the sanctuary. But in the ordinary signification of the term the sanctuary points to fellowship in worship, to a commonwealth of praise, to a common inheritance of grace—a great mystery, no doubt, but known well to those to whom God has given keys and promises and a sure word of prophecy. It is the religious man who should govern the State; it is the Church that should rule the empire. We have inverted things, and have gone to the marketplace to understand what can only be explained in the sanctuary. But the day is coming when the sanctuary, the holy, redeemed, blood-bought Church of Christ, shall tell the world what to do.

We might call on our way in the house of Canticles, the house of the love-dreams, and there in chapter 2:17 we shall read, "Until the day break and the shadows flee away." That is a grand "until." It is possible that the sun can find his way through all the gray cold clouds of December? Is there a day promised? Will the day break? Who ever heard the gates of the morning creak as they swung back on their golden hinges? Who ever heard a tramping army bringing up the sun as if by strength of muscle? Who ever heard the stars make a noise? Yet through all this wondrous process of the suns there is a silent march, a silent incoming of the Messianic period, and when the day breaks upon the grave, the grave shall be as a cradle; and when the day breaks on sorrow and sickness, failure, disappointment, and manifold misery, we shall see the whole sphere of life in its proper colors, relations, and proportions and find that God has been busy in the darkness. God does wonderful things in the night time; what He has done in the sanctuary of densest darkness we shall never know till the shadows flee away; then we shall find that all the while He has been building a palace for us, a right glorious and royal house, and making things ready for our souls away beyond the humble paths of the stars which now we think a long way off, but we shall think them a longer way off still when we get above them and look down on them with a kind of gracious contempt of their twinkling and quivering lamps. Hope on! There is a word in the wintry air, a song in the wintry night—"Until!"

Paul's idea of "until" was a coming to the measure of the stature of perfect men in Christ Jesus. Perfect does not mean what is often supposed to mean and what people get up more or less futile and senseless meetings for the purpose of promoting. There are no perfect men in that narrow sense. There is probably no sin greater in its possible implications than sinlessness as it is narrowly and imperfectly understood. Not until resurrection has done for the body what regeneration has done for the soul shall we know the meaning of "perfect" in its moral and spiritual sense. Meanwhile, it may signify the culmination of a new period, the advancement, chapter after chapter, of a new book, promotion after promotion to school after school in the higher academies of creation; it may mean as much as can be done here and now, but not perfection except as the end is the beginning of another period. The Bible ends, Revelation can only begin. Sometimes we have heard our dear little children say that they have finished school. We know the sense in which those dear little hearts use the word school. We can never get beyond the school of God, but we may go from class to class, from grade to grade, and on the conclusion of each grade, we may say, So much is perfect; that is done, but it is only done as a pedestal is done on which the statue is to stand, or is only perfect in the sense in which a field has been sowed with good seed which will come up thirty, sixty, a hundredfold. And so, as experience is multiplied by experience, and as consciousness is added to consciousness, we may seem at each particular crisis to be so far perfect. But the perfection is away beyond the sanctuary of the sun, away in the city which has no temple, because the whole city itself is but a temple: no paradox in words. We must die to see it, and we shall see no temple because the whole heaven is one vast radiant house of God. Brothers, let us cheer ourselves with this "till" and "until." Do not let us rush at hasty judgments; let us practice a religion of repose, let us exemplify the piety of rest. And when people ask us the vain question when will we reach the last perfection, we shall say, The hour is hidden with God, but the promise is that we are to wait until Shiloh come.

Words for Preachers

A wicked priest is the worst creature upon God's earth; no sin is so black as that shall appear from under a white surplice. Every man's iniquity is so much the heinouser as his place is the holier. The sin of the clergy is like a rheum, which rising from the stomach into the head, drops down upon the lungs, fretting the most noble and vital parts, till all the members languish into corruption. The lewd sons of Eli were so much the less tolerable by sinning in the tabernacle. Their sacrifices might do away the sins of others; no sacrifice could do away their own. Many a soul was the cleaner for the blood of those beasts they shed; their own souls were the fouler by it. By one and the same service they did expiate the people's offenses and multiply their own. Our clergy is no charter for heaven. Such men are like the conveyances of land, evidences and instruments to settle others in the kingdom of heaven, while themselves have no part of that they convey. It is no impossible thing for men at once to show the way to heaven with their tongue, and lead the way to hell with their foot.—*Adams, 1654*

As shell-fishes which breed pearls for others to wear, but are sick of them themselves; as a Mercury statue, which shows the way to others, but stands still itself; or as a whetstone, which sharpens the knife, but is blunt itself: thus many men, like Plutarch's Lamiae, have eyes for abroad, but are blind at home, are wise for others, but not for themselves. "If thou be wise," saith Solomon, "be wise for thyself." It is not enough for a man to do good to others, though he could to all, if he remain an enemy to himself: he must be like a cinnamon tree, which lets not out all its sap into leaves and fruit which will fall off, but keeps the principal part of its fragrancy for the bark which stays on; like a tree planted by the water side, which, though it let out much sap to the remoter boughs, yet is specially careful of the root that it be not left dry. And to speak truth, what profit would it be to a man, if he could heal and help all the sick men in the world, and be incurably sick himself? If he could get all the men on the earth, all the angels in heaven to be his friends, and have God still for his enemy? If he could save others, and then lose his own soul; to be like the ship (Acts 27) broken to pieces itself, though it helped others to the shore? Or like those that built the ark for Noah, and were drowned themselves: this is to have the cares of Martha upon him on the behalf of others, and never mind that one thing of Mary, the care of his own salvation. —*Purchas, 1577–1628*

Prayer

Almighty God, we thank Thee for all special mornings and tender memories and morning stars that bring with them the dew of new ideas and new encouragements. We bless Thee that Thou hast broken up the currents of history and given each a peculiar significance. Thou hast made many beginnings and many endings, and endings that are themselves beginnings; we pray that we may have understanding of the times and interpret the periods as Thou dost mean them to be interpreted. May there be no foolish men who let the signs of the times and of the glowing heavens pass by unread and unheeded: may we have understanding of the times, may we hear the beating of the pulse, may we know the coming of God and of His invisible kingdom; and thus may we be succored and strengthened and mightily upheld in all the coming and going ages of time. We bless Thee for anything that brings to our heart's memory the birth of Thy Son; may He be born in our hearts the hope of glory, may each heart be a Bethlehem, may the Son of God be the child of every man, and the Son of God be the Savior of everyone; and thus shall we hold fellowship with the past and with the future, and shall realize the security and the blessedness of a complete citizenship. We thank Thee for whatever brings human hearts together in loving interest, in reciprocal solicitude, so that we may take interest one in another, and may extend help and loving sympathy one to another when the valley is very dark and when the mountain is very steep; to this end we bless Thee for Thine own house upon the earth; the tabernacle of God is with men; our little houses lean their walls against the rock of Thy sanctuary. May we never live outside Thy temple; may Thy sanctuary be in our thoughts night and day; may we love Thy Zion, and steadily and faithfully work for the interests of Thy kingdom. We give Thee thanks for all the blessings of the year; by-and-bye we may give Thee thanks for all its withering sorrows; meanwhile, we think of the brightness and the sun and the gladness, and bathe ourselves in the joy of those who have greater joy than we ourselves can realize. Hence we bless Thee for all young-heartedness, for all true festival of love, for all the delights of those who have met kindred souls on the pilgrim way and have united themselves one with the other to complete the journey to the skies. We thank Thee for all who have prospered in business and have remembered the Lord in the high noon of their success. We pray for those who have been desolated and sorely stricken and utterly bereaved, and have been made to drink the bitterness of Thy waters; enable such to remember that Thou didst open all the fountains, whether bitter or sweet, and that Thy purpose has not yet come to the morning dawn. Enable us, therefore, to sustain ourselves in holy promises and prophecies, and to rest quietly while others can sing loudly and sweetly. We remember now many who are desolated by reason of the ravages of war; we think of lonely homes, of widows and orphans and childless parents, and we commend the whole case to Thee, Thou God of battles and Thou God of love. Many questions are too high for us, much knowledge lies beyond the reach of our feeble minds; but we can pray for faith to leave all in the hands of God, and for patience to wait the unfolding of Thy will. We thank Thee for all Thy love, we trust Thee in all Thy providences, we say, Clouds and darkness are round about Thee, but righteousness and judgment are the habitation of Thy throne; in these great sanctuaries, hidden in the eternal rock, we abide and wait, not knowing God, but knowing His Son Jesus Christ, who is able by the power of the Holy Spirit to reveal Him unto hearts that wait for His coming.

We tarry for a moment at Bethlehem. We tarry forever on Calvary. Amen.

28
Till and Until (II)

Preached on Sunday Morning, December 24th, 1899.

Let us continue as far as possible the discourse which we began on Thursday, studying the "Till" and the "Until" of prophecy and providence and soul-sustaining promise. We swept over considerable space on Thursday; there remains some ground yet to be traversed. The till and the until of time, the point that seems to go beyond time, to anticipate ages that are hardly yet reckonable within the four corners of the calendar of time. We could not live without the till and the until of the Divine book. Sometimes the period is far off; sometimes it is tomorrow; yet we could not live without it, though it be ages away beyond the arithmetic of counted centuries. Nor could we live without that event which is going to take place in the tomorrow of imagination. "Day" seems to mean, if strictly limited to itself, despair, then suicide–the last of the sacraments and the best; then we see a light just on the mountain top; it may be but a candle-gleam, but it is a gleam; meanwhile, all light is poetry and liberty and strength. When naturalists have written all they have to write about the great mystery and action of light, they have only written a preface to a course of sermons. There are moral uses of light, poetries of light, paradises in every star-ray and in every blink of the sun.

Let us add to our list of untils. Ezekiel has a grand until or till–the words are the same in meaning. In Ezekiel 21:27 we read, "Until He come whose right it is"–to save, to reign, to direct, to take the whole ribbons into His own hands and drive the chariot of the universe as He pleases. What a word of cheer, encouragement, and

279

most blessed and inspiring assurance! There is always One coming "whose right it is." He does not come in an apologetic attitude with a compromise from some threatened power, with a proposition that this and that should be divided between light and darkness; He comes with right. Nothing is settled until it is settled right. Do not believe that hush is peace; do not believe in any peace that is not built on righteousness. Understand, however, the largeness of that word righteousness; it is not my right, your right, the right of some third or unknown party, a selfish and limited right; it is a righteousness that involves the very nature and essence of the Deity. What is a crooked plumb line? Nothing, worse than nothing. What if we trifle with the joint of the square and give it a little tip to a hardly measurable angle? Will it still be a square? No. You killed the square when you changed the angle Geometry is sensitive; mathematics will not bear to be affronted; mathematics will have an avenging visitation upon those who trifle with rectitude. The arithmeticians say that figures, poor plain figures, have affections. Who could have thought that an arithmetician could have dreamed so deeply? He looks as if he himself were but a superficies, and sometimes he gets into such ecstasies as to speak about the passion of numbers and the affections of numbers; then he becomes religious, and builds what small altar he can with his brickdust. On what do the ages feed? On the promise that One is coming who will bring right with Him, and who will reign because He is right; who will sit upon a throne that cannot be torn down, because it fits into the whole scheme of things and is the part and the coronation of processes immeasurable and inconceivable. This will get rid of many paltry, petty, and insufficient teachers of compromise and balancing and settled covenantings and perfidious double commissions, taking alike from the buyer and the seller, and considering that all is going well because nobody knows anything about it. Nothing goes well that is in itself wrong. There is a tumbling day, a day of upset and ruin. "Be sure your sin will find you out!" thunders through the universe, and no man can cough it down. If we could get rid of the notion that we have to handle and to settle things we should be greatly strengthened and greatly relieved. There is next to nothing that we have to handle. Some people can scarcely handle their own raiment; some persons need trainbearers to carry their poor skirts; and men are soon bereaved, stripped, and depleted of every high ambition and crafty cunning policy, and are left on the roadside with coronets that never ruled and with ambitions that were but decorated abortions. Those who live by faith live in peace; they are perfectly sure that all things work together for good to them that love God; and nobody loves God who does not love the right, who does not love righteousness, and who takes a little, narrow, parochial, selfish view of things. We are so soon overdone; we write fables and draw pictures about a man who tried to carry a globe on his shoulders. Why, it is but a poor bean, nay, it is but a poorer pea which he carries, and not all worth mentioning in any catalogue of the stars. We are tempted to think that nearness is bigness, and we forget that there is One coming, coming with the clouds, coming with the morning, coming after the shortest day has had its little dark reign; coming, and coming to remain by force of right. I wish men would not tinker with things; that they would simply know their limitations; that they would go into the sanctuary of God, and sit there; and if they cannot speak they can be silent, and if they cannot sing they can speak, and if they can neither sing nor speak they can have wrought in them by the mighty power of the Holy Ghost the miracle of patience. Is it nothing to have had all these men about us who have said "till," "until"–the men of eyes who have seen the far-off light and interpreted it to those of us who dwell in the shaded valley?

There are wondrous instances of "till" and "until" in the New Testament. For example, in Matthew 2:13, "until I bring thee word." That is a new scheme of lodgment. How long have I to remain here? And the angel says, Until I come back. I want to be moving. Sit still! I do not see why I cannot proceed further. Wait until I bring thee word in thy little business, thy little household environment, thy limited village or limited circumstances; lodge there until I bring thee word: I will not forget thee: God knows the address, He never forgets an address, He never mixes in indiscriminate confusion the dwellings of those who love Him with the dwellings of those who despise Him: wait until! Thank God for that "until"! It is itself a limitation. While it appears to be the indication of a great space or a great time, it fixes a point of return, of deliverance, of liberty, of light. Oh, it is so long! So it is; but the length of the waiting is part of the education of the soul. When shall I see him, see her, again? Could I not see for one little golden hour in the week? I ask no more. And the angel said, Remain until I bring thee word; I watch all the dressing and preparation and equipment; I know when spirit should meet spirit, when alliances should be completed or renewed; when the veil should be blown to pieces or withdrawn like a curtain of film; I understand the counsel of God in this matter; stop until—until—until.

The apostles were not men much given to a very high order of patience. Like ourselves, they always wanted to be doing something. Some men cannot be really happy unless they are doing a little; it may be only opening and shutting an umbrella, but they must be at it, you cannot keep their hands off it. Well, they were made so, and God will read such riddles to us when we have nothing better to do than to listen to their reading. The apostles were men of this sort: Wilt thou at this time restore the kingdom unto Israel? Wait; it is not for you to know the times and the seasons. What shall we do when we are bereaved of our Lord? Tarry in Jerusalem. How long? Until ye be endued with power from on high. What are we to do in the meantime? Do nothing. We think we can be doing something. You think wrongly. Do not do anything in your own strength, because you will only live to apologize for having done it. Do not imagine that you see anything as it really is; the secret of the centuries is with God. Tarry ye in Jerusalem until you get the power. There is no mistaking power. The difference between one man and another often is that one man can do it, and another man cannot do it; and the great mischief is that the man who cannot do it is tempted of the devil to believe that he could do it as well as the other man. We have to wait until there is a great flood-tide of power, a conscious access or accession of strength; when that mighty power comes upon us, then we may go forth and do the Lord's will. Waiting is education. We are taking in elements of strength when we hardly know that we are doing so. But one clear day at the seaside when the wind is coming over the sea sometimes makes an old man young again. What has he been doing? Nothing; and doing everything by doing that nothing: putting himself into right relation, waiting for proper opportunities, lying sweetly, softly, dreamily in the arms of God, the Father-Mother; next day he enters upon a renewed inheritance of energy; all the time the kindly wind was breathing into him new power and displacing old weakness. Tarry ye until you are conscious of power, not of power only, but of power from on high; that is, not only a certain degree of power, but a certain quality of strength; then go forth, and no man shall be able to stand against the hosts of the Lord. Oh, this neglect of the Spirit, this disregard of the Fountain of energy, this broken and hesitating companionship with the angel powers of the universe, who are waiting to nourish us and cherish us and nurse us out of our infirmity into God's own true strength. We think we are making progress when we are only going round and round a circle. You cannot teach the right idea of progress to some persons. A man does not go across the Atlantic by walking round and round the main-mast; that is not the action which is progress; there is an action that has no forwardness in it. God Himself takes us through the right exercises and keeps us on the right line. But we cannot wait for the power. We think we have the power, and therein we become weak as other men. Where the power is really given there is no mistake about its quality. You cannot explain it; all power is a mystery, except the merely mechanical power; but the dynamic power, the inside, or what we may term the almost spiritual power, who can understand or interpret? Yet there is no mistaking its effects; its energy is indescribable, but patent and indisputable. The Church will not wait for power; the Church wants to mechanize its own strength, to get up its own new little program of progress: and the Lord Himself watches such poor little paper kingdoms take fire, go up into smoke, and fall back into dust. The Church of Christ today and everyday ought to be the mightiest force in the world. It has all the elements, all the promises; it has not the faith. It proposes and compromises and begs pardon of the devil and hopes he is not unduly inconvenienced. What becomes of such a church? Wreck, ruin, oblivion, or contempt.

The Apostle frequently uses the word "till" and "until"; notably in 1 Corinthians 11:26, "show the Lord's death till He come." There are so many double sentences in Holy Scripture, and so many people have never noticed them. They are too busy with their Christmas beef to read the word of the living God. These Biblical double sentences are great jewels, and we are not forbidden to decorate with such ornaments. Hear David, the greatest master of plaintive poetry that the world ever knew; saith he: "I shall go to him, he shall not return to me." There is the double action. I always want to reverse that sentence that I may feel more acutely the tenderness of its meaning: He shall not return to me, but I will go to him. The assurance that I will go to him makes him live in the very grave; I am moving in a curve unknown to geometry, we shall come face to face in the by-and-bye. So when Paul tells me about my Lord's death he hardly gets the word out of his mouth until he says, "till He come." That is the true rhetoric, the divine eloquence, the substantial and indestructible logic. We do indeed show forth a death, but we only show it forth until it be turned into life, until it be forgotten and the grave is destined to be forgotten, and one day the new earth may not remember that ever a grave was cut in the old earth. If in that day we should ask for reminiscences of the grave, the new earth will be stupefied by our very inquiry, it will not know what language we are speaking. Death, grave, loss, pain—is there any interpreter who will tell me, poor old earth, what these words mean? And lo, there shall be no interpreter. The language was only invented that it might be forgotten.

I notice that the Christian pulpit has suffered a severe loss within the last few days by the withdrawal from these gray scenes of time of Dwight Lyman Moody, known to all the Christian Church as a devoted, faithful, and successful evangelist. Mr. Moody was a strong, capable man. Like a wise man, he knew his limitations, and he worked within them; he never wanted to be somebody else, it was enough that he knew his talent, whether one or two or five, and with whole-heartedness he gave himself to the highest of all work. There was a time when I was slightly disinclined to have much commerce or communion with Mr. Moody, because I feared he was a man with only one set of sympathies. When I met him in his own house in America that feeling was instantaneously and completely dissipated; I found he was a big man, a man of wide views and wide sympathies, and that he only needed more light, or the opportunity of enjoying more light, in order thoroughly to enter into his privileges. He was preeminently, within his own limits, a preacher. Do not be misled by the word preacher, because it admits of several definitions, or, perhaps, many definitions have been unduly thrust upon it. I could not imagine Mr. Moody taking out of his satchel or pocket an elaborate essay which he was going to read to a stupefied and bewildered audience. He spoke right out of his heart, and grammar had sometimes to take care of itself, and logic had sometimes to get out of the way. But it was the Gospel Mr. Moody preached, a living, comprehensive, divine, everlasting Gospel. What is that Gospel but a great welcome to the human heart to come to the living Christ and receive the assurances of pardon and growth and happiest destiny?

Having a little feeling of hesitation as to whether he and I lived under the same firmament so far as theological views were concerned, I did not hasten to his house. Feeling that I was loitering by the way, he came to fetch me; that was extremely and beautifully

Moody-like. He had a good deal of the disciplinarian and even of the soldier in his constitution. So he came to the hotel, about a mile away from his house, and said I must come at once. We all went with him. It was a simple, homely, comfortable, farmlike home on the hillside, a room on the right hand and a room on the left, and both the rooms and the passage included some of us could put into one of our London houses. Mr. Moody beckoned me into a little room which he called his study, and taking two books out of his shelves he said, "Look at these." I looked at them. "Open them," he said. I opened them, and I found marks, notes, special indications of careful perusal; little sentences were marked that I should have thought Mr. Moody would have never noticed. And then said he to me, putting back these two volumes of "The People's Bible" into his shelves, "I never travel without these, and these books have done more for me than any other books of the kind I ever read." After that I could not suspect him of any tendency towards narrowness or exclusiveness, because I know that in "The People's Bible" there is room for everybody who is earnest in spirit and lovingly waiting for the consolation of Israel.

From that moment I knew more of the man. I examined some of his work. I was taken down to his great school, almost a university in outline. When I considered what he had been doing along those lines I could not there and then, one sunny Saturday afternoon in Connecticut, but thank God for the man and his service. He brought some thirty or forty of his girls to sing to us at his front door, and when they were singing "We shall know each other better when the mists have rolled away," the tune sort of limped, and he said, "Girls! sing up, or Dr. Parker will think you are frightened of him." Then they all sang like so many birds, and it was a scene my wife and myself never could forget.

A few days ago we heard that Mr. Moody was dead; I remembered that sunny afternoon, I remembered that he alone of that little company was not the only one who was dead, in the little human sense of the term. My wife was fond of his ministry, nor was she the less fond of some of his, shall we say, less conventional ways of doing things. Not knowing who she was, at one great London meeting he seized her by the arm and said, "Are you for Christ?" And she was once at a great Salvation Army meeting, and something of the same kind occurred. A sweet little Salvationist came and said to her, "Are you saved?" and she said, "No, but I am being saved"— the true grammar and the true theology. May God raise up many men like Mr. Moody, strong, simple, unselfish men, who will teach us how to make the best of our time, and to be ready when the Lord comes!

Prayer

Almighty God, we thank Thee for the good news of the world, we bless Thee that there is now a gospel in the air, a great voice of love, a great cry of welcome from the heart of heaven. We bless Thee for the mysteries of the great Redemption; we cannot penetrate them, but we can feel their holy awe and their inspiring energy. We live in mystery; for we live and move and have our being in God. Teach us, we humbly pray Thee, the limits of our understanding; may we know where to stop, how to listen, and how to pray. Teach us that secret things belong unto the Lord our God, but the things that are revealed belong unto us and to our children, that we may do all the words of the holy law. We bless Thee for a song in the night season, for a sudden gleam of light that pierces and disperses the darkness; may we often see that beam of light in our own spiritual experience, lest we sink in dejection and die in despair. It hath pleased Thee to create a great ministry of darkness; Thou dost come unto Thy servants in a thick cloud, Thou dost take them away into a mountain apart where there is no noise, where no tumult is known, and there in the holy loneliness Thou dost communicate Thy law and whisper of Thy coming kingdom of redemption by blood and enthronement by right of love. We thank Thee for all holy memories, we bless Thee for historical days, and count them among our jewels; we often recount them, we obey the inspiration of reminiscence, and go back over long-gone yesterdays and centuries that we may thus fortify ourselves for present stress and pain by a review of Thy wondrous providence. We cannot fail if we pray. Didst Thou not say in the oldest of the times, "Thou shalt remember?"; and did not Jesus Christ Thy Son, our Savior and Priest, say, "Remember?"; and did He not give us a cup and say, "Remember me?" We bless Thee for the faculty of memory; may we go back upon all the centuries which Thy great judgment has set up in awe, and the glorious centuries which Thou hast set forth in light. Coming back from these holy sanctuaries, we shall be strong and full of hope and tender-hearted, because of overflowing gratitude. This Christmastide we would remember. Lord, help us to exercise our spiritual memory. Amen.

29

Personality

Preached on Christmas Morning, 1899.

And it was noised that He was in the house—Mark 2:1.

No matter who else was there; if Jesus Christ Himself was not there the house was of no consequence. There may have been fifty people in the house, but if He was not there the whole fifty could not make up for His absence. It was always noised, reported, published when Jesus Christ was in the house. Everybody seemed to know it as if by intuition or instinct; there was a balminess in the air, and a strange weird kind of feeling in the very wind. If you had asked people to explain this in words they might have felt some difficulty in doing so. So it is with us; we know a great many things without being able to tell why or to explain how, or to reduce the gracious and inspiring intelligence to language. If the one person is not there, what does it matter who else may be there? It is always one person that unites and accentuates all other persons, and turns the multitude into an aggregate friendship; but without that one person, explanatory, luminous, all-uniting, what is the multitude but a mob? It is one person that creates the house, that creates our interest in certain affairs, private, social, public; there is always one life we wish to please, there is always one peculiar and special approbation we wish to realize; the praise of such a one is worth a whole theater of others. This principle, which we all know in daily practical life, was peculiarly realized in the case of Jesus Christ. He went to be guest, but He soon became host; He went to receive, but

He soon realized Himself in His character, meant to be such from all eternity, and became the giver. It was noised that He was in the house, and thenceforth that house, however small, obscure, humble, became the central point of the town or the village or the universe.

How wondrously strange it is, this whole mystery and action of personality! You had a great number there? Yes, but—What made the town so fair, what turned the whole mob into a company of apostles and friends, what made the world tolerable, bearable, what saved it from being an inconceivably painful tragedy? And you mustered in great thousands to see the great hero leave his native shores; did you? Yes, we did. You do not seem to be very gratified or pleased about it? No, we are neither gratified nor pleased. Oh, tell me why! There were fifty thousand people there; that was enough? No; the hero did not come; he changed his plan, he went by another route. But were you not satisfied to behold fifty thousand people? No. You understand that? Perfectly. That is exactly what happened in the case of Jesus Christ. No matter who was there, or who was not there; if He Himself was not present the whole occasion lost its genius, its accent, and its poetry. It is one man that brings the fifty thousand together. I wonder if I could make this quite clear to the youngest and slowest of my hearers. There was a wonderful man who played wonderfully upon a wonderful instrument; they say he sometimes played upon one string only; and a Welshman told a friend of mine that he went to hear him. The Welshman himself was a player upon the violin, and said he, "We were all jealous and envious of this long greasy-haired Italian, and we said, 'What can Paganini do more than we can do?' and there he stood before us, and we said, 'That is Paganini, what can he do more than we can do?' But he lifted up his bow and brought it down, and, my word, sir! it was like a shower of music from heaven, sir!" He cut off all their heads, poured them all into a common basket, and gave the basket to anybody that would take it. I want thus to illustrate even to the youngest what is meant by personality—the one soul that creates an interest in other souls. That was peculiarly the case with our Lord Jesus Christ. He it is that unites the universe, and makes the universe worth keeping up; otherwise, it would exhaust itself and go away in fire and cloud and a horrible noise. Read what the apostle Paul says in his great epistles to the Colossians and to the Ephesians, wherein he represents Jesus Christ as being before all things and above all things, and the explanation and glory and crown of all things; as if to remove Him were to shatter the universe, which He used as a garment in which He might go forth more or less visibly to itself. We will never get rid of personality. There is a section, whether great or small I heed not, of people who would like to get rid of what they call individuality. You cannot get rid of it; it is written and unwritten, it is a decree from the beginning; it would suit them to get rid of individuality because they might in some cases get rid of responsibility, and then there is always some little streak of comedy lying in the very middle of a tragedy. When they got rid of individuality they would be as good as anybody else. Blessed be God, there are some things which even the meanest insects cannot do, and to get rid of individuality would be to impoverish and enfeeble the world. Today we gather around the greatest Individuality ever known, the Personality that explains all other life, and that brings with it a promise, a discipline, a blessing, and a destiny.

It was noised that He was in the house. This Christmas morning we may say, It was noised that He was in the world. Never forget that there was a great noise made about this birth. One angel began it, and suddenly there was with the angel a multitude of the heavenly hosts, singing and shouting and praising God, and saying, "Glory to God in the highest!" and all heaven throbbed and quivered under that triumphant anthem. Jesus Christ, then, did not come noiselessly into the world; so far as He Himself was concerned, there was little or no noise, but the moment it was hinted that He was in the world-house, the earth, a visible manifestation of the invisible Deity, there was noise enough, musical noise, a great multitudinous acclaim.

There are some times when people cannot be silent; indeed, there are some times when silence would be a species of blasphemy. Jesus Christ Himself said, If these little ones were to hold their tongues, the very stones would cry out. Enthusiasm has its day, its place, its elevating and inspiring influence. Never have much social commerce with indifferent people, with people who can turn away from a great piece of music and ask how you are. As if it mattered how you are or how anybody else is amid the entrancement and the passion and the transport of a wondrous revelation. They say there are people who after the greatest possible religious service can tell you what the weather was last Wednesday. Ah me—it is so hard to live. They are not caught in the whirlwind of the great cry and welcome and gospel of the heart of God. I suppose such people must live, or the marketplace would come to bankruptcy.

It was noised that He was in the world to bring you good tidings of great joy; for unto you is born this day in the house of David a Savior, which is Christ the Lord. And all heaven was not orchestra enough to announce the infinite blessing. Have we ever been caught in that passion, or are we only those cold-blooded folks who have to be carried in the ship as ballast?

It was noised, not only that He was in the world, but presently that He was the foremost Man in the world. In a sense the only man, because without Him there could be no life. People began to say concerning Jesus, "Never man spoke like this man." He became the pronoun that stood for the only noun there is, the Deity. And on another occasion the people said, "It was never so seen in Israel." That is personality, that is something characteristic and divine and highly accentuated. The people knew what they were talking about; the history of Israel was the only history with which they were really familiar, and they said, looking upon the works of Jesus and listening to His words, "It was never so seen in Israel." And thus little by little He stands apart in a dignified, majestic, divine isolation. It was not that Jesus Christ spoke, but that He so spoke that no other man ever spoke like Him. When Nicodemus came to Him, he did not say, Rabbi—or Teacher—Thou doest miracles. That would have been a poor speech; the tribute was in the descriptive word which the master in Israel used: "Rabbi, we know that Thou art a teacher sent from God; for no man can do"—miracles? No, but—"these miracles that Thou doest"; this peculiar kind of miracle, this miracle *sui generis*—"except God be with him": it takes the Godhead to create flowers like these. Thus it was the individuality or personality of the man. Nor did the people care so much about the miracles when they came to their own better understanding; they idealized the miracles, they lifted them up to the level of their proper significance, and they said in effect, These are not miracles only, they are blessings. No man can work a miracle, blessing, except God be with him. Conjurers enough, sleight-of-hand has outrun all the words, and now puzzles the infancy of the generations and makes a livelihood out of the puzzling; but there are no blessings in these necromancies and conjurings. When Jesus Christ did a miracle it was never to show the power, it was always to confer the blessing. That separates Him from all the miracle-mongers and Egyptian astrologers and ancient necromancers: He chose to do or to confer His blessings in that peculiar and striking form.

It was noised that He was in the house, and the world; that He was not only in the house-world or world-house, but that He stood alone in it and gradually drew away from all other men that He might ascend the throne which He created. But in a sweet domestic sense it is often noised that He is in the family circle, in the little house, in our house where the cradle is, and where the little schoolbooks are scattered about, and where the aged folks are that are now wondering what there is just across the river. It is noised that Jesus is in this house or that house; the one may be a little thatched cottage, the other a great mansion, almost a palace, with great grounds around it; and Jesus can be equally in both. How so? How so?—as the sunshine is; the sunshine visits the little thatch-roofed cot, and the sunshine pronounces its silent blessing on the proudest roofs of the proudest people.

Is it noised that Jesus Christ is in our house? What do they say? They say, knowing our family life, that Jesus is in that house because of its order, its temper, its resignation, its whole method and economy of existence; they say that only the presence of Jesus Christ in that house could have made such a death. There never was a deathbed scene like it except under the same circumstances, the same deep consciousness of the same majestic and tender Personality. They say that Jesus was so visible in that house to the heart of faith and to the heart of love that the people could not sing but sob a hymn over the dear departed. They say that the joys were greater than the sorrow. Who did it? Take that wine to the master of the feast and say, "Who made this wine?" and you will be told that never such wine was tasted before, that there has been a great miracle wrought. These are the proofs and illustrations of the presence of Christ, in the heart and in the house, and no amount of argument, contention, can get rid of those solemn, profound, inspiring experiences which enable the bereaved to cry, O Death! where is thy sting? O Grave! thy victory? Produce it! We smite thee on the face, and defy thy cruelty.

One day it will be noised that He is on the throne. It was noised that He was in the house, it was noised that He was in the world, it was noised that He was the chief speaker and the chief miracle-worker of the world, and it shall one day be noised with the voice of thunders and tempests and great whirlwinds that He is on the throne. Tempest shall tell it to tempest, and ocean to ocean, and world to world, and planet to planet; and there shall go forth a great, grand, solemn cry, The kingdoms of this world are become the kingdom of our God and of His Christ. And they shall cry in every tongue, Hallelujah! and Bethlehem shall culminate in Heaven.

Words for Preachers

Husbandmen, when they are disappointed of their expected harvest, have not any to recompense their loss, but all is gone, both seed and labor; but notwithstanding the labor of the minister doth not profit with men, in respect of their incredulity, yet hath he his reward in heaven.
—*Cawdray, 1609*

A graceless, inexperienced preacher is one of the most unhappy creatures upon earth: and yet he is ordinarily very insensible of his unhappiness; for he has so many counterfeits that seem like the gold of saving grace, and so many splendid stones that resemble Christian's jewels, that he is seldom troubled with the thoughts of his poverty, but thinks that he is "rich, and increased in goods, and hath need of nothing," when he is "poor, and miserable, and blind, and naked."—*Baxter, 1615–1691*

And he that sits at home may study geography, and draw most exact descriptions of countries, and yet never see them nor travel towards them; so you may describe to others the joys of heaven, and yet never come near it in your own hearts: as a man may tell others of the sweetness of meat which he never tasted; or as a blind man, by learning, may dispute of light and of colors, so may you study and preach most heavenly matter, which yet never sweetened your own spirits, and set forth to others that heavenly light, wherewith your own souls were never enlightened, and bring that fire for the use of your people that never once warmed your own hearts. If you should study of nothing but heaven while you lived, and preach of nothing but heaven to your people, yet might your own hearts be strangers to it. What heavenly passages had Balaam in his prophecies, yet little of it (it is likely) in his spirit. Nay, we are under a more subtle temptation than any other men, to draw us from this heavenly life. If our employments did lie at a great distance from heaven, and did take up our thoughts upon worldly things, we should not be so apt to be so contented and deluded; but, when we find ourselves employed upon nothing else, we are easier drawn to take up here. Studying and preaching of heaven is liker to a heavenly life than thinking and talking of the world is, and the likeness is it that is like to deceive us. This is to die the most miserable death, even to famish ourselves because we have bread on our tables, which is worse than to famish when we cannot get it; and to die for thirst while we draw water for others, thinking it enough that we have daily to do with it, though we never drink it to our souls' refreshing.—*Baxter, 1615–1691*

Prayer

Almighty God, our Father, we bless Thee for the ministry of reconciliation. It is a ministry of Thine own; by Jesus Christ, in whose name we approach Thee, we have received the atonement; we are now by Thy grace and by such faith as Thou hast enabled us to exercise, no longer twain, but are in very deed one with God. There is one God, and one Mediator between God and man, the Man Christ Jesus. He is our Daysman, He is able to lay His hand upon both and to make reconciliation. By none other have we received the atonement. We gather in the name of Christ, in the name of Christ we pray, in the name of Christ we hope. Thou hast brought us to our last weekday service in another year; all things seem to have upon them the image and aspect of death. This is a dying time; we think of it as a sleeping hour: the earth is at rest; behold, there will presently come upon the face of the land we live in a great vision of light and a great sense of warmth, and the flowers will come back, and we shall forget they have ever been away. We thank Thee for all seasonable suggestion, for a gospel of the year, for a gospel of the day, for a sweet, tender music that belongs to the special morning, whether it be a morning in winter or a morning in the glowing summer. Thou hast a word for every hour, for every soul, for every occasion. We come to Thee, therefore, in this the closing time of another year, and we feel tenderly, gratefully, yet profoundly solemn. The Lord gave and the Lord hath taken away the year. We cannot get it back to remedy its wrongs, to obliterate its false records. God pity us, seeing that we pray, in all these glooms, in the name of Jesus Christ, in whom there is no darkness at all. Amen.

30

Reconciliation After Conversion

Preached on Thursday Morning, December 28th, 1899.

Reconciling the world unto Himself. . . . Be ye reconciled
to God—2 Corinthians 5:19, 20.

This paragraph is full of the word and of the idea reconcile or reconciliation. "All things are of God, who hath reconciled us to Himself"; He has given unto us the word or the ministry of reconciliation; He has given us our instructions, written us our gospel, expressed it in words we cannot fail to remember: knowing "that God was in Christ reconciling the world unto Himself." And more than that: He "hath committed unto us the word of reconciliation," as if it were a continual word, a living word, a word that belongs to the very air we breathe; it is a ministry, a stewardship, a charge, a responsibility; so that the ministry has never to ask, What have I to do? The ministry has to do a certain thing, profound, far-reaching, much-including; the ministry has to declare and preach and expound and enforce the word of reconciliation. If you ask us who we are and what we are, I will tell you: "Now then," after all this, "we are ambassadors, ambassadors for Christ." It is as if "God did beseech you by us and through us: be you reconciled unto God": be at one with God, be at peace with God; let there be no war or discontent, let there be no evil reproach or upbraiding, but a complete, solid, continual oneness with the Eternal Spirit. That is grand. There is something then for the ministry of Christ to do, something definite, something beneficent, something positive, and in its way something final; this, however, being one of the finals in which we shall find new beginnings, germs, and starting-points of new and un-dreamed growths and advances.

There are two reconciliations, if I may so put it, and I shall not be deterred by pedantry from so declaring my gospel. There is a rec-onciliation before conversion, necessary to conversion, and in itself a species of complete conversion; there is another reconciliation, which seems to me oftentimes to be harder, deeper, as it were more exacting; a neverceasing reconciliation; a reconciliation of growth, progress, advancement, perfectness. We have all, it is but reasonable to suppose, passed the first conversion or the first reconciliation; we carry no arms against God, no gun, or saber or sword or cruel spear; we do not dare the Almighty to battle. I hear as it were the clash of falling arms, which, being interpreted, means, We fight no longer against our God; we say to Christ, Galilean, Thou hast con-quered. We do not declare war against the Lord and against His anointed, saying, Let us cast their bands from us. We are no more scoundrels, ruffians. We may have passed into a still more danger-ous state, and it is that second reconciliation which unmans and overpowers me. Have we received the second reconciliation? Some Christians do not hesitate about talking concerning the second blessing. It is a richly evangelical term; we have no need to be ashamed of it or to apologize for it. I will venture to ask, Have we received the second reconciliation? Are we far away from the gate of Damascus, where our wrath was hot against the Lord and against His Christ, and have we passed into serener conditions, into a no-bler and ampler, a saintlier and tenderer manhood? "Be ye recon-ciled to God." I am not addressing a gang of opponents of the Lord; I will not treat my audience as if they had gathered them-selves together for the purpose of opposing the Most High; they have done nothing of the kind. And yet I may venture, first to ad-dress myself, and then through myself to address them in some such terms and tones as these: We have passed from open, bitter, hostility against the Lord and against His throne, but are we yet fully reconciled to God? I am not; I sometimes am; like yourselves, I have mountain moments, times when I can see afar, when rivers are threadlets in the sand; stormy seas are not to be heard in such sacred altitudes: but there is a coming down again, times of peevishness and unrest and self-regard and almost self-idolatry; an atheism within a theism, an atheism within the sanctuary; the sanctuary without them, but a secret hard coldness or distrust, and sometimes an active suspicion against things, against the shaping and the managing of things, as if I could do it better. I have received the first reconciliation, as you have; let us together unite in thanking God that we are not as we once were; we are washed, we are cleansed, we have passed the gate of the first catharism, and now we sing Christian hymns and psalms and spiritual songs, and call ourselves a congregation of believers. And yet it is possible to be this honestly and joyously, and to have moments in which we feel that it might have been otherwise, and sweeter and better, and the hymn is sung to notes, but not to music; we have the form, we may not have the power of unity with God, an acquiescence in His holy will. You see partly now what I mean by the second reconciliation, which is impossible without the first, but which ought to flow from the first as a matter of natural sequence, and indeed is so flowing; and God who inhabiteth eternity is patient with us in all the repairing and rectification and critical attention and self-distrust and self-laceration which must follow as indeed a happy sign of growth in the divine life.

We are reconciled to God in the matter of sin, through our Lord Jesus Christ, but are we reconciled to God in the matter of providence? Do we think it enough to cast off the old nature as to sin in its common or usual acceptation, and do we follow the soul back and back and back, until we get at the nearest point to spirituality, and say, You are right in the main, you are right in the mass so-called, but are you quite at one with God in the order of His daily providences? There is self-examination there. No man must lecture another upon that topic; the preacher must be severer with himself than with any of his hearers. I am reconciled as to what is customarily called sin; I pray, I pray in the name of Jesus Christ our Lord, I pray at the Cross, I love to dwell on the great mystery of the great Savior: but am I reconciled to God in the way in which He is managing my life? Could I not have done better, could I not have ordered things more proportionately and satisfactorily in the great world, could I not have snubbed the wicked with a sharper reproach, and could I not have lifted up the righteous to a more visible altitude of eminence and acceptance with God, and would I have allowed that little cradle to be emptied? Could I have allowed some invisible hand to pluck the child from the mother's breast and almost laugh in the mother's face? I am reconciled as to great, rough, coarse sins; I have my hymn-book and my psalm-book, and I gather with the people of God, and call myself reconciled to God through Christ: and that is right and most true as a matter of history and experience open to daily and indisputable confirmation; I know it. But am I reconciled to God when He sets up a sick-chamber in my house, and says to me, Keep the key of this door yourself, make this your school-house, offer your prayers within these shades and glooms, and offer them joyously, make your very suffering a sacrifice and offering of praise? We may not have reached that second reconciliation in its fullest and best sense, but we may be growing towards it; every time we turn the lock of that sick-chamber we may say, God pity me, God help me to pray more fully and richly today than I was able to pray yesterday, and so enlarge my horizon that I shall give things something like their intended proportion, and catch the meaning of the Divine going even in silence, when nothing can be heard but the dropping of tears.

We are reconciled to God in the rougher sins and the initial sins, but what about God's discipline with our souls? Are we reconciled to God in the matter of discipline? Is discipline a Bible word? Could you at this moment answer this question definitely? Sometimes people think discipline is a dictionary word, or a made word; but somehow this great vessel which we call the Bible has caught all the language and all the words in their best and deepest meanings; and the word discipline is in the Bible. You know that the promises are there, you have marked your Bible in some bright color that your eye may easily alight upon the promises; will you look into your Bible presently, and say if you have marked the word discipline with a black line? Are you not a little too fond of the promises, because you only understand them in their literal sense and in some sense of immediate comfort? Do you accept the promises as a species of discipline? That is what the apostle did; he said, "Having therefore, beloved, these promises, let us—" then he stood in military altitude and stature, and delivered as he never failed to deliver some exhortation towards cleanness and holiness. Some of us cannot read the promises except in the sense of their being so much spiritual confectionery. Believe me, they are not; such encouragement means increase of strength; consolation means enhancement of virtue or manliness; not a getting rid of the burden, but such an increase of the strength that bears it as to make nothing of it. What does a giant know whether he is carrying a pebble or two more or less? His strength is the central question with him.

Are we reconciled to God in the matter of discipline, which sometimes means rebuke; which sometimes means that God will not see us today in the way we like best; which means that sometimes the morning order is to go into wildernesses and far-off places where there is no bread and where the water is but liquid poison, and we may have to go there for a time to learn a particular but necessary lesson in the school of bitterness. We have had fathers in the flesh and teachers who have been strict disciplinarians, and we almost resented their military, their Spartan discipline at the time, but we have lived to thank God for such kindly-meant severity; it kept us at our work, it taught us our weakness, it showed us the possibility of our strength; it, along with other elements and ministries, in the providence of God, made us men. Are there any men made now?

Are we reconciled to God in the distribution and in the allotment of talent and position and prize of a social kind? If so, we
have got rid of the devil jealousy, envy. Are we reconciled to God
when we see that the man standing next us has got five talents, and
we have got but two? I do not ask whether the man who has the
five talents is reconciled to God in the matter of distribution of possession and prize; my concern is about the man who has the lower
number, who has only the two, or the one, or the one and a half—
that most difficult of all possessions in which the one and a half is
oftentimes so nearly two as to vex itself and find fault with God.
This is a sore trial to the flesh, this is indeed severe discipline. Why
is one man low down, and another man high up? Why is one man
a musician, but not a vocalist? Why are we so near being at the top,
and yet just one stride short of it? And is it enough to know that
God has done all this, and do we say, He who set the stars in their
places has set men also in their position? It is hard, sometimes it
seems unjust. Then the enemy says, Of course it is unjust; you
ought to feel and to express it and to act upon it; you never can
turn things of this kind into prayer, quoth the devil; you ought to
turn these things into criticism and into condemnations of what is
roughly and often falsely called providence; why, continues the
devil, there is no such providence, it is a rough-and-tumble life, first
come, first served; it is the man who makes for the uppermost place
that gets it. The Christian in his best moments knows better than
that; there is an allotment, an allocation and distribution of power
and talent and genius and position and all manner of good gifts,
and we have not received the second reconciliation until we can say,
It is the Lord, let Him do what seemeth good in His sight. A philanthropist visiting one of our deaf-and-dumb institutions ventured
upon a question on the blackboard, for which he could have apol-
ogized, and yet he seemed to be unable to control himself when
the suggestion came to his mind, and he wrote, "Why were you
born deaf and dumb, and I was born to hear and speak?" These are
the questions that test our Christianity in the aspect of the second

reconciliation. And one of the inmates of the sacred home stepped forward, took the chalk, and wrote under the question this answer: "Even so, Father, for so it seemeth good in Thy sight"—an answer that made the deaf-and-dumb world hear and speak in the largest and best sense. If we could only get into the second reconciliation, as we got into it what wondrous results would follow! What would such second reconciliation do for us? It would put us right in our relation to God, so that we should say, Thou art the giver, I am the receiver; Thou doest as Thou wilt among the armies of heaven: Thy will be done as in heaven so on earth. We never can get into that mood of submission, which is more than submission, until we get into the very heart of Christ and drink at the very fountains of His love. It is not submission in the sense of a grievous must or a fatalistic necessity; it is acquiescence, consent. Even so—a kissing of the hand that gives all the favors to the lowly universe.

When we enter into this blessing and security of the second reconciliation we shall have peace, we shall know that it is all right because God did it. That is the supreme miracle of the Holy Ghost. Observe, there are miracles wrought by Christ, and miracles wrought by the Holy Spirit, and Jesus Christ prepared us for those spiritual miracles by performing some of them Himself, and giving us a hint that this is the kind of miracle that He meant from the very first. They are no miracles that relate to the body, its bones, its diseases, its limitations, and its infirmities; these are but initial or elementary, alphabetic and outline miracles; the great miracles are spiritual and belong to another region of divine sovereignty, and if we receive the second reconciliation we shall have peace because God does it all. Did He send that fell disease into the family? Yes, He did. "Shall there be evil in the city, and the Lord hath not done it?" There cannot. How timid souls have been frightened at that text and timid preachers who have avoided it! Can there be evil in the city and the Lord not have done it? Can there be a devil in the universe, and the Lord not have created him? No. All things are of God. The explanation must come by-and-bye. The last thousand years have given us many explanations, the next thousand will give us still more; and we must not allow that there is a power in the universe that can outwit God, that can intercept His designs and frustrate them. See what the enemy is doing to Job, the poor, crouching, helldog that said, May I touch him? Yes, but let his life alone. He could not move without permission. There is a great mystery there which no words can ever explain, but I would rather take the mystery of the divine sovereignty in all its completeness than put God on half a throne and some demon prince on the other half. I believe God; I believe that the grave will be explained, I believe that death is a riddle which God set and God alone can answer. Lord, increase our faith!

When we enter into this second reconciliation we shall get the best out of life, and until we enter the second reconciliation we shall not get the best out of life; it will be a mere scramble for existence, it will be a misreading of the divine purpose, and it will be a great heat and unrest and irreligious tumult, until we get to the center of things and know that God is bringing us into the second reconciliation, so that in presence of the wilderness and the serpent and the great sea and deep river we shall be able to say, I can do all things through Christ which enableth me. The impious man is never happy, the jealous man cannot have an hour's peace; he tries to turn his jealousy into laughter, but the merriment dies on his livid lips. He says, Jealous, forsooth! What is there to be jealous of? In that hour Satan has won his triumph. May we pray God to give us a right acceptance of His will, a profound interpretation of His providence, and a tender anthem-singing acquiescence in all His decrees and all His purposes; then shall we be reconciled unto God, then shall we be able to say, Not my will, but Thine be done. Do not trust in the wisdom of the wise men or in the understanding of man's prudence, for that understanding the Lord hath said, with a promise that is also a threatening, shall be hid, obscured. It is His delight to turn the interpreters who have not learned His spirit upside down and to make them the laughingstock of the pious creation.

I do not ask, Have we received the first reconciliation? I end where I began. I will not say, Are you a converted sinner? You are. I do not believe in evangelistic services, so-called, that limit themselves to only one aspect of the divine reconciliation. The one aspect is necessary to the completion of the other, and Christians need to be evangelized. I bethink me of what the Spirit gave me to say a moment ago, to my great surprise, of atheistic theism, of being an atheist in the sanctuary, of having a God, not on paper only, but in vocal psalm and triumphant hymn, but none in the soul of the soul. Men, that is what we want, a revival of spiritual, penetrating, profound faith in God, a faith which enables us to say, All things work together for good to them that love God; come what may, God will see that His purpose is vindicated at the last, and when the hurly-burly's done and the battle's lost and won, it shall be Christ that shall be seen on the throne; we shall see no man, save Jesus only.

Part II

Prayer

We bless Thee, Thou Father in heaven, for everything that enlarges our life and brightens our outlook and makes us more what Thou didst intend us to be. For worship and song, high thought and deep devotion, we thank Thee as for the ministries that feed and enlarge the soul. We bless Thee for Thy house, for Thy book, for Thy name; Thou hast surrounded us with blessings, Thou hast multiplied Thy lovingkindnesses and Thy tender mercies. We worship Thee, we bow down before Thee, we lovingly and adoringly call upon Thy name. All this we do in the name of Jesus Christ, Thy Son, our Savior, our only because our infinite Savior. It does us good to mention His name; the utterance of it purifies our lips like a warm coal hot from the altar; when we speak of Jesus we become new men, conscious of new creation and of a possible resurrection, and our whole heart is lifted up with gladness when we have mentioned the name of the Savior. It is the name to sinners dear; it is the name that Thou hast entitled sinners to mention; there is no other name given under heaven whereby we can be saved but the name of Jesus Christ of Nazareth. May we find heart-room in the house of our Father; may we say what is in our heart while our Father inclines His ear; may we keep nothing back from the hearing of God. If we dwell upon our sins it is only that we may dwell still longer upon what Jesus Christ did for the sins of the world; night and day would we exclaim, Where sin abounds grace doth much more abound. We live in the "much more" of God's redeeming love. We bless Thee that our eyes have seen and our hands have handled of the Word of life given for the life of the world by the loving heart of God. May we be led further and further into the innermost sanctuary of Thy light and love and grace; may we see more clearly than we have ever seen that God is love. Thou art a God of judgment and of fierce wrath, and the pestilence and the darkness and the arrow that flieth by day and by night are all Thine; yet God is love. Thou didst not mean us to dig graves in the earth, but our sin has dug them; we dig the graves, Thou dost cause the flowers to bloom. God is love; we will say so with all the houses of history, all the great tabernacles of testimony; with them of old will we unite our voices and say, though mayhap with sobbing hearts, His mercy endureth forever. Wilt Thou pity Thy poor Church, O Thou who didst redeem her with blood, and crown her with more than fine gold? She is divided and torn, and she belittles herself, and has taken to herself a narrow language and a strange tongue, and has lost the music of her virginity as Thou didst espouse her at the Cross. Lord, pity the poor Church, intoxicated, delirious, proud, vain, foolish with excessive folly; man excommunicating man when man's greatest grace is to hold his tongue. Wilt Thou look upon the earth in its sad condition? Oh the misery! Oh the unspoken grief, the unuttered and inconceivable sorrow! In every house there is a shadow, in every great soul there is a lament which dare not utter itself in words. In every cradle there is a hope, a promise, the beginning of a song; and yet the cradle but rocks itself into the tomb. Oh the pain, the misery, the wild dolorous sense of loneliness and desolation! Wilt Thou hear Thy people when they say, Thy kingdom come? Thou art preparing for the coming of Thy kingdom, now by peace, now by war, now by great loss of blood, and now by shattered ambitions, and now by gentle breathings of human love. Thy kingdom is coming. Come, Lord Jesus, come quickly! Amen.

1

Christ's Legacies

Preached on Sunday Morning, January 21st, 1900.

I give—John 14:27.

We are in spirit gathered around the Son of Man almost at the very moment of His exit from this scene of earth and time. He is, so to say, making His will; in modern phrase, He is disposing of His possessions, He is devising and bequeathing legacies. We may easily and happily imagine ourselves to be present at the distribution of His property. In a sense we can readily understand the Savior is His own executor; again and again He says, "I give." We want to know what it is that He gives, and to whom He gives it, and for what purpose He bequeaths it. Surely this is an interesting spectacle and a thrilling engagement. The Son of God is just about to leave the earth, and He calls His friends together, and through them He calls the Church of all coming ages, and He devises and bequeaths and endows and enriches with both hands and with His whole heart. We should delight to be present when such a testator devises His property.

The words now quoted from the Gospel of John may be regarded as a motto rather than a text. It is a motto pointing towards detailed statements; the particulars of the devising in which Jesus Christ is now at this historical moment engaged. Every word of His was always more precious than jewels; if possible the closing words are more precious than any that went before them. There is a softness, a light, a starry gleam about them which almost compels us to mix our metaphors and devise new ones, that we may represent the feebleness of our impoverished expression. Let us be as near Him as we can that we may hear the will. It is not the will of some dying plutocrat or pauper. It has nothing to do with gold and silver and houses; it has to do with blessings, comforts, inspirations, and assurances that exhaust all language and turn the soul into one fervent dream and brilliant but speechless imagination. His voice will be low and tender, but well heard if well listened to. We could hear much if we listened much.

Hear these beautiful words spoken by the Son of Man: "I have given you an example." He took a towel and girt Himself, and took a basin filled with water, and He began to wash the feet of the disciples, and He wiped them with the towel with which He was girt, and then He said, "Ye call me Master and Lord: and ye say well; for so I am. If I then, your Lord and Master, have washed your feet; ye also ought to wash one another's feet. For I have given you an example." We have nothing to do with the literal illustration. We deprive ourselves of the greatest spiritual blessings by insisting upon the literal word and the literal instance. The example was not one of feet-washing, it was one of humility, condescension, brotherly service, willingness to help, accounting everything dignified and beautiful that was inspired and illustrated by the Lord. The poor are always with us, and we can joyously endure their presence and can even cultivate their companionship; but the literalists are always with us, and they spoil the prayer, and tear the music out of the holy psalm, and turn the heavens and the earth into one grim cloud of praise. What we have to learn is the inner lesson, the everlasting truth, the spiritual purpose of the living God. In this instance Jesus Christ did not institute a sacrament, He cultivated a spirit, a temper of the heart, a disposition of the soul; and we wash one another's feet when we are willing in Christ's name and for Christ's sake to do everything in our power to help those who are round about us. "I have given you an example": a million golden pounds would poorly express that gift and bequest. It is in our power to bequeath an example of purity, tenderness, sympathy, condescension. He dies rich who can leave to his children and to his neighbors an honorable, beautiful example.

That is one clause of the will which we are now reading.

Another clause reads thus: "My peace I give unto you; not as the world giveth give I unto you; peace, My peace, divine peace, I leave with you." He does not distribute His clothes, He distributes His soul. That is the will! Blessed are they who are included in this devising and bequeathing. I know of no man who is excluded from this will, if he be of a broken heart and a penitent spirit. Peace knows nothing of panic. The whole world is nearly every morning thrown into panic by bubbles that are wafted over by the wind from far-away countries or countries near at hand. It seems to be a patriotic intelligence that frets itself to death about what it has nothing to do with. Does it not seem patriotic to fall into hysterics and shout incoherently about things that are not half understood and in which there is oftentimes nothing to be understood? The soul that lives in God knows nothing of panic; the soul that tabernacles with the Most High is not at the mercy of a newsboy; the soul that lives with God in Christ says, The Lord reigneth; He has a great purpose and design which He will work out and none can hinder; the proud shall stoop under His rod, ambition shall be disappointed, and self-idolatry shall be crushed, and the kingdom of God figured by that blue summer sky shall come more and more, until there be no room for darkness, and until the habitations of cruelty are torn down and scattered to the wind. "How is it that ye have no faith?" That is the wonder of the soul of Christ. We can imagine in what tone of voice He uttered the inquiry; He was perplexed and disappointed, He was sore wounded in the heart, He said again and again, "How is it that you have no faith?" Where the peace of God is there is no fear, there is no night, there is no more sea, there is no more death. We may have to wait, but the peace of God gives us the power to wait. Waiting is not a grace, it is a virtue; it is stronger than a grace, and then it grows up from being a virtue to becoming a grace in the divinest and most supernatural sense. So that effort becomes easy, labor rest. This is a great miracle, to be interpreted and enjoyed only by experience. Why art thou cast down, O my soul? Why art thou disquieted within me? Hope thou in God, for thou shalt yet praise Him who is the health of thy countenance and thy God. The Bible has been pleading with us for many a day to sit down.

The third clause of the will is a very tender one: "I will not leave you comfortless; I will send you another Paraclete, Advocate, or Comforter: if I go not away the Comforter will not come unto you, but if I go away I will send Him unto you; He shall not speak of Himself, He shall take of the things that are Mine and show them unto you, and He will lead you into all truth; He will show you things that are coming, He will bring all things to your remembrance whatsoever that I have said unto you." These will be the festive times, the consciously realized Holy Spirit. I will not leave you orphans; I go away that I may be nearer to you; I come down upon you through a wider gyration and sweep of energy and influence; you cannot understand this; I am patient with you, saith Christ; I know your infirmity, I know you are still in the flesh, I know you are guided by your few poor senses that were only meant from the very first to be elementary and initial; I understand your whole case; by-and-bye you will understand what it is to be nearer when you are further. This is not a question of physical measurement; you will understand in due time if you be patient, if you pass through the costly school of experience, what it is to have more by having less, and to win the life by losing it. I know, continues Christ, that all these are contradictions to you now; you cannot bear all I have to say to you in your present degree and state of education; by-and-bye you will begin to see what I mean when I tell you that I go away that I may help you. All this is dead against our rules of language and our poor little mud-grammar house; that miserable building wholly of our own doing cannot hold the sun; we mistake the ceiling for the sky, and we think the window is the horizon. Nothing can get us out of these fallacies but prolonged, bitter, diversified experience; nay, nothing can deliver us from these terrible imprisonments but the Cross. When we are crucified with Christ, we shall rise with Christ, and our words are sown in corruption, but are raised in incorruption. The resurrection penetrates all things and gives all things true and beautiful their divine embodiment and expressiveness. We are in the age of the Spirit; we are now realizing this special covenant in the will of our Lord Jesus Christ.

Still there seems to be something more in the will if the reader would but continue his recitation of its terms. There is another clause: is it not the sweetest clause of all? "I will come again, and receive you unto Myself." The will would now seem to be complete. We can live upon a promise spoken by such lips; but we shall have to live a long time before we can understand these little words, "I will come again." You think you understand them because their meaning is on their face. It is not. The meaning of God is never on the face of things. A lily requires an interpreter; a blade of grass requires an angel to unfold its meaning to the observing eye. "I will come again"—in a thousand ways, in My own way; not at all of necessity in your way, or through the channel of your imagination; I will come in My own way and be there if you will look for Me. I am always there; My coming is from the beginning and is eternal; it is in your consciousness that the miracle must take place. If it were possible for us to open the eyes of the blind man he would not create the sun, he would behold it; the sun has been there through all the centuries, but the sight to see it has not been there. To the man whose eyesight has been recovered it will seem as if the sun had been just made, but a moment ago rounded and hurled into its place by the infinite energy of God. The recovered blind man would be at perfect liberty to say this, for it is in this way that the matter represents itself to his newly awakened consciousness, and indeed to his newly completed personality. If he started the matter—call the matter an argument—from the standpoint of his own consciousness and experience, who would blame him? Your room at darkest midnight has all the furniture in it and all the pictures, but you cannot see one of them; would you therefore say that furniture and pictures are not there? To that depth of folly you would never descend; you want the light, you may have the eyes, but the eyes without the light are helpless. Now the light does not create the pictures, it simply enables you to see them. The light has never left us—"Lo, I am with you alway unto the end of the age"; He is a God nigh at hand, and not afar off. He is accessible and approachable every moment of the day, but we are not always equally sensitive to His presence. What we therefore have to pray for is that we may be made sensitive so that we may feel the air, and feel the air within the air, and learn little by little this great word, "God is a Spirit."

The Lord Jesus said very nearly at the point of His leaving, handing them a morsel of the supper bread and a drop of the wine which they had been drinking at the supper, "Do this in remembrance of Me." And what a mystery we have made of it! And what a complication! What a battlefield, and what noisome controversy has arisen from this simple exhortation! It does not read to me like a command; I hear the sound of entreaty in the expression, "Do this in remembrance of Me." It was not a sacrament, it was not an ecclesiastical or official feast; we have degraded the simplicity of that action; and we have degraded everything we have touched; the moment we pluck a flower we kill it. The Lord and the disciples were at the common feast, the love-feast, and in a moment as it were Jesus signalized that feast by asking His disciples to sanctify all bread and all wine, all eating and drinking; every meal we take should be the Lord's supper in its highest significance. It was so understood in the Church; for seven hundred years there was nothing like what we call the Lord's supper; for seven hundred years the Church did without it. It is only true in the sense in which it is an act of the heart; love awakening its own memory, gratitude stirring up its own consciousness, and going back to the old, old time while the Roman gallows were standing to receive the body of the Son of God. Let all eating and drinking be sacramental; let every time man and wife clasp each other's hands be the wedding day, the new wedding with the old blessing; let every ring that is on the finger be a wedding ring; let every mouthful of bread we take be the Lord's body, taken by faith; thus let us live in Him and on Him and through Him, and thus let Him come again and receive us unto Himself. Poor Church! By poor Church I mean all the Christian communions with their diverse denominations and badges and banners and rag flags; I do not refer to any one single communion, but all these communions have gone a-whoring from their sweet Lord, and have made themselves gods of their own invention in the form of ceremonies and statutes and diverse observances; all of which the apostle seems to throw away with almost avenging hands as though they concealed and degraded the simplicity of the Lord.

The Lord who made the will designs us all to partake of it. Not one soul is left out of Christ's testament. There is something for everyone. The more faith, the more blessing; the more trustfulness in the Spirit and in the love of God, the greater the religious enjoyment. In this way nothing is to come between us and the Lord Himself. I am not to be introduced to my Lord, except by my sin; I do not want a man's letter, my own leprosy is enough; and if I may but touch the hem of His garment I shall be made whole. And we shall thus grow towards simplicity, all ecclesiastical manufactures will be taken away, and God and man shall stand as it were face to face—the face of Sin looking on the face of Love, and the finger of Mercy pointing to the Cross. How simple, yet how profound! This is what we need; this is the vital matter. If all people would believe this there would be new heavens and a new earth, and every day would be midsummer day.

Prayer

Almighty God, our hearts go out to those who are on the field of battle on both sides, and we pray that reason and righteousness and humanity may triumph. We are all in Thine image, men; may we see the image of God in one another, and may the time come when men shall put up their sword into its sheath, for they that use the sword shall perish by the sword. Pity us, Lord, in this time of darkness and grief, and sore loss. God save the Queen! And look upon our opponents in the field of battle, many of them wise men and strong, with an honorable family record. The Lord send us relief in some way on both sides, so we may see our way to peace, to the best patriotism, to a divine philanthropy. We ask it in the name of Christ, and especially when we ask Thee to pity those who today are widows and orphans through no fault of their own. May the grace of our Lord Jesus Christ, the love of God our Heavenly Father, and the fellowship and comfort of the Holy Ghost abide with us through the night till the shadows flee away! Amen.

Words for Preachers

A pastor's life should be vocal; sermons must be practiced as well as preached. Though Noah's workmen built the ark, yet themselves were drowned. God will not accept the tongue where the devil has the soul. Jesus did "do and teach." If a man teach uprightly and walk crookedly, more will fall down in the night of his life than he built in the day of his doctrine—*Owen, 1616–1683*

The faithful minister is strict in ordering his conversation. As for those who cleanse blurs with blotted fingers, they make it the worse. It was said of one who preached very well, and lived very ill, "that when he was out of the pulpit, it was a pity he should ever go into it; and when he was in the pulpit, it was a pity he should ever come out of it." But our minister lives sermons. And yet I deny not, but dissolute men, like un-skillful horsemen, who open a gate on the wrong side, may, by the virtue of their office, open heaven for others, and shut themselves out—*Fuller, 1608–1661*

The preacher stands up before his audience to proclaim salvation and offer pardon to the guilty—to the guiltiest, by the blood of Jesus. By all that is sacred and holy, by all that is tender and terrible, by love to God and regard to themselves, he urges on them its cordial and immediate ac-ceptance. Yet how often do the vacant eyes, and unmoved demeanor of hearers—so unlike persons under sentence of death getting tidings of a pardon—remind him of the question, Shall horses run upon the rock, shall a man plow there with oxen? A very profitless field! Time, besides shedding snows on our head, draws furrows on our brow; but it is not over bald mountain brows that the husbandman guides his plow. Culti-vating the soil of the valley, he leaves the rocky summits to the eagle, to mists and clouds and roaring tempests. Bolder than he, the preacher of the gospel casts the seed of the word on stony hearts. Why not? Has not God encouraged him, saying, Is not my word a fire, and hammer to break the stone in pieces? Yet, alas! how often does the result of his most solemn, most startling, most searching appeals but show that he has run his horses on a rock, and plowed there with oxen!—the only feeling elicited, temporary—like the spark which the horse's hoof strikes from the rock; dying the instant of its birth—*Guthrie*

Prayer

Almighty God, Thou hast set us amid wondrous surroundings, now summer, now winter, now the cold blossoms of snow, and now the warm blossoms of June. We hear music without words, and words without music, and there is a sound in the air as of strife and wrath and hell moved to its depths. Now there come to us angel voices, as if babes were singing and bringing gladness into our hearts in wondrous ways. Such is Thy providence—a daily parable, a daily pain, a daily resurrection with its accompanying song. May we be of steadfast mind, that we may note these things, and read the unwritten word, and deeply consider when our hearts are in sore trouble or in a very tempest of gladness. The Lord is round about us, and within us, and Thou dost set us behind and before and lay Thine hand upon us; Thou dost consider man as if he were a subject worthy of Thy thought. What is man? Sometimes so little, oftentimes so possibly great. We have come to thank Thee for all Thy wondrous kindness, so great that we have called it lovingkindness, as if it were kindness upon kindness, like summer swiftly following summer without any winter between. We have come to sing of household mercies and of household judgments; for Thou hast made the desolate alive with joy, and Thou hast turned the song of those that were of proud and ungrateful heart into a great silence. This is Thy way, Thy wondrous untold way. We have lived long enough to believe this, we have studied Jesus Christ long enough to know that all things are working out to the eternal summer. Thou hast made some sad halting-places by the way; Thou hast done some things we could not have done even to dogs. We know not the meaning of anything just now, but Thou hast hidden a promise in our heart, and our hearts already see the dawn beyond the darkness, and we see the darkness fleeing away as with the speed of shame. Thou art teaching us these things outside Thy Book; then when we come to read Thy Book we find them all confirmed by the holy Word, yea, and all predicted and sealed with the sovereign seals of Thy court, and made sure to us forever in Christ Jesus. All that we know of Thy government we know through our Lord and Savior, in whose name we approach Thee. He spoke familiarly of Thyself, called Thee Father; He spoke about the bosom of God and the Son that lay therein in eternal peace and safety; He promised us great things in His name, and in Thine; yea, He pledged the Deity to resurrection and immortality and heaven and service unspeakable. All these years we have been trusting to such promises; they have yielded us great fruit, they have stirred us as with heavenly inspiration, they have enabled us to defy the enemy, and to ask Death for his sting and the Grave for his poor victory. Thou hast done great things for us in Jesus Christ our Lord: He is the Amen of God, He is the Amen of our hearts, He writes and reads and interprets and applies the covenant. We stand in Christ Jesus; in Him we cannot fail. How many are our complaints and are our murmurings, our sore griefs and tender sensitive misery! Behold, we represent them all: the child is in great pain or in great danger; the old man is laying aside his staff and his sandals; the busy man has just heard that a brother man in merchandise has been struck dead as by an invisible ax. In the midst of life we are in death; we have great fears about one another which we may not speak; we tell lies to one another by speaking words of cheerfulness which our hearts refuse to believe. Thou knowest the mystery of pity, Thou art the author of that great riddle, and Thou wilt not condemn us with all the austerity of Thy righteousness. The prodigal is far away, further away today than ever before, quite beyond the reach of our hesitating prayer, but not beyond the reach of the mercy which endureth forever. If any man's way is hard and on the sunless side of the road, or up a steep hill where everything is against him, Thou canst bring to bear upon him influences which will throw down all difficulties and lift up hopes downtrodden. If any man is beset as with seven devils, so that he cannot wholly utter the prayer that he would utter if he could, the Lord be merciful to him lest at last the devil should be successful. We gather all our sick folks together, them that are faint and weary and in a hopeless condition, paralytic, apoplectic, and those who have diverse diseases, and we lay them all at Thy feet, Thou Healer of the world. The Lord comfort those who are in special sadness because of the torment of fear, because of great weakness and sinking of heart; the Lord lay His hand on the dumb and those who are too sorely driven to be able to complain of their misery. It is a sad world; Thou didst make it, and Thou didst not make it sad; Thou hast brought into it redemption and deliverance, new mornings and new summertimes. The Lord hear us and pity us even in our best estate. Amen.

2
Things No Man Could Say

Preached on Sunday Morning, January 28th, 1900.

I say unto you—Matthew 5:20.

Things which no man would say or would be allowed to say and retain any reputation for sanity or truthfulness. There are things which we cannot say, as certainly as there are things which we ought not to say. There is a language of profanity or obscenity; we do not allow ourselves to speak it; just as certainly as that, there is another language religious, pious, which we cannot use, which we would not use, which no apology, how full soever, could excuse us in using or for having used. Observe that there is an environment or liberty of language. The agricultural laborer uses only three hundred words. He is not forbidden to use four hundred or a thousand, but the agricultural laborer is limited, perhaps he has had no opportunity of acquiring other words; we therefore do not blame the agricultural laborer because he is shut up within such narrow verbal confines. Then there are other words we dare not use, because of their moral rottenness. Were a man to use such words in society, society would either expel him or abandon him. How so? Are they not all words? Yes, they are words, but words not to be used by self-respecting or reverential men. There are those who have broken limits and freely intersperse their common conversation with vulgarisms and profanities; such people have no standing; society is revolted. Society may not condescend to show at the moment its true estimate of such unholy customs, but society will take care to abstain from the company and fellowship of persons who have so stigmatized themselves as unworthy of notice or confidence or respect. So we come into the very highest class of language, and there we find ourselves either shut up or severely limited; we have to explain ourselves when we use certain most religious words; we say, "If we may be permitted to say so," or we parenthetically observe, "If we may borrow so great an expression." We feel that we are in an Eden of language of which we may taste of only one tree. In the first instance we might partake of all the trees but one, but we are now in a paradise of which we may not partake of one tree without express permission or special explanation and apology.

Yet we are now face to face with a Man who used all the vocabulary of God, a Man who never hesitated to use the language which God alone, according to our interpretation, has permitted Himself to use. It is not poet's license; no poet is licensed to be blasphemous; the court of heaven issues no licenses to blasphemers. Jesus Christ set aside all the great teachers of history; He said, "It hath been said to you by them of old time . . . but I say unto you." No man is at liberty to set aside the great teachers and founts of historic wisdom, knowledge, and experience, unless he can produce a special authority for such supersession. There are some things which cannot be done; no man, let us repeat, can stand up and say, I sweep away all the founts of morality, all the springs of ethical teaching, all the intellectual philosophies of the ages, I simply sweep them away. No man is permitted to do that. Here is a Man who in effect said, You must take the law from My lips. We want to know how He establishes His authority, so to say; there must be an authority that we can investigate. All the sources of His authority are open to us, and it can be proved within a very limited compass that this Man had a right to use the words, and it is the business of this discourse to prove unmistakably, emphatically, without the possibility of doubt, that He had a right to use the words which set Him at the head of all history and set Him forth in heaven and earth as the Maker of all things new.

Begin where you like, the evidence is forthcoming and is unique. Let us hear Him in one of His simplest speeches; simplest, that is, when looked upon superficially: "I am meek and lowly in heart." No man has a right to say that; to say "I am meek" is to prove that the speaker is not meek; to claim lowliness may be to abandon it. Never forget the ironies of history. You should study the great figure of speech called irony and its special uses throughout the whole biblical record, in which things are said by way of mockery, in which things are said to prove that they ought evidently not to be said. Consider what it is for a man to stand up in any company of his fellows and to say, "I am meek and lowly in heart"! Not a soul would believe him; there is a human instinct, an unwritten transcendental human intuition that says to a speaker, No, for if you were so you would not speak thus; you would leave us to discover your meekness and your lowliness of heart.

Take another instance, running on the same line: "I will give you rest." This a word that no sane man can utter if he be only a man. If we could really get at his roots and beginnings, if we could dig into the very bed of his genesis and get down to the very protoplasm of his social beginnings, we should be able to bring evidence to bear upon the presumptuousness of any such offer. Who knows the meaning of rest as Jesus Christ used that pregnant word? No man can give another man rest; he can lull him, soothe him, administer opiates to him, and bring to bear upon him the influence of chemical anodynes; he cannot give peace, rest fullness of peace. Jesus Christ said that He would give the world rest; He challenged all the weary and heavy laden to come to Him and take away rest, leaving behind them only their burdens. If He said so, we must challenge Him for His proofs. He will supply them this morning, here, now, and undeniably. Let us wait.

No man is at liberty to say, "I and my Father are one," no matter in what sense he uses the terms. We will not endeavor to take away their natural and proper meaning; we will not suggest parentheses or mental reservation; we insist upon the words being accepted precisely as they were uttered; and no man is able to say with truthfulness, "I and my Father are one." How does he know that? If he can speak familiarly of the Father he must be the Father. If he is speaking with limitations he is speaking unfairly, because he has not hinted at any limitation in the great deliverance which he has just made. He cannot come in an hour hence and say, I meant in my degree. You did not say that, you misled us, you lied; therefore you have taken away your own right to come back with amendments and explanations; you must not assail the very foundations of human reason and human consciousness, human aspiration and instinct, and then come back in a month to explain that you did not mean it just in that sense. But you said it just so, and we risked our souls upon it. No man has a right to trifle with the common language. If He had said this only once some crafty mind might have endeavored to explain that the words are perhaps the interpolation of a careless scribe. But Jesus Christ said nothing only once. Hear the statement, and I will refer you to the proofs. There is not a word, so far as I have been able to search the record, which Jesus Christ ever uttered that He did not always utter; not necessarily in the same form of words, but as to the same substance and emphasis and responsibility of meaning.

Take this instance: "I and my Father are one." If that occurs only once perhaps it was introduced surreptitiously, but it does not occur only once; for the same lips said: "He that hath seen Me hath seen the Father." No man in this congregation would be allowed to say that. In saying it he would instantly destroy his own reputation; what this congregation signifies includes the whole world and all the ages. Fix your mind upon the picture. A man arises anywhere, under any sky, and in any language, and says, He that hath seen me hath seen God—hath seen the Father—hath seen the One Father. A man may have said that, but he called down upon himself the ridicule of all who heard it; he did not seek the faith of the world, he tempted its distrust and its derision.

Hear Him once again, as we might hear Him in every day of His life: "I will raise him up at the last day." A man cannot say that, and be only a man; he is a lunatic, he is the devil, or he is God. You cannot make a commonplace of him; you find no place in history that he can occupy. "I will," there is personal, definite, sovereign decree, purpose, or resolution; "raise him up," perform the crowning miracle, make him again with ennobled powers; "I will raise him up"–that young man, comparative boy, youth, some thirty years of age, without social credentials, without any appearance that would favor his empty declaration. The Jews were perfectly right in taking up stones to stone him; it was the only right and proper thing to be done if he were what they supposed him to be; stone is the natural reply to such insanity. "At the last day," meaning, I will be there; whenever the last day may come, centuries or millenniums hence, I will be there, and I will undertake the responsibility of re-establishing this man in conscious life and in individual and social responsibility. If any man were to arise in this audience and say, "I will raise him up at the last day," he would be taken out–the modern and natural form of stoning. No man has a right to blaspheme, nor has any man a right to make promises which he cannot fulfill. We condemn this policy in commerce: if a man's note is returned, that man is degraded, distrusted, marked, proclaimed a commercial leper. We cannot allow, therefore, any man in history to stand up and say, "I will raise this or that man up at the last day"; he must not avail himself of the condition or concealment of countless centuries; we must not allow the centuries to create a glamour around this man's name; we ought to be just to the centuries; we ought indeed to be present in mind, in judgment, and in conscience at the very moment the speech was made, if it were made five thousand years ago. We have no right to interpret such a text at the end of fifty centuries, covering the text itself with the aureole of superstition, with the haze and the glamour of something that cannot be proved. The historian, to be just to the occasion, must live himself backwards all the fifty centuries, and get beside the man really to interpret him. Can any man in the world stand this test? Not one. If any man has uttered these words he was less than a man or more than a man; and you cannot find a middle place for him.

These are some of the passages. Now these passages put Christ in this position; they utterly discredit Him; He is the victim of His own pretensions; He has discrowned Himself in the presence of sober-minded, honorable criticism. If He had claimed less He might have received more. He would sit down nowhere but on the throne. A man may easily cut up his own claims and pretensions, and may be burned by lighting his own certificates and credentials, and go up with them in their own smoky evaporation. But if the words are true they make Jesus Christ more than a man and better than a man; and you cannot remove those words from the record without removing Christ with them. Let us clearly understand that; you cannot take out all these self-assertions and self-revelations, and still leave the Christ on the record. Jesus Christ was made by these very claims, or He has no standing in history; it is when He separates Himself from other men that He becomes in very deed the Christ of God, the Darling of the Father. Do not suppose that you can retain all these and idealize them. Who is this marvelous little man who has taken out a license to idealize things?—a man who dresses himself well, and feeds himself well, and keeps up a large estate, and does diverse things which attract the attention of the world for a moment or two, and who says that all these things must be taken of course in an ideal or transcendental way. We say, My little sir, who are you, where did you come from, and whither are you going? Nay, stop, that would be to make too big a figure of him—go on, and never let us see you again.

Now these things cannot be the utterances of an insane man, because of the discipline which follows them. The longer I live the more I see the argumentativeness of discipline. I find that discipline is the seal and corroboration of all merely intellectual reasoning. Others I can read because they do not ask me to do anything. When I was comparatively young I bought the last and largest work of the last and greatest English philosopher, and I said, Now I will find all these things out. I read his first chapter, some eight-and-forty crowded octavo pages, and I could have read them everyday in the week, and have done nothing. I could have written marginal notes upon those pages, and never lost a night's sleep for any poor dying little child; I could have read all the words, and looked up everyone of them in the dictionary—for the very last greatest of the dictionaries would be required for the purpose of elucidating these wonderful polysyllables—I could have done all that, and stopped the pension which I was paying to poverty. I cannot read the Sermon on the Mount and be the same man after it I was before reading it; I am better or I am worse. This Man of Nazareth calls upon me to do, to go, to heal, to teach, to preach, to forgive, and to be known by the stigma, the brand of the Cross, or the burden thereof. The one thing that Jesus Christ will not allow me to do with Matthew, Mark, Luke, and John, the fourfold record of His life, is to read them, and praise them, and say what wonderfully limpid minds they had, and how very deeply they were fascinated by this marvelous Carpenter. Jesus Christ will not allow such reading or such annotation; His word is, Crucify, cut off, pluck out, forgive. Oh the last, the climacteric word! He who does not forgive can never enter heaven. I could read, either originally or by translation, all the ancient philosophers, and spend my night in the bed of lust, or spend my night with Bacchus, the drinking god; but I cannot read a chapter of my Lord's speech without feeling that I must be holy if I would be acceptable by God, and that I can only be made holy in one way. Sanctification does not come by diverse and by contradictory processes. I feel that to be a just criticism upon the New Testament, and especially upon the Gospels. Is there no argument in this? Christ could not have been lunatic, because He was beneficent; Christ must have been divine, because He was a disciplinarian of a kind the world has never provided before. That is the argument. I could idealize, but I have to give my loaf to the hungry. Is that idealism? I could say that of course He was really a very beautiful character, quite a jewel creature, quite a beautiful flower in the garden of history. But He says, "Forgive." That kills my little theory! I say He was a delightful man to listen to, because never man spoke like this man in the mere manner of His utterance, so sweet, so tender, so gracious. But said He, "Love your enemies." Ay! No lunatic ever talked like that. "If thine enemy hunger, feed him." That is a strange lunacy, if lunacy at all. He says, "Follow Me." I say, Lord this I will gladly do; I shall be pleased to do it; I love Thee; I love Thy young-heartedness; I am charmed by something that I see in Thee that I see in nobody else; I will follow Thee with pleasure. "Take up your cross before you come." That alters the case! He might have had me as a follower, but He demanded that I should bring a cross with me; so I consulted with the flesh, the world, and the devil, and the indifferent Christian—which is the worst species of opponent the Lord ever had—and we agreed that if we could follow Him without a cross we should be glad, but He said, "Except a man take up his cross, he cannot be My disciple." This was no mere man. Call Him incarnate Satan, and you may have some kind of defense; call Him God manifest in the flesh, and you have a grand support in the book of God; but never attempt to make a mere man of Him, for then you insult God and misunderstand His Son.

I know the difficulties of this position from a social and ecclesiastical point of view. It would be comfortable and socially easy to sit down beside a man who denied the Lord's deity, and say we are practically one. We are not; we are separated by infinity. The man who says Jesus Christ was only a man may be right; the man who says Jesus Christ was Emmanuel, God with us, in Him dwelt all the fullness of the Godhead, bodily, may be right; but they cannot both be right. And I ask you to form your own judgment, to read the Book, to study deeply and lovingly the mind and heart of Christ. It would be socially reputable to forget the difference, between the one conception of Christ and the other, and might bring with it a little popularity for the moment; but there are times when we must be faithful to our convictions even at the risk of being called narrow and prejudiced. Such little crosses I could carry as a handful of chips, they are no crosses. But when it comes to saying to Christ, "My Lord and my God!" I accept the responsibility of that faith. I want in that faith to die.

Prayer

Almighty God, Thou hast called us in Christ Jesus to a great fight. Fight the good fight of faith, is Thy word from heaven, and when Thou speakest such a word Thou dost mean to supply the necessary grace. Thou dost not command without at the same time finding the strength; Thou dost not vex and mock Thy creatures; Thou speakest great words and givest them great commands in order that they may test the fullness and sufficiency of the eternal grace. May we put that grace to the test, may we lean upon it the whole weight of our souls, not attempting to protect ourselves at any single point, but trusting the whole necessity to the unfailing, condescending grace of God. Thou hast called every soul to battle, Thou hast not exempted one of Thy people from the great strife, but Thou art able to do exceeding abundantly above all that they ask or think; it is when they are sorely put to it that Thou showest the wealth of Thine own resources. We are all tried, tested, some are sorely torn, and others are deeply wounded; they have got past the period of tears and are now in the agony of silent grief. Thou hast a message for each, Thou hast a cordial for every soul; no man need leave Thy throne unblessed, Thou living, loving, all-saving One. We have been taught to say this because we have companied with Jesus, we have caught His breath upon our cheeks as we have lingered near Him, and the very music of His soul has passed into our hearts as we have tarried at His feet. We ask everything in His name and for His sake, without whom there is no Christian prayer, but by whose blood we enter into the holiest and bring out with us into the common air and the common light some great support and some healing grace. If Thou hast been hard in Thy providence upon some men, it is that Thou mayest show them exceeding great and tender love. They have wondered about the harshness of God; their song has been of judgment; they have not yet been able to sing of mercy, but one day Thou wilt enable them to sing of Thy mercy also, and they will say in their new song, He hath done all things well. Prepare us for the great fight, for the daily struggle, for the nightly wrestling, for the hand-to-hand work that comes in this great battlefield of life. Amen.

3

The Whole Armor of God

Preached on Thursday Morning, February 1st, 1900.

Ephesians 6:13–18.

No man could have invented this expression. It brings with it some sign and token of its divine origin. The most of things that are in the Scriptures are things that never would have occurred to the mind of man. Hence I stand by the old argument that the Bible is a book which no man could have written if he would, or would have written if he could. The uniqueness is part of the argument. "The whole armor of God." Is there any mere poetry in the word whole? Is it employed or introduced in order to perfect a rhetorical climax? or is there great weight of meaning in the word whole? Is it the emphatic word in the exhortation? or are all the words on one high level?–the monotony not of weakness or weariness, but of completeness. We must revert to our own spiritual experience if we would receive a sufficing answer to these inquiries. Could we do without the word whole? What does the word whole stand for in this connection? It stands for completeness; there must not be one piece of the panoply overlooked, nor must the places and arrangements of the armor be for a moment changed or otherwise related. The provision of the divine grace is complete; we are armed from the head to the foot, there is no unprovided place or spot in all this divine clothing with spiritual steel. But is there any meaning in the word whole? Yes, there is great meaning in that word. Consider what the exhortation would be without the word whole, complete, entire; it would be a different command or exhortation; the military tone would be taken out of it. It would sink into a very poor admonition. There is a kind of gentle severity in the very language, and specially in that one word "whole armor." Consider what it would be if we missed any one of the pieces. A man is panoplied all over except the helmet. Then he is doomed, no matter how muscular he may be, how alert, how determined. Suppose a man is panoplied all over except the shield. He is lost, no matter what his sword may be or his helmet of brass; if he has no shield his heart is exposed. Suppose a man is armed all over except the sword; the foe mocks him, asks him to produce his sword of straw, laughs at him. Does the foe deride him simply because he is wanting in one solitary piece of armor? That is precisely what the foe does. The armor is not to be looked upon as consisting of pieces; although it is given in detail, it is only given in order to mark the solidity of the unity of the panoply. The armor is only enumerated that it may be totaled, brought to one grand fitness.

Many persons are armed in places. If nine points out of ten are attended to, these people suppose that they are very well provided for, but they are not. You have shut up all your castle, every window, every door, except the postern gate, the little gate behind, the small door that a small burglar may pass through. All that is wanted is not an army of burglars, but one little child-burglar that can creep through an unguarded pane of glass. Enough! The castle is in the hands of the thief. How noticeable it is that people are very fond of pet graces and favorite virtues, and how they dangle these before the eyes of these poor creatures who are not similarly created or provided for at those special points. It is heart-sickening, it must hurt the Savior! How the mean creature who does not thirst for strong drink mocks the poor creature who, under the pressure of three generations, burns to drink the fire-fluid! The Pharisee holds himself erect and says in the audience of the people, I do not need stimulants, I have no craving for strong drink! Other people can surely do as well as I can. Hold thy tongue, thou servant of the pit!

Thine own brother mayhap may have an unquenchable fire in his throat, for which he is not so broadly responsible as may be supposed at first sight. The generations come up again; we reap old harvests; our forefathers are living in us; they heat the blood; they should be twice damned. "The evil that men do lives after them." So it is through the whole gamut of human experience and spiritual utterance; we are apt to be proud of the particular part of armor which we have, and to torment other people because they are not equally strong at the same points, though they may be stronger at other points in the clothing of the divine panoply. Let us be merciful, let us be tenderly gracious; the people who are more easily tempted than we are know it, mourn it, cry over it in unknown places and in darkened hours; too well they know their weakness and their shame. Do not let us who are not tempted in such directions hold ourselves up as stupendous models of behavior in some other direction. A man may not be drunk, but his soul may be steeped in covetousness, which is worse than drunkenness. A man may not be led away by his passions, but he may be greedy, selfish, self-considering, proud, and pride is worse than any sin that stalks about the city in the night-time. We condemn sin at wrong points, or we exaggerate some sins and practice others. Hence the beauty, the force, the necessity, of the expression or commandment, "Put on the whole armor." Every inch of it, be equally strong at every point; ay, and it will take thee all thy time to panoply thyself in the steel of God. The Christian life is a hard life; when it is otherwise it is not the life Christian. Jesus Christ laid down this condition at the very first; He said, The badge of all our tribe is a Cross; every man must bear his own cross, every man must carry the cross at the heavy end. Except a man carry his cross daily he cannot be My disciple; he may have some kind of unpractical admiration of Me, he may even say very fine and attractive things about Me, but he knows nothing about My salvation; that salvation represents a garden of agony, a cross of shame, a brand of dishonor in the eyes of the world. Who then can be saved? That is no question for us; that is not our inquiry. When we do put it in our heat and ignorance Jesus says, Strive ye to enter in at the strait gate; do not inquire how many people can get in at the strait gate and walk along the narrow road, but strive ye, every one of you, as if ye were the only creature in the universe to enter and to walk along and to fight the devil day by day. What wonder that the Christian religion is not popular, and that Jesus Christ is at the foot of the list of the religions of the world? Herein is that saying true, He that is first shall be last, and he that is last shall be first. The statistical tables will be reversed and are being reversed with every process of the sun.

If we look at this panoplied man we shall find that he is a living parable. Many written parables have fascinated our imagination and delighted our hearts, and even comforted our hearts in times of sore distress, but here is an incarnate parable, a living picture of the complete man. Everything upon the Christian man has a meaning. We know what this is in ecclesiastical attire. It is foolish to mock such attire and to ignore its possible and even holy symbolism. You inquire the meaning of this part of the apparel, and the explanation is given to you. It is symbolic; it is nothing in itself, and if it were taken away from the rest of the attire what would it be but a piece of cloth or linen, or silken ribbon, or dumb drapery? But set in its place, interpreted by the truly ecclesiastical genius, it has a meaning, and a meaning not to be despised; but if the meaning be exaggerated or misplaced, then it will become an offense. The captain of the ship will tell you, as I have heard him say, Every passenger who comes near me when I am standing looking over the sea says, What is the meaning of this chain, captain? what is the meaning of this arrangement for turning the machinery? The captain may well get wearied and tired of answering such questions, for they occur day by day, and on every voyage, on the voyage out and on the voyage in; the same ignorance asks the same questions and the same petulance gives the same keen and almost resentful or uncivil replies. Carry the idea up to its highest levels and meanings, and the signification is this, that everything that is provided for the Christian's attire or accouterment is symbolical, is a sign, so that the man thoroughly equipped for the fight is a living parable read by well-trained eyes. The parables flush with beauty, listen to them as a voice, they tremble with ineffable music. We are much too material in our construction of things. Of course we have signed a very serious article of religious confession against materialism, and having signed the clause condemning materialism we go out and practice it. So many people get rid of things by signing them away. Many persons would be very religious if their signature could be accepted as a sacrifice. That is where the point of agony occurs. If by signing any number of credenda we could be enrolled as Christians we would sign at once; we are always prepared to sign, and we are exceedingly hard upon the man who will not attach his signature to the same credenda. But signing is not crucifixion, and except a man take up his cross—not write his name—he cannot be My disciple. Christianity is known by its hands and its side; no wound-prints there, must mean no Christ in the heart. Of course this doctrine will empty the churches; praised be God, it will drive people away who ought never to have been there. But if some remain they will be of the real quality, and the real quality is always in the majority; not in a majority numerical, but in a majority spiritually energetic, influential, and sovereign.

It is wonderful in reading over this panoply to discover how much of it is meant for defensive purposes. It is not all meant for aggression. Christianity is both aggressive and defensive. It is astonishing, I repeat, how much of the Christian armor is for purposes defensive. The helmet does not fight, it protects; the shield does not aggress, it secures, defends, protects the very heart of the warrior. We need a great deal of defensive armor. The devil is wily. If there is one little heel spot missed in the Christian Achilles that little vulnerable heel will be found out and some great assault will be made upon it; mayhap the injection of some deadly poison; and injections are not accompanied with noise or with an uproar that is supposed to betoken heroism and angry strife; injection may be silent. The morphia is inserted with hardly any sense of pain, the digitalis makes no noise when it gets into the life and helps the poor laboring breath. So there are many noiseless temptations, there are many assaults that are not suspected; and therefore this saying is true, What I say unto one I say unto all, Watch; resist the devil, and he will flee from you. But to be called to all this arming and watching and fighting and agonizing expectancy, is this the way to life eternal? Yes, and other way there is none.

It is very noticeable that a great deal of this combat is what may be called hand-to-hand strife. It is not a discharge of ball and other missile over a space of miles; it is wrestling. Two men do not wrestle when they are standing five miles apart, nor a mile apart, nor a yard apart. It is when they are grappling, one with the other, seeking for the tightest place, watching every movement of the antagonist, anticipating and discounting it; the uplifting that there may be the downcasting. Sometimes the Christian warfare is just as hand-to-hand and arm-to-arm as this. Jacob wrestled; we speak and sing of wrestling Jacob. The record says, "Now there wrestled with him," and the wrestlers were so near to one another that the one touched the thigh of the other, and it shrank, and the muscle shrunken abides there till this day to tell what angel tussles there have been in the dark nights of spiritual experience.

It is not enough to watch the agonies which other men undergo. We cannot always follow even our own brother into the dark Gethsemane. Every man must fight his own battle. We can help him up to a given point. It is the same with what men call grizzly, gruesome, cruel death. You can accompany a sufferer it may be in some cases up to the very last half-hour, or the last fifteen minutes, or the last five minutes, but he must go the rest alone. No two souls ever go together within a certain compass of time; it may be shorter, it may be longer, but there is a period in which the whole action becomes solitary; there is no discharge in that war. There is apart from Christian sympathy and succor but one relief I have ever found, and that relief is this, that I too must go alone; that is a relief. How easy to die! How hard to live! How delightful to breathe the last breath away! How terrible to turn from the chamber in which the victory has been won and to go out into some other room desolate with unutterable misery! And as in the hour and article of death there is this hand-to-hand wrestling with the great foe, so all through life there are days when nobody can be with us, hours when we are most social when we are most lonesome, strange gray times when our dearest surviving friend would hurt us by the very breath that is balmy with blessing. So we find in this great combat the lonely hour, the sacred strife, the contest that has not help given to it except from God; and God is most when we need Him most.

Is this armor all to be turned against the enemy? No; it is to be turned, so to say, but to say it with tenderest reverence, sometimes against God. How so? The proof is here: Having equipped yourselves, then follows the command or exhortation, "Praying always with all prayer and supplication in the Spirit, and watching thereunto with all perseverance and supplication for all saints." Does the Lord make an armory that can be employed against Himself? Yes, in a certain sense, but that sense must be very carefully and even tenderly distinguished and discriminated. The action is this: "The kingdom of heaven suffereth violence, and the violent take it by force." And God, having armed the men, says, Now come and take My kingdom. God is willing to be overthrown. The angel was willing that Jacob should throw him as it were in some great struggle. This is part of the condescension of the divine mercy. Sometimes a father wants even baby to deal some heavy blow of tenderness upon him; he means to yield only to force in a certain construction of that term. And God says, Now that I have given you the whole armor, the entire panoply, now come and let us fight, and you shall win, you shall overthrow Me in the agony of prayer. Do not go to God to fight Him in your own strength and in your own panoply, and say, Now I have made ample preparation for taking the fort of heaven. No man can ever take the celestial fort; it must be surrendered by God in answer to prayer. He waits to be gracious,

He waits for you to take it; He says, Come and prove the armor with which I have clothed you; prove Me now herewith, saith the Lord, and see if I will not open the windows of heaven and pour you out a blessing, river upon river, until you are not able to receive it. He clothes us with armor that we may, so to say, violate His very presence. He waits to be violated. He watches the whole movement. He loves His children. He loves them to win in the great contention.

Prayer

Almighty God, will it please Thee in the name of Jesus Christ our Savior to meet us in Thine own house, before Thine own altar, and within the shadow of the one Cross? We need some such meeting, for our hearts are aching with grief, and our lives are overshadowed by threatening clouds. Wherein we have been frivolous and self-sufficient, let the Lord have mercy upon us and turn our hearts to soberness of thought, to religious considerateness, so that we may know our way and our standing before the Lord. We have done grievously, and grievous is the harvest of our doing; we knew it was bad seed we were sowing in God's field, and now we have to reap and to consume the poison. God is not mocked, Thy law abides amid all the changes of incident and circumstance; the way of the Lord cannot be hindered: whatsoever a man or a nation soweth, so shall the reaping be. For a time we think we have deluded God, and behold, Thou wast waiting for us with an uplifted sword, and Thou hast smitten us sorely and proved that we are but frailest men. The Lord help us to read the lesson well, to ponder it deeply, and to apply it fearlessly; then out of repentance and broken-heartedness the summer of Thy love shall return, and all the sky will be cloudless. Thou hast an appointed way, and an appointed time, and an appointed house: who are we that we should sin against God with a lofty hand and escape all the divine judgments? Behold, Thou art inflicting great suffering; it would be cruel if we did not deserve it; Thou hast thrown down our idols, and Thou hast taken Thyself and Thy smile away from us, and now life is cold and desolate, and the country totters into ruins. We come before Thee with humbleness of mind, with utterest self-humiliation, and say, one and all, as a man, as a family, as a people, We have done the things we ought not to have done, we have left undone the things that we ought to have done. If Thou hast shattered our pride, we deserved it; if Thou hast torn our nest to pieces and scattered it on the flying wind, behold, did we not provoke the Lord to this instance of helping and healing wrath? Dost Thou not destroy that Thou mayest reconstruct, and are there not more houses still and larger into which our souls can flee? We have been fools before God, we have

340

betaken ourselves to holiday-making and to recreation and to pleasure and to self-indulgence, and have never named the name of God. O pity the foolish people! Pity the nation that has kept its catechism and lost its faith! Behold, we stand before God who can hardly stand because of loss of strength. This we say individually: for Thou hast turned our house upside down and poured Thy snow upon its central fire; and Thou hast taken the summer light from our window, and not a bird makes its voice heard in the forsaken garden. We say this as families: for we have turned out the Lord, and banished His book, and laughed at His ministries, and denied His providence. The Lord pity us! And then we shall become men again, and get back to the old discipline and faithfulness and reality of manhood, and then the Lord will arise for us and Zion shall be the comfort of the world. The Lord look upon us when we confess our sin, and the Lord mercifully hear us when we return thanks in feeble voices and hesitant hearts, it may be, for His mercy and His lovingkindness. Oh that we had hearkened unto Thy words! Then the summer had never left the garden; oh that we had lived and nestled in the heart of God! and then the winter would be as the summer, and the long night a long sweet rest. I will arise and go to my Father! is the utterance of the prodigal nation, and will say unto Him, Father, I have sinned against heaven and in Thy sight, and am no more worthy that I should stand foremost amidst those who profess Thy name. Do not destroy us utterly, leave us a nail in Jerusalem; do not blow out the last wailing candle. God pity us, not only for our fathers' sake and the graves that make the jewels of the country, but pity us for Christ's sake, seeing that He redeemed the world with blood. The Lord comfort us exceedingly, wherein our hearts are sore, wherein our lot is difficult, wherein the cup Thou hast given us to drink is exceeding bitter. O Jesus, Lamb of God, hear each man when he says in his heart, Let me lean my little cross against the Tree on which Thou didst die! Amen.

4

How Not to Pray

Preached on Sunday Morning, February 4th, 1900.

Only this once—Judges 16:28.

We have heard these words until we are heartsick of them. It seems as if such words could not be done without in the history of human experience. How words fall into base and false familiarity; how soon expressions lose their originality; how in a moment everything seems to become stale! Yet there are some words we cannot do without; we know they are lies, we mean them at the time, or at least we think we mean them; and lo, in a little while the remembrance utterly fades, and we come back upon the old spot with the old hammer, with a false repercussion, with a smiting that we promised should never be renewed.

Samson would gather himself up for a grand final effort; he said in effect, O Lord, the Philistines have taken away mine eyes, I am no longer what I was, I am no longer a prophet and servant of Thine, I am no longer a judge in the country, I am a poor fool; I gave up my secret, I was fallen upon by cruel wretches, they are laughing at me and mocking me with a most bitter sarcasm; Lord, remember the old days, direct my hands, some of you, to the pillars on which this house stands, and now, Lord, this once, the last time, give me back the old Samson, and I will tear these Philistines down as a palace might be torn down by an earthquake: Lord, this once, only this once; I pray Thee let the old strength come back, and I will be avenged for my two eyes. It was very natural, it was most human, it was just what we would have done under similar circumstances, and therefore do not let us laugh at the dismantled giant.

Let us accommodate the passage, so that it may become a lamp which we can hold over various points of life.

"Only this once": forgive me, I will never ask it again, this is the very last time; I have no excuse, I did the evil deed, I wrought the deed of shame, I spoke the false word, but I am getting old, and I shall not trouble my family much more or much longer; give me the final pardon; I seem as if I could not do without it; it seems as if I had it I would die easily and triumphantly; I do not deserve it, but add one more to your forbearances and your gentle judgments and your soft-hearted acts of true clemency and pity; I will never ask again, but pardon me this one time. You know that speech; it is now a stale speech in your ears; you have pardoned seventy times seven, and another pardon is requested with the promise that it shall be the last. You know it, in the case of your son, your daughter, your best friend, the life from which you hoped the most, and that life has come in with its last and last and last, until you have proved it to be a lie. Is it not so with ourselves? Ought not the remembrance that this is a self-accusation to moderate our judgment of others? This is the very thing we have done in the case of the divine Creator and Redeemer of the worlds; we have told Him that we would never repeat the sin. He asks us to repeat the necessity, He loves, He lives to give; we cannot go to Him too frequently with our hunger and our thirst; He says, Blessed are they that hunger and thirst after righteousness: for they shall be filled. It is not of our necessity we go again, but for the very self-same sin we did last week, and we will do tomorrow. Life is critical. I am sure I thought I would never do it again, I did in my heart's heart; I said this shall not occur again; then I told a blacker lie than ever, and put myself more thoroughly into the devil's service, and I found after reveling a whole night with the devil and awakening with a tormenting headache, that it was the headache I was sorry for, not the broken law. If I could have awakened with all my passions still alive and still in their acutest state of sensibility I never would have prayed; but when a man is self-hit, self-scourged, and so to say, strange as the paradox may appear, downtrodden by himself, he will say anything, he will endeavor to impose upon Omniscience. There is no telling what a fool a man may be. Do not mock at the other man; this is no animadversion upon other people, it is first and foremost a grinding of the speaker's own heart to powder, to dust. Do not think of the other man, say to your own heart, looking so to say straight into it, It is you—coward, false soul!—it is you that I am speaking to.

And then we have it again in the daily cry from familiar voices, Deliver me out of this perplexity only this once, no more; I will never ask for deliverance again, I will take the literal consequences: nay, I will pray to go to hell rather than come back to be delivered. And the fool means it; he thinks he will be brave next time; the dog that has in theory died upon a hundred dunghills will come back that he may perish where he has often perished before. You know this in your own family, in your own soul, in your own son, daughter, best friend. Only this once, this other ten pounds, this other acceptance of a bill; this once screen me, and I will never, never return. You know the cry. Which of us has not in his desk a hundred promises that this shall be the last solicitation of love? So we have not fallen upon some out-of-the-way text, we have come squarely down upon a common experience; nay, not common only, but universal, beginning with every man's own self. You have said so to God; many a time I have said so with a lion's confidence, with a face uplifted so often to the heavens that it has forgotten the art of blushing. We say again and again, Lord, let Thy providence help me in this case, only this once; this is really the final perplexity of my life; I am very ill, and I am afraid of the other world; I have suffered much on account of it in a dream but yesternight; I saw the unveiling of the invisible world, I heard the groanings of the lost, in my dream I saw thousands of men mad, lost, could not find their way back again, walking in circles when they thought they were walking in straight lines; I heard the cry for water, and the water had fled away. I do not want to die just now; if Thou wilt give the doctor great success and turn the herbal medicines of the field into sacramental wine, I will never grieve Thee more; only this once! And I promised God many things; I said I would love His Church, I would support His altar, I would vindicate the Cross; I would take up a new line and become a new man if He would but relieve me this once. He did, and the devil has never had a sturdier soldier. Oh the pity of it! The utter, utter sadness of it! What wonder if there runs through the whole Bible the wail, "The heart is deceitful above all things, and desperately wicked"? We would rebuke the other man if the way were not barred by self-accusation.

Now let us note three things about this prayer. First of all, the prayer was to the true God. It was not offered to an idol or to a graven image of any kind or to a mere filmy ideality, a shadowy half-something that was wraith-like, apparitional, but not nameable or not approachable in any suitable and substantial way. This prayer went up directly in the line of the true throne. It was the Lord God of Israel, it was the cry of necessity to the Giver of all good. Know then that we may be praying to the right God; that is no guarantee that we shall get the answer which we desire. You may read the right book and get nothing out of it. Not every man who reads the Bible receives a revelation, or has the slightest idea that there is a revelation of a spiritual and effective kind in the whole range of holy Scripture. Hear what the man will say: I am sure I have done my best; I have taken down the Bible, I have turned over its leaves, I have punctuated its beautiful literature with scalding tears, and I have prayed almost all night, and I prayed to God the Father in the name of God the Son; and this morning I feel no deliverance. The right God does not make the right prayer; the prayer is in the spirit, in the will, it is in the temper or disposition of the heart; it is in the self-crucifixion of the soul: not a cry, but a sacrifice.

What ailed this poor prayer? What was its mortal disease? The mortal disease of this prayer uttered by Samson was that it was offered in the wrong spirit. It is the spirit that determines the quality.

"That I may be at once avenged of the Philistines for my two eyes." It was a prayer for vengeance. That prayer comes easily to the natural spirit. We love to magnify the individual, and to think that individualism is personality. What grave mistakes we make in our verbal definitions! A man will say that he stands up for personality, when he knows nothing about it. He is standing up for individuality, his own little miserable self. Personality is an inclusive term, bringing with it sovereign rights on which God will bestow sovereign recognitions. Do not imagine that when you magnify your individuality you are maintaining the doctrine of personality. Personality is a wide and pregnant term, connoting and consolidating many diverse elements and making of them one temple-like unity, having one divine purpose. Here is a man who comes forward to avenge his personal or individual or physical loss; in that spirit a man cannot pray. What he says may have the form of prayer, so to say the likeness of prayer, and may have about it something of the shape and tone of prayer as it might be uttered in a church and under holy environments and circumstances, and yet the man may not be praying, he may be in reality simply and deeply cursing. You can pray prayerlessly; you can have a creed without having any faith; you may shut yourself up within the mechanical forces and all their applications, and yet not know that you yourself are carried about in diverse circles by a law which mechanics cannot touch, much less rearrange or modify. A curse is not a prayer; an imprecation is not part of the great liturgy in which all redeemed souls ought to take part, and are called upon as a solemn obligation to take part. Herein is it true that aspiration is not prayer. There are many people who are perfectly willing to aspire who are not willing to pray. Prayer is self-slaughter, insofar as the will and the supreme desire of the heart may be concerned. Prayer is self-renunciation; prayer says, Lord, Thy will be done, not mine. Thus the divine will is done by consent human and divine, and is the law, in its own degree of the universe; the soul then falls into the rhythmic movement of the creation, and the man is translated out of individuality into personality in its broadest definitions, and he is part and parcel of the great unity which swings like a censer round the altar divine.

In the third place this prayer was answered, but answered in judgment. Samson had his way, but his way killed him. God has many ways of answering prayer. One sad case is recorded which will at once occur to your memory: "He gave them their request; but sent leanness into their soul." They had their way, and lost it; they got what they wanted, and it poisoned them; they turned the egg which they coveted into the scorpion which stung them to death. How marvelous it is in all this process that Samson still had within him what I may call a spark of vital faith. He knew he had lost his opportunities, and forfeited his privileges, and betrayed his trust; yet he knew something higher than all this, namely, that God lives, and that God is a God of judgment, and that the way of God shall yet prevail upon the earth, be human circumstances and conditions what they may. He made the most of that vital spark; he could have described himself as Peter described himself on another occasion: Lord, Thou knowest all things, Thou knowest that—bad as I am, deserving of damnation as I am, having committed the unpardonable blasphemy, having set myself at the head of the traitors of creation—Thou knowest that Peter loves Thee. But Samson might have said, Do not upbraid me; I have played the fool before God, I yielded up my secret, I parted with my strength, I ceased at once to be a judge in Israel and to be a child of God; but there is one last lingering flash of faith, and I want to turn that last lingering flash into works, into actions, into palpable and crushing results. Samson was then at the very height of his will; he then touched the sublimest personality of his own consciousness, and he was dealing not only with his enemies, but with the enemies of the Lord—bigger enemies than Samson realized them to be—and he tore down the pillars, and killed more in his death than in his life. We will not say anything about Samson's character, we have too much to say about our own; it does not do to stretch our hands across the centuries that we may smite some downtrodden man, but we must begin at the house of God. The judgment must begin in every man's own secret soul. But this we may say; for the eternal comfort of the race it is written according to the blessing pronounced by father Jacob, "Gad, a troop shall overcome him: but he shall overcome at the last." So we come upon the familiar thought of intermediate and final victories. Gad, my poor, poor son, a troop shall overcome him, but he, my son Gad, shall overcome at the last. When they think he is dead he will spring to his feet; when they report it in pagan uncircumcised cities that Gad is dead, Gad will rise and whet his sword and challenge the enemy to a deadlier combat. Do not pronounce upon intermediate failures; there may be many of them, and yet there may be conquest at the last.

So it shall be with our poor hearts. Yes, we were caught in all the sins; the decalogue was flying round us in splintered, shattered pieces, the devil was triumphing over us, but we overcame at the last. It was a long time in coming, but the purpose of God cannot be set aside, and if we diligently, humbly, and reverently entreat the divine presence, and if we be heartily ashamed of our sins, and name them one by one in the face of the noonday sun, and smite upon our hearts and say, "All these sins are ours, and we repent them," who can tell whether God will be gracious unto us, and give us a nail in His tabernacle, and one small place in His great providential plan? We have sinned, we have done the things we ought not to have done. As a nation we have sinned; I do not see that our cup of iniquity could hold one drop more; with the West of London as a consolidated Sodom and Gomorrah, with corruption in high places chargeable, and justly chargeable, with every form of iniquity and pestilent misbehavior, it is not for us to fall back upon a history we have dishonored, it is for us to go forward to a throne that is still a throne of mercy. We are not to be ashamed to confess our sins in the face of the nations. God will see to the answer to such confession. Do not talk about pride and self-respect and conscious loss of dignity. Lose your dignity, but save your souls!

Prayer

Almighty God, all things are in Thine hands, and we rejoice in Thy gracious sovereignty. Thou dost appoint men their places, their goings out and their comings in, yea, their risings up and their sittings down; it is all of Thy doing and all under Thy oversight, and our hearts when they are sober are also glad. Thou dost permit us to tell what we would like, and Thou dost rebuke the prayer while yet it trembles on our lips. We have learned to know that this is best. Once we thought Thee hostile; now we know that rebuking is part of Thy love, that anger is an aspect of the Divine solicitude. We are poor scholars, and dull at the best, and we complain that the light is poor and will not permit us to see all Thy writing; we blame Thee when we should blame ourselves; we are borne before the wind of our own ignorance when we should lie down at the feet of God and humbly cry, Thy will be done. But Thou knowest our frame, Thou rememberest that we are dust, a wind that cometh for a little time, and then passeth away; Thou wilt not batter us down by Thy thunder or dazzle us by Thy sudden lightning. We are but men, partly dust, and partly inspired by Thyself, yea, in some degree we are in the image and likeness of God. It is so wonderful, so distressing, so full of tragedy and awful pain. Yet Thou hast given us some power of dreaming and hoping, and seeing in the dark, and marking the outline of wraiths and specters and strange filmy things. Oh that we could rest in God through Jesus Christ our Lord; oh that we could simply throw down our burden at Thy feet or wait for the strengthening of our back that we might bear it with less difficulty! The Lord be pleased to hear us in all the utterance of our desire after completer resignation, deeper, tenderer submission to the Divine will; then time shall be nothing and succession shall be unknown, and we shall be as those who are unclothed and wait upon Thee in the invisible and the eternal. As we pray at the Cross we pray in confidence, and we mention our sin that we may forget it or remember that where sin abounds grace doth much more abound, and in the name of the blood of the Son of God we cry for pardon; for we have done the things that we ought not to have done, and we have left undone the things that we ought to have done, and we say from our hearts in trembling and in awe, God be merciful to every sinner! Amen.

5

Prayers That Must Cease

Preached on Thursday Morning, February 8th, 1900.

Speak no more unto Me of this matter—Deuteronomy 3:26.

"The prayers of David the son of Jesse are ended." There are prayers that must not be prolonged. We have wearied God, we are talking unwisely to Him; we think we are praying when we are only aggravating Divine providence; it would be the supreme mercy if we could only learn to hold our tongue. It is as if God had said, We have had enough of this matter; this is mere ignorance or selfishness; this is no piety, it is anything but piety; thou art now talking wordily and ineffectively, and nothing can follow such talk as this but bitter disappointment; drop it! This is a great and blessed mystery in the Divine sovereignty and providence of the world. Some people you cannot get to be still; your only hope of partial safety is in not allowing them to begin; by all means prevent them from opening their lips; if you once permit them to begin, they will never imagine that it can be possible that you would wish them to end.

A remarkable instance is that of Moses. There was a longing in his courageous, kingly old heart to go over and to go into the land. "I pray Thee let me go over and see the good land that is beyond Jordan, that goodly mountain and Lebanon; I have had a long hard time of it; who could repeat the miserable experience I have had with this wild, unchastened Israel? Do let me go over and see the end of it all, which shall also be the beginning of it all, as sunset seems to hide in its radiant heart white and glorious sunrise." The Lord said in effect: Moses, we have had enough of this; let there be no whining and no continuance of this poor mean prayer; speak no more to Me of this matter; the arrangement is complete and final; fall into My hands, having first encouraged Joshua, thy successor, who has not done one hundredth part of thy work; but I have a meaning in this; speak no more about it. Hence we come almost abruptly upon the subject of stifled prayers, prayers cut right in two, a most tragic and heart-paining bisection of our prayer. We thought we might talk always to God, but herein we are rebuked; we have been offering, mayhap, poor prayers, mean, worthless, superstitious or superficial prayers; we have not gone deeply down into the root and life of the matter; and God seems to say, For My sake, drop it; speak no more about it. "The Lord was wroth with me for your sakes, and would not hear me," would not heart even me after this lifetime of priestly solicitude and fatherly intercession. Thus we are driven to consider whether there may not be some prayers that ought not to be prayed, and thus we are further driven to consider whether we may not have sinned in prayer; for if some people begin there is no getting rid of them anymore. Oh for the genius of silence! Oh for the prayer that often has no words, a great dumb, piteous look that says nothing, but leaves everything, Canaan and all its beauties, to the decision of the sweet, tender, all-loving Father-Mother. It is difficult for some people to think they can pray if they do not talk. Prayer is not understood; it is supposed to be a little process in mendicancy, a sort of occupation of a poor blind man seated at the roadside and holding out a hand. It is prayer that is not understood. It would be well for us if we could stifle some of our prayers. We say in the sanctuary of an unbroken silence, I would like to go over, I should very much like to see him, her, it, the man, the woman, the city; I should greatly like to gather a plenteous crop of that field on which I have bestowed so much pains; I would like to see God if He would but shapen Himself into visibleness. We may say all that if we will only undertake to choke it down and never let even a dog hear that we have committed such foolishness, trembling on blasphemy.

What are the prayers which ought to be stifled, and of which God wishes to hear nothing more? They are selfish or self-considering prayers, which never find their way into heaven. No nail could carry them up so high, no eagle-nail so strong in pinion could lift up the burden of such worthless prayers to the threshold of heaven. They are self-considering, they are little peddling, meddling prayers, utterances of ignorance and self-concern. The greatest men in the Church have sometimes prayed such prayers, and God has in His own way rebuked them; sometimes quite sharply, at other times with a hesitating anger as if it would rather turn into love than proceed into deprecation and denial. Yet there is the great principle, that some of our prayers are like dead birds that fall because they bruise themselves against the ceiling without ever getting out into the fresh air, much less winging their flight into the blue sky. For example, here is Moses saying, "Let me go over." He is so little as that! After all his Herculean labors, after all the experience of an unprecedented life, he wants just one last little sweetmeat. He is very old; I think I should have granted the prayer, because I am as old and feeble and poor as Moses at his worst. But God would not hear it; God had other ideas and purposes. I think all the Church would have said, Moses must pass over; surely he must pass over first, surely he must pass over amid resounding bands of triumphal music, and all Israel must go mad with joy when the old man sets his feet on the green sward of Canaan. We have many programs which God does not countersign; we are fecundant in the manufacture of suggestions and programs. We can make programs without ever wetting our feet; we can sit at our own fireside and dream programs and write out a list of new year's honors and distribute them with quite royal bounty; but God says when we have finished the programs and handed them up for the divine signature, No more of this; I have had enough of this; this is not the right way. Oh, what things God does! He will kill an old man; He will thrust the last dart through the very soul of His most faithful servant; He will be cruel if we measure Him only by a foot rule or by such space as the naked eye can encompass. We must wait for the revelation, the result, the last beam of light, and then mayhap it may be seen even by Moses that it was better to be buried on Nebo than to be a pioneer in Canaan. Leave God to work out the chastening and perfecting of our character. That is piety, though the price may be a furnace, or a cross.

And Elijah had his little prayer. Elijah thought he would live on his own resources, and Elijah came to partial, to intermediate, but not final ruin. Said the old grand prophet: Release Thy servant; I have had a long, weary, exhausting day; I seem to fall asleep over my work, I who was once so alert that the night had difficulty in conquering me and subduing me into slumber; I nod at noonday and fall asleep when I ought to be at my very busiest engagement and exercise; Lord, release me, for I am tired. And the Lord rebuked him, and said He would hear no more of such praying; that the fire had gone out of the prayer, and the altar held nothing but cold white ashes; and the Lord took other means of refreshing the exhausted prophet and recalling the long gone youth of his soul: Arise, eat, speak the word that I shall tell thee, and if it will encourage thy poor old heart to know that thou art not alone, then be it known to thee, thou son of flame, that I have seven thousand men, who despise Baal and will not kiss his impotent hand.

Then we find Paul praying just the same kind of useless and fear-burdened and fear-shadowed prayer: I prayed the Lord Christ that he would take away the thorn; no thorn in history was so long and so sharp as mine, and it pierced its way through as if into the very center of my heart, and I said once and twice and thrice, Lord, remove this cruel thorn, and He would not, He specifically declined to remove the thing that was killing me; but He said, My grace is sufficient for thee, and until that hour I never knew the meaning of the word sufficient: I felt I could bear a thousand thorns, and in the strength of that assurance I rose, and almost challenged the thorns to tear me, and let my blood flow out in a libation of love to God. How fond we are of these little self-regarding prayers! One of

the things we shall have to repent of someday, when we are bigger
and wiser souls, will be our prayers. We argued before the throne so
poorly; we dragged our poor little selves into God's sight, as it were,
and said, See this emaciated life, and pity it, and give it decent burial even in the wilderness; only let me get rid of it, it is so like what
I think hell must be. To repent of our prayers, to recall the paltry intercessions of our ignorance and our poverty—who can enter into
the mystery of that experience? May God give us time for oblitera-
tion; the Lord enable us to have a sufficient number of days in
which to erase our prayers; oh for the rubber that can get at that
mean ink and drink it out so that God Himself, were it possible,
should not see again the tracing of our mean, graceless hands.

Then, secondly, there are prayers that minister subtly but surely
to intellectual or social vanity. A man will set himself to pray for
knowledge of the future. The future has always been fascinating to
a certain type of imagination. If we could only find out, without
other people being also able to find out, what is coming tomorrow!
There is a field for fancy! Can we not devise some method of pea-
counting or stone-carving or wood-carving or sign-making by which
we could report the morrow? These poor, occasionally lying boys
that call out today's paper—if one could rise and call out with confidence and with adequate proof of his veracity tomorrow's paper!
It looks as if it would do no harm if we could see into the mystery
called tomorrow; but it would do nothing but harm. A day at a
time is enough for us; we know our own intellectual vanity and
selfishness well enough to know that it is better for us to be sent
home in the evenings and shut up in the security or even in the
dungeon of darkness. Yet if you analyze human mind and action
you will probably discover that the most of people are living in tomorrow; they are not the less certainly living in it that they are not
aware of the fact. In a certain sense it is perfectly right that we
should live in the future, but with resignation, with confession of
ignorance and dependence, with constant looking to the Divine
hands for guidance and to the Divine eye for light. Thus it is that

posterity draws us on, strange as the paradox may appear while it lingers in mere words; it is tomorrow that helps us to live today, it is heaven that makes earth tolerable. Yet we are here on delicate ground, we must take care, we must not press the Lord too far; He will give us just as much time as is useful to us or can be turned to useful purposes in the interests of others. The longing, this desire to penetrate the future, is the desire to succeed in intellectual speculation, the desire to get the newest view, the unheard-of interpretation, the set of combinations that will produce a totally variant condition of historical development and social responsibility; to be delivered from ignorance, to have a secret key opening into secret places, to be enabled to enter into sanctuaries from which the general mass of mankind may be considered to be excluded; to have special certificates and special endorsements and professional dignities and professional remunerations, solaces, and rewards; to constitute ourselves into classes so that we can exclude a large number of persons, in which the high priest is the Pharisee who is not as other men, certainly not as this publican. The Lord will not hear us; when He does admit anybody into His more secret chambers it is the babe. What babe ever took up any room, or were we not so fond of the babe that we imagined it occupied no place at all, but was just as welcome as a sunbeam and as little likely to incommode us in the matter of space? "Father, I thank Thee that Thou hast hidden these things from the wise and prudent, and hast revealed them unto babes." "Of such is the kingdom of heaven"; that is my reason for baptizing them; that is all the certificate I want. I do not write to any registrar to ask him how old this baby is, because I know the older he is the worse he is. "Of such is the kingdom of heaven." They brought their little children, and in all time little have either given us the secret of God or have largely been the medium through which we have in some way, ideal, poetic, literal, received the seals of the kingdom. Lord, make us babe-like; give us the child-heart, and seize us while we are thus remade young before we have time to make fools of ourselves and heretics!

There are prayers that do not involve thorough renewal and submission of heart; they are anecdote prayers, little pottering prayers about fine days and fine harvests and rain and diverse little comforts that are specially and locally desired and needed; it will require all the grace of God to turn these whinings into real and effectual prayers. There is no prayer worth praying that does not aim at the submission of the human will to the divine—"Nevertheless, not my will, but Thine be done." That is true prayer, and prayer, we have often said, that is always and necessarily, when offered in the right spirit, answered and glorified. We may make our prayers sources of profit, or we may regard them, not altogether with frank outspokenness, but with deep, secret, subtle intent, as a species of investment. Some of us have been guilty of this. It is a mean but ever-disappointing exercise and attempt to enlist God on our side. We cannot get away from the notion that God is specially interested in us at the expense of some other man. You cannot eradicate out of this heart of yours the notion that God has a special liking for you and your parish and neighborhood and country: God will be sure to hear the Briton. Is He not the God of the Boer as well as the God of the Briton? Is He not the God of the Briton as well as the Boer? Does He reign in His heaven to make paltry distinctions among the people who owe themselves to His creative power and providential care? Beware how you make selfish prayers, investing prayers, profit-seeking prayers.

I must say, though at the risk of incurring disrepute, if not hostility, which I despise, that the debate the other night in the House of Commons upon the condition of affairs made me sore and sick at heart. It was a mean debate on both sides, a paltry, worthless, atheistic debate, unworthy of the occasion, unworthy of the awful tragedy that is involved, unworthy of a proper appreciation of the broken hearts on both sides, occasioned by this diabolic bloodshed. In the debate there was not a religious voice heard in the whole utterance, but one. The greatest speech of the debate was in one word. It was made by Mr. Healy, one of the brightest intellects of the century. When challenged to say to whom are the Boers looking for support, he said, "God." It did my heart good—poor, old, withered, disappointed heart—to hear that sacred word. They should have turned the Houses of Parliament into a sanctuary when they debated upon action that involves the making of thousands, if not tens of thousands, of widows and orphans and desolated homes. They might have discussed the matter as politicians *plus* Christian citizens and Christian believers. If a man of weight and authority had stood up there and said, with the fervor of a man hardly dead yet, a memory and an inspiration still, "We do not love war, we hate war, we feel that we have been driven into a combination of circumstances in which war is more or less inevitable and unavoidable, but we say to Boer and to Briton, we want the war honorably and righteously ended," that man's words would have rung round the earth and have awakened a response that would have had happy results. What caviling! What neat little essays, grammatically correct, small-boy exercises in English composition, little nagglings one with the other, assurances that if something had been done on Wednesday instead of being done on the previous Saturday, then the Government would have been worthy of confidence! But I look in vain for grand, fundamental, all-encompassing principles, and an enthusiasm so religious that it must have affected hearts in England, in Africa, and in every other part of the world.

These are the prayers that I do not care for, namely, the ordered prayers and the scheduled prayers and the atheistic debates, and the great care so to speak as not to mention the name of the Ruler of the universe. Brethren, I was ashamed of it all, on both sides, as mean, inhuman, contemptible, disastrous. I will not have it therefore that human nature belongs either to this country or to that country exclusively and specially. God is no respecter of persons; in every nation he that feareth God and worketh righteousness is accepted of the Almighty Father. We must broaden our petitions, and become more human that we may become more divine. Then let us leave our prayers, and if we have offended God by ignorant desires and superficial intercessions and supplications, let us clothe ourselves in sackcloth and ashes. For my part I do not hesitate to pray for all classes and conditions of men, for all foreigners so-called, for all heathen and pagan nations, and I look upon the whole population of the globe as the children of God. To charge God with partiality is to degrade Him. God is no respecter of persons, but He is a respecter of character, He respects righteousness, obedience, virtue, purity, self-sacrifice; and He accepts these as certainly from the Boer as from the Briton, as certainly from the Malagasy as from the Red Indian, as certainly from the civilization of Europe as from the heathenism of the islands of the sea. Surely better days are coming; surely we shall drive out all these politicians and only readmit them on proof of character. I pray God to dissolve both Houses of Parliament, and never to reconstruct them except on a basis of a love of righteousness and adequate proofs of Christian intelligence. I do not want mere politics-mongering; I want humanity, the next word below divinity. My dear friends, I do not care one iota whether you applaud me or dissent from me, except in the degree that I am always pleased when great principles are preferred to petty policies.

Prayer

Thy people cry unto Thee, O God, in the name of Jesus Christ their Savior, humbly desiring to offer Thee some gift of praise in return for Thy boundless mercy and most loving kindness. It is in their hearts to be grateful: how can they be false in presence of all Thou hast done for them in Thy blessed and most merciful providence? Sometimes we give ourselves to review, we go back to our earliest days, watch Thee taking us into Thine arms and guiding us and upholding and protecting us according to our necessity; then our hearts glow within us; we say, Surely the Lord who hath brought us thus far will take us still further and bring to happy issue all His thoughts and purposes concerning us. We turn our eyes to the Cross and see all Thy love there; that is the heart of God; we see it bleed for us, and we hear the gentle, gracious voice which says, The blood of Jesus Christ cleanseth from all sin; and herein is that saying true, There is a fountain opened in the house of David for sin and uncleanness. Thou hast surrounded us with Thyself, with all the tokens of Thy presence and love; we would be blind of heart not to see them; sometimes we seem to see them altogether; then the floods lift up their voice and the thunders are raised to music, and we would praise the Lord with our whole breath and with all the fire of a redeemed life. We bless Thee for high religious emotion, for great depths of tenderness, for manifold and sustaining experience; sometimes we bring into our song the very furnace itself, and the great trial, and the forty days in the wilderness when we are face to face with the wild beasts. It is a wondrous life; it is Thine own doing, Thou Doer of all the true marvels. We say again and again as we reap the crop, This is the Lord's doing, this also cometh from the Lord of hosts, wonderful in counsel and excellent in working. Thou dost write Thy name on the fields, Thou dost sign each season as it comes and goes claiming it as Thine own and as a fulfilled covenant. Now we are with Thee in the wintertime, when we have to look upon the cold snow and feel the piercing wind; and we want to be able to say that God who made the summer made the winter also. Why should we not round off our song and the utterance of our trust? Why should we have but a partial faith or an occasional uplifting of the soul to God in Christ? Wilt Thou not be with us in our deepest consciousness all the year through, so that we shall sing our psalm in midwinter and our anthem when the summer is at its glowing height? Thou knowest that we are slow of heart and dull of understanding, and we bless Thee that Thou dost not reject us though we are faint and feeble and our knees knock against one another as we half trust Thy providence. Forgive us our atheisms; they are partial and transient, but they are facts; oh! that we might be delivered from all negation and half trust and daring denial, and that we might wholly, absolutely throw our souls into Thy keeping, Shepherd of Israel, Redeemer of man. We commend one another tenderly to Thy care: those who are feeble and old, those who are sick of heart, and those who are weary of life and would gladly dig their grave in the snow. And we commend unto Thee those who are great-hearted, full of loving thoughts, seeking out the blind to lead them, and the lame to give them a lift on the rugged way. We bless Thee for sanctified riches, and for uncomplaining and trustful poverty, and for all the people who teach us great lessons in the field of labor, in the furnace of suffering, in the activities of daily life. The Lord be round our houses; who can rock the cradle but those who love Thee, Father of all? Be with the physician and with the nurse, with those who are weary of the day and wearier still of the night; be with hearts that are killed with anxiety, wondering what the next news will be, those whose very lives are shaken and tortured and most sorely tried. If the Lord will thus in the name and for the sake of Jesus Christ hear our prayer and answer it, we shall not know this to be winter, but through the snow we shall see the warmer blossoms. Amen.

6

By What Authority?

Preached on Sunday Morning, February 11th, 1900.

Showing by the scriptures—Acts 18:28.

Man must have some kind of authority. He must assume something; he must begin. The proof is not always in the beginning palpable and undeniable; the beginning contains the end, but until the end is reached we do not know the full value and true force of the beginning. What is there in all your life which does not rest upon an assumption? The whole scheme of life seems to rest upon some airy, beautiful, fragile bubble. You think at a certain part of your process of life that you are acting upon definite proof and authority; but you are doing nothing of the kind; you are basing your whole selfhood upon an assumption. The very first line of your spiritual algebra reads: Let this or that symbol represent or in the meantime be equal to the unknown quantity of which we are constantly and sometimes peevishly in quest. You must have something, if it be no better or stronger than a cobweb, to begin with; the cobweb has to prove itself in a long process; in the first instance it must be assumed. Who are these that cry out so loudly for authority and write books upon it? Everything is its own authority, or there is none, and everything must prove its own authority or fall, or be nonsuited in the court of commonsense and true wisdom. If that could really be understood and applied, it would alter the whole face of things. We do not go far enough back, we take a great deal for granted which is not literally and verbally provable; but if we accept the assumptions, and so to say presume upon them and act as if they were true, we give them a chance to prove whether they are true or not. The poor algebraic x has a hard time of it in the first three or four lines of the equation; it is nobody, it is nothing, it is less than anonymous, it is a mere convenience, something to which something else may be attached; and the process goes on line by line, combination by combination, until the poor struggling humble x of the first line stands out in plain strong arithmetical figures at the last. Yet, in the process specially referred to, you could not have undertaken two lines without the x, which only assumed or represented something which it knew nothing about. Yet there are persons who are always asking for our authority. If that foolish question were permitted we should destroy the whole fabric of things. The assumption must prove itself; things are not done from the outside; all things worth doing are done from the inside. Those of us who are more foolish than others are looking far away for someone to come and prove something we are struggling with. The great voice from heaven says, Let the thing you are struggling with prove itself, or cast it out. So in the Church and in the marketplace and in the academy and in all the large schools of training, we are dealing absolutely with assumptions and with nothing else, until the assumptions work themselves into such combination and issues that we begin to feel the whole process to be ghostly, weird, spiritual, yet most substantial and invulnerable in practical logic. There are many persons who never become religious because they say, What is the authority?—as if the authority were outside, and had a postal address and must be approached by way of deputation. Everything has in it its own proof, or proof it has none. Upon that as Christian teachers and thinkers we venture without throb of heart-misgiving to build the whole Christian argument and appeal.

You cannot intellectually prove the existence of God, but you can prove it by living it. You must not go to the library for many learned books whereby the existence of God is logically established. God is in you, or to you He is not God. God comes through the

consciousness; sometimes almost an argument, often a dream; sometimes a madness, a peculiar inexplicable process, and as the Apostle
John says, we know that we know—a double affirmation, and oftentimes without explanation in mere words. Do not be disturbed because some man, who was born stupid and will probably die insane,
comes and asks you what is the seat of authority in religion. As if he
had some authority in arithmetic. He has no standing in arithmetic;
there is no standing in arithmetic but the standing of assumption or
consent of minds. Arithmetic is sometimes simply a document as
between parties, saying, Let it be understood that this figure and that
figure added together mean another or third figure. But it has to be
assumed; there is no revelation upon arithmetic, the multiplication
table has nothing behind it but a human consent, and the days or
months have to live the beggarly life of being permitted to live. And
yet those of us who are on the Christian side of things are called
upon to prove all we say in a certain way, or it will be discredited,
and people will arm themselves against it under the name of unbelief
or infidelity. O thou fool! Everything has in it its own proof, or there
is no proof.

Now we can stop at many points and illustrate this. What do
you suppose is the probable age of this pebble which I have just
picked out of the brook? I ask you, geologist, and the geologist
replies as if he knew all about it: I think you must at least take it for
granted that this pebble has been in existence two million years.
What is your authority for saying so? The reply is, The general authority is the result of our investigation into the duration of the
scheme of things which goes by the vague name of nature; we take
into account rocks, formations, laminations, strata, and other long
names that you probably as a tyro have never heard of. And I reply
that having heard of them at this very moment I simply wonder
what they are. Nature is old, we feel that too true; but Nature never
gives us her real calendar. We have almost in our most insinuating
and persuasive way invited dear old mother Nature to put her name
in our little birthday book, with the suggestion that she might add

the year in which she was born. But she never does that. She writes Nature in a bold Roman hand, and when we look for the date we want she is as mysterious as she can be. Yet we trust the age of nature; we argue from it, we say, Let it be granted that this occurred under such and such circumstances, and under such and such accumulations of periods of duration. But that is imagination, hypothesis, conjecture; the proof of which, if any proof there is, will be found a long way off. Yet all we can do in many cases is to argue upon assumption. That is how you brought up your little child. You assumed that the little creature was sane. What an act of faith! But you never regarded it as such. The other thing had to be proved; not the sanity, but the non-sanity had to be proved. That is how we ought to approach all great subjects—to assume the great, the noble, the true, the profound, the beneficent, and if there be anything on the other side let it come out slowly, and let it be received with hostility, with angry unbelief; the mother says, I will not believe that my babe is insane. What is it that tempts us always to begin on the negative side, and to say, There is no God, there is no Bible, there is no inspired record—we who would not for the world at first believe in the deficiency, mental or bodily, of our own little child? Change the center of gravity, change the mental and moral standpoint, and though we have written it down in words that a negative cannot be proved, yet let it be one of those negatives that we insist upon being proved before we treat the little suckling child as the beginning of a babbling idiot. Better prove the other way; if at last you have to give in, crying, oh the sorrow of it, and the bitter misery! Let it be wrung from you by evidence which you cannot deny.

From the beginning God has been endeavoring to incarnate Himself in various proofs and authorities suitable to the growing mind of man. So He has made all nature a parable, a panorama, an open secret; upon every door of nature He has written, Knock, and it shall be opened unto you. Then came a book, The Book, the Bible or Revelation. For God's sake and your sake, give it a fair chance! Let it prove its irreligiousness or its insanity, but remember that it is a book that wants to do you good; therefore it may have come from a good source. If it were a book of dreams and imaginings only you might receive it as such, but it is a book of discipline, a book of army orders; no soldier is to invent his own book; whatever the book may be, it tries to do us good, to dry our tears, to direct our way, to sustain us in our misfortune and distress; yea, it holds a lamp above the grave and frightens death into deeper gloom. Let it therefore have a fair chance. After the book comes Manhood, which is, so to say, the result of the book. The book has been sown as seed in our minds and hearts, and after it has come to fruition we have manhood. So the incarnation advances from nature to intellect, to character. It is a progressive revelation; it proves itself by itself. Revelation which is true never goes backward, it always has some larger kingdom, it always preaches a warmer, a larger welcome to the growing mind and the enlarging heart. These are the proofs. Let it be assumed that the Bible is the book of God and spoken by God, full of God, leading to God; let that assumption be nothing but an *x* to work with, but let us try how that assumption works out; then we must believe, commit ourselves to certain propositions and doctrines, receive a certain testimony and witness into our hearts; then we must indicate a certain discipline of humiliation, depletion, bereavement, mockery, disappointment; the whole time hearing a voice saying, Hold on, be faithful unto death; do not let go; keep the commandments, follow the Christ, though it cost thee right hand and right eye; persevere. Then see what the upshot is; what are the sheaves we have brought, what the tokens, the signs, the proofs or the disproofs of our spiritual education; and I now say in view of human history and Christian experience that the result of that assumption, faithfully believed and faithfully carried out, is manhood, virility, and masculine nobleness. We began with an assumption, we proceeded to a conviction, we ended with a new manhood.

How profitable it would be if instead of going to the library to borrow a very large book to prove that Christ is the Son of God, and that Christianity is the sum of all virtue and spiritual excellence, we would simply go down where the work has been realized and brought into eloquent and impressive life. We do not need the book to prove the argument; the argument proves itself. If I were called upon to prove the truth of Christianity, I would lock up the library, and say to those who longed for elucidation or confirmation, Come with me, and I will show you some folks who ten years ago were little better than cannibals, men and women who had outlived their humanity, who had succeeded in obliterating the image of God from their very faces. Such and such agencies were brought to bear upon them, such and such gentle ministries operated upon their life; little by little the light broke, questions were asked, experiences were realized, services were offered; and one day all these folks seemed to see each other with new eyes; women had a new value, children became unspeakably precious, a sense of responsibility arose in the hearts in question; people began to ask how they could help one another to carry a burden, to bear a grievance, to sustain a sorrow, to make up for bereavement; little by little the sun came into the place from which he had been banished, little by little the woman gave glints and gleams of some hidden angel that was awakening in her womanly heart, and they are there today. And you ask, By what authority? The people themselves are the best answer. And having shown you this proof I turn upon you, and if with fierceness and abruptness, it is because of my glowing gratitude to the God that redeemed these souls, and I ask, Where are *your* proofs? What has your non-religion done for the world? what has your unfaith done for little children, suffering women, toiling men, broken hearts? I challenge you.

This is how the line of proof develops itself; probably altogether an assumption at first; something that was to be taken for granted, something about which we said, Now, this is only an assumption, what is called a conjecture or a hypothesis; we say nothing about it at this stage of the inquiry, but let it be granted, and then what comes out of it, and necessarily comes out of it, and partakes of its own quality? What is it? Man! I have seen no other religion produce anything like this; other theories I may have intellectually accepted on approbation for purposes of speculative inquiry and titillation, but I have seen this Christianity do such things, and do such things by the very necessity of its own nature; I have seen this decalogue work such and such results, and these beatitudes realize themselves in such and such forms of heroism and martyrdom, patience and beneficence, that I have living, breathing, imperishable proofs and authorities.

That is my stand as a Christian minister and as a Christian thinker. I am quite prepared to displace the Bible, but not until you have put a better in its place; I think that is fair. I am prepared to pray at another altar, but not until you have given me reason to do so larger than at this moment I can believe. To show that we do not hold the Bible as a fetish, we say we are ready to give it up today if you will replace it by a better. I am no fetish-worshiper. I do not care for the pulpit as a mere platform or rostrum; but you must show me an instrument or medium by which I can do better work or better serve my day and generation, and tomorrow you will find my pulpit vacant. The Christian position is absolutely unassailable. Ignorant men may have ignorantly defended it, but if you will consult those who have lived the Bible and companied with the Lord Jesus, and have seen morning, noon, and night His hands and His side, they will tell you what Jesus Himself tells us; standing up in His meek majesty and majestic meekness, He said, "Believe me for the works' sake." Could man, rational man, desire a better proof? When I go astray into a far land, and think I can invent a new religion or can elect a morality better than the morality of my mothers' Bible, I do not go to hear a very learned lecture by a very dim-minded man who can hardly make out his own manuscript. I go where my wife went, to some simple-minded, kindly, gracious fisher-folks on the northeast coast, men who have been, as they are not afraid or ashamed to say, converted, and I listen to their singing, and to their ungrammatical English, and to the outpouring of their spiritual experience;

and I say, I will arise and go to my Father, and will say unto Him, Father, I have sinned, and am no more worthy to be called Thy son. By what authority? By the authority of these men and women, by the authority of their homes, by the authority of their lives. Whatever made these men and women what I know them to be is the religion which I voluntarily and spontaneously and rapturously receive and believe, to live with, to die with. Young soul, when asked for authority, go to living instances, and stand by them. Whoever made the blind man see I will receive with gratitude, with adoration; and though at first I may be timid, yet in my timidity I will whisper, My Lord, my God! Then in ten years I will say the same words, but more loudly, and then at calm, expectant seventy I will say them with all the thunder of my gathered energy, My Lord and my God!

Prayer

Almighty God, we thank Thee for the providence of time. Thou dost preside over the moments and over the ages. Thou dost sit upon the circle of eternity, and nothing happens without Thy wise and loving will. It is a comfort to know that the very hairs of our heads are all numbered, that none of our steps will slide if so be we take hold of Thy hand and accept the guidance of Thine eye. The Lord is our strength and our salvation, our infinite sufficiency, and our immortal hope. Hitherto the Lord has led us, upheld us with the arm of His might, and comforted us with the solaces of His love. Thou wilt not forget the past, Thou wilt make all Thy promise sure to those who put their faith in Christ and live according to Thy will. It is our joy to know that everything about us is known in heaven; we can hide nothing from the searching eyes of Thy judgment of the pitying look of Thy love. It is enough, it is balmy as a summer morning, it is tender doctrine, divine supervision, and continual watchfulness. May we live and move and have our being in God, may we take nothing into our own hands, may we fall into the loving arms of the mighty God of Jacob; then shall we be assured and very steadfast, yea, as one of the rocks which Thou Thyself hast set in the earth, we shall be no more afraid, nor shall the spirit of depression overwhelm us. Surely then, living in God through Jesus Christ our Lord, we shall say, All is well, when the whole sky is a dark cloud. So let it be, Thou Father of spirits and Redeemer of the souls of men. Amen.

7

The Providence of Time

Preached on Thursday Morning, February 15th, 1900.

When the time was come—Luke 9:51.

If we look carefully into things, we shall find that every matter is related to a plan, a method or scheme of life. Time has hitherto been treated in the sacred record almost with contempt; it is spoken of as so transient, so empty, and our very life as measured by time is as a post hastening on his way, is as a vapor rising up to be blown away by the wind. What is our life as measured by time? A breath, a gasp, nothingness. Yet here we have time elevated into a kind of significance and special importance. "When the time was come": cannot man hasten the time? That man can never do. Cannot man hasten the coming of the summer? Not by one hairsbreadth. Is it not in the power of man to say to the snow, Be melted and flow away in fertilizing rivers among the valleys and the meads and the fair gardens? The snow does not know the name of man. The Lord keeps all the great opportunities and appointments in His own hand, and He will not allow the most scientific and painstaking of us to interfere for one moment in the degree in which His providences shall ripen and take effect. We are no doubt, when we measure ourselves, great men, and we are gradually, with a fine and most appropriate dignity, getting more and more control over the laws of nature. Yet a snowfall delays the express, and, in effect, looking at it poetically, says, You shall not go today. We are the men who are making such great strides and noble and sure advances in the paths of science; yet the rain will wet through our most scientific man, and bring on pneumonia. It is so comical, and yet it is so sad, that man persuades himself that he is getting higher up the ladder in this matter of acquiring a wider knowledge of the laws of nature. It is exactly the same with the laws of time. We can light a conservatory fire and hasten the ripening of sundry flowers and fruits, but we can light no fire that takes effect upon a landscape and turns a wilderness into a garden of roses. If we could but know our limitations and quietly work within them, we should live in a holy and quiet sanctuary, we should not attempt to hasten anything; we should remember a great and most profound text, "He that believeth shall not make haste": he will leave the clock in the hands of God, he will permit the sovereign One to fix the moment of maturity and the fruition of holy prophecy. Yet man is most impatient. Where he can, as he vulgarly says, hurry up anything, he does not spare the lash: what a mercy of mercies it is that he cannot hurry up the sun, or the spring, or the summer! Why, he would lash himself to death! How great, how tender the mercy that keeps man in a certain little place, and smiles with a fine contempt upon his endeavors to get more and more control over the laws of nature. There is a great moral lesson here, which we shall discover if we study the providence of moments.

This or that action, says the divine Ruler, shall be done at such and such a time; it shall not be done one hour before the appointed moment; all the kings in the world cannot hasten the chariot-wheels one hairsbreadth; we simply have to stand still and see the divine movement and watch the palpitations that make the very clouds of mystery alive as if a heart were throbbing within their folds. Jesus Christ was very careful in pointing out this matter of providential time, and so was the apostle Paul. Jesus Christ said, "Woman, what have I to do with thee? Mine hour is not yet come": it may come at any moment, but that moment itself has not yet arrived; we must not forestall or anticipate. Who but some subtle imp ever suggested the notion of mortgage in any form but especially the idea of mortgaging time? Who can borrow from the day that is yet to come? Who has any right to pledge unborn time? It may never come, or he who pledges it may never see it come. "Boast not thyself of tomorrow; for thou knowest not what a day may bring forth." Thus Jesus Christ says again and again, if not in so many words, yet in substantial and spiritual effect, "Not yet"—"Mine hour is not yet come"; "Father, the hour is come." He watched it descend like a falling jewel from the bright heavens. It was an hour of sorrow, but it came from the place of joy; it was an hour born in heaven, and let down with its tragic Cross to the waiting and trembling earth. This is the point, that the time is fixed: "Is there not an appointed time for man upon the earth?" His rude violence would become a sin, if he would plunge himself into eternity; he must carry his murder with him and answer for it yonder. If we would live and move and have our being in God, we must wait for the hour for closing the weary eyes and stepping into the newly arrived chariot from heavenly places. We would hasten the coming of that chariot if we could, but our discipline lies in the fact that we must not even wish to hasten it. That is where the Cross with all its misery of agony, and yet its latent mystery of hope, enters into our poor life. It is so arranged by the eternal One, that I must not wish my black deliverer to come, though I perspire blood and though I cannot straighten my back to receive again the blazing of the sun upon my face. Yet there is a voice—oh that wondrous mystery of voices!—which says, Son, thou mayest not even wish for the ending of thy pain. Nor must we wish for the moment of our coronation. Jesus Christ was ready to show the world all His miracles; He was prepared from eternity with all the wonders which were to accompany the Messianic reign. Yet Jesus Christ waited for the moment, Jesus Christ tarried for the divine will; Jesus Christ said, Mine hour is not yet come, I am watching, I am waiting, I am neither wishing nor praying, I am simply awaiting the ripening of time, the almost visible presence of the one moment that is critical and agnostic. We are too small to live as Jesus did; we can only hope and pray to live in the direction of His life, to show what we would be if we could but for this sense of death that outruns the summer and this sense of incompleteness that mocks our most aspiring ambition.

Something is to be learned from the almost taunt with which Jesus Christ replied to the scribes and Pharisees upon one occasion; said He, "Your hour is always ready." That is the distinction between philosophy, and impatience or ignorance. Your hour is always available; it came from nowhere, and it is not going anywhere in particular; it is something that comes and goes bubble-like, but how it rose, how it burst, and how it was forgotten are matters of no concern to the sorrowing heart of the world. You have no forethought, no afterthought, no sense of the relation, fitness, and spiritual music of things; so you can at any moment do what you want to do, only the thing you want to do is not worth doing, because it goes not back into the eternal or forward into the everlasting. We know what the meaning of such personal hastiness and impetuosity is. There are people who always want us to be doing or going on. To that poor ridiculous game has the worst species of irreligiousness, namely, the pietic species, brought the civilization and the religion of the world! There are persons who are never happy except in a noise; there are souls that think nothing is going on unless they themselves are the chief part of the noise. They do not understand the mystery of silence; they enjoy a conversation in the degree in which they take a leading part in it. They declare afterwards that the meeting was most interesting and most profitable; when they did not speak, the meeting was not worth attending, and the whole outlook of civilization hungry and poor. We have not learned what it is to have a little sanctuary into which we enter and hear only that which cannot be heard, and are delighted and thrilled by the wordless music. That kind of realization belongs to the higher life; it may take us seven years and more to enter into that high tabernacle of God; when we enter it we shall know that silence may be the purest music, and that rest is the last expression of energy.

The apostle Paul also made observations upon this matter of moments of time. Said he, in 1 Corinthians 4:5, "Judge nothing before the time." If we could be kept to that rule what generous judgments we would often pronounce! We should be no longer censorious, vengeful, resentful; we should wait for the signal from heaven. When all is known much will be forgiven. You cannot even in your confession tell your priest everything. Even when you think you have emptied your memory of its last recollection you have not begun the real story. You are not understood because you cannot explain yourself; if you are charged with this or that sin or offense, it may be broad black crime, you cannot always tell exactly and exhaustively how it came to be; you would have to go over the centuries and dig up your grandsires and call them as living witnesses to say what lives they lived. There is a descent of poison, there is an old, old acridness traceable two centuries since or ten centuries ago. Only God knows how your blood came to be so compounded; only the Eternal knows this blending of juices and acids and this quickening of poisonous and pestilent desires; leave the judgment in the hands of God. "Judge nothing before the time." When He who broods over the earth knows all about us, which He does from the beginning, I wonder not that He says, "The first shall be last, and the last shall be first," for the kingdom is not divided and there is but one King. Beware of ill-timed judgments; beware of hasty speeches upon other men's conduct; beware of that foul Pharisee who thanks God that he is not as this publican. When the two histories are searched into and lifted up into the light, what if the publican have the crown and the Pharisee be not in the broad heaven at all? Therefore judge nothing before the time. Wait another moment; by the next post we may get the explanation; in a moment more the light may flash. Great things are done in great moments. "Let there be light," and there was light; no chronometer could measure the distance between the fiat *Lux!* and the shining glory. Judge nothing before the time. Never pretend that you know more than you do know; never give people the impression that you could say a great many things if you were not so religiously reticent and so piously and exorbitantly as it were silent and forbearing about matters; do not give the impression that some other man owes his life to you because you could tell this and that. If you say so I would, with the open Bible before me, and the roof of God's house over me, pronounce you coward.

Do we not sometimes admit the principle of providential moments even in our own speeches and actions? We say, "There is a tide in the affairs of man which taken at the flood leads on to fortune." Why not take the tide an hour earlier? Because there is a law of tides. Why not wait until we can approach the tide in leisurely and impressive dignity? Because there is a law of tides; the law of tides imposes upon us the duty of taking it at the flood. We atheistically speak of the lucky moment, or even the psychological moment; whatever we say in description of the moment, it is better for us to recognize the great religious fact that there is a moment when a thing is in season, another when it is out of season; there are opportune moments, and moments inopportune, and upon this basis of critical speciality is the providence of God conducted. Oh, if I could rest upon that great truth I should be a man again with sevenfold strength, and with most precious, yea, with unquenchable hope, but the tempter says, Try it now! and his now is not God's now; so my foot slips, and I fall from the pinnacle and am dashed almost to pieces on the rocks below. Of course you and I would like this or that to happen today; we say in our ignorance and impatience, Why does it not happen at this very moment, or in an hour or two? If we had the ordering of things we should arrange that this matter should mature and fructify by sunset, or we should identify it with the more poetic time of sunrise; why is it not according to our will? Because we are not God. We must be taught in some way, probably by lash and scourge and disappointment and contempt, that there is only one God, and that His will is sovereign, is supreme.

It is curious and affecting to see how men try to make time. Often we attempt to create opportunities and to fix the responsibility of their occurrence upon God. "When a convenient day was come," we read in the history of the king. "A convenient day"—a day when things came together, and because we wanted them to come together we thought they came providentially; the atmosphere was, so to say, propitious; the appointment lay in this or that direction, and it really seemed as if we could see the very hand of God in it. Oh the foulness of the human heart! Oh the wickedness of the human soul! We want a thing to be done, and we make the doing of it convenient—all the radiating lines coming back into the center, and seeming to say in their consolidation that this is the hour which God appoints. Do not interfere with God, do not endeavor to be under-deities, small minor gods; leave all in the hands of Him who is Father, Redeemer, and Spirit of all light and holiness. "When a convenient day was come" Herod arranged that this and that should be done; we make our own conveniences and charge them upon God; we arrange our little plans, and then say that we never had anything to do with them.

It is almost impossible for some men to keep from palpable lying. They seek for appointments, they move heaven and earth to get the appointment, and when they succeed in getting the appointment they solemnly declare that it was most providential, and came upon them with perfect surprise. How hard not to lie! We make certain arrangements for meeting certain persons that we may prosecute certain purposes upon which we have set our hearts, and then we say, How providential! That we should meet at this hour and at this place does really seem as if this thing were from heaven. It was all arranged; by prompting, by suggestion, by letters, by diverse subtle and inexplicable missions and methods everything was so arranged as to culminate in this meeting; and then we say, What a surprise, and what a providence! Oh, it is so hard not to lie!

Said another man, "When a convenient time is come—when I have a more convenient season—I will call upon thee"; resolving in his heart that no such season should ever occur. When I have a more convenient season I shall be glad to see thee; thou hast put my soul through the fires of hell; thou hast tortured me; I must get rid of this man; I cannot rudely say I will never see him again, I know what I will do, I will say, When I have a more convenient season I will send for thee; and thus may give the impression that I was delighted with his discourse. He reasoned of righteousness, temperance, and judgment to come, and he spoke with great force, and I wished him to receive the impression that my wife and myself were very much impressed and greatly pleased by his wonderful discourse—the Lord send him out of my way forever! Men can make it convenient to go to church, or they can make it extremely inconvenient to go and hear the word of the Lord. There are times, of course, when circumstances do seem to combine against the most honest desire, but there are other occasions when we can so arrange matters as to make our convenience the standard of the divine purpose. Let every man examine himself, let no man judge another. Saith one man, I must so arrange matters that I can do this or that on Sunday; on no account would I take an hour of my own time, but probably I shall not be missed if I do not go to the assembly of the people of God; I will cut an hour out of the consecrated time, and then say that it was most convenient, or to go would have been most inconvenient. Oh depart, and let thy children not know thee, because thou art a leper white as snow! It is a terrible thing to live under the criticism of God; it is a fearful thing to fall into the hands of the living God; we should pray for an honest heart and an honest speech, and pray to be delivered from the tyranny of subconscious lies: that is to say, lies which are so deep down in our hearts that we almost persuade ourselves that we are true men and not false.

What then are we to do? The answer is that if we are in Christ Jesus, without whose precious blood we can have no communion of the heart with the living God, we have simply to accept the discipline of waiting. We must learn to do without some things; we must be taught, though the lesson be most painful and severe, that

we may look at some things without touching them. We are trained
by a great vision of possibilities, yet the Lord does not permit us
to carry out the possibilities into effect. Think what it must be to
the soul to see the things that might have taken place, the persons
towards whom we might have stood in another and happier relation! Within such souls or within such environment are we trained
to self-abnegation, to self-crucifixion. Why may not this be done?
Because it is not the will of God. How easy it would be for such
and such complications to take place, issuing in such and such fe-
licitous results; why may not the combination be effected? Because
it is not the will of God. When I want to give up my pastorate and
seek for something more congruous with the spirit of my ambition
or even my more or less innocent hope, why should I not just force
the door, and then vanish as if I had not been near it? Ought not a
man to use the means in order to secure the end? Not until he has
obtained God's permission. Such and such a place is open: why
may I not look after it, and get half a dozen friends to write to the
place about me, saying how admirably adapted I am to that very
position? And then for me at a congratulatory meeting to assure the
people that I had no idea whatever of any such thing coming to
pass. This may be the same in statesmanship, in the craft of politics, in commerce, in all the departments of life. I may want to be
member of Parliament for such and such a borough, and get certain people to write to me and to write to the borough, and if I
should happen to be elected I could go down to the borough and
say that the very idea of being entrusted with the representation of
such a constituency simply never occurred to me. O the danger!
The temptation! The pits that lie hidden on life's rugged road! The
Lord's Spirit go with us, and point out the death-traps, and save us
from this awful ruin. I will trust in Christ, I will say to my Savior,
Still lead on; through desert or through gardenland, still lead on;
through deep waters, through rocky places, still lead on; through
flowery gardens, through balmy air, across velvet sward, still lead
on; and let me do nothing before the time.

Prayer

Almighty God, Thou dost work in the great field, and the tares may be Thine as well as the wheat; we cannot tell: who can follow all the way of the Lord, and say, Behold, this is the doing of heaven, and this the doing of the pit? Can there be evil in the city, and the Lord not have done it? Is Thine a limited sovereignty, or dost Thou include the devil and all his angels? Have we lost our hold upon God, and art Thou punishing us by diverse illusions and schisms and heterodoxies which we trace to men, not knowing that the Lord may be the author of delusions? It is all so strange, so weird, so vexing to the heart. Thou dost give us up sometimes to the working of our imagination, Thou dost abandon us to the idolatry of our own will; we do things we did not at first mean to do, and then we trace them to the enemy. Behold us, O Lord, and bring us back to simplicity and sincerity and young-heartedness, and deliver us from the delusion and the lie of the day. Behold us, we humbly pray Thee, as we tarry at the Cross; we want to be good and wise and right, and we do not want to overload the devil with responsibility. The Lord send us a searching into our own hearts with one of the Lord's own candles. Amen.

8

The Genesis of Delusions

Preached on Thursday Morning, February 22nd, 1900.

I also will choose their delusions—Isaiah 66:4.

They will think it is the devil, but I am behind it all; they will ascribe it to some peculiar condition of the brain, and they will endeavor to trace that condition to indigestion, to the wrong food, to a mistake in choices and fancies; they will never suspect that I am in it. We are not worshipers of a limited Sovereign; the universe is not split up into sections, God presiding over, it may be, the larger section, and the devil presiding over the remaining fraction. Yet it would seem as if this was the religion of some people; what wonder if they are disturbed and perturbed and dealt with vexatiously, the whole process ending in confusion twice confounded? They do not know the central reality of things; they have no faith; they have a kind of meager and struggling sentiment, but a deep, living, eternal faith they have not; and they cannot have until they get back to the center and metaphysic of things. It is no use preachers coddling up people who ought to be stripped and sent into the open air when the barometer is very low. But we cannot get to these great heights all at once. It will be our delight, in the hope that it may be our profit, to show that delusions are sometimes falsely estimated and falsely treated. Once we should have been shocked to have heard even in the most secret whisper that God had anything to do with men's delusions; are we any hardier now? Have we a stronger grip of things? I was once so severely dealt with by a man who saw in a prayer which was offered in this place the words, "Disgrace not the throne of Thy glory." He wrote to the journals about it, he almost, according to his own estimate of things, overwhelmed me; he was irate beyond all the heat known to the thermometer; he could not control himself; he gave away the accusing pamphlet at this front door. I do not wonder if he died a bankrupt if he threw his money away in that sort of fashion. What, said he, shall it be permitted that a man shall stand in a Christian pulpit, and say, "Disgrace not the throne of Thy glory"? I had no answer but one; I simply said, You must fight it out with Jeremiah, and not me; I was simply quoting the prophet. The man thought I was inventing something out of my own mind, and he charged me with blasphemy. What a mercy it is that there are not many such fools! Be very careful how you contradict certain men; they may have a rod up their sleeve or a dagger; let someone else contradict them first, and you see how it goes on. And so when we hear that God will choose their delusions, how shocked we are, and how pained, and how distressed! Yet here is the text in Isaiah 66:4, "I will choose their delusions"; they shall be idiots of My own making, stumblers and gropers for whose existence I am responsible.

The apostle uses the word which we have correctly translated delusion: "For this cause God shall send them strong delusion, that they should believe a lie" (2 Thess. 2:11). The apostle Paul was not so dainty and whimsically sensitive as we are; his God ruled the heavens and the earth, little time and great eternity. And he said that the object of this delusion was that "They all might be damned who believed not the truth, but had pleasure in unrighteousness." We should carefully consider the exact terms used by the indignant and ever-majestic apostle. God shall send them strong delusion, that they should believe not *a* lie, as it is written in this English, but that they should believe *the* lie–the lie of the day, the popular lie. Every day has its own lie; it may be war, or gambling, or atheistic prosperity, or materialism; and people rush to the lie of the hour as if it were a revelation and should be accepted as such without further inquiry. Notice how true it is that every day has its heresy, its lie, its devil. Why do we deprive ourselves of spiritual blessing and profit by imagining that all the things that are written in the Bible were limited to the time in which the Bible was written? Why do we not realize that the Bible is published every morning in anticipation of every newspaper, and that it travels not on wheels of iron to distant and out-of-the-way places, but travels with the light, ay, and is there before the light has well begun its quick journey? Persons sometimes imagine that they have no time to read the Bible early in the day, because they are so anxious to get through the newspaper before they get to business; not knowing that the Bible is the original newspaper and has all the news of the day in it.

"I also will choose their delusions"—their devices, their imaginings, their new brain conditions and brain expressions; I will take the whole case into My own hands, and even that will not drive the whole of them to see that there is a God. I will trouble their dreams. Dreamland is part of the acreage of the universe, and all the universe is God's; I will send cruel and punitive nightmare upon these people; they have abandoned Mine altar, they have taken to their own ways, and I will trouble all their dreams and all their fancies, and they will think that they have created the whole intellectual creation thus established among them out of their own wit; they will publish poems in their own names; they will write and dictate and sell nightmares, and call them original productions. Has God any amusement in the heavens? Can God smile? He gave man a facial muscle that has nothing to do but to smile, and was not man made in the image and likeness of God? We cannot understand these things nor properly define and limit them; and yet we sometimes in our most exalted moods wonder about certain things and suggest poor but tentative answers. A dream may be a delusion. You may rely upon dreams as you have done for many centuries; there are interpreters of dreams; we say that a dream after midnight means one thing, and that a dream ought to be laid upside down, and that we are perfectly sure that there is something in the dream because it was so startlingly vivid—so startlingly vivid that when we were consciously awake we looked around to see if all the *dramatis persona* were not standing round the bed. We trace these dreams to our late meals or to our undigested food, or to some memorial of the trouble which passed over our outer life during the common day. Does it never, never occur to us that God is the author of dreams, that God has worked wondrous things through the dream miracle, that God has associated Himself in history with the springs which He caused to fly in the darkness and unrest of the night? God may be the author of heterodoxy; God may have His own reasons for punishing some men by giving them over to a strong delusion, so that they oftentimes, being very young, inexperienced, and living at other persons' expense, may contradict all the old divines and flick their fingers in the face of the whole Church. It may be in some deep interior sense that God is in it; the persons who are afflicted with this heresy will not always see it to be the case. Sometimes men take a little pleasure in being thought to be heretical, because it is so fresh, so intellectually fresh, so damp with originality, so dewy with impossibleness. There are some persons who know just where orthodoxy begins and heterodoxy begins; they are exceedingly penetrating persons who have taken out a blank license and signed it themselves, and are operating upon it as if it were a charter granted by the chancery of heaven. Why do we not sometimes pensively and broken-heartedly wonder if some of our fancies and conceptions and theories of things may not be delusions sent upon us by the punitive ministry of the living Father, that through the wilderness of delusion we may be scourged by hunger and thirst in the direction of the home city where the Father waits surrounded by a plenteousness of bread? Many persons are great at expelling other people from the Church. There are people who can expel a soul from the visible Church of Christ, and go home and make a good supper. Oh the broken-heartedness of it and the unutterable sorrow! After that expulsion we should be drowned for many an hour in the bitter waters of penitence.

Apply this to your own family; do not shrink from applying it
to the eccentricities and arrancies of your own sons and daughters.
Who knows what they may have done to have brought this state of
mind upon themselves? And who can tell but that God is training
them by these odd out-of-the-way courses that there is no place like
home—the faith-home, the house of God, Bethel. God may sometimes allow a man to feed on the east wind in order to teach him
that in the east wind there is no nutrition for his soul.

When does God choose for us our delusions, intellectual devices, and mean and false-tending imaginings and nightmares?
Often when we have sinned away our privileges. We have attended
church so long as to have become quite familiar with it, with a familiarity of that kind which breeds, if not contempt, at least indifference. A man may have sat through a ministry thirty years long,
and have remained a hard heart at the last. A man may boast that
he sat under the brilliant ministry of teacher, and the instructive
teaching of another expositor, and under the comforting ministry
of one tender-hearted as Barnabas; and yet when we come to ask
him concerning the result of it all we may find him under the spell
of a delusion which keeps him out of the Church and makes him
an alien and a stranger who ought to have been like a child at
home. It is a dangerous thing to have too many spiritual privileges;
such an abundance of opportunity of understanding somewhat of
the kingdom of God may tell against us in the judgment. Every sermon ought to be to us as a spiritual miracle, every exposition of
the divine word should be as a new sign and token in the morning
heavens; every sweet hymn we sing should be another baptism of
reviving dew. This must be so because the Bible itself is so. No man
has read the Bible through. Of course there are some dear sweet
souls who imagine that they have read the Bible through once a
year for many years; in their own sense of the word that may be
perfectly true, but it is a poor sense, an unworthy sense. There are
some of us still struggling in the Pentateuch and still in the four
Gospels, and others who are still in the Epistle to the Romans, with

very little hope of ever getting into the wonderful land of the Apocalypse. It is the heart that reads; it is love that tarries at the feet.

When we have trusted our own imaginations God may have turned imagination itself, our finest faculty, into a delusion. When the imagination carries us too far God simply breathes upon us, and it becomes a delusion; He takes the poetry out of it, He robs day of the morning light, and that which might under some circumstances have been to us as wings, great strong pinions that flap themselves in the upper airs, yea, even at the gate of heaven, may be turned into a poor cripple, a mean dreamer, a man who is the victim of his own misguided impression. God often chooses our oracles for us or our delusions for us when we seek for guidance at forbidden oracles. There are many such oracles at human disposal. One man has his dice-box, and says, If I turn up such and such numbers I will know what to do. Another man says, If I can invent a system of casting lots I shall be able almost to outwit God Himself, and to know the divine mind before the mind has been consulted. I think I shall go to spirit-rapping and to table-turning, and to all the various sorceries and witcheries with which poor human history is crowded, and I will draw a lot or consult an oracle for myself; and God in His anger may say, Let it be so; and thus He may permit, He never enjoins, such courses, until the heart has proved its own moral idiocy and is led to cry out for the true Oracle, the living and the infinite wisdom.

God always sends us delusions when we undertake the management of our own lives. A man thinks that he will undertake everything on his own account and do it in his own strength, not knowing that he has no account and that he has no strength but such as may be given to him by a condescending and loving God. We are not self-complete; we belong to other lives, we are part of the great household. God will not send the sanction or the comfort of His benedictions upon persons who isolate themselves and who undertake to do all that requires to be done without the communion of saints and the masonry of regenerated hearts. We belong to one another. Your child may have the wisdom today, the wife may have it on another occasion, you yourself may be the chosen instrument through whom God has sent His message for the day. Let there be no self-idolatry, no self-containment, and no self-limitation. We have come to the Church of the firstborn, to an innumerable company of angels, to the millionfold of the Cross and army of the spirits, and we must in all things ask God, just as little self-distrusting children would ask father or mother, what is to be done next. Never make any plans when you come into the distribution and direction of your higher life. "Go to now, ye that say, Today or tomorrow we will go into such a city, and continue there a year, and buy and sell, and get gain: whereas ye know not what shall be on the morrow." Drop your plan-making: for what is your life? It is a vapor that cometh for a little time and then vanisheth away.

Then what are we to do? We are to go back to God; we are to live and move and have our being in God; we are to have a sanctuary in the rock; we are to possess the key of a chamber in high places into which we can retire prayerfully, lovingly, and penitentially, there to learn what God would have us do on this particular day and at that particular hour. Then we shall have no delusion; God will say, They are returning; they have found no bread in the wilderness; their misery is crying out for the living God; there are tears in their poor eyes; I will meet them, and hold out my heart to them, and wave them back to the only hospitality that can furnish and sustain the redeemed soul. We must have no double purpose in life. That is the mischief, and that indeed is the ruin of many a practice; we do not tell the truth; in other words, we do not love and live the truth. When Jesus Christ said in His sermon, Let your Yea be yea and your Nay nay, He preached a doctrine that would revolutionize society, and destroy all the haunts of hypocrisy and self-seeking.

Yet we may gabble over the words as if they meant nothing; on the contrary, they mean everything, even those simple words go into the heart of reality and pronounce judgments in the court of righteousness. I must have no double purpose in coming into the pulpit or in opening the pulpit Bible, or God will even allow me to stray, and possibly He may order me astray that He may humiliate me and show that the nimbus which is round about my poor failing head is no crown, but a twisted twine. We must have no double purpose in speech; we must never say one thing and mean another; we must be sincere, flawless like porcelain even when the sun shines through it; we must be as the seamless chrysolite; we must impersonate the righteousness of God. Then we shall have no delusions, but a simple, beneficent, grand policy, which will end in great harvest fields here and eternal summer yonder.

And we shall escape delusions if we use our own experience of deliverances for the benefit of other people. He that converteth a sinner from the error of his way shall cover a multitude of sins, yea, shall save a soul from death. You will get your religion back again in proportion as you preach it. If you would have a living church at home you must go into all the world and preach the Gospel to every creature; afterwards you will return to your home-church, to fathers, mothers, sisters, brothers, old pastors, and friends, and say, We have seen great things on the mission field, we have because we gave, we lived the Gospel, loved it, preached it, and hastened from shore to shore to tell it to every listening soul, and therefore we have had more ourselves. Ah me, that a man should sit in this pew or in that, and know a good deal about the Gospel, and never mention it to another human creature! What would be said of a man if he, having a panacea for some bodily ill, heard of another person suffering from that ill, and never mentioned the panacea to the suffering creature? Cry shame upon him! He is a murderer.

Prayer

O Thou that hearest prayer, to Thee shall all flesh come. Thou hast spoken great words respecting all flesh, all men, all nations, all tribes. We do not understand the wholeness of Thy love; it shall be revealed to us little by little; meanwhile we talk of our nation and our people: not knowing that the earth is the Lord's and the fullness thereof, and Thine the fullness of the sea. But Thou dost train us day by day and little by little, a lesson at a time, and a precept as we are able to bear it. We are young and small and often ignorant, and our wonder is, as the light increases within the temple of our mind, that Thou dost not hold us in derision. We are of yesterday and know nothing; we cannot see before us; to the blind there is no light, there is no summer glory. Yet Thou dost in Christ Jesus Thy Son, in whose name we pray and in whose name alone we find acceptance, teach us little by little that other people are Thine, that Thou dost carry the whole world, yea, and the whole universe, in Thy warm bosom, where it finds its summer and its rest and its growing power. If we confess our sins, Thou art faithful and just to forgive us our sins. That is not enough for us, we cry for more; we would that all evil might be destroyed, that we might be cleansed from all unrighteousness; not only pardoned, but sanctified, entering into the larger temple and catching all the larger meanings of Thy love. Oh! that we might be delivered from the bondage of little things, from mean endeavors and paltry occupations, and be brought into the liberty of Christ Jesus our Lord, where we might see all things in their relation and in their unity. Teach us that we shall find everything in Thy holy Book; may we search the Scriptures that we may find the Christ, from the first page to the last; and while we are searching may Jesus Himself draw near, and begin at the beginning and go through the whole process, until our hearts glow like a conscious summer. Amen.

9

Working Towards Ideals

Preached on Sunday Morning, February 25th, 1900.

For all nations—Mark 11:17.

"All nations," "of all nations." It was a great reading of the Scriptures; this was a thunder sermon. The butchers had not ears to hear
it; they were a grim, gruesome mob, gruesome as their trade. Yet "of
all nations" does not express the true accent, purpose, and the music
of that wondrous discourse. "For all nations" would be better than
"of all nations." The temple was built for all people that on earth do
dwell. Perhaps the people who built it did not understand this in all
the fullness of its meaning. A building is to many persons only four
walls and a roof; they do not see the poetry or the ideality of the
structure; consequently we have an abundance of houses, and only a
home here and there. Homes are not made of bricks. We read in
Mark 11:17: "My house shall be called of all nations"; we should
read, "My house shall be called for all nations"—the home of homes,
the house built for everybody, my Father's house. Whoever found
Christ's name associated with a little paltry patriotic idea? Jesus
Christ was no patriot, Jesus Christ was a philanthropist; the Son of
God was no politician, He was a statesman, He grasped the whole
situation, and allotted to everyone east or west, north or south, what
was proper to the occasion and the environment. Some people never
see the ideal of things; they are afraid of what they call mysticism,
idealism; they are poor self-starved literalists, and the Bible slips out
of their hands because it was made by a mechanical process. The

smallest little hut on the barest hillside in which a hymn of the heart is sung is a great ideal. Persons who can only live under big roofs of course smile at it and point towards it with a walking staff, and pucker up their unintelligent faces as they leave the thing behind them. Jesus Christ goes after these people and scourges them, lacerates them, says, It is written, My house is a house for all nations, and the little house you have just passed with a sneer is a miniature sanctuary or temple or heaven. Some people never saw the sun in a dewdrop. Pity them! They are not all poets, else how could some of them follow the occupations which yield them no livelihood?

Jesus Christ looked over all the walls of the temple and the outside parts of the temple, the low walls that marked definitions of space and in a certain sense of consecration and proprietorship. These traveling cattle-dealers and poulterers had gathered within certain spaces that were supposed to be not consecrated; there they sold pigeons and lambs, animals for sacrifice; all sorts and conditions of social status were represented there, the rich Jew and the poor Jew, and some outsiders that could hardly be classified at all. The men who were poulterers and cattle-dealers fixed themselves within certain boundaries almost in the Jewish temple itself; they went as near to the temple proper as they possibly could. When Jesus Christ came and saw the scene His great young heart was sore as with a new wound. How had these men been talking? We may paraphrase their tavern speech in this way: Surely we can have our counters spread out here; there are people here who have diverse standards and denominations of money; they will want the big money changed into little money, and we can sell these pigeons and fowls and lambs, and be quite a convenient medium of commerce between one set of persons and another; and we can do all that within these almost Gentile spaces, those outer courts, these annexes and appendages, and there can be no harm in our making a little marketplace here. But when the Son of God came He recognized the temple in its unity, the temple in its ideality, in its high poetic spiritual meaning, and, making a lash, He scourged these fellows from the purlieus of the holy place; for, said He, My Father's house is for all nations; every bit of it is sanctified, every stone has been purified in the fire of the divine acceptance; be off! Go! And the thong made itself heard in the air. What a blessed and comforting thought that Jesus Christ saw the whole house, the whole idea, and that He foresaw a day when that idea would spread among all nations, and king and peasant of this land and of that shall be equally welcome and equally recognized as members of the Father's household. When did you ever find the Lord Christ associated with a little idea? You have your little dreams and you have also your little prejudices which you call your patriotisms, and you have your little bags of self-conceit which you call your consciences; you have and we all have our half notions and imperfect purviews, and we think that we could manage everything perfectly with a strong handling, with a penetrating perspicacity. We make an idol of a nation and think our idolatry is patriotism. Within a given line that may be well enough, but it must be recognized as belonging only to a definite boundary. The earth is the Lord's and the fullness thereof, and not a drop of the ocean but would reflect the glory of His image. We need to keep long company with the dear Christ to know the meaning of things.

Now in this instance Jesus Christ accuses the intruders, and those who permitted the intrusion, of narrow-minded ideas, and He accuses them of being imperfect and misleading interpreters of the divine revelation and purpose. To have Jesus Christ read the Bible with us; that would be educational, spiritual instruction, divine inspiration. He would take us into the roots of things. He would get behind the north wind of words and fill us with the spirit of wisdom and of grace. It is a comforting thing if some dear old preacher will begin the Bible with us, meekly saying as becomes the dignity of a great soul, I will tell you as far as I am able to do so what God has taught me about His own book. What a delight it would have been to me as a young, struggling, groping preacher if some sweet-souled

Samuel or even Elijah had said to me, Before you go out to deliver
the message, let us read it together; I being the older man can tell
you what I know about this message, but we must not rely upon
any man's word; every morning we must meet before the dew is
off the grass, and the first thing we do is to pray; I will pray sometimes, and then you will pray at other times, and we will read the
holy message together; and when the Spirit has interpreted the message to our poor waiting hearts we will go out, the old man and the
young man, and tell others what we have seen and heard and
known, felt and handled of the Word of life, and great shall be the
harvest-time. Will not our venerable ministers and scholars and
practiced suppliants take others by the hand and say, Let us read
the message together; God wrote it; we have not to invent a gospel,
but to preach one, and we have not to hear what other men think
about the gospel, we are to study the gospel itself, and to receive
auxiliary comment and hint within its own proper lines, and be
grateful for it as the best which such expositors could give us. Let us
live inside the sanctuary; do not let us have two things to do in
life; let us be men of one purpose, one consecration, one sacrifice
of blood. Jesus Christ alone can interpret the Cross; Jesus Christ
interprets the Scriptures by interpreting the context. The context is
the greater text. The context is the text without which the limited
text can never be understood. Every leaf traces the milk of its sustenance to the root; not only does the great branch do this, but the
tiniest little twig that trembles in the breeze would seem sometimes
almost to be peeing over the big branches and to be looking down
to the root, and then to be saying, I am still here, think of me, I
belong to you; without your hidden, vital root, I could not tremble
in the breeze, I could only die and be blown away by the wind. Ay,
amen, so be it, thou little trembling leaf, thou toy and pet of the
zephyr, thou art part and parcel of the biggest oak that grows in
Bashan. Jesus Christ in interpreting the Scriptures would take away
from us many of our favorite little texts. There are some persons
so fearfully and wonderfully made that they have constructed de-

nominations upon half a sentence. Such people are not above reason or below reason, they are simply outside reason, and I have no time to tarry with them in their progress to oblivion. To hear the true interpreter read the Scriptures! When Jesus Christ wanted to explain an event that occurred say the day before yesterday, what do you think He did? He began at Moses. What preaching was this! That preaching would not be tolerated now. The great biblical preachers are on the shelves of our libraries. Many persons in a great haste to get nowhere tell us that the minister must have preached at least three-quarters of an hour. What a mercy they were not on the way to Emmaus, for then the Preacher spoke the whole eight miles, and the people were not tired when He was done; their hearts were aflame with love, and they said in their souls, Who is this? He carries the whole heavens in the brightness of His eyes and in the balminess of His breath.

And Jesus Christ, in the next place, included the whole human race in the temple idea. God never commanded any temples to be built for twos and threes, and to end their purpose in these trivial numbers. When He saved the twos and threes it was that He might save the world through them. Sometimes the number was very small, but it was a vital number; there was enough saved, sometimes called the remnant, out of which to get the biggest forests that ever waved on the hillsides of the world. He said He would save a city, He would save a remnant, He would save one little child, He would save eight persons, He would save an Isaac; He would do a wonder of this kind, but always having before His eyes the world, the whole world, all nations, every creature. That is the divine love, and it is useless our endeavoring to whittle it away by verbal criticism and by some monstrous display of our ignorance or our selfishness. Whenever God did a little thing it was the beginning of a great thing; and we have sometimes attempted to stop the process and to begin the interpretation before the text has been announced. You find it in the first chapter of Genesis. Oh, when shall this old heart of mine get through that first chapter? Never. And so few people read it. The great Creator said that this or that had the seed in itself. What a revelation! What a new book! Here is the ear of corn. No. But I have it in the hollow of my hand. You have not, in the little narrow verbal sense which you are tempted to attach to that fact. He who has an ear of corn in the hollow of his hand has the harvest of the world; he who has an acorn has Bashan; he who has the cedar's seed has Lebanon; he who has a place in which to pray has a place that will expand until it takes in all nations. What then becomes of any little notion along the religious and especially along the Christian line? All Christians should be great men, all Christians should have great minds because they have great subjects, and the subject and the mind are related to one another in a sense congenital, and therefore when fair play is done to the subject the mind will grow, and when the subject is fairly treated the subject will grow, and by-and-bye there will be a new map without frontiers, a globe beautiful as the flawless crystal, all love, pureness, beauty, heaven. To be associated with the development of such ideas we ought to be really men of energetic minds and of high quality of soul, because we are not set here to prop up some little idol of an idea, but to declare the heavens, and to declare the God of the heavens, and to show that the crimson of one blood makes the whole sky rich with divinest color. No man can injure the Christian idea in all its loftiness and comprehensiveness so much as the man who professes it and does not in any degree understand it. There is a process among some communions called joining the church; many persons are under the idea that when they have joined the church they have concluded their Christian education: whereas when our notion is large enough and clear enough we shall see that when we have joined the church we have only in a certain sense begun our education. Who are the people who grumble about the church idea and the church theory and the church conception? The same people who grumble about their food. Who are the people who grumble about their food? The men who do not work, lazy, indolent, self-destroying men. If they were out a couple of hours on the hills before their breakfast was partaken of that breakfast would soon become an almost sacrament; it would be such an answer to hunger, such a reply to necessity, it would unite them with the all-giving heaven. Have no connection whatever with these grumbling people that are not satisfied with the Anglican idea or the Presbyterian idea or the Congregational idea, and who would like to have a denomination made to order, and made while you wait. They degrade the Church, they do not see in the simple bread which a mother may have broken the broken body of the Lord, nor do they see in the ruddy juice a drop of the infinite Heart. If we could get rid of these people the Church in its largest interpretation might make some progress.

If we take this principle and carry it round the whole area of human life, it will be a light to lighten the narrowest mind. We are to regard the child in the light of his manhood. We are not to trifle with children, saying they are but a few years old, and it really does not matter what we say in their presence or what we do; they are children and they cannot understand the case, and if the child has a little ownership in this or in that it can make no particular matter that we should take it and use it for some other purpose, because the child really does not know what we are doing. And then the dear Christ takes cords and binds them together, and makes a thong of them, and lays it righteously upon our back, and says, Is it not written that of such is the kingdom of God? See the man in the child; see all the rights of property in any little bit of string which the child calls his own; see the citizenship of heaven in the child nestling trustfully in your breast and heart. Thus take the larger view; thus interpret all things ideally and transcendentally. Look upon the heathen in the light not of their barbarism, but in the light of their possible civilization, what they may be someday. People to whom you sell what rubbish you can get rid of, and whose goods you are glad to take in return, gold or diamonds, as the case may be, will one day by Christian influence be enlightened and educated, and turning back the pages of their history, so to say—I speak in a figure, but you follow my meaning—they may discover that we have been burglars who lived in palaces; what if their anger should then rise against us because we sold them guns that would not shoot and took back from them such diamonds or other property as we could in any way secure for ourselves? Do not sneer at the black man, he may have a white soul. Do not say, This man is a foreigner, and therefore we may treat him offhandedly and discourteously. One day the word foreigner will be blotted out of all language, and man to man shall brother be. What a day of judgment may then arise, except the magnanimity of the man we despised shall forbear to recall the contempt and the injury which he suffered at our hands. Do not look upon the ward in chancery as a mere creature protected by certain duly appointed officials whose main object it is to pluck the bird as thoroughly as it can be until hardly a feather is left. That ward in chancery belongs to society; the humblest ward in chancery should be the child of the age, the child of the country, the child of the divine protective providence.

I beseech you, therefore, not to take little, narrow, and contemptible views of things, but always to follow Christ in His great broad luminous interpretations. Thus we may incarnate and expound by our daily life the great principles and the holy expectations which are the very marrow and sustenance of our souls. Never so live that in ten years the person we have attempted at least nominally to help shall find out that all the time we have been doing him secret injustice. Let me say to myself in the name of Christ and under the very shadow of His Cross, This child thinks I am an honest man; this child's life is in a secondary sense entrusted to my custody and culture; now how much more can I do than the mere letter of the law expects me to do? Can I carry up law into love? The father of the child was my friend; instead of taking some green wreath of flowers to lay on his grave, I will do an extra service to his little child, I will try so to live that when the child has come to years of discretion he will find it no violence of language to call me his father. That would be Christian; that would be the spirit of the Cross;

that would be the sacrament of love. Do not let us bind ourselves by the mere letter of the law, but say, What did God mean when He laid down this law? He meant it to be an expression of love; bare law as a mere group or clump of letters will not do for me since I have known Christ; I will so treat this child that when all the children, mine and this other man's child, shall have grown up together, they will hardly know which is which, and they will all know that there is room enough in this great big heart for each of them to pillow his weariness on my sympathy.

So Jesus Christ interpreted the temple; He would have everybody under its shining roof and itself under the roof of His own love. I preach no local Christ. I preach no patriot Christ. He—my Lord, my Savior—He called the Gentiles, and I am one, to enlarge the temple, and found a seat for me. He said "the world," and therefore I have some chance. He teaches "all nations," and if I cannot sit at the high table and hear all the greater lessons I can say, The dogs eat of the crumbs that fall from the Master's table.

Prayer

Almighty God, we confess that we have mocked Thy prophet, and that we have done despite to Thy Son and to Thy Holy Spirit. We have not understood the day of our visitation; we were busy here and there, and let the King pass by; we knew not the things that belonged to our salvation; we mocked the prophets; we said, Precept upon precept, and here a little and there a little, and a line here and a line there; we imitated their voices and mocked their accent and threw back their message in their faces. We have done the things that we ought not to have done, we have left undone the things that we ought to have done; oh that we had hearkened unto Thy messenger, that we had accepted Thy terms of reconciliation and peace! Then had we been strong men in Thy sanctuary, and as pillars in Thy temple. Behold our weakness, our want of gratitude, our indolence, and pity us from Thy great heart, Thou that didst redeem the world. We have been living among little things, we have not accepted the higher companionship of the angels and the spirits of just men made perfect; ours has been a life on the surface, we have not sought for the former and the latter rain, the upper and the nether springs, the morning and the glorious noonday; we ought to have been so great, so noble, the very princes and sons of God. May we not begin the better life today? May we not go in quest of holy things and reverently appear at the doors of the inner and upper sanctuary? We are moved to this prayer by the Cross, by the spirit of the Christ, by the blood of the Victim-Priest; Thou wilt hear it in heaven Thy dwelling-place, and answer it with a great forgiveness. Amen.

10

The Verifying Faculty

Preached on Thursday Morning, March 1st, 1900.

This is the rest wherewith ye may cause the weary to rest; and this is the refreshing—Isaiah 28:12.

The Bible is always talking in our mother tongue. The oldest and greatest of the prophets spoke in language which almost children can understand and appreciate. Take such words as "weary": the child knows what it means when it sees its father returning from the fields and stretching himself in token of fatigue. And "rest," the little word needs no translation; and "refreshing," the very word which an apostle uses in later times when he speaks of "times of refreshing," new showers, larger rains, food in the wilderness, water among the rock. "This is the rest, this is the refreshing": it is undoubted, it brings its own evidence along with it, it needs no witnesses and no certificates and no chemical tests. It makes its gospel known, and the world says, Well, master, thou hast said the truth; this is right, the heart feels it, the inmost soul is grateful for such proclamations.

A wonderful thing is this verifying faculty that is in every man, the faculty by which we know whether a thing is true or not; a marvelous remainder of the Deity. He had almost been shattered, He had nearly been driven away wholly and absolutely from the human soul; and yet there lingers one faculty, instinct, power of testing, which says without words to the listening and wondering soul. This is right, that is wrong; this is gospel, that is superstition. A voice no

other man can hear, only the soul can say in sacred monologue,
That is it, this is the Christ, this is real preaching, this is the message
that comes from God; there is no earth taint in this high wind that
blows down from the fragrant paradises and the upper liberties of
the universe. That verifying faculty is in the body as well as in the
soul; perhaps we can first familiarize ourselves with the verifying
faculty in the body. My anxiety is to deliver these great words, and
all the tribe to which they belong, from merely superstitious or
even theological uses, and to show those who study the Bible with
me that we have in our body and in our common life and in our
common sense the beginnings, the germs, the protoplasm of the
kingdom of God. Why will men flee away to some intangible
cloud, and call that theology? Theology is in every red drop of
blood that is in our arteries; the true theology is part of the very
soul we breathe, it is the sign and proof that we had a great origin.
Has the body a verifying faculty? The body has five faculties that
are verifying, critical, judicial. The nostril—where does that word
nostril occur? Where I have told you that everything occurs, in the
book of Genesis, and ye will not, yet stiff-necked and uncircumcised in heart, read it. What does the book of Genesis say about
the nostril? It says that God breathed into Adam's nostril the breath
of life; and it is still there, the breath that knows which is good
food, which is bad food. Yet men deny or doubt the existence of
God, not knowing who formed the nostril and breathed into it the
breath of life. Yet I see the merchantman applying his nostril to this
or that food which he would dispense to the public. What is he
doing? He is studying one of the elementary chapters in theology.
No man gave himself his own nostril; the nostril is, so to say, outside the man, and is revealing to him the difference between health
and disease, foul air, fresh air, the air that has death in it, and the
other air that is warm with summer and alive with the wind of
health. So that the term verifying faculty ought not to be so strange
to us. And the eye is also a verifying power; if we may personate it,
the eye says, This is beauty, this is loveliness, this is proportion, this

is statuesque music, this a poem in stone, a song in color. Close your eyes, and the whole thing is gone; recall the verifying faculty, and behold what a universe we live in—even that small part of the universe which comes within the range of the naked eye! So with the other senses. The fingers, representing touch, go before us and make inquiry and prepare the way; they are as messengers which prepare the way of the soul.

Therefore, grouping all these instances together, we ought not to be so very much surprised by the use of the word verifying faculty, or claiming and endorsing faculty, so that a man is enabled to say again and again, This one thing I know; what I do not know is your lucubration and your polysyllabled cant. So must we speak to the dear little souls who tell us even while we have blinded ourselves at the eyes of light that we might see with the eyes of the soul that this is all superstition. That is an easy way of getting rid of things that trouble us. Nor would I be severe with the youth who calls his father's religion superstition; there is a time in life when we really are sincerely fond of talking about things we do not understand; there is also a time of life, a kind of bank holiday of the soul, when nothing but polysyllables will give us any sense of manhood. Be patient; this whole matter will yet come right; who is there among us who has not passed through that measles period? If I heard a man more than forty-five years of age telling me that he once had the measles, I would cut the conversation short. So with the days when we regarded the great idea of religion as superstition, something that had in it nothing that was really valuable or that could be subjected to crucial test; we have outlived that period, and we must be patient with those who are still in it; the stairway to heaven, though golden, is spiral and long, and everyone is not on the same rung. Let us be forbearing and magnanimous.

What is true of the body with its five senses should be true of the soul. Why? Why should we hesitate to give things their larger interpretation? We have five senses or verifying faculties for the guidance of the body, and we are left absolutely without any verifying

faculty for the guidance of the soul. That is impossible. We believe
that the soul knows when it hears the truth. We have a feeling
which cannot be explained in words, it may be psychological or
metaphysical, but it is in the soul, a faculty or voice which says, Beware; there is danger ahead; suspect this proposition; do nothing
without further thought, and see that thou do nothing on a proposition which troubles the conscience and makes the soul narrower
and less liberal in its conceptions and active issues of service and
beneficence. This is the doctrine which the apostle Paul laid down
when he said "the natural man receiveth not the things that are of
the Spirit of God: for they are foolishness unto him: neither can
he know them: for they are spiritually discerned," tested, or verified. Why do not men carry these points of science into the higher
life? The nostril says, having detected the quality of certain food,
No! touch not, taste not, handle not. On whose authority? Mine.
Who art thou? The nostril. Whence camest thou? Into me God
breathed the breath of life; and I tell thee, O wayfaring man, ad-
venturous, reckless soul, beware! Why should it not have its coun-
terpart in the nostril of the soul, in the eye, the touch, the taste,
the hearing of the soul? To have a body sentient and a dead soul inside it is to have a very beautiful and costly casket with a handful of
rubbish inside. We could not believe it, our sense of proportion
would reject it; we say, This is not harmony, this is not music, this
is not the fitness of things. We would rise up in indignation and
disappointment, and we should be quite right in so doing. Never,
therefore, consult the natural man as to spiritual verities and spiritual realities; the natural man has nothing to do with such quantities and forces. My teaching is that we are not to go to the natural
man to give us any opinion whatever about true religion. The man
himself knows nothing about it; he has not passed through the
great, deep, sorrowful, joyous experience. He may have his opinions. Who wants them? He may have his views and his fancies, but
he himself would not be responsible for them if a flood came. If
you asked him to attach responsibility to his views, he would in-

stantly repel the suggestion and leave you to go to hell alone. Only go to the spiritual man for spiritual counsel, sympathy, and direction. Go to wisdom for counsel and to experience for sympathy.

We have in the text, therefore, an exercise of what may be called the verifying faculty. We may take it by a very slight accommodation in that sense and way. "This is the rest, this is the refreshing." We know when an answer suffices a question. Explain that psychological fact to me. Take it in so small and insignificant a matter as a conundrum. You have heard the riddle? Yes. You have heard twenty guesses made concerning the riddle? Yes. Do any of them satisfy you? No. Here is the right answer, and the moment you hear the right reply you say, So it is, that is good; undoubtedly the answer is sufficing. Note what the case really is; you have heard twenty answers, and you have rejected them all; some of them are rather clever, acute, *ad rem;* yet there lingers in the mind a doubt about the whole twenty; but now that the real answer is given there is a unanimous verdict in favor of its sufficiency. You have had experience in so trivial a matter; yet it is not a trivial matter if considered in all its implications and practical uses; it means that there is in man a power or faculty or sense which says, That is right. Hear Christ's answer to the outside scribe. A man said to the great Teacher, Master, which is the first and great commandment? Jesus answered, Thou shalt love the Lord thy God with all thy heart and mind and soul and strength. The scribe said, Well, Master, Thou hast said the truth. The man knew it in his heart; he knew that was the right answer to the great riddle. And the Bible alone gives you the all-sufficing answers to the all-including enigmas. Why fool away our time by asking adventurers and empirics to give us answers, when the Bible overflows with them, and our verifying faculty takes up the answers one by one and says, This is right, this is the voice of God, this is the outlined kingdom of heaven?

Take for example the question of consolation. You are told that you live in a system of law, that you are encaged or enmeshed in a great scheme of fatalism, and that things come and go, and we must accept them either in their going or their coming. Are you satisfied? You say to such visitors from far-away countries, Miserable comforters are ye all! Away with you! For my soul loathes this evil meat which you set before it in its hunger. Who told you that these conceptions were wrong? You told yourself; the verifying faculty within you said, All that may in a certain measurable and momentary sense be more or less true, but it does not touch my hunger, my thirst, the sore of my heart, the agony that looks death into me. I believe in inspired experience; there comes a time when life so pulses and suns itself before a man's consciousness and a man's imagination that he himself has within his very soul the pleading and illuminating and solacing Spirit of God. Let some one come to you from the fountains divine, from the wells of salvation, and that man's coming is itself a blessing, his very way of listening is itself an answer which your grieved heart understands. When he says, "I will never leave you or forsake you," you look up in hope of seeing a radiant presence more beautiful than the presence of an angel, and when he says, "I have been with thee in six troubles, and in seven I will not forsake thee," you say, Lord, this is what I have waited for; it was the seventh wave I feared; the six billows have gone over me, but when I saw the seventh swelling into terrible strength and grandeur I was afraid between its coming down upon me and this voice I have heard, the comfort of God; and now I have no fear of even the seventh wave, it will thunder on the shore and dash itself into helpless bubbles, but I, trusting in God, shall remain unharmed, untouched. When the man who has the divine counsel says to you that all our afflictions work for good if we accept them in the right spirit, when he says, "They are not afflictions to be despised, to the poor suffering body they are very hard, why I have passed through just such afflictions as you are now passing through, and I never felt the dear Spirit of Love that died for the spirit of man so near me and so tender as when I was in that great strait," you say, Abide with me, stranger, preacher, pastor, abide with me, come in and break bread with me, and do not go away until I know that thou art a teacher sent from God. This is the exercise of what we have termed the verifying faculty in the body taking its proper place and function in the culture of the soul.

Now take it, secondly, in the matter of repentance. The prophet was offering this people in the context a very great offer. They were all drunk; they were all babbling mockers; when the prophet went among them, they derided him; they had a gift of mimicry, took up his cry, and said in words which no English can represent, Precept upon precept, precept upon precept; line upon line, line upon line; here a little, and there a little. It was mockery, it was chattering back the man's counsel into vulgar response. The words cannot be Englished, they cannot be uttered, and if they were uttered they could not be reported and printed. Yet these are the words which we quote, not intelligently, not knowing anything about the meaning of them—"Precept upon precept, and line upon line." We are quoting the words of drunken fools, thinking that we are quoting the words of the prophet, if not of the Lord; whereas these drunken, lustful, shameless men were mocking the sermon, mocking the preacher, mocking his looks, mocking what they would call his mannerisms—Ha! What again? Are we imbeciles, are we little children, that thou art so mumbling, Precept upon precept, precept upon precept; and line upon line and line upon line; here a little and there a little, here a little and there a little—over and over again—begone! And the drunkards laugh as only drunkenness incarnate can laugh.

Yet the Lord made a great offer to them, He offered to teach them knowledge and to understand doctrine; He said to them, I will give you another opportunity: this is the rest wherewith ye may cause the weary to rest—repentance, be sorry in your soul's soul on account of your sin. We know at once that the answer is right. Only repentance can touch sin; it is not something on the surface that can be removed by a mechanical act; sin is in the soul; sin is so to say in the very tissue of the spirit; it is a grief against God and a grief in God's own heart, and God's only answer to sin is creating the possibility of true, profound, poignant and sufficient repentance.

Repentance is not an intellectual assent to a misunderstood dogma; it is the slaughter of the soul that the soul may live, it is the soul laid upon the altar that afterwards it may in the grace of Christ and faith in His gospel stand erect in a new manhood, in a new creation. If this is so, the answer is fundamental, vital, it goes to the very root and the very core of things. Such is the position and such is the claim of the Gospel, that it never cries Peace, peace, where there is no peace, it never daubs the wall with untempered mortar; it will have it out with the soul. Then began Jesus to preach and to say, Repent!—a word which the Church is in danger of forgetting, and, forgetting that word and all its implications, she loses heart and power and is numbered with the commonplace and the competitive.

Take it in the matter of obedience. Obedience is God's way to refreshing; obedience opens the fountains; obedience points the way that will conduct you to the living wells of the living water. This is the rest—repentance; this is the refreshing—obedience; go back to God and find what you want. When you have lost your jewel, you must find it. Fool is he that goes a million miles away from the place where the jewel was lost in the expectation that he will find it in some other universe. The soul sinned against God, and the soul must by God's own grace and righteousness put itself right with God. That is never done in public; that is a secret, sacred act. Enter into thy closet, and when thou hast shut the door, pray to thy Father which is in heaven, and thy Father which seeth in secret shall reward thee openly, and there in the humblest obscurity He will open the well of living water and give thee refreshment.

Then we take it, finally, at the very grave itself. We come to that awfulest of all sights, the descent of the coffin, the moment of intolerable agony, the dumb farewell, the speechless withdrawal; and there comes a loving voice which says of those who are interred in the hope of the Christian resurrection, This is the rest whereby He causes the weary to rest: he, she, is going to rest, to the last sleep, the holy slumber, out of which only one voice can awake her: this is the rest, this deep cold hideous thing, the grave, this is the rest.

Then the soul catches the fire of God; it says in words that cannot be heard, O grave, where is thy victory, thou cruel monster, thou terrible thing? It has no victory; she has found in thee the pillow on which she can rest her weariness. And this is the refreshing; this tomb is not a grave only, it is a well, a well of living water, and in a mysterious, ideal, but not the less influential and effective sense, those who go down into the grave in the spirit of Christ and in the spirit of His Cross find below it the rockspring of which, if a soul drink, it shall thirst no more. In My Father's house, said Christ, are many manses. On this text we have already spoken in this pulpit—not terrified by mansions, but, translating the word properly, manses, man's houses, refreshment rooms. Jesus translated into our mother tongue, says, In My Father's house are many refreshment places, many refreshment houses, into which we can go, in which we tarry a little while and take what food we need; in My Father's house are many stopping places, lodgings for the night; away in the morning, for the morning beam is a call to further progress. The prophet offered them the true rest and offered them the right refreshing, but they would not have it; the word to them was still, Precept upon precept, precept upon precept; line upon line, line upon line; here a little, and there a little. And they sent and fell backwards, and were broken and snared and taken, and they are the fools of the universe today. What shall our answer be to the great prophetic appeal, "This is the rest, this is the refreshing"? Bless God for this demonstrative pronoun, the living *this;* it is one of the treasures of the soul. This God is our God, He will be our refuge forever and ever; this is the victory that overcometh the world, even our faith; this is the way, walk ye in it; this, said the seraphic poet, this is the God we adore, our faithful, unchangeable Friend—not a vague deity, an indefinite deliverance and redemption; but this specially and emphatically indicated, this, this is the God; not a shapeless shape, but a definite and living and loving presence. This is my God, this is our God, and we will trust Him.

Prayer

Almighty God, wherein we have forgotten Thee, and have suffered for our forgetfulness, do Thou in Thy great mercy through Christ Jesus our Lord forgive us all our sin. We confess our sin, we do not hide it even from ourselves, from God we cannot hide it; we have done the things we ought not to have done, for our sins we are heartbroken. We bless Thee for the house of prayer, for the open altar, for the daylight opportunity and freedom round about us calling us to nobler manhood and to richer service. The word is not so small as we thought it, it is a gate that opens upon other worlds that cannot be measured, neither can they be numbered, for they are as mansions in the Father's one house of stars. We bless Thee for everything that expands the mind, that gives us deeper consciousness of true freedom, and that leads us away from things narrow and little and insufficient. We now can say, because of the liberty Thou hast given unto us in Christ Jesus, Lebanon is not sufficient. Once we thought Lebanon very great, and we gathered under the shade of its cedars with somewhat of awe and fear; now we think nothing of that little tuft of trees, for we have seen the Lord, and our souls have become acquainted with the liberty of His righteousness and love. We bless Thee that we can trample the earth under foot; we thank Thee that time and space, always evil when not rightly known, are no longer of any consequence to us, for we revel in the presence of God, the Infinite Light, the Eternal Peace. Truly our history has been a history of sin and shame, and Thou hast plowed us as with hot iron, and Thou hast stricken us through and through as with darts of fire; and we deserved every pang of pain, for we have sinned against light and love and mercy, we have scorned the tears of God. And behold, Thou didst send a famine upon us, Thou hast filled up the wells, Thou hast bidden the fountains to cease, the rivers Thou hast sent off in evaporation, so that in the morning we found them not; we thought we would prevail over Thine anger by sending our little ones to the well and finding water for us; but, behold, they have all come back poor, white-faced, disappointed little ones; and there is no grass. Let us fall into Thy hands, we pray Thee in the name of Jesus, and at the

Cross of Christ, and give us that grace of repentance which keeps back nothing of sorrow that it may tell Thee in floods of tears how grievous is our sin and how bitter our sorrow. The Lord will then send us all the wells back, and every fountain shall spring up, and the maidens of Israel shall sing the great national anthem and say, Spring up, O well. Amen.

11
Bible Wells

Preached on Sunday Morning, March 18th, 1900.

Spring up, O well—Numbers 21:17.

The children of Israel had been having a hard time. This is the way in which God makes men, by driving them from pillar to post, by making them to live a long time in tents, and by commanding them to take up their tents and go on, no matter where; not for them to know, it is enough that God knows. Afterwards they will know and talk about it, and write stories for their children regarding their wonderful campaign. The children of Israel pitched in Oboth; and they no sooner got to Oboth than they went on further; and they had not settled down there until they removed and pitched in the valley of Zared; and thence they removed and pitched on the other side of Arnon, a place in the wilderness coming out of the coasts of the Amorites. Then they went to Beer, a very singular but most historical and enchanting place; it was the well whereof the Lord spoke unto Moses, Gather the people together, and I will give them water. Cannot men live without water? Why, it is a mere nothing, and yet the world could not go on long without water. It could go on forever without wine. "Gather the people together, and I will give them water," and when they got the water Israel began to sing, saying, "Spring up, O well; sing ye unto it." You cannot regulate the song of the people; they will sing when they want to sing—God bless them! There is an enthusiasm that cannot be mechanized; there are times when we ignore all leaderships and batons and signals, and the great gushing, loving, grateful heart makes for itself a national anthem, and none can hinder. This was the national anthem, if I may so say, of old Israel, and you cannot improve upon it today under any complete and grateful review of life. Hear the song in part: "The princes dug the well, the nobles of the people dug it." The nobles of the people dug the well with their scepters and their fine instruments; and that is the right use of all things golden, silver, or jeweled. How foolish we are and altogether unpoetical when we stand with staring eyes and open gape looking at some staff or scepter or jewel thing in a glass case, bearing this legend, "Touch not"! Then has the nation come to a pretty pass when its kings' things are locked up in a tower and locked away beyond utility or usefulness. Blessed are the people who can say concerning nobles and princes and mighty men, when the well was to be dug, they used their signs of rulership and office, and the golden scepter was not too fine a bauble to use in digging a well that the people might be saved from death. What wonder that the maidens of Israel kept up this sweet song! It is in the air even yet. Woe betide any nation that forgets the memory of its well-diggers; they are the greatest men living.

He digs a well who teaches a child to read. You have made that child independent. Of course it may fritter away its dowry, it may disinherit itself or turn to perverse uses the greatest gifts of God and of society; upon that side of things we make no remark. But dig a well of letters, of learning, historical wisdom, and tell the child that such a well belongs to himself, not the less that it belongs to a great host of other people. The sunshine belongs to everybody; the sunshine is for me, and not for me, and most for me when most for all. Such is the mystery of the divine beneficence. Jesus died for me, but not for me in any narrow sense, but for the whole world, and therefore for me; for I thus get advantages which I could not otherwise fully and permanently realize. Oh, those singing maidens who by instinct or some kind of divine faculty catch the poetry of occasions, those singing hearts that hear, and then echo, and then repeat in broader note and phrase all the meaning of God as He lays the foundations of the earth, and puts above all things a roof of more than gold! What should we do without poetesses, the poets, the seers, who see everything by apparently looking at nothing? "Spring up, O well." How utterly poetic; to the prosaic mind, how absurd, these maidens singers saluting, hailing, welcoming a well. They could not help it, for the Holy Ghost was in them, and the thing that was born of them in lofty song was the creation of the Holy Spirit. Probably it would be better for some purposes to keep the non-poetic people alive by educating them the whole seven days in the week, they are apt to be great nuisances. Therefore we want the church, the sanctuary, the altar house, where all things are made into manhood and vision and power of realizing God. Possibly it may be of some consequence to have people reckoned as live members of society who have no windows in their life-houses, who worship a little starveling deity called reason, a small thing that is really satisfied with board wages and generally a starvation allowance, who thinks that to have the multiplication table is holiday enough and recreation sufficient. But we want another tribe of men, great singers, great deliverers, translators and poets, and men who insist upon it that before we rose this morning they were out and on the wet dewy mountaintops, and that there they saw the Lord. Madmen, of course! Awfully destitute of proper appreciation of the multiplication table, but still singing through our poor prosaic hearts a trill that does us good. Whenever you see a well, sing a song; whenever you see streams widened by velocity of pace, hastening down the face of the hills, sing a doxology; and thus be wise, thou seller of merchandise.

How many wells are mentioned in the whole Bible? We cannot pretend to count them. Sometimes the well is in the singular number, and frequently the word well swells into the plural number, as if it became a gathering of waters and a meeting of singing streams. We find one wonderful well in Genesis 21:19: "And God opened her eyes, and she saw a well of water." It was there all the time, but the eyes were not there. But had not the woman eyesight? Yes, of a bodily kind; but all that is sensuous ought to be typical and sacramental. "And she went, and filled the bottle with water." She only took a bottleful when she might have had a whole well. We might have more gospel if we had more capacity; sometimes we need a greater boldness that we may test the generosity of God; for saith He to those who draw from His wells, Bring another vessel, another, another; until the recipient says, Lord, I have been looking for more vessels, but I cannot find any. It is the receiver that gives in, not the Giver. She "gave the lad drink"—water drink, the true drink, the wine of heaven, in which no man ever found murder, lust, shame. "The lad"—that is a generic designation, taking in all the lads of the world; but in this particular instance she gave a nation drink, she nourished a nation in her bosom. Poor Hagar did not know the well was so near. But what do we know? If we have studied even elementary things, we shall find that God has left nothing in the singular number. If you find poison, you may be quite sure that a bush or two from where you found the poison you will find the antidote. The devil has always been hunted by the Savior. Alas! it is the devil we meet first. Whatever you want you can have by the mercy of God and the presence of the Spirit in your own soul either by way of initiation or secondary suggestion, by the specific faculty or by the great power of conscious dependence upon God. You need not go beyond your four walls for anything you want that appertains to the real and vital culture of your own immortality. John the Baptist gave all the people a great well. They were wondering what they should do, who would come next, what the development of force would be, and especially who he would be, whatsoever his name, who would play the part of goel or deliverer or nearest kinsman. John said, "There standeth one among you whom ye know not, he it is." Poor, poor fools! We have been stretching our necks over seas and wildernesses when the thing we were in search of was within the compass of our own shadow. Arise! Be thyself! Look with the eyes of the soul.

A great range of subject is started by this Hagar's well, covering such suggestions as the unexpected supplies of life. We were at our extremity, and that extremity became God's opportunity. Also referring to the unexpected deliverances of life. We say it is always the unexpected that happens. "And, when Herod would have brought him forth, the same night," the angel of the Lord got ahead of Herod. But it came just as near as that, namely, "the same night"; not two nights before or a week in advance. Herod was allowed to make a fool of himself to the uttermost possible extent; so to say, the Lord fooled him to the top of his bent, and then when he would have gone forth, there was nothing to go for. This has happened in my case, it has happened in your case; this is a vital extract from the history of conscious and especially of religious experience.

Then the subject further suggests the unexpected friends, the human wells that occur or arise in life. This man will befriend me when I am in difficulty? Where is he? Gone. I am sure that I can apply to such an old comrade when this poor head fails and this poor hand can no longer serve itself; I will go in quest of him. And lo, he does not know me; he knew me when I was young and strong and prosperous. Yet I have friends and deliverances and supplies: how did I get them? You did not get them, God sent them; and the same night when Herod would have brought you forth to your mockery and contempt and derision, so far as society was concerned, the Lord sent His angel, and the chain melted at his touch. What did the Lord do to Hagar? Simply opened her eyes. Our eyes are not open. We think we see the things that are round about us, but there are not things round about us. That would seem to be a ridiculous speech, but it is real gospel. There are two great enemies we have, and they mislead us when not put in their right relation, and these two enemies are time and space. We make a great deal of them, we write books about them, we conduct examinations as if they were reality; and yet there is no time, and there is no space, except in some such limited view as actually would go almost to the length of destroying the very things which we think are proved. There is no church round about us at this moment, in the sense in which we read the term church, namely, a building, a structure, a thing measurable and appreciable, and that could be sold by auction. In the very narrowest sense such a structure is enclosing us now, but in reality the true meaning is within that and beyond that, and so much within it as to rend it, and so much beyond it as to cover it with the derision of the universe. What we want therefore is eyesight, the power of seeing things behind things and within things, and the power of denying the existence of anything that is measurable and tangible. Hagar was taught that if she would only open her eyes she might have seen God.

And there is a curious little idyll about a well in this same book of Genesis—24:13: "Behold, I stand here by the well of water; and the daughters of the men of the city come out to draw water." They will all come to the well. You may not meet them in the field or in the wood or on the broad wayside; only now and then people come to such places or pass through them; but the well—that is the point of union, that the wedding-ring place. Perhaps we may meet these fair daughters of men in the gardens of spices. Perhaps not; now and then they may be there, and we may be fortunate enough to catch a vision of such living beauty, but I can promise you nothing positive about that. We may find them in the cornfields. Well, the cornfields are a kind of annual festival, there is a time when the cornfields are thronged with people; but I cannot make you any definite promise about meeting the persons you are in quest of even in the cornfields, but I can promise you that all the city will be at the well. What! Is it water—so simple and poor a thing as water that will bring men together? Many a man has been in such straits for want of water that he would have emptied his pockets if you would have given him one vessel full of spring water.

We must watch for signs. The man who is speaking here is a man who knows well where men will be and women and little children; he knows that all the parish will bank at the well. Everything depends upon the well of living water: watch therefore long enough and you will see him, you will see her, and through him or her you may see God, for God is at the well, He sits by the well. So Samaria's daughter may catch that wondrous eye-flash, she will look for some great vision. When Jacob came to what is to me the most interesting period of his life, namely, when he came to the blessing of his sons, he was quite overcome when the name of Joseph occurred to him: "Joseph is a fruitful bough, even a fruitful bough by a well, whose branches run over the wall" (Gen. 49:22). Why were the branches so alert, so sweetly ambitious, so determined to see what was on the other side of the wall? Because of the well; the roots of the bough were comforted by the well; no man needed to water this bough; God had planted it by the well that never evaporates. Some men are specially environed; you cannot get at them. How gladly would cruel souls get at such men and tear them to pieces as the vulture tears his prey! But the men themselves cannot be touched. No jealousy, envy, cruelty, pious savagery of any kind can do them the slightest possible harm. You know it, we all know it; history is full of it; that is election, that is the concrete instance and demonstration of divine sovereignty. What some men would have given if they could have indirectly killed you! Instead of that they never even scratched you. What prevented their vengeance taking effect? Because your bough was planted near a well; it drank the living water, it was nurtured by the milk of the breast of the man-woman God. You cannot be fair to your own history and deny divine providence; you are a criminal sevenfold dyed in iniquity if you can stand up and assert that God has failed you in any crisis of your life. As for my own life, I see God everywhere. I must let Him alone, I may spoil His ministry.

I read of a curious instance of a well in 2 Samuel 17:18, "They went both of them away quickly, and came to a man's house in Bahurim, which had a well in his court." Is it a fine house? I do not care; what I want is the well. Is it a large and beautiful house? These are trivial questions to me, I want the well. Where is the well?

It is in the man's own court, he has resources at home; he need not go out for water. In a very large sense we might have almost completeness of life at home. Some men could not live alone, they would call it solitary and lonesome, and they would be afraid of the silence. You know persons who dare not be in the house by themselves; what poor creatures; how little they know of the universe; what a poor definition of solitude is theirs! You know such persons; they are waiting for the glare of night's poor swaling gas; they must be out; the moment the drum sounds they begin to be happy. Can such people be saved? The preliminary question is, What is there to save?

Here is a corresponding well mentioned in Proverbs 5:15, "Drink waters out of thine own cistern, and running waters out of thine own well." Have a city of the mind. There is an atheistical fidgeting; there is a yearning or a solicitude after outward things that would make the sacrament you drank in the morning of no effect. Can you not live on that sweet sacrament? Can you not listen and hear the winds? Can you not close your eyes and read the Bible of the shadows? Poor beyond all poverty ever experienced by man is the soul that has no well in itself, the soul that is not independent of the holiday and the red flag and the blare of trumpets. "If thou knewest who it is that saith unto thee, Give me to drink, thou wouldest have asked of him, and he would have given thee living waters, spring water, springing up into everlasting life." Again, have a city of the mind.

Does any other well occur to you? The greatest well of all. Jesus sat thus by the well, Jacob's well, Himself a deeper well, Himself, indeed, the creator of that well. Do you not read in the prophets this wondrous expression, "The wells of salvation"? It is a beautiful picture. Men are drawing water out of the wells of salvation, and as they do so they sing a sweet song unto the Lord; for who can be silent in the plash of living streams? Is it possible for us to make nothing of those wells? Alas, it is possible; this is the Lord's complaint against His people; He said, My people have committed two evils: they have forsaken Me, the Fountain of living water; and that is not enough, they have hewn out for themselves cisterns, broken cisterns that can hold no water. You no sooner put the water into the cistern than it leaks away drop by drop, little by little, hardly a measurable quantity at any one time; but incessancy is the secret of ultimate depletion and humiliation. A man does not throw his religion away in one act of insanity; he does not rise up and say, I call the nations to witness that I abandon all faith and all prayer, and I abandon God Himself. It is rarely thus proclaimed, but little by little, a little cooling, a deepening indifference, an almost immeasurable alienation, dropping one service on the Sabbath, taking less interest in benevolent occupation, being more and more taken up by frivolous entertaining, evanescent things preoccupying the mind to the exclusion of the great verities that used in the older, brighter time to dominate it. This is the way, little by little, a drop at a time, and in a year, or a year multiplied by seven, and you may stand up a naked atheist, if not a blaspheming rebel. The Lord save us, the Lord keep us near the place of the holy well, the Lord enable us to drink deeply of the living river. Then shall our fruit be abundant in season and out of season; we shall be evergreens, amaranths that no famine can wither.

Prayer

Almighty God, wilt Thou condescend to show us the meaning of all mountains and rivers and wells and fields? Some of us have never seen the meaning of them; we have written their names on legal paper, but we have not caught the fragrance, the music, the poetry. Wilt Thou now show us somewhat of the higher significance of things; may we awake from time to time here and there to say with wonderment and appreciation, How dreadful is this place! This is none other than the house of God, and this is the gate of heaven. Hitherto we have but seen the rocks, we would now see the gate; heretofore we have only seen forms and shapes, we would now see the house, the home, unbuilt by hands, but sheltering all who put their trust in God. We humbly pray Thee to show us the meaning of everyday events; we have treated them frivolously, we have not gathered them into one poem pattern, we have not united the story of the day in manifold paragraphs and made of it a gospel sweet as the love of God. Oh that we had seen things and heard them and understood them in some part! For then had we been at rest, and our souls had not been troubled by the little things that move those who have no city of the mind. Come to us, we humbly pray Thee, in the name of the Cross of Christ the infinite Savior, and show us that every lily has a meaning and every fowl flying in the midst of the firmament has a gospel in its mouth. Amen.

12

Bible Mountains

Preached on Thursday Morning, March 22nd, 1900.

As the mountains are round about Jerusalem, so the Lord is
round about His people from henceforth even forever
—Psalm 125:2.

Why this "henceforth," as if a new thing had occurred in history, as if an unexpected Bethlehem had just heard an unexpected song? The Lord has always been round about His people; they could not have lived one moment without Him: all things are from eternity. God elected His Church before He formed the world. In God are no beginnings and no endings. We need such terms in all their clearest and broadest significance, because we are so little and frail and so apt to lose our memory; but when it comes to looking into the real state of affairs, the essential plan and purpose of God, then all things are just as old as God is; form and color and incident may vary, but the spirit and poetry of things came up with God, and they are from everlasting to everlasting, because that is the measure of the Divine duration. We have already lectured upon the seedling parables of the Bible; we have been apt to think that the parables were features of Christ's ministry, and in a certain sense that is true; but parables are from the beginning, like all poetry that is true and all truth that is poetic and admitting of parabolical expression. Some have found parables and the all-inclusive parable in the book of Genesis itself; I think we could find it there if we were to look for it carefully; probably the word parable would better fit the whole occasion than any other word. "And Jesus answered and said." What is the Genesis equivalent? "And God said." They have always been the great speakers, the only speakers, the speakers whose speeches were pregnant with all things living, true, beautiful, and of useful account. Here is a seedling parable: "As the mountains . . . so the Lord." Jesus Christ founded His parables upon those lines. "As"—then an interval—"so." So to say, God has built Himself upon us, having first built us upon Himself, so that all the wise talking and sweet singing of creation would seem to embody themselves in parables indeed in the bulb; now in the tiny seed small as a mustard seed, and now in great pictures that want the firmament for a canvas. "As the mountains." The Bible handles all big things, all things majestic and stupendous, and makes but small letters of them in its great literature of the sum total of things. The mountains are the capital letters of the landscape. Do you know what initial letters sometimes cost? Meissonier began his great career, or almost began it, by getting a fee of five guineas for an illuminated initial letter. The mountains are illuminated capitals, the hills are the aristocracy of the fields. And yet the fields are oftentimes more fruitful than the hills; in many an inventory the hills are practically thrown in; it is on the meadows and on the valleys that the gold lies.

Are there many mountains mentioned in the Bible? Are they lumped under one generalization? They are not so massed, they are spoken of in detail, as if each were almost a living thing or a living church or pillars of some vaster edifice. Shall we take a few of those mountains in their parabolical significance? May we not bring them usefully into the whole action of our daily life and service and suffering? Some mountains are red with blood, some soft with dew, but both the hills were set up by Him who buildeth all things. Who can forget Mount Moriah? Who could pronounce that sweet word frivolously? All the hillside is alive with thoughts, and the thoughts are almost winged things, fluttering and flying and shaking from their wings great suggestions and pensive yet triumphant memory. It was Abraham who said to the young man who followed him and his son, "Stand you here while I go up and worship yonder." Some worship must not be intruded upon; there is a place for solitary communion with God, and the footfall of the dearest friend would disturb the spirit of the holy occasion. The two travelers climb the hill; the younger one wants to speak, as youth always does, and at last he summons courage enough to say, "Behold the fire, the wood, and the knife, but where is the lamb?" Isaac missed the meaning. Men do not know the meaning of their own questions; no preacher sees all the rings that form and widen on the lake of his audience at the time when the sermon splashes into the middle of the pool. Abraham said—it was the greatest thing that had yet been said in human story—"God will provide Himself a lamb." We know the rest of the narrative; enough for us that we tarry for a moment on Moriah, and see the poem of sacrifice, the first Gethsemane, the great surrender of the human will to the will of God. Yours has been a poor landscape if there is no Moriah. I want to hear what you can tell me about your Lebanon and all the hills silvered and carpeted, so to say, with tiniest flowers, each a diamond in its own way; but when you have shown me all these acres of hill I ask, Is there not another? We always seem to know when we are mocked by incompleteness. All these sons are noble stalwarts; but is there not another? Yes, there is one, quite young; he can be of no account in this purpose of heaven. Said the prophet, Bring him, we must have the whole number; the tribes of God are twelve, and though the kingdom was rent they come up again as a solid twelve; produce him, send for him, though he be in farm or field or far-off colony. He came, he was the king in the purpose of God. So with all these mountains we instinctively ask, Is there not another? And we discover that other in the hill of sacrifice, the mount of surrender, the place where a human will was laid down to be murdered.

Is there not somewhere a hill of fellowship, a kind of council-chamber amid the rocks, a high place where certain men that seemed to be the very pillars of society are closeted? Yes, there is a hill of that kind. What is its name? Tabor. You love the name. Are not names as birds that sing their own songs? Do you not realize even in Tabor solemnity, possibility, suggestion? Who was on Tabor? Moses and Elias and Jesus. There must be hills that are as council-chambers in the Church and in the individual heart, Tabors on the top of which the most eloquent must be silent, and therefore the more eloquent. We may learn new languages on that hilltop, and yet through all the languages there may run a tone as of our mother-tongue. There are languages that we seem to know without learning them, just as there are songs which we are quite sure we heard in some other and fairer world, where the notes run out with a clearer tone and mean more than they can mean among these gray lingering clouds. Moses and Elias and Jesus had an equal number of listeners. Never take more people with you than you can possibly do without. There are hours when small numbers are great numbers, and when great numbers are so great that they become mobs and crowds, a tumultuous ochlocrasy, concerning whose uproars the great historic voice says, "Why do the heathen rage, and the people imagine a vain thing?" Let communion stop short of outcry; let communication be done in whispers, not the whispers of mere timidity, but the other and better whispers of genuine reverence. So to Moriah we must add Tabor.

Are there any other severe mountains in the Old Testament? Yes, there is one severest of all; surely this mountain is nought but rocks; you could not plant the simplest flower in those crannies so high and solemn. I refer to the mount Sinai, the mount of law, the mount where the eternal righteousness was, so to say, born in this bitter, gruesome Bethlehem. For law must descend into letters; the law is nothing if it have not its acts and statutes and decrees and memoranda and marginalia, meaning much to the trained eye, but nothing to the eye untrained. Law has its Thou shalt, Thou shalt not—go, come, stand, sit down; a high imperative with some tone of cruelty about it. Law limits man, and thus gives him freedom; law builds man a cage, for it is all the space he can make use of in certain relations, and enough for him if the cage be so barred that through it he can see the sunshine and the moon-poetry of night. Jesus Christ said, I am not come to destroy Sinai, but to fulfill it; I am not come to destroy the law, but to accomplish it; I am not come to destroy the root and the branch, but to bring them to fullest fruition, so that there shall be the joy of plenteousness and the grace of a divine hospitality, in the north and in the south, far away on either side even until the whole earth become an obedience of love. Some persons think they have outlived the commandments; they think vainly and most impiously. The commandments ought never to be out of sight; I would show them in golden letters in every sanctuary, an appeal to the conscience, a kind of visible demonstration of the presence of the Deity, an embodiment of the spirit of truth. He is either a great man or a small one who is independent of the commandments. We may in some way plant beautiful flowers on the grim hill; that is surely not forbidden; or we may by the providence of God so enlarge the plain into garden land as to include the mountain; let it stand, but give it a new and blessed environment.

We tremble before Mount Sinai; all the incidents seem to be of a frightsome kind. If even so much as a beast touch the mountain he shall be thrust through with a dart. Have we not come upon better times? Have we not lived in a quieter light? Can we not do better with the dawn than with the thunderstorm? All this may be so, blessedly, inexpressibly so; but we must have the rock, and its companion law, and in our yearning after something quieter we may find our holy prayer lovingly and sufficiently answered by taking a glimpse at another mountain. What mountain is that? It is Mount Hermon. "As the dew upon Hermon." Dew is often to us more acceptable than lightning and snow and crushing tempest, though all these may be sanctified and ennobled by the great voice of law and claim of righteousness. "As the dew upon Mount Hermon." Is there not dew upon every mountain? Yes, there is upon every mountain more or less, now or then some morning dew. Sometimes the dew is not spoken of; there is a time when we need something, so to say, deeper and fiercer than dew; so we do not read about the dew that was on Mount Moriah, nor do we read about the dew that was on Tabor, and certainly we never saw any dew upon Sinai, but the dew was there in each case all the time. But who does not know that there are hours when certain thoughts take a predominant position, when a signature for the day makes the character and history of the mount itself? We do not see all things always even as we travel up the same hillside; now it is jeweled dew, now a wind that may overthrow us, presently a cloud that establishes sudden night upon the mountain brow: who can tell what it will be? The mountain has its changes, its new characteristics, so that sometimes we cut out faces in the rock, and now and then we see personalities in the cavernous places, now and again we think we heard voices, and we are sure of it, and we are not to be laughed or mocked out of it. The mountains have their diary of change.

Can there be more mountains in this mountainous land of the Bible? Yes, a hundred more; we can touch but two of them. There is a mountain I should like to see; it is the mount of vision from one of whose peaks men catch glimpses of the land they long to go to. It is Mount Nebo. I would not care to see the specific and nameless grave amid the solitudes of Nebo, it would be enough for me to know that one sorely tried life climbed the steeps of Nebo that he might catch sight of another land, while Jordan rolled between his poor old heart and that green Canaan. There are such mountainous times in the history of our souls. The Lord says, You shall not go into Canaan, but you may climb Nebo, and you may find a resting-place there, a soft bed for a tired body; as for the other place, you must take it in symbol; do not suppose I am disappointing you by not showing you what you call green and lovely Canaan; I will save all that, and you shall go in directly with a most startling immediateness from weariness into eternal rest, into the Canaan of which the greenest of your sunny fields is but a poor symbol.

It was so on Mount Olivet. Jesus climbed that Olivet hill that He might leave it forever behind Him as a mere letter or a term in geography. The ending-place was the beginning-place in the history of Christ; He did not end on Olivet; Olivet was to the dear Savior a beginning, the point at which He started, a point therefore never to be forgotten. Blessed are they who climb Olivet, for they shall not die. The most beautiful sentence in the whole history of burial is to be found in connection with this same Olivet, as also in connection with old Nebo. Moses we know nothing about as to his death or his burial-place, and Jesus did not die on Olivet, but ascended; herein is the poem complete, the poem of Moses and the Lamb. Nebo and Olivet shoulder each other in the memory of a common and most blessed and significant history.

You can see all these mountains without going from home. There may be something in change, no sensible man would deny that for one moment, but as a matter of fact you can see all the mountains of the Bible without going out of your own sunny garden. You find these mountains in the clouds; but who cares for clouds? Who reads the poetry of the clouds? Yet all the Alps are there and all the Indian hills, and all the rocky places and snow-clad places, and all the places that seem to turn a little from you that you may see the places that are beyond them millions of miles beyond their snowclad shoulders. But some people would almost rather die than not see the Alps, if they can only be seen after the payment of so much money and the endurance of so much discomfort; then they think they have seen the mountain. I have seen them many a year in the sky, and we have sung together and talked together, and as it were wept together for very joy. What personalities we have seen just above the clouds! How often in the eventime have we almost heard the vespers of the upper church. If you would simply stretch yourself out on your native earth and exclude that earth and look at God's beautiful morning heavens, you would see all the mountains that are charged with messages to your poor life.

And is there not a place called Mount Calvary? There is not; all the best historians tell us that there is no such place as *Mount* Calvary. We sing with more or less of ignorant joy that "There is a green hill far away"; we are too much taken up with the tragedy to study the geography. But there is no Mount Zion. What we call Calvary is a plain, yea, a flat place, and yet it was higher than all the mountains; its history lifts it above all competition as to majesty and grandeur and fruitfulness. Enough for us that there is a Cross, blessed Cross, dreadful, holy, tender Cross. In my hands no price I bring, simply to Thy Cross I cling. Moses went up into the mountain to commune; Jesus went up into the mountain to pray; what is the difference? It is still Moses and the Lamb, Genesis and the Apocalypse, or whatever other book may ever duly terminate the Book of books. What am I to do? Speak some sweet encouraging word to me, O thou preaching man, say something that I can recollect, that I can treasure in my heart as a living jewel of speech. Is that the desire? The answer is at hand. The text we have found in Psalm 125, the text you ask for is in Psalm 121; let us read them together. "As the mountains are round about Jerusalem, so the Lord is round about His people from henceforth even forever." "I will lift up mine eyes unto the hills, from whence cometh my help. My help cometh from the Lord, who made heaven and earth." Hills, mountains, sanctuary places—they enrich the world. Blessed is the man who has eyes to see what is on the mount, if not at the top yet at the foot.

Words for Preachers

As a bird bringeth all kinds of food to her young ones' nest, and is nothing the better herself thereby: so some do only learn that they may immediately teach, not seeking thereby to amend and make themselves better.—*Cawdray, 1609*

The preaching of the law is necessary to true conversion. A man will never be taken off from the opinion of his own healthfulness but by the preaching of the law. The law shows men what they are, what they may expect, etc. The fallow ground of the heart will never be broken up without the plow of the law (Jer. 4:3). The plow of the law must go and make deep furrows before the seed of comfort be cast in. Though the preaching of the law does not convert, yet it helps forward conversion, inasmuch as it works that preparatory work without which conversion ordinarily is not. As the needle makes way for the thread, so the law makes way for conversion.—*Robinson, 1559*

Take heed to yourselves, lest you should be void of that saving grace of God which you offer to others, and be strangers to the effectual workings of that gospel which you preach; and lest while you proclaim the necessity of a Savior to the world, your own hearts should neglect Him and you should miss of an interest in Him and His saving benefits! Take heed to yourselves, lest you perish while you call upon others to take heed of perishing! And lest you famish yourselves while you prepare their food. Though there be a promise of shining as the stars to those that turn many to righteousness (Dan. 12:3), that is but on supposition that they be first turned to it themselves: such promises are meant, "caeteris paribus, et suppositis supponendis." Their own sincerity in the faith is the condition of their glory simply considered, though their great ministerial labors may be a condition of the promise of their greater glory: many a man hath warned others that they come not to that place of torment, which yet they hasted to themselves; many a preacher is now in hell that hath a hundred times called upon his hearers to use the utmost care and diligence to escape it. Can any reasonable man imagine that God should save men for offering salvation to others, while they refused it themselves; and for telling others those truths which they themselves neglected and abused? Many a tailor goes in rags, that maketh costly clothes for others; and many a cook scarcely licks his fingers, when he hath dressed for others the most costly dishes. Believe it, brethren, God never saved any man for being a preacher, nor because he was an able preacher; but because he was a justified, sanctified man, and consequently faithful in his Master's work.—*Baxter, 1615–1691*

Prayer

Almighty God, we have come to seek living water. We seek it from Jesus Christ, in whose name we pray; He will give us spring water. We come that our thirst may be assuaged, that all our desires after God may be abundantly satisfied. We have heard that the river of God is full of water; we know that the streams of the river cannot be dried up; there is a river the streams whereof shall make glad the city of God. Blessed is the man who delighteth in Thee as known in Jesus Christ our infinite Savior; he shall be like a tree planted by the rivers of waters; of the drought he shall know nothing, of the summer heat he shall be unaware. We have come therefore to seek water not at Jacob's well, but at a deeper, higher spring. In coming to these wells of salvation we come with rejoicing; the sound of the flowing water makes us glad; these streams are music; we would sit down beside them and rest, we would drink of them and lift up the head by the way and be glad as with a joy that must shout for very joy. Thou hast fed us and refreshed us and kept us all the way; Thou wilt keep the old the few remaining days, and the young Thou wilt make glad with a father's generous promise. We have committed two evils; we have forsaken Thee, the Fountain of living waters; and we have hewn out unto ourselves cisterns, broken cisterns that can hold no water. All we like sheep have gone astray, we have turned every one to his own way; but by Thy grace we have returned unto the Shepherd and Bishop of our souls. We have done what we ought not to have done, and we have been stung by disappointment, morning, noon and night, and we have thrust our sickle into a harvest of darkness. We are ashamed of our sin, we hardly bring Thee souls at all, so withered are we by sin, so desolated by crime. Our desires have been evil, our thoughts have not been heavenly, and we have suffered at the root and core of our being because there has been a cankerworm testifying against us and threatening us with further ruin. But, coming in the name of Jesus, we come with a name that must prevail; He lived and died for man; for man He rose again, and is at this very moment pleading for man in the courts that cannot be seen. Deliver us from the great temptation to put away from us the unseen and invisible;

may we close our eyes that the eyes of our souls may be opened, and may we see with the eyes of faith and love God Himself, Thy very self, Thou bleeding Heart, Thou commanding Voice. We have been betrayed by our senses, we have been led astray by a perverted fancy, we are following a dream to which there is no reality; and we confess it all, and pray for the mercy of the Cross. Thou knowest us altogether: which is our terror and our joy, for if there is ought in our souls struggling after God Thou seest it and Thou dost reward us with the sunshine of Thine appreciation; and what there is ill in us Thou knowest altogether how it came to be there, for we have had fathers of our flesh, we have grown up out of a thousand ages, we are the last weeds of innumerable summers that have been wasted. God pity us and take us to the mountain where the sanctuary is, or to the valley where the thorn grows, or to the wells where the water flows that means the cleansing of the soul. The Lord's pity be round about us, the Lord's tears be shed upon our lives and very hearts, and let our prayer prevail in heaven because it is inspired and ennobled by the name of Jesus, Son of God. Amen.

13
Bible Valleys

Preached on Sunday Morning, March 25th, 1900.

The valley of Berachah—2 Chronicles 20:26.

We have been spending some time among the caves of the Bible, and the fields and the wells and the mountains of the Bible. We have thus been able to compile a kind of religious geography. Let us now look at the valleys. The word valley is a poem in itself; it is associated with a great deal that is beautiful, comforting, and that gives the soul a sense of security and plentifulness. The Bible is full of valleys, as it is full of wells. You know this beautiful land of the mountain and the stream and the great flood and the green sward and the unexpected garden and the great and terrible wilderness— oh, that world of sand, that foe that mocks the spring, and smites the summer as a woman might be smitten on the cheekbone. What is this valley of Berachah? In some senses I do not care much for it; I know it means the valley of blessing, and that the people, in whom I have not the slightest confidence at all, sang themselves hoarse in the valley of Berachah because they were fed like oxen that were to be slaughtered. I suspect some things, I have no respect for anthems simply in themselves considered; I must know their history, their meaning, their ultimate purpose. We sing lies. Perhaps even a dumb man might try to sing or growl a little if he were singing over gathered prizes and golden things and manifold riches. That is what the people were doing in the valley of Berachah. To me their blessing goes for nothing until I have deeply inquired into the motive of the hymn, the intent and the genesis of the ringing psalm. It was all right enough within given limits, but the limits themselves were wrong. No doubt there had been great victories, no doubt Jehoshaphat and his people came to take away the spoil of them that had been overthrown; and they found abundance of riches, and they stripped the dead bodies of their precious jewels, and stripped the jewels off for themselves more than they could carry away; and then they began to sing. I listened with reluctance to their selfish psalm. God might see some good in it; God sees good wherever it exists, in how poor soever a form. Sometimes the goodness is like a little starveling thing that has got no blood, no fire in the eyes, and no real trust in the soul—a kind of living, self-vexing speculation. Who would not sing in carrying off all these precious jewels? There is a better time for singing than the time of all this commercial aggrandizement and secular comfort. One little song of patience is worth the whole of this blaring noise; a sigh may be vaster in its meaning than an anthem; yet there was a victory; the victory was in some sort divinely guided and secured. There are fruits of war which may be legitimately gathered by those who have won them by strategy or skill or sharp sword; all that may be true, but I do not care for a national anthem that may not be through and through nationally honest. I never like to hear an atheist sing; it hurts me like a saw. Atheistic nations, not atheistic in formal creeds and ecclesiasticisms, should take care how they add to the guilt of atheism, the guilt of falsehood.

There is another valley mentioned in Numbers 32:9—"the valley of Eshcol." What valley is that? 'Tis the valley of grapes and summer fruits, all of which we may pluck, because it is the intent of divine love that we should possess ourselves of such luxuriant vineyards. Do we not suddenly come upon the grapes intellectual, social, educational, spiritual? Is not hunger itself often surprised by unexpected plentifulness? Yet sometimes men cannot believe even in this uncrushed wine of the grape; they will hasten home and say, Do not, we beseech thee, venture in that direction; grapes enough there may be, even to abundance, but we had better remain where we are; can a man live upon grapes? We cannot deny the purple fruit, yea, some of the people have brought large bunches of the grapes to show us what a fruitful land is beyond; but on the whole is it not better to remain where we are? On the other hand, having gotten into a land of grapes, our colloquy may proceed in a disastrous strain, having in it nothing of the hope and cheer and music of the coming day. Had we not better sit down by these grapes? We cannot tell what there may be beyond the river or on the other side of the mountain; here, you see, we have grapes enough; until we have drunken of this wine why should we strike our tents and go ahead? We may pervert some little mean proverbs of our own, and say, "Better bear the ills we have than fly to others that we know not of." We have grapes today: why should we care about tomorrow? We are tempted to go a flight higher, but who knows what is up there, or a league further on, but who can tell what lion may be in the path? Here let us rest like cattle that have browsing enough. Thus enthusiasm is killed, and all daring, high exploit, and noble endeavor. Ambition may be perverted, but ambition may be one of the forms or aspects of inspiration. It is the future that draws us on, it is the prophetic assurance of some fiery man that a mile further on and we shall have *it* that keeps the world young and keeps the rust away. Poor fools they are these prophets! They are always raving about the years that are coming; they say they see them; they are perfectly sure that as yet we know nothing about summer or harvest or gladness; but there cometh a time when the land shall be a land of summer and the sky an infinite benediction. Had a prophet ever a comfortable day in his whole life? Was a prophet ever able to gather his mantle around him, and say, This is perfectly sufficient; we will call this the millennium? Never true prophet. There have been liars enough who would have sat down anywhere if they could have found enough to eat and to drink. You cannot silence the divinely inspired and most restless man. We could rouse him and say, Now, why not be content? Why not rest and be thankful? Of course there may be higher heights and wider landscapes, let us admit all that for a moment; but why worry ourselves about it? There may be something beyond the grave; when we die we shall see what there is. Perhaps not; there is a right way of dying; there is an atheist's snore that never wakens in any land of summer. The world is kept going by its young folks; this is a young man's world. We do not want a young man of seventeen to talk as if he were an old man of seventy; we want him to tell us that the great Eshcol has not yet been reached, that we know nothing about what grapes really can be, and as to size, and as to quality and lusciousness: come! Tomorrow we may find the great fruits of the orchards of God. Young men must be cheered along this line; they must not be discouraged by those who cry out, Peculiarity, eccentricity, something about very sensational. The world has been kept going by what foolish people would call sensationalism. The very persons who now wrap their rugs around them and enjoy the immediate comfort of the day owe the very rugs in which they wrap themselves to the sensationalism of a former time that could not be kept back from the wilderness or the jungle or the faraway land, no, not kept back by the roaring sea and the tempest that seemed to be an embodied destruction. Do not live yourselves down into saplessness and reluctance to move; let the dog gather itself into comfort before the blazing fire, but as for you young souls, just bringing in upon us a new era, stand up, go forth, and return not but with the prey. It is a pity that some men allow themselves to become so exceedingly old; you need not attempt to guess their ages except you begin at the humble unit of one hundred; now then add to that unit what you like, because the souls to whom immediate reference is made have no tomorrow and no land grape-growing and far off. And it is easy for some persons to come and sanction such indolence, but we want the true spies that say to us, We have seen a land worth going to; it grows life, it is warm with summer, it is boundless with an illimitable hospitality. Young souls, do not be frightened by the man sitting next you, for he is no man, he is hardly a figure in wax.

In Hosea there is a glorious valley—"the valley of Achor" (2:15). What is the meaning of Achor in this connection? What is its broad significance, without going into the immediate geographical detail? What is the broad spiritual interpretation of Achor? It may be given in two little words, each word a syllable, one of the words a letter: "a door of hope." Behold, I have set before thee a door of hope; I have given thee a new beginning, new chances, new opportunities, new mornings; this is not the end, this is the beginning; there is the great wall, go grope in blindness, but with fingertips that can see; thou wilt in that great blank wall find a door; it is there, I made it, I made it for thee; I know the blankness of the wall, but on my word go thou forth and grope for the door, the Achor that will give thee visions beyond big as horizons, big as firmaments, big as outlined heavens: go forth in the spirit of hope. We are saved by hope. We are not saved by depression; probably depression never did anything for any man; sometimes there rushes through the heart quite a quickening stream of red blood, the meaning whereof is that there is even now something further to be done, and we are the men to do it. Tennyson speaks of our blood or lives or hearts being thronged with the pulses of the spring. For a few weeks cold east wind, the breath of the devil, may keep back such thronging and such sense of infancy and growing manhood and new opportunity; but the spring is coming, she cannot be finally delayed, she is a maiden with a purpose, she has messages from God, she will surely come. Do you say so with your hearts? Yea, verily with a heart that has felt the bitterness of life and the joy of the Holy Ghost, and that heart says, that taking the year together, there is not more night than day. Let us sometimes go to the Church of Hope, where the preacher is a singing man, where he speaks in poetry and music of the highest kind, who every now and then comes upon a door, and says, That is the door; open it, and proceed. Beware of melancholy, the deathly, the manhood that has been degraded into a sepulcher. The voice of the Christian religion is a voice of hope. Realize that, and live as if you believed it.

There is a new beginning for you if you please to avail yourself of it. I have heard your story about lost opportunities and a wasted life and failure upon failure, and I have heard your dreary talk about having lost your spirits and being no longer able to take any interest in life. That is atheistic controversy; you had better know it, it spoils your life, it spoils your home, it casts a dreary, cloud-shadow upon your whole environment; it is killing your wife, or killing your husband, or blighting the primrose of the childhood that is under your roof. What the preacher is set to do is to proclaim the door of hope; salvation by hope, hope that is in Christ Jesus our Lord. I know how bad you have been, I know that you have been as bad almost as I have; but there is still something of the sunny day left. When you want to sink down and fade away, that is a temptation from the devil; when you get a glimpse of youth, when you feel a throb of returning energy, that is the Son of God. Be a man; believe that the enemy thou hast not killed today thou wilt of a true certainty slay tomorrow.

In the book of Isaiah we have a beautiful valley; in chapter 22:1 we read about "the valley of vision." That is a large valley, that valley is worth living in. To live with people who have always seen new lights, new possibilities, and new and brighter interpretations than have ever been realized before; that is companionship, that is resurrection. Who cares for these dullards who never see new lights, new companions, and the outlines of new springs and summers in the morning sky? What a poor life it is to live without vision! How small the life whose facts, often so miscalled, are never completed by dream. It is poor living without a dream ministry. You do dream—why not dream in the right way? We could have a stomachic dream, for which we must take medicine in the morning, when we might have a spiritual dream that renews the soul's health and lifts fact into true poetry. There was a young man who had a very poor little world. I want all young souls to hear about this young man. I tell no anecdotes, I am not telling an anecdote now. This young man had only one set of eyes; he went up to his master and said, The end has come; you see the enemy on the hillside there: what can we do? We are at the length of our tether, we had better surrender. The old man who never was in a passion except when he was in one—not one of those little creatures that have continual excitement without any spiritual madness—said, Lord, open his eyes! That is all. The young man became instantly an inhabitant of the valley of vision or the mount of illumination; the moment his spiritual eyes were opened he found that there was a circle within a circle, that the prophet was girdled with fire, that the angels were nearer than the enemies. They always are; why not believe it?

In Isaiah 28:1 we come into "fat valleys." The poor drunkards were all lying down dead drunk and choked and suffocated with their own wine of fatness. They were pampered creatures; their soul was subordinated to the body, they were all flesh and next to no spirit. You cannot mistake the real drunkard; every pore of his skin is drunk, every action of his body is a reel; he breathes wine, exhales poison. There are fat valleys that have no fatness of the true sort. Then there are valleys that are spiritually rich with all manner of nutritious food. There is a wine that has no intoxication in it, there is a wine that does not carry the seal of death. Into those fat valleys, and not into the other, may God lead us.

Can Ezekiel be alive and not take his position in this great question of valleys? Ezekiel saw a valley, it was a valley of dry bones. Read chapter 37:1 and the context. It was an awful valley, a valley of dead men's bones, a valley of death, filled not with the sheeted dead, but with those that had, so to say, been blown to pieces by some great wind of contempt; and the Lord said, "Son of man, can these bones live?" And the son of man said, "O Lord God, Thou knowest." The wisest answer to every divine inquiry: refer the question back; let Him who propounds the problem solve it.

I wish we could read all about the valleys. There is a beautiful historical expression upon which we have already preached: "So we abode in the valley." We wanted to climb the green banks and get up to the points and coigns that catch the earliest kiss of the sun, but seeing that it was better for us to take another course, seeing that we had better obey God than obey our own fancy or whim, we abode in the valley. Abode in a dark, cold place? No; you are misinterpreting the word valley when you attach such epithets to it. I read of other valleys. The valleys are covered over with corn. That is never said about the snow mountains. Have the valleys no compensations? Is sickness itself without advantages? When you are weak are you not sometimes strong? The valleys for the oleanders and the vines and the crimson beauty; and the snow for the edelweiss—poor little flower, yet a brave little thing that outwits the ice. Where did you get the little flower from? I know not that I have seen anything sweeter for many a day: what is it? The lily of the valley. Tell me there is no compensation in poverty, in sickness, in weakness, and even in failure and disappointment? It was in the valley that the lily grew. But the valleys are not the subjects of prophecy, no poetry has been written about the valleys? Wait! "Every valley shall be exalted." What do you say now? "And the rough places shall be made plain, and the crooked shall be made straight." Why? For the Lord is coming, and His kingdom is a kingdom of beauty.

Prayer

Almighty God, we thank Thee in the dear sweet name of Christ that we have heard things which are from above. We know them by their bloom, their music, their fragrance; we say to Jesus Christ Thy Son, No man can do these works except God be with him. We humbly pray Thee to give Thy word still broader witness; let men begin to feel in these latter times that there is no voice like Thine. We have been heedless long, and mistaken noise for music; we have lived in a confused uproar, all the time being partly conscious that we have not heard the true voice and the true music. May we begin to hear the voice now, may man after man say to Jesus, Son of Mary, Son of God, never man spoke as Thou speakest. May we hear all His tones, may we make room for them in our hearts, that they may have a stilling effect upon the tumult and the sealike uproar. We give ourselves morning by morning into Thy charge; we join the innumerable company of angels and the holy ones invisible; we would be numbered with those who stand before Thee and carry the seal of Thine election. Watch our lips, keep Thine eyes upon our mouths, lest we see evil and admire it and begin to sing the praise thereof to unholy listeners. O come to us in the day of danger and the night of darkness, in the seastorm time, and keep us and humble us and chasten us and sanctify us by the Holy Spirit. Unto the Father and the Son and the Holy Ghost, Three in One, One in Three, never to be explained, but ever to be adored, be all the kingdoms and all the glories. Amen.

14
Bible Seals

Preached on Thursday Morning, March 29th, 1900.

Set me as a seal upon thine heart, as a seal upon thine arm—
Song of Solomon 8:6.

"He that hath received his testimony hath set to his seal that God is true." How often does that word seal occur in the whole Bible? What does it mean? All things have significance. The value is often wholly in the meaning. The thing itself may be small enough, so small as to be almost beneath notice, if the question be one of magnitude and appraisement. We must look at the biblical seals just as they come and go; we must as commentators have much license in the matter of accommodation. Some of the meanings are obvious; some are implicit, they have almost to be dug out as if men were searching for silver and for hidden silver. Sometimes the seal applies to God and sometimes to the Church, sometimes to the foundation and sometimes to the internal spiritual witness; we will not stop to discriminate transient uses, we shall pause here and there to wonder what the little seal really means—a little tracing in gold letters written from different points of origin, sometimes from the right hand to the left, so that when any stamping has to be done we may find on the stamp the right succession of the letters. Sometimes in old story they will be like two lumps of clay, but without those balls of clay your paper would be of no use. When you write your check, which is the valuable part of the oblong document? Is it a check for £2,000? If so, of course the value of the check is in the poetical expression £2,000; never did any Shylock pronounce ducats so sweetly as we could pronounce pounds if we got them on the right conditions. But are you sure that you have named the word or words giving real value to the piece of paper? If you think the value is in the sum, you are wrong. The value is in the signature. But would I not be well off if I had a check unsigned–a check for not less than two thousand pounds? No, you would not be well off if you had nothing but that blank check. The signature gives the value to everything: to the conveyance of the little freehold estate that you bought the other day. Show me the deeds: how elegantly written, how perfectly distributed over the face of the document! These deeds are of great value. Before I commit myself to that statement I must see the deeds; if there is no signature to the deeds, you may as well give them away, there is nothing in them until the signature and the seal are placed where they ought to be, and after you in the presence of witnesses mayhap have signed the deeds, or they have been signed on the other side with the magic words, "I deliver this as my act and deed." Now the document acquires value. Many persons have carried their Christian profession just up to the act of signature, the act of sealing, and their profession comes to nothing. You may be sacramentarian or non-sacramentarian; on that matter you may please yourselves, I have no time to discuss it; but you must go through the sacrament of signing, sealing, or the paper is valueless. You are going out of the country for a few months, and you wish to empower someone to transact your business for you, and you have given some man what you call power of attorney; let me see it. This is no use. Why not? It is not signed. But what can there be in a mere signature? Everything is in the signature. Why, the document to be of any real value must be signed with your own hand. There are some ways of making up for lame and infirm people, but speaking the general rule on matters of negotiation and commerce, the signature must be done by your own hand; and probably somebody will have to stand near you to testify that it was done by no other man's hand. They will not–may I speak it with some hesitation, because I am going to inflict a great suspicion on the human race—they will not allow you to sign any important and binding document with the aid of a typewriter. You can write all you please to write with your typewriter, but not the signature. If the signature means little or nothing, you may write it with a typewriter, or get somebody else to sign it for you and to initial the signature, no doubt; there are many ways of helping lame dogs over stiles; but if the document is to be of any real binding legal force it must be signed by your own hand, you must give the name or give your mark, or in some way indicate that you have signed it with your blood or self or soul. What, is it so important a thing that it may be written with blood? Yes, symbolically, significantly; in the soul of it; it is red blood ink that gives value to your signature. So it is in wider spheres and in more spiritual relations. The covenant between God and His people is written with blood; the seal which we carry is a seal which has blood in it, at least by implication. We are saved by blood. There be those people so unholy in their daintiness that they do not like the word blood. They do not understand the sorrow of the universe, they do not know that sorrow is life, soul, blood, the blood of sprinkling, and the blood of sacrament. I revel with holy delight in my sweet Savior's words, which bid me eat His flesh and drink His blood, and not perform something mechanical and without the deepest and most solemn and even tragic significance.

In choosing this as our text we are not making vivid—a process which is often allowable in pulpit exposition—a peculiar or distinctive word; we are engaged upon the unfolding and expansion of a long golden chain. This is a text of links, this is a polysyllable of love, this the endless word, because pointing to the endless life. Would you hear a little of the drip, drip of the music of the sealing? Why, I could begin anywhere, but we might begin in Job: "He commandeth the sun and sealeth up the stars," as if they were quite little morsels of jewels, and He gathered them into one slender batch and tied some jeweled seal to them, and said, These are my jewels, to be gathered up on a given day. Or Isaiah: "Seal the law among my—" and then comes a New Testament word. The New Testament in Isaiah? Why, certainly. The New Testament is in Genesis. What is that completing word in Isaiah? Read the text again, and we will conjecture, now that you have given us the key, that the word is in the New Testament and in the very first part of the New Testament: "Seal the law among my disciples." We are familiar with the word; when we first read it we did not know the meaning of it, but we read on through Isaiah and Jeremiah and Ezekiel and Daniel, and right away through into Matthew, and there the word disciples occurred, and then it often occurred, and then we thought we had always known the word—so ungrateful is man. And Job: "My transgression is sealed up as in a bag": I cannot deny the transgression, God hath produced the witness against me; the Lord could open the bag and shake out the black transgressions, the unholy jewels, and call my attention to the horrible proof of the horrible accusation. And there are books we cannot open. Curiously, our eyes have always been turned towards a book that we could not open and no man could open; we were sure the book was there, and we knew of a certainty that it was a most important document, and we said, Who shall open that book? And a voice loud as thunder said, Fear not; the Lion of the tribe of Judah, He shall open the sealed book and read mysteries and make them sound as if they were poems in our mother tongue. And in the Epistle to the Romans Paul speaks of circumcision—a mere flesh-cutting in itself—as a seal of righteousness. Some people never get further than the knife; some people never see the lancet beyond the lancet, the brighter, keener, blade that cuts strange words into human life. And Paul in writing to Timothy of course uses the word seal: "Having this seal, The Lord knoweth them that are His." And what about Jesus Christ Himself? Can the Apostle John, who had the privilege of His breast, tell us anything about this Son of God? And John answers in these words: "For Him hath God the Father sealed." It is God's doing; this is the Lord's doing, and it is marvelous in our eyes. And is there not another seal still? Yes, there is another seal, and it is Paul who reveals that seal in his great epistle to the Ephesians, for he assures those people, "Ye were sealed with that holy Spirit of promise." Then they are All in it–all the Deity? Yes, God, and the Son, and the Spirit; and you cannot get rid of these three Forces, this One-Three number, this Three-One power.

Thus the word seal is used in many significations, and the text now before us is not to be employed wholly in any one direction; we are to accept the image and apply it according to varying experience; we are to study the morning in order that we may shape out the day; we must ask where the wind is before we dare go out in such and such garments. It is the sun that tells you what to eat and drink and wear. Oh, how independent we thought ourselves! That we could say what dress we would put on, and of what food we would partake, and of what vessel we would quaff in order to satisfy our thirst; whereas it is all a question of the sun; let him retire behind his clouds and keep there for days, and it is one thing; let him come forth rejoicing like a strong man to run a race, calling in silence for the whole firmament to prepare the way of the light, and it is another. Yet we think we are very independent. We are when the sun will let us be.

Wonderful wearing of a seal is this in the Song of Solomon 8:6– "Set me as a seal upon thine heart, as a seal upon thine arm." The whole idea of the gospel bondage–sweet, sweet slavery!–is in that symbolism. Where must the seal first be? "Upon thine heart." Begin at the heart if you would begin wisely; begin metaphysically, begin a long way from the visible, the concrete, and what is called the practical–poorest, meanest of the little heaps of dust that gather around the feet of our pilgrimage! Begin far away. You can always tell, perhaps almost by the voice, whether a man has come up a long way to face this subject, or whether he is making observations upon it that are of the nature of mere obiter dicta, little passing extemporaneous remarks, never thought of by the speaker and never remembered by the hearer. The great comings have been from eternity. Who is this

that cometh up from eternity, with dyed arments from Bozrah, he
that is red in his apparel? Whence obtained he that red dye? We are
plunged into the abysses of the past eternity. So we must have
Christ in the heart, a great secret, a solemn yet joyful silence. Christ
and the heart must have tender communion; they have festive times
that are not marked on the calendar; they muse together, they ask
questions of one another, then come more nearly near; in the soul
there is a mystic wedding without which any other wedding is blasphemy, an oath broken at the altar. The Scripture gives us a large
use of the word heart; it is not mere emotion or affection. "Thou
shalt love the Lord thy God with all thine heart and soul and mind
and strength": the word heart as used here is not a physiological
term, it does not refer to that little muscle we call the heart, and
which we can cut out and put in a bottle; it means the whole nature, soul, spirit, conscience, imagination, and the inmost desires
after light and life and fellowship. Seal mine heart, stamp my whole
nature with the stamp of heaven. I cannot read that stamp until it is
brought to bear, as we have already said, upon the molten wax or
the molten heart; then that which once looked written in the wrong
direction is brought down, and henceforward it is written from the
left to the right, and on to the right, and still on to the right, an endless hallelujah. The heart is the true character: "As a man thinketh in
his heart, so is he." Not what we say in open ordinary conversation,
not what we do in the plain gray daylight of these under skies, but
what we think without saying; when we look at a man without the
man seeing us except in the crude flesh, and thinking he detects a
smile wreathing itself around the supple lips: whereas in our heart
there is a smile, but of contempt and depreciation. As a man, therefore, is in his heart, or thinketh in his heart, so is he in reality. The
Lord seal mine heart, set His seal upon my affections, desires, imaginations, and aspirations; then I shall be true through and through,
my nay will be nay, and my yea will be yea, and there shall be no
breach between mine honor and my fear of social criticism—the
deadliest, meanest nettle that grows in the hedgerows of the world.

Then set thy seal upon mine arm or thine arm: there is a time for protest, confession, public profession of the Eternal Name; there is a ministry of symbolism, there is a way of walking that means that the pilgrim has a sanctuary in view; there is a mysterious influence upon the attitude, the figure, the dress, the whole tone and speech of the life. What is it? We often call it the profession of the name of Christ. Some of us would perhaps under certain circumstances turn our clothing so that we could conceal the seal from everybody; and there is a way to be equally detested, and that is an opening and showing the seal as if making an investment and testimonial and credential of it. There is another way, the way of true modesty, gentle but invincible love that is not ashamed of Jesus or ashamed of the Christian seal. I call for more open, loyal profession of the Son of God.

> Ashamed of Jesus! sooner far
> Let evening blush to own a star.

Have we the seal? The order of the sealing cannot be reversed. We have a miserable trick of inversion. There is a sequence of things, there is a logic of events; things do not happen oddly and eccentrically and unaccountably; there is a stern law of logic: first the heart, then the arm; never, never first the arm, then the heart. The heart will show itself on the arm; the inward and spiritual grace will show itself by outward and visible works, great and beneficent realities. O man of God, never lower thy flag in the presence of the enemy. If you have a conviction, be true to it; though it be not my conviction, it is your conviction wrought out by careful study, verified by deep experience, vindicated by a course long continued of self-sacrifice and honorable service; cling to it, and thou shalt, my brother, be respected by every man who respects truth and adores God. Long, long ago, quite in the time of the old, old folks, people used to speak about adhering to their church; some spoke quaintly about joining the church; others gladly availed themselves of sacred ordinances whereby they might testify from personal experience that God is good and His grace an unfailing fountain of sympathy and helpfulness. Then there came over the times a most cloudy atmosphere; tongues that were once eloquent with honest confession of Christ began to say less and less about the Savior and His Gospel; then they said they had ceased to speak so much because religion was too sacred a thing to be spoken of. It was a lie, the devil's miracle! Show me a mother who is regarding her baby as too sacred to be spoken about, and you show me a woman that I will forever avoid.

What seal have we? What seal has my poor life? Have I ever spoken coldly of my Savior? Has there ever been any mistake as to which side I was upon? Did some person or persons merely suggest, This fellow was also with Him? And did I try to alter the accent of my voice in order to escape suspicion? Did I throw myself into some momentary disguise that I might escape the censure, the acrimonious word, ay, the ax and the saw of persecution? Have I been faithful to my trust? Do I go home and stab myself with a sword two-edged because I was a coward when I ought to have been a hero? Did I sell my Lord for thirty pieces of silver and throw the seal away lest anybody should think I was other than a man of the world and a reveler in poison cups? Do not let us condemn one another; let him that is without sin cast the first stone. I would pray for the modesty that wears the seal right openly, and for the modesty that expresses the loyalty—grand, invincible, unchangeable—of the heart conscious of its redemption by the precious blood of the Son of Man, the Son of God.

Prayer

God be merciful unto us and bless us, and cause His face to shine upon us; God be merciful unto us, sinners! We have broken Thy law, we have defied Thee to Thy face, we have turned our back upon Thee, we have resented Thy reigning over us. Pity us, notwithstanding all! We are foolish and we are wicked, and we know not that which concerns truly and forever our peace and our progress. Thou knowest our frame, Thou rememberest that we are dust: what are we but as a wind that cometh for a little time, and then passeth away? What is our life but a vapor, here a moment and gone? We are as a post passing through the hills and the valleys, hastening upon His errand saying, The King's business requireth haste. We are of yesterday and know nothing. The Lord pity us, and spare us, and let our cry reach His heart, for we are but children of time. Yet we can pray unto God in the name of Jesus Christ; so we are more than the children of time. Thou hast set eternity in us, Thou hast given unto us the music of the everlasting; we know it and feel it and express it, and then we fall back into the commonest mortality. God pity us! What fools we have been! Oh that we had hearkened unto Thy law and kept Thy commandments! Then had our peace been as a river, and our righteousness had been as the waves of the sea. We cannot recover the past, we are helpless as to yesterday; but the blood of Jesus Christ Thy Son cleanseth from all sin; He can go back through all our yesterdays and cleanse them and make them as vessels meet for the Master's use, and can gather up all the scattered days and shape them into one meaning and crown them with one glory. What wonder if our trust is in the Lord, and our expectation from Him that built the heavens? We have no resources; our inventions are many, but poor; we must go back to Thyself, up to Thy throne, and follow out all Thy law by the help of the Cross of Christ Jesus our Lord. Pity us, pity us! We live in Thy pity, we have no hope but in Thy tears and all that those tears mean. Yet Thou art our Rock, and our Refuge, and our Shelter, our Hiding-place, the Church in which we find shelter, asylum, and rest. The days of our years are few, they are but a handful at the most. O be not angry with us, nor plead against us with Thy great power; for who can stand against the thunderbolts of God? May we come to Thee through the Cross, and whisper in Thine ear that we want mercy, and that we die but for the Cross. Amen.

15
Threescore Years and Ten

Preached on Sunday Morning, April 8th, 1900.

The days of our years are threescore years and ten
—Psalm 90:10.

A mere handful, not worth talking about, coming and going and vanishing, and leaving hardly any trace on the memory, but many scars and wounds on the heart. I have no intention of speaking what is known as a conventional sermon; I cannot keep myself sufficiently under control for that. I have wasted seventy years of life, wasted nearly all the days. I have had glimpses of better things and made some efforts after them, but, taking them as a whole, I am ashamed of them, and wish, with some reservations, that I had never lived them. "Would you live your life over again if you could?" Not for ten thousand worlds, every world a diamond. "Has it been so very disappointing and bitter?" Much more so, with exceptions, marked, brilliant, emphatic, forever memorable, the roots and sources of new hymns and psalms and hallelujahs greater than ever blown by the trumpet. But it is on the whole sad enough, mysterious. Why is it so? The little child dying before it has uttered its first word, and the old man sighing to be released, and God reigning over all. They say God is love; this is said by millions of grateful hearts and voices, and I gladly join that infinite chorus: still we sometimes feel so sad that the thorn lives longer than the rose.

And yet the whole ever-shifting mysterious thing we call life is full of hope and parable and morning; still there is the morning star, that child of hope, that center and source of infinite light. There is not a heart here in all these multitudes of people that has not been broken or will be broken. Every man is on the way to his own grave; yea, though he be laughing at the graves of others or heeding not that they are passing by him in blackness, the dead that are going to be buried, yet the fool is on the way to his own last freehold. Oh! That men were wise, that they understood these things, that they would consider the latter end, bring it to bear upon the mutations and the disappointments and sorrows of the present time, and thus secure balance and massiveness and mute music.

There are three things that keep always before me, and that give me a measure of steadiness, and that keep me from suicide; I will tell you what they are, and they may be of help to you sometimes when your knees give way and you are reeling as if drunk, but not with wine.

(1) The first idea that comes to me in these moods is that life is short—yet so long. It is a contradiction in number; it is a paradox in reality. How short our life is! A flash—gone! How long! When will this black-robed procession unwind itself and get around the road and pass the corner that we may not see it any more? Yet life is short; for it is like unto something that is evanescent when it is treated of aright. It is a post among the hills and the valleys; it is a smoke rising up and fading away; a wind that comes for a little time, and then passeth on to blow on other acres and other worlds. What is life? An evaporation, something always going. Now there are some persons that would call this pessimistic. But they do not know what they are talking about. We must be pessimistic before we can be optimistic. We must get down, down, before we can really begin under the divine handling and shaping of things to get up into shape and structure and palace-like magnificence and beauty. Do not put much trust in people that are afraid of the melancholy, that say, Pass on, pass on, another dance! Put no trust in these fools; they live in giddiness, in tramping and stamping, in leaping up and down, in forgetting themselves, in murdering God.

Believe me, they are not optimistic; they are bubbles that rise and gleam and perish, and are forgotten. Yet life, I repeat, is short; short to look back upon, long to look forward to in some aspects and from some starting points. When we were children, how long it was from one Christmas to another! Now we speak of next Christmas as if it were here and simply waiting to be called at the tinkle of a bell. But life being short means a great deal. This is not a commonplace platitude. We think that if a man should say in a great high pulpit, "Man is mortal," that he is speaking a platitude. He is speaking all mysteries in one. We are the platitudes if we make a platitude of so profound an observation as the mortality of man. How suggestive it is! If life is short, what are the best things in it, the wisest, the deepest? Let me get hold of them. If life is short, what is the most important thing to be done? There are things to be done that are of varying importance and degrees of value; tell me, O sir, if thou knowest, which is which, where is the accent, the emphasis, the responsibility; I do not want to fool away my time, I want to get hold of the most living, pulsing, throbbing moments, and get out of them what immortality I can. If life is short, then I think it will be wiser on my part to leave the mysterious alone; I think so. Why so? Because life is short. We cannot do everything: we had better, therefore, make a selection, and attend to those things we can get hold of, and work to the soul's best advantage. Why should I, with so few days at command, trouble myself seriously and to the possible destruction of my soul by constructing theories about the constitution of the Godhead? Why should I break up my life by trying to reconcile the various theories of the creation and existence of the universe? I have not time; if I had talent, genius, inspiration, in these directions, I have not time, I am but a pilgrim, I can tarry but a night: O tell me what is the thing to be done now? So many people are mooning away their time as if they had a whole eternity to spend, and they pay so much attention to things that can help the individual soul but little if any at all, and they neglect the weightier matters of the law. Tell me that my age will be ten thousand times ten thousand years, and I say, My brothers, halt! Let us look into this weed: how did it come to be what it is, what other weeds are there round about its neighborhood, what is the relation of these various and apparently competing weeds; and halt, let us gather a thousand little shells from the seashore, and number them, and appraise them, and wonder about how long they have been in their evolution. There might be some little grain of sense in that, but when you tell me that the days of our years are threescore years and ten, I must reconsider the whole calculation, and get to understand if I can which is the more important, which the most important, what is the thing to be done now.

What is your life? Seventy years. Nothing of the kind; this is quite a poet's mistake. My life threescore years and ten? Oh no, no. What are you up to about five? Well, not much. There may be five years struck off the seventy for many purposes of life; now you are sixty-five. How much of your time do you spend in sleep? Why, I am told that from six to eight hours out of the twenty-four should be given to sleep. Why, that is a third of your lifetime. And what is the third of sixty-five? And deduct that from sixty-five; why, the days of your years are getting down to about forty. And how many of those days and years will you spend in weariness and weakness, under the doctor's care and the nurse's attention? And you think the business in the City is in great danger because you are not there. What does that bring your life down to? It takes off some years. So it may. And then you have what you call your holidays and recreations—yes—when you are supposed not to be strenuously engaged in life, but to be recruiting and renewing and gathering up your strength for some further effort. How does your age stand now? You began with a store of threescore years and ten, according to poetic license; where are you now? So this little quantity is encroached upon sometimes, turned to waste: and what time have we for the deeper thought concerning the deeper life? Well, we are so busy that we have abolished family devotional exercises; our fathers used to be given to that sort of thing, but now—the train, the bus, and I am due in the City in an hour. How much time is there for the really important and solid thinking that ought to form part of every life that aims to end in something worthy of manhood?

That is the first thought that gives me steadiness. Life is short; therefore I can intermeddle with only a few things; therefore I had better consider which are the truly great and worthy things; therefore I must buy up the opportunity, redeem the time, and make the most of this dower more than gold with which God has blessed my personality. Then life is so long. Oh, when will the reunion take place? When will the children be here again? And even if I have to meet her at the train or at the coach, will I know her very clearly? She will be so tall, so changed; she is leaving her girlhood and childhood behind her: surely that is not the child I came to meet; I do not quite recognize her. How then does the recognition take place? On her side? She recognizes you; middle-aged men do not change so much as the girl changes. There are shaping and settling times in life, and then there is a period in life, say from figure one to figure three, where little change takes place, and in that period we think we are getting rest and hope: whereas it may be but a kind of daylight slumber, a forbidden and interdicted dream. Poor man! Think of thy life: what a small thing it is and how great, greater than the sun. Pascal said, "I am greater than the sun." How so, philosopher? "The sun," replied the sage, "could fall and crush me, but I am greater in that I should know that I was overpowered, but the sun would not be conscious of victory." Our greatness is in our consciousness, its largeness, its intelligence, its sanctification; that is how we stand.

(2) And not only is life short, but life needs help. The strongest man will say that; however rich a man is, he cannot do without some other man. There are times when it is so dark that even the outputting of the hand is a gospel. Oh to feel a holding hand, a familiar grip! It makes the darkness light; it brings sustenance to the soul. We cannot do without one another. The weakest may help the strongest. Paul said, "Brethren, pray for us." There is the mightiest man in the Church asking some man and woman heart to pray

for him, when the water is deep and cold and the night so dark. It is a wonderful thing this, that we all need help, if not today, yet tomorrow. A man has ten thousand acres, and yet he feels sometimes as if the hug of a little child round his neck would be worth the whole ten thousand ten times over. The man cannot live upon acres; the man cannot live upon balances at the bank; he does not despise any of them, but he puts them into their right place, and he says, "Oh for the touch of a vanished hand and the sound of a voice that is still!" And sometimes he thanks his little lonely fire for throwing shadows on the wall which he can turn into pictures, into more than animated photographs. Let the very humblest man know that he may one day have it in his power to help the very strongest man he has ever known. It may not be in any grand and dramatic way. A child can open the gate for a horseman; a mouse may let a lion at liberty; and the very poorest creature can put a terrible check upon atheism. A poor woman left with her eight children and hardly a crust in the house or a coal in the grate may fall apraying, and open the Bible at some grand psalm, and wet it with her tears, and pledge God to it. And somehow, she could not tell how, but somehow the angel came and help arrived, and the darkness was mitigated, and the morning dawned upon the far-off hills, and she took heart again; and boy after boy went out and turned out to be good and helpful and useful, and at the end of a long period of trial she says to the atheist, "What has your no-God done for you, you fool? This is what my living God did for me; what has your no-God done for you?" And before you can destroy that woman's argument you have to destroy that woman's character. She is living; she is there to sign, seal, deliver, corroborate.

That is the second thought that comes to me, that life needs help and true sympathy, just a hand to ease in an extremity.

(3) And a third thought is that no help that can be given to man is so gracious, so complete, as the help that is given by the Son of God. On these three grounds I stand; millions stand on the same grounds and praise the same Savior. Jesus Christ comes to us when

other people are engaged with the feast and are pledged to the dance and have no time for old sorrow and wordless misery. Jesus Christ says, "Call upon Me in the day of trouble"; nobody else will want to see you; call upon Me; look in your diary, and you will find the day of trouble is a disengaged day, a vacant line; others will come to you on all the other days, but call upon Me, and I will fill up that space for you. Jesus Christ will go where no one else can go. Jesus Christ discusses with us, so to say, the very deepest subjects; Jesus Christ never shrank from any topic. There are those about us who say, Do not mention that, if you please, for that is very ghostly; what do you think of the weather? What is the prospect for the crops? When is the next merry-making to take place? O tell me, and do not talk about these subjects! Never trust such people with a single coin of the realm; they are rotten; they have no souls; they have outlived themselves. Believe in the people who believe in tears and tenderness and healing sympathy; they are your real friends and your best friends and your truly approachable friends, and the greater they are the more approachable they are. Jesus Christ never casts any of His trusting ones off. The devil is always getting rid of his clients; he does not know them after a certain time; when they have drunk themselves up to the point of satiety, he shakes them off; he says, These fools! I need not trouble about them anymore; let them go into the gutter, and into any river the gutter can find a channel into; I must be after the young, the fresh, and the beautiful, and those who are comparatively inexperienced, and I am content to let the others alone. I have seen a man who represented millions rot, and I should have considered it a dishonor to have been called in to inter his bones; I would not be called in; there is a pestilence, a reek, that it is dangerous to go near. But Jesus Christ has gone to people who have had one foot in hell; to one man He said, Today thou shalt be with Me in the unseen, the Hadean world, the paradise that can only yet be dreamed about. Jesus Christ can give comfort when no other one can give any consolation. Oh, He has a sevenfold voice! I have heard Him, so to say, when He has spoken to scribes and Pharisees, so that they have gotten angry with Him to the point of madness and murder, or have been insulted and affronted and humbled, and have gone out like stricken dogs. I never knew Him so gentle in His voice as when He spoke to people that had got wrong and who knew it, and who came near Him thinking that they could elude His eyes and yet steal His virtue; but they could not. He said, Rise—mother, sister, friend—rise, thy faith hath saved thee. People went up to Jesus Christ fifty and sixty and seventy years old, and came back from the touch of His robe, children in their teens, so vernal looking, so tender, so recruited, so renewed. And He is the same living Christ today, and as near to us as ever He could be in the flesh, yea, more nearly near, for He is nearer to us than we ever could be to ourselves.

> Happy, if with my latest breath
> I may but gasp His name;
> Preach Him to all, and cry in death,
> "Behold, behold the Lamb!"

I have seen the Savior in sick-chambers these fifty years of ministry; I have met Him again and again, as it were, by appointment of His own making, and I have seen Him in the sick-chamber—no woman so gentle, no nurse so careful, no doctor so healing. He enters the sick-chamber without opening the door; He considers the fever that is burning the patient, and says, No noise must be made here. So the Savior came into the room as the light came. Who ever knew the sun to thunder at the window, and say, I want to come in? No one. O the might of silence, O the poetry of stillness! He has always been gentler to the patient or sufferer than to anyone else in the room. Only the dying have seen Death. We think we have seen Death, but we have not. To us he comes as King of Terrors; he is going to commit robbery on our own premises, he is going to impoverish us. But how easy to die! It is the living that is the hard part. When such friends die, who has really died? We will say with the great poet that when such friends part 'tis the survivor dies.

Words for Preachers

It is happy for him that teacheth others, to be himself righteous. It is absurd in him that stammers, to teach others to speak plain. Great learning and good living are a fair couple, a fit match; it is a pity to part them. —*Adams, 1654*

That preacher who presseth a duty (though with never so much zeal), but doth no chalk out the way how it is to be done, is like one that brings a man to a door that is locked, and bids him go into the house; but gives him no key to open it; or that sends a company to sea, but lends them no chart by which they should steer their course.—*Gurnall, 1617–1679*

The praise of a good speech standeth in words and matter: matter, which is as a fair and well-featured body; elegance of words, which is as a neat and well-fashioned garment. Good matter, slobbered up in rude and careless words, is made loathsome to the hearer; as a good body, misshapen with unhandsome clothes. Elegancy without soundness is no better than a nice vanity. Although, therefore, the most hearers are like bees, that go all to the flowers; never regarding the good herbs, that are of as wholesome use as the other of fair show; yet, let my speech strive to be profitable, plausible, as it happens. Better the coat be misshapen than the body.—*Hall, 1574–1656*

As a careful and skillful surgeon, who, having patients that are diseased with sundry grievous wounds and sores, and having provided drawing plasters and corrosives for the same, doth not commit them to his patients, that they should lay and apply them to their sores and wounds, lest they should withdraw and keep back the same plasters from their sores and wounds, and so seek to free themselves from the smart and grief which would ensue and follow upon the laying to of the said plasters and corrosives to their festered sores and wounds, and therefore he will not trust them therewith, but doth himself both lay and apply the same plasters and corrosives to their sores, and will himself cut out the corrupt and rotten flesh that groweth to their wounds: even so it is not enough that a preacher should deliver unto his auditors and parishioners a general doctrine, and so leave the application thereof to themselves, for (as it is commonly said) that which is spoken to all is spoken to none; but he ought so to apply his doctrine, that everyone of his hears may have his portion, and thereby well perceive that it is spoken to them—as the prophets and apostles have done.—*Cawdray, 1609*

Prayer

We trusted that it had been He which should have redeemed Israel; and, behold, He is on the Cross, helpless as the thief on either side. There is a dead trust in our hearts, our ambition is perished; we thought it had been He which should have redeemed Israel; and, behold, we have gathered at the festival of sorrow. What shall we say? For we had trusted that it had been He which should have redeemed Israel. We hear the cry, He saved others; Himself he cannot save. We see men wagging their heads at Him; already His head has been bruised by the cruel thorn. We are taunted; we have nothing to say; we were His followers, and we trusted that it had been He which should have redeemed Israel. Give us patience to wait, and give us strength to drink this cup of bitterness. What is Thy world as we see it at present but a great feast of sorrow, a festival of bitter aloes? Behold, our souls are stricken with distress and misery. Thou dost drink of the cup first, and then Thou dost pass it round; now my turn, now his turn, now hers, now the child's, and the cup goes round till every throat swells because of that wash of poison. Hear us in our ignorance; stop not our wailing misery, for the very wailing does us good. Help us to wait today, and tomorrow, and the third day; then perhaps we may see the rising glory, the descending and eternal kingdom. Amen.

16

The Christian Idea of Death

Preached on Good Friday Morning, April 13th, 1900.

To die is gain–Philippians 1:21.

I think the text would read more strongly if we were to omit that intruded "is" in both cases. Let us delete this intrusive verb, and look at the text in this naked English: "For me to live–Christ, and to die–gain." That is nobler poetry; that is a better scansion of the poem. O Death, thy sting? Strike out the "where is." Grave, thy victory? It is a giant's taunt, and terrific and derisive challenge and rebuke. "To die." Why does man talk about death? He knows nothing concerning it but what he has been told or what he has seen; he goes wholly upon observation and report. Yet man thinks he is familiar with death and knows its secret. No living man knows what death is; do not speak of it; we do but show our ignorance; we cannot now rise to the height of that great argument. We say, looking at our dying friend and at those who watch the solemn scene, Poor man! I am sorry that he is about to sustain this great loss. We know nothing about it. We are sorry for his impending dissolution. That may be atheistic talk, a proud and ignorant vanity. Who dies? The living. They say it is sweet and easy to die; preparation can be made for dying, the bed can be tossed into softness, and applications can be made to the icy feet or the burning head. Something can be done for the dying; but what can be done for the living, for the desolate one who has to be turned out of the room, so to say, where the great sacrament of death is administered? And what has he to go

461

to but to an infinite darkness, an emptiness that cannot be described? He left the room—he left heaven. No man has seen death except the dying man. That is an infinite comfort to those who think tenderly and solemnly about final catastrophes. We look on and see nothing but paleness, weakness, utterest exhaustion, and watch the panting, panting, panting breath. What do we know what the panting heart saw, what reminiscences it called up, what old familiar faces gathered in cloud outlines before the closing eyes? Who can tell? Let sanctified fancy, led and sustained by inspired revelation, lead the way, and see what it may of heaven in this dying which is gain. What made us take this high view of death? The death of Christ is the answer. That death explains all other death, enriches it with all manner of possibility. If Christ died, then . . . and after that "then" a whole heaven of dream and a whole Canaan of certainty may come.

A most curious mind is this of the Apostle Paul. He thinks aloud while he is apparently only writing with his hand or with the hand of another man. This is a monologue, this is the soul overheard, caught in its most secret and sacred whispers; what a privilege that we may hear the greatest soul that ever lived in the Christian Church talking! "For me to live is Christ, and to die is gain": I am in a strait between two, having a desire to depart and be with Christ—that is what I want, it is far better—nevertheless, to abide in the flesh is more needful for you; I know that; I am in a strait between the two; to die might be gain, not to me, a poor dying man, but to the cause. Some promote the cause by dying for it; it was so Christ lifted up His Cross, until its magnitude turned the firmament into a cloud, and its glory abashed the sun. We think our work is done when we die; probably in this matter, as in many other matters, we are quite wrong; it may be that by dying in harness, being brave to the last, and working the furrow only halfway through or wholly through, we are doing more by dying than we could do by living. Let our ignorance hold its breath, let our impiety dismiss its crude and often blasphemous dreams and anticipations, and let God have His own way in His own Church among His own people. It might be a cowardly thing to desire to die if by dying we mean getting out of it, shaking it off, having nothing more to do with it, with its anxiety and its burdensomeness and its agony; that would be cowardice, and we should put Christ to a blushing shame if we talked so and yet professed to be the followers of His Cross. To die may be the greatest contribution we can make to the faith which we have endeavored to express in words, and which now we must in one gigantic final effort endeavor to express in sacrifice.

The religion of Christ is a grand religion to die in. It is so fearless, it is familiar with the spirit of eternity; it has grown the soul into a reverent familiarity with things big as infinity and glorious as incarnated light. This is the sign of our growth, that the things which once affrighted us now exercise upon us all the subtle power and fascination of a charm or spiritual enchantment. Once we feared to look upon a dead body; in the England that I can remember the poor dead flesh was set in a dark room, with a few dim-lighted candles just to mitigate the darkness; and there were watchers, people who sat up all night near the dead or near the chamber where the dead were coffined; everything was in a sad, hopeless hush; few dare go near the dead. We have not so learned the Christ; the death-chamber has been turned into the center of the house, the only bright spot in the whole habitation. What may we not learn from that image of triumph and that image of rest? That is the natural fruition of true faith in Christ, who "both died, and rose," as if the dying and the rising were part of the same act, hardly a pause between the going and the coming, the departing and the return. So the literature of experience has undergone a new punctuation. We breathe better than we used to breathe when we speak the music of the Word of God; we take more time, we take a deeper inspiration, and while we are deepening the inspiration, behold, the miracle is wrought, and the breath which we expected to expend in some threnody upon desolation and loneliness we spend on the All hail! And behold, we face the Christ we missed but for a moment. So it is in its own sense and way with our human fellowships and disfellowships, with our comings and goings, with our wedding today and our desolation tomorrow; we must breathe better, with a deeper wisdom, with a firmer grasp of the facts and realities of human experience. Death is full of visions; we have caught some of them on the face immediately after the last breath has been expended. If we had eyes to see, we should notice on that whitening face a trailing glory. The vulgar eyes cannot see it, the swine eyes of the field can look upon no such sight, but the radiant eyes of the soul, washed by the tears of grief and made beautiful by the expectancy of hope, can see even on the paling face where the glory was, outlined angels, in the last sacramental moment.

Christian death is full of brightness that living eyes cannot see, and full of hope that this poor, struggling, hesitating, self-contradicting experience of ours cannot adequately spell or interpret as one interprets who has the gift of telling what a dream is. We must be very careful therefore how we interpret the experience of those who die. Blessed are they that die in the Lord, for they rest, and their interpretation follows them, and we, too late, see meanings in things we did not understand and in actions which we were ignorantly inclined to resent. When we know all we shall forgive all and ask that all may be forgiven. There is not a wretch among those out of hell who has not some redeeming point. God can see it, Christ created it, the Holy Spirit will work upon it, and I know not what may take place between the here of time and the there of eternity. I repeat, therefore, that the Christian religion is an excellent religion to die with. It is hopeful, confident, poetical, expectant; it hears voices that the dull ears of the body cannot hear, and it sees sights hidden from the eyes of the flesh. The history of Christian dying would be the most thrilling history in literature. But it cannot be written, we can only see a verse or a chapter here and there, and from these broken fragments we may infer somewhat of the dignity and the restfulness and the triumph of dying in Christ. Weep for yourselves, do not weep for the Christian dying. It is quite right for you to weep, because you are still in the body; you are still environed by the world, the flesh, and the devil; your nerves are exposed to rough winds and to touches that have no gentleness in them; cry, relieving your misery by the rivers of your grief, but do not grieve for those who have gone. They are not the authors of misery, they are the inspirers of wisdom and confidence and hope.

Some will say this would be delightful and most gratefully acceptable if it could be proved. I can prove every word of it, and will prove it now. There is no difficulty about the proof. If we have been thinking so, then we are worse infidels than we imagined. All this poesy, Christian reverie, and marvelous transcript of the soul can be established upon a rock of facts, and by the help of God I will so establish it in a few moments. The question which is imaginatively put to the preacher is this: How can you prove that the Christian religion is a great and sufficient religion to die in? My immediate, emphatic, final reply is: Because it is an excellent religion to live in. The life interprets the death. The life is the standard of everything. You want a basis of facts? You shall have it; in the name of the Father, and the Son, and the Holy Ghost, you shall have it, and you shall not leave this opportunity of seeing somewhat of the kingdom of heaven, saying that this matter has not been proved. You may tell lies, but not here; you cannot lie your way out of this great argument, the argument of life. What is it, then, that precedes and prepares for the great triumph, the triumph of Christian faith? The discipline of faith destroys the idea of its being a fancy. You have talked much about the reverie, but not a word about the discipline. That is where you go wrong, by looking at a hemisphere instead of looking at the total globe; you took the matter in parts and patches, and not as a grand and completed and reticulated mosaic composition, marvelous in its parts and in its combinations. What is this Christian discipline? I will tell you. I will ask you to admit this if you are logically inclined, though logic is often a lie: If the end which we can test is good, the end that we cannot yet test is likely to be good too. That ought to be perceived by the very slowest minds.

To enjoy a Christian death we must first live a Christian life. But will not a Christian life be all sunshine? Far from it. Is there not only one season in the year of Christian life, and is not that season summer? No, no; there is a fourfold season in the Christian life, and we must go through the whole process if we would reach the happy end. Is not this Christian life fanciful, sentimental, and indeed, quoth my lord, in his velvet slippers and on his hair hearthrug—is not this a little what we call superstitious? No, and I will prove it. You sitting there under your gilded ceiling, never having done a day's work in your life, never having divided a meal with a fellow pilgrim, never having known the pinch of poverty and the desolation of orphanage, you sitting there and saying, Is not this a little superstitious? Why, sir, you are an insult to society; you are a blot upon the world of God. It is not for you to bear witness in this court, no counsel for plaintiff or for defendant has ever asked you to enter the witness box and swear that you are about to tell either truth or lie; you are not wanted in this argument, you are out of it. What, then, is the argument from the Christian life of belief? How does the Christian life begin? It begins in repentance, and penitence is no superstition; when a man's heart is broken because of the wrong he has done, do not call it superstition. The man says, I have broken the commandments of God; I have broken human hearts; I have insulted holy memories; verily I have done the things I ought not to have done and I have left undone the things that I ought to have done; I know it, and I condemn myself, and I curse myself, and I dare not look up into the blue vault of heaven, for its very holiness of life would rebuke me and strike me dead; God be merciful unto me a sinner! Is that superstition? Will you gather up your warmed and coddled feet, and drink your reeking liquor and say, After all there may be a good deal of superstition in the Christian religion? Are you so far lost to sense of right and justice, and historical reality and human experience as to tell that lie over again? Have you no knowledge of human misery, human tears, human broken-heartedness? Have you not been touched by your own son's return to his father's backdoor, because he dare not come in at the front door, crying in the cold chill of the night, "I have sinned against heaven and in thy sight, and am no more worthy to be called thy son"? Take your pipe out of your mouth, and throw your liquor away, and go and tell the boy of your own blood and muscle that he is a little superstitious. You cannot; you will fling everything away that you may be able to get at him, and throw your arms around him, and reinstate him, and he shall be the dearer to you because of his penitent misery.

What after penitence? Self-crucifixion. How long shall the self-crucifixion last? Forever, throughout all earthly life, through the whole circle of the little forever of time as we know it. Will not God forgive a man? Yes, but the man cannot forgive himself; that is where it is. The heart is still broken that you broke. But I have prayed to God and besought His forgiveness, and I think He has extended pardon to me. Not unless you first ask pardon of the broken heart; you cannot be serving the devil in one corner, and going and asking God's forgiveness in the other. It must be an out-and-out affair this, a thorough down-to-the-base-line affair; there must be no keeping back; a clean breast must be made of it, and the parties that have been injured must be told about the injury, and asked to exercise forgiveness upon you, the wretch of wretches, because you desolated a life and ruined a home. Is this a sort of superstition? Dare you mock us by using that interdicted word? We did the sin, we have told about the sin, we have kept back no part of the price, we have fallen flat dead down before the sinned against, and have said, Forgive us for God's sake and Christ's sake, and we will spend the rest of our days in trying to heal the wound we inflicted. Do not call that superstition, if you please, or you will hurt the heart of the whole world, and you will prove yourself unworthy to abide in a world which you have thus wounded by charging upon it hollowness, insincerity, and falsehood.

Well, then, suppose we have repented of our sins, and sought forgiveness through our Lord Jesus Christ; suppose we have seen our own unworthiness and have been penitent in consequence, and suppose that we have utterly and absolutely received absolution from those we have wronged because we have first received it from the God we have dishonored, does it rest there? No; we shall get all the superstition out of it presently; the rest of the forgiven life has to be spent in the devoted and unselfish service of other people. You thought it was reverie, you thought it was rhetorical transport, you even hinted that there might be a streak of sentimentality about it. We shall thrash that out of you before we have done; we have got you to confess your sin and your shame, and we have driven you to God in Christ for the pardon of your sin, and we have made the rest of your life an endeavor to repair the injury you have done; and now we say, Every man is your brother, and the lower he is, the more gentle you must be to him; you must go out after that which was lost until you find it, you must think better of every other man than you have ever thought, and you must devote your life to the poor, and sit up all night with the lonely one who is in the last valley; and when he is gone, you must take care of his children; you must see that they do not want; the case that you know not you must search out, you must be eyes to the blind and feet to the lame, and hands to those that are helpless. Now, sir, say is this a religion to be flouted as sentimental and somewhat superstitious?

And I will add one more word—that you cannot do all these things of your own strength. This is not a mechanical arrangement; morality is not an attitude. We have lost our sense of the moral by our use of the remoter word, the ethical. We must get back to right, wrong, and not lose ourselves in new terms and ways and ideas and clouds. O hear me, angels of God, devils in hell, men upon the earth! This is not a religion to be taunted with being a transport, a reverie, or a dream.

Words for Preachers

I do not hesitate for a moment to give it as my opinion that what may be called the alarming style of preaching is most adapted to convert the impenitent. I do not mean gross and revolting descriptions of eternal torment, nor the carrying out into minute detail what may be called the material and corporal representations of the punishment of the wicked. This is offensive and disgusting, and generally defeats its own purpose, especially when done, as is often the case, in a harsh, cold, and unfeeling manner. What I mean by alarming preaching is an exhibition of the purity and unbending strictness of the law, together with such a method of applying this strict rule to the heart and conduct of the individual sinner as is calculated to awaken and startle his conscience; a faithful portraiture of the heinousness of sin, stripped of all the excuses which our deceitful nature is so skillful in framing for its defense; a careful discrimination between mere reformation and a renewed heart; the indispensable necessity of regeneration, and the absolute certainty that every man will perish who dies without it; a solemn manifestation of the immaculate holiness of God, and of His retributive justice in the punishment of the wicked; an impressive description of the solemnities of judgment, together with a chastened but awaking account of the torments of those who reject the sacrifice of Christ and refuse the offer of mercy. These are the subjects explained and enforced in suitable language, with close application to the heart, pungent appeals to the conscience, and with an affectionate, earnest, solemn manner, that are likely to arouse the careless and convert the sinner. I do not mean, of course, that we should make such topics the incessant subjects of our ministerial addresses. A perpetual denunciatory strain would at length render those for whom it was intended carelessly familiar with the terrors of the Lord. The timid would come at length to listen to the most appalling tempest without alarm if it always thundered. But what I mean is, that while a minister's habitual strain of preaching should be so discriminating as to leave no unconverted sinner at a loss with whom to class himself, whether with believers or unbelievers, it should not infrequently contain those allusions to, and descriptions of, the wrath of God, which, like the distant rumblings of the gathering and approaching storm, should drive men to the refuge provided by infinite mercy in the Cross of Christ. No one will flee for shelter who does not see a tempest at hand; and then only will the shelter be valued when the storm is believed to be coming. That this style of preaching has been the most useful could be easily proved by an appeal to the history of the Church.–*James*

Prayer

Behold is Thy hand wide open to us today, and Thou art as it were waiting to make our souls glad and enlarge the light of the morning. How good is God! And what wonder that men should say of Thee, God is love? For the victory is so overcoming, triumphant, that we have no memory of assault or danger or momentary overthrow. We bless Thee for these special mornings, these Eastertides, that come variously and when they will, not at our asking or bidding, but at Thy sending; may we say to Thee, Send more of them, for our hearts are often in the valley, and there is no fountain to give us water. Thou knowest our frame; Thou rememberest that we are dust; we are a wind that cometh for a little time, and then passeth away, and Thou art very merciful and pitiful, even so that mothers stand back and wonder at the tears of God. We thank Thee for all Thy love and care; we bless Thee for every Easter morning; we thank Thee for every bird that makes the morning glad with song. Thou hast done great things for us whereof we are glad; we knew it must come, from our reading of Thy wondrous Word, that some Man must arise to fight death and overthrow the monster. We were watching for His coming; we thought we heard His footsteps; far away there seemed to be some sound of a new footfall: for one said, Thou didst not leave my soul in hell, neither didst Thou suffer Thy holy one to see corruption; and another said, I know that my Redeemer liveth, and that He shall stand at the latter day upon the earth. We heard these voices, but we did not see the Deliverer, but in these latter days we have seen Him, within these handful of thousands of years we have beheld the victory over death. We are redeemed by His blood; we are inspired by His Spirit; Christ hath abolished death; Christ hath brought life and immortality to light in the Gospel. It is the religion of the morning star, the religion of new hopes, of dawnings, of coming things, of the beginning of the end and the end of the beginning: an infinite and blessed mystery. Thou hast brought us round to another Eastertime; so we get younger and younger by this revolution of the years, and presently we shall be where there is naught but youth, the oldest being the youngest and the youngest the oldest, and all ages lost in a great commonalty of rest and love. To some the year has been a year of weariness; some have nearly committed suicide through the pressure of despair—that chief of the fiends of hell; and some have said, though they had the harp in hand, My feet had well-nigh slipped, I had nearly gone over the brink; for I saw strange things, yea, as if life itself had been abandoned of God and wickedness were triumphant; but I have come to the sanctuary-house today with my harp still in my hand, and it is in this house God will teach my fingers the way of music. And some have grown flowers all the year round; if they could not grow them outside, they have grown them inside; they have had the flowers; the whole year, notwithstanding snowing and blowing of mad winter, has been a year of flowers and one continuous summer delight. We are all here before God to speak each in his own tongue, the tongue of his despair and sorrow and mystification, and prosperity and thankfulness, and we are but one Man, though many men; we represent one humanity, the humanity Thou didst shape into Thine own likeness as far as omnipotence could go. Oh the ruin of it, the black sin, the self-idolatry, the madness and the dance in the pit! But Jesus is a name of redemption, recovery, restoration; He creates us anew, creates us according to the infinite purpose of the Divine love. It is enough. Oh let the whole April sky shake out of its lap all the blessings we can hold! And today we will bless Thee for the Savior who died and rose and revived. Amen.

17
Eastertide

Preached on Easter Sunday Morning, April 15th, 1900.

Christ both died, and rose—Romans 14:9.

How singular is the genius of man! How odd is man wholly and all the year round! What a half-mind he has! He has no difficulty about that Christ died; there he may be said to be almost orthodox: he is a poor creature who has no patches of piety about him. It is when we come to the "and rose" that man shows how little of a man he can be. Keep him to little things, and it is wonderful how big he is upon his own scale; take him out into wider areas where the horizon is the fence that shuts in his own fields, and if you do not watch him with many tigers and wolves, he will be an infidel; he seems to like that kind of luxury. Oh keep him to little things; let him have his Noah's ark and his toys and his bricks, and let him build them and throw them down and build them up again; and what a wonderful genius is man! But keep him away from the poetry, the ideality, and the divinity of "and rose." Because he never rose he thinks no one else could ever rise. He is just like a water-tank; every plumber knows that water cannot rise above its own level. So there is man, a believer and a denier. He is absolutely certain that Christ died; there he would accept a challenge to public discussion, he would be armed with Roman authors, historians, and poets, and he would delight to encounter the man who denied that Christ died. He has classic proof: he calls pagan witnesses. Now take him to the other court; he has neither law nor philosophy; he is weak as other men. Oh keep him in the lower court; away down, further down, and he can argue where nobody disputes; he is no chancery lawyer, he knows nothing of the black letter law of the Eternal. The Apostle Paul had no doubt about the resurrection of Christ; he says, "Christ both died, and rose." No question ever occurred to the early Christian mind as to any difficulty about the resurrection: the event was so new it would be like disputing the dew of the morning; there is was, the thing was immediately present; it was a new eye in the midst of things looking over all the cloud and through it, and testifying to a new and glorious power. Paul turned the resurrection of Jesus Christ into an argument, and into a poem, and into an inspiration. He lived on it, he risked the whole Christian fabric upon the resurrection: "If Christ be not risen from the dead, then is our preaching vain," and that would be nothing; but "your faith is also vain," you are harboring a dead trust; you are mocking your own soul.

Jesus Christ died on Friday and rose again on what we call the Sunday, and we have by the providence of God, ever good and large, gathered around an empty tomb, and then around a risen Lord. I would be beautiful if in the hands of a true artist to compare the Friday and the Sunday. They belong to one another; the Sunday would not be half so bright but for the Friday. Your joy would not be so exquisite if there were not a historic background of tears and sorrow and speaking silence. That work was apparently well done on the Friday. That is what we call root-and-branch work. Why do the heathen rage? They are going to put an end to this sort of thing in Judea and in all the world; they are going to stamp it out. Poor stampers! Poor feet that stamp on such granite! The work, let us keep in view, of the Friday was well done; it would have required mechanical force to get any nail out. This was no work of trifling. Are you sure the arrangement is satisfactory as to this malefactor's crucifixion? Yes, we are quite certain. You speak hoarsely. We speak truly; every nail is fast to the wood, and the wood is no cedar; the whole thing is ready; we have caught this man at last, and we will stamp him out. That is better, I like that ascending inflexion. You are sure that it is all right? Quite right; before sunset he will be utterly dead. But may they not be making some arrangement of a kind that is open to suspicion? No, have you no fear about that; ha, ha! why, they have all forsaken him, and fled; all his friends have gone downhill; so there is no fear; this thing will in a few hours be stamped out. So far, so good. We have made an end of this business; we have stamped out a character, we have wrecked a claim; we have killed a bastard royalty; home! and let the wine be generous in quantity and quality. That was no lost Friday, that was no jerrywork, that was not done by men who wielded the hammer reluctantly and wanted to flee anywhere in order to play at football; this was workmanship; this was reality. That was Friday. We felt all along that this wonderful problem of Death (spell it with a large capital) had to be faced sooner or later; it was wearing out the patience of the world; it was mining the towers which men had built; it was blighting the generations that seemed to be just peeping up above the horizon line; at last men's hearts got weary; they did their best to turn old age into poetry; they wrote letters and essays upon it; one of the most refined of the Romans wrote a book upon old age; they have watered that ivy very much, and they have dreamed dreams about it, and they have told the old man that he was looking younger than ever—so softly and tenderly do men lit when they want to beat off the ogre Despair that threatens a man's life and joy. Yea, and also long before these refined classic writers spoke about old age there was a man who said, I know that my goel liveth; these boils are cruelly painful, my house is blown down and all my children are swept away, but I know that my redeemer liveth. He kept the fire as bright as he could on the altar of hope. Another said, Thou didst not leave my soul in hell, neither didst Thou suffer Thine holy one to see corruption. But the battle had not yet been fought; the world has always had a singing hope at its heart, a harp-playing power, a voice that could sing though it was often damped with tears, and there was sometimes in that thrilling voice a note of fatigue; still, it was there, and it kept the world alive.

Now there is some great fight being fought this Friday. They have nailed His hands, and they have nailed His feet, and they have pierced His side, and the environment seems to vindicate and justify their villainy. It is all over; Job would withdraw his faith, and David would cease his song. Rest awhile, pause for a day or two; never hasten God; never try to force your own destiny; be great by being quiet. Now comes the day on which everything will be silent. It must be so, because this is the third day that the Malefactor Himself indicated. He was always so bold. He did not say, I will rise in three centuries, when you will all be dead and no man will be here who could charge Me with My own words; He said, On the third day I will rise again. It was a fair challenge, square, complete. When was Jesus timid, cowardly, uncertain? When did He, if not prevaricate, yet seem to handle words with such tricks of magic as to perplex and bewilder those who heard them? Never. He said before the Friday, The Friday is coming, my friends, I warn you of it; I go to Jerusalem to suffer many things of the scribes and the elders and of the chief priests, and I go to be killed, and on the third day—He knew that the hearts were breaking that loved Him, and that the third day was about as long as they could keep up at all even in solitude and secrecy and even under the apparent abandonment of their own faith in His personality and purpose. But on the third day they will give way. The soul can only hold on for a given time: if the next post but one does not bring that letter I shall die. "As it began to dawn toward the first day of the week." He did not keep them long waiting on that day, "it began to dawn"; it is not said that it fully dawned, it predawned, it sent forth itself in a kind of mimic dawning; it would require the eye of an expert look-out on one of life's ships to see that dawning. But it is always so in Christianity; it is always after its fullest noonday beginning to dawn; it never exhausts its hope; its trumpet has always another bold tune in it. It seems sometimes as if the faith were overthrown, but "it began to dawn toward"—there was a great silent wondrous onward movement. Enough! Where God begins He continues, He completes. So there was that morning a hailing. Hail! It was one of the last words His own ears had heard but a few hours ago: "Hail, King of the Jews! Hail!" and He said, All hail! Stop, stand still! This is a great day in Israel and in the world.

So we meet on resurrection morning. We know that Christ died, we may as certainly know that Christ rose. This is part of a great evolution, part of a great demonstration of Divine energy which no man can comprehend and which no man can arrest. We can do nothing against the truth, but God hath been pleased to permit us to do something for the truth. What can man do? He can kill every minister of truth, but he cannot kill the ministry. When will we look, at the right points? Is the missionary dead? Yes, but missions are still going on, and nothing can hinder their advance. Is not that the blood of a head that has been clubbed to death by Rarotongan savages? Yes, that is the blood of the martyr of Erromanga. Is mission work therefore done? No, it is beginning to dawn toward—You can kill the minister, but not the ministry. When I was but a boy I was preaching in a little village, and while I was talking, I had no doubt with great energy and possibly with some incoherency, a drunken brawling man shouted, "We will stone you out of the town!" And I, at eighteen, said, "You can easily stone me out of the town, but you cannot stone the truth out of the town." You can kill the man, but not his work; you can crush the minister, but not the ministry; you can destroy the instrument, but not the music; you can cut off all the branches, but the root remains. Ay, but we can go down to the root too. Yes, to that root, but I am speaking about the root metaphysical, the Root of roots, the Thing, the Force, that cannot be got at, that no ax can find, and no digger can sink ground enough to discover the roots and all their fibers. So there is a root not to be touched, and out of that root there shall bud a stem more beautiful than flowers, more majestic than oaks and proudest cedars.

They did a great work on Friday. Oh no, no work at all. They secured their case certainly. Not at all; the wicked man secures nothing but his own destruction, and wickedness never triumphs except in its own overthrow. In the degree in which man, woman, child, cause, church, institution, is right, in that degree it is invulnerable; you can only confer upon it the opportunity of proving its own resurrection. It is well for us to know there are some things we cannot do. We cannot put down any really earnest, true, and divinely inspired ministry, whatever that ministry may be, in the pulpit, in the press, in the senate-house, in the family, or elsewhere. It is well, therefore, for us to know that there are some heights we cannot reach. Height is a religion. The best of us would not be half the man he is if there were no heights beyond his climbing, and if he did not know of the existence and reality of the heights, and pay them the tribute due to their unscaleable altitudes. There are some who want to do without religion. So be it; it is no business of mine to force religion upon anybody. In fact, if you wanted to do without the sky, well, so be it. Grow your flowers without the sky. Could we not grow flowers without the sky? Never. Could we not create flowers without the sky? Never; all flowers come out of the sky. But can we not light lamps? Yes, but the lamps in all that makes them lamps come out of the sun, and the sun out of the bosom of God; and all things lie there, all these infant constellations lie in that all-feeding breast. You have tried to put down some good man probably. You will not succeed. You have demonstrated against some man. What became of your demonstration? Did anybody pick up the stick of that rocket? Not a boy on the earth cared to pick up such dirty cinders. It is therefore, let us say over and over again, something to know that there are some things we cannot do.

"Christ both died, and rose, and revived." That word "revived" comes in like a freshet into a channel that has been waiting for the rising of the river. All the channel has been so droughty, so barren, and all the land round about has suffered from it, but there is a freshet rising, and that freshet represents true revival, relifeing. And so Christ said before the Friday, "I am come that they might have life, and that they might have it more abundantly," like wave on wave, billow chasing billow, until death was ashamed and overthrown, was lost, was swallowed up in victory. Why will not men remember that there are two very trying periods in the development of truth? There are periods of apparent stoppage. We call such periods dark ages; we say, It is no use any longer prosecuting this mission of truth; the people will not have it, the nations are dead, and it is whipping a dead horse to try to move this idea of ours into further action. There are therefore periods of stoppage in the development of truth. Then there are periods more trying still; I name them all under the one designation periods of transition, where the case is neither here nor there, definitely and finally, but it is both there and here, both here and there, both coming and going, advancing, receding, and men do not know where they are; they ask for the old landmarks, and the oldest inhabitant is dead, and there is no voice in the ear. The dear old Book is now in a period of transition, but it has come out of so many periods of transition that I am not giving myself a moment's heartache about the issue. It would never do for those who profess to have been companying long with Christ themselves to get into a period of transition. What a ministry that would be! There must always be a ministry of advance, a ministry that throws the fighting line out fifty yards further ahead, or fifty miles. The leaders must not give way. Think of a man preaching who is in a period of transition! And he admires himself for being in that period, and treats himself to many a birthday cake because he is in a period of transition; and the people all get to know about it, and they get into great anxiety about it, and the man himself knows it, and he says this should be expected; he is now in a period of transition. Let him trance as much as he likes! I am in no period of transition if the question is, Is God love? Yes. Did Christ die and rise and revive? Yes. The transition, so far as I know anything about it, is in incidentals, accidentals, occasionals; but the steady, ascending, triumphant movement is in no state of transition, except it be transition to pass from the lower to the higher, from the human to the Divine, from earth to heaven; and that transition does not pule and whine, and seek pity, and go into occasional headaches that it may be bathed by gentle hands. That is not the transition that requires such poor nursing. Grow in grace, but while you are growing be strong. This is the case with Christianity. Jesus Christ is now discarded by many people. He is. I hear them putting the nails into His hands. I hear the splash as of red water; that is the puncturing of His side with the spear. They have left His Church. They will come back again. They say it is all superstition, and man is very glad of any plea that will exempt him from the discipline he dare not face. I want my young friends to stand fast in the Lord. It is not the business of every man to answer questions. There are questions which can only be answered by experts, but whether I love my mother is not one of them, and whether I love my Savior is not a question which some expert can answer. I must answer it myself.

Prayer

Almighty God, may we know our limits, and abide within them as within a habitation planned and roofed by Thyself. May we know how frail we are, may we not exaggerate ourselves and thus forget God, may we remember that it is the Lord that reigneth, and that His throne is set upon pillars that are built on the rock. Keep us without our right as Thou hast defined it; may we leave behind us the things that are forbidden, or if we touch them may we be so filled with Thy grace as to be able to defy their seductiveness. Thou hast put us in a strange garden, and Thou hast hedged us in, and every leaf is a watching eye, and all things are known to Thyself. We are so forgetful; we think we planted the garden, and set the hedge, and that we can do what we like with the green leaves, so foolish are we and ignorant; we do not see the red flame of the sword, nor do we see the movement of the cherubim and the seraphim. We live on the dust; we build ourselves streets, and call them beautiful; we think not of Thy sky star-lighted and a great height that may not be touched; so we grope and stumble into the grave. Oh that we knew that Thy throne is established in the heavens! If we could but know that all things are settled and ordered and sure, and that we have nothing to do with them but to obey and to aspire and to pray, to love and to serve, to suffer and to triumph in Christ! We need these teachings every week, everywhere, specially in the city that is the greatest disturbance in our lives. We bless Thee for a quiet hour, for a shelter inviolate; we thank Thee for a refuge and a sanctuary in which the Lord Jesus is, with all His wounds, with all the mystery of His priesthood, with all His offers of grace and all His infinite solaces and delights. May we meet Him in His own appointed place, and tarry till we forget the time! Amen.

18

The Boasting Ax

Preached on Thursday Morning, April 19th, 1900.

Shall the ax boast itself against him that heweth therewith? or shall the saw magnify itself against him that shaketh it? as if the rod should shake itself against them that lift it up, or as if the staff should lift up itself, as if it were not wood
—Isaiah 10:15.

Is this a Divine interruption? Has the previous speaker talked too much and made an utter fool and atheist of himself? Who had been talking? The king of Assyria. Who interrupted him? The Lord: "I will punish the fruit of the stout heart of the king of Assyria, and the glory of his high looks." What had the stout heart of the king of Assyria been saying–anything modern, by anticipation? Let us hear: "By the strength of my hand I have done it, and by my wisdom; for I am prudent: and I have removed the bounds of the people, and have robbed their treasures, and I have put down the inhabitants like a valiant man: And my hand hath found as a nest the riches of the people: and as one gathereth eggs that are left, have I gathered all the earth; and there was none that moved the wing, or opened the mouth, or peeped." It was time someone interrupted a monologue so swollen, so tumid, so utterly blasphemous and diseased. The meaning of the text is always in the context; the context is the best commentary upon any text. Whatever you younger preachers do, never fail to read and carefully study the context. Here you have a proud Assyrian thinking that he has done everything, offering incense to himself, building an altar to his own glory and his own fame; and he is broken-in upon and thrown down, and there he lies in the dust of contempt. "I will stain the pride of all glory." That is the declaration of the Lord. We have the same thought in the New Testament; for the Testaments are one in all their great moral distinctions and all their great lines of moral movement. "Let him that thinketh he standeth take heed lest he fall." If any man think he knoweth anything, he knoweth nothing as he ought to know it. Be humble under the hand of God, thus making prayer of the meanest petition, "Thy will be done on earth as it is in heaven."

How many ways are there in which this text could be applied? To God, to man, to society, to destiny. This great pregnant inquiry seems to hold within itself all solemn questions, and to answer them one by one with appropriate dignity and with efficient energy. What say you? Shall we gather under it? We may find ourselves in an asylum, lighted by the sun, whose air is full of the peace of God.

"Shall the ax boast itself against him that heweth therewith? or shall the saw magnify itself against him that shaketh it?" Is there not a philosophy of things and a subtle poetry, an obvious and self-vindicating fitness? Is there not a place for everyone? Is everyone in that place? Does the saw ever mistake itself for the sawyer? And does the rod ever spring up and say, I am no wood, I am as good flesh as you are? Is the whole universe, so far as we know it, an adventure, an empiricism, a happy-go-lucky construction, no man knowing which shall be up and which shall be down? Is it a system of confusion, whose only sun is the midnight, or is everything planned, designed, fitted into its own proper place? And what would be the issue if we accepted, not nominally but with all our heart and soul, the sovereignty of God? The acceptance of the Divine sovereignty would make all things new: no more war, no more clamor, uproar and tumult forgotten, and sorrow and sighing would flee away. But we won't. Every man is God, and not the less so that he shudderingly denies the statement. But we believe a good many things we do not formulate; we are cunning enough to drop the use of words when such use might bring us under severe stricture and encroach upon our means of obtaining a livelihood—that odd creature man is not without a certain degree of self-reserve and cunning. What would be the result if we accepted the glorious doctrine of the sovereignty of God? The first result would be great personal peace. Do you know what a murder would be committed if we accepted the sovereignty of God? So far as we are concerned, the devil would be killed; there would be no more devil, envy, jealousy, and clamor and evilspeaking and backbiting all would die as by a lightning-stroke. Then what would society do? If we could not find some fault with the sermon or with the speaker of the sermon, why go to church? Then we could not backbite one another just a little; the salt would have lost its savor so far as social intercourse is concerned. And all envy, restlessness, petty ambition, selfish aspiration, mean calculation would be blown out of the way as by a great wind from heaven. But we won't accept the sovereignty of God that would rule all things into peace and unity and music. If I could accept the sovereignty of God really and truly I should know my limitations and not find fault with them. The mischief is, not that we are unaware of our limitations, but that having found them we bruise ourselves in futile endeavors to enlarge them. Now, do what the saw may, it never can be the man that wields it. If the saw could know that really and truly, it might do great and useful work, and never have a dream of trouble. I must accept the sovereignty of my Father, and thus get rid of a great many ambitions, self-exaggerations, and assurances never spoken, that I may be better than you are. A man would not say so for the world; no, this odd creature man is really not destitute of cunning. He can denounce most when he praises most; he can be most bitter when he is most sweet; yes, he is cunning. The magistrate cannot always catch him; he is a poor thief that can be caught.

What would be the result if we had among us through and through a most hearty and loyal and loving reception of the great doctrine of Divine sovereignty, the great doctrine that all things are settled and decreed and arranged? In that doctrine I do believe with my whole soul, though I have had in a sense to pay my soul as the price of its own faith. The second result we should have would be great social harmony. That is the great solution of all our social squabbles. Many have sought to handle society by means of programs. Society is never to be efficiently and redeemingly handled in that way. But man must have some holiday; if he were always working and praying might not life to some kinds of temperament be rather dull and melancholy? So man will now and again take to program-making, and his great scheme is to persuade the saw that he is as good as the sawyer, and the saw is willing to believe him. Where you have willingness to believe, progress, at least nominal and superficial progress, is easy. Accept the sovereignty of God; accept the great doctrine of personal, daily beneficient providence, and all your social troubles are at an end. This is the Bible method, and the Bible is one of the oldest of the books. We have among us a kind of thing called pantheism which is distributing its aphorisms and apophthegms without knowing that they were all distributed in India two thousand five hundred years ago. It would be a pity to know that, because it would be bad for trade. You can never get rid of the saw and the sawyer, the ax and the hewer, the clay and the potter. You must always have in society the great man, and the little man, and each in his own place may be equal in importance to the other. Mark the definition; everything depends upon the definition: each in his own place. But you cannot get rid of the classification of men; you cannot write men up; it would never be possible for any number of men to lift any little man so high up as to make a great man of him. Great men are not made; they come up from the Eternal. They cannot explain themselves; they are mysteries to their own consciousness; in the degree in which they are truly great and noble are they truly great in humility and gentleness and beneficence. The giant talks less than the dwarf. You can never get rid of the superior, and the inferior. It is no use saying that they are of equal value. I know that the man with whom I am conversing is a thousand times my size; I do not need to be told to fall down before him in lawful homage, I do it instinctively–Hail, king! When we lose the spirit of social reverence, I do not care how much uproar we have, for uproar can never make up for the absence of the music we have banished. But it is no shame to be less than some other man. The man who has more than I have has more responsibility, more will be expected of him, a heavier bill will be brought in for his discharge. So must we all think of the various distributions and classifications made by the sovereignty of God; and the man who has five talents, the man who has two talents, and the man who has one talent must all get together and see what is the best thing to be done, how individuality can flow into harmony or union, and how union can fall back upon individuality with cheer and appreciation and inspiring courage. You cannot get rid of the leader and the follower; these things are not of our invention. We think that we made so-and-so leader. Quite a delusion. God is behind everything, around everything, and above everything, and it is God that worketh in you. You may contravene Him; you may disobey Him; you may for a moment thwart His plans and violate His idea of social architecture: still remains true the gracious saying, The Lord buildeth all things, and the city is unwatched that is neglected by His hands.

If we could really believe these elementary truths we should have a great unit in society. Man did not make society, and man cannot destroy it; man did not make mystery, and man cannot solve it, unless by God's enlightenment and special permission. The scientific man has told us that an atom of iron may be a more complicated system than any that can be found in the stars. Of course it is difficult for us to understand this, but the man of science does not ask us to understand it, and he does not care whether we understand it or not; for the man of science several days in the week has a very real contempt for the other man. It is not whether we will accept these things or not, we are bound by these limitations; what we have to do is to accept the situation, to say, The Lord reigneth; He did not make me to speak or to sing or to paint or to write immortal verse, but He made me thus, and so, and set me in this corner to do the best I can under His blessing: enough! Is there not a way of enlarging an environment? Certainly; there are two ways. The first way is the break-down way, utterly defying and despising it, and getting it out of the road by taking a short cut. The second way is to work within the environment so lovingly, patiently, and self-disregardingly, that God will come to us one day, and say, Son, thou hast been faithful over a few things, I will make thee ruler over many things. That is legitimate promotion, elevation, enthronement. Never take to the rough and atheistic plan; it always ends in darkness and disappointment; but let me humbly wait where I am, and when the Lord sees that I can do a little more than I am doing now He will say to me, Thou hast been faithful over a few things; I will make thee ruler over many things. That is the great law of true expansion and true liberation.

Out of this acceptance of the Divine sovereignty comes a grand religious brotherhood, as well as a deep satisfaction and noble peace. God did it all. Here is a man talking that has really a fresh-air talk, a south-west wind the blowing of which brings gospels with it. Saith he: God did it; God does everything in love; God does all things; there is not a blade of grass in all the acreage of the globe that does not owe its individuality to God; the great God taketh care of the fowls of the air; He knows their names; He knows their wings; He calls some of the wings pinions that can carry the eagle away until the rock becomes a speck; and some of the wings are but pulses, little bits of sunshine, little blobs, but wondrous little creatures they are, who make the best of their way through the air with such poor instruments. You have seen the blackbird listen for his worm; the blackbird does not see the worm, he listens for it. If we listened, we might hear God. I often watch my neighborly blackbird, and I love to see him turn the worm into a song. That is a surprising resurrection. God has placed me in a lower place than another man, and sometimes the devil says to me, You are just as good as he is—throw a stone at him; you are just as good as he is—

write an anonymous letter about him. The devil says, What business has he to be up there, and you have to be down here?—heave a half-brick at him. Poor devil! He never had a noble conception, a grand idea; he is a liar from the beginning and a murderer.

Now we must have a scepter, a throne, a king. We as Christian students and believers have accepted the idea that God reigns, and by God we mean the loving, personal, redeeming God, the God incarnate in Christ Jesus, the God of Bethlehem, of Calvary, and of Olivet, the priest God, who loved us, who gave His Son to save us. That is what we believe; and, believing that, out of it comes a whole philosophy of daily life, of social responsibility, and of all manner of well-regulated and harmonic action. Now which is the greater—for we must have great and small; these distinctions are not of our own making—which is the greater, I will ask you, the man who wrote the book—being *Paradise Lost* or Homer's *Iliad*—the man who wrote the book or the man who bound it? I wonder if you could constitute yourselves into a committee and appoint a sub-committee in order to return an answer to that inquiry? Which had the greater mind, judging both men from the evidence that is accessible? The one man wrote the book, the other man bound it; the book has achieved universal and imperishable fame, and the book-binder has—been paid. Which is the greater? Oh, tell me! The picture or the frame-maker? If I could invite you to a grand exhibition of all the paintings of the year, and if I could also ask you to attend a complete exhibition of all the frames that have been made during the year, to which exhibition would you go? But is not one man as good as another? Why not go and see the frames? They are all gilt, and they are all shapely, and they are all made by very expert and efficient workmen; now will you go to see the pictures or the frames? I need not wait more than one moment; you have answered before the question was put. There is a spirit in man, and the inspiration of the Almighty giveth him understanding. You want the pictures, the genius, the flame Pentecostal, the mystery of harmony, perspective, color, the silent oratorio.

And so we can carry the matter into a higher level, and say, Which is the greater, the father or the child in arms? Who will answer questions regarding the house, regarding its sale, its occupation, its decoration, its management, the father or the child in arms? Whom would you consult, the expert or the layman? There are experts in all trades, occupations, businesses, and professions, and there are men who know nothing about these occupations and professions, and they are appropriately called laymen. Now if you were really ill would you send for the physician or the blacksmith? You are a socialist, and you say one man is as good as another. It is folly, falsehood. Why, there was a trial some time ago about some postage-stamps, and there was only one man in the world who could settle the case. And yet one man is as good as another! The expert was called in, and he held up the sheet and applied his lenses, and read the mystery which the lay eye could not see, and then he said, This is genuine. There was no appeal. Could I not have done that? One postage-stamp is the same as another to me, but this man is an expert, and judge and jury could say nothing against his decision. And one of her Majesty's justices told me the other day that it is perfectly possible to distinguish one kind of stitching from another. Who did this stitching, the woman A, or the woman B, or the woman C? There is a signature of stitching; that signature can be discovered and verified; no other woman would do this stitching exactly as the stitcher herself did it. And yet to you and me all stitches seem to be much about the same. But there is a distinction in everything; there is a signature all through and through. They are prosecuting some poor people, I see, who think they can read the lines upon the human hand. Let them read them. I do not want them read, and I do not believe in their palmistry, but if that is just as far as they have got, why find fault with them; why stop them? If a man has a dream, let him tell it. I may not have time to listen to it, but I would leave him all the space there is to tell the dream in. And that is the only way to put down bad preaching. Do not put it down by thumbscrews and by axes and blocks, but come and say to the man, Now what is your thought, let us hear it; you shall have time and opportunity, tell it. And in many cases you will find the heretic will talk himself back into faith. Never expel the heretic; you magnify him and you make a martyr of him; but take as much faith as he has and work upon that, and by magnanimity and nobleness and charity endeavor to win the man's confidence, and mayhap he who for a moment was a heretic may for the rest of his life be an apostle of the faith.

Then let us beware of second causes in providence, let us beware of second causes in religion, and let us beware of second causes in destiny; and let us accept the old, old doctrine of the sovereignty of God, and when we are in darkness, let us seek the altar, the Cross, and pray. How long? Till the light comes. All night Aquinas knelt alone; why should I be outdone by his saintly patience? I too will wait, wait, wait upon God, and I will say, Feed my heart. After many days He will find me still praying. Still? Not attacking another thing until I have got the answer to this importunate, earnest prayer. Go to, men, women, children, preachers, hearers; go to; for God waits, and if we wait upon Him, we shall grow, not towards old age, but towards youth and immortality.

Prayer

Almighty God, do Thou pity us and visit us with Thy salvation, and give us continual assurance that Thou art near us; otherwise we shall faint and be as dead men on the ground. We can only live in Thy Spirit; our time is worthless but for Thine own eternity; take up our handful of days into Thine eternity, and bathe them with the glory thereof, that we may be no longer as those who grope in darkness and inquire of one another in the twilight. We would walk in noonday; our whole lives would be bathed in the summer sun of Thy love. Oh that we knew our calling in Christ! Oh that we might be no longer slothful and sluggish servants, but alert and wise, full of wakefulness, answering every sign in Thy condescending heaven, and showing how ready we are by the power of Thy grace to run the way of Thy commandments. Oh that we had hearkened unto Thee long ago! By this time we had been men stalwart and giant-like, and none could have stood before us because of the indwelling of our God. But we have compromised and made truces, and we have endeavored to work with both hands; we have looked unto the heavens, and then we have looked unto the earth, and we have wondered whether we could manage our own lives by a poor, mean, shallow cunning in which there is no divinity. Then again we have repented and fallen upon our knees and cried unto God at the foot of the Cross, if haply after all we might become men, strong men, valiant, the whole life a ringing anthem, the whole breath a tender hymn. We have heard of Thy kingdom and of its coming, and we have heard of great voices being lifted up in heaven to proclaim the descending and ascending sovereignty of Thy Son. We believe it, we live in it, our souls take fire again at this holy torch, and behold we stand fronting the world, the flesh, and the devil armed with all the sufficiency of God. We pray Thee to waken up Thy Church, poor, dead, sluggish, slumbering Church, having ten talents and using only one. Oh that Thou wouldst revive us, bring back to us the old vitality and the infinite passion and the real consecration! We long for that day; sweep out of the way whom Thou wilt, only let that day come; and the earth shall know when the summer sun is at the zenith. Amen.

19
Spiritual Discernment

Preached on Sunday Morning, April 22nd, 1900.

Ye can discern the face of the sky; but can ye not discern the signs of the times?—Matthew 16:3.

How wonderful is this half-growth of man! You think if he can know so much, it would be quite easy for him to turn over the page and to read the longer words. But it is not. There seems to be an almost arbitrary stopping-place in growth, whether it be growth of the body or of the mind or of business; the question applies to all the directions and evolutions of life. You can get so far; how does it come that you cannot get further? One thing is meant to lead to another; where we end we should begin. We should only finish the Bible in order to begin the revelation. Men may be clever in one direction, and all but fools in another. It does not follow that because a man is a good judge of a horse that therefore he ought to give you an opinion about your destiny as a man. This puzzled and perplexed the Son of God; for said He, How is it that you can go so far and stop dead there? You say about a boy, He is going to be extremely clever. I am not so sure of that; I have known very clever boys stop short and become quite ordinary without there being any apparent reason for the stoppage. I have known quite ordinary and commonplace boys suddenly develop and become wise and strong, full of virtue, full of life, insomuch that people have said, Surely this is the boy we knew some ten years ago, and then he was so dull and almost stupid; he seemed not to have a word to say for himself, but to retire into some congenial shadow. How is this? We have prophesied of some boys that they would become the chiefs and leaders of their day, and behold, they have dropped off into commonplace and obscurity, halting there for a moment on their way to oblivion. How is it that a man can be so clever in one direction, and be utterly useless in another? That this is so is written upon the broad sheet of daily life; there is no questioning of it, it is a fact, and a pregnant fact, and we ought to apply that fact as a standard in measuring our own abilities, our own vocation, and our own responsibilities to society.

Jesus Christ found that He was in the midst of a number of weatherwise people; they were quite experts in the reading of the cloudy signs, they knew what the weather would be today and perhaps tomorrow, and they published their forecasts of the weather; but when it came to higher reading, reading on another level, they were as moles and bats from whom the genius of daylight penetration had been withheld. Do we make one another up? Do we hold varied trusteeships? And are they brought under one grand obligation, so that we may, thus supplementing one another, constitute a great social unit? Are there not really readers of the clouds and readers of the unseen? Could they not meet now and then in common counsel to see how things stand and what the general outlook is? They must not despise one another; for one man can do this, and another man can do that, and neither man can do both. So that we are mutual trustees, we supplement each other; if we could enter into the spirit of this arrangement, we should have brotherhood, free, frank interchange of opinion, and work together in a great and beneficent association. Some things are common to us all, and at points hardly calculable we break off from the common holding, and each becomes a freeholder by himself and in himself, as it were directly holding the land of his genius and power from the great Creator. Strange as it may appear, there are some things that belong to us all, things in which we have a common right. We do not understand this. Every man thinks that surely he has a right

to smoke in the open air. Now that is the only place where he has
no right to smoke; because the air belongs to the little child, and
the old man, and the sick, and the feeble; it is the great benediction
belonging to us all, and no man has a right to spoil it. Who would
have thought of this? The thing is absolutely preposterous on the
face of it, says the man who thinks about nothing but himself, and
is content with that small subject. There are things that belong to us
all—the great sunshine. O poor unwashed hands of the child, put
yourselves out into this great bath of light and glory, and enjoy
yourselves in this great gift of day. Blessed be God, no man can
build high enough to build out the sunshine. Man in some forms
and phases has built a good deal. One gang of men undertook to
build a tower which should reach unto heaven: I have not heard of
its having put on the copestone. Heaven will not be too nearly approached by any of your building. And today, vernal day, day of
violets and sweet flowers, goes so to say all over the earth, saying,
today as everyday, Come out into the light, and enjoy yourselves
with a wise dance and the holy sacrament of thankfulness.

But while we recognize these great common gifts, we recognize
also a partition of ability, so that one man is an expert along line A,
and another man is an expert along line B, and each must work out
his own vocation. As there are great commonwealth blessings of
nature, so there are great republican blessings in moral and spiritual regions. God did not intend any man to be born a slave. Liberty belongs to every responsible creature; his responsibility will
limit and define his liberty, and thus give him the very best of it.
Liberty that wantons itself into license really conducts itself into
the worst bondage. Regulated liberty is freedom. God means every
soul in this sense to be free. God did not intend any man to be
born into hatred, either to hate or to be hated; God meant us all to
be the great children of His great love. Love is not confined to this
place or to that; there is love in the very darkest parts of the city.
Love is not bidden or commanded to come into the heart; love is
there natally, originally, and wants only to be awakened; and

hands—poor hands and arms on which there is no fatness or signature of prosperity—are put out in the dark to find the child to hug. There are common instincts, common privileges. And yet singular to say, and yet necessary to say, there are limitations which are round about the individual, so that he has his talent, his two talents, his five talents, himself not to be numbered with other men in certain great generalities. The individuality of the soul is never lost; it is never drowned in the river of mean compromises; it should stand forth individual and yet associated; a great personality, yet part of a greater humanity. To combine the whole and the part, the great universal gift and the special endowment: this is the problem, and Christianity alone sufficiently and finally solves it.

We make great limitations of our own; we ought to know something about this problem of definition or boundary. We are quite learned in frontiers, in social and moral as well as natural geography. How is it, saith the Spirit of Christ, that you are so expert in definitions and limitations, and rights and wrongs, in all lower things, and can ye not discern the higher limitations which often mean the higher and wider opportunities? We have a great law of trespass; on the matter of trespass we are quite experts. We go to the expense of printing or otherwise inscribing boards two feet by eighteen inches declaring that no trespass is permitted in these fields—"By Order." Has a board like that been put up by order? Yes. How is it that ye can print and paint these little boards guarding a few handfuls of sod from trespass, and can ye not see that in the wider moral regions there is a great sovereign law of trespass, a warning that whosoever violates this or that boundary a serpent shall bite him, or his own conscience shall torment him as with the lash and sting of living thongs? How is it that we can be so clear upon the protection of our property from trespass, and yet we leave all the gates of the soul open, so that as many as like may come in and make a playground of our hearts? Wise along one line, fools along another! A man who would be irritated by the fact that some half a dozen little boys had climbed over his five-barred gate and stolen a few crabapples from his plantation would be astounded if he were told by some preaching man that possibly he had left his whole soul open to temptation, seduction, suggestion, and that thieves of a spiritual kind have robbed the orchard of his heart. How is it? My Lord crucified, how is it?

We have a very stringent law against forgery. Of course all decent people tremble at the very word; and yet—my Lord, how is it? These same people will take any number of forgeries along the line of faith, spirituality, deception, cunningly devised fables whereby the devil violates the sanctuary of the soul and befouls the fair half of a redeemed world. What a fuss men make when their names are forged; how they run hither and thither to rectify it; in what wild amaze they look out if haply they can detect the man who forged a signature. All that is right; within its own limits it is perfectly right; no wise man attempts to dispute it; but why be so very alert upon the matter of forging a signature, and yet allow yourselves to be set down in the national statistics as what you are not? Why not be consistent? Why not be as eager-minded at one part of the great question as at another? How is it that ye can read the signs of the weather but cannot read the signs that are written in the inner air, the mystic signs, the dreams that tell of the greater realities? The law says we must not vitiate the air. What a fussy law it is! and it can only be by some Act of Parliament that the air is kept from certain kinds of vitiation. Your neighbor cannot do just what he likes on his own property because he may create a nuisance whereby your property would be prejudiced. O ye hypocrites! saith Christ, how is it that you are so anxious about the air that is natural and so careless about the moral atmosphere? Any drunken, disgraceful being can befoul it with oaths. You would not permit a brick chimney to be built within a certain number of feet of your front window, you have nothing to say to the people who are blackening the air with blasphemy and soiling the summer with vile words. Some of you go into little parliaments and grate on the question of sanitary regulations. They say, Vote for A, and sanitation! How is it that you vote for the amendment of drains, and take no interest in the destruction and afterward the reconstruction of the foulest of sewers, the human heart? Have you no province there? Tell God so; do not beat my poor cheek with such foolish observations. What, have you no influence upon the higher sanitation? Can you not by speech or example show what a foul thing it is to have a cathedral built by men who blaspheme one part of the day and drink themselves into stupidity on the other? This applies to all work, to all engagements, professions, and responsibilities of every kind. The great point of the argument is exactly the point of the text, that men are great in the weather, but in nothing else; great judges of the external, and no judges at all of the internal and spiritual; foolish men who think that by adding a few inches to the width of a wall they can build out the cholera and also build out the angels. Why not be consistent all round? Why not aim at least to be as eager on moral and religious questions as on questions of mere politics and mere social economies and arrangements?

By the text we are entitled to enlarge what we can see into what we cannot see except by the vision of the soul. Here is a great lesson in inductive reasoning. Because such and such is the direction of the wind an such and such are the indications of the clouds, therefore we shall have such and such weather. Quite right; I do not oppose your forecasts; but why not carry up the idea, and endeavor to reason concerning the things you see with the eyes of the heart in the spiritual realm, and draw your inductions according to the great basis of fact, phenomena, and experience available to every student who faithfully and humbly and lovingly endeavors to discover the will of God? There is a spiritual barometer; there is a spiritual thermometer; there are many ways appointed and therefore approved of God by which we can put this and that together and draw wide inferences from great spiritual premises. If we had eyes to see, we should know that from the beginning God has a certain purpose and will surely accomplish it. That purpose is a purpose of beneficence. Jesus Christ says the fields are already white unto the harvest;

Jesus Christ reasons from the lilies and from the fowls of the air to the great paternal providence of God over every soul of man. It is not everyone who can get the oak out of the acorn. You cannot get it out with a clasp knife; you may not take a pair of garden shears and cut the oak out of the acorn; none of our little cutting, if you please, none of our mischief-making, no taking to pieces the organ to see where the music comes from, no vivisection of the poor shrinking human heart to know where are the springs and by what issue it finds its way out into the world. There is a way by which we can find the oak in the acorn; we must, so to say, marry the acorn to the sun, to the earth, to the great chemistry of nature, and then we must simply but hopefully wait. It is often the waiting that kills: the fighting is a holiday, the waiting is slow murder.

Yet we must observe the line of limitation even here. We must not imagine that we can see things which are forbidden. There is no meaner trade than fortune-telling, yet there is not a man in London that would not succumb to it under certain circumstances. I know that many will rebel against this sentiment, and therefore I am quite sure that I am right in advancing it. You have to get the proper bribe gathered, then my lord Haughty will succumb, but it must be under certain circumstances because his respectability must be protected and his signature at the bank must still be valid. Now if considering these things you can arrange a little movement by which he can have his fortune forecast, especially if you can say to him that almost presently his ship will arrive with a hundred thousand pounds, and that almost before he can turn round the world—dead, stupid world hitherto—will recognize his greatness and send him to the Upper House direct, he might smile at the forecast, but deep down in his heart he says he would not wonder if there is something in it! How can such a world be redeemed? It may take countless millenniums to effect the redemption of such a world.

We must recognize the fact that there is a difference in sight. We recognize this in the sight of the bodily eyes; why not recognize it in the inner and truer sight of the soul? Can you read a placard fifty yards off? Your answer is, I certainly cannot do so. Are you entitled from that consciousness to declare that there is not a man in the world that can read it? You have to admit that there is sight longer than yours. Can you read the Bible without lenses, glasses, or mechanical aids of any kind? You may possibly reply, Certainly I cannot do so. Does it therefore follow that no other man can read it without such aids? In a moment you say that to make any such contention would be simply absurd. That is right: why not apply that fact to a higher level, and find for it a broader and deeper interpretation? As a matter of fact some men can pray with great fluency and comprehensiveness, and other men cannot; some men can write books, and other men cannot; some men are prophets who can see afar, and others never had a dream in either eye. Why not admit this, and then apply it to the lives and ministries of all the great men in the Bible who have under Divine inspiration interpreted to the world the will of God? You cannot read a letter from your own child without saying, "Where are my spectacles? I cannot read this: anybody seen my spectacles?" and your own companion will say, "Give it to me, I will read it for you." Which of you is right? or is there any real difference between you as to merely physical gifts? But when you come to the interpretation of moral and spiritual truths, then the prophet makes himself felt; he says, I will interpret the will of God by the power of God that is upon me and within me. For no prophet speaks out of his own wisdom; he speaks according to the inspiration of the soul by the God whom we recognize and adore as the Holy Ghost. We must therefore listen to the higher voices. We are at liberty to test the spirits whether they are of God; that may often be a bounden duty which we cannot shirk under any plea or pretext. Yet there remains the great fact that we have a book which is filled with holy messages from the holy God, and these have been so often confirmed that their very confirmation becomes not only an argument but a starting-point of the most profound and elaborate reasoning. If any man has read the Book of Genesis aright he knows that there is a book coming that shall be full of anthem, song, and triumph; for the kingdoms of this world have become the kingdom of our God and of His Christ. He read that in the very first verse of the Bible if he was a prophet when he read that opening verse. There is a great philosophy of implication; one thing means another, points to another, and gives assurance of another. Nothing ends in itself. Created is a word that does not end in creation. Created is a polysyllable, a literature, a grand theology. When God created, He meant that not a hair should be uncounted, not a sparrow fall without the Father.

I am not ashamed to say that, having just passed the threescore years and ten; I am still an Evangelical believer. If this were my last testimony as a public preacher of the Kingdom of God, I would declare that the Evangelical faith, as learnedly and experimentally interpreted and practically applied, answers more questions, solves more problems, settles more difficulties, and opens up vaster vistas to the religious imagination than any faith or any theory ever submitted to the confidence of mankind. We want more definite assertion of definite principles. I do not believe in narrow dogmas, in literal imprisonment; I believe in the great bed-rock of truth, and over it the great sky of religious imagination and spiritual interpretation. I believe that all life is a great problem and a great parable, and I am sure that there come times in the history of the soul when nothing but the Cross—deride it who may—can touch the agony of our life. Believe a man who has seen a great deal of human experience, a man who has known difficulty and strenuous effort, and unrelenting and unrelaxing devotion to what he believes to be true. I have been a man of war from my youth; I have feared the face of no man. I have believed my cause to be righteous. I may have spoken unadvisedly; I may, on the spur of the moment, have selected words which I would not in calmer leisure have selected; but I will say this: that nothing but the Cross of our Lord Jesus Christ can follow a man all day and all night, up the hill and through the valley—nothing will stand by him in such steadfast purpose and friendship as the love of God as seen in Christ Jesus the Lord. I tell the generation of preachers yet to come, if my words should be preserved for their attention, that they can preach all their little theories and read all their elaborate and soulless essays; they can be as literary and ingenious and even poetical as they please, but if the Cross be not the staple of their ministry, their congregations will turn away as hunger turns away when stones are offered it instead of bread.

[*Extract from speech delivered by Dr. Parker at the reopening of Paddington Chapel, April 24th, 1900.*]

Prayer

Almighty God, how long have we to live? Is there not an appointed time to men upon the earth? Is not the grave of the strongest man already dug? We know not what Thou dost do in the night time. We cannot tell how near the rising of the tide is; we have our poor geographies and calculations, but no man may take his pencil and paper into Thy kingdom and add up the movements and totals of things. Thou leadest men by a way that they know not, yea, the blind by paths in which they need not stumble. Would that we had faith enough to trust ourselves entirely to Thy care and Thy keeping so that we have no thought of our own concerning a day so near as even tomorrow! May we live short lives, and therefore happy ones and useful; may we receive the seal of Thy love every morning and hold it as a sacred trust until the time of the coming of the evening star; then may we lay ourselves down in peace and in safety, knowing that it is the eye of the Lord that watches through all the hours of darkness. One dieth in his full strength, being wholly at ease and quiet; another dieth in the bitterness of his soul and never eateth with pleasure; some are subject to bondage through a lifetime in fear of death. Such is the life we lead, a wondrous troubled, joyous life, full of starvation and festival, despair and hope, a living daily terrible self-contradiction. Blessed are they who hide their handful of years in the years that are at the right hand of the Almighty; may we bring our time to rest its fevered self in the coolness and the calm of the divine eternity. Oh that men were wise, that they understood these things, that they would consider their latter end, that they would be no longer fools, but wise men bent on wise journeys, so that at the end they may glorify God, magnifying His name with many praises, and loudly singing the providence which has been their salvation. Thou knowest our frame; Thou rememberest that we are dust, poor sensitive, shrinking things without the heroic temper, without the daring spirit, afraid of our own shadows, afraid of the rustling in the twilight in the summer hedges. Oh that we had lived in God as He is known in Christ Jesus, the Christ of the Cross, the Jesus of Bethlehem and Calvary! Then had we come into a great estate of honor and peace and quiet confidence, and we should have shown in all the ways of our daily life that they who trust in the Cross, in the God and Savior of the Cross, have an infinity of calm, a tranquility akin to the peace of God. Amen.

20
Fewness of Days

Preached on Sunday Morning, May 6th, 1900.

How long have I to live?–2 Samuel 19:34.

I have been almost forced into this text because during the last few days people have been dropping down dead at my feet, without a moment's notice, but with a lifetime's preparation. I think some four of my friends have dropped down dead within a few days–ministers, fathers, men of position, and men exerting the most benign and sacred influence in life; and they have been struck down suddenly as a thunder-shower strikes the young flowers of the spring. So that again and again a weird voice has come singing round about me, "How long have I to live?" There is no answer to the question; the cleverest man among you cannot offer even a conjecture, much less a solution, to some of these tragical problems of life. All men live in uncertainty. A man is afraid that he will not live long enough to sign his own will. It is after he has given instructions to prepare the will that a curious feeling comes over him, implying that he may not be able to sign his own testamentary dispositions, and then an aggravating and most cruel voice says to his heart, Then whose shall those things be that thou hast stored? Why, thou wilt die intestate, and the court will distribute thy rubbish. At other times man is so egregiously foolish that he never thinks of his life or of his death or of his will or of his family. They say he was a most loving man. Where is the will? The loving man made none. Call that love? It is frivolity, it is madness.

While these dear friends, some of them yet unburied, are lying as to the body dead around me, I thought I would ask you to join me in asking this question, each for himself, "How long have I to live?" There is one answer that can be given with painful definiteness and certainty: we have not to live long; there is no length in life. The man in the text who asked this question is described as "very aged." How old was he? He is "a very aged man." Well, how old was he? He was "fourscore years old." Why, the roof he lives under is older than that; there is an old oak-tree chest outside his bedroom window double his age. "A very aged man . . . fourscore years old." What is that? A melting snowflake, a swiftly passing shuttle, a shadow chased by the sun, chased into non-existence. Oh that men were wise, that they understood these things, that they would consider their latter end! Oh that men in all their adding up and multiplying and dividing, and all their little clever tricks in the first four rules of arithmetic, would say, each for himself, "How long have I to live?"

A very beautiful little story is this, told a thousand times and yet young as the morning dew. David had been chased about by a most cruel disloyalty and unfilial ingratitude and rebellion; things had gone very hardly with him; when he was in the very depths of despair a rich old Gileadite took compassion on the king, and said: I have fruit and bread and wine and stores diverse and useful; come to me; bring thy following with thee; what is a king if he cannot feed another king, and what is a rich old man really worth if he is not prepared to give all he has to what he believes to be a good cause? The times got better, the long-tarrying sun came round and lighted up the fortunes of David, and David was going back to Jerusalem. David was not ungrateful, he remembered the rich Gileadite, and he said, Barzillai, come with me, come with me to Jerusalem; I am going back over the Jordan, and there will be a great reception and an endless festival; now renounce everything, and come and live with me in Jerusalem. David was always lavish both in love and in revenge; David did nothing by halves. The man

who wrote the Psalms for the centuries told his own son Solomon
to bring certain men's gray hairs, reddened with their own blood, to
the grave. How contradictory is man! He writes psalms that startle
the heavens with their glory and high music, and then he writes as
with a dying, trembling hand his will: See that Joab be stabbed,
murdered, cut his throat, crush him, bring him to a great clot of
blood, and bury the beast with curses. Perhaps it takes the one man
to make the other. Psychology is very wonderful. Some men never
would have written so eloquently or spoken so forcibly in the cause
of right if their tempers had not been capable of being turned into
very distressing use in other directions. We must be careful how we
condemn men; we ourselves may come into great condemnation.
God has made man in His own image, and of God we read, "God is
love . . . God is a consuming fire."

Nay, said trembling Barzillai, my lord, permit me to beg off; I
am old, and I have got used to my own city and my own folks; as
for these poor old bones, they are not worth thinking about, but
God has so made us that we must think about them, and I should
like these poor outworn old bones to be buried near my father and
my mother; beside—beside, what is the use of it? How long have I to
live at fourscore years? I am this day fourscore years old; and can I
discern between good and evil? Can thy servant taste what I eat or
what I drink? can I hear anymore the voice of singing men and
singing women? Let thy servant, I pray thee, turn back again, that I
may die in mine own city, and be buried by the grave of my father
and of my mother. Here is a young man who will represent me well
enough; he has all his life to live; he wants the mirth-song and the
dance and the timbrel, the great king's feast; let him go. Young folks
should marry young folks and should live their own life, but I, poor
old inhabitant of Gilead, I do not want to be a burden even to the
king: farewell; let me go. And Barzillai returned. The king had kissed
Barzillai and blessed him, and the little tragedy was at an end. How
glad we are that we did not go with some folks! It was a great temptation; my feet had well-nigh slipped, my soul had well-nigh given

itself away; the bribe was so great, Jerusalem and the palace and the smile of the king and no work and nothing to do but linger out my golden eventide. You are glad that you did not go with certain people at certain times. Do I not speak directly into the very center of your experience? You were just about to go, and by a hairsbreadth you escaped going; you have been thankful ever since that that hairsbreadth intervened. It was a strong temptation at the time. What, you said, another thousand? Yes, and another ten thousand, and another ten thousand upon that, and another ten thousand. And a voice said, Deafen thine ears against this seductive appeal; there is death in this bribe; renounce it; go home poor. You heard the better voice and you went back to your own little Gilead, and you said it was better, and that somehow by mystic influence you had never missed the money, and you are a stronger man today than you would have been if you had taken it. You did not argue on the ground of age, but you argued upon some other ground, and no matter what that honest ground was, your argument prevailed and you are happy today.

Suppose we accommodate this inquiry of Barzillai, and apply it here and there along the sensitive line of our ever-changing life. It may do us good; we may be the better for cross-examining ourselves upon this matter of the possible or probable, certainly incalculable, period of life.

"How long have I to live," that I may make the most of what remains? That is a very proper question; we ought to ask ourselves that question every day. To make the most of what remains. What does remain? No man can tell. A breath. Where is your friend? He is dead. What thine hand findeth to do, do it with thy might; he that does it quickly does it twice. You have no time to lose; you have been haffling with yourself for the last six days, and you are six days nearer your end. Shall I do this deed of charity, or shall I not? Do it! I have had some thoughts of helping my friend in his distress, but I am just hesitating. You may hesitate too much and too long; do it now, and then think about it. You were going to do so many things for your friend, for your family, for your minister, for the country, for the world, for the heathen, always being on the point of almost doing it. And one of the uncounted and uncountable darts of God struck you, and now you are not sure that you will live long enough to sign your own will. Foolish man! You should have written it twenty years ago; you have no right to tempt the Lord your God. There is only one time, and that time is mentioned in the Bible, and that is the only available and sure time, and I can tell you when it is. When is the only available and sure time? Now! The Bible keeps that great dummy clock, and it stands at Now! Now is the accepted time; now is the day of salvation. And you propose to make up some part of the leeway that you may make the most of what remains? Let me see, how many years have you given to the devil? Fifty. And you suppose that fifty more remain? Very doubtful. Would it not now be well to make the most of what remains, to do the rest in gold, diamonds, and precious stones of every name? You may not be here next Sunday, I may not live to preach this evening; we had better be doing something. What say you? Is not this wisdom? It is wisdom in secular things, why not in spiritual things? It is right in the matter of the health of the body, why not right in the matter of the health of the soul?

"How long have I to live," that I may set my house in order? You want a little time for preparation; you do not want to be hastened away so as to leave many things unarranged and unprovided for. What a beautiful thing it is to be able to stand over the grave of your friend, and to say, He did what he could; he was a sweet, heroic, valiant soul; in his own little way and sphere, take him for all in all, he was a man; we ne'er shall look upon his like again; so gentle as a father, so faithful as a friend, so wholly excellent and estimable in every capacity and aspect of life. If you want to set your house in order, make a just will. I know of no sweeter reading–and I myself have no recollection of ever having been named in a will, so I can speak the more without prejudice–I know no sweeter reading than a will after which men say, That is just, that is wisely conceived;

the man makes no demands upon revenge; he does not use any instrument of retaliation; he was a great-natured man, and he has disposed of everything justly; he was a righteous man. You do not want to be driven out of the world leaving everything unarranged, leaving your whole life's career in chaos. You do not know how much time remains; there may be still time to send for the solicitor or the representative of your family, the man on whose judgment and fidelity you will so largely depend. Why have you made no arrangement, no preparation? Are you going to leave a lawsuit to your family? Shame! But if I send for the solicitor, I shall feel I am going to die. That is old woman's nonsense; it does not suit your manhood at all. The arrangement for your latter end, whether it be legal, moral, social, whatever the arrangement may be, should be done calmly, with great deliberateness, and with a conscious realization of the Divine presence. If I could tell you today that you have one hundred years yet to live, the case would be different; but, sir, O sir! Hear me; you may die today.

"How long have I to live," that I may do the most important things first? There is a gradation in importance: some things are important; others are more important; others again are most important, are indeed of superlative and inexpressible importance. That is a graduated scale which commends itself to common sense: why not apply it in all the regions and outgoings of life? It is not enough to be busy; you must be busy at the right time, in the right place, and in the right work. To be busy is nothing; it may indeed be an aggravation of your unwisdom. What is the most important thing to do? I will not leave the most important undone or unconsidered. Have you been doing important things, Mr. Husbandman? Yes, I have been doing most important things. What have you been doing? This is the time for sowing seed; this is preeminently the time for seed-sowing. What have you been doing? I admit that seed-sowing is of great importance, but I have been spending the last six weeks in cleaning my windows. Was there ever such a fool on the soil? It is important to clean windows certainly; it is important to make a highway for the light, no doubt; but at this particular time the thing important above all things is to sow the seed now. I am sure I have been exceedingly busy in cleaning all those windows. You have been busy at the wrong thing, busy at the wrong time, busy at the wrong place; to be busy is not the thing, but to be busy in a right way at the right time, and to be doing the right thing, and the only thing to be done in that one pregnant moment. How this would change our life! how this would rearrange all our plans! And is it not the way of common sense? If it is the way of common sense in the matter of husbandry, it is surely the way of common sense in the culture and preparation of the higher nature. I have in all these years met so many busy people—people that were always in a state of perspiration and excitement, and really were fatiguing themselves by continual, absolutely uninterrupted business. My friend, what about? Everything depends upon your answer to that. I know you have been busy, but you may have been so busy as not to be able to do anything; you may have been so fogged up that you did not really know which is the door and which is the window of your house. But you have been so busy, so active, and there is no keeping you still; your poetical wife said, There was really no getting him to sit down. I am sorry. Oh, that he had sat down for a long time! So many people are busy here and there, and letting the King pass by; so many people are busy that they never heard the prophet; they had heard something of him, but the great Ezekiel himself they never saw, the man of fire, the man all wings, the dweller in the heavens and on the earth; and when he had gone they said in a kind of gossipy cheerfulness that they never heard him. What have they been doing? No one knows; but so busy, so energetic, so active. But they might have heard Ezekiel and seen the prophet that read the colors of the amber and the fire and the motion of the wheel, but they never saw him. Oh that men were wise, that they understood just when to sow the seed, when to take the tide at the flood; oh that men were wise, that they bought up the opportunity as they would buy up a wedge of gold! The complaint is not that the men are indolent, but that they are industrious at the wrong point and about the wrong thing. Lord, give me a wise and understanding heart that I may be busy about Thy business; then Thou wilt write what epitaph my industry and faithfulness may deserve.

"How long have I to live," that I may pay all that I owe? This is not a question of money only, it is a far greater question. What do you owe to your family? Have you spoken enough to your boys? Have you been a boy with them, so that people have sometimes been uncertain which is the boy and which is the father, so united and harmonious and mutually completing are your lives? Have you kept other vineyards and failed to keep your own vineyard? Have you been so busy about the committee and with the Sunday-school and the church organization and all the diverse charities connected with the church that you are almost a stranger at home? How much owest thou to the past? Pay the bill of thy neglect, and take a receipt from the hand of God.

There we are face to face with the great fact that we may die at any moment; therefore we should ask the question, What is it to live? How long have I to live? I reply by asking another question, What do you mean by living? Do you mean eating, drinking, self-indulgence? Do you mean neglecting all things spiritual, invisible, and eternal? Then you and I are not attaching the same definition to the word *live* or *living*. To live means to live the life of faith, to live the loving life of trust in the Son of God and obedience to His Cross and to His will. We only live as we live and move and have our being in God. The life of the body is nothing; it perishes while we enjoy it or while we use it. "How long have I to live," O poor soul of mine? Dost thou ask me such question as a Christian preacher? Ask it again, and assure me that thine heart is in the piercing interrogation. How long have I to live? The answer is from the Christian pulpit: Forever.

Prayer

Almighty God, Thou art gentle unto Thy creatures with a great gentleness. Thou dost stoop to the lowliness of their condition; Thou dost fill the vessel of their unbelief; Thou dost answer the cry of their perplexity. Thou art indeed a great and terrible God: yet who is like unto Thee in pity and mercy and the fullness of tears? God is a consuming fire—God is love. We know it all, we can explain but little of it; we know the meaning of the fire and the meaning of the love, and we know that sometimes they are both the same thing. But we cannot see afar off; no man hath seen the tomorrow that is hidden in God's eternity. Make us humble, dependent, yet expectant. We thank Thee for Thy way of education; it is like the way of no other teacher; Thou dost train us by a way that we know not, and Thou dost lead us by the same way, and Thou dost separate between the know and the know-not as with sunbeams. O, how strange is Thy way! How heavy Thy rod, yet how gentle Thy hand! We cannot tell the meaning of all this; we are like poor outsiders who have not seen the inside of the house of God and its great meaning. May we wait; may we be sure that Thou art love; then we can live, though all waiting is hard to men made like ourselves. We are impatient, fretful, too easily disappointed; we hear the tender cry in the air, How is it that you have no faith? When we might have a whole heartful, and by the power of the Cross and the sanctification of the Holy Ghost might rule the world, the flesh, and the devil, and subdue them under our feet. Lord, increase our faith! Amen.

21
The Point of Perplexity

Preached on Thursday Morning, May 24th, 1900.

We cannot tell what He saith—John 16:18.

That is a point in the history of the soul which often passes without recognition. We are great on infidels; we deliver courses of lectures upon blatant and vulgar infidelity; some men have made their reputation along those lines. And others are great on triumphant faith; some ready skillful writers have written hymns of victory for the use of the Church in its highest mood. We thank God for such poets and prophets. But the we-cannot-tell period—has that period any lyrist, any poet of high and worthy aim? We are all now and then in the we-cannot-tell period, and has any man arisen to turn our cannot-tell into some kind of joyous and hopeful psalm? Will you kindly suspend your lectures to absentee infidels, and come to these poor souls who are fumbling and groping and crying, We cannot tell whether this should be, or that should be, or whether we are now going exactly to the right or somewhere to the left. What a field there is unoccupied for the souls in the cannot-tell period! We dare not mention it even in prayer; and yet here we are with all these problems round about, all these great unsolved enigmas, yet we would like to know what the answer is. Sometimes, perhaps, our prayer descends to prying, and then God cuts it in two with a sharp wind. But there is a desire that is holy; there is a going round and round problems and looking at them with a wonder that is almost an answer, with a great and delicate expectancy which mounts sometimes as high as prayer. You know how skillfully you have answered the unbeliever, you have ground him to powder, you have cut him into small pieces, you have scorned him and driven him away, and have had no mercy or pity on his unbelieving soul. Have you any genius left that you can expend upon the fumblers and gropers who believe that at any moment they may see the Lord, and get the key from His girdle, and go up and down opening the secret drawers in the marvelous cabinet of mysteries? These men are not unbelievers; they are not to be treated with contempt or with neglect; they are earnest men, and they see a great deal further than many men who condemn them. Yet they have quite a large bundle of problems, and they are saying to one another, Do you know anything about this? Have you one little trembling ray of light like the trembling of the receding star? No, I have not. Have *you?* Well, but yesternight, I thought I saw some light on that problem. I am going to watch tonight specially; tonight I may see that star that seems to light all the other stars; come, watch with me: who knows what we may see tonight? Mark all the periods through which the poor soul passes. There is a great period of downright unbelief, in which man has no faith but in his own disbelief; he denies the Bible, he denies God, he denies the Cross, he denies all the religious possibilities and prophecies, and he seems to grow proud of his unfaith. There is no mistaking that man. We have all passed through that period; we have been dead in trespasses and sins, and we have seemed to take a kind of gleeful delight in our want of faith. We are not in a negative relation to the great verities, but at the period now within contemplation we simply repudiate them, scoff them, yea, we would break them in pieces like a potter's vessel if we could. We have passed through that rude, miserable state of semi- if not total idiocy. There are men who are still in that period of development; they smile, if they do not broadly laugh, at the idea of an inspired book, actually translated into our mother tongue, and as to entering the sanctuary of God and taking part in simple, holy exercises of worship, such an idea would be utterly beneath their intellectual dignity, as they themselves measure it. I say that regarding that class of persons we have no doubt, and they need have no doubt about themselves; their position is defined, rampant, outrageous.

Then there is another kind of faith; I will call it, if you please, for want of a happier term, faith *minus*. It is not without positiveness; it has a certain fleeting life of its own; yet in the statement of the creed there is a great disjunctive which separates the parts, dividing them almost asunder. That state of mind was beautifully represented by the dear, sweet creature who uttered the creed of the whole Church, in some of its moods, when he said, "Lord, I believe; help Thou mine unbelief." That is what I say when I hear all the creeds of the churches. I do not believe in creeds written and subscribed and sworn-to and forgotten. Yet when I read these gatherings up of holy words, and feel as it were the pulses of the ages trembling in those syllables I say, Lord, I believe; help Thou mine unbelief. I have sung this creed to Thee, but I do not believe it all, and I would gladly believe a great many things which I have not yet received into my faith; Lord, I believe; help Thou mine unbelief, that it may be sphered out into a great planet-like faith, a complete star and glow of confidence intellectual and spiritual.

See how we advance! The first man a blatant unbeliever, rejoicing in his want of faith, and contemning with cold, cruel scorn the men who do believe. Then we come to faith *minus*, faith that would eke out its own unbelief, and failing there would seek the Lord's aid in eking it out. Do not treat these people unkindly, because if you treat them unkindly you treat them unwisely and unjustly; they want to pray as much as you pray; they would like to live on the mountains, right away on the hilltops, which catch the first kiss of the morning sun; they cannot climb so high just yet; we must go down to them, and say that presently, it may be, in the power and grace of God and His Christ, they will be up to the very gate and portal of the morning, the gate which has a precious stone, and there they will see Aurora in all her bridal beauty, and she will kiss them because they are seeking her love and benediction. Do not boast of your semi-faith; let there be no boasting. Some men make a kind of god of their infidelity. They do not know that they are molding a little clay deity of their own, but they are doing so nevertheless; they have their own little ways of worship and their own petty and futile deities, and there is a subtle possibility that a man may be hawking round his semi-belief or his semi-unbelief and may be seeking to attract attention by his quavering but most conscious unbelief. Beware of that state of mind. O, be frank, white of heart, really candid, spiritually bright because all the colors are blent into one beauty of holiness.

And then we can go into another region and find a man who is no infidel, but a plain doubter. There are so many cattle in that pen that I should like to have them carefully counted before asking much about them. But there are the doubters: can we not send them away on some long excursion; can we not bring to bear upon them all that is kind and all that is intellectually superior; and thus treat them according to the grade of their unbelief? We cannot. Some men make a religion of doubt. When a man calls himself an honest doubter, I always ask in a polite voice and tone for his references. An honest doubter? No honest man calls himself honest; the moment he begins to tell me that he is now speaking honestly I know that he never did speak honestly, because honesty, transparency, speaks like a little child, speaks exactly what is the truth at the moment, and is not afraid of being inconsistent because it talks differently at seven to what it did at three years of age. I say to this boy, You are inconsistent; when I last saw you, you were just three years old, and you talk quite differently today; and therefore I charge you with inconsistency. There is an inconsistency of growth. I find the brick wall where I left it; I never find the young growing tree just where I saw it last; there is another leaf a little further out, there is a branch struggling to be just as long and strong as any other branch. That is the inconsistency I love, the inconsistency of growth, evolution, development, progress. Grow in grace and in the knowledge of our Lord Jesus Christ. Beware, however, of being a sort of doubter that requires to be often invited out to tea to have itself relieved by kind and misunderstanding friends who whisper, Sh! I think he is improving. There are some infidels who become the more infidels the more that they are infideled. If you would let them alone they would soon come in for something substantial and nutritious to eat. Have the gospel ready, the high verities, the great house of God filled with the bread of the Father, and when you hear a tap on the door, fly to open it, and bid the knocker welcome to the feast of Christ's body and blood and heart and atoning love.

Thus we have had these three people before us—the disbeliever, and the believer *minus,* and the doubter, who calls himself Thomas, greatly to the disgust of the original Thomas. And then we come to the great, the supreme act of belief itself. I have been waiting to see that lovely face; I knew it would come—belief, trust in God, really going over to the Almighty through the Cross and by the power of the Eternal Spirit. What a face is the face of Faith! How it glows like the morning, beams and gleams like June's brightest noontide, and what a summerlike freshness and abundance there is about the faith that conquers and works by love! Said Christ to one poor soul, "Believest thou that I am able to do this?" And he said, "Lord, I believe." Enough! The miracle was done while the man was breathing his confession. That man had no greater figure in history by which he could stand than the figure of Abram when the Lord said unto him in a night watch, Behold these things; look up: canst thou count their number? as their number is so shall be the number of thy seed. And Abram is reported to have believed God. Now there arises the Abram of the New Testament, who says, "Lord, I believe." Then be it unto thee as thou wilt; take what thou canst of heaven; be a man in thy faith.

But now we come to the class of the text, "We cannot tell what He saith"; we come to the point of perplexity. It may be thus, or it may be so: what thinkest thou, John, James, Peter? Are you all silent? So am I. "A little while, and ye shall see Me; a little while, and ye shall not see Me, because I go unto the Father." What is this that He saith? We cannot tell what He saith. We are at the cannot-tell period. No infidels are we and no doubters; it is still *He*—that wondrous pronoun that gathers into its ample meaning and its glowing love all the nouns that have ever represented Him in the grammar of history. What is this that He saith? We cannot tell what He saith. It is still He, the living, beautiful One, the brother-sister, the man-woman of the race, who carries the crown and a Cross, for He is the Lord that saved the world.

Many of us are at this poin; we cannot explain the words of Jesus; we are glad that many of them are yet without explanation; we have no confidence in those people who know all about it, as they would vulgarly say. We want to have knowledge enough to make us silent; we want to know enough that we may pray in a humble tone. There are persons who know all that the Almighty thought in the counsels of eternity; there are people who can write it all down in plain black ink and make other men swear to it, or cast them out as heterodox and an unbelieving and noisome nuisance. I do not want to belong to that class. I am rich in having a revelation concerning large parts of which I say, I cannot tell what they say. "All that ever came before Me are thieves and robbers." What is this that He saith? "All that ever came before Me are thieves and robbers." Well, Moses came before Him; many of the great teachers and moralists came before Him: what is this that He saith? All that ever came before Him are thieves and robbers? We cannot tell what He saith. But He said so much other than this that the greater quantity helps to relieve the darkness of the smaller, helps indeed to make that smaller a puzzle for the education rather than for the destruction of faith. "All that ever came before Me." What was the year in which Plato came? And what was the year in which the great Latin moralists taught? What was the age in which the great Moses read the tables of the law to the people? My good people, you are altogether on the wrong track of inquiry. "All that ever came before Me" is not a clock phrase, is not a time quantity;

any man that sets himself "before" Christ, in front of Christ, who attempts to supersede Christ or to render Christ unnecessary, he is a thief and a robber, whenever he lived, and even if he be living today. And there are men who set themselves before Christ this morning. But they cannot live; place after place they haunt is given over to the spiders; there is not enough in their poor weazened faith to pay the ground rent. They cannot live. If you have faith as a grain of mustard seed you can live, and no intellectual dandy can put you down in the long run. What lives is faith. What is faith? Life in God: "He that liveth and believeth in Me shall never die." What is this that He saith? All men that live and believe in Him shall never die? We cannot tell what He saith; Peter, James, John are going over the first line—Paul, do you know what He means— "He that liveth and believeth in Me shall never die"? My dear ones, say you, thinking of husband or wife or child or friend or pastor, surely lived and surely believed, and yet they are dead: what is this that He saith? "He that liveth and believeth in Me shall never die." That word "die" has puzzled the ages; like all the other great words, it occurs first in the book of Genesis, and it has been a fruitful source of mischief because of misunderstanding all these ages. No man can explain fully and exhaustively the word die; it is a dead language, an unknown tongue. And yet now and again we seem to feel that it is still alive and has meanings in it that we can at least dimly apprehend. But death is often an abused and often a mis-used word. Why, I heard of death. What have you heard of death? I heard that death is swallowed up in victory. "He that liveth and believeth in Me shall never die."

"Except a man eat My flesh and drink My blood, there is no life in him." What is this that He saith? "Eat My flesh, drink My blood"—what, can this Man give us His flesh to eat? What ignorant questions we ask; how wanting in spiritual imagining, in that great dream power of the soul that escapes merely circumstantial theol-ogy and enters into the very heart and breath of God. How can this Man be in twenty different places at once, in two thousand different places at once? How can He be here and yonder, miles away at the same time? He said to us in the very first interview we had with Him; "The Son of Man which is in heaven." Yet we were standing looking at Him, He was sitting on the earth, and He said the Son of Man is in heaven. How can He be both on earth and in heaven at the same time? Because He was the Son of God. "Lo, I am with you even unto the end of the world,"—wherever you go in My name I go with you. A perplexity in merely human words; no perplexity at all in the glow and triumph of faith.

So then we come again, you see, to the point of perplexity. There are scriptures we can hardly read, let them alone for the time being; there are other scriptures that we can only partially explain, and we go to them now and then to see if the buds be opening and if we can inhale fresh fragrance in the King's garden; there are other passages that mothers can speak to children, and children can understand by their hearts, and in these passages we revel and triumph and hold sweet sacrament. Why do you not confine yourselves to those things that you can really take hold of and apply and profit by? Why will you be endeavoring to read books you cannot read? Let them alone; not forever, mayhap, but for the time being, and keep to your psalm, your sweet Jesus words, to the smile of the Master, to the encouragement of the apostles. I hope someday some strong man, who is ready to be slain by the Church, will arise, and read us the Bible by the distribution of progressive steps so that we shall end with Moses, and thus understand what Moses meant; go back to roots and origins and plasmas, and thus interpret the Old Testament by the New and the New by the Old, and find that they are the same sacrament, and the same Testament, and the same covenant with the souls of men. But we are so timid. Every man that has yet risen to do something in the world has been killed. Be perfectly sure of that, and be quite sure that ye will rise again in the proportion in which you are true, in which you have anticipated the time and rode three centuries in the van. But O, before it comes to pass what ostracism, what starvation, what gathering-up of robes and passing-by of those who have not the same flame or the same sight and passion of faith!

Now how did Jesus Christ treat this point of perplexity? First of all, He did not rebuke it; He said, What ye know not now ye shall know hereafter: I keep a great school known by the name Hereafter, and you will be promoted to that higher school in due time; do not expect to do everything in twelve hours; do not expect to do everything within the little span of your life; hereafter ye shall see; hereafter ye shall know. I have many things to say unto you, but you could not bear them now; why, you could not even hear them now; you would not understand them now; for My revelation is gradual and progressive; it is like the path of the just man, shining more and more unto the perfect day, and we forget that we ever saw the gray, cold time of winter. He does not do away with the point of perplexity; He says, it is good for you to have this puzzle; work away at that in the meantime; do not be impatient, do not tear the organ to pieces in order to see where the music comes from, and do not be taking up the roots of the flowers to see how the roots are getting on. Simply wait; O, wait upon the Lord; wait patiently for Him, and He will come with the morning star. Yes, Jesus Christ satisfies perplexity with a promise: Not now, but in another time.

Are we at the cannot-tell period of Christian experience? Well, men have been there before us; Jesus Christ noted the people who were at that point and treated them with great gentleness, with ineffable love. Hear the soliloquies of perplexity; hear the moan of the non-understanding of some words that He saith: Why am I so unfortunate? I pray seven times a day with my window open to Jerusalem, but no white dove comes to me with an answer from the gardens of God. O, why am I so outrun and overborne with business and trade and competition? There is always one man gets in before I get down to the troubled pool. O, what is this that He saith? I seem to have taken hold of one end of the promise, but I am unable to take hold of the other end of the promise. O, why so poor, so harassed; and my next-door neighbor has plenty, and a man just within sight of my window has abundance upon abundance, and I live all day and all night in the cold companionship of poverty. O, why am I so bereaved? Why may I not have had that life spared to me? It would have done God no harm; it would have done me an infinite good, so far as I can see the case at present. I cannot tell what He doeth, I cannot tell what He sayeth. O, how is this? Jesus understands the perplexity, and He is going to make that perplexity an education and a comfort and a triumph, and I will one day have to ask His pardon for misreading His words and misinterpreting His providence. We cannot tell. Hereafter, the explanation long delayed will be forthcoming. Then we shall praise the Lord in a great thunder song, one emulating the other to be the louder and the sweeter in the great anthem.

Prayer

Almighty God, Thou hast undertaken the conduct of our life, and we will not through unbelief interfere with the action of Thy providence. We will go up the hill and down into the valley as Thou mayest decide, into the wilderness or the garden as Thou dost please, where the fresh fountains play or where there is no water for our thirst. Thy will be done; pay no heed to ours. Thou knowest Thine own end and purpose, and Thou wilt bring all things to bear thereupon; may we learn the piety of silence; may we speak not while the Lord is present; may we be dumb before the Most High, and commit our way into Thy hand. We bless Thee for many shinings of the morning; we thank Thee for many a golden hour; we remember that we have walked by the blue sea when there was no storm upon all its waters. We remember too that Thy way towards us has been full of mystery, and yet we dare not question Thee; we had a question upon our lips, but we stifled it; Thou didst give us the victory which overcomes, even faith upon faith which means assured triumph. We nearly asked Thee; we were on the point of breaking silence; sometimes we could hardly keep in our breath, for it was hot with riotousness, and behold, the spirit of unbelief did drive us into the wilderness so that we were tempted of the devil. Thou hast tried us sorely; we have nearly fallen upon those things which Thou hast taken away, and nearly have we cried that Thou shouldst not have them. Thou hast given unto us bitter bread; Thou hast given unto us also waters of sorrow; Thou hast sometimes seemed to us to be very hard in Thy judgment, and to have lost Thy mercy and Thy tears. We have cried out bitterly against Thee; we dare not always put our bitterness into words, but it was none the less bitter. We said, Why is this? we said. O Lord, how long? And we nearly hurled great questions at Thee which would have been as blows in Thy face. Oh, how narrow is the road; how strait is the gate; how difficult is the path! But seeing that the end of all is righteousness and purity and heaven, we will endeavor to be men in Thy spirit and by Thy grace, and not complain. Thou knowest the wildness of our grief, the scorching heat of our misery; Thou interpretest all the unspoken desires, and sometimes

Thou dost secretly answer the problem that is too much for our faith. Yet, remembering all this, and quietly receiving it as from the Lord, we will recall the sunny days, the earlier times, when Thou wast more manifestly with us, when Thou didst shine upon us as the morning shines upon the opening flowers. This is the miracle of Thy Cross; this is the great wonder of Thy love. O Thou Man, Son of man, whose seals are five red wounds, torn and gashing into the flesh, let every blooddrop of Thine be an encouragement to us. The Lord hear us, for there must be something in this wild woe after all; we must wait in the appointed Jerusalem, till shall come the interpreting Spirit and the delivering Lord. Amen.

22

Unspoken Inquiries

Preached on Sunday Morning, May 27th, 1900.

Jesus knew that they were desirous to ask Him—John 16:19.

He saw their lips shape into a question. But they dare not go any further. This presents Christ to us in a most interesting and pathetic aspect. He knows the unspoken prayer—blessed be God! There are prayers we dare not put into words; there are wonders and problems to which we dare not give expression. We do not know one another sufficiently, or we would know that behind many an utterance of faith there is a deep moan of unbelief. We put our best selves forward on many occasions, and we do so without pretense or conceit; we try to think ourselves into better selves, and in advance we speak the great words we shall one day speak as part of the current experience and reality. Sometimes we store our prayers; they are the prayers that are going to be answered in a month, perhaps next year; we have many entries into the execution of which we have not yet come. We have pledged to meet the Lord under a hawthorn bush, in a wide green field, in some little bay by the sea that nobody knows of but ourselves. We must not be taken just at the moment as always realizing the high triumphs which we venture to express in words; they are the triumphs that are going to be, the victories of the long-coming tomorrow. We can only enter into these mysteries and eternities by prolonged, deep long-suffering and long-torturing experience.

The happiness is that Jesus Christ knows all about this; He knows the questions we would like to ask, how many they are, how urgent.

This is the comfort, that Jesus knows every one of them. Is there not some significant smile of all-love and half-pity upon His face as He watches the prayers we dare not pray, as He sees the questions struggling and choking in our very throats, and yet we dare not give them audible utterance? We are two men; we are dual, bivalvular, binary stars, contradictions, mutual self-completions, and a mass of paradox and inconsistency. The comfort of it all is that Jesus knows it all. We can almost penetrate His thought, He has made us so familiar with the method of His pity. Poor disciples! And yet we are just like them; our experience is identical with theirs. Oh the questions we would like to ask! Yet we feel that the asking of them would be an act of impiety; we seem to feel as if the asking of a question would be an act of bankruptcy in the great course of a living faith, and as if, asked we such questions, we should give up all the old things, all the old resounding psalms, all the venerable creeds and holy verities on which our souls fed long, long ago. Yet we want to ask the questions, and Jesus knows that we are desirous to ask them. Let us watch Him coming along; He may interpret our attitude and give it words. The Lion of the tribe of Judah hath the power to open all seals; He may rend the seal of our ignorance and our agonizing desire. Let us tarry awhile here and there. Jesus will find us out, and we can so look that He will understand the expression, and so kind is He that He may find words for our silence and our distress.

Jesus finds us sitting by the grave, and He knows that we are desirous to ask Him, and we dare not. So we can only look, but what a look it is! How it tears the heavens in twain, how it pleads with the eloquence of miserable silence! He pauses, He draws near; He also looks as well as we do; there is a masonry of facial expression; He knows the meaning of the dumbness, and knows that it is the biggest eloquence we ever poured out of our lips, and yet we dare not but restrain the growing flood lest we should grieve Him by unintentional impiety. Dare you ask Him? You are on terms of great familiarity with this Jesus who is now almost bending over us—dare you tell Him our desire? The grave is so little, and it is the first grave we ever dug in our house; it is the burial-place of a little flower I am desirous to ask Him why the flower ever budded; I am desirous to ask Him how He thinks we can partake of the sacrament of silent misery when we go back this summer afternoon to our lonely home. Dare you ask Him, wife?—a woman hath greater power than a man. Jesus knows that we are desirous to ask Him, and as to the disciples so to us He says, "Do ye inquire among yourselves of that I said, A little while, and ye shall not see Me: and again, a little while, and ye shall see Me?" He begins, thus He gives us liberty; now let the flood of our questions rush upon His attentive ear; something may come out of this interview. Always let Jesus begin; He knows when to open the holy conference; He pities the silence that is killing us. Other people have a good many collateral and indirect comforts and solaces, but we had only this one; when that one went all went. The man who has only one ewe lamb is not to be thought of as one of the people who have flocks that make the hillsides alive; the man who has only one fig-tree is not to be treated as a man whose figs and olives and vines are not to be counted in human numbers. Can Jesus reach a case like mine? you say. Yes, He can; there is nothing we ever suffered that He has not suffered, only a thousand times more intensely in all that strains the very nerves of the soul. If anyone else has suffered this, I have already divided my misery; find me my companion-sufferer; Jesus knows that I am desirous to ask Him, and perhaps through this companion He may send me an answer: O come thou, sent by the Son of God. You do not know how much of real comfort and strength you would part with if you asked all your questions in plain words. There is a comfort in reservation; reticence has its own sanctuary into which it retires as into a deeper self-preservation. Sometimes misery is the very jewel of joy. We cannot teach these things in a school, we cannot take pence and shillings for the teaching of such meanings; we must live them, and come out of them as strong men, and then we shall know they cannot be taught in words.

Jesus Christ is coming this way today; let us be found reading His holy book and stopping at the difficult places. He comes; I see Him but a yard or two away; now you look quietly and intently at the hard places; find them all out, mark them with markings of the hand and of the heart, and be speaking them—sh!—just as He passes; He will know that we are desirous to ask Him. Let us not be fools who look only at the hard places, and think they are the whole revelation; there is a better method. We should look at the words we can understand, and then at the words we cannot understand, and He may find us just between the two points: who knows but that He may explain His own word? Never man spoke like this Man. The oil of grace is poured into His lips; He can speak to misery as if He had lived with it all His life, and He can, as we have just said in a recent exposition, touch a wound without hurting it. Many of us are at the hard places of the Bible; we are desirous to ask the Writer of the holy book, and we dare not put the question; but He knows that we are desirous to ask Him. Sometimes, instead of answering us directly, He quietly, as a summer breeze might do it, turns over the page, and then there are words that a child cannot misunderstand, great full-blown promises: I will never leave thee, I will never forsake Thee. We can understand that. There are passages I cannot understand, and therefore I will not go and interrogate them and waste my spiritual energy in endeavoring to level them down to my poor mode of speech; I will go back to that further promise, I will make myself quite at home in the jewel-house of heaven; I will make myself rich with the exceeding great and precious promises with which God has supplied the storehouse of the Church. Why should I be so perverse as to go to the hard texts which I never can understand, and leave all the texts that a child might comprehend? I will feed upon the bread, though I cannot understand the process of germination; I know the true bread, and I know that it alone can satisfy mine hunger. Why should I trouble myself about chemical questions which I have not learned or which I have not intellectual capacity enough to penetrate and comprehend? Very often Jesus

Christ does not answer the hard text, but He simply turns over the page, as I have already said, and almost finger-marks it, as who should say, That is the answer; what more you want will come in life's far-off tomorrow; meanwhile here is a question bathed in the sunlight and seen at the noonday of conscious love.

That is what I am endeavoring to do as a preacher of the Word. I do not understand the Bible; here and there I understand a little part of it, and to that little part I cling with all the intensity of my love. Do not expect anybody to be able to explain all the mysteries of divine revelation; otherwise you would reduce the exposition of the Scriptures to a science or a fine art, or a priestly trick, or something that can only come by great intellectual expertness: whereas the Word of God is not that hard text or the other; it is something that breathes through all the texts, hard and simple, and unites them into one grand, luminous, sympathetic, redeeming revelation. Do not suppose that preachers have no biblical difficulties. I am standing in a harvest field full of such difficulties; I am no priest; I am a fellow-student; I am a brother suppliant; if I have lived a little longer than some other men, and I am able to explain a passage here and there, so be it; that is lovely; that is true cooperation of soul. Let us set aside all the very hard passages and say, When the Lord comes, He will throw light upon them all, and until He does come He has given us passages enough to be going on with—bread passages, and gifts of living water, and consolations that can hunt every misery out of the soul and fill the soul with morning light, which is morning hope.

So, if we review the whole scheme and economy of life, there are many things we would like to ask Jesus. How is it that this man prospers, and he never prays? How is it that I have to make all my life a hard study so as to keep out of debt and misery, and I try to pray? Jesus knows that I am desirous to ask Him; I want to know about the mystery of the divine going; I want to know why the garden of the atheist brings forth flowers abundantly, and the garden of the suppliant has not a single flower within its four borders. I should like to ask my Lord that question, but I do not know how to put it; I might imperil my own faith by inquiring into the metaphysics of other people's unbelief. Oh, if He would start the subject I would tell Him about twenty whose lives are complete mysteries as viewed from a Christian standpoint; they bet and gamble and swear, and riot and revel and dance, and cannot get through their money. I would tell Him then of the poor woman who cannot make money enough to pay her rent. If He would begin the subject! He may do some day; then I will venture upon it, and embrace the opportunity of having all my doubts cleared up, and I will be glad to have some divine illumination upon the plan of providence. Meanwhile I am an Asaph with a song he dare not sing, a harp he dare not use, a question he may not ask.

The very desirousness to ask is a proof of the existence of some faith in the soul. That is a delightful and most vital point. Our very perplexities may be evidences of our faith. If we had no faith, who would care to ask any questions about this chaotic, tumultuous world? Why not join in the uproarious atheism and get what gladness you can out of it? It is because there is something tugging at the heart; it is because there is a pleading voice saying, Do not give up faith; many things are but for a moment; life has its visions filmy and transient; you cannot give up your faith without giving up your very soul's soul, the very innermost plasma of being. It is everything to keep that wondrous belief. Take it with all the possible questions and stings and miseries. You must have manifold experience of life, and there is nothing that can so surely and completely support and sustain you as the faith that the outcome of the whole chaotic movement will be a palace, a temple of the holy presence. You do not want to ask every question today; you do not want to consume this morning all the bread you have in the house; you lay up in store; you say, There is a future, and we must make some provision for it. Now in the spiritual world there is a future, and we must be prepared to wait for it. Tarry ye in Jerusalem until ye be endued with power from on high. When the power comes you will know it: flame has a way of making itself known.

Unasked questions need not mar believing prayers. After all, the unasked questions may not be necessary to the edification of the soul. God may educate us by not allowing us to tell everything we want to tell. Self-control is the last result of true power. Not to ask may be to ask. Sometimes not to pray may be the best prayer. This is a great mystery, but I speak concerning Christ and the Church. Oh, if He would begin! He will someday, and it will be a long day, a day without an evening star. The child does not cast away the home letter because there is a word here and there which he cannot make out; nor does the child depreciate the letter because he has now and then, it may be, to go to the dictionary to find out the meaning of some word. Why, the mother may have put those words in on purpose; she said in her heart, He is fond of looking up the dictionary, now this will give him a chance; I put in a long word where I might have put a short one to educate the child, to excite his attention, and to lead him into further inquiry. Sometimes I myself write a letter—nay, many times; it is one of my eccentricities—all badly spelled; I know what interest it will excite at the other end. I spell receive with *ie,* and believe with *ei,* and with all sorts of little orthographical tricks, I fill up the page. The child at first is amazed, exclaims indeed what a bad speller I am; then at the end of the letter I say, "Please excuse the spelling," and the child thinks that I have been up to something. And so I have, and for his sake; because in a postscript I say, "Will you be good enough to mark all the misspelled words in this letter, and let me have it back again?" What do we know about the home scheme of Providence, the upside-downness of many things, the eccentric plan of no-plan? All these things may come to be revealed to us by-and-by, and then we may find that all the while the Lord has been educating us, arresting our attention, asking us to pay attention. The Lord's way must be done; it is the best way: trust Him!

Now desire may mean life. A dead body does not desire; the living body does desire, and must have its food, its water, and its due attention. Desire may mean inspiration, as who should say on the part of God, Let it be so that this soul may inquire and be cheered and fired into the exercise of nobler energy. Sometimes it may mean trust. I will trust him where I cannot trace him; he is out of my sight now, but he will return. This providence seems very hard, but the Lord doeth all things well. That is true confidence. As we have had occasion to see before, many people never trust their friends; they call them friends and then distrust them. Thus, a man being my friend, and being charged with something—any fool can charge or accuse another—am I to say, Is that possible; he must have forgotten himself for the moment; he must have been over-powered by a sudden temptation; I will ask him to explain the whole thing to me? Never! Ask my friend to explain? Then he is no longer my frien, he is outside my trust. I say to the accuser, Never! It is a lie you have heard! Yet there are many loose-jointed friends who believe anything that is bad. They would believe that you, the senior member of the church, had stolen a horse yesterday if they were told so. What wide, soft, flabby mouths they have! Tthey could swallow a sack, instead of standing up and saying, No! I know nothing about your miserable case, but it is a lie. That is trusting a friend, not setting him upon his trial and interviewing him with the intention of finding out whether he did it or not.

Prayer

Almighty God, in Thee is no death. In the Lord our God there is no darkness. Jesus Christ has come to give men light, and to give men life more abundantly, yea, wave upon wave of life, yea, immortality. We bless Thee that we live in Christ; this is eternal life, to know Thee, the only true God, and Jesus Christ whom Thou hast sent. May we seek for no other life, for other life there is none; behold, the soul that sinneth it shall die. May the Savior's reproach never fall upon us, Ye will not come unto Me that Ye might have life. May we all hasten to the Savior day by day, yea, at dawn and at eventide may we repair to the Fountain that is full of life; thus may our eternity in Christ be established, and our immortality become an immediate and blessed possession. We thank Thee for all thoughts that lift us above the time-sphere and above all space, and that connect us with the kingdom of Thine eternity, Thou Everlasting One, and may enter into the mystery of Thy being that is neither night nor day, but one eternal Now. Deliver us from vain thoughts and little thoughts, and all thoughts that vex and torment the mind and prevent its carrying out its great purpose in the love of the Cross. Be Thou our guest, our abiding one; take up Thine abode with us, and fill our hearts with Thine own heaven. We have come for a little rest; we have retired from the hot footpath, from the thoroughfares of commerce, and we have come into the sanctuary that we may wait a little and tarry before God in expectant prayer. Behold, we remember that now there came a great wind from heaven and shook the place where Thy loved ones were assembled; may we become prepared for the outpouring of the Spirit, and through Jesus Christ our Savior, whose five wounds are five seals, may we expect the Spirit and be ready to receive the glory. Amen.

23

Devourers and Endeavorers

Preached on Thursday Morning, May 31st, 1900.

It devoured men—Ezekiel 19:3.

It was a beast, and yet it devoured men—men that were intended in the divine purpose and love to be sons of God. It was no ordinary quality of men that this beast learned to devour; the message is delivered to "the princes of Israel." "What is thy mother?" A woman—degraded, beastialized. "A lioness . . . and she brought up one of her whelps; it became a young lion, and it learned"—a word to be specially noted—"to catch the prey; it devoured men." The whole lamentation is allegorical. Never omit the ideal from your criticism. We may unduly exalt the ideal or parabolical, or we may unduly repress it, and, shutting it out of our purview, we may starve our highest faculties and get nothing out of the Bible but letters, syllables, written and printed in iron and in ink.

"It devoured men." That is an allegorical lion, a beast that lived long ago, a beast that is dead. There you mistake the whole case. This ravenous lion is not only a lion now, but the beast is alive in every one of us. We go to sundry gardens and other public resorts to see the lions; how lost to the true sense of things are men who think that lions in their truest meaning are beasts in cages that may be visited at so much per head. Sir, you—madam, you, have a beast in you; you are beast—and God. This is the diagnosis which I have made of my own heart; I know I have a devouring beast in me that wants to devour my prayers before I have uttered them; I know there is a bloodsucker in my heart that wants to drink the red blood of my devotion before I can possibly pour it out as an oblation and token of homage before my redeeming God. Why do we not look upon the Bible as published today? Why think of Ezekiel, with all his allegorical wheels and visions and parables and dreams—why think of him as a character belonging to a hoary antiquity, a time that was exciting enough in its own way while it passed over the surface of the earth, but now dead and gone? It is not so. If your Bible is only a letter, I have no wonder at all that you have lost it. People may misplace things, people may put them where they cannot find them again. Why? Because they are things, something to be handled and looked at and moved about. But who can mislay himself? Who can mislay his own soul? Therefore it is that the Bible is the newest book in all the world; it has in it all news; it contained all the intelligence before the intelligence was so to say created by fact. Men will not believe this; they are going in quest of new information and confirmation, whereas the whole thing, the whole human history, is in the Bible. How many of these people before me, Thou God that piercest the heart, have really read the Bible this morning; I mean much of Thy book, quite a considerable portion of Thy revelation? I do not ask Thee who has glanced at the book and read the shortest psalm, but who has this morning bathed himself in the Bible river?

There are two classes in the world at this moment—why should we not recognize them both, and apply and store such practical truths as we may be able to realize? There are two classes going forth this morning and every morning; one may be called, what they call themselves indeed, Endeavorers; the other, wanting to imitate their name and almost forge the label of God's wine, call themselves Devourers. There they are, and you can follow which band you please—endeavorers, devourers—and you cannot belong to the betwixt-and-between party. Perhaps you would not like to belong to the endeavorers, because that name may have to your perverted taste somewhat of cant and infatuation about it, and you want to see how the idea goes on before you join it, and you will join it most lovingly when it does not need you. There are many persons waiting to applaud me as soon as I become a very great man. Then they are my friends; they always were my friends; they had not said much about it perhaps, but they always had a warm side to me, and if ever I became a millionaire twice over and were the prime favorite of the throne, why, of course they knew me. So it is with my religious programs, conceptions, and policies; when they establish themselves in public confidence and reputation, then perhaps there may be some dainty souls that may offer a rejected patronage. And you do not perhaps, on the other hand, like to belong to the devourers; you would not like to imagine that any of your faculties could possibly be so vulgarized and prostituted as to become associated with the awful process of devouring anybody. But you want to belong to the between class, neither an endeavorer nor a devourer. And yet you must be one or the other. God has but two hands, and it is to the right or to the left, and we must by the grace of God or under the temptation of the devil decide which—but one it must be.

What remark occurs to you when thinking about the devourers? A very commonplace remark, but only commonplace because it is profoundly true. The devourer always takes the easy course. That is why I contemn him. God never takes easy courses. Jesus never took an easy course. That is one of the reasons why I from a merely literary point of view delight in the conception of the Jesus of the New Testament. From the very first He would do hard work; He said He would save the world. There are some propositions that glorify themselves by their very boldness. Audacity may be an element and a seal of subdued and holy ambition. The devourer takes an easy course: he suggests doubts; he says, My friend, you take that potion I hold in my hand; it can do you no harm, and it may do you great good; it will cool thee and lull thee and rest your fevered body; you take this; you need not take much at first, or at last; only, take it. The devourer suggests—always does at least when he wishes to be almost pious in the esteem of his victims—that we or they should not do things. It is a negative policy; the tempter whispers that upon the whole it may be safe not to do this or that. The devil is a coward; he slinks and sneaks and hides himself, and comes out at calculated moments and meets lone lives when they are wandering around the garden of beauty and squats on the shoulder and whispers this or that—something easy, tempting, flattering, no harm in it. He never yet said to any loving soul, You have a hard time of it, and I have come to help you. He loves no man; therefore do I with some hot iron, plucked from his own fire, brand him, and send him out with the disfiguring stigma upon his cruel face. Nothing is easier than to destroy, to devour, to consume. How long did it take men to build the minster or the abbey? The abbey took two hundred years to build; give me one half ton of gunpowder or one barrel of dynamite and I will blow it to pieces in a night. Is it possible to blot out the work of two centuries in an hour or two or in one dreary night? Yes, it is quite possible; there is nothing so easy as to destroy, and that is the part which the devil has undertaken because he is a coward, an utterly mean soul. But he would not destroy an abbey, a minster, a sanctuary made beautiful by art? Yes, he would destroy it; he hates all beauty; he loathes the morning star; he would gladly pluck the star of the evening from its setting and crush the jewel under his cruel foot. To destroy, therefore, I repeat, is the easy course.

That is how the devil succeeds so often with young and trustful souls. He says he loves them; he can greatly comfort and enrich them; he can satisfy their ambition, and he can make the way up the steep quite easy, and the young soul will find at the top of the ascent everything—throne and crown supremacy, dominion, and rest, and honor, and as for riches, they are to be had not for the asking, but for the taking, and taking such riches is no burglary; and he says to the young soul, Come! as if inviting the young soul to a festival on the top of the sunny mountains. My son, if sinners, or the devil, entice thee, consent thou not. Nothing is easier than to disfigure. Go to the academy, and in its proudest moment you can spoil the whole of it; you can either set fire to the picture, or you can dip the broad brush in some liquid that will almost immediately erase the proudest figure and the sunniest landscape so that before the evening men would say, Where is the academy? Gone, devoured, disfigured, destroyed. It is the same way with character. My young darling soul, there is a lion which will devour men; it may be lust or drink or ambition or meanest selfishness. It means thee no good; it will smile upon thee and lure thee and promise thee anything to get thee out, away from father, mother, and altar, and sacred association that it may destroy thee. Be warned.

There is another passage in this book of Ezekiel which is of the same tone. That passage speaks of men who are "skillful to destroy." We have had that text; we spent a morning long years ago in meditating upon these words—skillful to take things to pieces, to injure the soul, to make mantraps and soul-snares. There are devils who are experts in the destruction of men, not violent opponents, but eminently skillful, almost artistic. O, they can paint well and plead eloquently and insert the poisoned sting without your feeling the puncture. What is the other class? Endeavorers. And the endeavorer has chosen the hard work. What work has that shepherd chosen who but now took to him his staff and his lamp? He went out: why did he not stay in his own little cottage that dark night and make himself comfortable? Why does he rise and proceed notwithstanding the biting wind and the starless cloud? Because, he says, I have lost one of my sheep, and I must go out to seek it until I find it. That is hard work; therefore it is likely to be good work; it denotes and specifies certain elements and qualities of soul that are more precious than rubies. He will not find warmth in his bed or comfort in his little well-sheltered house; nay, he says, there is one lost, and I go till I find it. That is heroic; that is divine. Whether is easier, to pull down a house or to build it? You could employ quite unskilled people to tear your house to pieces. Here, men, take it down, blow it up, wheel it away. But to put your house up again requires thought, calculation, endeavor, some sense of proportion, and mute music, and to make it so beautiful as to be almost a home as well as a house; that requires energy, skill, devotion. Whether is easier, to make a ladder or to make a character? Whether is easier, to tear a ladder to pieces or to build up a manhood? That building up of manhood means culture, real intelligence, noble, manly sympathy; yea, and it means some sense of the divine presence and touch and inspiration; it means nurture, culture, little-by-little service, nothing seen, quite imperceptible for a long time. The husbandman may have lost patience, but when he sees the first green blade pushing through the black earth, he takes heart again; he multiplies the little blade of corn into a stalk, into ears of corn, into golden harvests, and he feels almost as if the little pricking blade were itself a harvest in miniature.

Now Jesus Christ always undertook hard work, always gave Himself for the life of the world. Said He on one graphic and ever-memorable occasion, Who hath touched Me? The disciples say, Seest Thou how they throng and press upon Thee, and sayest Thou, Who hath touched Me? Of course they have all touched Thee; certainly a great number of people have touched Thee. Nay, said He, one has touched Me for virtue hath gone out of Me, and I am less a man than I was, and yet more than a man, for the giving has been a receiving and the parting of strength has been an accession of power: who touched Me? Who has the electric hand that plucks virtue from the craspedon of Christ? Some people think all touches are alike; there are persons who think that all voices are alike; they say, We can hear you without your speaking so loudly. They do not understand what music and significance there may be in loudness. We do not want an organ that can just make itself heard; we want to make the walls hear it, to make the roof hear it, and the foundation, and we want to receive from that thrill and uplift a sense of dominance, which is sense of God and His heaven. So many men think they have touched Christ when they have only approached Him with a cold, unbelieving, ceremonial hand. What did Jesus Christ undertake to do? He undertook a work which at once seals His deity. I am tired of hearing many people speak about the divinity of Christ; that is in some cases a very elastic and unreliable word. I want to hear men say with their hearts that they believe in the Godhead of Christ; that indicates His real nature, His true power, and His indefeasible ability and right to save the world. He who can save the world is God.

What did Jesus come forth to do? He said, I am come to seek and to save that which was lost. Is that easy work? Does that mean a long all-the-year-round holiday? Does that mean fine raiment and abundance of food and overflowing enjoyment, and entering so passionately into the life of the people as to lose your individuality in their commonplace? It does not. To seek and to save the lost is an action which I will not reduce to a dogma because over dogmas men fight, but I will ask you to consider it for a moment as a conception of power, a possibility in the brain of a madman. O, tell me what does this madman propose to do? He proposes to save the world. Then He is no madman. I proceeded forth and came from God for this purpose, said my Lord and Savior.

We have in the first instance a devourer of men; in the second instance we have a Savior of men. Which are we going to follow? Which will really do us good? Which will talk to us upon the greatest subjects? Let us listen to the conversation of both and determine by the tone of the conversation which is the devourer and which is the endeavorer or savior. You can know the moral meaning of a tone; you have nouse enough to detect insincerity even under its most skillful concealment and variety of mood. You know counterfeit coin from the real coin of the realm, and *vice versa*. The heart knows the Gospel. The listener listens after he has been consciously awakened to his bitter, awful sinfulness, and he says to himself, Which of these two men will do me good? One is a devourer; he says, Do not believe it, never mind the future; this so-called sin is only an invention of certain vague persons and ministries; do not rack and vex your soul about your sin; come away, I will give you a liquid which if you quaff deeply will make you quite a happy man again. No; my heart tells me that you are a liar. What does this man say who is a Savior? Come unto Me, all ye that labor and are heavy laden, and I will give you rest: if any man thirst, let him come unto Me and drink. I am the way, the truth, and the life; if any man will be My disciple, let him take up his cross and follow Me. O, this is health; there is health in the man's voice; there is health in every offer He makes. He wants to give me relief from my burning thirst, He wants to give me rest, He wants to introduce me to the Father, and He does not lay down easy and tempting terms; the price is the Cross. His discipline proves His theology. Which shall we follow, brethren? Let us make up our minds. The beast is there; your adversary the devil goeth about like a roaring lion seeking whom he may devour, and there is nothing so easy as to devour. It required God to create man. A devil can devour him.

Prayer

We bless Thee for this Pentecost. May the power of the Spirit dwell in us and be upon us; may there be a glow and a brightness as of heavenly fire round about our life. May we be known by fire; may men be assured that we have been with the Holy One because of the glow that is in our hearts and the fervent charity which makes our lives felt as a great and gracious power. We bless Thee for the Holy Spirit, the unseen, yea, the invisible never to be seen, always to be felt—a great Presence in the heart and life, giving us joy and peace in believing, and raising our Christian character to its supremest point. We thank Thee for the Holy Ghost as the interpreter of Christ; He takes of the things of Christ and shows them unto us; He does not speak of Himself; whatsoever He hears that does He report to our souls, so that we are kept in touch with heaven and with the eternal counsel. O wondrous privilege, ineffable delight, heaven begun! O that men were wise, that they understood these things, that they might know that all things grow up from the visible to the invisible, and thus return to their source. We have stopped intermediately and befooled ourselves by worshiping the things that are seen; we have mistaken bigness for greatness, and nearness for importance; we have not seen the Lord with the eyes of purity, with the heart of tenderness, and with the spirit of love. We have beheld the outside, and have made an idol of it, yea, a graven image, and a thing to be bowed down unto. We have heard the gentle voice, the spiritual music, saying unto us, God is a Spirit. But we have not received the gospel; we still look at things visible, and touch the things we can lay our hands upon, and we are as fools before God. Men have sought to build Thy temple of wood and of stone and of things that could be appraised in plain figures; they will not hear the sweet, tender spirit which says, The kingdom of heaven cometh not by observation, by ritual, and ceremony, and church-going, and altar-building, but is a great mystery of the heart, a wondrous kingdom absorbing the whole life, and turning its love into sacrifice and service for others. Pity us, Thou God of mercy; we have clothed our nakedness, and we have thought we could clothe God also. Thou didst intend us to be simple and true and beautiful, pure and flowerlike through and through, but we have debased ourselves and brought a manhood to Thee that requires Thine own blood to redeem. O the pity of it and the heart-soreness! God be merciful unto the foolish men that have misrepresented the kingdom of God, and have not known that it is invisible, ineffable, eternal. Amen.

24
Spiritual Diversity

Preached on Whit-Sunday Morning, June 3rd, 1900.

The vessels being diverse one from another—Esther 1:7.

At the great feast vessels of gold were given to the dazzled guests. It was a great feast: "When he showed the riches of his glorious kingdom and the honor of his excellent majesty many days, even a hundred and fourscore days." Then the king made a feast unto the people. He did not care who came; he was in a lavish mood, and said, Let everybody take what he wants. And there were given to the guests to drink vessels filled with wine, vessels of gold. Silver went for nothing; and the vessels were diverse one from another, no two alike, the kind of thing that pleases men in their low estate. To think that no two vessels were alike! There was wonder; there was glory. Poor things! O sad and heart-wearing to live within the cackle and the noise of such poor creatures! As if this were something new, as if the king had hit upon an original idea and were the patron of great novelties. O the pity of it and the heartache! As if this were something new! Why, this was from the beginning of the creation. There is another King that has no two cups alike, that has made or created millions upon millions of cups and vessels, and never repeated the plan. But who would think of going to God for originality? We go to the shop windows for the latest novelties. That God should have allowed such creatures to prowl about His universe! No two grassblades are alike. Things that seem to be identical are diverse one from another, and we never see the diversity; nay, some hearts are so made that they would constitute this as a charge against God, that He does not repeat the same thing, but makes sameness into variety, and monotony into great delights of music. It is so terrible to live with the vulgar. Through and through the whole economy of God as we know it by revelation, observation, and experiment, the great principle of novelty prevails.

What wonderful things we read about this in the New Testament! Who would ever think of going to the New Testament for anything original? But the time will come when Jesus will have His turn. I find that the other originals grow stale; custom stales their finite and abominable and miscalled variety. Jesus Christ has no two vessels alike in His beautiful palace-church. When He went up on high, "He gave some, apostles; and some, prophets; and some, evangelists; and some, pastors and teachers . . . till we all come in the unity of the faith, and of the knowledge of the Son of God, unto a perfect man, unto the measure of the stature of the fullness of Christ." No two Christians are alike, and they do not understand this, and therefore they get into controversy and build themselves up into little sects and denominations. We must recognize the sovereignty of God in all this variety. That is the thing we neglect to do. "All flesh is not the same flesh, but there is one kind of flesh of men, another flesh of beasts, another of fishes, and another of birds"; and God can go on through all eternity making all these over again without any reference whatever to what we ourselves have seen and catalogued. Poor man! He can catalogue his originalities. "There are also celestial bodies, and bodies terrestrial: but the glory of the celestial is one, and the glory of the terrestrial is another. There is one glory of the sun, and another glory of the moon, and another glory of the stars: for one star differeth from another star in glory." Now where is Ahasuerus and his palace and his feast and his little cups that are diverse one from the other? Yet you hear more of the king than you hear of God, and you speak more of the king than of God; though you drink His sacrament and drench yourselves with His blood, you never mention His name six days a week. O the unutterable sadness of it! No two blades of grass are alike. They seem to be alike, but there are instruments that can detect differences. Yet we pine for something new and stretch ourselves in lassitude, we who might live in the innermost places of the palace of God, we who might see the blood flowing through all the veins of all the little summer flowers, for all blood is red if we can see it aright, and the flowers are full of blood.

The text is, "The vessels being diverse one from another." There is a principle in this statement; let us find that principle and fear not to apply it. No two men are alike. Yet we speak of men as if they were one. They are one, but not in likeness. The root lies deeper than the appearance; the root is unity; the evolution is variety; but the variety does not destroy the unity. The great thing to be done is to realize unity in diversity, and diversity in unity. Why judge one man by another? I suppose it is one of the small entertainments which a man can have at small expense. You cannot praise one without trying to dispraise some other man. This is our rule of criticism, and we call it judgment by relativity, criticism by relation. Man is fond of making words like relativity. A man might lounge in his armchair with some sense of having deserved it after making a word like relativity. So we cannot exalt Paul without depressing Apollos, and if we say a word in favor of Apollos we almost instantly withdraw it by saying that in many respects he is quite inferior to Cephas. Why not judge the man by what he is, and let the other man alone? Why say that this or that man is very noble, but he is an inch shorter than another man who lives over the hill? What do we want with that other man at this moment? We do not know him; we do not ask for him; why not take a man just as he is, and thank God for him? That would never do; all things would then be so dull; there would be no spunk in conversation if we could not reduce somebody. To this, O Christ, has redeemed manhood come, that it cannot praise the sun without insulting the moon!

There are no two sins alike. No two men sin in just the same way. Wherein is the satisfaction or the subtle delight? It is in this, that I can thank God that I do not sin as my neighbor sins. There is some originality about my iniquity; there is no originality about the other man's iniquity. He who is strong at one point seeks to magnify his strength by comparing it with the weaknesses of other men. We do not like to sin as other people sin. One man can sin broadly, roughly, and with some sense of publicity and dominance, as if he defied the eyes of critics. Him we deem very coarse clay; we leave that man in the hands of the police, and we who left him in the hands of the police sin on the sly. We keep the Sabbath by drawing down the blinds and drinking whiskey behind them. But that is not vulgar; that is well-guarded sin, and we wipe our lips with a red-hot hand and look out behind the blinds to see if anybody is breaking the Sabbath. We are all sinners; all have sinned and come short of the glory of God; all we like sheep have gone astray, only every one in his own way and according to his own taste and fashion; but the thing to be recognized is this, that we are all sinners, one as big as another and as guilty and as red-handed and as deeply in need of the Cross. It will be a long time before we can get the people to believe this, and therefore a long time before the Gospel can make any real progress in the world; because men will draw sin in various lights and shades, men will draw sin gradedly, little step after little step; and one man will be very proud if his gray is not as dark as another man's black. Put them, gray and black, right in the front of the white-faced sun at noonday, and tell me whether the sun can distinguish between the one and the other or will permit any broad and vital distinction to be made. Judging ourselves by ourselves, we are respectable; one man is a magistrate on the bench, and another man is a prisoner in the dock, and in God's sight they may be both in the dock. What is the dock? Who made it? Who had any right to make it? And what is respectability? Is it the texture of a coat or the quality of a character? It is when we get into these religious places, into these innermost sanctuaries, where the eternal lamp burns in continual beauty, that we begin to see that we are all sinners. There is none righteous, no, not one. It is enough to make a man think of suicide to see the smug sinner in his velvet condemning the poor homeless sinner on the open street doing his sin in the sight of the sun. We want the inner criticism. No two sins are just alike; they are various in measure if not always various in quality, and are to be judged by the temperament of the men. When all is known, much may be forgiven. Who knows all? What a life you have had! Maybe I speak to some poor stranger friend. The drink curse has been in your family for scores if not hundreds of years, and you are the last representative of a genealogy of drunkenness; and men turn up their faces and turn away their smile from you because you are reaping a harvest which other men sowed in years far-gone. Good God, Thou gentle One, full of mercy, full of tears, Thou knowest how it is that I have come to be so bad a man. Pity me! For the Cross still stands in the Calvary of Thy memory.

Men believe in different ways. We are not all equally gifted in faith. "Him that is weak in the faith receive ye." You have been made strong that you may help the weakness of other men. Do not boast of your greatness and your orthodoxy, your Pharisaic pride and pomp, but wherein the Spirit of Christ has laid hold on you and made you very strong in faith and mighty in prayer, remember that you are trustees of these abilities and privileges, that you may use them for the sake of the poor, the outcast, and the weak. Who uses his strong faith in that way? There are some men who are gifted with a nose for heterodoxy, with a nostril that can smell heretical doctrine across a sea. Poor creatures! I would myself shut them all up in prison and feed them on bread and water until they cried for mercy because of their hard-heartedness towards men who were struggling with doubt, crying in bitterness of soul, Lord, I believe; help Thou mine unbelief. I have seen a spiritually minded man expelled from a Christian assembly because he could not pronounce the shibboleth of that gathered throng of nominal Christians.

When he had been voted out, the assembly seemed to fall into complacency, as if it had done a great duty, and the learned, noble, benevolent, devout soul was left, so far as that gathering was concerned, to go to the devil. But God heard that they had cast him out, and met him at the door, and gave him sunshine, a year's value of light for one short day. Be sincere, earnest, through-and-through men of God, and no matter who casts you out. Let casting-out be the last work of the Church. It is our business as representatives of Christ to keep as many in as possible, and never to put one out unless forced by an irresistible compulsion. That would be heaven.

It is easy to add, but most necessary, that men work in different ways. The vessels of gold are diverse one from the other even in this matter of work. But if you do not work in my way what becomes of you? When will people let other people alone? When will they recognize individuality of conscience? When will they give men credit for doing the very best according to their ability? If I am a Sunday-school teacher, and you do not teach in the Sunday-school, consequently I expel you. If I do certain work which you never attempt, of course I suspect you and distrust you. If I do not subscribe to the charities which your support, then of course I must be a ridiculous and intolerable character. When will we remember that the vessels of God are diverse the one from the other, that each man must be himself and work in his own way according to his own ability; remembering all the time not to make himself offensive to people who work along other lines and policies? Read the sixteenth chapter of Paul's Epistle to the Romans for a specimen of the discriminating judgment. See how he handles the case with a master's handling. He mentions those who labor in the Lord, and then he mentions and sends salutations to others who labor "much" in the Lord, and that "much" split up the Church. Why should these people be said to labor much in the Church while I am only said to labor in the Church? I consequently never speak to these people.

And shall it be said without fear of giving offense that no two men preach alike? Let us thank God for that! If all men preached alike, nobody would go to church. We live by diversity, but our delight should be to turn our diversity into unity without destroying the diversity—a moral miracle, indicative of the presence of the grace of God in the heart ruling with sovereign power. One saith, I am of Paul; and another, I am of Apollos; and another, I am of Cephas. Was Paul crucified for you? That is the determining question. The man who has suffered for you ought to be most valued. Not the man who has amused you or titillated you, but the man who has in a well-understood sense laid down his life that he might help you; that is the man, whether of this nation or that, whether of one creed or of another, who deserves to be hailed and blessed as an apostle of the Cross. We have often had occasion to remark upon a foolish criticism which the world cannot really shake off. We speak of a minister or preacher, and describe him as "without the learning of Pusey," "without the rushing rhetoric of Melville," "without the extemporaneous epic power" of the man on this side of the river or on that side. Suppose that this poor unfortunate man should be as learned and as polished and as eloquent and as rhetorical and as critical as all other men, he would want a pulpit seven times the size of this to hold even part of him. Why can we not take the individual gift and say, Blessed also be God for this holy and winning speech? And why not recognize the sublime fact that all ministers are needed to make up the ministry? Then should we have more charity and more appreciation and more sympathy. There are diversities of operations, but the same Spirit.

Now this gives us the right idea of unity. The Church may be united, though it may appear to be superficially divided. In my judgment, and I make this the basis of my teaching, the Church of Christ is united. When people are talking about the reunion of Christendom, I do not understand their foreign language. Christendom was never divided, except in a nominal, formal way, in a way quite mechanical. It has never been divided so long as it has held to the Christ. It is not the creed, but the Christ that unites men in one massive and indestructible Church. We must allow each other his way of looking at things. Every man must read the Bible according to his own capacity, his own intelligence, and his own opportunity. The point at which we are united is not in our commentaries, but in our inquiry and searching into the mystery of the divine word. If we are all really in quest of the revelation, we shall soon see that merely literary and scholastic questions adjust and determine themselves. All the denominations are one, yet no two of them are alike, and they are utterly diverse one from another as to framework and purpose and methods of doing things. Find the unity in the Christ, not in the formula or the ritual. When this idea is fully realized, the churches will have great rest. We are appointed to different functions, we are gifted in different degrees and measures; but there is one Lord, and He must judge and settle all. What did you think of that music? Well, I liked the clarinet best. But the clarinet is not a band; you want to pick out little whistles and constitute each whistle into a band or an orchestra. That is the little mischievous trick that we are about. No one instrument is a band; no one instrument is all instruments: no man is all men, and no child of the family of seven is the whole family. Why not look at things in their proper units? There may be a thousand units, and all the units may be required to consolidate one unity. Love the band, the great torrent of eloquence; be thrilled by the united instrumentality and the united vocalism of the entire performance; receive the whole and speak of the whole in its totality, not in its broken fractions. Let us speak of man in the same way.

What a brotherhood there would be among us if we all recognized this principle! No two experiences are alike. We are at liberty to talk one to another, but we are not at liberty to judge one another in this matter of spiritual experience. I remember spending many cloudy and stormy days in my teens when I unfortunately got hold of a book called "Grace Abounding to the Chief of Sinners," by John Bunyan. It was a book that had been misunderstood; let that be said in justification of Bunyan's memory. He depicts himself in that book as worse than the worst sinner that religion had ever dreamed or imagined, and I thought I had to pass through all that heart-searching and heart-breaking, and I did not feel that I had, outwardly at least, been so vile and detestable a character; and therefore I felt as if I could not repent in the right way. So I stood outside the gate crying bitter tears because I had not sinned according to the magnitude and quality of another man's transgression. You must live your own life; you must measure your own environment. Education, parentage, a thousand opportunities and ministries enter into the complicated question of condition and environment. There are some before me who do not need to pass through what Bunyan represents himself as having passed through. You have had godly parents; you have seen piety at home; you have been gradually, gently led by green pastures and still waters. The opening of your religious life has been more like a dawn than an earthquake, or some tempestuous action of the sea. You seem almost to have grown up in an atmosphere of prayer, and you wonder to hear that anybody can be irreligious; you are surprised that anyone can keep outside Christ's sanctuary. I do not expect you to pass through the same experience that Bunyan passed through, but I want you to love the Savior. "A flower, when offered in the bud, is no vain sacrifice."

Prayer

Almighty God, Father of mercy, God of grace, may we join the whole company of heaven in praising and magnifying Thy holy name. Behold, this will do our souls good; we shall thus be lifted up above the wind and the dust and the cloud, and see the fair land, the birthland of summer. If we groan in great heaviness of heart, Thou knowest why; if our heads are bowed down as if seeing below the ground we stand on, as if in search of the grave for that which is there, Thou knowest why we come on the first day of the week, early in the morning, to find the Lord wherever He may be found. We thank Thee for all angel voices that say when we look into the grave, He is not here, He is risen; He is among all vitalities, Himself the most vital of all. May we hear the angel voices and respond to the celestial music. We thank Thee that now and again we do see somewhat of the light with which Thou art robed; in God there is no darkness, as there is no death. Yet sometimes we are afraid, and we are seized as if by a great shock, and, behold, we cannot recover ourselves, for the tempest is hard against us. Then we know not God, nor do our hearts consider how great the Lord is, and how gentle and how full of tenderness and tears. May we always have the right view of our Father; may we know that God is love. We have cried out because Thy bolts have pursued us and there was no refuge, and we have cried on the hillside because we could not screen ourselves from Thy sheets of rain. Yet all the while Thou wast seated above us in love and tenderness and daily care, and we knew it not. The Lord pity us because of our blindness, because of our atheism even in the midst of our prayers. We know not the truth as it is; we do not touch the eternity of God; we are poor, sunken, because sinful, depraved, and lost; we are not the men Thou didst make us. Pity us in our grievous fall! When there was no eye to pity and no arm to save, Thine eye pitied and Thine own arm brought salvation; and now and again we have a great living consciousness that though we had gone astray we have returned unto the Shepherd and Bishop of our souls. We bless Thee for a high experience, for a broad and brilliant religious outlook; we thank Thee for those tidal times of faith wherein we have no fear, no doubt, no hesitancy, but are in very deed, in the grace that is in Christ Jesus, the sons and daughters of God. Thou hast given us bread, and we thought we grew it in our own fields; Thou hast given us wine and oil and an abundance of summer fruits, and we heeded not the Giver. The Lord pity us, for it is the evil nature that rises against the good. Wherein we have been mean and miserly, God's love forgive us if it can; wherein we have been quarrelsome and evil-disposed, fretful, altogether out of good keeping and out of good conduct, the Lord pity us, for we make fools of ourselves seven times a day. Wherein we have been hard upon any human creature, the Lord soften our hearts, and say unto us, With what judgment ye judge ye shall be judged. If any man have a quarrel against any, may the oldest be the first to forgive, and may the youngest sue for pity. Thou knowest how short our day is, how near is the rising of the evening star. May we then, gathering together in the time of the shadows, know how God has been good to us all the day, and may we fall into each other's arms of forgiveness and comradeship and brotherhood, and thank God for the Cross that has redeemed the world. Amen.

25
The Master Key

Preached on Sunday Morning, June 10th, 1900.

God is love—1 John 4:8.

What is the Bible in one sentence? What is theology in one breath? There may be words enough, a thousand thick on every page, and yet there must be one living sentence somewhere that will contain and suggest and glorify the whole. What is that sentence? Some of us are not prepared to take the Bible as a whole; it is too much for us, written by so many scribes at so many different times that we have not mental training enough to grasp the whole question at once. Is there not a little Bible, a Bible of bibles? Cannot you find one sentence that gathers up all the other sentences into itself? We have it in the text, "God is love." That is the Bible. Why should you and I, imperfectly trained and very infirm in intellectual compass and grasp, attempt to sit upon high judgment seats, and take in the whole Bible, and pronounce upon it with the authority and fluency of ignorance? This is the little Bible, or the sum-total Bible; this is the seed that holds all the trees of Eden, all the oaks of Bashan, and all the cedars of Lebanon. Why should you and I permit ourselves to be the victims of people who are altogether impossibly clever and who have undertaken to settle everything about the Bible in its totality? I want my little Bible, my all-containing Bible, my one pregnant sentence; enough for me; all the notes of music come out of that one tone. Give me a Bible that I can carry with me in the memory of my heart; give me a Bible that will interpret all the rest of the Bible, making it perfectly simple and clear and credible. Strange it is, and foolish to innocent insanity sometimes, and to criminal insanity in other instances, that men who cannot really read the Word–Hebrew, Greek, Chaldaic, Syrian, what you please–should undertake to have an opinion! My lords, think of the idiots! I want some miniature Bible; I want a star that holds all the other stars in some mysterious way. Here it is in the text; it has been waiting for us all these years, and we have never really read it aright. "God is love." That is the master-key, if I may change the figure, that wonderful key that can open any door, that one key that can open seven locks at once. Until we get hold of the master-key we shall have little infidels and small tom-thumb unbelievers, who want to stretch themselves into things much bigger. Get the master-key, and all will be well. There is a pass-key or a pass-word, an open sesame, a talismanic touch, or look or sign, and all things fly open, and seem to say in their opening, Come, and welcome; the fields are yours, and the palace is your sanctuary.

Here is all we want. Here we have three words, which are three syllables, and they are bigger words than all the piled words of the most elaborate dictionary ever constructed. These are the words out of which all the other words come. No man invented this word. It has become so familiar now that we do not know its meaning, but if we could throw ourselves back mentally and spiritually to the right standpoint, we should know that it did not lie within the compass of human genius to invent any of these words. We take the words for granted; we speak the word *God* as if we knew all about it, and the great verb *am, is,* as if it were one of a dozen verbs of equal merit; and *love,* which the boldest lexicographer has never successfully defined, we roll glibly off the tongue. We have all things in three syllables. Here is the Bible reduced to the smallest possible verbal scale, and yet losing nothing of the stellar glory and the infinite compass of the evolution of the Divine idea.

The use of this text is not to be found in its own verbal exposition. This is a text that is to be carried all over the Bible; this is the commentator of the whole Scripture. Turn over a page—where is the lamp? That is Bible reading. You fail to expound the Scripture because you have lost the lamp. Do not suppose, then, that "God is love" is a text that can be explained in one discourse or explained in all the discourse ever poured from the fluent tongue of eloquence. Never read a chapter without lighting the lamp and putting it just over the chapter you are reading. What is your lamp? "God is love." Good! Now read on, and all things will give up their secret at the touch of the gleam of that magic lamp. You have been bewildering yourself, have you, about the authorship of this and that book, about the continuity and the apparent self-contradiction of some of the historical writings, have you? Did you read the whole under the light of the lamp? You are not sure, but I am sure because if you had taken the lamp with you, you would have seen everything, or have been enabled so to treat it as to take away all the intellectual hostility and all the moral perplexity!

The lamp! We might take it with us now and look at a few passages in the light of this gleaming candle of God. Take this awful text: "In the day thou eatest thereof thou shalt surely die." He threatens the man whom He has made! He does not. The lamp! Now read under the light of the lamp, and you will find that this is no threat; this is no uplifting of the arm of Jehovah, as who should say, Take care what you are about, or one mistake on your part and you are a dead man. God never learned that savagery of tone; God speaks in another music. These were hard words, no doubt, to the man who heard them for the first time. Why speak to a man almost on his first day of conscious manhood about dying? Why begin with foreign languages? Yet, properly read, it is the language of love, and that is never foreign; it is the tender language of solicitude. When you point out to your dear little child that if he goes into a certain place he will be injured, you are not threatening the boy; we cannot say, Why speak to the dear little boy in that tone? You properly reply that the tone is an expression of solicitude, anxiety, tenderest love, saying in all the music of the parental heart,

Take care! if you go down there you will be perhaps injured, something may meet you there that will frighten you; if you once go into that den or jungle where the wild beast is, you will be torn to pieces: take care not to go in that direction. That is not threatening; that is loving, caring-for, going-out-after, with tender desire and anxiety. So I take my lamp text, "God is love," and hold it all above the story of Eden, and behold, I know that God has made all things good and designed all things in love, and that the very voice of warning is a new accent in the music of sweetest, tenderest care.

Let us hold the lamp over another text that is almost too terrible to read. May I read it in a genteel assembly? shall I not be hissed out of the pulpit I degrade if I read this text?—"The wicked shall be turned into hell, and all the nations that forget God." I admit that it is possible so to utter these words as to import into them a false meaning and a false tone, but I insist that it is also possible to read them to make them about as tender words as can be found in the whole compass of inspired revelation. This is not wrath, it is pleading. It is the expression of solicitous love: as who should say, My dear soul, do you really know what wickedness is? Do you know what it means, what it involves, and what it really must come to in the bitter end? No, I thought it was a philosophical question. It is not; it is a question of moral harvest, moral issue, a question of the inevitable. Do you know what it is to be wicked? I have studied moral philosophy. You will not find it there. Where can I find it? Mainly in your own heart, in what is called consciousness, self-consciousness, self-analysis, deep self-knowledge. No mere system of philosophy ever eventuated in such a proposition as that "The heart is deceitful above all things, and desperately wicked." That was only found out in the most agonizing moment of human tragedy. No man ever invented that saying; he had not mental compass and strength to invent it or to express it. You must live some texts if you would get at their meaning. Here, then, God is not in a petty fume; He is not, as we should say in human terms, shaking His fist above the human race and saying, I will have you! Depend upon it; you shall come to ruin for this. There is no such tone in the divine voice. The Bible is a book of tender music, generous, strenuous warning: My child, take care; if sinners entice thee, consent thou not; if they make thee big promises, saying, There is much gold in this; come, toss the dice; there is a fortune in this trick, consent thou not; for this house goes down to the pit, and this wickedness spends its holiday in hell. O don't, don't! Let me throw mine arms around thee; son of my heart, consent thou not. It is a father pleading with the son; it is not a father threatening the son; and the son would have a right to say, if he were not so warned, You never told me of this; you never gave me a hint of what this would come to, you kept silence when you knew I was being seduced and tempted by a thousand malign influences, and you never spoke a word about hell or the pit or the endless fire. That would be an accusation to be hurled at the head of the father. So here, in one of those so-called rough imprecatory passages, wherein God is supposed to be very wrathful and very stormy, here, we find the very heart of love; in the midst of all this warning there is one large tender tear that wets the cheek of God. Do not believe those persons, therefore, who point out the imprecations and denunciations, and wish you to believe that all these things are indications of the wrath of God. Hear me, they are not; they are indications of the love of God; God in His mercy thinks it right to tell us what the harvest of sin-sowing is, and if He had never told us, how could He judge us? And if He had never told us and attempted to judge us, what a standing-ground we would have for self-vindication, how we might charge Him with injustice for having kept back the secret of the evolution of moral processes. We go to the judgment with our eyes open; we go to perdition with the Scriptures written in plainest language of entreaty and love.

The lamp! What is this? "It shall be more tolerable for Tyre and Sidon in the day of judgment than for you." "God is love." He does not judge promiscuously or indiscriminately; there is not one lot for all; if a man has begun with much, much will be required of him, and if he has begun with little, he will be judged accordingly. The heathen man who never heard of the Christ is nearer heaven than the man at the high end of London town who has been brought up in the Church, who has been trained under the very shadow of the altar, and has heeded none of these things, but has deliberately hurled them back in the face of God and said, I will not have Thee to reign over me. The little child who has never seen a real living blade of grass will not be judged like the child that has been born in luxury and who could take a long walk around his father's estate, and who yet has despised the goodness of God and never suffered it to lead him to repentance. They cannot be judged alike. Jesus Christ has laid down this law; He says, There is not one judgment for all; there is a judgment for each; all the circumstances will be taken into account, all the environment will be calculated and set forth, and will be treated as an element or a factor in the great judicial process. If the mighty works which have been done in you had been done in Tyre and Sidon they would have been on their knees centuries since; having sinned away the greater mercies, you have dug the deep hell.

Take another passage. I am endeavoring to vindicate the goodness of God in passages that appear to be somewhat terrible and somewhat opposed to what we regard as the true nature and quality of a Divine Being. Here is a prophet who is about to be sent forth, and the Lord gives him His prophecy before sending him out, and He says to the prophet, "Say to the wicked, It shall be ill with him." Is that a threat? It is not. By reading it in a loud and strident tone you have missed the music of the message. This instruction might have been whispered to the prophet; it might have been whispered with a voice choked with tears. O tell the fool that he is an enemy to himself; it will not be ill with him because I determine it so to be, but because of the very necessity and philosophy of the case: men cannot gather grapes of thorns or figs of thistles; there is a harvest law; there is a marvelous process of cause and effect, incoming and outgoing, a wonderful reciprocal action between the outward and the inward. Say to the wicked—take him aside; take him to thy very heart, O thou prophet of heaven—and say to him, Man, it shall be ill with thee if thou dost fight against God; my son, why kick against the pricks? He who fights lightning loses the battle; he who would upset the moral and spiritual system of the universe is bringing down upon himself a stone which will grind him to powder. O tell him—say—arrest him by name, plead with him, tell him, God is love.

So I come back to my little Bible, my three syllabled Bible, the Bible that holds all the Bible. When I come upon a great and awful mystery, I call for the lamp, and it has a way of throwing its beams down into the deepest cavities. I have held it over the grave. This epigrammatic sentence fits all graves, it fits all cemeteries; it is the word that is written on the portals of the churchyard, "God is love." I have seen a strong man reel over his son's grave as if he would plunge himself into it, for there was nothing worth living for after that one boy had gone. He was not in a mood to hear any preaching; he was not in a condition to hear even the gentlest tone; he must be watched; we must wait for him; he must feel it like a man before he answers it like a man. It will be no use speaking to him today; he sups sorrow; nay, he does not sup it, he gulps it, he drains the dish of grief at one great gulp. We must call upon this man tomorrow; we must be remote; we must learn in God's grace how to touch a wound without hurting it. Next week perhaps we may meet him, and even then we must hold ourselves remote, and yet be near at hand, and when the lull comes, the only sentence the man can bear, and at first he may receive it with unbelief and partial scorn, is, "God is love." It does not seem like it. No, it does not. I feel inclined to deny it. I do not wonder; your grief is exceeding great; but—God is love. Who says so? I do. On what authority? My own experience; I have dug a grave as deep as you, and I thought just as you are thinking now; I said there are a thousand happy families, and one of the children might have been taken, but I had only one. That was a thousand strokes in one laceration, and I, brother in grief, fellow-mason in tears, I say, God—is—love. Let us meet again when we are both quieter.

From *The British Weekly,* June 14th, 1900:

I have never seen a congregation more moved under Dr. Parker's preaching (writes a correspondent) than during the delivery of his sermon last Sunday morning. He is continually surprising his hearers by new glimpses of divine truth and new applications of Scripture. On Sunday morning his text was "God is love," and these three words were used as a lamp in the light of which difficult passages in the Bible were read. Instances were given, the last relating to death. As he hinted at his own experiences the emotion of the congregation deepened, and became almost uncontrollable, when, having said, "I have dug a grave as deep as you, yet I can still say, 'God—' " there came a painful pause, so prolonged that it seemed the sentence would remain unfinished. When at last Dr. Parker recovered himself and completed the quotation, a great many people, men and women, had their handkerchiefs to their faces.

Prayer

Lord God Almighty, if we tell the story of Thy goodness, where shall we begin or end? Thy mercy is from everlasting to everlasting upon them that fear Thee, and to those that call upon Thy name Thou art all attention, loving, generous attention, forgiving sin, receiving penitence, and returning prayers back in multiplied blessings. Let all the houses of history cry, His mercy endureth forever. There is no counting Thy mercies; Thy lovingkindnesses are more than the sands upon the seashore. Verily God is love; there is no limit to Thy compassion and Thy care. Because Thy compassions fail not we are here today, living witnesses to the loving care of the living God. Again and again Thou dost remind us by Thy love of Thy great majesty, and Thou dost remind us of Thy great majesty by Thy tears, Thy tenderness, Thy more than motherly compassions. Behold, we are here before Thee to worship God, to call mightily upon His name, and to show as it were by the shedding of our blood that through Jesus Christ our Lord there is no limit to our obedience and to our joyous, grateful service. Amen.

26
Mistaken Views of Religion

Preached on Thursday Morning, June 7th, 1900.

But he said, Ye are idle, ye are idle; therefore ye say, Let us go and do sacrifice to the Lord–Exodus 5:17.

That was Pharaoh's rough-and-ready and foolish estimate of religious aspiration and service. In this matter Pharaoh lives today. There are many people who cannot understand the utility of religion; they think religious people are always going to church, and no good comes of it. We must put up with these things; we have to bear many reproaches, and this we may well add to the number without really increasing the weight or the keenness of the injustice. Pharaoh said, Ye are idle, ye are idle; I will lay more burdens upon you; so you want to go and pray, do you? I will see to it! It is because you are lazy men that you pretend to want to go and do sacrifice to the Lord; I see through you; you cannot deceive Pharaoh; I know the meaning of your hypocrisy; I will have more bricks out of you, and you shall have no straw, and I will punish your religion by making you do more work in the brickfields.

Sometimes great men are mistaken, and sometimes they are unwise, and at no time do they really comprehend, if they be outside of it themselves, the true religious instinct and the true meaning of deep religious worship, ceremony, and service. The spiritual has always had to contend with the material; the praying man has always been an obnoxious problem to the man who never prays. The praying man is an enigma. When he hastens to prayer people who do not understand him, think that he is hastening to the indulgence of the downy bed, the feathery pillow; he is calling it worship, but in the soul of it it is nothing but sheer laziness. We have had to bear the reproach of the supernatural; we have had every spiritual word we have ever uttered mocked and thrown back as it were in our very faces, and we shall have to bear the discipline of misconstruction right away down to the end of life's chapter, short or long. That some men should be trusted with the function of criticism—whether of men or books or religious service, or preaching, or what else—the pity of it is as sore as a wound! They will not hold their tongues; they will not spare their folly; it trickles or it swells into streams, or rises into torrents; it cannot be really helpful. We live under each other's criticism; every man is perfectly sure that the other man is not perfect. The worst of it is that there is so much error at the heart of the criticism, so much want of sympathy and appreciation; the critic is not *en rapport* with the author, speaker, server, actor, whatever the name may be by which the Christian instinct and its operations become known. You cannot really judge a man unless you can see into his very heart; you cannot read the book of an author whom you dislike. I have returned books which have been sent to me for criticism because I did not like the authors, and I could not do the authors justice, and rather than sit behind an inky veil and say something that was perhaps unfriendly, if not even positively hostile, I thought it better to send the book back, and tell the sender of it in the first instance to get somebody to criticize the book who either knew nothing about the author or could really and truly appreciate him. I hold that to be a just course under all circumstances. You cannot be at church unless you are in church, and many persons are at church as a mechanical action who are not in the sanctuary, in the very soul and innermost holy of God's house; they are there in the body, but the soul is away, out of atmosphere, out of touch, and the whole thing may be the perpetration of a great villainy. Pharaoh knew nothing about the religion of Israel; he worshiped in other directions if he worshiped at all. He could not understand this longing for the sanctuary, this heart-hunger for the old psalms and the old way of doing things, this cry of the historic heart. Away! said he. Let me hear no more from you; I see through all your hypocrisy; you want to get a day's holiday or three days' march into the wilderness, but I will take care you do not enjoy yourselves after your own fashion; get to your brickfields, and if you want to pray and sacrifice, make more bricks. Pharaoh does not speak a strange tongue; it is exactly what is being said today. Men cannot rise above their own level. The fool must be a fool though you pass him through a mortar; he will come up again even under the influence of the pestle his old wearisome and burdensome self. Only they know what prayer is who themselves do really and agonizingly pray; only they know what it takes out of a man to go through a religious service who can shed such nerve blood and never energy on the same consecrated ground. If we could understand one another better, what an increase of brotherhood there would be, and what a mutual lightening of burdens and dispersion of Christianity! To some people the Apostle Paul was mad. There is a great scarcity of crazy people today; they have nearly all become mechanically sane in the sense of having lost their divinity and quenched their force. The great thing in many cases today is to say to one another, Sh! The old wind of Pentecost, the old enthusiasm that made the Cross a power, has died down to an annual examination of each other's orthodoxy. Oh the sadness of it! Oh the new, new tragedy!

How few of us understand really the sacrifice which is implied in true spiritual worship or service! I am told that it is possible for a man to preach three times on a Sunday. I am inclined to the opinion of John Wesley, one of the greatest philosophers as well as theologians that ever lived; said he, A man may preach once, and may do something a second time, if he preach twice; he can only chatter the third time on the same day. It is nothing to some people to estimate a sermon; they imagine that a man has only to open his mouth and let the bird fly out, and they will say, Well flown! not

knowing that he has come up from midnight sanctuaries to proclaim morning gospels. It is an awful tragedy to preach, or to serve
the living God with living blood in any form. What a destruction
of nerve force! Yet a gentle brother, who married well and did little,
called upon me and said that I could easily get down to his "place"
after the Thursday morning service and preach at his "place" at
three o'clock! He could have done it, and come back again, but
then the people never would have allowed him to preach here. Our
religious service, whether in the pulpit or out of it, in the press or in
the family or elsewhere, is nothing if it be not a sacrifice, a shedding of blood.

So you want to go to sacrifice unto the Lord, do you? You are
idle, idle; back to your bricks, and make more bricks, and you shall
have no straw, and I will put a thicker thong into the hands of the
taskmaster, and I will teach you—I, Pharaoh, king of Caesars, will
teach you—better than to run away from your work under the pretense that you are going to be very religious.

So this opens up the whole subject of work and its meaning,
spiritual worship and its signification, heart-sacrifice and its story in
red, reeking blood. Who is the worker—the architect or the bricklayer? I never hear of the architects meeting in council for the purpose of limiting their hours or increasing their bank holidays. The
bricklayer is the worker; so it seems; in a certain aspect he is the
worker; but how could he move without the architect? St. Paul's
Cathedral or St. Peter's did not move from the bricklayer to the architect, but from the architect to the bricklayer. Who had the
worry, the anxiety, the nights' sleeplessness, the weary, solicitous,
critical calculation, and thinking and comparing and estimation of
forces? It was the architect, who apparently was doing nothing—just
walking about in a black coat, and so far as the bricklayer could see
he might as well be ten miles off. But bricklayers are not the final
court of appeal. Why does not each man occupy his own place
with honor and with sincerity and with a true appreciation of the
other man's place? In the beginning was the Logos—everywhere;

not the mechanic, not the artisan, but the Logos. What is the Logos? The Word. And what is the Word? The Thought. And what is the Thought? God. In the beginning God created the heavens and the earth. So by a true analysis we get back into word, scheme, plan, dream, specification, suggestion—the Logos, Jehovah, Eternity. All the churches that are true came up from God with Edom from Paran, the nameless, from everlasting. Do we, then, mock at the labor that is meaner than the great profound thought? No, indeed; the architect cannot do without the builder, any more than the builder can do withoiut the architect; they are workers together; and this is the true idea of society, each man having his own talent, making his own contribution, working under his own individual sense of responsibility, and all men catching the spirit of comradeship and of union and cooperation, united in the uprearing of a great cathedral, a poem in wood and stone, a house of the living God.

Where is the severe strain felt, in the muscle or in the brain? You can take hold of your muscle. As the blacksmith said to the northern cobbler, showing his great muscle, "Thou cannot grow that upo' water." That is to say, you cannot grow such a thick iron muscle on water; get back to your porter and your whiskey and your other assistants of that kind. Where is the burden felt—on the muscle or on the brain? Who has the hard work to do, the blacksmith or the thinker? I insist that no class of men on the face of the earth can have any right to get together and call themselves invidiously, the working classes. We are all workers, and we are all members of the working classes, and the word working must be redeemed from its unjust limitation; and the prime minister and his gardener must both, each hailing the other as a working man, be glad that the apportionment of capacity and of service is with the living Creator. It is worry that kills a man, whether he be blacksmith or prime minister, whether he be author, merchant, preacher, it is the worry of it; it is the nightmare of wondering how we can get both ends to meet. It is that troublesome action upon the brain that puzzles a poor creature up a rickety pair of stairs how to live on nine shillings a week with five and sixpence of it to go out in rent; it is the worry, the solicitude, the care, the cancering anxiety; and only they know it who have passed through the process; and the greatest sympathy is due to those who are troubled by many cares, who are beaten and pierced by many solicitudes and anxieties. How are they distributed? All over the human area. Every man has his anxiety; every poor heart has its own special misery; every heart is broken in some way. If we could realize that and constitute ourselves into a brotherhood of sympathy, it would be better for us, and they that are strong would bear the burdens and the infirmities of those that are weak. Do let us understand one another. Jesus had compassion upon all men because He knew all men—knew them at the root, knew them at the core, knew them before they knew themselves. "Casting all your care upon Him"—why?—"for He careth for you." Sympathy asks you to allow it to share the burden. If we care for those who are in distress, our service to them will not be a burden, but in some way a delight, and in exercising our opportunity we shall in a high degree know what Jesus did when He carried the Cross that He might save the world.

Insincere religion is idle. People who go to church when they do not want to go—that is idleness, and that idleness will soon sour and deepen into blasphemy. Going because I suppose we shall be expected to go—that is idleness and weariness. That cannot apply to people who come to a Thursday morning service at twelve o'clock in the day; they do not come because they must go or people will wonder where they are. No, they must want to come; they must earnestly desire to be there: hence the delight, the joy of jubilee, to preach to folks who are there because they want for the time being to be nowhere else. Insincere religion—would God we could get rid of it! Would God the people who do not want to come to church would stay away! They hinder the kingdom; they hurt the wounds of Christ. Let us be sincere, and defy the world. Decorative religion is idleness. When religion is turned into a mere fad or fancy or something aesthetic, then it becomes idleness, and it entitles itself to the rebuke of Pharaoh and of Christ. There are people who would make religion into an art; there are some persons who have almost succeeded in turning the pulpit into a profession. I believe there may be found a man here and there, quite an eccentric creature, who would speak about the ministry of Christ, the ministry of all churches, as one of the learned professions. My God, it is not that; whatever it is, it is not that in their evil sense of the words. No man can make a minister; no man can make a poet or a prophet; this is God's work; this is work not made with hands. Man can light a fire in his own parlor stove, but no man can create a Pentecost. Yet the ministry is a learned profession! Thou hast given me the tongue of the learned that I may speak a word in season to him that is weary. There is a learning of the heart; there is a skill of the soul; there is a university of the midnight sorrow and the morningtide sight of God. Do leave God some room in His own Church.

Do we not read further, "Be fervent in spirit, diligent in business, serving the Lord"? Yes, but the expression "diligent in business" in that text is not a commercial expression. "Diligent in business" in that verse has to do with a higher commerce. Those who only read the Bible superficially and in order to forget it, say, Remember the words "diligent in business." If some people would quote Scripture, it would be a great relief. "Diligent in business" in this text means diligent in spiritual commerce, creating a great business between heaven and earth, a great spiritual sea on which are passing cargoes of spiritual commerce, holding great intercourse with heaven, praying without ceasing, sending out the ship of prayer, expecting the ship of reply. That is diligent in business in the apostolic sense as indicated in this passage. "Knew ye not that I must be about My Father's business?" The word business there is not commercial; the revisers of the translation of the New Testament have wisely changed the whole expression: Knew ye not that I must be in My Father's house, about My Father's house. Do you not know the true address of the Christian? Wherever the Christ-follower is—in the kitchen, in the house of commerce, on the thoroughfare, on the sea—he is about his father's house. For the temple of the Lord is no mud hut built of certain dimensions; it is the roofless, the immeasurable, the heavenly.

Now if there are any persons who do make an idleness of religion, let them be rebuked. I am afraid some people do make an idleness of religion. Wherein that can be shown to be true, let it be condemned. Am I too practical a man? Mayhap. Do I cry out for square justice? I hope so. And when I see at eight o'clock in the morning young people dressed up and running about to this church or that chapel, I wonder what the mother is doing at home, and I say in my heart, God forgive you! You have left your own mother to make the bed and get the breakfast, and you are going about to do something decorative. I say the wrath of God is upon you if you are doing what you think is justice on the one hand by doing grievous injustice on the other. If you can say, "This ought ye to have done, and not left the other undone," there I am one with you; but I do not like my mother to be left at home to brush my boots or wash my collar, while I go out to show other people how drunkenly pious I am; I will remain at home with the old mother, and I will help her so that we can both go presently, both go together, mother and son, and enjoy the delights and the quietness of God's dear house. I should be a persecuting old prophet if I had my way and dare cry out against these things. I long to do it; sometimes in various relations of life all I want to do at the moment is to cry, Shame! And it would be good preaching.

Let us, then, not care what Pharaoh says, but examine our own hearts. The name typified by Pharaoh has given me an opportunity of cross-examining myself, and I will say, Pharaoh, thou thinkest I am idle, and therefore I want to be religious; I wonder if Pharaoh is right; he is a very astute man, he has great councilors about him; he has a great country to administer, and there is a light in those eyes sometimes that suggests that he can see a long way into a motive. I never thought this would come to pass, that Pharaoh would say to me that I am an idle hound, because I want to go and serve the Lord. Is Pharaoh right? It is lawful to learn from the enemy, and if Pharaoh has fixed his eye upon the blemish in my life, if he does see the hollowness of my heart, well, I will think over what the king says. We may learn some things from heathenism. But if I can, by the grace of God, assure myself that by the Holy Spirit I am really sincere in wanting to go to this sermon, this sacrament, this prayer; if I know through and through, really, that I do want to go and serve God, the gates of hell shall not prevail against me.

Prayer

Almighty God, we thank Thee for all Thy love and tender care, for Thy help when we are helpless, and for the light that shone upon us when we thought the whole day was swallowed up in night. We bless Thee for counting us when we thought we were left out of the number. Thy mercy endureth forever. Behold, Thou dost see in us what we cannot see in ourselves. Why didst Thou redeem us, Thou mighty One, at the price of blood? Could no lower sum be made to effect the unworthy purchase? Could not silver and gold buy such dead things as we? Yet we are redeemed with the precious blood of Christ. What dost Thou see in us? What but Thine own image and likeness, shattered and degraded and despoiled unspeakably, but still there. May we regard Thy view of us as a call to better life, larger labor, more sacrificial obedience and love. We bless Thee for the Book in which all the names are written, and for that other book which is the book of life, the wondrous book in which names are written as it were in red blood; they cannot be blotted out; these writings are the writings of the hand of God. Before eternity Thou didst see us one and all, there is nothing new to Thee, nor is there anything old. Thou seest the whole scheme and purpose of things as existent in the divine mind long before time chimed its fleeting hours. Oh that we might stand in the years that are at Thy right hand, and through the power of the Cross and grace of Christ realize that we are sons of God, children of light, songs of the morning; then there should be no more depression and no more discouragement, and as for death, it would be swallowed up in victory. Amen.

27
Outside Friends of Jesus

Preached on Thursday Morning, June 14th, 1900.

Whence knowest Thou me?—John 1:48.

"I am not a public man, I take no part in demonstrations, I fly no flag; I am a quiet man; I should have rested under the figtree if I had not been called suddenly and perhaps somewhat abruptly; whence knowest Thou me?" Suppose we wanted to make out a list of Christians, how would you proceed? Imagine that I have by your own consent and appointment been chosen to ask you to furnish me with a list of Christian citizens and their families, how would you proceed? What have you done? Have you attempted what I asked you to undertake? Show me the result. I have examined all the church rolls and all the baptismal registers, and this I think you will find to be a tolerably complete register of Christian citizenship. Is that the way to get the answer to my inquiry? Who wrote the church rolls, and who had any business to write them? And who wrote the baptismal registers, men or women or children? And who bade the writers undertake their task? Who shall count the flock of God? Men are always endeavoring to do the impossible and sometimes to do the absurd. Make a list of Christians? Only one pen could write that register, and that pen is the pen of God. Who will take the census? Ah me! And who is it that creates quite a little public uproar about taking the religious census? Who can do it? Only in some lame and imperfect way can a scale of figures be drawn up, and that by hands that tremble as they write it, conscious as it were of their own infirmity and inadequacy. Who can count the flock of God? But it pleases man to write out little lists of the Christian population; it pleases man, little, fussy, fretful man, to be writing out lists and registering statistics and telling us who are good and who are not good. What would some men do if they could not in some way or other take the census? But who can count the flock of God? And who has made us constables that we should watch the church door and say who shall enter and who shall not enter? And I saw, and behold the books were opened. Then the registers are kept in heaven? Surely so. All the registers? Yes, all the registers. You see those books spread out there? Yes. Well, wait one moment. And another book was opened. Who knows but that another, and another? The registrar is God. The Lord knoweth them that are His; He seals them, and the color is red.

Jesus Christ was always surprising His disciples by saying to this or that man whom the disciples did not know, Let him come in. The disciples sometimes gave the Master sour looks, yea, looks of distrust and utter unbelief regarding His judgment of these people. They would have turned them away; they turned the children away, and when you turn the children away, you turn the mothers away, and when you turn the mothers away, you turn the fathers away. They were great at turning away people. Jesus Christ said, Let him come. Lord, what! This man? Yes, this man; let him come. But we know something about him. I know more than you know. Before any Philip among you saw this man I saw him, the shadow of the fig tree could not conceal him; let him come. If this be done, who knows how many people may be included in the love of Christ that we never thought of in that connection? Who can count the flock of God? See how they pour down the hills and rise up out of the valleys, an exceeding great host, elect, chosen, fore-ordained, children of eternity. Yet there are some persons who think they know who are fit to come to the Lord's table and who are not. They are the persons who know exactly how many persons the Church of God can hold. Their temple floor is only so many hundred yards long and so many hundred yards wide, and beyond that accommodation all is outside. Outside what? Even some of us may be inside and may hardly know it. There is a word of cheer for you this hot noontide in the City of London. We may hardly venture to claim to be inside, yet we may be there; His mercy whom we adore as God endureth forever. The Lord of the feast will find room for all His guests, and the guests shall be thousands of thousands, squared and cubed up to ever-enlarging numbers—persons who have never entered into the imagination of sectarian or bigoted minds to conceive as being elect of God. What if at one time we shall wonder rather at the number of the elect than at the number of the rejected, if such there be in a universe the name of whose Creator is Love? The disciples knew who should come on and who should be driven off. They imagined themselves very great and expert disciplinarians: Master, we saw a man casting out devils in Thy name, and we forbade him, because he walketh not with us. Who could believe it? With "us"! It is dangerous to give some men privileges; it is perilous to entrust some men with honors. They soon set themselves up into an entity called "us." A man may be an almost decent man when he is let alone by himself, but the moment he joins half a dozen other men, where is he? The history of bigotry is a history of ignorance. When we know each other better, we shall hasten to each other in confidence and love and mutual emulous honor, because we are made one not by our own cleverness, but by the redeeming grace and cleansing blood of the Son of God.

Take this very man Nathanael: How do I come to be known and known by name by Thee, Thou new Man? How is it? Jesus knew him before he was born; Jesus knew us all before we were knowable. He never pleaded being an agnostic in relation to us. It suits our little tiny vehement vanity to be agnostics in relation to God, but God has never been an agnostic in relation to us. Consider that as a conception in poetry and magnify it beyond all other poetry ever known among men. Take it as idealism, transcendentalism, apply to it what flashy name you please; there remains the central fact: in the conception of the Bible we have never been absent a moment from the consciousness and the love of God. Thus Jesus Christ surprises everyone who comes to Him. He mentions the name, refers to family circumstances, quotes some instance of domestic history, recalls to the mind some tender providence. The Lord Jesus works wonderful miracles in reminiscence, so that memory is His first resurrection ground; He blows the trumpet, and dead memory gives up all that it had forgotten even of the love of God and the tender mercy of the Most High, and we see new lights flashing upon the dead past. Nathanael was recognized as "an Israelite indeed." It was Jesus Christ's way; He made much of encouragement. Some of us might have been further on in life if our friends had encouraged us more, spoken to us more kindly, given to us a better view of our abilities, and had said to us sometimes when we were in the deep dark valley, Cheer thee! It will be morning presently; come, come, it is in thee to be a bigger man, yet cleverer, nobler, better; come, no hangdog look, but lift up thine eyes and behold; it is night, but night is the time of stars. So on another occasion Jesus Christ dined with a man chief among the publicans and rich; that was all he was at the beginning of the feast. Wondrous things occur at the supper table of the Lord; when Jesus is your guest, He may knight you on the spot; when you entertain such Royalty, you acquire ineffable honors, new names, uppermost crowns. What is this man your Master, whom ye call Christ, ought to have known, and what manner of man is this; he is chief among the publicans; he is rich; he tyrannizes over the people; your master if he were a good man would not have dined with Zaccheus. And the Lord stood up and knighted him with the sword of heaven, and said, Forasmuch as he also is a son of Abraham. Dead memories revived, old associations quickened, forfeited privileges restored, man awakened. Zaccheus, thou also art a son of Abraham. Who shall count the flock of God? Give me back that list you wrote. Is the name of Nathanael on it? No. The name of Zaccheus? No. Take it back and count better.

And once Jesus treated men in clumps and groups; He enlarged the unit from individuality to family. Once He put up so to say a whole family, and said, This is the larger unit; we are advancing from personality or individuality to the family, and by-and-by we shall go to the country, and by-and-by to another country, and on, and on, till all flesh shall see the glory of the Lord. It was His way. And Jesus loved Martha and Mary and Lazarus. Have you got these people down on your list? No. Take it back and write it better. Miss Nathanael, an Israelite indeed; miss Zaccheus, a son of Abraham; miss Mary, Martha, and Lazarus, the whole little family of Bethany! Tear up thy list; let God be registrar. So we are speaking now about what we may call the outside friends of Jesus. We are at present not dealing with the esoteric and inward, and if we may so say the special, but we are dealing with people who were never thought of at all in their relation to Christ. As if there could be anybody out of relation to the Son of man! They came from odd places; they came in eccentric ways. One of the outside friends of Jesus was a mere listener, but he listened well, and when the Master had made him an answer, he said with spontaneous, glowing, grateful enthusiasm, "Well, Master, Thou hast said the truth." Have you got that man on your list? No, I have not got that man on my list; I have been to the church rolls and the baptismal registers and the religious census as appointed to be taken by government. And you have missed Nathanael and Zaccheus and Lazarus and the listening scribe! What a poor list is yours! Tear it up; it is fit only for the burning. So while we are talking, let me say again and again, about the outside and unrecognized friends of Jesus Christ. Shall this man enter into our sanctuary? Yes, he is a member, and his name has been on the communion roll for some years. Is that the reason why he should enter? Yes. It is a poor reason. And there was a ruler that came to Jesus by night. Perhaps he had more time then; *came to Jesus* is the point; *by night* is the accident. Come by day, or by night, and welcome all. We do not expect everybody to come in the broad noontide and to be of the proportions of a giant or the dignity of a hero; we expect every poor heart to come just as it can according to its own pain and conviction of sin and weariness and sense of self-helplessness. There is only one way to God; there are a thousand ways to Christ. And Joseph of Arimathea, it is well we cannot put him upon the list. Why not? Who made you keeper of the list? If God puts him on the list there he must remain, and though we may unanimously–how the poor Church was wrecked itself on that word unanimously!–reject him, you cannot put him out; he is still there, and will recur, and then recede, and then return. If God has chosen him, why bruise your poor knuckles on the eternal granite?

Now let me say there is nothing to be proud of in ignoring the Church. Understand that all these men have not ignored the Christ or stood outside of Him on purpose. They did not exhibit hostility to Him in the case of Nathanael, Zaccheus, Nicodemus. There is room in the Church for all. Let us drop the qualifying word which is often put before the word Church–as the Church of Rome, the Church of England, the Scottish Church, the Irish Church, the Congregational Church, the Nonconformist Church. Oh, when it comes to the higher life and work, take a spade, not a pair of scissors, and cut off all these qualifying terms, whether they go before the noun or after it, and throw them away; they are fit only for the burning. There is a spiritual Church; there is a mystical Church; there is an invisible Church. But I think if I may trust to my memory for a moment, there are churches enough for everyone of us to find a place in somewhere. What an odd man he must be who wants to have a whole church to himself! I think if you were to go carefully through the Church as to its names and divisions and subdivisions, its unions, synods, assemblies, congresses, and more and more, and then etc., etc., until the whole page is filled with them, I think you might surely find one of them that would give you just the accommodation you are looking for. But if not, then heave out a tub of your own and sail on it. There is no peculiar virtue in a man not belonging to a denomination. He must be very supersensitively and absurdly conscientious, or very degradedly bigoted and self-satisfied, if he cannot find room in England, in Great Britain, in America, just to unite himself in Christian fellowship to somebody of well-meaning and hard-working Christians.

There is no warrant, in the next place, for making the Church exclusive. We ought rather to err, if we err at all, on the side of hospitality and inclusiveness. We ought to be prepared to differ in opinion; we ought also to be prepared to agree in everything but opinion. If I tell you that such and such was your opinion six months ago, you say, Well, a good deal has happened since then. I will join you at the point of stability; I will join you not at accidental and changeable points, but at the point of firmness and everlastingness, and we will tabernacle together in the infinite temple whose name is God-is-love. It was Jesus Christ's way to recognize people that nobody else recognized. He offended the Jews greatly and frequently in this matter. He was the most fearless speaker whose name has been recorded in human history; He was always offending the bigotry, the prejudice, and the ignorance of such. He said, There hath not returned to give glory to God save this stranger. That is the same idea—outside people, unrecognized people, and such people surprising the inside people by acts of gratitude and faithful service. Once the Lord Jesus quite offended a number of people by a parable. He said in what we know as the parable of the Good Samaritan, "And a certain Samaritan came where he was." We do not understand the puncturing force of that expression; there was an insult in it, there was a challenge to the Jews, for the Jews had no dealings with the Samaritans, and it was a Samaritan of whom Jesus said, "But a certain Samaritan came where he was." The supposed favorites of God fall back and a stranger was chosen as the jewel of the occasion. All this was adumbrated, wondrously foreshadowed, in that wondrous prayer which Solomon offered at the dedication of the Temple; he said, "And when the stranger"—I thought it was going to be a bigoted temple, a place built for Israel alone; and yet Solomon said, "And if the stranger . . . and the stranger." And the stranger was recognized even before the temple of Solomon, his name is in the decalogue, this wondrous figure of a man that was coming, coming, coming. And the time shall come when there shall be no strangers; there shall be no more strangers, foreigners, but brothers, sisters, part of the whole family in heaven and on earth. Towards that consummation all history tends; because history is in the soul of it the revelation of God, the outshining and forthgoing of His benign, benevolent, redeeming providence. Get thee home, stranger, outsider, and say thou hast today heard a man who declared that Jesus Christ has outside, un-recognized friends, and who told thee that thou might be one of them. Then fall on thy knees and say, God be merciful to me a sin-ner! Then, having received thy pardon, go forth and testify to Christ, and witness for Him, and find the fellowship with which and with whom thou canst most familiarly, tenderly, and profitably associate.

Prayer

What is our life? It is even as a vapor that cometh for a little time, and then vanisheth away. We all do fade as a leaf, and at the best we are as a shock of corn fully ripe, ready to be gathered into the garner; but it is nothing. Our days are threescore years and ten, and if by reason of strength they be fourscore years, yet is their strength labor and sorrow, for it is soon cut off, and we fly away. Thou art training us in the shadow school; Thou art making patterns in the clouds, and showing them unto us; Thou knowest that we are here but for a little while, and Thou dost call upon us in Thy mercy and love to redeem the time, to turn the hours into gold, and to give time what we can of the dignity of eternity. This is Thy call in the soul; it moans in us like a great hill wind blowing from afar, rich with messages, some of sorrow, some of joy. Oh! that men were wise, that they understood these things, that they would consider their latter end, and that they would no longer play the fool, as if they had eternity to waste. May we be wise men, considerers of the time, merchants in buying up the opportunity and turning it to the best account; then when the last call comes, it will be a call to supper, the supper of the Lamb, the feast of the heavens, the banquet of higher, fuller service. Let the young be young as long as they can, and may old age have in it some bloom and touch of youth; but may we know that we have this young-heartedness only because of Jesus Christ, the Child that died for us. We bless Thee every day for Jesus; we call Him with Thine own Word the Morning Star, and we receive Him into our hearts as a pledge that we shall never die. He that liveth and believeth in Me shall never die; yea, if he were dead, he shall rise again and be clothed upon with the robes of resurrection and belong to a kingdom of priests. For these hopes we bless Thee; we need them every one, for there is enough in the cold earth-air to chill the soul and to drive us back and to quicken our unbelief into a great rebellion. Lord, increase our faith; may we meet life like men, men of God, men of faith, men full of the Holy Ghost. Enable us to trample upon circumstances; may they not overcome us; may we overcome them; this is the victory that overcometh the world, even our faith. When the temperature is low, cold, and wintry, draw very near us, thou Sun of right-eousness in whose wings alone we can find healing. When we are in weak-ness and sorrow, and when we are living under a great fear which we dare not communicate to the dearest heart we know, then be our society, Thou who sittest up the whole night with those whose hearts are sore. When we are troubled and perplexed, the Lord give us power to consider things wisely and well, and to set up a time of balances and measures so that we be no longer fools in the handling of our own lives. The Lord speak com-fortably to those that are bowed down, and to those who are weary of life, and asking many a time in the dark night hours, When will it be morning? For the Lord Christ's sake hear us when we ask Thee to turn our sick chambers into temples and churches and sanctuaries of the Pres-ence. Amen.

28

The Fading Leaf

Preached on Sunday Morning, June 17th, 1900.

We all do fade as a leaf—Isaiah 64:6.

The danger is that we mistake all such texts as commonplace. It is a great peril to suppose ourselves so familiar with any text that we really need no further exposition or application of its inward and spiritual truth. There is no commonplace in such a sentence as "We all do fade as a leaf." It is a text for the day; it is a parable for the hour. Interpreted poetically, it can never be stale. We may pervert the richest truths and treat them as if they were commonplaces, but the blame is in us and not in the truth. I could not but hear this little angel text singing to me ever since I heard that dear Mrs. Gladstone passed away. We cannot account for these visitant singers; we do not know who sends them, but we know who sends them primarily, for every good gift and every perfect gift is from the Father of lights. So the texts come singingly; they do not wait for the audience. The birds in all these June trees never say to one another, Is the audience fully gathered? They care nothing for the audience; they do not want your audiences and your cheers and your encores; they never ask you for a favor. These June birds sing by laws and impulses and motions over which we have no control, and the psychology of which we could never explain. So it is with the text; it comes at the time; it sings its sweet song of heaven, and then vanishes to make way for some other song-teacher. The text applies to old age that would perhaps rather be gathered to the grave like a shock of corn fully ripe. But what is fully ripe, and who shall say when a life is fully ripe and when it is not? Is there not a ripeness of youth, a ripeness of quality as well as a ripeness of quantity? May not seven golden days be a longer time than seven barren years? These things we must live; let God be teacher, let the Holy Spirit, who makes all the summer the soul can ever know, work His miracle of song and light and completeness.

I think we should notice lives that pass from our poor eyesight—persons who have been great as women, wives, mothers, healers, and who have made the world-house worth living in. O man, thou art a clumsy fool compared with any woman that knows how to handle a house without fussing about it. We are so tempted to run after the romantic, the spectacular, the demonstrative, that we often leave out of account the souls that have made us, the influences that have charmed away the devil. We like something stupendous; we love to have twentieth century funds, and oh into what sweltering excitement we work ourselves when we hear that other people have contributed them. It is so un-Christlike, such a horrible affront on Calvary and its Cross, all this romance. If people would give a stated sum out of each year's income, say one tenth, every year would produce five times more than any twentieth century fund ever produced. But who will do that? It is commonplace. There is the answer, Do it systematically, unfailingly, on the first day of the week, and we should have revenue enough for all purposes. But we do not like these inner and spiritual modes of working. No!—a dinner—champagne—loud cheers—another thousand! O Thou sweet Jesus, no wonder Thou dost turn away Thy marred face and seek the wilderness. But you do not know really how to reckon your income? You reckon it for the queen, why not for the King? But we like that which is romantic, obvious, dazzling, prodigious. And so, following out the same line of thought, we write long books about what we call great men and their great doings. And all this is right; we wait for the books; we are thankful for them because they may be instrumental in our higher education, and they may bring to us inspiration, impulse, encouragement, stimulus, just what we need in many a laggard mood. But there are lives that have no biography, though they may be among the most fruitful of lives. I think Mrs. Gladstone's life was one of these—full of kindness, sunshine, sympathy, gentleness. I have seen her close at hand, and have been affected and stimulated by her sweet and most motherly presence. I dare only speak as an onlooker, but what little onlooking I have been able to do has been to my own heart most elevating and sanctifying. Such a woman sweetened the atmosphere; her very presence drove away unholiness and every suggestion of it and created a disinfecting light as well as a luminous glory. What it must be to be in one's eighty-ninth year as she was, and to look back so far and to be unable to find out any one mischief, injury, or infelicitous mark! This must be a triumph of the sweet grace of Jesus Christ; the whole life-line a line of light. I saw her when she went into the Abbey on the occasion of Mr. Gladstone's never-to-be-forgotten interment. She walked as if she were keeping an appointment, went with some spring and energy and expectancy, as one who had said in her heart, I must not be late; I must not keep him waiting. I saw her when she returned, and she was alone—a bride without a bridegroom, a widow old as her age, and yet a gleaming, beauteous light flooding the whole countenance. On Tuesday next she will be taken back, and the wedding will be completed. What we want to feel more and more is how much we are indebted to people who have no outstanding and demonstrative fame, but the greater renown of making other lives rich and happy, and turning the whole house and home into a picture of sunshine. We may all excel in some degree along this line; we can all make somebody else happy; some in this way, some in that way, but we can all live, the very smallest and humblest of us, so as to be one day missed. We may by the grace of God and the charity of our renewed lives so live as to leave a great vacancy in at least one or two hearts. That is fame, and all other fame is a bubble and a vanishing smoke.

"We all do fade." Yet we do not believe it. We see how another man is failing, fading, aging, and we remark to one another when the man is not there, I saw a great difference in him; he was much older looking than when I saw him last; I saw that the experience through which he had been passing had wasted him a good deal. And do you know, observing and talkative critic, that the same thing was observed in your own case by another person? We all do fade; we all age. I thought I saw in his attitude and motion a stoop like the stoop of fatigue. Did you? That is the very thing he thought he saw in you who think yourself so young and lithe and alert; I heard a man say about you the other day that he was under the impression that you had aged a good deal. "We all"—it is the common fate; it is the common destiny.

What wonderful reading there is in the Bible about this departure of men! Some of the Old Testament words make me at once sad and glad; notably this—a text I can never pass over without a tear—"Joseph died, and all his brethren, and all that generation." Poor scribe! He began well; he pointed out that one man had died—"And Joseph died"—he had time to write that line; he thought he was the biographer of the world. Yet presently he says, "and all his brethren." Why not name them one by one? O, they die so fast I have no time to give the details, the names, and therefore I group them together and say, "all his brethren." What more? "And all that generation." He who began to individualize, who began to say in his biographical capacity with the simple unit of individualism, is obliged, so quickly does death follow his writing, to shut up his sentence with "and all that generation." The unit changes; we speak of a dying individual, then of families, then of generations. The invisible cruel archer shoots so fast that a generation is gone before the names of the brethren can be recorded. Nor dare I pass this text without meditating upon it with tearfulness, for after all he was a great man, a prince and a great man, a king and a great man; and this is the record, "So Saul died, and his three sons, and all his house died together" (1 Chr. 10:6). Why not read it again? It is such a pregnant record. How hurried must the historian have been, how assured that if he did not make haste there would be a thousand more men carried past him dead. "So Saul died, and his three sons, and all his house died together." Where is king Saul? Gone; his three sons? Gone. Any remnant of his house? Gone. You know how a shadow goes; shadows leave no imprints.

These may be commonplaces, but they are the commonplaces we need to remember. Do not debase the divine poetry of providence into commonplace by saying that you knew all that very well—talking to me as if I did not know all that before. Sir, you never knew it; a man talking so can know nothing; he is a fool in the sanctuary, and the altar shudders when he nears it. All that generation of workers. They were a fine strong old tribe; I knew some of them well; they were stalwarts; they were genuine men; they lived for the church; they delighted in the courts of the Lord, and they never said they were done. "All that generation." They were severe; oftentimes we passed them as a set of austere old gentlemen, but they made England. All that generation of givers. They were noble souls; they said everything they had belonged to Jesus Christ. We have reversed their way of looking at things; I am not sure that their way was not the right way. They said, All this gold is Christ's; I suppose we must live while we live now—how little of this can we take for living purposes? They took as little as possible, and invested all the other in the bank of God. When I came to London, Samuel Morley, one of the true children of God, said to me, "Call upon me for anything you want in beginning this great work of yours in London." All that generation of workers, givers, and types of men—great trustees and stewards of the divine will. Some of their sons survive and wear the paternal mantle with great grace and dignity, but many of them do not, and many men who have been made by the old process have abandoned it for the new trick. I will not speak of them; hounds that ought not to have a name! All that generation—the old-fashioned, the well-tried, the well-instructed and deeply experienced souls. They were not so very glaring and attractive, but they made England. Yet these men have successors, and some of their successors are quite equal to any of the predecessors; the work has been varied, not ended; it is the same work conducted under different conditions. Yet though there be differences of administration there should be one spirit, and that spirit a spirit of consecration and love, simplicity, devotion, obedience to the spiritual, the unseen, and the eternal. I delight to think that though many have faded away like the leaf, there are today as good men, as good workers, as good givers, as good types and examples as ever lived since the days of Bethlehem. Yet it does us good to visit the old places, the old graves, and to take up the old books. I have books that I look at sometimes, curiously bound books, sort of binding in sheepskin; curious old type—my father's edition of Boston's Fourfold State. Who dare be found reading that book today? Yet it is fat with the fatness of Christ; it was written by a man whose heart was in the heart of Christ; you will have some difficulty in finding an edition of it; it is not the kind of book that is sold in tens of thousands, but if a dozen men in this congregation or any other congregation should read it, study it, and inwardly digest it, they would make their influence felt as spiritual powers; they would be as living rocks and as throbbing, glowing pillars in the house of my God.

"We all do fade as a leaf." So I must make the best of my dwindling opportunities, and this should be the lesson to the youngest leaf among us. Even now in this mid-June what do you find? All the laburnums nearly or many of them on the ground, all that golden water; the flower of the laburnum tree has dripped, dripped, dripped, and the golden water, as the German calls it, is lying very largely on the ground. Dear, sweet yellow flower, the canary of flowers and trees, thou hadst but a short day, but now that I crush thy yellow beauty under foot I will say to myself, "We all do fade as a leaf"; and thus in thy dying, thou laburnum, shalt teach me lessons about the measurement of time and the duration of life and the duty of making the best of present opportunities. We could all make somebody happy while we live; not always by leaving money, but by giving pleasure, giving sympathy, by showing that we are not indifferent to the distresses and the necessities of other people. Believe me, there is no virtue in social indifference: as who should say, Make the best of it for yourselves. Grander man is he who says to the virtuously poor, I cannot help you much, but I will help you all I can. You do not know how long you will have the opportunity of helping. Once I knew a man whom I thought quite equal to king Saul; and his grandchildren have come to beg at my door; this morning I have a letter respecting one of his grandchildren who would like to be housed in some refuge for indigent gentlewomen. The wolves of sons which that man had tore the flesh off his bones, wrecked his house, and others have to suffer for their cruel villainy. We know not what shall be on the earth. Do good to seven, and withhold not a portion from eight; for thou knowest not what shall be. Showers soon swell into deluges, and winds rise into storms; that which but an hour since was blue as the bluest of morning azure may in a few hours more be dark with storm and big with tempest. Do not let us mourn the past, but ennoble the present, and by ennobling the present prepare for the fruition and harvest delight of the future.

We have all done wrong. We all do fade as a leaf, and we all do sin as the prodigal son. If I have been hard with any man—I thank God I cannot remember an instance of hardness, and I say this to His glory and not to my own praise—but if I have been hard with any man, it was a pity, a sad and terrible pity, a great solemn degradation of manhood. If I have been hard with any human creature when I could have been gentle, then I have dishonored the Lord; I have misinterpreted the Gospel, and I am a base man worthy of the pit. You never had such an opportunity in your life for showing the divine Christ as when another man said to you, I did you wrong—will you pardon me? That was your chance; then you might have been a great man. It was not a time for snarling and reproaching and waking up sharp memories, it was a time for tears and sobbing and heartbreak and outgoing of the soul to the man who asked to be pitied and pardoned.

"We all do fade," and our time fades; our years crumble away, and the man is now digging the grave I shall lie in next week. This is the view of life to take, so as to make the best of the golden but passing moments. And if we live in the right way and fade according to the gentle laws of nature, what is it but to fade into immortality—to languish into life?

Prayer

Almighty God, Thou dost lash us with the thong of questioning. Thou dost pour out Thine inquiries upon us like a torrent, and we have no breath to reply; Thou dost speak about strange times and far away spaces, and behold, when Thou dost lay the lash upon us we gather together as it were at the heel of God. Yet how boastful we are, how full of pride, how utterly fuming, and how we bow down to the spirit of vanity. Teach us that if any man think that he knoweth anything, he knoweth nothing as it ought to be known; he that is least in Thy sight is also greatest. Teach us to hold our tongues; oh that we could behave ourselves in Thy presence and not return Thy questionings in our own vain form. If Thou wilt give us grace to say, "I was dumb because Thou didst it," Thou wilt work a miracle in us by the power of the Holy Ghost. We cannot tell what Thou doest; who can follow all Thy way? Who can keep pace with the lightning flash that goeth from one point to another in a moment? Teach us our littleness, and in our littleness may we find our greatness: blessed are the meek, for they shall be great inheritors, and all things they can bear and carry well will come to them and ask for acceptance. We thank Thee that Thou hast made us inquirers; now do Thou make us inquirers that are reverent and humble and meek-minded, for Thou dost temple with those who are of a broken heart, and into the contrite spirit Thou dost come with the quietness of light. The Lord help us through this wondrous, weary, painful, glorious life; teach us that our days are but as a handbreadth, and may we work well within the limited space. We look unto Jesus, the author and finisher of our faith. Lord, increase our faith, and thereby increase our best knowledge; enable us to see more and more into the mystery and meaning of the Cross. At the Cross we stand; we cannot explain it, we receive it, and we would work and suffer in the spirit of it. Amen.

29
Humbling Questions

Preached on Thursday Morning, June 21st, 1900.

Art thou the first man that was born?—Job 15:7.

What cutting and snubbing questions there are in the Bible!
What a whip it is; how we are lashed like hounds! It will be profitable from time to time to study some of the humbling questions
of the Bible. In fact, are there any other questions than those that
are humbling in the whole compass of revelation? How can this
Book hope to make itself popular? It is flattery that gathers popularity, at least for a time; how can this man Christ Jesus ever expect
to make Himself popular when He says His badge is the Cross, the
daily Cross; the Cross not of dramatic conception and speculation,
but of real blood-suffering? This is not a Man to make Himself popular. He cuts down to the root of things; we heard indeed early concerning Him that the ax was laid to the root of the tree. Everybody
about Him seems to ask the same question, having drunk of His
Spirit and caught the holy contagion of His moral fury. "O generation of vipers, how shall ye escape the damnation of hell?" This was
not popular preaching, and the church ought not to be a popular
resort. Let those go to bands and parades and demonstrations and
fools' merriments who want to be popular, but keep far away from
Him whose every question is a whip.

"Art thou the first man that was born?" Eliphaz plays questioner
to Job; he pelts him well. "Wast thou made before the hills? Hast
thou heard the secret of God? What knowest thou that we know

not? What understandest thou, which is not in us? With us are both the grayheaded and very aged men, much elder than thy father. Is there any secret thing with thee?" And thus he mocks him. Job might have borne all this interrogatory chastening and whipping, this question-scourging, this new and biting discipline, if it had been confined to Eliphaz the Temanite; but later on another questioner comes to him, and beats him and lashes him without sparing, and pours upon him torrents of contempt. So that Job's few days undergo such a shrinkage that he feels as if he had never been born. "Art thou the first man that was born?" Art thou Adam that we have read about? Hast thou lived all the centuries, and gathered all their wisdom? Speak up! Yet it does us good to have these humbling questions put to us now and then, while we are dressing and while the man-servant is there, and the maid-servant, and all the jewel box is being opened, and all wild preparation is being made for outshining the stars of night. It does us good now and then for an imp or some demonlike thing to be squatting near our ear and saying, Who art thou at the best? And canst thou see tomorrow? Knowest thou that thou shalt come home tonight filled with envy and jealousy and maddened because of disappointment? And thy days how many? Art thou as old as England? England was once a swamp. Boast not of thy ancestry, for thou hadst none but a handful of mud; have no pride in these poor jewels, for they may all be stolen tonight. Thieves are members of a learned profession. What hast thou at the best that thou hast not received? Oh, why not kiss the hand of the Giver and know that in the sight of God the ornament of a meek and quiet spirit is of great price? Why not now begin to learn the higher, deeper, broader wisdom?

We may have humbling enough if we would but attend to the case. It is when we put our fingers in our ears and draw down our eyelids and think that all is going well that we enjoy a moment's game, speculation, and a species of criminal luxury. If we would see in every bad man our brother, in every Cain a man that wants to murder us and a Cain that is in very deed in ourselves, were he but awakened, we should have reason enough to walk softly all the days of our lives. And what are we at the best? The worm has already whetted the appetite that is to be sated on our proud flesh. It were well for men now and then to think, consider out things together, and make arithmetical calculations as well as spiritual outlooks, forecasts, and holy speculations.

When the poet accompanies himself upon a harp, he had to buy the very harp that he makes eloquent. The man that made the harp probably never played; he made harps for other people. You would say the man who can make a harp must be a harper. As well say that the carpenter who made the ship is a navigator. It is very wonderful all this intertwisting and intertwining of men and men, trades and occupations and professions and gifts; it is a wondrous thing this social unit. We are very great in the individual unit; there we feel quite certain and quite strong and quite impious. The individual unit, the one-coated man standing before his own looking-glass, what is he? Why, in a spider's first string that he throws out to start his web from there are sixty strands. We are made for one another; one man is completed by another man. No one should despise anyone; there should be a sense of commonwealth and unity, and thus we should get from the unit of isolation the unit of society. No man thinking that he was the only man or even the first man that ever was born, but every man looking out for some other man, and being quite sure that he is there; though he be hidden for a moment he is there, and there for a purpose. What knowledge have we? Only what we have been told. We who despise authority live upon it. That is very like us. It is a marvelous thing that we gather ourselves together in great numbers in order to demonstrate against authority, and every man among us is living on the authority of another man. Do not tell him that, because it would spoil his demonstration, and he likes to throw his hat high in the air, and despise authority. The multiplication table is authoritative. Somehow or other it has come among us to be regarded as final; pity indeed it is that the first man that ever was born does not rise up and make a multiplication table of his own and insist upon everybody adopting it. But we despise authority; we hate that word; it touches our blood as the spur touches the blood of a high-bred animal; we cannot stand it, and yet we must submit to it and live under it, and we cannot cast it off without casting ourselves off at the same time. Have we any original knowledge? Who taught us the rules by which we regulate our speech? Did we invent them? No. Is it not open to every man to invent his own syntax? Yes, and it is open to every other man to laugh at him for doing it. There are very few things open to us except genuine humility and true, exact self-esteem in the sight of God, and a holiness that looks well, but oh so gray when foiled with the infinite whiteness of the ineffable purity of God.

"Art thou the first man that was born?" There must have been a first man. He might possibly have had some measure of independence from a merely superficial view of himself, but he had no real independence, he was part of the next man that was coming, and thus we belong to posterity as well as ancestry, and we hand on the life which we have often stained and spoiled. If I am not the first man that was born, if I am not the only man, then it follows that I must consult some other man. That is an extraordinary process. It is a process that goes on in every city and in every family all the time. The doctor sends for the doctor. One would think he might by this time have been too wise to do that, but he falls into the general superstition at least and sends for the doctor, and dies *secundum artem* and has a doctor's certificate that he died properly. I must consult some other man. Do I not know law enough to guide my own affairs? Possibly, and possibly not. You must consult some other man on certain things, even if after prolonged and wise consultation you adopt a policy gathered from the total council. We belong to one another. Your friend knows better than you do how certain cases stand, because you may be part and parcel of the cases, and he stands aside or at a proper distance giving them the right proportion, perspective, and color, and he, being a wise man, can tell you what to do, and you in your turn may be able to render the same service to him. We belong to one another. There is but one Man—multifold, but one. Thus self-conceit is smitten on the cheekbone; thus the back of pride is lashed with the thong of a true retribution and resentment; and thus and thus variously we are taught that no one man is all men, but that all men are one Man, and that there was but one fount of blood out of which all veins were filled, and there is but one fount of blood which can cleanse the putrid sinfulness and crime into which we have drawn and plunged ourselves by some act of awful, stupendous suicide.

Thus God makes one man debtor to another, and so creates mutual interests. When you "take a man in," using a commercial phrase, you do not enrich yourself. That is curious, but it is true. You enrich yourself apparently or for the moment, you increase your possessions for the moment at least; but you do not really enrich yourself, your soul, and there is no abiding, no durableness, in the stuff that you get with a thief's hand. Honesty is rich, economy is wealth; he who has few wants has many riches. We are, however, debtors to one another in a deeper and broader sense. The apostle said, "I am a debtor both to the Jew and the Gentiles,"—I am a debtor to everybody. Why so, Paul, and how? Tell me. Inasmuch as I have the Gospel and they have not yet received the Gospel, I am a debtor to every man who does not know the secret of the divine love, and I must away and tell him what I know and thus discharge the debt. If you know anything really wise and good that some other man does not know, and the knowing of which would enrich and dignify him, you are a debtor to that man; not a debtor in the financial or bookkeeping sense, but a debtor in the higher spiritual sense, that you know a secret or mystery the knowledge of which and the appropriation of which is eternal life. You are not to hold it as a secret; you are to dispense it as a blessing. Herein is the glory of the Gospel; it belongs to every man: "Go ye into all the world, and preach the Gospel to every creature," as if you were paying the creature a debt, and tell him that you are doing so. You are a trustee, a steward; you are in more than a fiduciary position, you hold the Gospel for the saving of the world. Go, tell it! Stop the winds till you fill them with this music; then let them go and carry it over all the wildernesses. How strange is man, how utterly peculiar! He thinks that he has some things of his own right, whereas he has nothing. May not a man do what he likes with his own? Certainly, but first find it. The moment that you have found anything that is your own, do what you like with it. What I hold in my hand is surely my own? No, your hand is not your own. What hast thou that thou hast not received? Trace things back, and you will be surprised to find—I am sorry to disappoint you, unless I can turn the disappointment into a blessing—you will certainly find that you are not the first man that was born. You talk as if you were. Yes, that is another thing altogether. You seem to receive your guests as if you were receiving so much disagreeable mud; but art thou the first man that was born? How we are thus cut up, snubbed, humiliated! Is there a sight more humbling in the world than to see a man take on the airs of a peacock? Why, his very tail is not his own. We are born into furnished houses, yet we have the notion somehow or other that we furnish our own houses. We do not, in any true, deep sense of the term. We were born into libraries. Disraeli said that he was born in a library. That was literally true, but he was also born into a library. We are all inheritors, though we have paid probably in many cases no succession duties and no death dues. Milton was born before us, and Shakespeare, and the great poets, dreamers, writers, prophets; and we are born into these inheritances, and somehow think that we created them. We created nothing. Wise men who know much by calculation say that if you were three miles from your house and had to make an adequate road such as you find in civilized cities before you could get home, you would be seventy years in getting there. You do not believe it? I thought not, because I can see by your face that you do not believe anything. But wise men who make calculations and tabulate experiences and precedents made that statement, and thereby show us how much we are indebted to the men who came before us and made the road. It is enough for us to find fault with it.

We are debtors, therefore, let me repeat again and again, to one another, because the first man belongs to the second man, and the second man to the first man, and when a third man comes they will be divided and sub-divided, and when the three-hundredth man comes we shall begin to shape our relations and define our responsibilities, and make that marvelous star called Society, that no telescope can see thoroughly into and which no calculation can estimate at its full and enduring value. You sing? Yes, I sing a little. You make your own songs? No. Is it possible that when people get together in church they are not singing their own hymns? Not only possible, but it is a serious fact that all our hymns were written for us and we had but to learn them. Then we are not the first men that were born? No. And what is our relation to the first man? Debtors. And the coming men? Debtors. And we ourselves, what are we, pray say in plain, simple, motherlike English? Debtors. Then we belong to one another? That is philosophically and literally true; and what one man has another man may not have, and what one man has not another man may be able to supply. We are members one of another, like the jointed body. This is the Lord's doing, and it is marvelous in our eyes.

Applying this line of thought to the highest spiritual things, let us remember that we did not invent the Gospel. This is no modern thought; this is no yesterday's ware turned out of some oven in the manufacturing districts. This is older than man. The Cross is older than Adam; the Cross is just as old as the love of God. When you have fixed the date of the birth of the love of God, you have fixed the date of the meaning of the Cross. Yet if we come into historical times, say into Mosaic years, we shall find the Cross in the Book of Genesis; we shall find the Cross in the Book of Revelation. Jesus Christ is the Lamb slain from before the foundation of the world. Our temptation is to amend the Gospel, to add something to it or take something from it, or set our own finger-mark upon its beauty.

If we could but deliver the Gospel instead of attempting to invent it, we might do some good. "I delivered unto you first of all that which I also received." That was the apostolic declaration, and if we would be in the apostolic succession we must do exactly what the apostle Paul himself did: he "received" the Gospel and "delivered" it. That is all we have to do, or if we make any contribution to it, which we cannot make to its substance, but to its illustration, it must be the contribution of our own personal experience in agonizing prayer, in self-crucifixion, and in the dwelling with God in secret places where the fountains throw up their healing waters for our refreshment and our renewal. The Gospel is in every bush of the summer, in every bird of the air, in every act of suffering, in the vicarious mother and the vicarious father. These are parables given to us to help us understand the central Gospel, which is that Jesus Christ tasted death for every man.

Then as we are indebted to the past we should make the future indebted to us. There was an old maxim in the older political economy, which is not at all to be despised, that we ought to endeavor to make two blades of grass grow where one blade of grass grew before. The earth has brought forth no grass yet; all those green meadows we see are nothing but parabolic signs of the grass that is in the earth. Why, it is all grass, all nutrition, nutriment, food, sustenance; and when the people praise the Lord in a worthy song, adequate in compass, in tone, in meaning, the old earth will give us thirty harvests in one. We may live so as to be missed; we may offer a suggestion that will help the solution of the deepest problems; we can breathe a healthy breath, and a healthy breath is peace. Let us limit our mischievousness; let us do nothing to make men angry or to hurt poor human hearts, but let us so live that the house will feel very empty after we have gone. It will be an excellent discipline, a real good soul-schooling, if we can enter into this great scheme of questioning which is revealed in the Bible. "Where wast thou when I laid the foundations of the earth? declare, if thou hast understanding. Who hath laid the measures thereof, if thou knowest? Or who hath stretched the line upon it? Whereupon are the foundations thereof fastened? or who laid the corner stone thereof; when the morning stars sang together, and all the sons of God shouted for joy?" Where wast thou? O thou poor braggart, thou art of yesterday and thou knowest nothing. Canst thou see through one sheet of paper and tell me what is on the other side of it? No. Canst thou see through the film of the night and behold the morning before it hath risen upon the eastern hills? No. It behoveth thee, therefore, to be quiet and calm and to go to God with thy questions, and to hide thyself in the love and mystery of the Cross.

Prayer

We bless Thee, Thou Living One, that the songs of the Church are also our song. We sing of Thy mercy, and we say that it endureth forever. In the old, old time men sang of Thy mercy, and said, It endureth forever; in the ages that have yet to come men and women will sing of Thy mercy, and say, It endureth forever. We live in Thy mercy, we are the children of Thy compassion; because Thy tears fail not therefore are we spared. We do not keep ourselves; in ourselves we have no strength, and we have no resources; our sufficiency is of God; He giveth us all things richly to enjoy; we have nothing that we have not received. So we will say again and again with every sunrise and every sunset, His mercy endureth forever. Thou hast turned our very life into a song, Thou hast made midnight bright as noonday when we remember that Thy mercy endureth forever. We have sinned against God with a high hand, with an outstretched arm, with great rebelliousness; but Thy mercy endureth forever. Hear, we humbly pray Thee at the Cross, the sighing of each penitent heart which says in brokenness and self-helplessness, God be merciful unto me a sinner! Let there be a great sense of forgiveness among us; may we feel as if heaven had been opened from within, and that a great voice had said, Her iniquity is pardoned and her trespass is forgotten. If we could hear some such voice in our innermost consciousness we would sing a great anthem before Thee, loud and sweet and far-sounding, and the burden of it should be, His mercy endureth forever. We all need mercy; like sheep we have gone astray, we have turned every one to his own way. But is there not One that taketh away the sin of the world? Is His name not Jesus? Signifying that He shall save the people from their sins, is He not figured to us as a Lamb set apart as a sacrifice for the sins of the whole world? There is none righteous, no, not one; may not one man therefore seek to crush his brother offender; we are all in the same condemnation, now here, now there, now in this way, now in some other way, but there is none righteous, no, not one; priest and people are all cast down into the same condemnation; there is none righteous; the man who prays is the man who sins—may it be that the man who sins become

601

also the man who prays. Thus in this wondrous manifold life, now praying, now sinning, now hoping, and now black with unutterable fear, yet all the while the great process is going on, which means purity, morning, liberty, joy, and final heaven. Have mercy upon those who need it most, if any need it more than others. Thou lookest upon broken-heartedness and contrition; may we pay our vows unto Thee that we vow in the house of distress and in the chamber of desolation and darkness. They were great cries we uttered then, and now that we are freed again for a little time and are permitted to go out into Thine open air and bright sunshine, may we remember the vows of the darkened room. Pity us, for we are so soon cast aside as it were by our own hands, and we are swift to forget the very prayers that made us men. It is a sad world, a hard and costly school, and the Master's rod cuts to the bone. Oh! That we might remember something, that we may not forget everything, but bring out of the great brawl and strife some holy part and redeem it by daily sweet behavior. Look upon the old and the young and the little child we have left at home to sleep its religion while we come to utter ours. Be with our sick ones; Thou only canst heal; men can trifle with disease, but Thou canst heal it. And be with any who are in peril on the sea or who are in the far-away wilderness; let Thy love search them out, and not Thine anger, and may they also join the high chorus of the infinite hymn, saying, His mercy endureth forever. Amen.

30

A Pastoral Retrospect

Preached on Sunday Morning, June 24th, 1900.

I must put away the sermon I had prepared for this morning, and take it out of its resting-place some other time; for something says to me, It is not the right subject, and you can today make nothing of it. I am always thus led by the Spirit. I know that what I had prepared would be out of season, out of tune, out of the whole environment of this occasion, which neither you nor I make, but which was made by due fluxion and process of time, and I am full of the suggestion which the occasion brings with it. It is almost to a day thirty-one years since you and I were pastorally wedded at the altar. It was June and about this part of June, and certainly this is the Sunday in June, and the whole thing comes back upon me with such vividness and tenderness that I must get rid of it before I can go on with the usual plow, continuing the furrow we have been at these thirty-one years—a long furrow and deep and plenty of seed in it, not of our sowing, but of God's.

May I begin by asking you to cut off thirty-one years from your life? Where were you and what were you thirty-one years ago? They say that men who have sons and daughters growing up around them are more sensible of the flight of time than men who have no such living standards by which to measure and estimate themselves. I cannot speak for such men, for I have a great host of sons and daughters growing up around me in this house; and when I look at those who came to my ministry with their little hymn-books and standing on the forms or seats and lustily singing something or

603

other with the hymn-book upside down, it seems to me that I must have been too long in the world; for now they are fathers, mothers, people in office, in the City, in the suburbs, people of high responsibility, some of them of great character, others of overflowing usefulness in the Church; and here am I almost seeking an apology for being among living men. You must judge all things in their relation. Thirty-one years, and talking on the same subject all the time! We have never changed the theme; we have never changed the text. All the texts are one text; they all run back into the Cross, the sacrifice, the redeeming work of Jesus Christ, the marvelous and tender providence of God, counting the hairs of our head, numbering our steps, sending the sun blazing every morning upon our windows great and small. Thirty-one years of the Bible! No other book could be used in the same way and with the same high energy, taking the Church as a whole, but the Bible. It is in this way that the Bible proves its inspiration. We take out of it, and leave it as full as we found it. It is like the sun—always giving itself away, and today as bright as when it shone on Eden. This is the test of the book. Do not let us go to false and inadequate standards and ask little questions about great subjects. The Bible in its sufficiency, in its complete covering and encompassing of all human experience, is a book which needs no help whatever in the way of apology and vital sustenance from any man's ingenuity, erudition, or critical faculty. Let the Bible alone, let it do its own work in the training of families, in the direction of business, in the inspiration of life, and at the long end, in the sum-total we shall say, It was the Word of the Lord. It has proved itself to be such by its depth, its tenderness, its simplicity, and its ability to meet us in all the need and sorrow and pain and helplessness of this tragic life.

By the mercy of God, therefore, we have been able to keep to our one book and our one subject and steadily to work towards our one high purpose. What is that? The saving of men. There is no other object worth pursuing but to save a soul from death. Why, that is enough to challenge the highest powers of energy and the most blinding glory of wisdom. To have the satisfaction created in us and proved for us by the blessed Spirit of God that we have been enabled to help some poor soul—that is the golden and more than golden reward. Every faithful servant of Christ, be he ever so small and weak, may appropriate and enjoy this great reward which in itself is the beginning and assurance of a final coronation.

Where were you thirty-one years ago? Some of you were just beginning business, and you did not know whether it would fail or whether it would succeed, and you had to count every penny. That was not a bad time in life for you; it was a school time; it was a period of discipline. Everything under God's blessing depended upon your action just them. If you had been spendthrifts, if you had been self-indulgent, if you had cared nothing for either pence or pounds, you would not have been here today. I am speaking of course, to a certain section of the audience. You have labored faithfully and well, and you have shown great commercial sagacity, and above all great commercial integrity, and if you have thousands a year, I wish you had ten times as many thousands, because you deserve it all, and you would spend it all right well, and everybody about you would feel that your accounts and transactions were about where they ought to be, and there is a feeling of sunshine in the social air because you have been making so many people just as happy as you could possibly make them. That is the kind of prosperity that I pray for, that it may be doubled and multiplied by high figures, because everybody will directly or indirectly be the better for your prosperity. It may have gone otherwise with some people. They may have squandered the little they began with; it was only a hundred pounds or two hundred pounds, and you may somehow have got through the little sum, and yet nobody could directly fasten upon you a reproach that could be justified. You have been sweet-tempered, really amiable, of fine creamy disposition; I am not here to reproach any poor soul. But the fact is, you did not get up soon enough in the morning. Do not take it as a reproach or an impeachment because the gift of sleep has been given to some heads

in undue measure. You cannot call it a high crime and misde-
meanor, yet there it is. The other man was up before you, and that
is the reason why you did not succeed as you would like to have
done. Yet not a single man in society can point a finger of shame at
you. There are many ways of not doing a thing: the positive hostile
way which says in effect, I will not do it, and the indolent, indifferent, sleepy-headed way that says, Well, I fully intend to do it,
and I think probably I shall do it tomorrow, and if I do not do it tomorrow I shall do it very soon. Ah! That is one of the little foxes
that spoil the grapes. Still you are here, and still the lamp of hope is
not altogether quenched; friends have been raised up for you in
one way and another, and you are here to join the hymn of one-
and-thirty years' co-labor, and to say in loud, resounding tones, His
mercy endureth forever.

How many have we dropped by the wayside? I have a melancholy way of numbering the lost and the left. Some we left behind
because we really could not assist them, and many we laid in the
grave and flung a flower in the empty place. We wanted them to
go with us all the miles, and we wanted to lie down with them that
at one and the same moment we might enter into the vision of
light and into the ecstasy of the heavenly song. What I have seen in
those broad pews! I have a list of those whose faces once shone
upon me as I gazed from this pulpit. Some were old, and their
going was not dying. We do not say that the sun dies; he sets, he
passes beyond the one wave that he may rise in silvery brightness
on another wave, which he will do in due time. We thank God for
the aged who have died. They were each like a shock of corn fully
ripe, and they left their labors and their hallowed memories behind
them, and they will be inspirations and solaces to us right through
the late afternoon and far away into the darkening night. They were
your fathers. I remember your father sitting there, and I remember
your sweet mother looking at you while the service was proceeding
as if by a gentle look she could bind you to the altar and encourage
you to take up some deep vow and make it the keyword and the

light of your life. We have not lost them. We do not lose whom we remember; they abide with us, and they do much for us that we cannot follow in letters and set forth in visible figures. Blessed are they who live lives of holy sweetness and beneficence! I mean the folks that were not great folks, great energetic factors in social life, but who lived sweetly, helpfully, forgivingly; those who kept the door ajar for us when we were too late out at night, and who watched as if they had not been watching and took us in as if we had never been out. Oh the sweetness, the tenderness! I remember some instances perfectly, and they help a man to pray and to preach and to hope. My notion at the first was to dedicate or consecrate all the windows in this church that were of a memorial nature to the honor of decent, quiet, home-loving persons, whose fame was in the house, who made the house, and when they went the house went and the sunshine perished as before a great fear. That was my notion of the windows, to perpetuate the memory of home ones— my father, my mother, my brethren. I heard my various people say, I will put in a memorial window to that dear old mother soul. She could not believe that anybody ever put in a window for her, but I will, said the young mercantile man who was doing well in the marketplace. Her name was never in the newspaper until she died, but she shall be had, so far as I can secure the end, in everlasting remembrance so that when people ask about her they will discover, perhaps to their happy surprise, that this was put into the memory of one who made home happy and who made her husband rich without adding a penny to his store.

I have been confirmed in what has always been an impression and what has sometimes deepened into a conviction—I have been confirmed in my view that where the Gospel of Jesus Christ is preached with the energy of experience and the tenderness of sympathy and a right apprehension of the battle and misery of human life, there will always be a congregation to listen. When we came to this City, it was through an array of evil prophecies. There was practically nobody in the City; the few people that were in the City were so tired of it that they traveled by train and omnibus and tramway to the outlying green fields. It was impossible to get an audience in the City; on Sunday the City was doomed to desolation and silence and utter forsakenness in every aspect and meaning of that term. Yet we must come. Why? We could not tell; we had no list of reasons. We had no reason to leave another place where we were reveling in social fatness and prosperity. But there is a spirit in man; that spirit communicates with the Spirit of God and with all the gloom yet glory of destiny. We felt ourselves obliged to come. And we are ready to testify that it has only been the Gospel, nothing but the Gospel, simple, pure, practical, sympathetic, redeeming, that has accounted for these thirty-one years of really delightful experiences in the helping of our fellow men. I do not know that preachers ever hear much about their great discourses that are full of hard words and deep sayings, and are greater mysteries to the preacher than they can possibly be to the hearer; I do not know that preachers ever had any very great encouragement in the direction of making the Gospel difficult by turning it into a kind of paltry science and inflated idea of social reform and respectability. What we have heard has been that the prayer helped me in a difficulty, that the prayer lifted me out of the valley, that the reading of the Scripture was like the sudden illumination of an unexpected light flaring, flaming from the heavens and shining into all the nooks and corners of misery and despair. What we have heard is this, that some little sentence, some comforting word, has gone right into the heart, and by the power of God has created a new manhood and called forth latent energies, so latent as to have been unsuspected. This is God's way. He blesses simple things; He makes sacramental supper just out of bread men are eating at the time, and turns the sour supper wine into symbolic blood. We should be nearer God if we wished to be so. He is on the highway, He is in the marketplace, He is in every blade of grass, and when a bird sings in the high tree, so sings as to attract the attention of the heart and to make Misery dry away her hot tear, God is not far off.

We have nothing to do with the future, nothing to do even with tomorrow. We gave some eight-and-twenty thousand pounds directly and indirectly for the land on which this house stands. The City of London is a great and generous City, but it does not give its land away for nothing; even the City must draw a line somewhere. And within a fortnight we were offered forty thousand pounds for the plot of ground, but we were not land speculators. We wanted a sanctuary, we were in quest of a home for the church, and therefore we did not take the forty thousand pounds and go into the suburbs to preach and sing among green hedges and rival songsters in the woods and forests. We settled down in the City proper; we are in the City proper now. Though some wise man addresses a letter to me this very morning in which we are described as being in the West Center. We have not the honor of that W. Many men would give a great deal to be able to put the letter W anywhere on their letters. I sign N.W., but there is so much N in it that sometimes the W looks so small. But we are in the Eastern Center, we are in the City; and there is no place like it, and if I had to build in London, I would build in the City of London; if I had to rebuild this place and had all London at my disposal, I would put the same building up on the same lines of land. It was God, through Mr. Deputy Fry, then a high name in the City, who fixed this place for us, and He will fix all the places we want if we will let Him. But we must fuss and arrange and invent and plan and replan and plague our little brains with our own managements: whereas God says as it were within an inch of those same heads, If you would obey I would build, I would fix the bounds of your habitation, I would take care of things for you. But we won't let Him; and that is the worst species of atheism—to confess God, and take no heed of Him; to acknowledge on paper that there is a God, and never to attend to His statutes and commandments; to say in pompous form, "I believe in God Almighty," in the sense that I will never call Him into my counsels or attempt to invite His interposition in the providence of my daily life.

So far, I am here to say, He hath done all things well. We would like a word about the future, all of us, but we cannot have it. The future will, I am afraid, ruin some of us because we want to pry into it, and it is enwrapped in so many folds that it does not lie within the deftness and skill of human fingers to take off the folds and read the innermost legend and mystery. What will become of this or that when something else takes place? That is atheism, absolute and pestilent godlessness. What we have to do is to work up to the moment. Blessed is he who works up to the last moment. Some people wish for a long eventide. I pray, if I pray at all on that subject, not for a long eventide, but for sudden night.

Joseph Parker (1830–1902) was born in Hexham-on-Tyne, Northumberland, England to Congregationalist parents. Parker had little formal education in his childhood, but studied Greek and theology extensively on his own and preached his first sermon at age eighteen.

Parker married Ann Nesbitt in 1851, and in his early adulthood traveled and preached whenever the chance arose. At age twenty-two he joined John Campbell in London as an assistant at the Whitefield Tabernacle. Campbell powerfully influenced Parker's preaching style and his Christian life in general. The following year, Parker undertook studies at University College in London and assumed the pastorate at Banbury Congregational Church in Oxfordshire, where the church grew tremendously during Parker's years there.

In 1858 Parker accepted a call from Manchester's Cavendish Street Congregational Church. While there he continued his prolific writing and studying, and the University of Chicago conferred on him an honorary doctor of divinity degree. Five years later while still in Manchester, Parker's wife died, and left the once bold, boisterous preacher a more somber man.

Parker went to the Poultry Church in London in 1869 and there planned the construction of a new building—what became the famed City Temple—to accommodate the growing crowds. He preached every Sunday and Thursday there, and traveled to preach in other parts of England and Scotland throughout the rest of the week.

The Congregationalist denomination benefitted from Parker's leadership abilities as he served three times as chairman of the London Congregational Board and twice as chairman of the Congregational Union of England and Wales. He was a voice for social concerns such as liquor trafficking and aid for the needy, and he frequently donated to charitable causes.

Preaching was undoubtedly his passion; despite his immense popularity, Parker never lost sight of his motive. "I have nothing to preach to my fellowmen," he remarked, "if it be not the gospel of Jesus Christ and the doctrine of the cross."